THE CLAY SANSKRIT LIBRARY

FOUNDED BY JOHN & JENNIFER CLAY

WWW.CLAYSANSKRITLIBRARY.COM

WWW.NYUPRESS.ORG

First Edition 2006.

The Clay Sanskrit Library is co-published by
New York University Press
and the JJC Foundation.

Further information about this volume
and the rest of the Clay Sanskrit Library
is available on the following websites:
www.claysanskritlibrary.com
www.nyupress.org.

ISBN-13: 978-0-8147-9981-9 (cloth : alk. paper)
ISBN-10: 0-8147-9981-7 (cloth : alk. paper)

Artwork by Robert Beer.
Typeset in Adobe Garamond at 10.25 : 12.3+pt.
XML-development by Stuart Brown.
Editorial input from Dániel Balogh, Tomoyuki Kono,
Eszter Somogyi & Péter Szántó.
Printed in Great Britain by St Edmundsbury Press Ltd,
Bury St Edmunds, Suffolk, on acid-free paper.
Bound by Hunter & Foulis, Edinburgh, Scotland.

MAHĀBHĀRATA
BOOK EIGHT

KARṆA
VOLUME ONE

TRANSLATED BY

ADAM BOWLES

NEW YORK UNIVERSITY PRESS
JJC FOUNDATION
2006

Library of Congress Cataloging-in-Publication Data
Mahābhārata. Karṇaparva. English & Sanskrit.
Mahābhārata. Book eight, Karṇa /
translated by Adam Bowles. – 1st ed.
p. cm. – (The Clay Sanskrit library)
Epic poetry.
In English and Sanskrit (romanized) on facing pages;
includes translation from Sanskrit.
Includes bibliographical references and index.
ISBN-13: 978-0-8147-9981-9 (cloth : alk. paper)
ISBN-10: 0-8147-9981-7 (cloth : alk. paper)
I. Bowles, Adam. II. Title. III. Title: Karṇa.
BL1138.242.K37E5 2006
294.5'92304521–dc22 2006032852

CONTENTS

SANSKRIT ALPHABETICAL ORDER

Vowels:	*a ā i ī u ū ṛ ṝ ḷ ḹ e ai o au ṃ ḥ*
Gutturals:	*k kh g gh ṅ*
Palatals:	*c ch j jh ñ*
Retroflex:	*ṭ ṭh ḍ ḍh ṇ*
Dentals:	*t th d dh n*
Labials:	*p ph b bh m*
Semivowels:	*y r l v*
Spirants:	*ś ṣ s h*

GUIDE TO SANSKRIT PRONUNCIATION

a	b*u*t
ā, â	f*a*ther
i	s*i*t
ī, î	f*ee*
u	p*u*t
ū,û	b*oo*
ṛ	vocalic *r*, American p*ur*dy or English p*re*tty
ṝ	lengthened *ṛ*
ḷ	vocalic *l*, ab*le*
e, ê, ē	m*a*de, esp. in Welsh pronunciation
ai	b*i*te
o, ô, ō	r*o*pe, esp. Welsh pronunciation; Italian s*o*lo
au	s*ou*nd
ṃ	*anusvāra* nasalizes the preceding vowel
ḥ	*visarga*, a voiceless aspiration (resembling English *h*), or like Scottish lo*ch*, or an aspiration with a faint echoing of the preceding vowel so that *taiḥ* is pronounced *taih*[i]
k	lu*ck*
kh	blo*ckh*ead
g	*g*o
gh	bi*gh*ead
ṅ	a*n*ger
c	*ch*ill
ch	mat*chh*ead
j	*j*og
jh	aspirated *j*, he*dgeh*og
ñ	ca*ny*on
ṭ	retroflex *t*, *t*ry (with the tip of tongue turned up to touch the hard palate)
ṭh	same as the preceding but aspirated
ḍ	retroflex *d* (with the tip of tongue turned up to touch the hard palate)
ḍh	same as the preceding but aspirated
ṇ	retroflex *n* (with the tip

	of tongue turned up to touch the hard palate)
t	French *t*out
th	ten*t h*ook
d	*d*inner
dh	guil*dh*all
n	*n*ow
p	*p*ill
ph	u*ph*eaval
b	*b*efore
bh	a*bh*orrent
m	*m*ind
y	*y*es
r	trilled, resembling the Italian pronunciation of *r*
l	*l*inger
v	*w*ord
ś	*sh*ore
ṣ	retroflex *sh* (with the tip of the tongue turned up to touch the hard palate)
s	hi*ss*
h	*h*ood

CSL PUNCTUATION OF ENGLISH

The acute accent on Sanskrit words when they occur outside of the Sanskrit text itself, marks stress, e.g. Ramáyana. It is not part of traditional Sanskrit orthography, transliteration or transcription, but we supply it here to guide readers in the pronunciation of these unfamiliar words. Since no Sanskrit word is accented on the last syllable it is not necessary to accent disyllables, e.g. Rama.

The second CSL innovation designed to assist the reader in the pronunciation of lengthy unfamiliar words is to insert an unobtrusive middle dot between semantic word breaks in compound names (provided the word break does not fall on a vowel resulting from the fusion of two vowels), e.g. Maha·bhárata, but Ramáyana (not Rama·áyana). Our dot echoes the punctuating middle dot (·) found in the oldest surviving forms of written Indic, the Ashokan inscriptions of the third century BCE.

The deep layering of Sanskrit narrative has also dictated that we use quotation marks only to announce the beginning and end of every direct speech, and not at the beginning of every paragraph.

CSL PUNCTUATION OF SANSKRIT

The Sanskrit text is also punctuated, in accordance with the punctuation of the English translation. In mid-verse, the punctuation will not alter the *sandhi* or the scansion. Proper names are capitalized. Most Sanskrit metres have four "feet" *(pāda):* where possible we print the common *śloka* metre on two lines. In the Sanskrit text, we use French *Guillemets* (e.g. *«kva saṃcicīrṣuḥ?»*) instead of English quotation marks (e.g. "Where are you off to?") to avoid confusion with the apostrophes used for vowel elision in *sandhi*.

Sanskrit presents the learner with a challenge: *sandhi* ("euphonic combination"). *Sandhi* means that when two words are joined in connected speech or writing (which in Sanskrit reflects speech), the last letter (or even letters) of the first word often changes; compare the way we pronounce "the" in "the beginning" and "the end."

In Sanskrit the first letter of the second word may also change; and if both the last letter of the first word and the first letter of the second are vowels, they may fuse. This has a parallel in English: a nasal consonant is inserted between two vowels that would otherwise coalesce: "a pear" and "an apple." Sanskrit vowel fusion may produce ambiguity. The chart at the back of each book gives the full *sandhi* system.

Fortunately it is not necessary to know these changes in order to start reading Sanskrit. For that, what is important is to know the form of the second word without *sandhi* (pre-*sandhi*), so that it can be recognized or looked up in a dictionary. Therefore we are printing Sanskrit with a system of punctuation that will indicate, unambiguously, the original form of the second word, i.e., the form without *sandhi*. Such *sandhi* mostly concerns the fusion of two vowels.

In Sanskrit, vowels may be short or long and are written differently accordingly. We follow the general convention that a vowel with no mark above it is short. Other books mark a long vowel either with a bar called a macron (*ā*) or with a circumflex (*â*). Our system uses the macron, except that for initial vowels in *sandhi* we use a circumflex to indicate that originally the vowel was short, or the shorter of two possibilities (*e* rather than *ai*, *o* rather than *au*).

When we print initial *â*,	before *sandhi* that vowel was *a*
î or *ê*,	*i*
û or *ô*,	*u*
âi,	*e*
âu,	*o*

ā,	*ā* (i.e., the same)
ī,	*ī* (i.e., the same)
ū,	*ū* (i.e., the same)
ē,	*ī*
ō,	*ū*
āi,	*ai*
āu,	*au*
', before *sandhi* there was a vowel *a*	

FURTHER HELP WITH VOWEL SANDHI

When a final short vowel (*a*, *i* or *u*) has merged into a following vowel, we print ' at the end of the word, and when a final long vowel (*ā*, *ī* or *ū*) has merged into a following vowel we print " at the end of the word. The vast majority of these cases will concern a final *a* or *ā*.

Examples:

What before *sandhi* was	*atra asti* is represented as	*atr' âsti*
	atra āste	*atr' āste*
	kanyā asti	*kany" âsti*
	kanyā āste	*kany" āste*
	atra iti	*atr' êti*
	kanyā iti	*kany" êti*
	kanyā īpsitā	*kany" ēpsitā*

Finally, three other points concerning the initial letter of the second word:

(1) A word that before *sandhi* begins with *ṛ* (vowel), after *sandhi* begins with *r* followed by a consonant: *yatha" rtu* represents pre-*sandhi* *yathā ṛtu*.

(2) When before *sandhi* the previous word ends in *t* and the following word begins with *ś*, after *sandhi* the last letter of the previous word is *c* and the following word begins with *ch*: *syāc chāstravit* represents pre-*sandhi syāt śāstravit*.

(3) Where a word begins with *h* and the previous word ends with a double consonant, this is our simplified spelling to show the pre-*sandhi*

form: *tad hasati* is commonly written as *tad dhasati*, but we write *tadd hasati* so that the original initial letter is obvious.

COMPOUNDS

We also punctuate the division of compounds (*samāsa*), simply by inserting a thin vertical line between words. There are words where the decision whether to regard them as compounds is arbitrary. Our principle has been to try to guide readers to the correct dictionary entries.

EXAMPLE

Where the Deva·nágari script reads:

कुम्भस्थली रक्षतु वो विकीर्णसिन्दूररेणुर्द्विरदाननस्य ।
प्रशान्तये विघ्नतमश्छटानां निष्ठ्यूतबालातपपल्लवेव ॥

Others would print:

kumbhasthalī rakṣatu vo vikīrṇasindūrareṇur dviradānanasya /
praśāntaye vighnatamaśchaṭānāṃ niṣṭhyūtabālātapapallaveva //

We print:

kumbha|sthalī rakṣatu vo vikīrṇa|sindūra|reṇur dvirad'|ānanasya
praśāntaye vighna|tamaś|chaṭānāṃ niṣṭhyūta|bāl'|ātapa|pallav" êva.

And in English:

"May Ganésha's domed forehead protect you! Streaked with vermilion dust, it seems to be emitting the spreading rays of the rising sun to pacify the teeming darkness of obstructions."

"Nava·sáhasanka and the Serpent Princess" I.3 by Padma·gupta

INTRODUCTION

The Story So Far

The 'Maha·bhárata' (*Mahā/bhārata*) is the story of a war between two sets of royal cousins, the five sons of Pandu (the Pándavas) and the hundred sons of Dhrita·rashtra (the Dhartaráshtras). A series of events befalling their respective fathers leads Duryódhana, the eldest Dhartaráshtra, to dispute the right to succession of Yudhi·shthira, the eldest of the Pándavas. After a number of incidents that escalate the rivalries and tensions between the feuding cousins, the Dhartaráshtras challenge Yudhi·shthira to a fateful dicing match, which Yudhi·shthira promptly loses. Much to his great humiliation, he forfeits his sons, brothers and wife, whom he has staked along with himself. Though Duryódhana cancels the match, bad blood prevails between the cousins.

The Pándavas are challenged again. This time the stake is the kingdom or thirteen years in exile, twelve of which must be spent in the forest and the remaining year incognito in public. Yudhi·shthira loses the second challenge as well, and the Pándavas head to the forest. After thirteen years and many adventures, the Pándavas return to reclaim their rightful inheritance, only for Duryódhana to refuse to relinquish the throne.

The cousins now prepare for war, establishing their alliances and bolstering their armies. Their teachers, Bhishma, Drona and Kripa, will fight on the side of the Dhartaráshtras, while Krishna Vasudéva is chosen by the Pándavas. The subsequent eighteen-day war is tremendous and violent, almost voiding the earth of every warrior. When

Bhishma, the general of the Dhartaráshtra forces for the first ten days, is felled in fraudulent fashion, Drona takes over. Drona leads the army for the next five days, until he too is killed, also in a deceptive manner. The mighty Karna is the next champion to assume command of the Dhartaráshtra army. It is here that we take up the story. . .

Karna

WARRIOR-HERO?

In the long history of the 'Maha·bhárata'—through its transmissions, adaptations, regional variations and poetic re-imaginings—there is perhaps no more remarkable figure than the hero Karna. Variously and often simultaneously famous for his courage, strength, unstinting loyalty and profound generosity, as well as his bragging, narcissism, and bitterness, Karna has become—beyond the Sanskrit 'Maha·bhárata' and perhaps especially in more recent times—venerated as the ideal warrior-hero and model devotee, idealized as a class-warrior and even worshipped as a deity.[1] Yet if modern interpretations and developments of his persona and story sometimes take Karna far beyond the imaginings of the poets of the Sanskrit 'Maha·bhárata,' these developments remain deeply rooted in the characterization of Karna in the Sanskrit 'Maha·bhárata.' Widely recognized as a prime Indian exemplar of the tragic mode, Karna embodies that most modern of frailties: a deep and unresolved crisis over identity that everywhere and always defines and curtails his aspirations. Underscoring many of the episodes filling out Karna's life is the confusion—both his own and others'—over his proper social status; and this confusion bolsters a central theoretical construct of early Indian thought: the incontrovertibility and inevitability of an individual's position in the social world being defined by his or her birth and, in turn, the necessity of this definition to ensure a stable, manageable and predictable social structure. Most of the chief narratives rounding out the character of Karna play out, in one way or another, an aspect of Karna's compromised status resulting from the confused and hidden circumstances of his birth, and these in turn serve to play out the impossibility of avoiding (yet the temptation to avoid as well) what is represented as an inevitability: a person's position in a social code as that position is defined by the circumstances of their birth.

From the first significant encounter between Karna and the Pándavas the loyalties, dilemmas and tragic contours of Karna's life begin to take shape. Karna, the son of Radha and the charioteer Ádhiratha, traveled to Hástina·pura to receive weapons training from the brahmin warrior Drona ('The Beginning,' MBh CE I.122.47), as had the Pándavas, Káuravas (Dhartaráshtras) and other princes. Drona organizes a weapons' contest to show off the skills of his most eminent pupils, a tournament to which Karna is not invited.[2] Towards its end, and after the great Pándava warrior Árjuna has especially displayed his prowess, the loud sound of arms being slapped, a heroic gesture of battle, comes forth from the gate. Then,

Karna, that conqueror of enemy cities, entered the vast arena like a walking mountain, wearing inborn armor, his face bright with earrings, and armed with bow and belted sword. Of wide eyes and wide fame, child of a virgin, of Pritha (Kunti), and a portion of the hot-rayed sun, Karna was a destroyer of enemy hordes. His courage and strength the equal of a lion's, a bull's and a regal elephant's, and with splendor, beauty and luster like the sun, the moon and fire, this youth was as tall as a golden palm tree and as robust as a lion; his virtues inestimable, he was the glorious son of the Sun. ('The Beginning,' MBh CE I.126.1–5)

The gathered crowd receives him with awe and, in an imperious voice, he addresses his "unknown" (*a/jñāta*) brother Árjuna, bragging that he will better each of his feats. Granted permission by Drona, he matches each of Árjuna's deeds, and Duryódhana and the Dhartaráshtras, already rivals of the Pándavas, celebrate and embrace Karna and invite him to take pleasure in the kingdom of the Kurus. Momentously, Karna enthusiastically accepts, choosing friendship with Duryódhana and boldly asserting his desire to duel with Árjuna.

Árjuna feels slighted, however, and questions Karna's right to attend the contest. Swapping invectives and threats of death, the pair face off for a duel. Their divine fathers, Indra and Surya, fill the sky with squalls and light, mirroring the heroes' contest and favoring their respective sons; and Kunti—mother of both—realizes hidden truths and collapses in a faint. Then, in a fateful intervention just as the two mighty warriors are on the verge of releasing their arrows, Kripa announces Árjuna's lineage, and requests the same from Karna. Unable to truthfully answer, Karna hangs his head in shame, since it is part of the warrior ethos that like must fight with like. Árjuna is a prince; but who is Karna? Karna's new found friend, Duryódhana, leaps to his aid. There are three ways to be a king, he suggests, by birth, by being a champion (*śūra*) or by leading an army, and he promptly has Karna anointed as king of Anga, a region roughly corresponding to today's south-eastern Bihar. The new king asks Duryódhana what he can give him in return. Your "eternal friendship" (*atyantaṃ sakhyam*) he replies ('The Beginning,' MBh CE I.126.38), sealing a bond that will repeatedly find expression in deep affection and loyalty, but will also lead to horrendous destruction.

Yet at this moment of profound personal triumph for Karna, as he evidently becomes a king through merit, Ádhiratha, a humble charioteer and Karna's father, enters the arena. Karna immediately greets him with reverence and is embraced with love. However, the moment the Pándava Bhima realizes Ádhiratha is Karna's father, he mocks him as the son of a mere charioteer, having no right, therefore, to either fight Árjuna or rule a kingdom. Leaping to his defense once more, Duryódhana again preaches a liberal doctrine of class determinism.[3] Remarking on the mixed provenance of various powers, their teachers and even the Pándavas, Duryódhana suggests:

> *How could a doe give birth to this tiger who seems like the sun and who, with his earrings and armor, is distinguished by divine symbols?* ('The Beginning,' MBh CE I.127.15.)[4]

This rich passage sets in train events that have far reaching consequences. A warrior with all the markings of a great and mighty hero has entered the stage. Willing and capable of defying and dueling with the greatest of heroes, he establishes a deep and loyal friendship with the most contemptible of allies. Karna will join Shákuni and frequently Duhshásana in becoming one of Duryódhana's chief co-conspirators, seeking to counter the Pándavas at every turn. Yet Karna does not merely join the side of the Dhartaráshtras, he becomes their champion; it is by relying on him that Duryódhana thinks he can best the Pándavas.[5] From this point he is irrevocably estranged from the Pándavas, his half-brothers who—like him—are unaware that they share a common mother, Kunti. And while his birth parents—Kunti and the Sun god Surya—look on, he demonstrates love and loyalty towards his adoptive father, Ádhiratha, inevitably exposing the low status of his lineage. Ádhiratha is a *sūta*, a charioteer, and *sūta*s are born of parents from different social classes and consequently are excluded from the privileges and entitlements of true kshatriyas.[6] The stigma of Karna's status dogs his career, and he only truly transcends it in death. His enemies are all too ready to recall it; and, even after he discovers the truth of his birth, he never quite manages to overcome a bitterness that eats away at him and fuels his hatred for the Pándavas.[7]

THE ABSENT PÁNDAVA

It is typical of epic style that surprises are rare; dramatic tension lies, rather, in the anticipation of the inevitable unfolding of catastrophic and sometimes tragic events, as is certainly the case with Karna. Thus, by the time of Karna's arrival at the weapons' tournament, we have already been apprised of his birth story a number of times, though Karna has to wait for a much later occasion to be told the truth, and the other heroes even longer.[8] Kunti (Pritha) was the birth daughter of the Yadu chief Shura who, in honoring a promise, gave her to his childless cousin Kunti·bhoja.[9] A famous and irascible brahmin sage by the name of Durvásas came to stay in their house, and Kunti was charged with the duty of serving him with hospitality befitting his status. Taking care not to rouse his famous temper, she so pleased the sage that he gave her a spell with which she could call upon any god at anytime to father sons upon her.[10] Overcome with curiosity, the young virgin Kunti summons the Sun god Surya, who arrives in all his splendor. Though Kunti asks that Surya return from whence he came, the god refuses, and insists that he have his way with her, or else curse her, her father and the brahmin who gave the spell. She strikes a bargain with the god: if he returns her to a virginal state and her son is born with divine armor and earrings and has the god's magnificence, then she will lie with him.[11] He agrees and Kunti is miraculously impregnated by means of the god's *yoga*. In shame she hides the pregnancy, wishing to protect her relatives. In time and as promised, she gives birth to a broad-shouldered boy sporting a coat of armor and golden earrings. Kunti places him in a basket and sends him down a river. The *sūta* Ádhiratha and the beautiful Radha, a childless couple, pull the basket from the river and, in astonishment, discover a baby radiant with golden earrings and armor, surely "the child of a god" thinks Ádhiratha.[12] They adopt him as their own and he grows up to be a powerful warrior.

Karna is clearly no ordinary hero. The son of the Sun god Surya, his divine features distinguish him as a character of particular potency and importance.[13] In addition, as eldest of the Pándavas, he is a potential rightful claimant to the throne. Karna is only made aware of the true identity of his parents just prior to the war in a pair of sequential conversations, first with Krishna and then Kunti, who try to convince him to join his brothers the Pándavas.[14] Krishna offers him both Dráupadi and then the kingship, with Yudhi·shthira becoming his crown prince (*yuva/rāja*).[15] Kunti intones that nothing would be beyond a united Karna and Árjuna. But the efforts of Krishna and Kunti fail. Too much blood has been spilt and too many insults have gone unanswered for war to be avoided. And after enduring years of muddled torment as a mighty hero who—in the eyes of his allies and rivals alike, and perhaps in his own eyes as well—cannot quite overcome his apparently low birth, Karna cannot forgive being "cast aside" (*apākīrṇa*; *avakīrṇa*) by Kunti at birth ('Preparation for War,' MBh CE V.139.4, 144.5). He owes debts of love and loyalty to Ádhiratha and Radha, his adoptive parents who cared for him as their own; likewise, after enjoying the benefits of sovereignty among Duryódhana's lot (*kula*), he could hardly abandon Duryódhana now in his time of need. Karna is resolutely true to his word and his loyalties, and he will frequently repeat these reasons for his continued alliance with the Dhartaráshtras and devotion to his adoptive parents. But he is bitter too. Kunti's great "evil" (*pāpa*) in casting him aside has denied him access to the glory (*yaśas*) and fame (*kīrti*) that are the proper pursuits of heroic warriors. In acknowledging this loss, Karna is being true to his nature as a warrior hero, a hero who gives himself up to fate and who fights though he knows he cannot win.[16] Therefore, it is of little surprise that for Karna, writ large is the central 'Maha·bhárata' trope of the great battle as a grand sacrifice.[17]

Yet having rejected his birth siblings and thrown his lot in with the Dhartaráshtras, Karna is never quite at home with his allies. Despite his friendship with Duryódhana, his ascension to the kingship of Anga and his being lauded as a champion of immense proportions, the Kuru elder statesmen never truly embrace him. Dhrita·rashtra, father of Duryódhana, is wary of his son's dependence on Karna, and doubts that he has the qualities to bring success.[18] And the Kuru-gurus, Bhishma, Drona and Kripa, the Dhartaráshtras' allies in war, remain suspicious of Karna's origins and impatient with his bragging and moral shortcomings.[19] Despite his extraordinary abilities and the immortality that derives from his divine armor and earrings, Karna is a fallible champion, and his fallibilities manifest as personal failings. These fallibilities are especially evident in four key scenes that lead inexorably to the great war. In one of these Karna could be described as being on the side of the victor; in the other three he is clearly on the side of the loser. In each case, events take place that enemy and ally alike shall never fail to recollect.

A HERO FLAWED AND FURIOUS

The first of these scenes is Dráupadi's *svayam̥/vara*, at which the princess chooses her future husband.[20] Dráupadi, the daughter of the Panchála king Drúpada, is keenly sought by all the princes, and her suitors are set a task in which they must string an extremely stiff bow and hit a golden target suspended in the sky. All the princes and champions, Karna included, try and fail to string the bow. Then, disguised as a brahmin, Árjuna stands up and strides to the bow to the astonishment of the spectators, for whom a brahmin's participation is not expected. In an instant he strings it and brings down the target, for which he is rewarded with Dráupadi as his wife.[21] Furious that this upstart brahmin should take a kshatriya's due, the assembly of warriors erupts and attacks King Drúpada. Árjuna and Bhima, still in disguise, leap to his defense. A great battle ensues in which Karna and Árjuna duel. But, with Árjuna admitting to knowledge of the Brahma and Aindra weapons, divine weapons of immense power, Karna withdraws from battle, citing the invincibility of "sacred power" (*brahmā tejas*).[22] Árjuna's disguise as a brahmin brings into relief once again the problem of class identity. Not for the last time, an intentional muddling of class distinctions turns out to be Karna's nadir.

The second scene is pivotal in the epic and again features Dráupadi.[23] Lured into a dice game against Shákuni, a master dice-player and, next to Karna, Duryódhana's closest confidant, Yudhi·shthira wagers himself, his sons, brothers and even Dráupadi, and loses them all, leading, eventually, to the Pándavas' thirteen-year exile. Karna can scarcely conceal his delight at Yudhi·shthira's loss and hurls invectives at Dráupadi, calling her a whore (*bandhakī*) and slave (*dasī*) ('The Great Hall,' MBh CE II.61.35, 81; 63.1–4). He orders Duhshásana to strip her and the Pándavas, though Dráupadi, as it happens, is menstruating. Although Karna is on the side of the winner in this contest, in his humiliation of Dráupadi Karna has not merely exposed his bilious tendencies and acted—as the general consensus has it—immorally and without honor, he has also given the Pándavas reason to foster a special hatred towards him. Leading up to and during the war, this event will become, unsurprisingly, a most frequently recalled incident.[24] Even Karna's allies will remind Karna of his cruelty to Dráupadi in the assembly hall, and eventually Karna too will come to regret his behavior.[25]

The next two scenes involve humiliating defeats for the Dhartaráshtras, which, however, will be remembered especially as Karna's failures.[26] There are two famous instances during the Pándavas' exile in which Duryódhana and his allies seek to best the Pándavas, only to end up disgraced. Karna plays a key role in both. In the first, urging Duryódhana to pursue the Pándavas in the forest and mock their destitution, Karna suggests an expedition to inspect cattle stations as a ruse to avoid Dhrita·rashtra's disapproval at what is, after all, a rather self-indulgent exercise. In the forest, they encounter a horde of *gandharvas* who object to their presence and attack them. Karna's chariot is crushed in battle and he flees, leaving the Dhartaráshtras to an ignominious defeat. To compound matters, the Pándavas come to their rescue and secure their freedom.

In the second instance, the Dhartaráshtras venture on a cattle raid into the kingdom of Viráta where, as it happens, the disguised Pándavas have been spending their thirteenth year in exile. With the exception of Árjuna, the Pándavas (still in disguise) join the warriors of the kingdom in repelling the first wave of invaders led by Susharman, the king of Tri·garta, and are responsible for freeing Viráta, who had been captured. Duryódhana launches a second attack and drives away large numbers of cattle. Viráta's son Úttara recruits Árjuna—disguised as a eunuch dressed in women's clothes—to be his charioteer and goes out to meet the second wave of invaders. But once he spies the army, he panics and flees. Still in his skirt, Árjuna chases him and forces him back on the chariot. At first Duryódhana's warriors laugh at what is clearly a comic scene, but, noticing the eunuch's impressive build, they begin to suspect she is Árjuna in disguise, and tremble at the thought. Drona sings his praises as a warrior without peer, a point Karna and Duryódhana protest. Árjuna prepares for battle, while Karna brags that he will kill him, for which Kripa and Ashvatthámán (Drona's son) rebuke him for being a braggart and question his ability to oppose Árjuna. Árjuna battles the Dhartaráshtras and soon kills Karna's brother Sangrámajit; Karna then attacks him, but he too is overcome and flees. Árjuna duels with and defeats (but does not kill) Kripa, Drona and Ashvatthámán, before Karna attacks him again, goaded by Árjuna to prove his boasts. Dueling with words and weapons, they wound one another and Karna again flees the battlefield in defeat with Árjuna's scorn ringing in his ears. Árjuna proceeds to overwhelm all the Dhartaráshtras, and they retreat from battle.

The Dhartaráshtras' elder statesmen repeatedly recall these two defeats in the remainder of the epic. Along with his abuse of Dráupadi in the assembly hall and, occasionally, his failure to win her at her *svayaṃ/vara*, it becomes part of the stock of episodes drawn upon when Karna's bragging and failings are brought to the fore. Forever promising to kill Árjuna, Karna has earned a reputation for failing to deliver on his word, a perilous situation for a heroic warrior. Bhishma especially harbors a strong dislike for Karna, and rarely fails to recall these defeats on the frequent occasions that he finds reason to rebuke Karna or call his abilities into question.[27] In Bhishma's and Karna's touching rapprochement at the end of Book VI (*Bhīṣma/parvan*, MBh CE VI.117), Bhishma, lying fallen but not dead on the bed of arrows made for him by Árjuna, gives as motive for his repeated rebukes of Karna the destruction of Karna's fiery energy (*tejo/vadha*). This notion is typically associated with Shalya, as we shall shortly discuss, and essentially refers to the verbal haranguing and ridicule Karna is subjected to in order to undermine his confidence and reduce the ardor that compels his behavior. In destroying Karna's *tejas* (fiery energy), Shalya is complicit in Karna's defeat at the hands of the Pándavas. Bhishma's concerns, however, are less determined by revenge, and have more to do with controlling a dangerously impulsive ally, whose fiery temper, fueled by a profound sense of personal injustice, leads the Dhartaráshtras from one disastrous encounter to another.

MAKING KARNA KILLABLE

Karna's lack of self-restraint is, indeed, a leitmotif of his characterization in the 'Maha·bhárata.' Such behavior arises in part from his resentment at his personal vilification, as well as, we might speculate, from his missing out on a proper warrior's upbringing, which may have better directed his combative tendencies. But this impetuosity must also stand beside some remarkable examples of moderation that Karna exhibits at key moments, not least when he rejects Krishna's offer of the kingdom, and insists that Krishna keep his true identity secret from "honest" Yudhi·shthira, lest he refuse to take the mantle himself ('Preparation for War,' MBh CE V.139.21). In this, Karna displays a forbearance and insight that is typically missing from his youthful allies.

It is for such reasons that, despite Karna's failings and the fallibilities they expose, it is difficult not to empathize with him. As a social misfit and unrecognized kshatriya, one can easily understand the psychology that motivates his quest to prove himself the supreme warrior. But there is also a sense in which the cards are stacked against him. Karna will often refer to his own destiny as being ruled by fate; and other epic interlocutors will suggest the same.[28] But one can perhaps view the destruction of his *tejas* at the hands of first Bhishma and then Shalya as a metaphor for a broader pattern in the 'Maha·bhárata' that sees Karna divested, step by step, of all those things that make him not merely a warrior, but a hero touched by divinity. These incidents occur in a number of telling scenes in the 'Maha·bhárata' that, ironically, reveal a more sympathetic Karna than the one displayed in some of the scenes discussed above. Curiously, they also bring into play once again some interesting instances of intentional class muddling that underscore that the pack has been stacked against Karna, and that, in the end, Karna's birth will win out.

In the first incident, known as "The Robbing of the Earrings,"[29] Indra lends the Pándavas assistance by conspiring to divest Karna of the golden earrings and divine armor that render him invincible. Mirroring Árjuna's earlier success at Dráupadi's *svayaṃ/vara*—and recalling that Indra is Árjuna's divine father—Indra adopts the guise of a brahmin and begs Karna for his armor and earrings, knowing full well his reputation for generosity to brahmins. Despite being fore-warned of Indra's plan by his father Surya (though at this stage he is unaware that he is his father), Karna plans to give them to Indra in any case. In being true to his vow of generosity to brahmins (*dāna*) and preferring over his divine attributes (and recalling his complaint to Kunti discussed above) the glory (*yaśas*) and fame (*kīrti*) he will earn for giving them to Indra,[30] Karna reveals himself at his most kshatriya-like. Surya, however, does manage to convince him to ask for an infallible spear in return. Sure enough, when Indra comes to beg his earrings and armor, Karna assents to surrender them in exchange for the infallible spear. Indra agrees, but with the crucial restriction that the spear can only be used for one extraordinary enemy, to then return to Indra. The pact is made, and Karna, in an act of brutal self-mutilation that again speaks to his remarkable courage and generosity to a fault, cuts off his earrings and flays his skin to remove his congenital armor, and hands them over to Indra.

The one extraordinary enemy against whom Karna plans to use the infallible spear is, of course, his *bête noire* Árjuna. But again he is foiled, this time by the scheming Krishna. Manipulating Bhima's *rākṣasa* son Ghatótkacha[31] to attack Karna at night, when *rākṣasa*s are at their most formidable, Karna is forced to expend his infallible spear, which, as promised, kills Ghatótkacha and returns to Indra.[32] Krishna is delighted and claims Ghatótkacha's death for himself, since, he suggests, it was he who made Karna kill Ghatótkacha with his spear through a stratagem (*upāya*) by which he "cheated" (*vyaṃsita*) the spear ('Drona,' MBh CE VII.156.24, 27). Now that Karna's one use of the infallible spear had been expended, it could no longer be used on Árjuna; and, having divested Karna of the spear given to him by Indra, Krishna delights at his diminution to the state of being merely a man.[33]

If first Árjuna and then his father Indra can employ the guise of a brahmin to achieve their goals, different rules would seem to apply to the would-be-kshatriya Karna. In his time under Drona's tutelage, Karna requests that Drona teach him the Brahma weapon, a powerful and divine weapon.[34] Drona rejects him, however, for it can only be learnt either by a brahmin who has performed his vows or an ascetic kshatriya. Karna immediately takes himself to the Bhárgava warrior brahmin Rama Jamadágnya and, pretending himself to be a Bhárgava brahmin, requests that he stay there in his hermitage. While residing there, he wanders off and accidentally kills the cow that provides the milk for a devout brahmin's sacrifices.[35] Despite his apologies and offers of recompense, the brahmin is furious and curses him: while he battles with an enemy the earth will swallow up a wheel of his chariot and the enemy will chop off his head. Karna goes on living in the hermitage and, in due time, Rama is impressed enough with Karna to teach him the secret of the weapon. However, one day while they were roaming the forest together, a tired Rama falls asleep with his head in Karna's lap. While he sleeps, a worm creeps onto Karna's thigh,[36] pierces his flesh and drinks his blood. Unable to remove the worm for fear of waking his *guru*, Karna sits resilient and unmoving, despite the pain. When Rama is roused by a drip of Karna's blood, he is horrified to be so polluted. Realizing no brahmin could endure so much pain, he thinks Karna a kshatriya and demands he tell him the truth. Karna confesses to being a *sūta* and, in fury, Rama curses him to forget the weapon when he needs it most.

With the curses of the devout sacrificing brahmin and the warrior-brahmin Rama Jamadágnya, the divestment of Karna's extraordinary attributes that began with Indra's deceptive request for his earrings and armor is now complete. And while all this has taken place, his nemesis Árjuna has undergone the opposite transformation, a double movement nicely captured in the following passage from the twelfth book of the 'Maha·bhárata':

> *Because of the curse of the brahmin and of great Rama, because of the favor he granted Kunti, because of the magic of Indra, because of Bhishma's contempt, because of his half-description in the enumeration of warriors, because of Shalya destroying his fiery energy and because of Krish-*

na's scheming, Karna Vaikártana, the equal of the sun in radiance, was killed in battle by the wielder of Gándiva who had obtained the divine weapons of Rudra, the king of the gods (Indra), Yama, Váruna, Kubéra, Drona and the great Kripa. ('Peace,' MBh CE XII.5.11–14)

Yet in traversing the pathways from semi-divine hero to the most human of warriors, Karna shows himself to be a hero who, though fallible, cursed and tragic, is also accepting, mighty and courageous. If Karna has become merely a man, as Krishna noted in glee, Rama's insight into Karna's true nature strikes to the heart of the narrative's conceit. In these episodes, double standards, conniving divinities and vengeful brahmins stand in stark contrast to Karna's displays of generosity to brahmins, his remarkable physical ability and immense resilience and courage. And in these encounters, the truth of this wannabe kshatriya's birth is given its fullest expression. It is in this that Karna's life serves to demonstrate, perhaps more than any other hero in the 'Maha·bhárata,' that birth inscribes an inevitable destiny which, if momentarily tricked, disguised or denied, eventually wins out. And so we meet him in the *Karṇa/parvan*, bereft of his most remarkable attributes and weapons (bar one, a particularly potent arrow), but hell-bent on grappling with the Pándavas as general of Dhrita·rashtra's army.

Of *Sūta*s and Pseudo-*sūta*s: Shalya and Karna Wrangling Before Battle

STATUS ANXIETY

From the time of his initial encounter with Árjuna at the exhibition of arms, through to his encounters with various Kuru-elders and his final denouement at Árjuna's hands, Karna is forever engaging in verbal contests, bragging at his own prowess and predicting his adversary's demise. Such flyting, as it is known, in which warriors engage in verbal disputation prior to battle, is a typical feature of heroic epic.[37] One such instance forms the dramatic heart of the first volume of the *Karṇa/parvan*, as Karna and Shalya, the latter recruited by Duryódhana to be Karna's charioteer, engage in a flyting contest that is remarkable for both its vitriol and the extravagance of its ethnographic imaginings, and that leads, inexorably, to Karna's final duel with Árjuna.[38]

After Karna's first day as general of the Káurava army, which did not go well, the depleted and dejected Dhartaráshtras gather to discuss the next day's strategy. Karna notes the benefit that Árjuna has gained from Krishna's advice, and suggests that Shalya, the king of the Madras and uncle of the Pándavas through their father's second wife Madri, become his charioteer.[39] Shalya, Karna suggests, is superior to Krishna, just as Karna is superior to Árjuna. Duryódhana approaches Shalya and asks him to become Karna's charioteer, and Shalya responds in fury at the insult, since this would entail a mighty king being subservient to Karna, a lowly son of a *sūta*. Duryódhana flatters him, telling him he is superior to Krishna and Karna, and, in an attempt to assuage Shalya's concerns of serving someone whose status is lower than his own, casts doubt on Karna's birth as a *sūta*. The flattery wins Shalya over and he agrees to be Karna's charioteer on the condition that he can say whatever he likes to Karna and whatever he says must be forgiven.

With the terms agreed upon, they mount the chariot. But their personal differences begin to surface almost immediately.[40] Karna brags that he will kill the Pándavas, for which Shalya chastises him. Dire omens accompany their departure and, in a comic but portentous twist, their horses stumble. Karna launches into another long boast of his intentions to kill the Pándavas, which Shalya counters by praising Árjuna and abusing Karna; Árjuna, he asserts, will kill Karna. The two alternately abuse one another and boast about their prowess, Shalya placing emphasis on Karna's bragging and his inadequacy when compared to Árjuna (mentioning some of the failures we have already discussed above), and Karna questioning Shalya's moral adequacy, noting especially the depravity of his people, the Madras. They continue until Duryódhana finally brings it to a stop, and they turn their attention once again to the battle.

Our two protagonists, it is clear, are not particularly fond of one another. As we have come to expect in dealings with Karna, their antipathy centers on questions of status and identity. Shalya is quick to remind Duryódhana that he is a king proud of his royal lineage; it is an affront to his dignity and heritage that he should serve a lowly *sūta*, whose occupation and status as charioteer is determined by birth from parents of different social classes, and is indicative of social disorder.[41] For Shalya to be referred to as charioteer (usually *sārathi*, but once also *sūta*) could easily be (and clearly was) taken as being a slur on his family.

Yet despite the gravity of the insult, Shalya's opposition may partly be viewed as bluster. We shall shortly see that Shalya has already foreseen that he will become Karna's charioteer, suggesting that his present tirade is largely a face-saving exercise. There is thus an air of high farce in this passage that is only heightened by the lengths to which the antagonists (especially Karna) go to abuse one another. Such farce is evident in Karna, the pseudo-son of a charioteer, addressing Shalya—king, chariot-warrior and reluctant charioteer—as "charioteer," and Shalya persisting in addressing Karna—his mighty chariot-warrior and a king who could have been a greater king—as "charioteer" (*sūta*) and "charioteer's son" (*sūta/ja, sūta/putra*), though Karna is certainly no charioteer, and, as we know, not really a charioteer's son either. And to convince Shalya to take on the role, Duryódhana must make the unlikely case that a charioteer is in fact superior to his chariot-warrior which, despite his illustrious examples (Brahma as charioteer for Shiva; Krishna as charioteer for Árjuna), runs counter to all accepted standards of social custom. A knowing audience, one might imagine, would have pricked all these conceits and found humor in the farce.

If Shalya's anxiety makes an issue of class status, and evokes the social pathologies of confused social codes (*dharmas*) and classes (*varṇas*), Karna's referents are quite different. For Karna, of course, arguing from the basis of inherited status clearly will not work, since he can admit to none (though we know and he knows that he has some). Rather, Karna focuses on an issue mapped out already by Duryódhana during their first significant meeting at the weapons' contest: merit is earned through behavior. In a sequence of tall tales, Karna paints Shalya's people, the Madras, as thoroughly despicable, gluttonous, paying no heed to the dominant social code (*dharma*) of the time, and prone to drunkenness, sexual promiscuity and depravity.[42] The Madras hail from an area surrounding the five tributaries of the Indus River, an area on the margins of the geo-political center of northern India as described by Karna,[43] which forms the central arena for the events of the 'Maha·bhárata.' Told by women, children and old people to amuse themselves, and by old traveling brahmins at the king's court,[44] the tales evoke denigrating and gossipy stereotypes, and are suggestive of the inanity of the playground, or have, especially in the case of the bawdier stories, the whiff of the barroom. The stereotypes are informed by a distant familiarity, a word of mouth passing of lore that strengthens the center at the expense of the periphery. These are further narrative conceits—lightening the mood despite their derogatory content—as is nowhere more apparent than in Shalya's meager response to these tales making a mockery of him and his people.[45] For Karna the point of all this, beyond the perverse joy of telling bawdy and wicked tales at an adversary's expense, is that Shalya can neither discourse on morality nor question Karna's bragging or abilities, because he has no moral legitimacy of his own. Shalya is a reprobate, marked with the stain of his degenerate people, and incapable of participating in or commenting on the dominant socio-cultural codes of the center.

FRIENDSHIP AND ITS BETRAYAL

But if Karna and Shalya express themselves through a discourse of status anxiety, their enmity does have a history within the 'Maha·bhárata' which brings other factors into play. Near the beginning of the fifth book of the 'Maha·bhárata,' as each side commences their preparations for the war, Shalya sets out to join his nephews the Pándavas.[46] Hearing of this, however, Duryódhana arranges for lodging houses to be built for him along the way where he is honored by Duryódhana's ministers and provided with all manner of indulgences. Flattered, and thinking Yudhi·shthira had had them built, Shalya seeks to reward whoever is responsible, only to discover that it is Duryódhana. Offered a boon in gratitude, Duryódhana asks that he become commander of his army. Shalya has no option but to accept. Arriving at the Pándavas headquarters in Upaplávya, Shalya explains to Yudhi·shthira what had happened on his journey. But Yudhi·shthira is barely disappointed and immediately hatches a plan to take advantage of his uncle's alliance. Remarking that Shalya is "Krishna's equal" and that he will become Karna's charioteer, Yudhi·shthira asks him for a favor, to destroy Karna's fiery energy (*tejas*), a deed, he admits, that "shouldn't be done" (*a/kartavya*).[47] Shalya, knowing he will likely become Karna's charioteer, agrees to speak to Karna adversely (*pratīpa*) and hostilely (*a/hita*), destroying his pride (*hṛta/darpa*) and fiery energy (*hṛta/tejas*). And so, unlike Bhishma's essentially irenic attempts to quell

Karna's *tejas*, Shalya—motivated apparently by his outrage at the abuse suffered by the Pándavas, but acting at Yudhi·shthira's behest—sets out to destroy the Dhartaráshtras by making their champion Karna easier to kill.

In each of these incidents—Shalya's persuasion to be Karna's charioteer, the luring of Shalya to the side of the Dhartaráshtras and the appeal to Shalya to betray Karna—the key character flaw that Yudhi·shthira and Duryódhana (twice) exploit is Shalya's vanity. In the first and third instances, Duryódhana and Yudhi·shthira compare Shalya to Krishna, Árjuna's divine and manipulative charioteer whose interventions are crucial to the Pándavas' success. While the comparison serves to flatter Shalya, it is clearly contrastive, as indicated, for example, by Krishna ignoring the same tempting lodging houses that lead Shalya to offer Duryódhana a boon.[48] The comparison extends further, however, for the text continually draws comparison between Shalya and Karna on the one hand and Krishna and Árjuna on the other. That this comparison is parody is no clearer than when the horses' stumble as Shalya and Karna depart for battle (HILTEBEITEL 1990: 256–257).

Krishna's advice to Árjuna is always salutary, as Karna has noted. They are companions whose bond runs deep, famous as participants in one of the most celebrated products of the Indian literary imagination, the 'Bhágavad Gita' (*Bhagavad/gītā*), from the sixth book of the 'Maha·bhárata,' in which Krishna discourses at length to Árjuna to convince him to take the field of battle against his kin. While Krishna is the wise discourser on all things worldly and otherworldly, Shalya, as his direct counterpoint, converses with

Karna in order to undermine and misdirect. Thus while Krishna and Árjuna represent an amplification of the warrior/charioteer model, in which the charioteer at all times serves his warrior's best interests, Shalya and Karna represent its subversion. It is one of the tragic contours of Karna's life that, in seeking a companion capable of Árjuna's deep and lasting friendship with Krishna, he woos the one man who has already been turned against him. By the time that Karna suspects that Shalya is a Pándava plant, it is already too late, and Shalya is free, having obtained Duryódhana's and Karna's forbearance, to undermine Karna in whatever way that he can. It will be of little surprise to learn that, when Shalya lies dead on the battlefield, birds peck at his face and eat his tongue ('The Women,' MBh CE XI.23.4–5).

Though Karna and Shalya are often contrasting characters, their contrasts circulate around surprising similarities. Standing opposed in their anxiety over status and identity, this opposition suggests a comparable psychology that has its roots, perhaps, in each being a marginal character—Shalya, being from the land of the Madras, exists on the margins of the socio-cultural center of the Gangetic plains, and Karna is never quite a Dhartaráshtra or a Pándava. Both share a predilection for vanity, manifesting in Shalya's susceptibility to flattery and gifts of material wealth, and in Karna's tendency to boast and his disconcerting and narcissistic habit of referring to himself in the third person.[49] In addition, both side with the Dhartaráshtras despite sharing relationships of kin with the Pándavas. In their alliances, however, a telling contrast comes to light; a contrast that perhaps defines the key representational axis of the Karna and Shalya relationship. Karna proves himself time and again to be a remarkably loyal friend to Duryódhana, despite the fact that this loyalty will lead him—as he admits to knowing—to certain defeat and death. It is this loyalty that maintains the strength of his alliance with the Dhartaráshtras, despite the efforts of the Kuru-elders to disentangle this dangerous union, and stops him killing Shalya for his abuse.[50] Karna is, as HILTEBEITEL (1990: 260) has said, the "tragic model of true, loyal friendship." If Karna is remembered for his friendship, then Shalya is remembered for friendship's betrayal;[51] and through his treachery Shalya, "the betrayer of friends" (*mitra/drohin*), or, as Karna would have it, "the enemy with the face of a friend" (*mitra/mukhaḥ śatrur*),[52] becomes the exemplary traitor of the 'Maha·bhárata.' The alliance that his vanity has led him to contract with Duryódhana is no sooner made than betrayed, as he conspires with Yudhi·shthira—who nevertheless shall soon kill him on the last day of the war[53]—for Karna's, and consequently the Dhartaráshtras', ruin.

THE SANSKRIT TEXT

The following edition and translation is based on KINJAWADEKAR's edition of Nīlakaṇṭha's seventeenth-century "vulgate" version of the 'Maha·bhárata.' On occasion it was felt necessary to emend the text as presented in the edition available to me, usually due to a transparent case of typographical error, but also in cases where it seemed faulty or incomprehensible. In such cases, emendations have been made with reference to the Critical Edition (CE) and its extensive critical notes, and have generally followed variants from manuscripts of the same group within the genetic typology of the manuscript tradition. Emendations are marked in the Sanskrit text by an asterisk (*) and described in the notes.

Bibliography

SANSKRIT TEXTS

The Mahābhāratam with the Bharata Bhawadeepa commentary of Nīlakaṇṭha. [MBh CSL] Edited by PANDIT RAMACHANDRASHASTRI KINJAWADEKAR. 1979. 6 vols. New Delhi: Oriyantala Buksa Riprinta Karaporesana [1st edition 1936, Poona: Chitrashala Press].

The Mahābhārata. [MBh CE] Critically edited by V.S. SUKTHANKAR et al. 1927–66. 19 vols. Poona: Bhandarkar Oriental Research Institute.

Manusmṛti, with the Commentary of Kullūkabhaṭṭa. 1983. Edited by J.L. SHASTRI. Delhi: Motilal Banarsidass.

THE MAHA·BHÁRATA IN TRANSLATION

FITZGERALD, JAMES L. (trans. and ed.). 2004. *The Mahābhārata*, Volume 7 [Books 11 & 12 Part One]. Chicago and London: The University of Chicago Press.

GANGULI, KISARI MOHAN (trans.) [early editions ascribed to PRATAP CHANDRA ROY]. 1981–1982 (4th edition). *The Mahabharata of Krishna-Dwaipayana Vyasa translated into English prose from the original Sanskrit text.* New Delhi: Munshiram Manoharlal. [1st edition 1884–99.]

JOHNSON, WILLIAM J. 2005. (trans. and ed.) *Mahābhārata.* Book 3, *The Forest* (*Vanaparvan*). Volume 4. (Clay Sanskrit Library.) New York: New York University Press & the JJC Foundation.

MEILAND, JUSTIN. 2005. (trans.) *Mahābhārata.* Book 9, *Shalya* (*Śalyaparvan*). Volume 1. (Clay Sanskrit Library.) New York: New York University Press & the JJC Foundation.

VAN BUITENEN, J.A.B. (trans. and ed.). 1973–78. *The Mahābhārata*, Volumes 1–3 [Books 1–5]. Chicago and London: The University of Chicago Press.

WILMOT, PAUL. 2006. (trans.) *Mahābhārata*. Book 2, *The Great Hall* (*Sabhāparvan*). (Clay Sanskrit Library.) New York: New York University Press & the JJC Foundation.

SECONDARY SOURCES

BIARDEAU, MADELEINE. 1994. *Études de mythologie hindoue II: bhakti et avatāra*. Pondichéry: École Française d'Extrême-Orient.

DE BRUIN, HANNE M. 1998. *Karna's Death: A play by Pukalentippulavar*. Pondichéry: Institut Français de Pondichéry & Ecole Française d'Extrême-Orient.

DUMÉZIL, GEORGES. 1995. *Mythe et Épopée I, II, III*. Paris: Gallimard.

FELLER, DANIELLE. 2004. *The Sanskrit epics' representation of Vedic myths*. Delhi: Motilal Banarsidass.

HILTEBEITEL, ALF. 1980. 'Draupadī's Garments.' *Indo-Iranian Journal* 22: 87–112.

HILTEBEITEL, ALF. 1988. *The Cult of Draupadī 1. Mythologies: From Gingee to Kurukṣetra*. Chicago and London: The University of Chicago Press.

HILTEBEITEL, ALF. 1990. *The Ritual of Battle: Krishna in the Mahābhārata*. Albany: State University of New York Press.

MCGRATH, KEVIN. 2004. *Karṇa in epic Mahābhārata*. Leiden; Boston: Brill.

MONIER-WILLIAMS, MONIER. 1899. *A Sanskrit-English Dictionary, Etymologically and Philologically Arranged*. Oxford: Oxford University Press.

NANDY, ASHIS. 2001. 'The Journey to the Past as a Journey into the Self: The Remembered Village and the Poisoned City.' *An Ambiguous Journey to the City: The Village and Other Odd Ruins of the Self in the Indian Imagination*. New Delhi, Oxford University Press: 1–41.

OBERLIES, T. 1997. 'Pali, Pāṇini and 'Popular' Sanskrit.' *Journal of the Pali Text Society* 23:1–26.

OBERLIES, T. 2003. *A grammar of Epic Sanskrit*. Berlin: Walter de Gruyter.

PARKS, WARD. 1990. *Verbal Dueling in Heroic Narrative: The Homeric and Old English Traditions*. Princeton: Princeton University Press.

SAX, WILLIAM S. 2002. *Dancing the Self: Personhood and Performance in the Pāṇḍav Līlā of Garhwal*. New York: Oxford University Press.

SHULMAN, DAVID DEAN. 1985. *The King and the Clown in South Indian Myth and Poetry*. Princeton: Princeton University Press.

WOODS, JULIAN F. 2001. *Destiny and Human Initiative in the Mahā-bhārata*. Albany: State University of New York Press.

NOTES

1 See, for example, NANDY 2001: 24–41 for class conscious representations of Karna in modern film and literary re-workings of epic themes; McGRATH 2004: 226ff. for Karna as ideal warrior hero among Rajputs in western India; SAX 2002: 157–185 for Karna as deity in the central Himalayas of north India; SHULMAN 1985: 380–400, HILTEBEITEL 1988: 410–413 and DE BRUIN 1998 for Karna as hero and devotee of Krishna in South Indian traditions.

2 For this episode, see *Ādi/parvan*, MBh CE I.126–127.

3 *Ādi/parvan*, MBh CE I.127.11–14. Duryódhana's liberal attitude to social classes is, in the eyes of the epic poets, a marker of his essential corruption and one of the principal motivations given for the necessity of his demise. His attitude is representative of the breakdown of social order (*varṇa/saṃkara*) and customary behavior (*dharma/saṃkara*) that occurs when class divisions are not properly maintained.

4 Cf. *Karṇa/parvan*, MBh CE VIII.24.160 (CSL VIII.34.161, below).

5 The association between the Dhartaráshtras and Karna goes back to their births (McGRATH 2004: 28–29). The Dhartaráshtras' mother Gandhári, upon hearing that Kunti had given birth to a son "splendid like the sun," aborted the foetus that she had been carrying for two years. Before she could dispose of the resulting mass of flesh, Vyasa Dvaipáyana intervened and ensured that a hundred sons and one girl would develop from it (*Ādi/parvan*, MBh CE I.107). We do not know how Gandhári came by the information regarding Kunti giving birth, but this counts among a number of flirtations with the truth regarding Karna's true identity that are entertained by 'Maha·bhárata' characters (for others, in relation to Duryódhana see p. 19, in relation to Ádhiratha, see note 12).

6 Indeed, charioteers typically serve kshatriyas, a point that will cause Shalya, the king of the Madras, particular irritation when he is asked to become Karna's charioteer, as will be discussed below.

7 In *Strī/parvan*, MBh CE XI.21.1, as he lies dead on the ground, Karna is recalled as "unforgiving" (*amarṣin*) and "long angry" (*dīrgha/roṣa*). Cf. *Strī/parvan*, MBh CE XI.26.36.

8 Karna's birth is mentioned at *Ādi/parvan*, MBh CE I.57.82; 61.89 and 104, the latter containing the first extended account. A more thorough narration is in *Vana/parvan*, MBh CE III.287–293 (CSL III.303–309, JOHNSON 2005: 232–265). Karna's discovery of his parents' identity will be discussed below. The Pándavas are not told that Karna is their brother until after the war, in the last chapter of the *Strī/parvan*, which leads in to Yudhi·shthira's great lament for Karna at the beginning of the twelfth book of the 'Maha·bhárata,' the *Śānti/parvan*.

9 Shura was the father of Vasu·deva, the father of Krishna. Krishna, therefore, is the nephew of Kunti.

10 It is with the same spell that Kunti shall later, when the wife of Pandu, summon the gods Dharma, Indra and Vayu to father

Yudhi·shthira, Árjuna and Bhima, and Pandu's second wife, Madri, summons the twin gods the Ashvins to father the twins Nákula and Saha·deva.

11 In addition, Kunti was in her menses (*Vana/parvan*, MBh CE III.290.3; CSL III.306.3, JOHNSON 2005: 244–245), a state of impurity that forebodes the dramas that will beset her son.

12 *Vana/parvan*, MBh CE III.293.8 (CSL III.309.9, JOHNSON 2005: 262–263).

13 Karna's solar symbolism—which the epic poets never tire of referencing—provides a mythic underpinning to his rivalry with Árjuna, the son of the storm-god Indra, who is a rival to Surya in the earlier Vedic period of Indian mythology. This solar symbolism is discussed in DUMÉZIL 1995: 154–172 (paying particular attention to the Vedic connections), HILTEBEITEL 1980 (drawing an interesting contrast with Dráupadi, who is symbolically linked with the earth) and BIARDEAU 1994: 118 n. 85 (stressing his inheritance of the sun's fearsome aspect, which the sun displays at the destruction that closes an epoch).

14 For the episode with Krishna see *Udyoga/parvan*, MBh CE V.138–141, and with Kunti see *Udyoga/parvan*, MBh CE V.142–144.

15 *Udyoga/parvan*, MBh CE V.138.15–18. Karna would join the other Pándavas in sharing Dráupadi and become her sixth husband. The kingship offered is, of course, infinitely superior to the "little kingdom" Duryódhana grants Karna; the offer is for the overlordship of the Kurus. On this scene, see HILTEBEITEL 1990: 225–227.

16 For Karna's prediction of the Pándavas' victory, see, for example, *Udyoga/parvan*, MBh CE V.139.20; 141. On Karna and fate, see note 34.

17 See, for example, *Udyoga/parvan*, MBh CE V.139.29–57, where the metaphor is developed at length. Cf. Duryódhana in *Udyo-*

ga/parvan, MBh CE V.57.10–18. See SHULMAN 1985: 384–396; and, on the metaphor as it is developed in the 'Maha·bhárata,' FELLER, 2004: 253–293.

18 See for example *Vana/parvan*, MBh CE III.46.9–10, 35; 228.10; *Udyoga/parvan*, MBh CE V.22.7; 51.4–5; 128.3–8; *Droṇa/parvan*, MBh CE VII.110.1–5; *Karṇa/parvan*, MBh CE VIII.35.1–3 (CSL VIII.51.1–3, below).

19 For Bhishma's antipathy towards Karna, see note 28. For Drona, who often stands in support of Bhishma in his rebukes of Karna, see *Ādi/parvan*, MBh CE I.196; *Virāṭa/parvan*, MBh CE IV.37; *Udyoga/parvan*, MBh CE V.51.4–5 and 165.7–8. Kripa scolds Karna for bragging in *Virāṭa/parvan*, MBh CE IV.44–45 and *Droṇa/parvan*, MBh CE VII.133. One could add to this list Dhrita·rashtra's and Pandu's mixed-caste half brother Vídura, see *Ādi/parvan*, MBh CE I.197; *Sabhā/parvan* MBh CE II.61.81; *Vana/parvan* MBh CE III.5.14; and *Udyoga/parvan*, MBh CE V.35.66; 90; 142.

20 For this episode, see *Ādi/parvan*, MBh CE I.174–185.

21 In fact, Dráupadi becomes the wife of all five Pándavas.

22 *Ādi/parvan*, MBh CE I.181.20–21. While Karna's withdrawal may be interpreted as being motivated by his respect for brahmins (MCGRATH 2004: 81), it is notable that this did not stop Karna attacking Árjuna in the first place. Shortly afterwards, Karna is described as *śaṅkhita*, "disconcerted" or "alarmed." His withdrawal, therefore, seems to be motivated by a realization that he could not defeat the pseudo-brahmin warrior Árjuna armed with his divine weapons. Later, it is precisely the Brahma weapon Karna seeks from the brahmin warrior Rama Jamadágnya, as if to counter Árjuna's possession of the same weapon.

23 For the dicing episode, see *Sabhā/parvan*, MBh CE II.43–65.

24 See e.g. *Sabhā/parvan*, MBh CE II.72.17; *Vana/parvan*, MBh CE III.13.113; 28.8; 46; *Virāṭa/parvan*, MBh CE IV.45; 55; *Udyoga/parvan*, MBh CE V.29.36–37; 88.81; 157.1; 112.38–41; 168.9; *Karṇa/parvan*, MBh CE VIII.5.78–80 (CSL VIII.9.59–62, see below); CE 51.78–79 (CSL vol. II, 73.81–86); and, at his death, CE 67.1–4 (CSL vol. II, 91.1–7).

25 See, for example, *Udyoga/parvan*, MBh CE V.139.45; *Bhīṣma/parvan*, MBh CE VI.117.23 and *Karṇa/parvan*, MBh CE VIII.1.4–8 (CSL VIII.1.4–8, below).

26 For the first episode, see *Vana/parvan*, MBh CE III.226–243; for the second *Virāṭa/parvan*, MBh CE IV.24–62.

27 For Bhishma recalling these incidents, see *Vana/parvan*, MBh CE III.241.6–9; *Udyoga/parvan*, MBh CE V.21.16–21; 48.32–41; *Bhīṣma/parvan*, MBh CE VI.94.6–9 (cf. *Udyoga/parvan*, MBh CE V.61.15–17; 165.2–7 for other instances of rebuke from Bhishma). Others recall these episodes too, for example, Árjuna in *Virāṭa/parvan*, MBh CE IV.55.13–14 and Shalya in *Udyoga/parvan*, MBh CE V.8.32–34; *Karṇa/parvan*, MBh CE VIII.26.67–68 and 28.56–62 (CSL VIII.37.38–39 and 41.73–79, below). For the antagonism between Bhishma and Karna, see McGrath 2004: 100–111. This antagonism leads Karna to refuse to fight until Bhishma falls in battle.

28 In *Vana/parvan*, MBh CE III.240.19 and 32 the demon Náraka is said to incarnate Karna in order to kill Árjuna. In *Strī/parvan*, MBh CE XI.8.29 Vyasa tells Dhrita·rashtra that Karna (along with the other leading Dhartaráshtras) sprang up on earth for destruction. In referring to Karna's birth, *Śānti/parvan*, MBh CE XII.2.4 says "the child of a virgin was created, born for friction" (*saṃgharṣa/jananas tasmāt kanyā/garbho vinirmitaḥ*), the passive voice suggesting the hand of fate. On Karna's attitude to fate, see especially *Bhīṣma/parvan*, MBh CE VI.117, and the brief discussion in Woods 2001: 43–46.

29 *Vana/parvan*, MBh CE III.284–294 (CSL III.300–310, JOHNSON 2005: 220–275).

30 See his response to Surya at *Vana/parvan*, MBh CE III.284.23–39 (CSL III.300.23–39, JOHNSON 2005: 222–227).

31 A *rākṣasa* is a ferocious demoniacal being. The story of Bhima's marriage to the *rákshasi* Hidímba and the birth of Ghatótkacha are told in *Ādi/parvan*, MBh CE I.143. Ghatótkacha comes to be favored by the Pándavas. In *Ādi/parvan*, MBh CE I.143.38 he is described as having been created by Indra so that he might destroy Karna.

32 For Krishna's manipulation of Ghatótkacha, see *Droṇa/parvan*, MBh CE VII.147.31–52; for his actual spearing by Karna, *Droṇa/parvan*, MBh CE VII.154.51–63.

33 *Droṇa/parvan*, MBh CE VII.155.27: *so 'dya mānuṣatāṃ prāpto vimuktaḥ Śakra/dattayā.*

34 For the following, see *Śānti/parvan*, MBh CE XII.2–3. See also *Karṇa/parvan*, MBh CE VIII.29 (CSL VIII.42, below).

35 In the *Karṇa/parvan* version it is the cow's calf that is killed.

36 In *Karṇa/parvan*, CE 29.4–5 (CSL 42.4–5, below), Karna says that Indra had entered the body of the worm to thwart his attempts to gain the weapon.

37 See, in general, PARKS 1990, which focuses on flyting in classical Greek and Old English sources, but also includes a discussion of Karna and Árjuna. It is typical for disputants in a flyting contest to project "martial resolutions" (as PARKS describes it). In the Karna-Shalya exchange, the projected martial contest is not between Karna and Shalya (which Karna defers), but between Karna and Árjuna.

38 A duel that will occur in the second CSL volume of *Karṇa/parvan.*

39 Shalya's persuasion to become Karna's charioteer is found at *Karṇa/parvan*, MBh CE VIII.22–26 (CSL VIII.31–36, below), and includes the story of the destruction of Tri·pura in chapter 24 (CSL VIII.33–34, below).

40 For the following, the Shalya-Karna dispute proper, see *Karṇa/parvan*, MBh CE VIII.26–30 (CSL VIII.37–45, below).

41 See especially *Karṇa/parvan*, MBh CE VIII.23.28–38 (CSL VIII.32.40–50, below).

42 On this section, see also Hiltebeitel 1990: 272–278.

43 *Karṇa/parvan*, MBh CE VIII.30.60–62, 73–75 (CSL VIII.45.14–16, 45.28–30, below). This roughly corresponds to the "sacred geography" described by Manu and other ancient codifiers of custom and law. See *Manusmṛti* 2.17–24.

44 *Karṇa/parvan*, MBh CE VIII.27.71–72, 30.8 (CSL VIII.40.20–22, 44.5, below).

45 *Karṇa/parvan*, MBh CE VIII.30.83–87 (CSL VIII.45.40–46, below). Shalya does not deny that such things as Karna describes occur in Madra. Rather, he suggests that such things occur everywhere, and that a person is not necessarily marked by the vulgarity of their country.

46 For this episode, see *Udyoga/parvan*, MBh CE V.8. Shalya is brother of Madri, the birth mother of the two youngest Pándavas, Nákula and Saha·deva.

47 This is indicative of a central motif in the deaths of all four generals of the Dhartaráshtra army, for in each case the deaths involve sins. For the classic presentation of this motif, see Hiltebeitel 1990: 244–286. Yudhi·shthira will later feel great distress for his part in Karna's death, see note 8.

48 See *Udyoga/parvan*, MBh CE V.83; Hiltebeitel 1990: 241–242. On Krishna and Shalya, who are each related to one of

the Pándavas' maternal lines, cf. *Strī/parvan*, MBh CE XI.23.2, where Shalya is described as always vying with Krishna (see also the note to this verse in FITZGERALD 2004: 675).

49 See for example *Karṇa/parvan*, MBh CE VIII.30.6 (CSL VIII. 43.6, below); CSL 49.59, below (not in the Critical Edition); and CE 57.38 (CSL vol. II, 79.54).

50 *Karṇa/parvan*, MBh CE VIII.29.20–21 (CSL VIII.42.29–30, below), and CSL 43.7–9, below (excised from the Critical Edition).

51 On Karna, Shalya, friendship and its betrayal, see HILTEBEITEL 1990: 259–266.

52 *Karṇa/parvan*, MBh CE VIII.27.28 (CSL VIII.39.11, below). Cf. *Karṇa/parvan*, MBh CE VIII.27.68 (CSL VIII.40.18, below)

53 Further on Shalya, see MEILAND, 2005.

1–9
DHRITA·RASHTRA'S LAMENT

VAIŚAMPĀYANA uvāca:

1.1 TATO DROṆE HATE, rājan, Duryodhana|mukhā nṛpāḥ
bhṛśam udvigna|manaso Droṇa|putram upāgaman.
te Droṇam anuśocantaḥ kaśmal'|âbhihat'|âujasaḥ
paryupāsanta śok'|ārtās tataḥ Śāradvatī|sutam.
te muhūrtaṃ samāśvasya hetubhiḥ śāstra|saṃmitaiḥ
rātry|āgame mahī|pālāḥ svāni veśmāni bhejire.

te veśmasv api, Kauravya, pṛthv'|īśā n' āpnuvan sukham
cintayantaḥ kṣayaṃ tīvraṃ duḥkha|śoka|samanvitāḥ.
1.5 viśeṣataḥ sūta|putro, rājā c' âiva Suyodhanaḥ,
Duḥśāsanaś ca, Śakuniḥ Saubalaś ca mahā|balaḥ
uṣitās te niśāṃ tāṃ tu Duryodhana|niveśane,
cintayantaḥ parikleśān Pāṇḍavānāṃ mah'|ātmanām,
yat tad dyūte parikliṣṭā Kṛṣṇā c' ānāyitā sabhām,
tat smaranto 'nuśocanto bhṛśam udvigna|cetasaḥ.
tathā tu saṃcintayatāṃ tān kleśān dyūta|kāritān
duḥkhena kṣaṇa|dā, rājan, jagām' âbda|śat'|ôpamā.

tataḥ prabhāte vimale, sthitā diṣṭasya śāsane,
cakrur āvaśyakaṃ sarve vidhi|dṛṣṭena karmaṇā.
1.10 te kṛtv" âvaśya|kāryāṇi, samāśvasya ca, Bhārata,
yogam ājñāpayām āsur, yuddhāya ca viniryayuḥ.
Karṇaṃ senā|patiṃ kṛtvā kṛta|kautuka|maṅgalāḥ,
pūjayitvā dvija|śreṣṭhān dadhi|pātra|ghṛt'|âkṣataiḥ,
gobhir, aśvaiś ca, niṣkaiś ca, vāsobhiś ca mahā|dhanaiḥ,
vandyamānā jay'|āśīrbhiḥ sūta|māgadha|bandibhiḥ.

VAISHAMPÁYANA said:

After Drona had been killed, king, in utter despair 1.1
the kings went up to Drona's son* with Duryódhana in their lead. Mourning for Drona, their vigor sapped by despair and pained with sorrow, they sat around the son of Sharádvat's daughter.* Having consoled him for a short while with reasons consistent with learned texts, as night fell the princes retired to their own tents.

Those rulers of the earth, Kaurávya, could not find solace even in their own tents. Brooding on their terrible loss, they
were completely filled with sadness and grief. But, above 1.5
all, the charioteer's son,* King Suyódhana,* Duhshásana, and Súbala's immensely powerful son Shákuni dwelled that night in Duryódhana's encampment brooding over the troubles of the great Pándavas, such as when Krishná* was led to the assembly hall and tormented during the dice game. Remembering that and grieving, they were utterly despondent. And as they mulled over those troubles that were the outcome of the dice game, the night passed painfully, king, as though it were a hundred years.

Then, when dawn broke clear, they all observed the command of fate and performed the obligatory observance with the rite prescribed by rule.

Once they had performed the obligatory rites and recov- 1.10
ered their poise, Bhárata, they commanded that their horses be harnessed and went forth for battle—the auspicious ceremonies completed after they had made Karna general and honored the finest brahmins with barley-corn, ghee, bowls of yoghurt, cows and horses, golden collars and costly gar-

tath" âiva Pāṇḍavā, rājan, kṛta|pūrv'|āhṇika|kriyāḥ
śibirān niryayus tūrṇaṃ yuddhāya kṛta|niścayāḥ.
tataḥ pravavṛte yuddhaṃ tumulaṃ, loma|harṣaṇam
Kurūṇāṃ Pāṇḍavānāṃ ca paraspara|jay'|âiṣiṇām.
1.15 tayor dve divase yuddhaṃ Kuru|Pāṇḍava|senayoḥ
Karṇe senā|patau, rājan, babhūv' âdbhuta|darśanam!
tataḥ śatru|kṣayaṃ kṛtvā su|mahāntaṃ raṇe Vṛṣaḥ
paśyatāṃ Dhārtarāṣṭrāṇāṃ Phālgunena nipātitaḥ.
tatas tu Saṃjayaḥ sarvaṃ gatvā Nāga|puraṃ drutam
ācaṣṭa Dhṛtarāṣṭrāya yad vṛttaṃ Kuru|jāṅgale.

JANAMEJAYA uvāca:

Āpageyaṃ hataṃ śrutvā, Droṇaṃ c' âpi mahā|ratham,
ājagāma parām ārtiṃ vṛddho rāj" Âmbikā|sutaḥ.
sa śrutvā nihataṃ Karṇaṃ Duryodhana|hit'|âiṣiṇam,
kathaṃ, dvija|vara, prāṇān adhārayata duḥkhitaḥ?
1.20 yasmiñ jay'|āśāṃ putrāṇām samamanyata pārthivaḥ,
tasmin hate sa Kauravyaḥ kathaṃ prāṇān adhārayat?
dur|maraṃ tad ahaṃ manye nṛṇāṃ kṛcchre 'pi vartatām,
yatra Karṇaṃ hataṃ śrutvā n' âtyajaj jīvitaṃ nṛpaḥ.
tathā Śāntanavaṃ vṛddhaṃ, brahman, Bāhlikam eva ca,
Droṇaṃ ca, Somadattaṃ ca, Bhūriśravasam eva ca,
tath" âiva c' ânyān suhṛdaḥ, putrān, pautrāṃś ca pātitān

ments. All the while they were lauded with blessings for victory from the charioteers, panegyrists and bards.

Similarly, king, the Pándavas, their morning rites completed, quickly set out from camp resolved on battle.

The Kurus and Pándavas then resumed their tumultuous, hair-raising battle, each eager for victory over the other. The 1.15
two armies of the Kurus and Pándavas battled for two days during Karna's time as general, king. It was a spectacular sight!

Then, after he had destroyed a vast number of enemies in the battle, Vrisha* was felled by Phálguna while the Dhartaráshtras looked on.

Sánjaya then went quickly to Naga·pura* and related to Dhrita·rashtra everything that had happened on the plain of the Kurus.

JANAM·ÉJAYA said:

When he heard that the son of the river* and the great warrior Drona had been struck down, the old king, Ámbika's son, became terribly distressed. In such pain after hearing that Karna, who sought the best for Duryódhana, had been killed, best of brahmins, how did he hold his life together?
The king had fancied that hope for his sons' victory lay on 1.20
that man. When he was killed, how did that Kaurávya hold his life together? I reckon it's difficult to die—even when men are in such a crisis!—since the king did not give up his life once he'd heard that Karna had been killed. Similarly, brahmin, having heard that Shántanu's distinguished son,* Báhlika, Drona, Soma·datta and Bhuri·shravas, and other

śrutvā yan n' âjahāt prāṇāṃs, tan manye duṣ|karaṃ, dvija!
etan me sarvam ācakṣva vistareṇa, mahā|mune,
na hi tṛpyāmi pūrveṣāṃ śṛṇvānaś caritaṃ mahat!

VAIŚAMPĀYANA uvāca:

2.1 HATE KARṆE, mahā|rāja, niśi Gāvalgaṇis tadā
dīno yayau Nāga|puram aśvair vāta|samair jave.
sa Hāstina|puraṃ gatvā bhṛśam udvigna|cetanaḥ
jagāma Dhṛtarāṣṭrasya kṣayaṃ prakṣīṇa|bāndhavam.
sa tam udvīkṣya rājānaṃ kaśmal'|âbhihat'|âujasam
vavande prāñjalir bhūtvā mūrdhnā pādau nṛpasya ha.
saṃpūjya ca yathā|nyāyaṃ Dhṛtarāṣṭraṃ mahī|patim,
«hā kaṣṭam! iti» c' ôktvā sa tato vacanam ādade:
2.5 «Saṃjayo 'haṃ, kṣiti|pate. kac cid āste sukhaṃ bhavān?
sva|doṣeṇ' āpadaṃ prāpya kac cin n' âdya vimuhyasi?
hitāny uktāni Vidura|Droṇa|Gāṅgeya|Keśavaiḥ
a|gṛhītāny anusmṛtya, kac cin na kuruṣe vyathām?
Rāma|Nārada|Kaṇv'|ādyair hitam uktaṃ sabhā|tale
na gṛhītam anusmṛtya, kac cin na kuruṣe vyathām?
suhṛdas tvadd|hite yuktān Bhīṣma|Droṇa|mukhān paraiḥ
nihatān yudhi saṃsmṛtya, kac cin na kuruṣe vyathām?»
tam evaṃ|vādinaṃ rājā sūta|putraṃ kṛt'|âñjalim
su|dīrgham atha niḥśvasya duḥkh'|ārta idam abravīt.

allies, sons and grandsons, had been felled, he did not give up his own life. I reckon this is remarkable, brahmin!

Great sage, tell me everything at length. For I'm not yet sated as I listen to the great deeds of my ancestors!

VAISHAMPÁYANA said:

AFTER KARNA HAD been killed, great king, Gaválgana's 2.1
dejected son* then traveled through the night to Naga·pura using horses equal to the wind in speed. Having gone to Hástina·pura, in utter despair he went to Dhrita·rashtra's residence, which had been emptied of his kinsmen. Looking up at that king, whose vigor had been sapped by despair, he joined his hands together and honored him with his head lowered to the king's feet. And once he had properly honored Dhrita·rashtra, the lord of the earth, he gasped out, "Ah! This is wretched!" and then began this speech:

"I am Sánjaya,* lord of the earth. Are you content, sir? 2.5
Having brought about this disaster through your own failings, are you not now bewildered? Remembering the good advice offered by Vídura, Drona, Ganga's son* and Késhava* that you did not accept, don't you feel devastated? Remembering the good advice offered by Rama, Nárada, Kanva and others on the assembly hall floor that you did not accept, don't you feel devastated? Now that you recall your allies led by Bhishma and Drona who, intent on your well-being, were slain in battle by enemies, don't you feel devastated?"

To the charioteer's son* who had joined his palms together and spoken this, the distressed king, after sighing at length, then said this.

DHṚTARĀṢṬRA uvāca:

2.10 «Āpageye hate śūre divy'|âstravati, Saṃjaya,
Droṇe ca param'|êṣv|āse bhṛśaṃ me vyathitaṃ manaḥ,
yo rathānāṃ sahasrāṇi daṃśitānāṃ daś' âiva tu
ahany ahani tejasvī nijaghne Vasu|saṃbhavaḥ.
taṃ hataṃ Yajñasenasya putreṇ' êha Śikhaṇḍinā
Pāṇḍavey'|âbhiguptena śrutvā me vyathitaṃ manaḥ!
Bhārgavaḥ pradadau yasmai param'|âstraṃ mah"|āhave;
sākṣād Rāmeṇa yo bālye dhanur|veda upākṛtaḥ;
yasya prasādāt Kaunteyā rāja|putrā mahā|rathāḥ
mahā|rathatvaṃ saṃprāptās, tath" ânye vasu|dh"|âdhipāḥ;
2.15 taṃ Droṇaṃ nihataṃ śrutvā
Dhṛṣṭadyumnena saṃyuge,
satya|saṃdhaṃ, mah"|êṣv|āsaṃ,
bhṛśaṃ me vyathitaṃ manaḥ!
yayor loke pumān astre na samo 'sti catur|vidhe;
tau Droṇa|Bhīṣmau śrutvā tu hatau me vyathitaṃ manaḥ!
trailokye yasya c' âstreṣu na pumān vidyate samaḥ,
taṃ Droṇaṃ nihataṃ śrutvā kim akurvata māmakāḥ?
saṃśaptakānāṃ ca bale Pāṇḍavena mah"|ātmanā
Dhanaṃjayena vikramya gamite Yama|sādanam,
Nārāyaṇ'|âstre nihate Droṇa|putrasya dhīmataḥ,
vipradruteṣv anīkeṣu, kim akurvata māmakāḥ?
vipradrutān ahaṃ manye nimagnāñ śoka|sāgare
2.20 plavamānān hate Droṇe, sanna|naukān iv' ârṇave!

DHRITA·RASHTRA said:

"When the river's heroic son who possessed the divine 2.10
weapons was struck down, Sánjaya, and then Drona the superb archer too, I was utterly devastated! The Vasus' powerful offspring* struck down ten thousand armor-clad warriors day after day. When I heard that he had been killed here by Yajna·sena's son Shikhándin, who was protected by the Pándava,* I was devastated!

Bhárgava* gave a superb missile to Drona for a great battle. Rama* himself granted him the lore of archery when he was a child. Through his graciousness those great warriors, Kunti's sons* the princes, and other rulers of the earth, became great warriors. When I heard that Drona, a mighty 2.15
archer who was true to his promises, had been killed in battle by Dhrishta·dyumna, I was utterly devastated!

In this world there is no man the equal of those two in the four kinds of weapons; when I heard that Drona and Bhishma had been struck down, I was devastated!

When they heard that Drona had been killed, to whom no man in the triple-world is the equal in weapons, what did my sons do? And when the great Pándava Dhanan·jaya* attacked and sent the army of oath-bound warriors* to Yama's place, and when the Naráyana weapon of Drona's intelligent son had been struck down, and when my armies fled, what did my sons do?

I think they fled and sank into an ocean of grief when 2.20
Drona was killed, drifting as though shipless in the sea!

Duryodhanasya, Karṇasya, Bhojasya Kṛtavarmaṇaḥ,
Madra|rājasya Śalyasya, Drauṇeś c' âiva, Kṛpasya ca,
mat|putrasya ca śeṣasya, tath" ânyeṣāṃ ca, Saṃjaya,
vipradruteṣv anīkeṣu mukha|varṇo 'bhavat katham?
etat sarvaṃ yathā vṛttaṃ, tathā, Gāvalgaṇe, mama
ācakṣva Pāṇḍaveyānāṃ māmakānāṃ ca vikramam!»

SAṂJAYA uvāca:

«tav' âparādhād yad vṛttaṃ Kauraveyeṣu, māriṣa,
tac chrutvā mā vyathāṃ kārṣīr! diṣṭe na vyathate budhaḥ.
yasmād a|bhāvī bhāvī vā bhaved artho naraṃ prati
2.25 a|prāptau tasya, vā prāptau na kaś cid vyathate budhaḥ!»

DHṚTARĀṢṬRA uvāca:

«na vyath" âbhyadhikā kā cid vidyate mama, Saṃjaya;
diṣṭam etat purā manye. kathayasva yath"|êcchakam!»

SAṂJAYA uvāca:

3.1 «HATE DROṆE mah"|êṣv|āse tava putrā mahā|rathāḥ
babhūvur a|svastha|mukhā, viṣaṇṇā, gata|cetasaḥ.
avāṅ|mukhāḥ śastra|bhṛtaḥ sarva eva, viśāṃ pate,
avekṣamāṇāḥ śok'|ārtā n' âbhyabhāṣan parasparam.
tān dṛṣṭvā vyathit'|ākārān sainyāni tava, Bhārata,
ūrdhvam eva niraikṣanta duḥkha|trastāny anekaśaḥ.
śastrāṇy eṣāṃ tu, rāj'|êndra, śoṇit'|âktāni sarvaśaḥ
prābhraśyanta kar'|âgrebhyo, dṛṣṭvā Droṇaṃ hataṃ yudhi.
3.5 tāni baddhāny, a|riṣṭāni, lambamānāni, Bhārata,
adṛśyanta, mahā|rāja, nakṣatrāṇi yathā divi.

When the armies had fled, what was the color of the faces of Duryódhana, Karna, the Bhoja Krita·varman, Shalya the king of the Madras, Drona's son and Kripa, and of my surviving sons, and of the others, Sánjaya? Exactly as it all happened, son of Gaválgana, tell me about the valor of Pandu's and my sons!"

SÁNJAYA said:

"Once you've heard what has happened to the Kaurávyas because of your mistake, dear friend, don't be devastated! A wise man does not become devastated at fate. Since a
goal may be either destined or not for a man, whether it 2.25
has or has not been attained a wise man does not become devastated!"

DHRITA·RASHTRA said:

"I'm not overly devastated, Sánjaya. I reckon it was fated already. Report as you see fit!"

SÁNJAYA said:

"WHEN DRONA the great archer was killed, your sons the 3.1
great warriors became dejected and dispirited, their faces ill. All those weapon-bearers had downcast faces, lord of the people, and, looking about tormented by grief, did not utter a word to one another.

Seeing their devastated faces, Bhárata, your troops looked upwards repeatedly, quivering with distress. Having seen Drona killed in battle, lord of kings, their weapons slipped
from their fingertips, completely smothered in blood. Those 3.5
weapons still gripped, Bhárata, boding misfortune as they sank down, looked like stars sinking in the sky, great king.

tathā tu stimitaṃ dṛṣṭvā, gata|sattvam, avasthitam
balaṃ tava, mahā|rāja, rājā Duryodhano 'bravīt:
‹bhavatāṃ bāhu|vīryaṃ hi samāśritya mayā yudhi
Pāṇḍaveyāḥ samāhūtā yuddhaṃ c' êdaṃ pravartitam!
tad idaṃ nihate Droṇe viṣaṇṇam iva lakṣyate;
yudhyamānāś ca samare yodhā vadhyanti sarvaśaḥ.
jayo v" âpi vadho v" âpi yudhyamānasya saṃyuge;
bhavet kim atra citraṃ vai? yudhyadhvaṃ sarvato|mukhāḥ!
3.10 paśyadhvaṃ ca mah"|ātmānaṃ
Karṇaṃ Vaikartanaṃ yudhi
pracarantaṃ mah"|êṣv|āsaṃ
divyair astrair mahā|balam!
yasya vai yudhi saṃtrāsāt Kuntī|putro Dhanaṃjayaḥ
nivartate sadā mandaḥ, siṃhāt kṣudra|mṛgo yathā;
yena nāg'|âyuta|prāṇo Bhīmaseno mahā|balaḥ
mānuṣeṇ' âiva yuddhena tām avasthāṃ praveśitaḥ;
yena divy'|âstra|vic chūro māyāvī sa Ghaṭotkacaḥ
a|moghayā raṇe śaktyā nihato bhairavaṃ nadan;
tasya dur|vāra|vīryasya, satya|saṃdhasya, dhīmataḥ
bāhvor draviṇam akṣayyam adya drakṣyatha saṃyuge!
3.15 Droṇa|putrasya vikrāntaṃ, Rādheyasy' âiva c' ôbhayoḥ
paśyantu Pāṇḍu|putrās te, Viṣṇu|Vāsavayor iva!
sarva eva bhavantaś ca śāktāḥ pratyekaśo 'pi vā
Pāṇḍu|putrān rāṇe hantuṃ sa|sainyān. kim u saṃhatāḥ?
vīryavantaḥ, kṛt'|âstrāś ca, drakṣyath' âdya parasparam!›»

But, seeing your army standing by motionless like this, its courage gone, great king, King Duryódhana said:

'Relying upon your strength of arms in battle, good men, I challenged Pandu's sons to battle, and this battle has come to pass! With Drona killed everything seems hopeless; but warriors fighting in war are always killed. There is either victory or death for one fighting in battle. Should it be so strange in this case? Face all directions and fight!

Look at great Karna Vaikártana as that mighty archer 3.10
roams about in battle with his divine weapons! It is for fear of him in battle that Kunti's weak son Dhanan·jaya always retreats, like a small deer from a lion. It was by him, fighting by ordinary means alone,* that mighty Bhima·sena, whose power is like a myriad of elephants, was brought to this situation. With his unerring spear, it was he who killed Ghatótkacha in battle as he roared horrifically, though that hero knew the divine weapons and had the power of illusion. Today you will see in battle the unrelenting strength of the arms of that brilliant man whose vigor is irrepressible and who holds to his promises!

Let Pandu's sons see that the might of both Drona's and 3.15
Radha's sons* is like that of Vishnu and Indra! All of you good men are certainly able, even single-handedly, to kill in battle the sons of Pandu with their armies. How much more if united? You're strong and skilled with your weapons! Look to one another today!'"

SAMJAYA uvāca:

«evam uktvā tataḥ Karṇaṃ cakre senā|patiṃ tadā
tava putro mahā|vīryo bhrātṛbhiḥ sahito, 'n|agha.
saināpatyam ath' âvāpya Karṇo, rājan, mahā|rathaḥ
siṃha|nādaṃ vinady' ôccaiḥ prāyudhyata raṇ'|ôtkaṭaḥ.
sa Sṛñjayānāṃ sarveṣāṃ, Pāñcālānāṃ ca, māriṣa,
Kekayānāṃ, Videhānāṃ cakāra kadanaṃ mahat.
3.20 tasy' êṣu|dhārāḥ śataśaḥ prādur āsañ char'|âsanāt
agre puṅkheṣu saṃsaktā, yathā bhramara|paṅktayaḥ.
sa pīḍayitvā Pañcālān, Pāṇḍavāṃś ca tarasvinaḥ,
hatvā sahasraśo yodhān Arjunena nipātitaḥ!»

VAIŚAMPĀYANA uvāca:

4.1 ETAC CHRUTVĀ, mahā|rāja, Dhṛtarāṣṭro 'mbikā|sutaḥ,
śokasy' ântam a|paśyan vai, hataṃ matvā Suyodhanam,
vihvalaḥ patito bhūmau naṣṭa|cetā iva dvipaḥ.
tasmin nipatite bhūmau vihvale rāja|sattame,
ārta|nādo mahān āsīt strīṇāṃ, Bharata|sattama.
sa śabdaḥ pṛthivīṃ sarvāṃ pūrayām āsa sarvaśaḥ.
śok'|ârṇave mahā|ghore nimagnā Bharata|striyaḥ
rurudur duḥkha|śok'|ārtā, bhṛśam udvigna|cetasaḥ.
4.5 rājānaṃ ca samāsādya Gāndhārī, Bharata'|rṣabha,
niḥsaṃjñā patitā bhūmau, sarvāṇy antaḥ|purāṇi ca.
tatas tāḥ Saṃjayo, rājan, samāśvāsayad āturāḥ,
muhyamānāḥ su|bahuśo muñcantyo vāri netra|jam.
samāśvastāḥ striyas tās tu vepamānā muhur muhuḥ,
kadalya iva vātena dhūyamānāḥ samantataḥ.

SÁNJAYA said:

"After saying this, faultless one, together with his brothers your immensely powerful son made Karna general. Then, king, once he'd gained the generalship, the mighty warrior Karna loudly roared a lion's roar and attacked, furious in battle. Dear friend, he caused great carnage among all the Srínjayas, Panchálas, Kékayas and Vidéhas. Arrow volleys 3.20
appeared from his bow by the hundred joined nock to tip like a row of bees. After torturing the Panchálas and the bold Pándavas and killing warriors by the thousand, he was felled by Árjuna!"

VAISHAMPÁYANA said:

WHEN HE HEARD this, great king, Ámbika's son Dhrita· 4.1
rashtra thought Suyódhana already dead and, seeing no end to his grief, fell to the ground in anguish like an elephant bereft of sense.

When that best of kings fell to the ground in anguish, there was a great cry of pain from the women, best of Bharatas.* That sound spread out everywhere over the entire earth. Sinking into a terrible sea of grief, the Bharata women, traumatized by misery and grief, wailed in utter despair. And once she reached the king, bull among Bharatas, 4.5
Gandhári fell unconscious on the ground, as did all the women living in the palace.

King, Sánjaya then consoled those suffering and bewildered women as they continually shed many tears. But, though he comforted them, they trembled incessantly like banana trees thoroughly shaken by the wind.

rājānaṃ Viduraś c' âpi prajñā|cakṣuṣam īśvaram
āśvāsayām āsa tadā, siñcaṃs toyena Kauravam.
sa labdhvā śanakaiḥ saṃjñāṃ, tāś ca dṛṣṭvā striyo nṛpaḥ,
unmatta iva, rāj'|êndra, sthitas tūṣṇīṃ, viśāṃ pate.
4.10 tato dhyātvā ciraṃ kālaṃ, niḥśvasya ca punaḥ punaḥ,
svān putrān garhayām āsa, bahu mene ca Pāṇḍavān.

garhayaṃś c' ātmano buddhiṃ, Śakuneḥ Saubalasya ca,
dhyātvā tu su|ciraṃ kālaṃ, vepamāno muhur muhuḥ,
saṃstabhya ca mano bhūyo rājā dhairya|samanvitaḥ
punar Gāvalgaṇiṃ sūtaṃ paryapṛcchata Saṃjayam.

«yat tvayā kathitaṃ vākyaṃ, śrutaṃ, Saṃjaya, tan mayā.
kac cid Duryodhanaḥ, sūta, na gato vai Yama|kṣayam?
jaye nirāśaḥ putro me satataṃ jaya|kāmukaḥ;
brūhi, Saṃjaya, tattvena punar uktāṃ kathām imām!»
4.15 evam ukto 'bravīt sūto rājānaṃ, Janamejaya:
«hato Vaikartano, rājan, saha putrair mahā|rathaḥ,
bhrātṛbhiś ca mah"|êṣv|āsaiḥ sūta|putrais tanu|tyajaiḥ!
Duḥśāsanaś ca nihataḥ Pāṇḍavena yaśasvinā,
pītaṃ ca rudhiraṃ kopād Bhīmasenena saṃyuge!»

VAIŚAMPĀYANA UVĀCA:

5.1 ITI ŚRUTVĀ, mahā|rāja, Dhṛtarāṣṭro 'mbikā|sutaḥ
abravīt Saṃjayaṃ sūtaṃ śoka|saṃvigna|mānasaḥ:

And then, sprinkling the Káurava king with water, Vídura revived the lord whose eyes were wisdom.* After gradually regaining consciousness and seeing those women, lord of kings, the king silently stood up as though he was drunk, lord of the people. He brooded for a long time and sighed 4.10
continually and then condemned his own sons and praised the Pándavas.

Condemning his own judgement and that of Súbala's son Shákuni, he brooded for a very long time, trembling continually all the while. Composing his mind and filled with resolve once again, the king further questioned Gavál-gana's son, the herald Sánjaya.

"I have listened to this statement you've narrated, Sánjaya. Herald, why has Duryódhana not gone to Yama's house? My son who always longed for victory has no hope for victory. Tell me again truthfully, Sánjaya, this tale you've told!"

Spoken to in this way, Janam·éjaya, the herald said to 4.15
the king: "King, that mighty warrior Vaikártana* has been killed together with his sons and brothers, those mighty archers the charioteer's sons who put their lives at risk! And Duhshásana has been killed by the celebrated Pándava. And out of rage Bhima·sena quaffed his blood in the battle!"

VAISHAMPÁYANA said:

AFTER HEARING THIS, great king, Ámbika's son Dhri- 5.1
ta·rashtra, his mind feverish with grief, said to the herald Sánjaya:

«duṣ|praṇītena me, tāta, putrasy' â|dīrgha|jīviṇaḥ
hataṃ Vaikartanaṃ śrutvā śoko marmāṇi kṛntati.
tasya me saṃśayaṃ chindhi duḥkha|pāraṃ titīrṣataḥ!
Kurūṇāṃ Sṛñjayānāṃ ca ke ca jīvanti? ke mṛtāḥ?»

SAMJAYA uvāca:

«hataḥ Śāṃtanavo, rājan, dur|ādharṣaḥ pratāpavān,
hatvā Pāṇḍava|yodhānām arbudaṃ daśabhir dinaiḥ.
5.5 tathā Droṇo mah"|êṣv|āsaḥ Pañcālānāṃ ratha|vrajān
nihatya yudhi dur|dharṣaḥ paścād rukma|ratho hataḥ.
hata|śeṣasya Bhīṣmeṇa Droṇena ca mah"|ātmanā
ardhaṃ nihatya sainyasya Karṇo Vaikartano hataḥ.
Viviṃśatir, mahā|rāja, rāja|putro mahā|balaḥ
Ānarta|yodhāñ śataśo nihatya nihato raṇe.
tathā putro Vikarṇas te kṣatra|vratam anusmaran
kṣīṇa|vāh'|āyudhaḥ śūraḥ sthito 'bhimukhataḥ parān,
ghora|rūpān parikleśān Duryodhana|kṛtān bahūn,
pratijñāṃ smaratā c' âiva Bhīmasenena pātitaḥ.
5.10 Vind'|Ânuvindāv Āvantyau rāja|putrau mahā|rathau
kṛtvā tv a|sukaraṃ karma gatau Vaivasvata|kṣayam.
Sindhu|rāṣṭra|mukhān' îha daśa rāṣṭrāṇi yāni ha,
vaśe tiṣṭhanti vīrasya yaḥ sthitas tava śāsane.
akṣauhiṇīr daś' âikāṃ ca vinirjitya śitaiḥ śaraiḥ
Arjunena hato, rājan, mahā|vīryo Jayadrathaḥ.

"Dear fellow, having heard that Vaikártana was killed due to the poor leadership of my son who has not lived long, grief tears my guts apart. I want to bring an end to my pain! Cut away my doubts about this! Of the Kurus and Srínjayas, who live? And who are dead?"

SÁNJAYA said:

"King, Shántanu's majestic and unassaiblable son was killed after he'd slaughtered a mass of Pándava warriors
over ten days. Similarly, unconquerable Drona, the mighty 5.5
archer with the golden chariot, was killed from behind after slaughtering hordes of Panchála warriors in battle. Karna Vaikártana was killed after he had slaughtered half those troops left surviving by Bhishma and great Drona.

The powerful prince Vivínshati was killed in battle, great king, after destroying warriors from Ánarta by the hundred. And your son, the hero Vikárna, recalling his warrior's vow when he'd lost his horses and weapons, stood facing his enemies. Remembering his vow and the many terrible troubles
brought about by Duryódhana, Bhima·sena felled him. Vin- 5.10
da and Anuvínda, both mighty warrior princes from Avánti, went to Yama's home after performing a task that was not easy.

Ten kingdoms having the kingdom of Sindhu at their head were under the authority of a hero who obeyed your command. King, that powerful man Jayad·ratha was slaughtered by Árjuna after he defeated eleven *aksháuhini* armies* with his sharp arrows.

tathā Duryodhana|sutas tarasvī, yuddha|dur|madaḥ,
vartamānaḥ pituḥ śāstre Saubhadreṇa nipātitaḥ.
tathā Dauḥśāsaniḥ śūro, bāhu|śālī, raṇ'|ôtkaṭaḥ
Draupadeyena saṃgamya gamito Yama|sādanam.
5.15 Kirātānām adhipatiḥ sāgar'|ânūpa|vāsinām,
deva|rājasya dharm'|ātmā priyo bahu|mataḥ sakhā,
Bhagadatto mahī|pālaḥ kṣatra|dharma|rataḥ sadā,
Dhanaṃjayena vikramya gamito Yama|sādanam.
tathā Kaurava|dāyādo nyasta|śastro, mahā|yaśāḥ,
hato Bhūriśravā, rājañ, śūraḥ Sātyakinā yudhi.
Śrutāyur, api c' Âmbaṣṭhaḥ kṣatriyāṇāṃ dhuraṃ|dharaḥ
carann a|bhītavat saṃkhye nihataḥ Savyasācinā.
tava putraḥ sad" âmarṣī, kṛt'|âstro, yuddha|dur|madaḥ
Duḥśāsano, mahā|rāja, Bhīmasenena pātitaḥ.
5.20 yasya, rājan, gaj'|ânīkaṃ bahu|sāhasram, adbhutam,
Sudakṣiṇaḥ sa saṃgrāme nihataḥ Savyasācinā.
Kosalānām adhipatir hatvā bahu|matān parān
Saubhadreṇ' êha vikramya gamito Yama|sādanam.
bahuśo yodhayitvā tu Bhīmasenaṃ mahā|ratham
Citrasenas tava suto Bhīmasenena pātitaḥ.
Madra|rāj'|ātmajaḥ śūraḥ, pareṣāṃ bhaya|vardhanaḥ,
asi|carma|dharaḥ, śrīmān Saubhadreṇa nipātitaḥ.
samaḥ Karṇasya samare yaḥ, sa Karṇasya paśyataḥ
Vṛṣaseno mahā|tejāḥ, śīghr'|âstro, dṛḍha|vikramaḥ,
5.25 Abhimanyor vadhaṃ śrutvā, pratijñām api c' ātmanaḥ,
Dhanaṃjayena vikramya gamito Yama|sādanam.

In the same way, while following his father's command, Duryódhana's bold and battle-mad son was felled by Subhádra's son. And Duhshásana's heroic son, strong-armed and furious in battle, was sent to Yama's house by Dráupadi's boy after he came upon him.

The coast-dwelling Kirátas' ruler Bhaga·datta, the soul 5.15
of the law, a much esteemed and dear friend of the king of the gods, was a king always devoted to the warriors' law. He was attacked by Dhanan·jaya and sent to Yama's place.

And the very famous kinsman of the Káuravas, king, the heroic Bhuri·shravas, gave up his weapon and was killed in battle by Sátyaki. And Shrutáyus too, a leader of kshatriyas from Ambáshtha roaming about fearlessly in battle, was killed by the Left-handed archer.* Your ever impatient son Duhshásana, great king, battle-mad and skilled with his weapons, was felled by Bhima·sena. Sudákshina, king, 5.20
whose stupendous army of elephants numbered in the many thousands, was killed in battle by the Left-handed archer. After he had killed highly esteemed enemies, the ruler of Kósala was attacked by Subhádra's boy and sent to Yama's house. And having fought many times with the mighty warrior Bhima·sena, your son Chitra·sena was felled by Bhima·sena. The heroic son of the king of the Madras instilled fear among his enemies. That illustrious man wielding sword and shield was felled by Subhádra's son.

The equal of Karna in battle, Vrisha·sena had great en- 5.25
ergy, swift missiles and firm courage. While Karna looked on Dhanan·jaya attacked and sent him to Yama's house, as had been his promise after hearing about the death of Abhimányu.

nityaṃ prasakta|vairo yaḥ Pāṇḍavaiḥ pṛthivī|patiḥ,
viśrāvya vairaṃ, Pārthena Śrutāyuḥ sa nipātitaḥ.
Śalya|putras tu vikrāntaḥ Sahadevena, māriṣa,
hato Rukmaratho, rājan, bhrātā mātula|jo yudhi.
rājā Bhagīratho vṛddho, Bṛhatkṣatraś ca Kekayaḥ,
parākramantau vikrāntau nihatau vīryavattarau.

Bhagadatta|suto, rājan, kṛta|prajño, mahā|balaḥ,
śyenavac caratā saṃkhye Nakulena nipātitaḥ.
5.30 pitā|mahas tava tathā Bāhlikaḥ saha Bāhlikaiḥ
nihato Bhīmasenena mahā|bala|parākramaḥ.
Jayatsenas tathā, rājañ, Jārāsaṃdhir mahā|balaḥ
Māgadho nihataḥ saṃkhye Saubhadreṇa mah"|ātmanā.
putras te Durmukho, rājan, Duḥsahaś ca mahā|rathaḥ
gadayā Bhīmasenena nihatau śūra|māninau.
Durmarṣaṇo, Durviṣaho, Durjayaś ca mahā|rathaḥ
kṛtvā tv a|sukaraṃ karma gatā Vaivasvata|kṣayam.

ubhau Kaliṅga|Vṛṣakau bhrātarau yuddha|dur|madau
kṛtvā c' â|sukaraṃ karma gatau Vaivasvata|kṣayam.
5.35 sacivo Vṛṣavarmā te śūraḥ parama|vīryavān
Bhīmasenena vikramya gamito Yama|sādanam.
tath" âiva Pauravo rājā nāg'|âyuta|balo mahān
samare Pāṇḍu|putreṇa nihataḥ Savyasācinā.

Shrutáyus, a lord of the earth who had always borne a grudge for the Pándavas, was felled by Pritha's son* after he crowed about that grudge. Shalya's courageous son Rukma·ratha, dear friend, was slain in battle by Saha·deva, though he was his brother, the son of his maternal uncle. The old king Bhagíratha and the Kékaya Brihat·kshatra were both courageous. They were killed while advancing, though they were the more powerful.

King, Bhaga·datta's wise and powerful son was felled in battle by Nákula, who moved like a bird of prey. And 5.30
your grandfather, Báhlika, who had immense power and strength, was killed along with the Báhlika people by Bhima·sena. And the Mágadha Jayat·sena, the immensely powerful son of Jara·sandha, was killed in battle by Subhádra's great son. Your son Dúrmukha, king, and the mighty warrior Dúhsaha, both esteemed as heroes, were struck down by Bhima·sena with his club. Durmárshana, Dúrvishaha and the great warrior Dúrjaya, after performing a most difficult task, went to Yama's house.

Both the brothers Kalínga and Vríshaka were mad for battle. After performing a most difficult task, they went to Yama's house. Your minister Vrisha·varman was a hero pos- 5.35
sessing the utmost strength. Bhima·sena attacked him and sent him to Yama's house. Similarly, the mighty king Páurava, whose strength was like that of a myriad of elephants, was killed in battle by Pandu's son, the Left-handed archer.

Vasātayo, mahā|rāja, dvi|sāhasrāḥ prahāriṇaḥ,
Śūrasenāś ca vikrāntāḥ sarve yudhi nipātitāḥ.
Abhīṣāhāḥ kavacinaḥ praharanto raṇ'|ôtkaṭāḥ,
Śibayaś ca rath'|ôdārāḥ Kaliṅga|sahitā hatāḥ.
Gokule nitya|saṃvṛddhā yuddhe parama|kopanāḥ
te 'pāvṛttaka|vīrāś ca nihatāḥ Savyasācinā.
5.40 Śreṇayo bahu|sāhasrāḥ saṃśaptaka|gaṇāś ca ye,
te sarve Pārtham āsādya gatā Vaivasvata|kṣayam.

syālau tava, mahā|rāja, rājānau Vṛṣak'|Âcalau
tvad|artham ativikrāntau nihatau Savyasācinā.
Ugrakarmā mah"|êṣv|āso nāmataḥ, karmatas tathā,
Śālva|rājo mahā|bāhur Bhīmasenena pātitaḥ.
Oghavāṃś ca, mahā|rāja, Bṛhantaḥ sahitau raṇe,
parākramantau mitr'|ârthe, gatau Vaivasvata|kṣayam.
tath" âiva rathināṃ śreṣṭhaḥ Kṣemadhūrtir, viśāṃ pate,
nihato gadayā, rājan, Bhīmasenena saṃyuge.
5.45 tathā, rājan, mah"|êṣv|āso Jalasaṃdho mahā|balaḥ
su|mahat kadanaṃ kṛtvā hataḥ Sātyakinā raṇe.
Alambuṣo rākṣas'|êndraḥ khara|bandhura|yānavān
Ghaṭotkacena vikramya gamito Yama|sādanam.
Rādheyāḥ sūta|putrāś ca bhrātaraś ca mahā|rathāḥ,
Kekayāḥ sarvaśaś c' âpi nihatāḥ Savyasācinā.

Mālavā, Madrakāś c' âiva, Drāviḍāś c' ôgra|karmiṇaḥ,
Yaudheyāś ca, Lalitthāś ca, Kṣudrakāś c' âpy, Uśīnarāḥ,
Māvellakās, Tuṇḍikerāḥ, Sāvitrīputrakāś ca ye,
prācy'|ôdīcyāḥ, pratīcyāś ca, dākṣiṇātyāś ca, māriṣa,

Great king, two thousand Vasáti champions and all the courageous Shura·senas were felled in the war. The armored Abhisháhas, and the Shibis along with the Kalíngas, all excellent warriors, were killed while attacking, furious in battle. They who had always prospered in Go·kula were tremendously furious in battle. As those heroes retreated they were killed by the Left-handed archer. The many thou- 5.40
sands of Shrenis and the hordes of oath-bound warriors all went to Yama's house after attacking Pritha's son.

Your two brothers-in-law, the kings Vríshaka and Áchala, were killed by the Left-handed archer as they boldly advanced for your cause. The mighty-armed king of the Shalvas, a mighty archer 'Fierce' by name and deed,* was felled by Bhima·sena. Óghavat and Brihánta, great king, together showed courage in battle for their ally's cause and went to Yama's house. Similarly, lord of the people, Kshema·dhurti, the finest of chariot-warriors, was struck down
in battle by Bhima·sena with his club, king. And, king, 5.45
the immensely powerful, mighty archer Jala·sandha caused massive carnage and then was killed in battle by Sátyaki. The demon-lord Alámbusha, who traveled in a beautiful vehicle pulled by donkeys, was attacked by Ghatótkacha and sent to Yama's place. Those mighty warrior brothers, the sons of Radha and the charioteer, and the Kékayas as well, were completely annihilated by the Left-handed archer.

The Málavas, Mádrakas and aggressive Dravidians, the Yaudhéyas, Lalítthas, Kshúdrakas, Ushi·naras, Mavéllakas, Tundikéras, Savítri·pútrakas, those from the north, east,
west and south, dear friend, and hordes of foot-soldiers were 5.50
killed, and millions of horses and multitudes of chariots

5.50 pattīnāṃ nihatāḥ saṃghā, hayānām prayutāni ca,
ratha|vrajāś ca nihatā, hatāś ca vara|vāraṇāḥ.
sa|dhvajāḥ, s'|āyudhāḥ śūrāḥ, sa|varm'|âmbara|bhūṣaṇāḥ,
kālena mahat" āyastāḥ, kuśalair ye ca vardhitāḥ,
te hatāḥ samare, rājan, Pārthen' â|kliṣṭa|karmaṇā;
anye tath" â|mita|balāḥ paraspara|vadh'|âiṣiṇaḥ.
ete c' ânye ca bahavo rājānaḥ sa|gaṇā raṇe
hatāḥ sahasraśo, rājan, yan māṃ tvaṃ paripṛcchasi.
evam eṣa kṣayo vṛttaḥ Karṇ'|Ârjuna|samāgame!

Mahendreṇa yathā Vṛtro, yathā Rāmeṇa Rāvaṇaḥ,
5.55 yathā Kṛṣṇena Narako, Muruś ca Narak'|âriṇā,
Kārtavīryaś ca Rāmeṇa Bhārgaveṇa yathā hataḥ,
sa|jñāti|bāndhavaḥ śūraḥ samare yuddha|dur|madaḥ
raṇe kṛtvā mahad yuddhaṃ ghoraṃ trailokya|mohanam,
yathā Skandena Mahiṣo, yathā Rudreṇa c' Ândhakaḥ,
tath" Ârjunena sa hato dvai|rathe yuddha|dur|madaḥ,
s'|âmātya|bāndhavo, rājan, Karṇaḥ praharatāṃ varaḥ.

jay'|āśā Dhārtarāṣṭrāṇāṃ, vairasya ca mukhaṃ yataḥ,
tīrṇaṃ tat Pāṇḍavai, rājan, yat purā n' âvabudhyase.
ucyamāno, mahā|rāja, bandhubhir hita|kāṅkṣibhiḥ
5.60 tad idaṃ samanuprāptaṃ vyasanaṃ su|mah"|âtyayam!
putrāṇāṃ rājya|kāmānāṃ tvayā, rājan, hit'|âiṣiṇā;
a|hitāny eva cīrṇāni, teṣāṃ tat phalam āgatam!»

DHṚTARĀṢṬRA uvāca:

6.1 «ĀKHYĀTĀ MĀMAKĀS, tāta, nihatā yudhi Pāṇḍavaiḥ,
nihatān Pāṇḍaveyānāṃ māmakair brūhi, Saṃjaya!»

were destroyed, and fine elephants were slaughtered. Heroes with banners, weapons and wearing armored garments, who had toiled for a long time and had prospered by their skills, king, were killed in battle by Pritha's son who never tired of performing deeds. And others of boundless might were striving to kill one another. They and many other kings with their troops—about whom you question me—were killed in battle by the thousand, king. This carnage took place during Karna's clash with Árjuna!

Just as Vritra was killed by great Indra, Rávana by Rama, Náraka by Krishna, Muru by that enemy of Náraka 5.55
as well, and Kartavírya* by Rama Bhárgava, so it was that the battle-mad hero was killed in combat with his relatives and friends after he'd waged a great and dreadful battle in the war that bewildered the triple-world. Just as Máhisha was killed by Skanda and Ándhaka by Rudra, in a chariot-duel battle-mad Karna—the best of fighters!—was killed by Árjuna along with his ministers and relatives.

The Dhartaráshtra hope for victory and the cause of this quarrel, king, has been overcome by the Pándavas, something you once thought impossible, great king. As you were told by those kinsmen eager for your well-being, this horrific 5.60
disaster has come to pass! On account of your craving for the well-being of your kingdom-coveting sons, their behavior has not been good, and they have reaped this reward!"

DHRITA·RASHTRA said:

"YOU HAVE TOLD of those people of mine who were killed 6.1
in the war by the Pándavas, dear fellow. Speak, Sánjaya, about those among the Pándavas that my men killed!"

SAMJAYA uvāca:

«Kuntayo yudhi vikrāntā, mahā|sattvā, mahā|balāḥ,
s'|ânubandhāḥ, sah'|âmātyā Gāṅgeyeṇa nipātitāḥ.
Nārāyaṇā, Balabhadrāḥ, śūrāś ca śataśo 'pare
anuraktāś ca, vīreṇa Bhīṣmeṇa yudhi pātitāḥ.
samaḥ Kirīṭinā saṃkhye vīryeṇa ca balena ca,
Satyajit satya|saṃdhena Droṇena nihato yudhi.
6.5 Pañcālānāṃ mah"|êṣv|āsāḥ sarve yuddha|viśāradāḥ
Droṇena saha saṃgamya gatā Vaivasvata|kṣayam.
tathā Virāṭa|Drupadau vṛddhau saha|sutau nṛpau
parākramantau mitr'|ârthe Droṇena nihatau raṇe.
yo bāla eva samare saṃmitaḥ Savyasācinā,
Keśavena ca dur|dharṣo, Baladevena vā, vibho,
pareṣāṃ kadanaṃ kṛtvā mahā|ratha|viśāradaḥ,
parivārya mahā|mātraiḥ ṣaḍbhiḥ paramakai rathaiḥ,
a|śaknuvadbhir Bībhatsum, Abhimanyur nipātitaḥ.
kṛtaṃ taṃ virathaṃ vīraṃ, kṣatra|dharme vyavasthitam,
6.10 Dauḥśāsanir, mahā|rāja, Saubhadraṃ hatavān raṇe.
sapatnānāṃ nihantā ca mahatyā senayā vṛtaḥ
Ambaṣṭhasya sutaḥ śrīmān mitra|hetoḥ parākraman,
āsādya Lakṣmaṇaṃ vīraṃ Duryodhana|sutaṃ raṇe
su|mahat kadanaṃ kṛtvā gato Vaivasvata|kṣayam.

SÁNJAYA said:

"The courageous Kuntis, noble and powerful, were felled by Ganga's son, along with their followers and ministers. The Naráyanas, the Bala·bhadras and other heroes devoted to the Pándavas, the hero Bhishma felled in battle by the hundred.

Sátyajit, the equal to the Wearer of the crown* in battle with his courage and strength, was killed in combat
by Drona, who was true to his promises. The Panchálas' 6.5
mighty bowmen were all skilled in combat. After engaging with Drona, they went to Yama's house. Similarly, the distinguished kings Viráta and Drúpada and their sons were killed in battle by Drona while displaying courage for their ally.

The lad Abhimányu was the equal in battle of the Left-handed archer and as invincible as Késhava or Bala·deva, ruler. Skilled as a great warrior, after decimating his enemies and being surrounded by six superb warriors of the highest calibre who were unable to overcome Bibhátsu,* Abhimányu was felled. Great king, Duhshásana's son killed in combat 6.10
that heroic son of Subhádra* who adhered to the warrior's law though he was stripped of his chariot.

And the illustrious son of Ambáshtha, a killer of enemies surrounded by a great army, showed courage for the sake of his ally and attacked in battle Duryódhana's son, the hero Lákshmana. After creating immense carnage, he went to Yama's house.

Bṛhantaḥ su|mah"|êṣv|āsaḥ, kṛt'|âstro, yuddha|dur|madaḥ,
Duḥśāsanena vikramya gamito Yama|sādanam.
Maṇimān, Daṇḍadhāraś ca rājānau yuddha|dur|madau
parākramantau mitr'|ârthe Droṇena yudhi pātitau.
Aṃśumān Bhoja|rājas tu saha|sainyo mahā|rathaḥ
6.15 Bhāradvājena vikramya gamito Yama|sādanam.
sāmudraś Citrasenaś ca saha putreṇa, Bhārata,
Samudrasenena balād gamito Yama|sādanam.
anūpa|vāsī Nīlaś ca, Vyāghradattaś ca vīryavān,
Aśvatthāmnā, Vikarṇena gamito Yama|sādanam.
Citrāyudhaś citra|yodhī kṛtvā ca kadanaṃ mahat,
citra|mārgeṇa vikramya Vikarṇena hato mṛdhe.
Vṛkodara|samo yuddhe, vṛtaḥ Kaikeya|yodhibhiḥ,
Kaikeyena ca vikramya, bhrātā bhrātrā nipātitaḥ.
Janamejayo gadā|yodhī, pārvatīyaḥ, pratāpavān
6.20 Durmukhena, mahā|rāja, tava putreṇa pātitaḥ.
Rocamānau nara|vyāghrau, rocamānau grahāv iva,
Droṇena yugapad, rājan, divaṃ saṃprāpitau śaraiḥ.
nṛpāś ca pratiyudhyantaḥ parākrāntā, viśāṃ pate,
kṛtvā na|sukaraṃ karma gatā Vaivasvata|kṣayam.
Purujit, Kuntibhojaś ca, mātulau Savyasācinaḥ,
saṃgrāma|nirjitāl lokān gamitau Droṇa|sāyakaiḥ.
Abhibhūḥ Kāśi|rājaś ca Kāśikair bahubhir vṛtaḥ
Vasudānasya putreṇa nyāsito deham āhave.
amit'|âujā Yudhāmanyur, Uttamaujāś ca vīryavān
6.25 nihatya śataśaḥ śūrān asmadīyair nipātitāḥ.

Brihánta, a mighty battle-mad archer who was skilled
with his weapon, was attacked by Duhshásana and sent to
Yama's house. The battle-mad kings Mánimat and Danda·
dhara were felled in battle by Drona as they showed courage
for the sake of their ally. The mighty warrior Ámshumat,
king of the Bhojas, was attacked by Bharad·vaja's son* and 6.15
sent along with his troops to Yama's house.

And Chitra·sena, who lived by the ocean, Bhárata, was
violently sent along with his son to Yama's house by Samú-
dra·sena. Nila, who lived in the marshy lands, and powerful
Vyaghra·datta, were sent to Yama's house by Ashvattháman
and Vikárna. Chitráyudha fought in numerous ways and
caused immense carnage. He was attacked in various ways by
Vikárna and killed in battle. A man the equal of Wolf-belly*
in battle and surrounded by Kaikéya warriors was attacked
and felled by a Kaikéya, a brother felled by a brother. The
powerful mountain-man Janam·éjaya fought with his club
and was felled by your son Dúrmukha, great king. 6.20

The two Rochamánas, tigers among men shining brightly
like planets, were sent together to heaven by Drona with his
arrows. And kings fighting courageously, lord of the people,
went to Yama's house after performing most difficult tasks.
Púrujit and Kunti·bhoja, the Left-handed archer's maternal uncles, were sent by Drona's arrows to those worlds
gained through combat. And Ábhibhu, the king of Kashi
surrounded by many warriors from Kashi, was forced to lay
down his body in battle by Vasu·dana's son. Yudha·manyu,
whose vigour knew no bounds, and powerful Uttamáujas,
slew heroes by the hundred and were felled by our boys. 6.25
Kshatra·dharman and the Panchála Mitra·varman, Bhárata,

Mitravarmā ca Pāñcālyaḥ, Kṣatradharmā ca, Bhārata,
Droṇena param'|êṣv|āsau gamitau Yama|sādanam.
Śikhaṇḍi|tanayo yuddhe Kṣatradevo yudhāṃ patiḥ
Lakṣmaṇena hato, rājaṃs, tava pautreṇa, Bhārata.
Sucitraś, Citravarmā ca pitā|putrau mahā|rathau
pracarantau mahā|vīrau Droṇena nihatau raṇe.
Vārdhakṣemir, mahā|rāja, samudra iva parvaṇi,
āyudha|kṣayam āsādya praśāntiṃ paramāṃ gataḥ.
Senābindu|sutaḥ śreṣṭhaḥ śastravān, pravaro yudhi,
6.30 Bāhlikena, mahā|rāja, Kaurav'|êndreṇa pātitaḥ.
Dhṛṣṭaketur, mahā|rāja, Cedīnāṃ pravaro rathaḥ
kṛtvā na|sukaraṃ karma gato Vaivasvata|kṣayam.
tathā Satyadhṛtir vīraḥ kṛtvā kadanam āhave
Pāṇḍav'|ârthe parākrānto gamito Yama|sādanam.*
putras tu Śiśupālasya Suketuḥ pṛthivī|patiḥ
nihatya śātravān saṃkhye Droṇena nihato yudhi.
tathā Satyadhṛtir vīro, Madirāśvaś ca vīryavān,
Sūryadattaś ca vikrānto nihato Droṇa|sāyakaiḥ.
6.35 Śreṇimāṃś ca, mahā|rāja, yudhyamānaḥ, parākramī,
kṛtvā na|sukaraṃ karma gato Vaivasvata|kṣayam.
tath" âiva yudhi vikrānto Māgadhaḥ param'|âstra|vit
Bhīṣmeṇa nihato, rājañ, śete 'dya para|vīra|hā.
Virāṭa|putraḥ Śaṅkhas tu, Uttaraś ca mahā|rathaḥ
kurvantau su|mahat karma gatau Vaivasvata|kṣayam.
Vasudānaś ca kadanaṃ kurvāṇo 'tīva saṃyuge
Bhāradvājena vikramya gamito Yama|sādanam.

a pair of superb archers, were both sent to Yama's house by Drona. Shikhándin's son Kshatra·deva, a leader of warriors, king, was killed in battle by your grandson Lákshmana, Bhárata.

Suchítra and Chitra·varman, father and son and mighty warriors, were killed by Drona as those great heroes surged forward. Vriddha·kshema's son, great king, who was like the ocean at full moon, found the highest peace after attacking and losing his weapons. Sena·bindu's excellent son, a fine bearer of weapons, great king, was felled in battle by Báhli- 6.30
ka, a lord of the Káuravas.

Dhrishta·ketu, great king, the most excellent warrior among the Chedis, performed a most difficult task and then went to Yama's home. Similarly, the hero Satya·dhriti, after creating carnage in the war and showing courage for the Pándavas' cause, was sent to Yama's house. Shishu·pala's son Sukétu, a lord of the earth, slaughtered enemies in the war and was killed in battle by Drona. And the hero Satya·dhriti, powerful Madiráshva and courageous Surya·da-
tta, were struck down by Drona's arrows. And Shrénimat, 6.35
great king, after waging battle with courage and performing a most difficult task, went to Yama's home. Likewise the king of Mágadha, who knew the finest weapons and was courageous in battle, was struck down by Bhishma, king. Now that killer of enemy-heroes lies prone. Both Viráta's son Shankha and the mighty warrior Úttara went to Yama's house while doing an extraordinary deed. And as Vasu·dana created massive carnage in battle, he was attacked by Bharad·vaja's son and sent to Yama's house.

ete c' ânye ca bahavaḥ Pāṇḍavānāṃ mahā|rathāḥ
hatā Droṇena vikramya, yan māṃ tvaṃ paripṛcchasi.»

DHṚTARĀṢṬRA uvāca:

7.1 «MĀMAKASY' ÂSYA sainyasya hṛt'|ôtsekasya, Saṃjaya,
avaśeṣaṃ na paśyāmi kakude mṛdite sati.
tau hi vīrau mah"|êṣv|āsau mad|arthe Kuru|sattamau
Bhīṣma|Droṇau hatau śrutvā n' ârtho vai jīvite '|sati!
na ca śocāmi Rādheyaṃ hatam āhava|śobhanam,
yasya bāhvor balaṃ tulyaṃ kuñjarāṇāṃ śataṃ śatam.
hata|pravara|sainyaṃ me yathā śaṃsasi, Saṃjaya,
a|hatān api me śaṃsa. ke 'tra jīvanti? ke ca na?
7.5 eteṣu hi mṛteṣv, adya ye tvayā parikīrtitāḥ,
ye 'pi jīvanti, te sarve mṛtā, iti matir mama!»

SAṂJAYA uvāca:

«yasmin mah"|âstrāṇi samarpitāni—
citrāṇi, śubhrāṇi, catur|vidhāni,
divyāni, rājan, vihitāni c' âiva—
Droṇena vīre dvija|sattamena,
mahā|rathaḥ kṛtimān, kṣipra|hasto,
dṛḍh'|āyudho, dṛḍha|muṣṭir, dṛḍh'|êṣuḥ,
sa vīryavān Droṇa|putras tarasvī
vyavasthito yoddhu|kāmas tvad|arthe.
Ānarta|vāsī Hṛdik'|ātmajo 'sau
mahā|rathaḥ Sātvatānāṃ variṣṭhaḥ
svayaṃ Bhojaḥ Kṛtavarmā kṛt'|âstro
vyavasthito yoddhu|kāmas tvad|arthe.

Drona attacked and killed these and many other mighty Pándava warriors about whom you question me."

DHRITA·RASHTRA said:

"MY TROOPS HAVE lost their pride, Sánjaya. Now that 7.1
their chief has been crushed, I see no survivors among them. Now that I've heard that both Bhishma and Drona have been killed for my cause, there's no point to this no good life! For those two heroes were mighty archers, the very best of the Kurus. And I cannot suffer that Radha's son has been killed, though he was brilliant in battle, the strength of his arms the equal of hundreds and hundreds of elephants.

Since you tell me about those fine troops who've been killed, Sánjaya, you must also tell me about those not killed.
Who's still alive there and who is not? Among the dead are 7.5
those who you've named today. But even those who remain alive are all dead, that's what I think!"

SÁNJAYA said:

"The hero to whom Drona, the finest of brahmins, king, consigned the four kinds of great weapons—the extraordinary, brilliant, divine and manufactured—a mighty and skilful warrior with swift hands and hard weapons, fists and arrows, Drona's bold and powerful son is in position eager to do battle for your cause.

Hrídika's son from Ánarta, a mighty warrior skilled with his weapons and the finest of the Sátvatas, the Bhoja Krita·varman himself, is in position eager to do battle for your cause.

Ārtāyaniḥ samare duṣ|prakampyaḥ
sen"|âgra|ṇīḥ prathamas tāvakānām,
yaḥ svasrīyān Pāṇḍaveyān visṛjya,
satyāṃ vācaṃ tāṃ cikīrṣus tarasvī,
7.10 tejo|vadhaṃ sūta|putrasya saṃkhye
pratiśruty' Âjātaśatroḥ purastāt,
dur|ādharṣaḥ, Śakra|samāna|vīryaḥ
Śalyaḥ sthito yoddhu|kāmas tvad|arthe.
ājāneyaiḥ Saindhavaiḥ, pārvatīyair,
nadī|ja|Kāmboja|Vanāyu|jaiś ca,
Gāndhāra|rājaḥ sva|balena yukto
vyavasthito yoddhu|kāmas tvad|arthe.
Śāradvato Gautamaś c' âpi, rājan,
mahā|bāhur bahu|citr'|âstra|yodhī
dhanuś citraṃ su|mahad, bhāra|sāhaṃ
vyavasthito yoddhu|kāmaḥ pragṛhya.
mahā|rathaḥ Kekaya|rāja|putraḥ
sad|aśva|yuktaṃ ca patākinaṃ ca
rathaṃ samāruhya, Kuru|pravīra,
vyavasthito yoddhu|kāmas tvad|arthe.
tathā sutas te jvalan'|ârka|varṇaṃ
rathaṃ samāsthāya Kuru|pravīraḥ
vyavasthitaḥ Purumitro, nar'|êndra,
vyabhre sūryo bhrājamāno yathā khe.

Artáyani* is immovable in battle, a leader of your army and the foremost of your people. Rejecting his sister's* sons the Pándavas and intending to make his own words true after promising before Ajáta·shatru* to destroy the fiery en- 7.10
ergy of the charioteer's son in battle, Shalya stands firm—bold, unassailable and the equal of Shakra* in courage—eager to do battle for your cause.

With the noble Sindhus, mountain people, river people, Kambójas and those from Vanáyu, the king of Gandhára is in position together with his army, eager to do battle for your cause. Furthermore, king, his arms mighty, fighting with many different weapons and grasping his marvelous bow that can bear a massive strain, Sharádvat's son Gáutama is in position eager to do battle.

The prince of the Kékayas, a great warrior mounted on a chariot displaying a flag and yoked to the finest horses, is in position eager to do battle for your cause, Kuru hero. Similary your son, the Kuru hero Puru·mitra, mounted on a chariot that has the luster of the sun's fiery rays, is in position, lord of men, like the sun shining in a cloudless sky.

7.15 Duryodhano nāga|kulasya madhye
vyavasthitaḥ siṃha iv' ābabhāse,
rathena jāmbūnada|bhūṣaṇena
vyavasthitaḥ samare yotsyamānaḥ.
sa rāja|madhye puruṣa|pravīro
rarāja jāmbūnada|citra|varmā
padma|prabho, vahnir iv' âlpa|dhūmo,
megh'|ântare sūrya iva prakāśaḥ.
tathā Suṣeṇo 'py asi|carma|pāṇis,
tav' ātmajaḥ Satyasenaś ca vīraḥ
vyavasthitau Citrasenena sārdhaṃ
hṛṣṭ'|ātmānau samare yoddhu|kāmau.
hrī|niṣevo Bhārata|rāja|putra
Ugrāyudhaḥ, Kṣaṇabhojī, Sudarśaḥ,
Jārāsaṃdhiḥ prathamaś c', Âdṛḍhaś ca,
Citrāyudhaḥ, Śrutavarmā, Jayaś ca,
Śalaś ca, Satyavrata|Duḥśalau ca
vyavasthitāḥ saha|sainyā nar'|âgryāḥ.
Kaitavyānām adhipaḥ śūra|mānī,
raṇe raṇe śatru|hā rāja|putraḥ,
7.20 rathī, hayī, nāga|patti|prayāyī
vyavasthito yoddhu|kāmas tvad|arthe.
vīraḥ Śrutāyuś ca, Dhṛtāyudhaś ca,
Citrāṅgadaś, Citrasenaś ca vīraḥ
vyavasthitā yoddhu|kāmā nar'|âgryāḥ
prahāriṇo, māninaḥ, satya|saṃdhāḥ.

With his chariot adorned with Jambu river gold, Duryó- 7.15
dhana shone brilliantly like a lion standing in the midst of a herd of elephants. He is in position and will fight in the war. In the midst of the kings, that hero among men clad in armor the color of Jambu river gold is radiant with the luster of a lotus, like a fire with barely a wisp of smoke and as bright as the sun in the midst of clouds.

And so too Sushéna with sword and shield in hand and your son the hero Satya·sena are in position together with Chitra·sena, their bodies bristling with excitement and eager to fight in the war.

The modest Bhárata prince Ugráyudha, Kshana·bho-
jin, Sudársha, Jara·sandha's first son, Ádridha, Chitráyudha, Shruta·varman, Jaya, Shala, Satya·vrata and Dúhshala, are all in position with their troops, those chiefs of men. The ruler of the Kaitávyas has the pride of a hero and is a prince
who's killed enemies in battle after battle. With chariot and 7.20
horse and marching his elephants and foot-soldiers, he is in position eager to do battle for your cause. The hero Shru-táyus, Dhritáyudha, Chitrángada and the hero Chitra·sena, these chiefs of men are in position eager to do battle, proud champions who hold true to their promises.

Karṇ'|ātmajaḥ Satyasaṃdho mah"|ātmā
vyavasthitaḥ samare yoddhu|kāmaḥ.
ath' âparau Karṇa|sutau var'|âstrau
vyavasthitau laghu|hastau, nar'|êndra,
mahad balaṃ dur|bhidam alpa|vīryaiḥ
samanvitau yoddhu|kāmau tvad|arthe.
etaiś ca mukhyair aparaiś ca, rājan,
yodha|pravīrair amita|prabhāvaiḥ
vyavasthito nāga|kulasya madhye,
yathā Mahendraḥ, Kuru|rājo jayāya!»

DHṚTARĀṢṬRA uvāca:

«ākhyātā jīvamānā ye pare sainyā yathā|yatham.
it' îdam avagacchāmi vyaktam arth'|âbhipattitaḥ.»

VAIŚAMPĀYANA uvāca:

7.25 evaṃ bruvann eva tadā Dhṛtarāṣṭro 'mbikā|sutaḥ
hata|pravīraṃ, vidhvastaṃ, kiṃcic|cheṣaṃ svakaṃ balam
śrutvā, vyāmoham agamac choka|vyākulit'|êndriyaḥ.
muhyamāno 'bravīc c' âpi, «muhūrtaṃ tiṣṭha, Saṃjaya!
vyākulaṃ me manas, tāta, śrutvā su|mahad a|priyam.
mano muhyati c', âṅgāni na ca śaknomi dhāritum!»
ity evam uktvā vacanaṃ Dhṛtarāṣṭro 'mbikā|sutaḥ
bhrānta|cittas tataḥ so 'tha babhūva jagatī|patiḥ.

JANAMEJAYA uvāca:

8.1 ŚRUTVĀ KARṆAṂ hataṃ yuddhe,
putrāṃś c' âiva nipātitān,
nar'|êndraḥ kiṃ cid āśvasto,
dvija|śreṣṭha, kim abravīt?

Karna's son, the great Satya·sandha, is in position eager to fight in the war. And Karna's other two sons are in position, lord of men, with superb weapons and fleet of hand, their great army impenetrable by those of little courage. Together they are eager to do battle for your cause.

With these chiefs, king, and with other warrior-heroes who are boundless in might, the king of the Kurus is in position for victory like mighty Indra in the midst of a herd of elephants!"

DHRITA·RASHTRA said:

"The fine troops who still live you have named in turn. From the implications of these details, I understand it clearly now."

VAISHAMPÁYANA said:

Uttering this after hearing that his own army, which had 7.25
been scattered and its heroes slaughtered, still had some survivors, Ámbika's son Dhrita·rashtra then became confused, his mind in disarray with grief. And in confusion he said, "Stay a while, Sánjaya! After hearing about this massive misfortune my mind is in disarray, dear fellow. My mind is confused and I can't bear the weight of my limbs!" And once he said these words, Ámbika's son Dhrita·rashtra, the lord of the earth, was distraught.

JANAM·ÉJAYA said:

ONCE HE RECOVERED his poise somewhat after hearing 8.1
that Karna had been killed and his sons had been felled in the war, what did the lord of men say, best of brahmins? He suffered immense and tremendous sadness due to his

prāptavān paramaṃ duḥkhaṃ putra|vyasana|jaṃ mahat;
tasmin yad uktavān kāle, tan mam' ācakṣva pṛcchataḥ!

VAIŚAMPĀYANA uvāca:

śrutvā Karṇasya nidhanam a|śraddheyam iv' âdbhutam,
bhūta|saṃmohanaṃ, bhīmaṃ Meroḥ saṃsarpanaṃ yathā;
citta|moham iv' â|yuktaṃ Bhārgavasya mahā|mateḥ;
parājayam iv' Êndrasya dviṣadbhyo bhīma|karmaṇaḥ;
8.5 divaḥ prapatanaṃ bhānor urvyām iva mahā|dyuteḥ;
saṃśoṣaṇam iv' â|cintyaṃ samudrasy' â|kṣay'|âmbhasaḥ;
mahī|viyad|dig|ambūnāṃ sarva|nāśam iv' âdbhutam;
karmaṇor iva vaiphalyam ubhayoḥ puṇya|pāpayoḥ;
saṃcintya nipuṇaṃ buddhyā Dhṛtarāṣṭro jan'|ēśvaraḥ
«n' êdam ast'! îti» saṃcintya Karṇasya samare vadham,
«prāṇinām evam anyeṣāṃ syād ap'! îti» vināśanam,
śok'|âgninā dahyamāno, dhamyamāna iv' āśayaḥ,
visrast'|âṅgaḥ, śvasan, dīno «hā! h"! êty» uktvā su|duḥkhitaḥ
vilalāpa, mahā|rāja, Dhṛtarāṣṭro 'mbikā|sutaḥ.

DHṚTARĀṢṬRA uvāca:

8.10 «Saṃjay', Ādhirathir vīraḥ siṃha|dvirada|vikramaḥ,
vṛṣabha|pratima|skandho, vṛṣabh'|âkṣa|gatiś caran,
vṛṣabho vṛṣabhasy' êva yo yuddhe na nivartate
śatror api Mahendrasya vajra|saṃhanano yuvā.
yasya jyā|tala|śabdena śara|vṛṣṭi|raveṇa ca
rath'|âśva|nara|mātaṅgā n' âvatiṣṭhanti saṃyuge,
yam āśritya mahā|bāhuṃ vidviṣāṃ jaya|kāṃkṣayā

sons' disaster. Tell me what was said to him at that time, I implore you!

VAISHAMPÁYANA said:

After he'd heard about the death of Karna, it seemed unbelievable and miraculous, as bewildering to the world as the formidable ascent of Mount Meru. It was as incongruous as confusion in the mind of clever Bhárgava. It was like the
defeat of formidable Indra by his enemies. It was like the 8.5
sun of great brilliance falling from sky to earth. It was as inconceivable as the never-ending waters of the ocean drying up. It was as miraculous as the complete destruction of the earth, heavens, regions and waters. It was like the absence of consequences from acting either good or evil.

Thinking it over carefully and deliberately, Dhrita·rashtra, the lord of the people, thought of Karna's death in battle, "This can't be so!" and of the destruction, "This shall happen to other lives as well!" And he burned all the while with grief's fire as if his heart was melting. His limbs slack, sighing and despondent, Ámbika's miserable son Dhrita·rashtra uttered "Ah! Ah!" and wailed, great king.

DHRITA·RASHTRA said:

"Sánjaya, Ádhiratha's heroic son* has the courage of an 8.10
elephant and a lion. His shoulders are as wide as a bull's and he roams around with the eyes and gait of a bull. Like a bull before another bull, he never retreats in battle even when the enemy is mighty Indra. This young man is as hard as diamond! It is due to the sound of his hand on a bow-string and the howl of showers of his arrows that warriors, horses, men, and elephants cannot remain standing in battle. It was

Duryodhano 'karod vairaṃ Pāṇḍu|putrair mahā|rathaiḥ,
sa kathaṃ rathināṃ śreṣṭhaḥ Karṇaḥ Pārthena saṃyuge
nihataḥ puruṣa|vyāghraḥ prasahy' â|sahya|vikramaḥ?
8.15 yo n' âmanyata vai nityam Acyutaṃ ca, Dhanaṃjayam,
na Vṛṣṇīn sahitān anyān sva|bāhu|bala|darpitaḥ,
‹Śārṅga|Gāṇḍīva|dhanvānau sahitāv a|parājitau
ahaṃ divyād rathād ekaḥ pātayiṣyāmi saṃyuge!›
iti yaḥ satataṃ mandam avocal lobha|mohitam
Duryodhanam avācīnaṃ rājya|kāmukam āturam;
yo 'jayat sarva|Kāmbojān,
Āvantyān Kekayaiḥ saha,
Gāndhārān, Madrakān, Matsyāṃs,
Trigartāṃs, Taṃgaṇāñ, Śakān,
Pañcālāṃś ca, Videhāṃś ca,
Kulindān, Kāśi|Kosalān,
Suhmān, Aṅgāṃś ca, Vaṅgāṃś ca,
Niṣādān, Puṇḍra|Kīcakān,
8.20 Vatsān, Kaliṅgāṃs, Taralān, Aśmakān, Ṛṣikān api.
jitv" âitān samare vīraś cakre bali|bhṛtaḥ purā
śara|vrātaiḥ su|niśitaiḥ, su|tīkṣṇaiḥ, kaṅka|patribhiḥ
Duryodhanasya vṛddhy|arthaṃ Rādheyo rathināṃ varaḥ.
divy'|âstra|vin mahā|tejāḥ Karṇo Vaikartano vṛṣaḥ
senā|gopaś ca. sa kathaṃ śatrubhiḥ param'|âstra|vit
ghātitaḥ Pāṇḍavaiḥ śūraiḥ samare vīrya|śālibhiḥ?
vṛṣo Mahendro deveṣu, vṛṣaḥ Karṇo vareṣv api;
tṛtīyam anyaṃ lokeṣu vṛṣaṃ n' âiv' ânuśuśruma!

after relying on him with his huge arms that Duryódhana, wishing for victory over his enemies, began a feud with those mighty warriors, the sons of Pandu. How did Pritha's son kill Karna in battle? That tiger of a man was the finest of chariot-warriors, his courage impossible to overcome!

Proud of the strength of his own arms, he had no regard 8.15
for Áchyuta,* Dhanan·jaya, the united Vrishnis nor others. It was he who always quietly said to Duryódhana when he was despondent, deluded by ambition and sick with desire for a kingdom, 'I'm the one who in battle will topple together from their divine chariot the undefeated bearers of the Gandíva and Sharnga bows!'*

It was he who conquered all the Kambójas, Avántyas and Kékayas, Gandháras, Mádrakas, Matsyas, Tri·gartas, Tánganas, Shakas, Panchálas, Vidéhas, Kulíndas, Kashis, Kósalas, Suhmas, Angas, Vangas, Nishádas, Pundras, Kíchakas, Vatsas, Kalíngas, Táralas, Áshmakas and Ríshikas. 8.20
Once he'd defeated them in battle with swarms of well-honed and sharpened heron-feathered arrows, it was Radha's son, a hero, the best of chariot-warriors, who then made them tributaries for the benefit of Duryódhana's prosperity.

Knowing the divine weapons and full of fire, Karna Vai·kártana was a bull and the general of the army. Knowing the finest missiles, how was he killed in battle by his enemies, the courageous Pándava heroes? Mighty Indra is the best of the gods and Karna is the best of the best. There is definitely no other, no third, that we've heard of who's the best in all the worlds!

Uccaiḥśravā varo 'śvānāṃ, rājñāṃ Vaiśravaṇo varaḥ,
8.25 varo Mahendro devānāṃ, Karṇaḥ praharatāṃ varaḥ.
yojitaḥ pārthivaiḥ śūraiḥ, samarthair, vīrya|śālibhiḥ,
Duryodhanasya vṛddhy|arthaṃ kṛtsnām urvīm ath' âjayat.
yaṃ labdhvā Māgadho rājā sāntvamāno 'tha sauhṛdaiḥ
arautsīt pārthivaṃ kṣatram ṛte Yādava|Kauravān.
taṃ śrutvā nihataṃ Karṇaṃ dvai|rathe Savyasācinā
śok'|ârṇave nimagno 'ham, bhinnā naur iva sāgare.
taṃ Vṛṣaṃ nihataṃ śrutvā dvai|rathe rathināṃ varam
śok'|ârṇave nimagno 'ham, a|plavaḥ sāgare yathā.
īdṛśair yady ahaṃ duḥkhair na vinaśyāmi, Saṃjaya,
8.30 vajrād dṛḍhataraṃ manye hṛdayaṃ mama dur|bhidam.
jñāti|sambandhi|mitrāṇām imaṃ śrutvā parābhavam
ko mad|anyaḥ pumāl̃ loke na jahyāt, sūta, jīvitam?
viṣam, agniṃ, prapātaṃ ca parvat'|âgrād ahaṃ vṛṇe;
na hi śakṣyāmi duḥkhāni soḍhuṃ kaṣṭāni, Saṃjaya!»

SAṂJAYA uvāca:

9.1 «ŚRIYĀ, KULENA, yaśasā, tapasā ca, śrutena ca
tvām adya santo manyante, Yayātim iva Nāhuṣam.
śrute maha"|rṣi|pratimaḥ, kṛta|kṛtyo 'si, pārthiva.
paryavasthāpay' ātmānaṃ! mā viṣāde manaḥ kṛthāḥ!»

Uchchaih·shravas* is the best of horses, Váishravana* the
best of kings, mighty Indra the best of the gods, Karna the 8.25
best of those who fight.

Joined by heroic, capable and courageous princes, it was he who conquered the whole earth for the benefit of Duryódhana's prosperity. It was only after he'd won him over and made peace with him with friendship that the Mágadha king persecuted princely power with the exception of the Yádavas and Káuravas.

Now that I've heard that he—Karna!—has been killed by the Left-handed archer in a chariot-duel, I'm drowning in a sea of grief, like a shattered boat in the ocean. Now that I've heard that Vrisha—the finest of chariot-warriors!—has been killed in a chariot-duel, I'm drowning in a sea of grief as if boatless in the ocean. If I do not perish through such
sorrows as these, Sánjaya, I reckon my heart must be harder 8.30
than diamond, so difficult would it be to break.

After hearing about the annihilation of relatives, allies and friends, herald, what man in this world other than me would not give up his life? I choose fire or poison or to plummet from the summit of a mountain, Sánjaya, for I cannot endure these wretched sorrows!"

SÁNJAYA said:

"IN RADIANCE, in family, in fame, in austerity and in 9.1
learning, good people regard you as like Yayáti,* the son of Náhusha. You are the equal in learning of the great sages, king; you have done what had to be done. Console yourself! Don't despair!"

DHṚTARĀṢṬRA uvāca:

«daivam eva paraṃ manye. dhik pauruṣam anarthakam,
yatra śāla|pratīkāśaḥ Karṇo 'hanyata saṃyuge.
hatvā Yudhiṣṭhir'|ânīkaṃ, Pāñcālānāṃ ratha|vrajān,
pratāpya śara|varṣeṇa diśaḥ sarvā mahā|rathaḥ,
9.5 mohayitvā raṇe Pārthān, Vajrahasta iv' âsurān,
sa kathaṃ nihataḥ śete vāyu|rugṇa iva drumaḥ?
śokasy' ântaṃ na paśyāmi, pāraṃ jala|nidher iva.
cintā me vardhate 'tīva, mumūrṣā c' âpi jāyate!

Karṇasya nidhanaṃ śrutvā, vijayaṃ Phālgunasya ca,
a|śraddheyam ahaṃ manye vadhaṃ Karṇasya, Saṃjaya!
vajra|sāra|mayaṃ nūnaṃ hṛdayaṃ dur|bhidaṃ mama,
yac chrutvā puruṣa|vyāghraṃ hataṃ Karṇaṃ na dīryate.
āyur nūnaṃ su|dīrghaṃ me vihitaṃ daivataiḥ purā,
yatra Karṇaṃ hataṃ śrutvā jīvām' îha su|duḥkhitaḥ.
9.10 dhig jīvitam idaṃ c' âiva suhṛdd|hīnasya, Saṃjaya.
adya c' âhaṃ daśām etāṃ gataḥ, Saṃjaya, garhitām,
kṛpaṇaṃ vartayiṣyāmi, śocyaḥ sarvasya manda|dhīḥ.
aham eva purā bhūtvā sarva|lokasya sat|kṛtaḥ,
paribhūtaḥ kathaṃ, sūta, paraiḥ, śakṣyāmi jīvitum?

duḥkhāt su|duḥkha|vyasanaṃ prāptavān asmi, Saṃjaya,
Bhīṣma|Droṇa|vadhen' âiva, Karṇasya ca mah"|ātmanaḥ.
n' âvaśeṣaṃ prapaśyāmi sūta|putre hate yudhi.
sa hi pāraṃ mahān āsīt putrāṇāṃ mama, Saṃjaya.
yuddhe hi nihataḥ śūro visṛjan sāyakān bahūn

DHRITA·RASHTRA said:

"I reckon divine fate alone is best. Manly valor be damned!
It must be useless if Karna—who seemed like a *shala* tree!—
has been killed in battle. After that mighty warrior destroyed Yudhi·shthira's forces and hordes of Panchála warriors, scorched all regions with showers of his arrows and 9.5
confounded Pritha's sons* in battle like the Thunderbolt-
wielder* the demons, how is it that he's been slain and lies
prone like a tree broken by the wind? Like the far side of
the ocean, I see no end to my grief. My trepidation swells
relentlessly and my longing for death grows!

Now that I've heard about the end of Karna and the
victory of Phálguna, I reckon that the death of Karna is
incredible, Sánjaya! My unbreakable heart must surely be
as hard as diamond since it hasn't burst now that I've heard
that Karna, a tiger among men, has been killed. Surely the
gods decided long ago that my life be very long since I
remain alive here in utter misery after hearing that Karna has been killed. Sánjaya, destitute of friends, my life is 9.10
damned. Now that I'm in this contemptible state, Sánjaya,
I will live pitiably, lamented by all as dim-witted. Having
been esteemed before by all people, herald, how will I be
able to live while others deride me?

After tragedy, I suffer the disaster of this even greater
tragedy, Sánjaya, with the deaths of Bhishma and Drona
and then of the great Karna. I see no survivor now that
the charioteer's son has been killed in battle. For he was
the great safe shore for my sons, Sánjaya. That hero was
killed in battle as he discharged many arrows. Without that 9.15
bull of men, what's the point of me remaining alive? Surely,

9.15 ko hi me jīviten' ârthas tam ṛte puruṣa'|rṣabham?
rathād Ādhirathir nūnaṃ nyapatat sāyak'|ârditaḥ,
parvatasy' êva śikharaṃ vajra|pātād vidāritam!
sa śete pṛthivīṃ nūnaṃ śobhayan rudhir'|ôkṣitaḥ,
mātaṅga iva mattena dvip'|êndreṇa nipātitaḥ!
yo balaṃ Dhārtarāṣṭrāṇāṃ, Pāṇḍavānāṃ yato bhayam,
so 'rjunena hataḥ Karṇaḥ, pratimānaṃ dhanuṣmatām!
sa hi vīro mah"|êṣv|āsaḥ mitrāṇām abhayaṃ|karaḥ
śete vinihato vīraḥ, Devendreṇa iv' âcalaḥ!
pangor iv' âdhva|gamanaṃ, daridrasy' êva kāmitam,
9.20 Duryodhanasya c' ākūtaṃ, tṛṣitasy' êva vipruṣaḥ.
anyathā cintitaṃ kāryam, anyathā tat tu jāyate!
aho nu balavad daivaṃ, kālaś ca dur|atikramaḥ!
palāyamānaḥ, kṛpaṇo, dīn'|ātmā, dīna|pauruṣaḥ,
kac cid vinihataḥ, sūta, putro Duḥśāsano mama?
kac cin na dīn'|ācaritaṃ kṛtavāṃs, tāta, saṃyuge?
kac cin na nihataḥ śūro yath" ânye kṣatriya'|rṣabhāḥ?
Yudhiṣṭhirasya vacanaṃ, ‹mā yudhyasv'! êti› sarvadā
Duryodhano n' âbhyagṛhṇān,
mūḍhaḥ pathyam iv' āuṣadham.
śara|talpe śayānena
Bhīṣmeṇa su|mah"|ātmanā
9.25 pānīyaṃ yācitaḥ Pārthaḥ, so 'vidhyan medinī|talam.
jalasya dhārāṃ janitāṃ dṛṣṭvā Pāṇḍu|sutena ca
abravīt sa mahā|bāhus, ‹tāta, saṃśāmya Pāṇḍavaiḥ!
praśamādd hi bhavec chāntir. mad|antaṃ yuddham astu ca!
bhrātṛ|bhāvena pṛthivīṃ bhuṅkṣva Pāṇḍu|sutaiḥ saha!›
a|kurvan vacanaṃ tasya nūnaṃ śocati putrakaḥ.
tad idaṃ samanuprāptaṃ vacanaṃ dīrgha|darśinaḥ.

wounded by arrows, Ádhiratha's son fell from his chariot like a mountain peak shattered from the blow of a lightning bolt! Surely he lies on the ground oozing blood and making it beautiful, like an elephant felled by a huge ruttish elephant! The Dhartaráshtras' strength and the Pándavas' terror, Karna, the idol of archers, has been killed by Árjuna! That hero was a mighty archer who put his friends at ease. That hero lies prone like a mountain struck down by Indra!

And Duryódhana's plan is like going on a journey for a 9.20
cripple, like something a beggar longs for, or like drops of water for a parched man. A task thought out one way happens in another! Ah! Fate is powerful and destiny impossible to overcome!

Herald, was my son Duhshásana killed as he fled pitiably, his body and courage destitute? Did he not do wretched things in battle, dear friend? Was that champion not killed like the other warrior-bulls?

Like a moron ignoring the right medicine, Duryódhana always ignored Yudhi·shthira's words, 'Don't fight!' When the highly illustrious Bhishma asked for water as he lay on a 9.25
bed of arrows, Pritha's son pierced the surface of the earth. And seeing the stream of water produced by Pandu's son, that mighty-armed man said, 'Son, make peace with the Pándavas! For once the fighting ceases there shall be peace. The war must end with me!* Enjoy the earth with Pandu's sons as if you were their brother!' Not acting on his advice, my boy now suffers as the words of that far-seeing man come to pass.

aham tu nihat'|âmātyo, hata|putraś ca, Saṃjaya,
dyūtataḥ kṛcchram āpanno, lūna|pakṣa iva dvijaḥ.
yathā hi śakuniṃ gṛhya, chittvā pakṣau ca, Saṃjaya,
9.30 visarjayanti saṃhṛṣṭās tāḍyamānāḥ kumārakāḥ,
lūna|pakṣatayā tasya gamanaṃ n' ôpapadyate,
tath" âham api saṃprāpto lūna|pakṣa iva dvijaḥ.
kṣīṇaḥ, sarv'|ârtha|hīnaś ca, nirjñātir, bandhu|varjitaḥ,
kāṃ diśaṃ pratipatsyāmi dīnaḥ, śatru|vaśaṃ gataḥ?»

VAIŚAMPĀYANA uvāca:

ity evaṃ Dhṛtarāṣṭro 'tha vilapya bahu duḥkhitaḥ
provāca Saṃjayaṃ bhūyaḥ śoka|vyākula|mānasaḥ.

DHṚTARĀṢṬRA uvāca:

«yo 'jayat sarva|Kāmbojān, Ambhaṣṭhān Kekayaiḥ saha;
Gāndhārāṃś ca, Videhāṃś ca jitvā kāry'|ârtham āhave,
Duryodhanasya vṛddhy|arthaṃ yo 'jayat pṛthivīṃ prabhuḥ;
sa jitaḥ Pāṇḍavaiḥ śūraiḥ samare bāhu|śālibhiḥ!
9.35 tasmin hate mah"|êṣv|āse Karṇe yudhi Kirīṭinā,
ke vīrāḥ paryavartanta? tan mam' ācakṣva, Saṃjaya!
kac cin n' âikaḥ parityaktaḥ Pāṇḍavair nihato raṇe?
uktaṃ tvayā purā, tāta, yathā vīro nipātitaḥ.
Bhīṣmam a|pratiyudhyantaṃ Śikhaṇḍī sāyak'|ôttamaiḥ
pātayām āsa samare sarva|śastra|bhṛtāṃ varam.
tathā Draupadinā Droṇo nyasta|sarv'|āyudho yudhi,
yukta|yogo, mah"|êṣv|āsaḥ, śarair bahubhir ācitaḥ,

My ministers killed and my sons slaughtered, Sánjaya, I 9.30
have arrived at this crisis because of the dice match like a bird whose wings have been clipped! For, Sánjaya, just as a bird caught by excited young boys who cut its wings, knock it about and abandon it, cannot move because its wings have been clipped, so I also have become like that bird whose wings have been clipped. Ruined and without any purpose, lacking relatives and friends, dejected and subject to my enemy's will, to what place can I flee?"

VAISHAMPÁYANA said:

After lamenting like this, Dhrita·rashtra was then very sad. His mind bewildered with grief, he spoke further to Sánjaya.

DHRITA·RASHTRA said:

"He who defeated all the Kambójas and Ambáshthas, as well as the Kékayas; the powerful man who defeated the Gandháras and Vidéhas in war because it needed to be done, and then conquered the earth for Duryódhana's benefit; he was defeated in battle by the strong-armed Pándava heroes!
When that mighty archer Karna was killed in battle by the 9.35
Wearer of the crown, who were the heroes that survived? Tell me this, Sánjaya! Was he not alone, abandoned when the Pándavas struck him down in battle?

Good friend, earlier you described how each hero was felled. With the finest of arrows Shikhándin brought down Bhishma in battle, the best of all the weapon-bearers, though he did not retaliate. Drona had also laid aside all his weapons in the battle and, while absorbed in meditation, Drúpada's son Dhrishta·dyumna larded that mighty archer with

nihataḥ khaḍgam udyamya Dhṛṣṭadyumnena, Saṃjaya.
antareṇa hatāv etau, chalena ca viśeṣataḥ,
9.40 aśrauṣam aham etad vai, Bhīṣma|Droṇau nipātitau.
Bhīṣma|Droṇau hi samare na hanyād vajra|bhṛt svayam
nyāyena yudhyamānau hi. tad vai satyaṃ bravīmi te!

Karṇaṃ tv asyantam astrāṇi divyāni ca bahūni ca
katham Indr'|ôpamaṃ vīraṃ mṛtyur yuddhe samaspṛśat?

yasya vidyut|prabhāṃ śaktiṃ divyāṃ, kanaka|bhūṣaṇām
prāyacchad dviṣatāṃ hantrīṃ kuṇḍalābhyāṃ Puraṃdaraḥ.
yasya sarpa|mukho divyaḥ śaraḥ kanaka|bhūṣaṇaḥ
aśeta nihataḥ patrī candaneṣv ari|sūdanaḥ.
Bhīṣma|Droṇa|mukhān vīrān yo 'vamanya mahā|rathān,
9.45 Jāmadagnyān mahā|ghoraṃ Brāhmam astram aśikṣata.

yaś ca Droṇa|mukhān dṛṣṭvā vimukhān arditāñ śaraiḥ
Saubhadrasya mahā|bāhur vyadhamat kārmukaṃ śitaiḥ.
yaś ca nāg'|âyuta|prāṇaṃ, vajra|raṃhasam, acyutam
virathaṃ sahasā kṛtvā Bhīmasenam ath' âhasat.
Sahadevaṃ ca nirjitya śaraiḥ saṃnata|parvabhiḥ
kṛpayā virathaṃ kṛtvā n' âhanad dharma|cintayā.
yaś ca māyā|sahasrāṇi vikurvāṇaṃ, jay'|âiṣiṇam
Ghaṭotkacaṃ rākṣas'|êndraṃ Śakra|śaktyā nijaghnivān.

many arrows, raised his sword and killed him, Sánjaya. I've learned that when Bhishma and Drona were felled they 9.40
were killed opportunistically and, especially, by deceit. For the thunder-bolt wielder himself could not have killed Bhishma and Drona in battle by lawful means while they were fighting. About this I speak the truth to you!

But how did death touch Karna in battle—a hero the equal of Indra!—while he hurled many divine weapons?

It was he who, in exchange for his earrings, the Sacker of cities* gave the divine spear, a killer of enemies decorated with gold and flashing like lightning. It was he who had the divine gold-decorated arrow with the serpent's head, a fletched destroyer of enemies that lay in sandal powder once it had killed. It was he who disregarded the great warrior heroes led by Drona and Bhishma and learnt the horrifying 9.45
Brahma weapon from Jamadágnya.*

And it was that mighty-armed man who, seeing the men led by Drona turning away tortured with arrows, split Subhádra's son's bow with his sharp arrows. And it was he who laughed after violently stripping Bhima·sena of his chariot though he is indestructible, as quick as lightning and has the vitality of a myriad of elephants. And it was he who defeated Saha·deva with his smooth-jointed arrows and deprived him of his chariot but did not kill him out of compassion and his regard for the law. And it was he who, with the spear obtained from Shakra, struck down the demon-lord Ghatótkacha as he created thousands of different illusions while seeking victory.

etāṃś ca divasān yasya yuddhe bhīto Dhanaṃjayaḥ
9.50 n' âgamad dvai|rathaṃ vīraḥ. sa kathaṃ nihato raṇe?
‹saṃśaptakānāṃ yodhā ye āhvayanta* sad" ânyataḥ;
etān hatvā haniṣyāmi paścād Vaikartanaṃ raṇe!›
iti vyapadiśan Pārtho varjayan sūta|jaṃ raṇe;
sa kathaṃ nihato vīraḥ Pārthena para|vīra|hā?

ratha|bhaṅgo na cet tasya, dhanur vā na vyaśīryata,
na ced astrāṇi nirṇeśuḥ, sa kathaṃ nihataḥ paraiḥ?
ko hi śakto raṇe Karṇaṃ, vidhunvānaṃ mahad dhanuḥ,
vimuñcantaṃ śarān ghorān, divyāny astrāṇi c' āhave,
jetuṃ puruṣa|śārdūlaṃ, śārdūlam iva veginam?
9.55 dhruvaṃ tasya dhanuś chinnaṃ, ratho v" âpi mahīṃ gato,
astrāṇi vā pranaṣṭāni, yathā śaṃsasi me hatam.
na hy anyad api paśyāmi kāraṇaṃ tasya nāśane!

‹na hanmi Phālgunaṃ yāvat, tāvat pādau na dhāvaye!›
iti yasya mahā|ghoraṃ vratam āsīn mah"|ātmanaḥ.
yasya bhīto raṇe nidrāṃ Dharma|rājo Yudhiṣṭhiraḥ
trayo|daśa samā nityaṃ n' âbhajat puruṣa'|rṣabhaḥ.
yasya vīryavato vīryam upāśritya mah"|ātmanaḥ
mama putraḥ sabhāṃ bhāryāṃ Pāṇḍūnāṃ nītavān balāt.
tatr' âpi ca sabhā|madhye, Pāṇḍavānāṃ ca paśyatām,
9.60 ‹dāsa|bhāry"! êti› Pāñcālīm abravīt Kuru|saṃnidhau.
‹na santi patayaḥ, Kṛṣṇe, sarve ṣaṇḍha|tilaiḥ samāḥ!
upatiṣṭhasva bhartāram anyaṃ vā, vara|varṇini!›
ity evaṃ yaḥ purā vāco rūkṣāḥ saṃśrāvayan ruṣā
sabhāyāṃ sūta|jaḥ Kṛṣṇāṃ; sa kathaṃ nihataḥ paraiḥ?

And it was he who the hero Dhanan·jaya—terrified of
him in battle—did not engage in a chariot-duel for days. 9.50
How was he killed in battle? 'The warriors of the oath-bound hordes are always fighting me elsewhere; once I kill them I'll then kill Vaikártana in battle!' Under this pretense, Pritha's son avoided the charioteer's son in battle. How then did Pritha's son kill that hero, a killer of enemy-heroes?

If his chariot was not destroyed, or his bow not shattered, or if his weapons were not lost, how did his enemies kill him? For who could defeat Karna in combat while he shook his great bow and sent forth horrifying arrows and divine missiles in battle, that tiger of a man who was quick like a
tiger? Surely, since you tell me he's been killed, his bow was 9.55
splintered, or his chariot got stuck in the ground, or he lost his weapons. For I see no other way of killing him!

'I shall not wash my feet until I've killed Phálguna!' He was the great man who made this dreadful vow. It was for fear of him that Yudhi·shthira, the King of Law, a bull among men, did not sleep at all for thirteen years. It was after relying on the courage of that courageous and great man that my son* forcefully led the Pándavas' wife* to the assembly hall. And then in the middle of the assembly hall while the
Pándavas watched on, it was he who called the Panchála 9.60
princess 'Slave's wife!' in the presence of the Kurus. 'All the equal of barren sesame seeds, Krishná, your husbands are no more! Beautiful lady, serve a different husband!' It was the charioteer's son who had earlier addressed these cruel words to Krishná in the assembly hall. How was he killed by his enemies?

‹yadi Bhīṣmo raṇa|ślāghī, Droṇo vā yudhi dur|madaḥ
na haniṣyati Kaunteyān pakṣa|pātāt, Suyodhana,
sarvān eva haniṣyāmi. vyetu te mānaso jvaraḥ!
kiṃ kariṣyati Gāṇḍīvam, akṣayyau ca mah"|êṣu|dhī,
snigdha|candana|digdhasya mac|charasy' âbhidhāvataḥ?›
9.65 sa nūnam ṛṣabha|skandho hy Arjunena kathaṃ hataḥ?
yaś ca Gāṇḍīva|muktānāṃ sparśam ugram a|cintayan,
‹a|patir hy asi Kṛṣṇ"! êti› bruvan Pārthān avaikṣata.
yasya n' āsīd bhayaṃ Pārthaiḥ sa|putraiḥ sa|Janārdanaiḥ,
sva|bāhu|balam āśritya muhūrtam api, Saṃjaya.
tasya n' âhaṃ vadhaṃ manye devair api sa|Vāsavaiḥ
pratīpam abhidhāvadbhiḥ! kiṃ punas, tāta, Pāṇḍavaiḥ?
na hi jyāṃ saṃspṛśānasya tala|tre v" âpi gṛhṇataḥ
pumān Ādhiratheḥ sthātuṃ kaś cit pramukhato 'rhati.
api syān medinī hīnā soma|sūrya|prabh"|âṃśubhiḥ,
9.70 na vadhaḥ puruṣ'|êndrasya saṃyugeṣv a|palāyinaḥ!
yena mandaḥ sahāyena, bhrātrā Duḥśāsanena ca,
Vāsudevasya dur|buddhiḥ pratyākhyānam arocata.
sa nūnam ṛṣabha|skandhaṃ Karṇaṃ dṛṣṭvā nipātitam,
Duḥśāsanaṃ ca nihataṃ, manye śocati putrakaḥ.
hataṃ Vaikartanaṃ śrutvā dvai|rathe Savyasācinā
jayataḥ Pāṇḍavān dṛṣṭvā, kiṃ svid Duryodhano 'bravīt?

'If Bhishma who is celebrated in battle or Drona who is mad in battle will not kill Kunti's sons because they're partial to them, then I will kill them all, Suyódhana. Let go the fever in your mind! What can the Gandíva bow and those two huge and inexhaustible quivers do to my arrow as it rushes towards them, smeared with sandal and oil?' How 9.65
is it that he, whose shoulders were like a bull's, has now been killed by Árjuna?

And it was he who, ignoring the sharp sensation of arrows released by the Gandíva bow, stared at Pritha's sons and said, 'Krishná, you have no husband!' It was he who had no fear, even for an instant, of Pritha's sons, their sons and Janárdana,* relying upon the strength of his own arms, Sánjaya. I scarcely believe that he would even have been killed by the gods with Vásava* had they rushed on him and he opposed them! How, then, dear friend, by the Pándavas? For when he seizes his bow-string and touches it to his arm-guard, no man can stand against Ádhiratha's son. The earth might even be deprived of rays of light from the sun or moon, but 9.70
that lord of men who never flees in battle cannot be dead!

It was with him as collaborator, and his brother Duhshásana, that the stupid fool* approved the rejection of Vasudéva.* Seeing Karna fallen now, whose shoulders were like a bull's, and Duhshásana killed, I reckon the boy suffers. Once he heard that Vaikártana was killed in a chariot-duel by the Left-handed archer and saw the Pándavas winning, what did Duryódhana say?

Durmarṣaṇaṃ hataṃ dṛṣṭvā, Vṛṣasenaṃ ca saṃyuge,
prabhagnaṃ ca balaṃ dṛṣṭvā vadhyamānaṃ mahā|rathaiḥ,
parāṅ|mukhāṃś ca rājñas tu palāyana|parāyaṇān,
9.75 vidrutān rathino dṛṣṭvā, manye śocati putrakaḥ.
a|neyaś c', âbhimānī ca, dur|buddhir, ajit'|êndriyaḥ;
hat'|ôtsāhaṃ balaṃ dṛṣṭvā, kiṃ svid Duryodhano 'bravīt?
svayaṃ vairaṃ mahat kṛtvā, vāryamāṇaḥ suhṛd|gaṇaiḥ—
pradhane hata|bhūyiṣṭhaiḥ—kiṃ svid Duryodhano 'bravīt?
bhrātaraṃ nihataṃ dṛṣṭvā Bhīmasenena saṃyuge,
rudhire pīyamāne ca, kiṃ svid Duryodhano 'bravīt?
saha Gāndhāra|rājena sabhāyāṃ yad abhāṣata,
‹Karṇo 'rjunaṃ raṇe hantā!› hate tasmin kim abravīt?
dyūtaṃ kṛtvā purā hṛṣṭo, vañcayitvā ca Pāṇḍavān,
9.80 Śakuniḥ Saubalas, tāta, hate Karṇe kim abravīt?
Kṛtavarmā mah"|êṣv|āsaḥ, Sātvatānāṃ mahā|rathaḥ,
Karṇaṃ Vaikartanaṃ dṛṣṭvā, Hārdikyaḥ kim abhāṣata?
brāhmaṇāḥ, kṣatriyā, vaiśyā yasya śikṣām upāsate
dhanur|vedaṃ cikīrṣanto Droṇa|putrasya dhīmataḥ;
yuvā, rūpeṇa sampanno, darśanīyo, mahā|yaśāḥ,
Aśvatthāmā hate Karṇe kim abhāṣata, Saṃjaya?
ācāryo yo dhanur|vede Gautamo ratha|sattamaḥ,
Kṛpaḥ Śāradvatas, tāta, hate Karṇe kim abravīt?
Madra|rājo mah"|êṣv|āsaḥ Śalyaḥ samiti|śobhanaḥ
9.85 dṛṣṭvā vinihataṃ Karṇaṃ sārathye rathināṃ varaḥ,
kim abhāṣata Sauvīro Madrāṇām adhipo balī?

And after seeing Durmárshana and Vrisha·sena killed in
battle, after seeing his army routed and being slaughtered
by mighty warriors, and after seeing the kings turn back determined to escape and his chariot-warriors running away, 9.75
I reckon the boy suffers. He was poorly advised, conceited
and foolish, his passions out of control. Seeing his army
with its will shattered, what did Duryódhana say? Having
himself created this immense feud though he was restrained
by numerous allies—most of whom were killed in battle—
what did Duryódhana say? After seeing Bhima·sena kill his
brother in combat and drink his blood, what did Duryódhana say? Since he said in the assembly hall with the king
of Gandhára, 'Karna will kill Árjuna in battle!' when he was
killed what did he say?

Dear friend, after playing the dice game and deceiving
the Pándavas Súbala's son Shákuni was delighted back then.
When Karna was killed what did he say? Krita·varman is a 9.80
mighty archer, a great warrior of the Sátvatas. When he saw
Vaikártana killed, what did that son of Hrídika say?

Brahmins, kshatriyas and vaishyas seeking the lore of
weaponry are devoted to the teachings of Drona's intelligent
son. A youth endowed with good looks, he is handsome
and very famous. When Karna was killed, Sánjaya, what
did Ashvattháman say?

A teacher in the lore of weaponry and the finest of warriors, what did Sharádvat's son Kripa say, dear friend, when
Karna had been killed? The mighty archer Shalya, the king
of the Madras, is brilliant in battle. When he saw Kar- 9.85
na struck down while he was his charioteer, what did the
powerful ruler of Madra say, the Sauvíra who is the best

dṛṣṭvā vinihataṃ sarve yodhā vāraṇa|dur|jayāḥ,
ye ca ke cana rājānaḥ pṛthivyāṃ yoddhum āgatāḥ,
Vaikartanaṃ hataṃ dṛṣṭvā, kāny abhāṣanta, Saṃjaya?

Droṇe tu nihate vīre ratha|vyāghre nara'|rṣabhe,
ke vā mukham anīkānām āsan, Saṃjaya, bhāgaśaḥ?
Madra|rājaḥ kathaṃ Śalyo niyukto rathināṃ varaḥ
Vaikartanasya sārathye? tan mam' ācakṣva, Saṃjaya!
ke 'rakṣan dakṣiṇaṃ cakraṃ sūta|putrasya yudhyataḥ?
vāmaṃ cakraṃ rarakṣur vā, ke vā vīrasya pṛṣṭhataḥ?
9.90 ke Karṇaṃ na jahuḥ śūrāḥ? ke kṣudrāḥ prādravaṃs tataḥ?
kathaṃ ca vaḥ sametānāṃ hataḥ Karṇo mahā|rathaḥ?

Pāṇḍavāś ca svayaṃ śūrāḥ pratyudīyur mahā|rathāḥ,
sṛjantaḥ śara|varṣāṇi vāri|dhārā iv' âmbu|dāḥ,
sa ca sarpa|mukho divyo mah"|êṣu|pravaras tadā
vyarthaḥ kathaṃ samabhavat? tan mam' ācakṣva, Saṃjaya!

māmakasy' âsya sainyasya hat'|ôtsedhasya, Saṃjaya,
avaśeṣaṃ na paśyāmi kakude mṛdite sati.
tau hi vīrau mah"|êṣv|āsau, mad|arthe tyakta|jīvitau
Bhīṣma|Droṇau hatau śrutvā, ko nv artho jīvitena me?
9.95 punaḥ punar na mṛṣyāmi hataṃ Karṇaṃ ca Pāṇḍavaiḥ
yasya bāhvor balaṃ tulyaṃ kuñjarāṇāṃ śataṃ śataiḥ!

of chariot-warriors? All those warriors whose resistance was difficult to overcome who'd seen him struck down, and any kings who'd arrived to fight for the earth who had seen Vaikártana slain, what things did they say, Sánjaya?

Once the hero Drona had been slain—that tiger among warriors and bull among men—who led the forces in its various parts, Sánjaya? How was Shalya, the king of the Madras and finest of chariot-warriors, appointed Vaikártana's charioteer? Sánjaya,explain this to me! Who protected the right wheel of the charioteer's son as he fought? And who protected the hero's left wheel and who protected him from
behind? Who were the heroes that didn't leave Karna's side? 9.90
And who were the weak bastards that fled from him? And how could Karna—a mighty warrior!—have been killed amidst all of you together?

And when those mighty warriors the Pándava heroes themselves attacked him, releasing torrents of arrows like rain-clouds torrents of water, how did the finest of the great arrows, that divine arrow with the serpent's head, then become useless? Sánjaya, explain this to me!

I see no survivors among my army, Sánjaya, with its pride shattered now that its chief has been killed. Now that I've heard that the mighty archers Bhishma and Drona have been killed—both heroes giving up their lives for my
cause!—what point is there in me remaining alive? I can 9.95
endure no more now that the Pándavas have killed Karna, the might of whose arms was the equal of hundreds upon hundreds of elephants!

Droṇe hate ca yad vṛttaṃ Kauravāṇāṃ paraiḥ saha
saṃgrāme nara|vīrāṇāṃ, tan mam' ācakṣva, Saṃjaya!
yathā Karṇaś ca Kaunteyaiḥ saha yuddham ayojayat,
yathā ca dviṣatāṃ hantā raṇe śāntas, tad ucyatām.»

And when Drona was killed, Sánjaya, tell me what happened in that battle the Káurava heroes had with their enemies! And then please explain how Karna took up the battle with Kunti's sons and how that killer of enemies was then pacified in battle."

10–30

KARNA THE GENERAL, DAY ONE

SAMJAYA uvāca:

10.1 HATE DRONE mah"|êṣv|āse tasminn ahani, Bhārata,
kṛte ca mogha|saṃkalpe Droṇa|putre mahā|rathe,
dravamāṇe, mahā|rāja, Kauravāṇāṃ bal'|ârṇave,
vyūhya Pārthaḥ svakaṃ sainyam atiṣṭhad bhrātṛbhiḥ vṛtaḥ.
tam avasthitam ājñāya putras te, Bharata'|rṣabha,
vidrutaṃ sva|balaṃ dṛṣṭvā pauruṣeṇa nyavārayat.
svam anīkam avasthāpya bāhu|vīryam upāśritaḥ,
yuddhvā ca su|ciraṃ kālaṃ Pāṇḍavaiḥ saha, Bhārata,
10.5 labdha|lakṣaiḥ parair hṛṣṭair vyāyacchadbhiś ciraṃ tadā,
saṃdhyā|kālaṃ samāsādya pratyāhāram akārayat.
kṛtv" âvahāraṃ sainyānāṃ, praviśya śibiraṃ svakam,
Kuravaḥ su|hitaṃ mantraṃ mantrayāṃ cakrire mithaḥ.
paryaṅkeṣu par'|ârdhyeṣu spardhy'|āstaraṇavatsu ca
var'|āsaneṣ' ûpaviṣṭāḥ, sukha|śayyāsv iv' âmarāḥ!
tato Duryodhano rājā sāmnā parama|valgunā
tān ābhāṣya mah"|êṣv|āsān prāpta|kālam abhāṣata:
«mataṃ, matimatāṃ śreṣṭhāḥ, sarve prabrūta, mā ciram!
evaṃ gate tu kiṃ kāryaṃ? kiṃ ca kāryataraṃ, nṛpāḥ?»

SAMJAYA uvāca:

10.10 evam ukte nar'|êndreṇa, nara|siṃhā yuyutsavaḥ
cakrur nānā|vidhāś ceṣṭāḥ siṃh'|āsana|gatās tadā.
teṣāṃ niśamy' êṅgitāni yuddhe prāṇāñ juhūṣatām,
samudvīkṣya mukhaṃ rājño bāl'|ârka|sama|varcasaḥ,

SÁNJAYA said:

ON THAT DAY when Drona the mighty archer was killed, 10.1
Bhárata, and Drona's son, a mighty warrior, had his hopes dashed, and the sea of the army of Káuravas receded, great king, Pritha's son arrayed his troops and waited, surrounded by his brothers. Realizing that he stood nearby and seeing his own army fleeing, bull of Bharatas, your son turned it back with a show of courage. Making his army hold its ground by the strength of his own arms, Bhárata, and after battling for a very long time with his enemies the
Pándavas—who were ecstatic after fighting for so long and 10.5
achieving their goal—he began the retreat once they'd made it to evening.

After directing the troops to put aside their weapons, the Kurus entered their royal encampment and deliberated together on the most advantageous plan. Seated on the finest couches and most excellent seats covered in the best carpets, they were like the immortals on their comfortable couches! After addressing those mighty archers with sympathetic words of the highest beauty, King Duryódhana then said to them at the appropriate moment: "All of you, the finest of intelligent men, speak your thoughts without delay! What should we do now that he's gone? And, kings, what would be even better to do?"

SÁNJAYA said:

When that lord of men had said this, those battle-eager 10.10
lions of men then gestured vigorously in various ways while seated on their lion seats. Taking note of the gestures of those men who wanted to sacrifice their lives in battle and seeing

ācārya|putro medhāvī vākya|jño vākyam ādade:
«rāgo, yogas, tathā dākṣyaṃ, nayaś c' êty artha|sādhakāḥ
upāyāḥ paṇḍitaiḥ proktās; te tu daiva|samāśritāḥ.
loka|pravīrā ye 'smākaṃ deva|kalpā mahā|rathāḥ
nītimantas, tathā yuktā, dakṣā, raktāś ca, te hatāḥ.
na tv eva kāryaṃ nairāśyam asmābhir vijayaṃ prati!
10.15 su|nītair iha sarv'|ârthair daivam apy anulomyate.
te vayaṃ pravaraṃ nṛṇāṃ sarvair guṇa|gaṇair yutam
Karṇaṃ ev' âbhiṣekṣyāmaḥ saināpatyena, Bhārata.
Karṇaṃ senā|patiṃ kṛtvā pramathiṣyāmahe ripūn!
eṣa hy atibalaḥ, śūraḥ, kṛt'|âstro, yuddha|dur|madaḥ,
Vaivasvata iv' â|sahyaḥ, śakto jetuṃ raṇe ripūn!»
etad ācārya|tanayāc chrutvā, rājaṃs, tav' ātmajaḥ
āśāṃ bahu|matīṃ cakre Karṇaṃ prati sa vai tadā,
«hate Bhīṣme ca, Droṇe ca, Karṇo jeṣyati Pāṇḍavān!»
tām āśāṃ hṛdaye kṛtvā, samāśvasya ca, Bhārata,
10.20 tato Duryodhanaḥ prītaḥ priyaṃ śrutv" âsya tad vacaḥ
prīti|satkāra|saṃyuktaṃ, tathyam, ātma|hitaṃ, śubham,
svaṃ manaḥ samavasthāpya bāhu|vīryam upāśritaḥ,
Duryodhano, mahā|rāja, Rādheyam idam abravīt:
«Karṇa, jānāmi te vīryaṃ, sauhṛdaṃ paramaṃ mayi;
tath" âpi tvāṃ, mahā|bāho, pravakṣyāmi hitaṃ vacaḥ.
śrutvā yath"|êṣṭaṃ ca kuru, vīra, yat tava rocate!
bhavān prājñatamo nityaṃ mama c' âiva parā gatiḥ.

the king's face radiant like the morning sun, the teacher's son,* who was astute and clever with words, offered this advice:

"Passion, method, skill and prudence are the measures the learned consider effective; but they depend on divine fate. Our mighty warriors, god-like heroes of the world, were killed though they were prudent, methodical, skilful and passionate. But we should not despair at victory! With all 10.15
measures well executed, even fate follows regular paths. We should immediately consecrate Karna with the generalship, Bhárata. He is the best of men, possessing all types of good qualities. Once we've made Karna general, we will destroy our enemies! For that hero is exceedingly strong, skilled with his weapons, battle-mad and as insufferable as Yama; he can defeat our enemies in battle!"

After hearing this from the teacher's son, king, your son then entertained this deeply felt hope regarding Karna, "With Bhishma and Drona killed, Karna will defeat the Pándavas!" Taking this hope to heart and recovering his composure, Bhárata, Duryódhana was then pleased after 10.20
hearing those pleasing words of Ashvattháman which were filled with reverence and affection and were true, good for the soul and auspicious. Collecting his thoughts and relying upon his strength of arms, great king, Duryódhana said this to Radha's son:

"Karna, I know of your courage and your great affection for me. Even so, man of mighty arms, I will speak these salutary words to you. Listen as you wish and do what pleases you, hero! You were always the wisest man and my best means of success.

Bhīṣma|Droṇāv atirathau hatau senā|patī mama.
senā|patir bhavān astu, tābhyāṃ draviṇavattaraḥ!
10.25 vṛddhau ca tau mah"|êṣv|āsau, s'|âpekṣau ca Dhanaṃjaye;
mānitau ca mayā vīrau, Rādheya, vacanāt tava.
pitā|mahatvaṃ saṃprekṣya Pāṇḍu|putrā mahā|raṇe
rakṣitās, tāta, Bhīṣmeṇa divasāni daś' âiva ha.
nyasta|śastre ca bhavati hato Bhīṣmaḥ pitā|mahaḥ
Śikhaṇḍinaṃ puraskṛtya Phālgunena mah"|āhave.
hate tasmin mah"|êṣv|āse śara|talpa|gate tadā
tvay" ôkte, puruṣa|vyāghra, Droṇo hy āsīt puraḥ|saraḥ.
ten' âpi rakṣitāḥ Pārthāḥ śiṣyatvād, iti me matiḥ;
sa c' âpi nihato vṛddho Dhṛṣṭadyumnena sa|tvaram.
10.30 nihatābhyāṃ pradhānābhyāṃ tābhyām, a|mita|vikrama,
tvat|samaṃ samare yodhaṃ n' ânyaṃ paśyāmi, cintayan!
bhavān eva tu naḥ śakto vijayāya, na saṃśayaḥ,
pūrvaṃ, madhye ca, paścāc ca tath" âiva vihitaṃ hitam.
sa bhavān dhuryavat saṃkhye dhuram udvoḍhum arhati.
abhiṣecaya saināṅye svayam ātmānam ātmanā!
devatānāṃ yathā Skandaḥ senā|nīḥ prabhur a|vyayaḥ,
tathā bhavān imāṃ senāṃ Dhārtarāṣṭrīṃ bibhartu me!
jahi śatru|gaṇān sarvān Mahendro dānavān iva!
avasthitaṃ raṇe dṛṣṭvā Pāṇḍavās tvāṃ mahā|rathāḥ
10.35 dravisyanti ca Pañcālā, Viṣṇuṃ dṛṣṭv" êva dānavāḥ.
tasmāt tvaṃ, puruṣa|vyāghra, prakarṣ' âitāṃ mahā|camūm!

Now that both my generals, the supreme warriors Bhishma and Drona, have been killed, please be general! You are more powerful than those two! Those mighty archers were 10.25
old and they looked out for Dhanan·jaya. But I respected those heroes because of your advice, son of Radha. Bhishma, conscious that he was their grandfather, dear friend, protected Pandu's sons for ten days in the great war. And while his weapon was lowered, grandfather Bhishma was struck down in the great battle by Phálguna who had placed Shikhándin before him.

When the mighty archer had been struck down and lay upon the bed of arrows, you spoke to him, tiger among men. Consequently, Drona went before you. I reckon that he also protected Pritha's sons because they were his students. And that old man too was quickly killed by Dhrishta·dyumna. Now that I think about it, in battle I see no other 10.30
warrior the equal of you—your courage was unrivalled even be those two slain chiefs! Without any doubt, you alone can triumph for us, since, in times past, lately and in the period in between, you've done well for us.

Like a beast of burden, you ought to bear this load in battle. You yourself must consecrate yourself by yourself in the generalship! Just as the imperishable lord Skanda was the commander of the army of the gods, so you must sustain the Dhartaráshtra army! Destroy all our enemy hordes, 10.35
like great Indra the *dánava*s! Seeing you engaged in battle, as when the *dánava*s saw Vishnu, the great Pándava and Panchála warriors will flee. Therefore, tiger among men, you must lead this great army! While you remain standing,

bhavaty avasthite yat te Pāṇḍavā manda|cetasaḥ
draviṣyanti sah'|âmātyāḥ, Pañcālāḥ Sṛñjayāś ca ha.
yathā hy abhyuditaḥ sūryaḥ pratapan svena tejasā
vyapohati tamas tīvraṃ, tathā śatrūn pratāpaya!»

SAMJAYA uvāca:

āśā balavatī, rājan, putrasya tava y" âbhavat,
hate Bhīṣme ca Droṇe ca Karṇo jeṣyati Pāṇḍavān.
tām āśāṃ hṛdaye kṛtvā Karṇam evaṃ tad" âbravīt:
«sūta|putra, na te Pārthaḥ sthitv" âgre saṃyuyutsati!»

KARNA uvāca:

10.40 «uktam etan mayā pūrvaṃ Gāndhāre tava saṃnidhau,
jeṣyāmi Pāṇḍavān sarvān sa|putrān sa|Janārdanān.
senā|patir bhaviṣyāmi tav' âhaṃ, n' âtra saṃśayaḥ!
sthiro bhava, mahā|rāja! jitān viddhi ca Pāṇḍavān!»

SAMJAYA uvāca:

evam ukto, mahā|rāja, tato Duryodhano nṛpaḥ
uttasthau rājabhiḥ sārdhaṃ, devair iva Śatakratuḥ,
sainâpatyena satkartuṃ Karṇaṃ, Skandam iv' âmarāḥ.
tato 'bhiṣiṣicuḥ Karṇaṃ, vidhi|dṛṣṭena karmaṇā,
Duryodhana|mukhā, rājan, rājāno vijay'|âiṣiṇaḥ,
śāta|kumbha|mayaiḥ kumbhair, māheyaiś c' âbhimantritaiḥ,
10.45 toya|pūrṇa|viṣāṇaiś ca
dvipa|khaḍga|maha"|rṣabhaiḥ,
maṇi|mukt'|āyutaiś c' ânyaiḥ,
puṇya|gandhais tath" āuṣadhaiḥ,
audumbare sukh'|āsīnam āsane kṣauma|saṃvṛte,

the Pándavas, Panchálas and Srínjayas, their minds bewildered, will flee along with their ministers. Just as the risen sun burning with its own fiery energy completely drives away the darkness, so you must torment our enemies!"

SÁNJAYA said:

This was your son's fervent hope, king, that, with Bhishma and Drona slain, Karna would defeat the Pándavas. Taking this hope to heart, he then said this to Karna: "Son of a charioteer, once Pritha's son stands before you, he won't want to fight!"

KARNA said:

"Once before in Gandhára I said before you that I will 10.40
defeat all the Pándavas along with their sons and Janárdana. I will be your general! On this there is no doubt! Be strong, great king, and regard the Pándavas as defeated already!"

SÁNJAYA said:

Spoken to like this, great king, King Duryódhana then rose together with the kings—just as Shata·kratu* rose with
the gods—to honor Karna with the generalship—just as 10.45
the immortals honored Skanda. Then with Duryódhana in their lead and eager for victory, king, the kings consecrated Karna with the rite prescribed by rule—comfortably seating him on a seat made from *udúmbara* wood and covered with linen—with sanctified golden and earthen pots, with water-filled horns of elephants, rhinoceroses and great bulls, and others filled with jewels and pearls and pleasant smelling herbs, according to the rule prescribed in the scriptures and with well-prepared materials. Brahmins, kshatriyas, vaishyas

śāstra|dṛṣṭena vidhinā, saṃbhārais ca su|saṃbhṛtaiḥ.
brāhmaṇāḥ, kṣatriyā, vaiśyās, tathā śūdrāś ca saṃmatāḥ
tuṣṭuvus taṃ mah"|ātmānam abhiṣiktaṃ var'|āsane.

tato 'bhiṣikte, rāj'|êndra, niṣkair, gobhir, dhanena ca
vācayām āsa vipr'|âgryān Rādheyaḥ para|vīra|hā.
«jaya Pārthān sa|Govindān s'|ânugāṃs tān mahā|mṛdhe!»
iti taṃ bandinaḥ prāhur, dvijāś ca puruṣa'|rṣabham.
10.50 «jahi Pārthān sa|Pāñcālān, Rādheya, vijayāya naḥ,
udyann iva sadā bhānus tamāṃsy ugrair gabhastibhiḥ!
na hy alaṃ tvad|visṛṣṭānāṃ śarāṇāṃ vai sa|Keśavāḥ,
ulūkāḥ sūrya|raśmīnāṃ jvalatām iva darśane!
na hi Pārthāḥ sa|Pāñcālāḥ sthātuṃ śaktās tav' âgrataḥ
ātta|śastrasya samare, Mahendrasy' êva dānavāḥ!»

abhiṣiktas tu Rādheyaḥ prabhayā so 'mita|prabhaḥ
atyaricyata rūpeṇa, divākara iv' âparaḥ.

sainâpatye tu Rādheyam abhiṣicya sutas tava
amanyata tad" ātmānaṃ kṛt'|ârthaṃ Kāla|coditaḥ.
10.55 Karṇo 'pi, rājan, saṃprāpya sainâpatyam ariṃ|damaḥ
yogam ājñāpayām āsa sūryasy' ôdayanaṃ prati.
tava putrair vṛtaḥ Karṇaḥ śuśubhe tatra, Bhārata,
devair iva yathā Skandaḥ saṃgrāme Tārakā|maye!

and well regarded shudras celebrated the great man consecrated on that excellent seat.

After he had been consecrated, lord of kings, Radha's son, a killer of enemy-heroes, encouraged the foremost brahmins to speak with gifts of gold collars, cows and wealth. "Defeat Pritha's sons and Go·vinda* and their followers in the great war!" the bards and brahmins said to that bull among men.
"Kill Pritha's sons along with the Panchálas for our victory, 10.50
son of Radha, just as the sun rising always destroys the darkness with its formidable rays! For, those with Késhava are truly unable to look at your arrows once they've been discharged, just as owls can't look at the burning rays of the sun! Pritha's sons and the Panchálas cannot stand before you once you've grasped your weapon in battle, just like the *dánava*s before Indra!"

Once he had been consecrated, Radha's son, whose radiance had no limit, remained unequalled in beauty and radiance, like the sun in the western sky.

And after consecrating Radha's son in the generalship, your son, impelled by Time, then thought his own goal
accomplished. And after assuming the generalship, Karna, a 10.55
conqueror of enemies, commanded the horses be harnessed at the rising of the sun. Surrounded by your sons, Karna shone there, Bhárata, like Skanda when surrounded by the gods in the battle for Taraká!*

DHṚTARĀṢṬRA uvāca:

11.1 SAINĀPATYAM TU saṃprāpya Karṇo Vaikartanas tadā,
tath" ôktaś ca svayaṃ rājñā snigdhaṃ bhrātṛ|samaṃ vacaḥ,
yogam ājñāpya senānām āditye 'bhyudite tadā,
akarot kiṃ mahā|prājñas? tan mam' ācakṣva, Saṃjaya!

SAṂJAYA uvāca:

Karṇasya matam ājñāya putrās te, Bharata'|rṣabha,
yogam ājñāpayām āsur nandi|tūrya|puraḥsaram.
mahaty apara|rātre tu tava sainyasya, māriṣa,
«yogo! yogeti»* sahasā prādur āsīn mahā|svanaḥ.
11.5 kalpatāṃ nāga|mukhyānāṃ, rathānāṃ ca varūthinām,
sannahyatāṃ narāṇāṃ ca, vājināṃ ca, viśāṃ pate,
krośatāṃ c' âiva yodhānāṃ tvaritānāṃ parasparam,
babhūva tumulaḥ śabdo diva|spṛk, su|mahāṃs tataḥ.

tataḥ śveta|patākena, balākā|varṇa|vājinā,
hema|pṛṣṭhena dhanuṣā, nāga|kakṣeṇa ketunā,
tūṇīra|śata|pūrṇena, sa|gadena varūthinā,
śata|ghnī|kiṅkiṇī|śakti|śūla|tomara|dhāriṇā,
kārmukair upapannena, vimal'|āditya|varcasā,
rathen' âbhipatākena sūta|putro 'bhyadṛśyata,
11.10 dhmāpayan vāri|jaṃ, rājan, hema|jāla|vibhūṣitam,
vidhunvāno mahac cāpaṃ kārtasvara|vibhūṣitam.

dṛṣṭvā Karṇaṃ mah"|êṣv|āsaṃ,
ratha|sthaṃ, rathināṃ varam,
bhānumantam iv' ôdyantaṃ,
tamo ghnantaṃ, dur|āsadam,

DHRITA·RASHTRA said:

BUT AFTER KARNA Vaikártana had assumed command of the army, and he'd been addressed by the king himself with affectionate words fit for a brother, and after he'd ordered the arraying of the forces at sun rise, what did that very wise man do? Tell me this, Sánjaya! 11.1

SÁNJAYA said:

After they were apprised of Karna's plan, bull of Bharatas, your sons ordered the army's preparation to the accompaniment of joyful music. During that long last period of the night, dear friend, a great sound suddenly arose from your troops, "Get ready! Get ready!" A huge, chaotic sound that 11.5
touched the sky arose from there, of the finest elephants being organised, of chariots being fortified, of men and horses donning their armor, lord of the people, and of hustling warriors egging each other on.

Then the charioteer's son appeared with his gilded bow and his bannered chariot. Radiant like the spotless sun, it was equipped with bows and bore *shata·ghnis*,* small bells, spears, pikes and lances. It was fitted with defensive armor and a mace, and filled with a hundred quivers. Its banner displayed an elephant's girdle, its horses were the color of cranes and its flag was white. Karna was blowing his conch, 11.10
king, that was decorated with golden webbing, and shaking his great bow that was decorated with gold.

Once they saw that mighty archer Karna, the best of chariot-warriors, standing in his chariot as irresistible as the rising sun overwhelming the dark, dear friend, no Káurava

na Bhīṣma|vyasanaṃ ke cin, n' âpi Droṇasya, māriṣa,
n' ânyeṣāṃ, puruṣa|vyāghra, menire tatra Kauravāḥ.
tatas tu tvarayan yodhāñ śaṅkha|śabdena, māriṣa,
Karṇo niṣkarṣayām āsa Kauravāṇāṃ mahad balam.
vyūhaṃ vyūhya mah"|êṣv|āso makaraṃ śatru|tāpanaḥ
pratyudyayau tathā Karṇaḥ Pāṇḍavān vijigīṣayā.
11.15 makarasya tu tuṇḍe vai Karṇo, rājan, vyavasthitaḥ,
netrābhyāṃ Śakuniḥ śūra, Ulūkaś ca mahā|rathaḥ;
Droṇa|putras tu śirasi, grīvāyāṃ sarva|sodarāḥ,
madhye Duryodhano rājā balena mahatā vṛtaḥ;
vāma|pāde tu, rāj'|êndra, Kṛtavarmā vyavasthitaḥ,
Nārāyaṇa|balair yukto, go|pālair yuddha|dur|madaiḥ;
pāde tu dakṣiṇe, rājan, Gautamaḥ satya|vikramaḥ,
Trigartaiḥ su|mah"|êṣv|āsair, dākṣiṇātyaiś ca saṃvṛtaḥ;
anupādas tu yo vāmas tatra Śalyo vyavasthitaḥ,
mahatyā senayā sārdhaṃ Madra|deśa|samutthayā;
11.20 dakṣiṇe tu, mahā|rāja, Suṣeṇaḥ satya|saṃgaraḥ,
vṛto ratha|sahasreṇa, dantināṃ ca tribhiḥ śataiḥ;
pucche hy āstāṃ mahā|vīryau bhrātarau pārthivau tadā
Citraś ca Citrasenaś ca, mahatyā senayā vṛtau.
tataḥ prayāte, rāj'|êndra, Karṇe nara|var'|ôttame,
Dhanaṃjayam abhiprekṣya Dharma|rājo 'bravīd idam:
«paśya, Pārtha, yathā senā Dhārtarāṣṭr" îha saṃyuge
Karṇena vihitā, vīra, guptā vīrair mahā|rathaiḥ!
hata|vīratamā hy eṣā Dhārtarāṣṭrī mahā|camūḥ,
phalgu|śeṣā, mahā|bāho, tṛṇais tulyā matā mama!

there worried about Bhishma's disaster, or Drona's, or anyone else's, tiger among men.

Then, urging the warriors with the sound of his conch, dear friend, Karna drew out the Káuravas' massive army. Having arrayed the army in the crocodile battle array, Karna, a mighty archer and tormenter of enemies, went forth with the intention of defeating the Pándavas.

Karna was positioned in the snout of the crocodile array, 11.15
king, the champion Shákuni and the great warrior Ulúka at its eyes, and Drona's son was at its head. With all his brothers at its neck, King Duryódhana was in the middle, surrounded by his massive army. Krita·varman was stationed at its left foot, lord of kings, with the Naráyana troops and battle-mad cow-herders; and at its right foot, king, was the truly courageous Gáutama, surrounded by archers of immense power from Tri·garta and the south. Shalya was stationed at the left hind foot together with his great army gathered
from the country of Madra; and at the right, great king, 11.20
was Sushéna, who was true to his promises, surrounded by a thousand chariots and three hundred elephants. Then at the tail was a pair of immensely courageous brothers, the princes Chitra and Chitra·sena, surrounded by their mighty army.

As Karna, the finest of excellent men, marched out, lord of kings, the King of Law* looked at Dhanan·jaya and said this: "Son of Pritha, look how Karna has arranged the Dhartaráshtras' army for this battle, hero, and how it is protected by those mighty warrior heroes! Since the Dhartaráshtras' great army has few survivors, its most eminent heroes killed, in my reckoning, mighty-armed man, it is the

11.25 eko hy atra mah"|êṣv|āsaḥ sūta|putro virājate,
sa|dev'|âsura|gandharvaiḥ, sa|kiṃnara|mah"|ôragaiḥ,
car'|âcarais tribhir lokair yo 'jayyo rathināṃ varaḥ!
taṃ hatv" âdya, mahā|bāho, vijayas tava, Phālguna,
uddhṛtaś ca bhavec chalyo mama dvādaśa|vārṣikaḥ.
evaṃ jñātvā, mahā|bāho, vyūhaṃ vyūha yath" êcchasi!»

bhrātur etad vacaḥ śrutvā Pāṇḍavaḥ śveta|vāhanaḥ
ardha|candreṇa vyūhena pratyavyūhata tāṃ camūm.
vāma|pārśve tu tasy' âtha Bhīmaseno vyavasthitaḥ,
dakṣiṇe ca mah"|êṣv|āso Dhṛṣṭadyumno vyavasthitaḥ;
11.30 madhye vyūhasya rājā tu Pāṇḍavaś ca Dhanaṃjayaḥ,
Nakulaḥ Sahadevaś ca Dharma|rājasya pṛṣṭhataḥ.
cakra|rakṣau tu Pāñcālyau Yudhāmany'|Ûttamaujasau
n' Ârjunaṃ jahatur yuddhe pālyamānau Kirīṭinā.
śeṣā nṛpatayo vīrāḥ sthitā vyūhasya daṃśitāḥ,
yathā|bhāgaṃ, yath"|ôtsāhaṃ, yathā|yatnaṃ ca, Bhārata.

evam etan mahā|vyūhaṃ vyūhya, Bhārata, Pāṇḍavāḥ,
tāvakāś ca mah"|êṣv|āsā yuddhāy' âiva mano dadhuḥ.
dṛṣṭvā vyūḍhāṃ tava camūṃ sūta|putreṇa saṃyuge,
nihatān Pāṇḍavān mene Dhārtarāṣṭraḥ sa|bāndhavaḥ.
11.35 tath" âiva Pāṇḍavīṃ senāṃ vyūḍhāṃ dṛṣṭvā Yudhiṣṭhiraḥ
Dhārtarāṣṭrān hatān mene sa|Karṇān vai jan'|âdhipaḥ.

equal of grass! For only one mighty archer, the charioteer's 11.25
son, shines forth there; that superb chariot-warrior couldn't be defeated by any creature moving or not moving in the three worlds, including the gods, demons, *gandhárvas*, *kínnaras** and great serpents! Once you've killed him today, mighty-armed Phálguna, victory is yours, and my thorn for the last twelve years shall have been removed. Understand this, man of mighty-arms, and array the army as you wish!"

After listening to his brother's words, the Pándava with the white horses* arranged his forces against that army with the half-moon battle array. Bhima·sena was stationed on its left flank, king, and the mighty archer Dhrishta·dyum-
na was stationed on its right. In the middle of the array 11.30
was the king and the Pándava Dhanan·jaya; and Nákula and Saha·deva were behind the King of Law. And the two Panchála wheel-protectors, Yudha·manyu and Uttamáujas, while being guarded by the Wearer of the crown, did not desert Árjuna in battle. The army's remaining kings—heroes clad in armor!—were positioned each in their proper place according to their energy and their strength, Bhárata.

In this way the Pándavas arrayed their massive army, Bhárata, and your mighty archers fixed their minds on battle alone. When they saw your army arrayed for battle by the charioteer's son, Dhrita·rashtra's son* and his kin considered the Pándavas already killed. Similarly, when he saw 11.35
the Pándava army arrayed, Yudhi·shthira, a ruler of people, considered the Dhartaráshtras and Karna already slain.

tataḥ śaṅkhāś ca, bheryaś ca, paṇav'|ānaka|dundubhiḥ,
ḍiṇḍimāś c' âpy ahanyanta, jharjharāś ca samantataḥ.
senayor ubhayo, rājan, prāvādyanta mahā|svanāḥ,
siṃha|nādaś ca saṃjajñe śūrāṇāṃ jaya|gṛddhinām.
haya|heṣita|śabdāś ca, vāraṇānāṃ ca bṛṃhatām,
ratha|nemi|svanāś c' ôgrāḥ saṃbabhūvur, jan'|âdhipa.
na Droṇa|vyasanaṃ kaś cij jānīte tatra, Bhārata,
dṛṣṭvā Karṇaṃ mah"|êṣv|āsaṃ mukhe vyūhasya daṃśitam.
11.40 ubhe sainye, mahā|rāja, prahṛṣṭa|nara|saṃkule
yoddhu|kāme sthite, rājan, hantum anyonyam ojasā.
tatra yattau su|saṃrabdhau dṛṣṭv" ânyonyaṃ vyavasthitau
anīka|madhye, rāj'|êndra, ceratuḥ Karṇa|Pāṇḍavau.
nṛtyamāne ca te sene sameyātāṃ parasparam,
teṣāṃ pakṣaiḥ prapakṣaiś ca nirjagmus te yuyutsavaḥ.
tataḥ pravavṛte yuddhaṃ nara|vāraṇa|vājinām,
rathānāṃ ca, mahā|rāja, anyonyaṃ abhinighnatāṃ!

SAṂJAYA uvāca:

12.1 TE SENE 'NYONYAM āsādya prahṛṣṭ'|âśva|nara|dvipe
bṛhatyau saṃprajahrāte dev'|âsura|sama|prabhe.
tato nara|rath'|âśv'|êbhāḥ, pattayaś c' ôgra|vikramāḥ
saṃprahārān bhṛśaṃ cakrur deha|pāpm'|âsu|nāśanān.
pūrṇa|candr'|ârka|padmānāṃ kāntibhir gandhataḥ samaiḥ
uttam'|âṅgair nṛ|siṃhānāṃ nṛ|siṃhās tastarur mahīm.
ardha|candrais, tathā bhallaiḥ, kṣuraprair, asi|paṭṭiśaiḥ,

Then conches and kettle-drums, cymbals and *ánaka·dúndubhi* drums, and *díndima* and *jhárjhara* drums were pounded on all sides. From both armies thunderous rackets were raised, and a lion's roar arose from those heroes desperate for victory. And the sounds of neighing horses and trumpeting elephants and the sharp sounds of chariot wheels came forth, ruler of the people.

No one who saw Karna there, a mighty archer clad in armor and at the head of his army, Bhárata, recalled Drona's disaster.

Both armies, great king, were crowded with excited men. 11.40
Eager for battle, king, they were determined to kill one another with their might. Alert and furious after spotting one another there, lord of kings, Karna and the Pándava roamed about stationed in the midst of their forces.

And as they gesticulated, the two armies drew near one another and battle-eager warriors started forward through their flanks and outer flanks. Then the battle began, great king, of men, elephants, horses and chariots assailing one another!

SÁNJAYA said:

AFTER ATTACKING one another, the two massive armies 12.1
fought together, their horses, men and elephants excited and their splendor equal to the gods and demons. Men, chariots, horses, elephants and foot-soldiers of formidable courage then began brutally striking each other, destroying their bodies, sins and lives. Lion-like men scattered the earth with the heads of other lion-like men, their brilliance equal to a full moon or the sun and their fragrance the equal of a

paraśvadhaiś c' âpy akṛntann uttam'|âṅgāni yudhyatām.
12.5 vyāyat'|āyata|bāhūnāṃ vyāyat'|āyata|bāhubhiḥ
bāhavaḥ pātitā rejur dharaṇyāṃ s'|āyudh'|âṅgadaiḥ.
taiḥ sphuradbhir mahī bhāti rakt'|âṅguli|talais tathā
Garuḍa|prahitair ugraiḥ pañc'|āsyair uragair iva.

dvirada|syandan'|âśvebhyaḥ petur vīrā dviṣadd|hatāḥ,
vimānebhyo, yathā kṣīṇe puṇye svarga|sadas, tathā.
gadābhir anye gurvībhiḥ, parighair, musalair api
pothitāḥ śataśaḥ petur vīrā vīratarai raṇe.

rathā rathair vimathitā, mattā mattair dvipā dvipaiḥ,
sādinaḥ sādibhiś c' âiva tasmin parama|saṃkule.
12.10 rathair narā, rathā nāgair, aśv'|ārohāś ca pattibhiḥ,
aśv'|ārohaiḥ padātāś ca nihatā yudhi śerate,
rath'|âśva|pattayo nāgai, rath'|âśv'|êbhāś ca pattibhiḥ,
ratha|patti|dvipāś c' âśvai, rathaiś c' âpi nara|dvipāḥ.
rath'|âśv'|êbha|narāṇāṃ tu nar'|âśv'|êbha|rathaiḥ kṛtam
pāṇi|pādaiś ca, śastraiś ca, rathaiś ca kadanaṃ mahat.

tathā tasmin bale śūrair vadhyamāne hate 'pi ca
asmān abhyāyayuḥ Pārthā Vṛkodara|puro|gamāḥ.
Dhṛṣṭadyumnaḥ, Śikhaṇḍī ca,
Draupadeyāḥ, Prabhadrakāḥ,

lotus. And with half-moon arrows, broad arrows and razor-edged arrows, and swords, tridents and axes, they cut off the heads of those who fought.

The arms of those having long and strong arms felled by 12.5
others having long and strong arms glittered on the ground with their weapons and bracelets. With those quivering arms and bloodied fingers and palms, the earth looked as if it was scattered with dreadful five-headed serpents hurled down by Gáruda.

Heroes slain by their enemies fell from elephants, chariots and horses, just as the gods fall from their celestial vehicles when their merit has been destroyed. Other heroes were felled by the hundreds, crushed in battle by heroes stronger than they with heavy clubs, maces and iron bludgeons.

In that extraordinary battle, chariots were destroyed by chariots, excited elephants by excited elephants and horsemen by horsemen. Men lay prone in the battle destroyed 12.10
by chariots, as did chariots destroyed by elephants, horsemen by foot-soldiers, and foot-soldiers by horsemen; and so too chariots, horses and foot-soldiers by elephants; chariots, horses and elephants by foot-soldiers; chariots, foot-soldiers and elephants by horses; and men and elephants by chariots. With their hands, feet, weapons and chariots, men, horses, elephants and chariots created great carnage among chariots, horses, elephants and men.

While champions destroyed and slaughtered the army like this, Pritha's sons advanced on us with Wolf-belly in their lead. Surrounded by a massive army, Dhrishta·dyumna, Shikhándin, Dráupadi's sons, the Prabhádrakas, Sát-

Sātyakiś, Cekitānaś ca,
Draviḍaiḥ sainikaiḥ saha,
12.15 vṛtā vyūhena mahatā, Pāṇḍyāś, Colāḥ sa|Keralāḥ,
vyūḍh'|ôraskā, dīrgha|bhujāḥ, prāṃśavaḥ, pṛthu|locanāḥ,
āpīḍino, rakta|dantā, matta|mātaṅga|vikramāḥ,
nānā|virāga|vasanā, gandha|cūrṇ'|âvacūrṇitāḥ,
baddh'|âsayaḥ, pāśa|hastā, vāraṇa|prativāraṇāḥ,
samāna|mṛtyavo, rājan, n' âtyajanta parasparam.
kalāpinaś, cāpa|hastā, dīrgha|keśāḥ, priyaṃ|vadāḥ
pattayaḥ sādinaś c' ânye ghora|rūpa|parākramāḥ.
ath' âpare punaḥ śūrāś Cedi|Pañcāla|Kekayāḥ,
Karūṣāḥ, Kosalāḥ, Kāñcyā, Māgadhāś c' âpi dudruvuḥ.
12.20 teṣāṃ rath'|âśva|nāgāś ca, pravarāś c' âgra|pattayaḥ
nānā|vādya|dharair hṛṣṭā nṛtyanti ca hasanti ca.
tasya sainyasya mahato, mahā|mātra|varair vṛtaḥ,
madhye Vṛk'|ôdaro 'bhyāyāt tvadīyaṃ, nāga|dhūr|gataḥ.
sa nāga|pravaro 'tyugro, vidhivat kalpito babhau,
uday'|âgr'|âdri|bhavanaṃ yath" âbhyudita|bhāskaram.
tasy' āyasaṃ varma varaṃ, vara|ratna|vibhūṣitam,
tārā|vyāptasya nabhasaḥ śāradasya sama|tviṣam.
sa tomara|vyagra|karaś, cāru|mauliḥ, sv|alaṃ|kṛtaḥ,
śaran|madhyaṃ|din'|ârk'|ābhas, tejasā vyadahad ripūn.
12.25 taṃ dṛṣṭvā dvi|radaṃ dūrāt Kṣemadhūrtir dvipa|sthitaḥ
āhvayann abhidudrāva pramanāḥ pramanastaram.
tayoḥ samabhavad yuddhaṃ dvipayor ugra|rūpayoḥ
yadṛcchayā drumavator mahā|parvatayor iva.

yaki, Chekitána and the Dravidian division, the Pandyas, 12.15
Cholas and Kéralas—tall, broad chested, long armed and large eyed, sporting wreaths, their teeth red, their courage that of ruttish elephants, their clothes colorful and sprinkled with fragrances and aromatic powders, clenching swords, holding nooses and restraining their elephants—were equal in death, king, and never left one another's side. And other long-haired foot-soldiers and horseman with quivers full of arrows, bows in hand and chatting jovially, showed frightful courage. And still more heroes attacked—the Chedis, Panchálas, Kékayas, Karúshas, Kósalas, Kanchis, and Mágadhas. Their chariots, horses and elephants, and their su- 12.20
perb, foremost foot-soldiers, danced and laughed, spurred on by various musicians.

Surrounded by the finest mahouts in the midst of that massive army, Wolf-belly attacked your troops riding atop an elephant. That superb elephant was exceedingly fierce and properly caparisoned and appeared as brilliant as the house on the highest eastern mountain at the sun's rise. Its iron mail was the finest and it was decorated with the finest jewels; it was the equal in brilliance of a star-filled autumnal sky. Shaking his lance, wearing a stunning crown and finely decked out, Bhima seemed like an autumnal midday sun and burnt his enemies with his fiery energy.

Seeing that elephant from afar, Kshema·dhurti fervently 12.25
rode his elephant and, issuing a challenge, attacked that man more fervent than he. Suddenly a battle had begun between those two formidable elephants that were like a pair of massive forested mountains.

saṃsakta|nāgau tau vīrau tomarair itar'|êtaram
balavat sūrya|raśmy'|ābhair bhittv" ânyonyaṃ vinedatuḥ.
vyapasṛtya tu nāgābhyāṃ maṇḍalāni viceratuḥ;
pragṛhya c' ôbhau dhanuṣī jaghnatur vai parasparam.
kṣveḍit'|āsphoṭita|ravair, bāṇa|śabdais tu sarvataḥ
tau janaṃ harṣayantau ca siṃha|nādaṃ pracakratuḥ.
12.30 samudyata|karābhyāṃ tau dvipābhyāṃ kṛtināv ubhau
vāt'|ôddhūta|patākābhyāṃ yuyudhāte mahā|balau.
tāv anyonyasya dhanuṣī chittv" ânyonyaṃ vinedatuḥ
śakti|tomara|varṣeṇa, prāvṛṇ|meghāv iv' âmbubhiḥ.
Kṣemadhūrtis tadā Bhīmaṃ tomareṇa stan'|ântare
nirbibheda tu vegena ṣaḍbhiś c' âpy aparair nadan.
sa Bhīmasenaḥ śuśubhe tomarair aṅgam āśritaiḥ,
krodha|dīpta|vapur meghaiḥ sapta|saptir iv' âṃśumān.
tato bhāskara|varṇ'|ābham, añjo|gatim, ayas|mayam
sasarja tomaraṃ Bhīmaḥ praty amitrāya yatnavān.
12.35 tataḥ Kulūt'|âdhipatiś cāpam ānamya sāyakaiḥ
daśabhis tomaraṃ bhittvā, ṣaṣṭyā vivyādha Pāṇḍavam.
atha kārmukam ādāya Bhīmo jalada|nisvanam,
ripor abhyardayan nāgam unnadan Pāṇḍavaḥ śaraiḥ.
sa śar'|âugh'|ârdito nāgo Bhīmasenena saṃyuge
gṛhyamāṇo 'pi n' âtiṣṭhad, vāt'|ôddhūta iv' âmbu|daḥ.
tam abhyadhāvad dvi|radaṃ bhīmo Bhīmasya nāga|rāṭ,

Their elephants sticking closely together, both heroes brutally pierced each other with lances that seemed like rays of the sun and then bellowed at one another. Then they separated and careered about in circles on their elephants and both grabbed their bows and began to strike one another. Exciting people with their growling, the sounds of their arms being slapped and the buzz of their arrows everywhere, they each gave off a lion's roar. Both skilful with 12.30
their elephants whose trunks were raised high, those mighty men fought with their banners tossing about in the wind. They bellowed at one another after splitting each other's bow with a shower of spears and lances, like two clouds in the rainy season showering with water.

Then Kshema·dhurti wounded Bhima in the center of his chest with a lance and, as he bellowed, with six more in quick succession. With those lances sticking to his limbs and his body burning with anger, Bhima·sena looked as brilliant as the sun with its rays of light piercing through clouds.

Then with great effort Bhima hurled at his enemy a straight-flying iron lance that seemed the color of the sun. Next, bending his bow and splitting that lance with ten ar- 12.35
rows, the ruler of the Kulútas* wounded the Pándava with sixty.

Then the Pándava Bhima grabbed his bow that sounded like a thunder cloud and, as he bellowed, tormented his enemy's elephant with arrows. Tortured by Bhima·sena with waves of arrows, like a cloud stirred by the wind that elephant couldn't hold its position in the battle though it was firmly held. Bhima's formidable king of elephants attacked

mahā|vāt'|ēritaṃ meghaṃ vāt'|ôddhūta iv' âmbu|daḥ.
samnivāry' ātmano nāgaṃ, Kṣemadhūrtiḥ pratāpavān
vivyādh' âbhidrutaṃ bāṇair Bhīmasenasya kuñjaram.
12.40 tataḥ sādhu|visṛṣṭena kṣureṇ' ānata|parvaṇā
chittvā śar'|âsanaṃ śatror, nāgam āmitram ārdayat.
tataḥ kruddho raṇe Bhīmaṃ Kṣemadhūrtiḥ parābhinat,
jaghāna c' âsya dvi|radaṃ nārācaiḥ sarva|marmasu.
sa papāta mahā|nāgo Bhīmasenasya, Bhārata!
purā nāgasya patanād avaplutya sthito mahīm,
tasya Bhīmo 'pi dvi|radaṃ gadayā samapothayat.
tasmāt pramathitān nāgāt Kṣemadhūrtim avaplutam,
udyat'|āyudham āyāntaṃ gaday" âhan Vṛkodaraḥ.
sa papāta hataḥ s'|âsir, vy|asus tam abhito dvipam,
12.45 vajra|prabhagnam acalaṃ siṃho vajra|hato yathā.
taṃ hataṃ nṛ|patiṃ dṛṣṭvā Kulūtānāṃ yaśas|karam
prādravad vyathitā senā tvadīyā, Bharata'|rṣabha!

SAMJAYA uvāca:

13.1 TATAḤ KARṆO mah"|êṣv|āsaḥ Pāṇḍavānām anīkinīm
jaghāna samare śūraḥ śaraiḥ saṃnata|parvabhiḥ.
tath" âiva Pāṇḍavā, rājaṃs, tava putrasya vāhinīm
Karṇasya pramukhe kruddhā nijaghnus te mahā|rathāḥ.
Karṇo 'pi, rājan, samare vyahanat Pāṇḍavīṃ camūm
nārācair arka|raśmy|ābhaiḥ karmāra|parimārjitaiḥ.
tatra, Bhārata, Karṇena nārācais tāḍitā gajāḥ

that elephant, like a cloud stirred by the wind attacking a cloud driven by a mighty wind.*

Restraining his own elephant, with his arrows glorious Kshema·dhurti wounded Bhima's elephant as it attacked.
Splintering his enemy's bow with a well shot smooth-jointed 12.40
razor arrow, Kshema·dhurti then wounded that hostile elephant. In a fury, Kshema·dhurti wounded Bhima in the fight and struck his elephant wherever it was vulnerable with iron arrows. Bhárata, Bhima·sena's mighty elephant collapsed!

Leaping down just before his elephant collapsed, Bhima stood on the ground and he too crushed Kshema·dhurti's elephant with his club. Once Kshema·dhurti had leapt from that crushed elephant, Wolf-belly attacked him with his weapon raised and killed him with his club. Slain, he collapsed lifeless beside his elephant still holding his sword,
as if he were a lion slain by a thunderbolt collapsing beside 12.45
a thunderbolt crushed mountain.

Seeing that king slain who brought fame to the Kulútas, bull of Bharatas, your army became alarmed and fled!

SÁNJAYA said:

THE HERO KARNA, a mighty archer, then hammered the 13.1
army of the Pándavas in battle with his smooth-jointed arrows. Similarly, king, the enraged Pándavas, mighty warriors, struck your son's army in front of Karna. Karna also, king, tore apart the Pándava army in the battle with his iron arrows that, polished by artisans, seemed like rays of the sun. Elephants wounded there by Karna with iron arrows,

neduḥ, seduś ca, mamluś ca, babhramuś ca diśo daśa.
13.5 vadhyamāne bale tasmin sūta|putreṇa, māriṣa,
Nakulo 'bhyadravat tūrṇaṃ sūta|putraṃ mahā|raṇe.
Bhīmasenas tathā Drauṇiṃ kurvāṇaṃ karma duṣ|karam,
Vind'|Ânuvindau Kaikeyau Sātyakiḥ samavārayat.
Śrutakarmāṇam āyāntaṃ Citraseno mahī|patiḥ,
Prativindhyas tathā Citraṃ citra|ketana|kārmukam.
Duryodhanas tu rājānaṃ Dharma|putraṃ Yudhiṣṭhiram,
saṃśaptaka|gaṇān kruddho hy abhyadhāvad Dhanaṃjayaḥ.
Dhṛṣṭadyumnaḥ Kṛpeṇ' âtha tasmin vīra|vara|kṣaye,
Śikhaṇḍī Kṛtavarmāṇaṃ samāsādayad acyutam,
13.10 Śrutakīrtis tathā Śalyaṃ, Mādrī|putraḥ sutaṃ tava
Duḥśāsanaṃ, mahā|rāja, Sahadevaḥ pratāpavān.

Kaikeyau Sātyakiṃ yuddhe, śara|varṣeṇa bhāsvatā,
Sātyakiḥ Kekayau c' âpi cchādayām āsa, Bhārata.
tāv enaṃ bhrātarau vīrau jaghnatur hṛdaye bhṛśam,
viṣāṇābhyāṃ yathā nāgau pratināgaṃ mahā|vane.
śara|saṃbhinna|varmāṇau tāv ubhau bhrātarau raṇe
Sātyakiṃ satya|karmāṇaṃ, rājan, vivyadhatuḥ śaraiḥ.
tau Sātyakir, mahā|rāja, prahasan sarvato|diśam
chādayañ śara|varṣeṇa vārayām āsa, Bhārata.
13.15 vāryamāṇau tatas tau hi Śaineya|śara|vṛṣṭibhiḥ
Śaineyasya rathaṃ tūrṇaṃ chādayām āsatuḥ śaraiḥ.
tayos tu dhanuṣī citre chittvā Śaurir mahā|yaśāḥ
atha tau sāyakais tīkṣṇair vārayām āsa saṃyuge.

Bhárata, bellowed and slumped and wilted and staggered off in the ten directions.

While the charioteer's son destroyed that army, dear 13.5
friend, Nákula quickly attacked the son of the charioteer in that great battle. Bhima·sena repelled Drona's son as he carried out a gruelling task, and Sátyaki repelled the Kaikéyas Vinda and Anuvínda. The lord of the earth Chitra·sena repelled Shruta·karman as he attacked and Prativíndhya repelled Chitra whose bow and banner were beautiful. Duryódhana attacked Dharma's son King Yudhi·shthira, and Dhanan·jaya attacked the hordes of oath-bound warriors in a rage. Then, amidst the carnage of fine heroes, Kripa attacked Dhrishta·dyumna, Shikhándin assailed imperishable
Krita·varman, and Shruta·kirti Shalya. And Madri's glorious 13.10
son Saha·deva, great king, attacked your son Duhshásana.

The two Kaikéyas attacked Sátyaki in the battle, Bhárata, and Sátyaki enveloped the Kékayas with a luminous shower of arrows. Those heroic brothers brutally struck him in his heart, like a pair of elephants in a great forest striking a rival elephant with their tusks. In that battle both brothers, their armor completely shattered by arrows, pelted Sátyaki whose deeds were sincere with their arrows, king. Laughing and enveloping all areas with a torrent of arrows, great
king, Sátyaki pushed those two back, Bhárata. Pushed back 13.15
by torrents of arrows from Shini's grandson,* those two quickly enveloped the chariot of Shini's grandson with arrows. Splintering their beautiful bows, the much celebrated Shauri* then repelled those two in the battle with sharp arrows.

ath' ânye dhanuṣī citre pragṛhya ca mahā|śarān
Sātyakiṃ chādayantau tau ceratur laghu suṣṭhu ca.
tābhyāṃ muktā mahā|bāṇāḥ kaṅka|barhiṇa|vāsasaḥ,
dyotayanto diśaḥ sarvāḥ saṃpetuḥ svarṇa|bhūṣaṇāḥ.
bāṇ'|ândhakāram abhavat tayo, rājan, mahā|mṛdhe,
anyonyasya dhanuś c' âiva cicchidus te mahā|rathāḥ.
13.20 tataḥ kruddho, mahā|rāja, Sātvato yuddha|dur|madaḥ
dhanur anyat samādāya, sa|jyaṃ kṛtvā ca saṃyuge,
kṣurapreṇa su|tīkṣṇena Anuvinda|śiro 'harat.
apatat tac|chiro, rājan, kuṇḍal'|ôpacitaṃ mahat,
Śambarasya śiro yadvan nihatasya mahā|raṇe,
śocayan Kekayān sarvāñ, jagām' āśu vasuṃ|dharām.
tam dṛṣṭvā nihataṃ śūraṃ, bhrātā tasya mahā|rathaḥ
sa|jyam anyad dhanuḥ kṛtvā Śaineyaṃ paryavārayat.
sa ṣaṣṭyā Sātyakiṃ viddhvā svarṇa|puṅkhaiḥ śilā|śitaiḥ,
nanāda balavan nādaṃ, «tiṣṭha! tiṣṭh'! êti» c' âbravīt.
13.25 Sātyakiṃ ca tatas tūrṇaṃ Kekayānāṃ mahā|rathaḥ
śarair aneka|sāhasrair bāhvor urasi c' ārpayat.
sa śaraiḥ kṣata|sarv'|âṅgaḥ Sātyakiḥ satya|vikramaḥ
rarāja samare, rājan, sa|puṣpa iva kiṃśukaḥ.
Sātyakiḥ samare viddhaḥ Kaikeyena mah"|ātmanā,
Kaikeyaṃ pañca|viṃśatyā vivyādha prahasann iva.
tāv anyonyasya samare saṃchidya dhanuṣī śubhe,
hatvā ca sārathī tūrṇaṃ, hayāṃś ca, rathināṃ varau
virathāv asi|yuddhāya samājagmatur āhave.
śata|candra|cite gṛhya carmaṇī su|bhujau tathā

Then they grabbed two other beautiful bows and numerous arrows and quickly and thoroughly continued to envelope Sátyaki. Numerous peacock- and heron-feathered arrows were released by those two. Decorated with gold, they fell illuminating all regions. A darkness arose in that great battle because of their arrows, king, and the mighty warriors splintered each other's bow.

Next, great king, enraged and mad for battle, the Sátvata* 13.20
seized another bow and, stringing it for battle, severed Anuvínda's head with a very sharp arrow. His great head thick with earrings fell down, king, just like the demon Shámbara's head when he was killed in a great battle. Distressing all the Kékayas, it immediately went to ground.

Seeing that hero killed, his mighty warrior brother strung another bow and covered Shini's grandson. Pelting Sátyaki with sixty stone-sharpened arrows with nocks of gold, he mightily roared a roar and yelled, "Stand! Stand your ground!" And then the mighty warrior of the Kékayas 13.25
wounded Sátyaki in the chest and arms with many thousands of arrows.

His entire body wounded by arrows, Sátyaki's courage was true, king, and he was radiant in battle like a *kínshuka* tree in blossom. Wounded in battle by the great Kaikéya, Sátyaki sneered and wounded the Kaikéya with twenty-five arrows.

After destroying one another's beautiful bows in combat and quickly killing their drivers and horses, the two superb chariot-warriors denied their chariots came together in battle to fight with swords. Having grabbed shields inlaid with a hundred moons, their arms impressive and wielding fine 13.30

13.30 virocetāṃ mahā|raṅge nistriṃśa|vara|dhāriṇau,
yathā dev'|âsure yuddhe Jambha|Śakrau mahā|balau.
maṇḍalāni tatas tau tu vicarantau mahā|raṇe,
anyonyam abhitas tūrṇaṃ samājagmatur āhave,
anyonyasya vadhe c' âiva cakratur yatnam uttamam.
Kaikeyasya dvidhā carma tataś ciccheda Sātvataḥ,
Sātyakeś ca tath" âiv' âsau carma ciccheda pārthivaḥ.
carma cchittvā tu Kaikeyas tārā|gaṇa|śatair vṛtam,
cacāra maṇḍalāny eva gata|pratyāgatāni ca.
taṃ carantaṃ mahā|raṅge nistriṃśa|vara|dhāriṇam,
13.35 apahastena ciccheda Śaineyas tvaray" ânvitaḥ.
sa|varmā Kekayo, rājan, dvidhā chinno mahā|raṇe
nipapāta mah"|êṣv|āso, vajr'|āhata iv' âcalaḥ.
taṃ nihatya raṇe śūraḥ Śaineyo ratha|sattamaḥ
Yudhāmanyu|rathaṃ tūrṇam āruroha paraṃ|tapaḥ.
tato 'nyaṃ ratham āsthāya vidhivat kalpitaṃ punaḥ,
Kekayānāṃ mahat sainyaṃ vyadhamat Sātyakiḥ śaraiḥ.
sā vadhyamānā samare Kekayānāṃ mahā|camūḥ
tam utsṛjya raṇe śatruṃ pradudrāva diśo daśa.

SAṂJAYA uvāca:

14.1 ŚRUTAKARMĀ TATO, rājaṃś, Citrasenaṃ mahī|patim
ājaghne samare kruddhaḥ pañcāśadbhiḥ śilīmukhaiḥ.
Abhisāras tu taṃ, rājan, navabhir nata|parvabhiḥ
Śrutakarmāṇam āhatya sūtaṃ vivyādha pañcabhiḥ.

swords, those two were as spectacular on that great arena as powerful Shakra and Jambha* in the battle of the gods and demons. Then, maneuvering in circles in that immense battle, they suddenly came close to one another for combat and began expending enormous effort to kill one another.

Then the Sátvata split the Kaikéya's shield in two and the prince split Sátyaki's shield in the same way. After splitting that shield which was inlaid with multitudes of stars, the Kaikéya then maneuvered in circles, advancing and retreating in turn. As the Kaikéya maneuvered on that great arena
wielding his fine sword, Shini's grandson moved quickly and 13.35
split him with a blow. In that great tussle, king, the Kékaya was split in two in his armor, and that mighty archer collapsed like a mountain struck by lightning.

After killing him in battle, Shini's heroic grandson, the very finest of warriors and a scorcher of enemies, quickly mounted Yudha·manyu's chariot. Then, after once again mounting another well equipped chariot, Sátyaki blew away the massive army of the Kékayas with his arrows. The great army of the Kékayas, being slaughtered in battle, evaded their enemy in the battle and fled in the ten directions.

SÁNJAYA said:

IN RAGE, KING, Shruta·karman then assaulted the lord 14.1
of the earth Chitra·sena with fifty arrows in that battle. But, king, the Abhisára* assaulted Shruta·karman with nine smooth-jointed arrows and wounded his charioteer with five.

Śrutakarmā tataḥ kruddhaś Citrasenaṃ camū|mukhe
nārācena su|tīkṣṇena marma|deśe samārpayat.
so 'tividdho, mahā|rāja, nārācena mah"|ātmanā
mūrchām abhiyayau vīraḥ, kaśmalaṃ c' āviveśa ha!
14.5 etasminn antare c' âinaṃ Śrutakīrtir mahā|yaśāḥ
navatyā jagatī|pālaṃ chādayām āsa patribhiḥ.
pratilabhya tataḥ saṃjñāṃ, Citraseno mahā|rathaḥ
dhanuś ciccheda bhallena, taṃ ca vivyādha saptabhiḥ.

so 'nyat kārmukam ādāya vega|ghnaṃ, rukma|bhūṣaṇam,
citra|rūpa|dharaṃ cakre Citrasenaṃ śar'|ōrmibhiḥ.
sa śaraiś citrito rājā citra|mālya|dharo yuvā,
yuv" êva samare 'śobhad goṣṭhī|madhye sv|alaṃ|kṛtaḥ.

Śrutakarmāṇam atha vai nārācena stan'|ântare
bibheda tarasā śūras, «tiṣṭha! tiṣṭh'! êti» c' âbravīt.
14.10 Śrutakarm" âpi samare nārācena samarditaḥ
susrāva rudhiraṃ tatra, gairik'|ārdra iv' âcalaḥ.
tataḥ sa rudhir'|âkt'|âṅgo, rudhireṇa kṛta|cchaviḥ,
rarāja samare, rājan, sa|puṣpa iva kiṃśukaḥ.

Śrutakarmā tato, rājañ, śatruṇā samabhidrutaḥ,
śatru|saṃvāraṇaṃ kruddho dvidhā ciccheda kārmukam.
ath' âinaṃ chinna|dhanvānaṃ nārācānāṃ śatais tribhiḥ
chādayan samare, rājan, vivyādha ca su|patribhiḥ.
tato 'pareṇa bhallena tīkṣṇena niśitena ca
jahāra sa|śiras|trāṇaṃ śiras tasya mah"|ātmanaḥ.

Shruta·karman was then furious and, with a very sharp iron arrow, struck Chitra·sena at the head of his army in an exposed part of his body. Deeply wounded by that great man with that arrow, great king, the hero became faint and filled with despair!

But at that moment, famous Shruta·kirti enveloped that 14.5
lord of the world Shruta·karman with ninety arrows. After recovering his senses, the mighty warrior Chitra·sena splintered Shruta·karman's bow with a broad arrow and wounded him with seven more.

Grabbing another swift-killing bow embellished with gold, with waves of arrows Shruta·karman made Chitra·sena take on a wondrous appearance. Decorated with arrows and sporting a beautiful wreath, the young king was as handsome in that battle as a beautifully attired youth in the middle of an assembly.

Then that hero quickly wounded Shruta·karman in the middle of his chest with an iron arrow and yelled, "Stand!
Stand your ground!" Shruta·karman, now also wounded by 14.10
an arrow in battle, bled blood there, like a mountain of damp red ochre. His body smeared with blood and his skin colored blood-red, that hero was then radiant in the battle like a *kínshuka* tree in blossom.

Then rushed on by his enemy, king, raging Shruta·karman split Chitra·sena's foe-repelling bow in two. Then with three hundred well-feathered arrows he enveloped that man whose bow had been splintered and wounded him in the battle, king. Next, with another keen and sharp arrow, he
lopped off that great man's helmeted head. Chitra·sena's 14.15

14.15 tac chiro nyapatad bhūmau Citrasenasya dīptimat,
yadṛcchayā yathā candraś cyutaḥ svargān mahī|talam.
rājānaṃ nihataṃ dṛṣṭvā te 'bhisāraṃ tu, māriṣa,
abhyadravanta vegena Citrasenasya sainikāḥ.
tataḥ kruddho mah"|êṣv|āsas tat sainyaṃ prādravac charaiḥ,
anta|kāle yathā kruddhaḥ sarva|bhūtāni preta|rāṭ.
te vadhyamānāḥ samare tava pautreṇa dhanvinā
vyadravanta diśas tūrṇaṃ, dāva|dagdhā iva dvipāḥ.
tāṃs tu vidravato dṛṣṭvā nir|utsāhān dviṣaj|jaye,
drāvayann iṣubhis tīkṣṇaiḥ Śrutakarmā vyarocata.
14.20 Prativindhyas tataś Citraṃ bhittvā pañcabhir āśugaiḥ,
sārathiṃ ca tribhir viddhvā, dhvajam ek'|êṣuṇ" âpi ca.
taṃ Citro navabhir bhallair bāhvor urasi c' ārdayat
svarṇa|puṅkhaiḥ, prasann'|âgraiḥ, kaṅka|barhiṇa|vājitaiḥ.
Prativindhyo dhanuś chittvā tasya, Bhārata, sāyakaiḥ,
pañcabhir niśitair bāṇair ath' âinaṃ sa hi jaghnivān.
tataḥ śaktiṃ, mahā|rāja, svarṇa|ghaṇṭāṃ, dur|āsadām
prāhiṇot tava putrāya, ghorām agni|śikhām iva.
tām āpatantīṃ sahasā mah"|ôlkā|pratimāṃ tadā
dvidhā ciccheda samare Prativindhyo hasann iva.
14.25 sā papāta dvidhā chinnā Prativindhya|śaraiḥ śitaiḥ,
yug'|ânte sarva|bhūtāni trāsayantī yath" âśaniḥ.

brilliant head fell to the ground, as if the moon had inexplicably been expelled from heaven and fallen to the earth's surface.

As soon as they saw the Abhisára king killed, dear friend, Chitra·sena's troops quickly fled. In a rage that mighty archer then pursued Chitra·sena's army with his arrows, like the king of the dead* in a rage pursuing all beings at the end of time. Being killed in battle by your grandson wielding his bow, they quickly fled in every direction, like elephants burnt in a forest fire. When he saw them fleeing dejected at the victory of their enemy, Shruta·karman was radiant as he put them to flight with his sharp arrows.

After that Prativíndhya pierced Chitra with five arrows, 14.20
penetrated his driver with three and his standard too with one arrow. Chitra wounded him in his arms and chest with nine peacock- and heron-feathered broad arrows with brilliant tips and nocks of gold. Prativíndhya splintered his bow with arrows, Bhárata, and then struck him with five sharp arrows.

Then, great king, Chitra hurled his unparalleled spear covered in golden bells at your grandson. It was like a horrific spike of fire! Ferociously rushing towards him like a great meteor, Prativíndhya almost laughed and split it in two in
the battle. Split in two by Prativíndhya's sharp arrows, it 14.25
fell like a thunderbolt terrifying all beings at the end of an epoch.

śaktiṃ tāṃ prahatāṃ dṛṣṭvā, Citro gṛhya mahā|gadām
Prativindhyāya cikṣepa rukma|jāla|vibhūṣitām.
sā jaghāna hayāṃs tasya, sārathiṃ ca mahā|raṇe,
rathaṃ pramṛdya vegena dharaṇīm anvapadyata.
etasminn eva kāle tu rathād āplutya, Bhārata,
śaktiṃ cikṣepa Citrāya svarṇa|daṇḍām, alaṃ|kṛtām.
tām āpatantīṃ jagrāha Citro, rājan, mahā|manāḥ
tatas tām eva cikṣepa Prativindhyāya pārthivaḥ.
14.30 samāsādya raṇe śūraṃ Prativindhyaṃ mahā|prabhā
nirbhidya dakṣiṇaṃ bāhuṃ nipapāta mahī|tale,
patit" âbhāsayac c' âiva taṃ deśam aśanir yathā.
Prativindhyas tato, rājaṃs, tomaraṃ hema|bhūṣitam
preṣayām āsa saṃkruddhaś Citrasya vadha|kāṅkṣayā.
sa tasya gātr'|āvaraṇaṃ bhittvā, hṛdayam eva ca,
jagāma dharaṇīṃ tūrṇaṃ, mah"|ôraga iv' āśayam.
sa papāta tadā rājā tomareṇa samāhataḥ,
prasārya vipulau bāhū pīnau parigha|saṃnibhau.
Citraṃ saṃprekṣya nihataṃ, tāvakā raṇa|śobhinaḥ
abhyadravanta vegena Prativindhyaṃ samantataḥ.
14.35 sṛjanto vividhān bāṇāñ, śata|ghnīś ca sa|kiṅkiṇīḥ,
tam avacchādayām āsuḥ, sūryam abhra|gaṇā iva.
tān vidhamya mahā|bāhuḥ śara|jālena saṃyuge
vyadrāvayat tava camūṃ, Vajrahasta iv' âsurīm.
te vadhyamānāḥ samare tāvakāḥ Pāṇḍavair, nṛpa,
viprakīryanta sahasā, vāta|nunnā ghanā iva.

Watching as that spear was struck down, Chitra grabbed his massive club decorated with golden webbing and threw it at Prativíndhya. It killed his horses and driver in the great battle and, after crushing his chariot, followed them to the ground with a thud.

But springing from his chariot just in time, Bhárata, Prativíndhya flung his decorated and golden-staffed spear at Chitra. Chitra grabbed it as it flew towards him, king, and
then the proud prince hurled it at Prativíndhya. Striking the 14.30
hero Prativíndhya in the battle and wounding his right arm, that brilliant spear fell to the earth's surface and illuminated that place where it had fallen as if it were a lightning bolt.

Then in rage Prativíndhya hurled his lance trimmed in gold with the aim of killing Chitra. Splitting his body armor and his heart too, it quickly entered the earth like a great serpent entering its hole. Struck down by the lance, the king then collapsed, stretching out his huge muscular arms that seemed like iron bludgeons.

When they saw Chitra slain, your men, who were brilliant in battle, fervently attacked Prativíndhya from all sides.
Releasing various arrows and *shata·ghni*s having small bells, 14.35
they enveloped him like cloudbanks the sun. Dispersing them with a spread of arrows in the battle, that man of mighty arms put your army to flight, like the Thunderbolt-wielder the army of demons. Being slaughtered in battle by the Pándavas, king, your men were quickly scattered like clouds driven away by the wind.

vipradrute bale tasmin vadhyamāne samantataḥ,
Drauṇir eko 'bhyayāt tūrṇaṃ Bhīmasenaṃ mahā|balam.
tataḥ samāgamo ghoro babhūva sahasā tayoḥ,
yathā dev'|âsure yuddhe Vṛtra|Vāsavayor iva.

SAMJAYA uvāca:

15.1 BHĪMASENAṂ tato Drauṇī, rājan, vivyādha patriṇā
parayā tvarayā yukto, darśayann astra|lāghavam.
ath' âinaṃ punar ājaghne navatyā niśitaiḥ śaraiḥ,
sarva|marmāṇi saṃprekṣya, marma|jño, laghu|hastavat.
Bhīmasenaḥ samākīrṇo Drauṇinā niśitaiḥ śaraiḥ
rarāja samare, rājan, raśmivān iva bhāskaraḥ.
tataḥ śara|sahasreṇa su|prayuktena Pāṇḍavaḥ
Droṇa|putram avacchādya, siṃha|nādam amuñcata.
15.5 śaraiḥ śarāṃs tato Drauṇiḥ saṃvārya yudhi Pāṇḍavam
lalāṭe 'bhyāhanad, rājan, nārācena, smayann iva.
lalāṭa|sthaṃ tato bāṇaṃ dhārayām āsa Pāṇḍavaḥ,
yathā śṛṅgaṃ vane dṛptaḥ khaḍgo dhārayate, nṛpa.
tato Drauṇiṃ raṇe Bhīmo yatamānaṃ parākramī
tribhir vivyādha nārācair lalāṭe, vismayann iva.
lalāṭa|sthais tato bāṇair brāhmaṇo 'sau vyaśobhata,
prāvṛṣ' îva yathā siktas tri|śṛṅgaḥ parvat'|ôttamaḥ.
tataḥ śara|śatair Drauṇir ardayām āsa Pāṇḍavam;
na c' âinaṃ kampayām āsa, mātari|śv" êva parvatam.
15.10 tath" âiva Pāṇḍavo yuddhe Drauṇiṃ śara|śataiḥ śitaiḥ
n' âkampayata saṃhṛṣṭo, vāry|ogha iva parvatam.

As that army fled while being slaughtered from all sides, on his own Drona's son quickly attacked mighty Bhima·sena. Then a horrifying clash immediately began between those two that was like the clash of Vritra and Indra in the war of the gods and demons.

SÁNJAYA said:

THEN DRONA'S son, king, endowed with great speed and displaying skill with his weapon, wounded Bhima·sena with an arrow. After carefully observing all his weaknesses, that man with deft hands who knows a man's weaknesses assaulted him again with nine sharp arrows. 15.1

Covered by Drona's son with sharp arrows, Bhima·sena shone in battle, king, like the sun with its rays of light. Then the Pándava enveloped Drona's son with a thousand well-directed arrows and let loose a lion's roar.

After repelling those arrows with his arrows in that fight, 15.5
king, Drona's son sneered and struck the Pándava on the forehead with an iron arrow. The Pándava then bore that arrow protruding from his forehead, king, as a proud rhinoceros bears his horn in the forest.

A little flummoxed, Bhima showed courage in the battle and pierced Drona's persistent son in the forehead with three arrows. With arrows protruding from his forehead, that brahmin was beautiful, like the highest triple peaked mountain when rained on in the wet season.

Next, Drona's son struck the Pándava with hundreds of arrows, but, like the wind striking a mountain, he could not make him waver. Similarly, the excited Pándava could 15.10

tāv anyonyaṃ śarair ghoraiś chādayānau mahā|rathau
ratha|varya|gatau vīrau śuśubhāte bal'|ôtkaṭau.
ādityāv iva saṃdīptau loka|kṣaya|karāv ubhau,
sva|raśmibhir iv' ânyonyaṃ tāpayantau śar'|ôttamaiḥ,
tataḥ pratikṛte yatnaṃ kurvāṇau ca mahā|raṇe,
kṛta|pratikṛte yattau śara|saṃghair a|bhītavat,
vyāghrāv iva ca saṃgrāme ceratus tau nar'|ôttamau,
śara|daṃṣṭrau, dur|ādharṣau, cāpa|vaktrau, bhayaṃ|karau.
15.15 a|bhūtāṃ tāv adṛśyau ca śara|jālaiḥ samantataḥ,
megha|jālair iva cchannau gagane candra|bhāskarau.
cakāśete muhūrtena tatas tāv apy ariṃ|damau,
vimuktāv abhra|jālena, Aṅgāraka|Budhāv* iva.

atha tatr' âiva saṃgrāme vartamāne su|dāruṇe,
apasavyaṃ tataś cakre Drauṇis tatra Vṛkodaram,
kirañ śara|śatair ugrair, dhārābhir iva parvatam.
na tu tan mamṛṣe Bhīmaḥ śatror vijaya|lakṣaṇam,
praticakre tato, rājan, Pāṇḍavo 'py apasavyataḥ.
maṇḍalānāṃ vibhāgeṣu gata|pratyāgateṣu ca,
15.20 babhūva tumulaṃ yuddhaṃ tayos puruṣa|siṃhayoḥ.

caritvā vividhān mārgān, maṇḍala|sthānam eva ca,
śaraiḥ pūrṇ'|āyat'|ôtsṛṣṭair anyonyam abhijaghnatuḥ.
anyonyasya vadhe c' âiva cakratur yatnam uttamam,
īṣatur virathaṃ c' âiva kartum anyonyam āhave.

not make Drona's son waver in battle with hundreds of his sharp arrows, like a flood of water against a mountain.

Enveloping one another with their dreadful arrows, those mighty warriors were radiant—a pair of heroes brimming with strength and travelling on superb chariots. Both burned like a pair of suns setting off the destruction of the world, scorching one another with their excellent arrows that were like their own sunrays. Expending immense effort in that great struggle when in defense, or fearlessly engaged in attacking or defending with multitudes of arrows, those fine men roamed in battle like tigers, dangerous and rousing fear, their arrows like teeth and their bows like jaws.

Covered on all sides by dense masses of arrows, they 15.15
became invisible like the sun and moon covered by banks of clouds in the sky. Then in a flash the two foe-destroyers became visible, like Mars and Mercury freed from a bank of clouds.

In that terrible encounter taking place there, Drona's son circled Wolf-belly from right to left, covering him with hundreds of sharp arrows like a mountain being covered with torrents of rain. But Bhima didn't put up with this—appearing as it did like his enemy's victory!—and the Pándava then counterattacked from right to left too, king. As they attacked and retreated in different kinds of circular
moves, the battle of those two lions of men became riotous. 15.20

Careering along various courses and in circular maneuvers, they struck one another with arrows discharged from their full bent bows. And they both expended enormous effort to kill one another; and they both strove to strip one another of their chariot in that battle. Then Drona's son, a

tato Drauṇir mah”|âstrāṇi prāduś cakre mahā|rathaḥ;
tāny astrair eva samare pratijaghne ’tha Pāṇḍavaḥ.
tato ghoraṃ, mahā|rāja, astra|yuddham avartata,
graha|yuddhaṃ yathā ghoraṃ prajā|saṃharaṇe hy abhūt.
te bāṇāḥ samasajjanta muktās tābhyāṃ tu, Bhārata,
15.25 dyotayanto diśaḥ sarvās tava sainyaṃ samantataḥ.
bāṇa|saṃghair vṛtaṃ ghoram ākāśaṃ samapadyata,
ulkā|pāt’|āvṛtaṃ yuddhaṃ prajānāṃ saṃkṣaye, nṛpa.
bāṇ’|âbhighātāt saṃjajñe tatra, Bhārata, pāvakaḥ;
sa|visphuliṅgo, dīpt’|ârcir, yo ’dahad vāhinī|dvayam.
tatra siddhā, mahā|rāja, saṃpatanto ’bruvan vacaḥ,
«yuddhānām ati sarveṣāṃ yuddham etad iti, prabho!
sarva|yuddhāni c’ âitasya kalāṃ n’ ârhanti ṣoḍaśīm!
n’ ēdṛśaṃ ca punar yuddhaṃ bhaviṣyati kadā cana.
aho! jñānena saṃpannāv ubhau brāhmaṇa|kṣatriyau!
15.30 aho! śauryeṇa saṃpannāv ubhau c’ ôgra|parākramau!
aho! bhīma|balo Bhīma, etasya ca kṛt’|âstra|tā!
aho! vīryasya sāratvam! aho! sauṣṭhavam etayoḥ!
sthitāv etau hi samare Kāl’|ântaka|Yam’|ôpamau!
Rudrau dvāv iva saṃbhūtau, yathā dvāv iva bhāskarau,
Yamau vā puruṣa|vyāghrau, ghora|rūpāv ubhau raṇe!»
iti vācaḥ sma śrūyante siddhānāṃ vai muhur muhuḥ.
siṃha|nādaś ca saṃjajñe sametānāṃ div’|âukasām.
adbhutaṃ c’ âpy, acintyaṃ ca dṛṣṭvā karma tayor mṛdhe,
siddha|cāraṇa|saṃghānāṃ vismayaḥ samapadyata.
15.35 praśaṃsanti tadā devāḥ, siddhāś ca, parama’|ṛṣayaḥ,

mighty warrior, revealed his great missiles; but the Pándava
then repelled them in the battle with his missiles.

Thereafter a horrendous missile fight took place, great
king, like the horrendous conjunction of planets during the
obliteration of living things. Arrows released from those
two collided, Bhárata, illuminating all regions and your 15.25
army from all sides. Covered with masses of arrows, the
sky became horrendous, king, like the planetary conjunction concealed in a hail of meteors during the dissolution
of living things. A fire arose there from the collisions of
those arrows, Bhárata. With its blazing flames and sparks,
it scorched both armies.

*Siddhas** hastening there said these words, great king,
"Of all battles, lord, this battle is the most extraordinary!
All other battles are unworthy of even a sixteenth of its mag-
nitude! There will never be a battle like it again. Oh! Both
the brahmin and the kshatriya are endowed with knowledge! Oh! Both are endowed with valor and have formidable 15.30
courage! Oh! Bhima's strength is formidable and Ashvattháman is skilled with his arsenal! Oh! There is a hardness to
their valor! Oh! They have great skill! For both stand in battle like Yama as Time the destroyer! Both tigers among men
have taken on dreadful appearances in this battle. They're
like two Rudras! Two suns! Or two Yamas!"

Such were the words of the *siddhas* heard among the
assembled deities, from whom a lion's roar came forth again
and again. Watching the marvelous and inconceivable deeds
of those two in battle, the crowds of *siddhas* and celestial
singers were astonished. The gods, *siddhas* and great sages 15.35

«sādhu, Draune, mahā|bāho! sādhu, Bhīm'! êti» c' âbruvan.

tau śūrau samare, rājan, paraspara|kṛt'|āgasau,
parasparam udīkṣetāṃ, krodhād uddhṛtya cakṣuṣī.
krodha|rakt'|ēkṣaṇau tau tu, krodhāt prasphurit'|âdharau,
krodhāt saṃdaṣṭa|daśanau, tath" âiva daśana|cchadau,
anyonyaṃ chādayantau sma śara|vṛṣṭyā mahā|rathau,
śar'|âmbu|dhārau samare, śastra|vidyut|prakāśinau.
tāv anyonyaṃ dhvajaṃ viddhvā, sārathiṃ ca mahā|raṇe,
anyonyasya hayān viddhvā, bibhidāte parasparam.
15.40 tataḥ kruddhau, mahā|rāja, bāṇau gṛhya mah"|āhave
ubhau cikṣipatus tūrṇam, anyonyasya vadh'|âiṣiṇau.

tau sāyakau, mahā|rāja, dyotamānau camū|mukhe
ājaghnatuḥ samāsādya vajra|vegau dur|āsadau.
tau paraspara|vegāc ca, śarābhyāṃ ca bhṛś'|āhatau,
nipetatur mahā|vīryau rath'|ôpasthe tayos tadā.

tatas tu sārathir jñātvā Droṇa|putram a|cetanam
apovāha raṇād, rājan, sarva|sainyasya paśyataḥ.
tath" âiva Pāṇḍavaṃ, rājan, vihvalantaṃ muhur muhuḥ
apovāha rathen' ājau sārathiḥ śatru|tāpanam.

DHṚTARĀṢṬRA uvāca:

16.1 YATHĀ SAṂŚAPTAKAIḤ sārdham Arjunasy' âbhavad raṇaḥ,
anyeṣāṃ ca mahī|pānāṃ Pāṇḍavais, tad bravīhi me!
Aśvatthāmnas tu yad yuddham Arjunasya ca, Saṃjaya,
anyeṣāṃ ca mahī|pānāṃ Pāṇḍavais, tad bravīhi me!

then praised them and said, "Outstanding, mighty-armed son of Drona! Outstanding, Bhima!"

Injuring one another in that battle, king, the heroes glared at one another, raising their eyes in anger. Their eyes red with anger, their lower lips quivering with anger, their teeth clenched with anger, and their lips clenched as well, enveloping one another with torrents of arrows, the mighty warriors were clouds of arrows in battle, their weapons shining like thunderbolts. Perforating each other's standard in the great battle and wounding each other's driver and horses, they
tore through one another. Then, great king, in rage both 15.40
grabbed an arrow and quickly shot them, hoping to kill one another in that great battle.

Shining brightly, great king, the two arrows approached as fast as lightning and impossible to counter and struck the pair of them standing at the head of their armies. Brutally struck by those two arrows, from the force of each of them the two great men of courage then collapsed onto the floors of their chariots.

Realizing Drona's son was unconscious, his charioteer then carried him away from the battle, king, as the whole army looked on. Likewise, king, in the battle the enemy-scorching Pándava staggered continually and was carried away on his chariot by his charioteer.

DHRITA·RASHTRA said:

TELL ME HOW Árjuna's battle with the oath-bound war- 16.1
riors unfolded, and of the other princes with the Pándavas! And tell about the battle between Ashvatthámana and Árjuna, Sánjaya, and of the other princes with the Pándavas!

SAMJAYA uvāca:

śṛṇu, rājan, yathā vṛttaṃ saṃgrāmaṃ bruvato mama,
vīrāṇāṃ śatrubhiḥ sārdhaṃ, deha|pāpm'|âsu|ṇāśanam!
Pārthaḥ saṃśaptaka|balaṃ praviśy' ârṇava|saṃnibham
vyakṣobhayad amitra|ghno, mahā|vāta iv' ârṇavam.
16.5 śirāṃsy unmathya vīrāṇāṃ śitair bhallair Dhanaṃjayaḥ
pūrṇa|candr'|ābha|vaktrāṇi sv|akṣi|bhrū|daśanāni ca
saṃtastāra kṣitiṃ kṣipraṃ, vinālair nalinair iva.
su|vṛttān, āyatān, puṣṭāṃś, candan'|âguru|bhūṣitān,
s'|āyudhān, sa|tala|trāṃś ca, pañc'|āsy'|ôraga|saṃnibhān,
bāhūn kṣurair amitrāṇāṃ ciccheda samare 'rjunaḥ.
dhuryān, dhury'|êtarān, sūtān, dhvajāṃś, cāpāni, sāyakān,
pāṇīn sa|ratnān a|sakṛd bhallaiś ciccheda Pāṇḍavaḥ.
rathān, dvipān, hayāṃś c' âiva s'|ârohān Arjuno yudhi
śarair aneka|sāhasrair ninye, rājan, Yama|kṣayam.
16.10 taṃ pravīrāḥ su|saṃrabdhā, nardamānā iva' rṣabhāḥ
vāśit''|ârtham iva kruddham abhidrutya mad'|ôtkaṭāḥ,
nighnantam abhijaghnus te śaraiḥ, śṛṅgair iva' rṣabhāḥ.
tasya teṣāṃ ca tad yuddham abhaval loma|harṣaṇam,
trailokya|vijaye yadvad daityānāṃ saha Vajriṇā!

SÁNJAYA said:

King, listen to me describe how that battle took place of those heroes with their enemies, destroying bodies, sins and life!

When he entered the ocean-like army of oath-bound warriors, Pritha's son, a killer of enemies, threw them into disarray like a mighty wind the sea. With sharp broad ar- 16.5
rows Dhanan·jaya severed the heads of those heroes, their mouths seeming like full moons and their eyes, brows and teeth beautiful, and quickly spread the earth with them as if with stemless lotuses. With razor arrows Árjuna hewed off the arms of his enemies in the battle. Well-rounded, long, ample, adorned with sandal and aloe powders, clutching weapons and sporting leather guards, they seemed like five-headed serpents. With broad arrows, the Pándava repeatedly cut down their charioteers, standards, bows, arrows, bejeweled hands and horses yoked and not yoked. With many thousands of arrows, Árjuna sent their chariots, elephants and horses, together with their riders, to Yama's place, king.

Drunk with passion and bellowing at him like bulls for a 16.10
cow on heat, those furious heroes attacked that enraged man and struck him with their arrows—as he struck them!—like bulls lashing out with their horns. This battle between Árjuna and the oath-bound warriors was as hair-raising as that between the *daityas* and the Thunderbolt-wielder for victory over the triple-world!

astrair astrāṇi saṃvārya dviṣatāṃ sarvato 'rjunaḥ
iṣubhir bahubhis tūrṇaṃ viddhvā prāṇāñ jahāra saḥ.
chinna|tri|veṇu|cakr'|âkṣān, hata|yodhān sa|sārathīn,
vidhvast'|āyudha|tūṇīrān, samunmathita|ketanān,
saṃchinna|yoktra|raśmīkān, vivarūthān, vikūbarān,
16.15 visrasta|bandhura|yugān, visrast'|âkṣa|pramaṇḍalān,
rathān viśakalī|kurvan, mah"|âbhrāṇ' îva mārutaḥ.
vismāpayan prekṣaṇīyaṃ dviṣatāṃ bhaya|vardhanam
mahā|ratha|sahasrasya samaṃ karm' âkaroj Jayaḥ.

siddha|deva'|rṣi|saṃghāś ca cāraṇāś c' âiva tuṣṭuvuḥ;
deva|dundubhayo neduḥ; puṣpa|varṣāṇi c' âpatan;
Keśav'|Ârjunayor mūrdhni prāha vāk c' âśarīriṇī:

«candr'|âgny|anila|sūryāṇāṃ kānti|dīpti|bala|dyutīḥ
yau sadā bibhratur vīrāv; imau tau Keśav'|Ârjunau!
Brahm'|Ēśānāv iv' âjayyau vīrāv eka|rathe sthitau;
16.20 sarva|bhūta|varau vīrau Nara|Nārāyaṇāv imau!»

ity etan mahad āścaryaṃ dṛṣṭvā śrutvā ca, Bhārata,
Aśvatthāmā su|saṃyattaḥ Kṛṣṇāv abhyadravad raṇe.
atha Pāṇḍavam asyantaṃ amitra|ghna|karāñ charān,
s'|êṣuṇā pāṇin" āhūya prahasan Drauṇir abravīt,
«yadi māṃ manyase, vīra, prāptam arham ih' âtithim,
tataḥ sarv'|ātmanā tv adya yuddh'|ātithyaṃ prayaccha me!»

Completely enveloping the missiles of his enemies with his missiles, Árjuna quickly wounded them and took their 16.15
lives with his numerous arrows. Breaking their chariots into pieces, shattering their axles, wheels and three-piece bamboo struts, slaughtering their warriors along with their charioteers, destroying their weapons and quivers, completely tearing apart their standards, cutting their yoking-thongs and bridles to pieces, breaking off their guards and railings and removing their driver's seats, yoking-beams, axles and fellies, he was like the wind breaking up the clouds. Causing astonishment, Jaya* did this deed the equal of that of a thousand mighty warriors, a spectacle rousing fear among his enemies.

The celestial singers and the crowds of *siddha*s and divine sages sung his praises, divine drums boomed and showers of flowers rained down, and a disembodied voice said above Késhava and Árjuna:

"There are two heroes who always possess the beauty of the moon, the brightness of fire, the power of the wind and the majesty of the sun. They are Késhava and Árjuna! Those two heroes standing on the one chariot are invincible like Brahma and Ishána!* The finest of all beings, those two 16.20
heroes are Nara and Naráyana!"

Hearing this and seeing that great miracle, Bhárata, Ashvatthámán, who was well prepared for combat, attacked the two Krishnas* in that battle. Then, as the Pándava shot arrows that destroyed his enemies, Drona's son challenged him with an arrow in his hand and said as he cackled, "If you reckon, hero, that I've arrived here as a worthy guest,

evam ācārya|putreṇa samāhūto yuyutsayā,
bahu mene 'rjuno "tmānam,* iti c' āha Janārdanam:
«saṃśaptakāś ca me vadhyā, Drauṇir āhvayate ca mām!
16.25 yad atr' ânantaraṃ prāptaṃ, śaṃsa me tadd hi, Mādhava!
ātithya|karm' âbhyutthāya dīyatāṃ, yadi manyase!»
evam ukto 'vahat Pārthaṃ Kṛṣṇo Droṇ'|ātmaj'|ântike
jaitreṇa vidhin" āhūtaṃ, Vāyur Indram iv' âdhvare.
tam āmantry' âika|manasaṃ Keśavo Drauṇim abravīt:
«Aśvatthāman, sthiro bhūtvā prahar' âśu, sahasva ca!
nirveṣṭuṃ bhartṛ|piṇḍaṃ hi kālo 'yam upajīvinām;
sūkṣmo vivādo viprāṇāṃ; sthūlau kṣātrau jay'|âjayau!
yāṃ abhyarthayase mohād
divyāṃ Pārthasya sat|kriyām
tām āptum icchan yudhyasva
sthiro bhūtv" âdya Pāṇḍavam!»
16.30 ity ukto Vāsudevena, «tath"! êty» uktvā dvij'|ôttamaḥ
vivyādha Keśavaṃ ṣaṣṭyā nārācair, Arjunaṃ tribhiḥ.
tasy' Ârjunaḥ su|saṃkruddhas tribhir bhallaiḥ śar'|âsanam
ciccheda, c' ânyad ādatta Drauṇir ghorataraṃ dhanuḥ,
sa|jyaṃ kṛtvā nimeṣāc ca, vivyādh' Ârjuna|Keśavau,
tribhiḥ śatair Vāsudevaṃ, sahasreṇa ca Pāṇḍavam.
tataḥ śara|sahasrāṇi, prayutāny, arbudāni ca
sasṛje Drauṇir āyastaḥ, saṃstabhya ca raṇe 'rjunam.
iṣu|dher, dhanuṣaś c' âiv', jyāyāś c' âiv' âtha, māriṣa,

then with total conviction extend to me now the hospitality of battle!"

Challenged like this by the teacher's son* who was eager for a fight, Árjuna reflected at length and said this to himself and Janárdana: "I'm annihilating the oath-bound warriors, yet Drona's son challenges me! Mádhava,* tell me which of 16.25
these two should be pursued next! If you reckon it's right, let's rise up and offer him a rite of hospitality!"

Once this had been said, Krishna maneuvered Pritha's son, who'd been summoned with the rule of conquest, close to Drona's son, like Vayu carrying Indra to a sacrifice. Késhava saluted Drona's single-minded son and said: "Ashvattháman, remain resolute and quickly attack and withstand us! For it's time for dependents to repay their master's due. Conflict between brahmins is a subtle matter; but victory or defeat is the warrior's lot, and they are tangible! If you want to receive the excellent hospitality of Pritha's son that you so foolishly requested, remain resolute and fight the Pándava now!"

So spoken to by Vasudéva, that best of brahmins uttered 16.30
"Fine!" and wounded Késhava with sixty iron arrows and Árjuna with three. Furious, Árjuna splintered his bow with three broad arrows. Drona's son grabbed another, more terrible bow and, stringing it in an instant, pelted Árjuna and Késhava again—Vasudéva with three hundred arrows and the Pándava with a thousand. Then Drona's son, exerting himself and paralysing Árjuna in the battle, discharged thousands of arrows and then millions and then tens of millions. Dear friend, arrows flew from the quiver, bow and 16.35
bow-string, from the arms, hands, chest, mouth, nose and

bāhvoḥ, karābhyām, uraso, vadana|ghrāṇa|netrataḥ,
16.35 karṇābhyāṃ, śiraso, 'ṅgebhyo, loma|varmabhya eva ca,
ratha|dhvajebhyaś ca śarā niṣpetur brahma|vādinaḥ.
śara|jālena mahatā viddhvā Mādhava|Pāṇḍavau,
nanāda mudito Drauṇir mahā|megh'|âugha|nisvanam.

tasya tam ninadaṃ śrutvā, Pāṇḍavo 'cyutam abravīt:
«paśya, Mādhava, daur|ātmyaṃ guru|putrasya māṃ prati!
vadhaṃ prāptau manyate nau prāveśya śara|veśmani.
eṣo 'smi hanmi saṃkalpaṃ śikṣayā ca balena ca!»

Aśvatthāmnaḥ śarān astāṃś
chittv" âik'|âikaṃ tridhā tridhā,
vyadhamad Bharata|śreṣṭho,
nīhāram iva mārutaḥ.

16.40 tataḥ saṃśaptakān bhūyaḥ s'|âśva|sūta|ratha|dvipān
dhvaja|patti|gaṇān ugrair bāṇair vivyādha Pāṇḍavaḥ.
ye ye dadṛśire tatra yad|yad|rūpās tadā janāḥ,
te te tatra śarair vyāptaṃ menire "tmānam ātmanā!
te Gāṇḍīva|pramuktās tu nānā|rūpāḥ patatriṇaḥ
krośe sāgre sthitān ghnanti dvipāṃś ca puruṣān raṇe.
bhallaiś chinnāḥ karāḥ petuḥ kariṇāṃ mada|varṣiṇām,
yathā vane paraśubhir nikṛttāḥ su|mahā|drumāḥ.
paścāt tu śailavat petus te gajāḥ saha sādibhiḥ,
Vajri|vajra|pramathitā yath" âiv' âdri|cayās tathā.

eyes, from the ears, head, limbs, body hair and armor and from the chariot and standard of that expounder of the Veda. Wounding Mádhava and the Pándava with a massive spread of arrows, Drona's son was ecstatic and roared the sound of a massive rolling cloud.

Hearing his roar, the Pándava said to Áchyuta, "Mádhava, look at the malice the guru's* son has for me! He reckons that we're dead now that he's led us into this house of arrows. I'll destroy his plan* with my skill and strength!"

One by one the best of the Bharatas split the arrows cast from Ashvattháman into three parts, and then three more, and blew them away like the wind a fog.

Then, with his terrible arrows the Pándava once more 16.40
pelted the oath-bound warriors along with their horses, charioteers, chariots and elephants, and the divisions of foot-soldiers with their standards. People of every inclination that watched there reckoned that they themselves were covered with arrows! Arrows of various types were released in the battle from the Gandíva bow and slaughtered the men and elephants that stood within the range of a whole league. The trunks of elephants shedding ruttish excretions were severed by broad arrows and fell like massive trees hacked by axes in a forest. Afterwards, those mountain-like elephants collapsed along with their riders, like multitudes of mountains destroyed by a thunderbolt from the Thunderbolt-wielder.

16.45 gandharva|nagar'|ākārān, rathāṃś c' âiva su|kalpitān,
vinītair javanair yuktān, āsthitān yuddha|dur|madaiḥ,
śarair viśakalī|kurvann, amitrān abhyavīvṛṣat,
sv|alaṃ|kṛtān aśva|sādīn, pattīṃś c' âhan Dhanaṃjayaḥ.
Dhanaṃjaya|yug'|ânt'|ârkaḥ saṃśaptaka|mah"|ârṇavam
vyaśoṣayata duḥ|śoṣaṃ tīkṣṇaiḥ śara|gabhastibhiḥ.

punar Drauṇiṃ mahā|śailaṃ nārācair vajra|saṃnibhaiḥ
nirbibheda mahā|vegais, tvaran Vajr" îva parvatam.
tam ācārya|sutaḥ kruddhaḥ s'|âśva|yantāram āśu|gaiḥ
yuyutsur āgamad yoddhuṃ; Pārthas tān acchinac charān.
16.50 tataḥ parama|saṃkruddhaḥ Pāṇḍave 'strāṇy avāsṛjat
Aśvatthām" âbhirūpāya gṛhān atithaye yathā.

atha saṃśaptakāṃs tyaktvā Pāṇḍavo Drauṇim abhyayāt,
a|pāṅkteyān iva tyaktvā dātā pāṅkteyam arthinam.

SAṂJAYA uvāca:

17.1 TATAḤ SAMABHAVAD yuddhaṃ Śukr'|Âṅgirasa|varcasoḥ,
nakṣatram abhito vyomni Śukr'|Āṅgirasayor iva.
santāpayantāv anyonyaṃ dīptaiḥ śara|gabhastibhiḥ,
loka|trāsa|karāv āstāṃ, vimārga|sthau grahāv iva.

Dhanan·jaya rained down upon his enemies with his arrows, breaking into pieces their well-equipped chariots that were harnessed to well-trained horses, ridden by battle-mad men and seemed like cities of the *gandhárva*s, and slaughtered foot-soldiers and well-attired horsemen. With sharp arrows his rays of light, Dhanan·jaya—the sun at an epoch's end—dried up the vast unparchable oath-bound warrior ocean. 16.45

Again he wounded Drona's great mountain-like son with exceedingly fast and lightning-like arrows, just like the Thunderbolt-wielder moving quickly against a mountain. In rage, the teacher's son came at him and his horses and charioteer, eager to fight him with his arrows. But Pritha's son cut those arrows down. Ashvattháman was then totally 16.50
infuriated and hurled his missiles towards the Pándava, as if he was giving up his house to a learned guest.

Then the Pándava left behind the oath-bound warriors and assailed Drona's son, like a patron leaving behind a socially unacceptable petitioner for one socially acceptable.

SÁNJAYA said:

THEN BEGAN THE battle of those two whose splendor 17.1
was the equal of Venus and Jupiter, as if they were Venus and Jupiter in the sky on either side of a constellation. Scorching one another with burning arrows that were their rays of light, they were like a pair of planets following the wrong orbits and terrifying the world.

tato 'vidhyad bhruvor madhye nārācen' Ârjuno bhṛśam;
sa tena vibabhau Drauṇir ūrdhva|raśmir yathā raviḥ.
atha kṛṣṇau śara|śatair Aśvatthāmn" ârditau bhṛśam
sva|raśmi|jāla|vikacau yug'|ânt'|ârkāv iv' āsatuḥ.
17.5 tato 'rjunaḥ sarvato|dhāram astram
avāsṛjad Vāsudeve 'bhibhūte,
Drauṇāyaniṃ c' âbhyahanat pṛṣatkair
vajr'|âgni|Vaivasvata|daṇḍa|kalpaiḥ.
sa Keśavaṃ c' Ârjunaṃ c' âtitejā
vivyādha marmasv atiraudra|karmā
bāṇaiḥ su|yuktair atitīvra|vegair;
yair āhato mṛtyur api vyatheta!
Drauṇer iṣūn Arjunaḥ saṃnivārya
vyāyacchatas tad dvi|guṇaiḥ su|puṅkhaiḥ
taṃ s'|âśva|sūta|dhvajam eka|vīram
āvṛtya, saṃśaptaka|sainyam ārcchat.
dhanūṃṣi, bāṇān, iṣu|dhīr, dhanur|jyāḥ,
pāṇīn, bhujān, pāṇi|gataṃ ca śastram,
chatrāṇi, ketūṃs, turagān, rath'|ēṣāṃ,
vastrāṇi, mālyāny, atha bhūṣaṇāni,
carmāṇi, varmāṇi mano|ramāṇi,
priyāṇi sarvāṇi śirāṃsi c' âiva
ciccheda Pārtho dviṣatāṃ su|yuktair
bāṇaiḥ sthitānām a|parāṅ|mukhānām.
17.10 su|kalpitāḥ syandana|vāji|nāgāḥ
samāsthitā yatna|kṛtair nṛ|vīraiḥ;
Pārth'|ēritair bāṇa|śatair nirastās
tair eva sārdhaṃ nṛ|varā nipetuḥ.

Then Árjuna brutally wounded him with an arrow in the middle of his eyebrows. Drona's son shone with that arrow like the sun with a shaft of light raised high. Then, brutally wounded by Ashvattháman with hundreds of arrows, the two Krishnas were like a pair of suns at the end of an epoch radiant with garlands of their own rays.

With Vasudéva injured, Árjuna then released a missile 17.5
that had sharp blades facing every direction, and struck Drona's son with arrows that resembled lightning, fire and Yama's staff.

Ashvattháman, who had immense fiery energy and whose deeds were horrendous, wounded Árjuna and Késhava where they were exposed with well-constructed arrows that were extremely sharp and fast. Even Death* would fall if struck by them!

Árjuna repelled the arrows of Drona's battling son and, after enveloping that pre-eminent hero and his horses, charioteer and standard as well with twice as many arrows having fine nocks, fell on the army of oath-bound warriors.

With well-constructed arrows Pritha's son cut through the bows, arrows, quivers, bow-strings, hands, arms, weapons gripped in hands, parasols, flags, horses, chariot-poles, garments, wreaths, ornaments, armor, beautiful shields and all the handsome heads of his enemies while they stood by, unable to avert their faces.

Zealous heroes of men rode well-equipped chariots, 17.10
horses and elephants. Together with them those excellent men collapsed, destroyed by the hundreds of arrows discharged by Pritha's son. Severed by broad, half-moon and razor arrows, without relent those men's heads fell to the

padm'|ârka|pūrṇ'|êndu|nibh'|ānanāni,
kirīṭa|māly'|ābharaṇ'|ôjjvalāni,
bhall'|ârdha|candra|kṣura|kartitāni
prapetur urvyāṃ nṛ|śirāṃsy ajasram.
atha dvipair deva|ripu|dvip'|ābhair,
dev'|âri|darp'|âpaham atyudagram
Kaliṅga|Vaṅg'|Âṅga|Niṣāda|vīrā
jighāṃsavaḥ Pāṇḍavam abhyadhāvan.
teṣāṃ dvipānāṃ nicakarta Pārtho
varmāṇi, carmāṇi, karān, niyantṝn,
dhvajān, patākāś ca tataḥ prapetur,
vajr'|āhatān' îva gireḥ śirāṃsi.
teṣu prabhagneṣu guros tanū|jaṃ
bāṇaiḥ Kirīṭī nava|sūrya|varṇaiḥ
pracchādayām āsa, mah"|âbhra|jālair
vāyuḥ samudyantam iv' âṃśumantam.
17.15 tato 'rjun'|êṣūn iṣubhir nirasya,
Drauṇiḥ śitair Arjuna|Vāsudevau
pracchādayitvā divi candra|sūryau
nanāda so 'mbhoda iv' ātap'|ânte.
tam Arjunas tāṃś ca punas tvadīyān
abhyarditas tair abhisṛtya śastraiḥ,
bāṇ'|ândhakāraṃ sahas" âiva kṛtvā,
vivyādha sarvān iṣubhiḥ su|puṅkhaiḥ.
n' âpy ādadat saṃdadhan n' âiva
muñcan bāṇān rathe 'dṛśyata Savyasācī;
rathāṃś ca, nāgāṃs, turagān, padātīn
saṃsyūta|dehān dadṛśur hatāṃś ca.

ground, shining with crowns, wreaths and ornaments, their faces like full moons, suns and lotuses.

With elephants that seemed like the gods' enemies' elephants, the heroes of the Kalíngas, Vangas, Angas and Nishádas then attacked the immensely fierce Pándava, aiming to destroy that destroyer of the pride of the gods' enemies.

Pritha's son hacked the armor, shields, trunks, handlers, standards and flags from those elephants. Then they collapsed, like the peaks of a mountain struck by lightning. Once they had been crushed, the Wearer of the crown enveloped the guru's son with arrows the color of the morning sun, like the wind enveloping the rising sun with huge banks of clouds.

After repelling Árjuna's arrows and enveloping Árjuna 17.15
and Vasudéva with sharp arrows, Drona's son bellowed like a rain-cloud in the sky enveloping the moon and sun at the end of summer.

Again attacking him and your troops and tormented by their weapons, Árjuna suddenly created a dark mass of arrows and wounded them all with arrows that had fine nocks. No one could see the Left-handed archer on his chariot grabbing, nocking or releasing his arrows; yet they did see chariots, elephants, horses and foot-soldiers with their bodies pinned together and destroyed.

samdhāya nārāca|varān daś' āśu
Draunis tvarann ekam iv' ôtsasarja;
teṣāṃ ca pañc' Ârjunam abhyavidhyan,
pañc' Âcyutaṃ nirbibhiduḥ su|puṅkhāḥ.
tair āhatau sarva|manuṣya|mukhyāv,
asṛk sravantau, Dhanad'|Êndra|kalpau;
samāpta|vidyena tath" âbhibhūtau
hatau raṇe tāv iti menire 'nye.
17.20 ath' Ârjunaṃ prāha Daśārha|nāthaḥ:
«pramādyase kiṃ? jahi yodham etam!
kuryādd hi doṣaṃ samupekṣito 'yaṃ,
kaṣṭo bhaved vyādhir iv' â|kriyāvān!»
«tath"! êti» c' ôktv" Âcyutam a|pramādī
Drauṇiṃ prayatnād iṣubhis tatakṣa.
bhujau varau candana|sāra|digdhau,
vaksaḥ, śiro, 'th' âpratimau tath" ōrū,
Gāṇḍīva|muktaiḥ kupito 'vikarṇair
Drauṇiṃ śaraiḥ saṃyati nirbibheda.
chittvā tu raśmīṃs turagān avidhyat,
te taṃ raṇād ūhur atīva dūram.
sa tair hṛto vāta|javais turaṃgair
Drauṇir dṛḍhaṃ Pārtha|śar'|âbhibhūtaḥ
iyeṣa n' āvṛtya punas tu yoddhuṃ
Pārthena sārdhaṃ mati|mān vimṛśya,
jānañ jayaṃ niyataṃ Vṛṣṇi|vīre
Dhanaṃjaye c' Âṅgirasāṃ variṣṭhaḥ.
niyamya sa hayān Drauṇiḥ, samāśvāsya ca, māriṣa,
rath'|âśva|nara|saṃbādhaṃ Karṇasya prāviśad balam.

Quickly nocking ten of his best iron arrows, Drona's son speedily released them as if they were one. Five of them wounded Árjuna and five arrows with fine nocks pierced Áchyuta.

Struck by those arrows, those foremost of all men who were like Dhánada* and Indra flowed with blood. Others there reckoned that those two had been killed in the battle, overcome by that man whose knowledge was complete.

The lord of the Dashárhas* then said to Árjuna: "Why 17.20
are you fooling about? Kill this warrior! Ignored he could do evil, just as an illness might become dangerous if left unchecked!"

Uttering "Very well!" to Áchyuta, that meticulous man diligently carved up Drona's son with his arrows. Provoked in that battle, with sheep-ear arrows released from his Gandíva bow he wounded Drona's son in his chest, head, and incomparable thighs and his two great arms smeared with sandal water. After cutting their reins he wounded his horses, and they then carried Ashvattháman a very great distance from the battle.

Thoroughly overcome by the arrows of Pritha's son and carried away by his horses that were as swift as the wind, Drona's thoughtful son, the best of the Ángirases, pondered awhile, and did not want to return to again do battle with Pritha's son, realizing that victory was a certainty for the Vrishni hero* and Dhanan·jaya. Drona's son, restraining his horses and consoling himself, dear friend, entered Karna's army that was teeming with chariots, horses and men.

17.25 pratīpa|kāriṇi raṇād Aśvatthāmni hṛte hayaiḥ,
mantr'|âuṣadhi|kriyā|yogair vyādhau dehād iv' āhṛte,
saṃśaptakān abhimukhau prayātau Keśav'|Ârjunau,
vāt'|ôddhūta|patākena syandanen' âugha|nādinā.

SAṂJAYA uvāca:

18.1 ATH' ÔTTAREṆA Pāṇḍūnāṃ senāyāṃ dhvanir utthitaḥ
ratha|nāg'|âśva|pattīnāṃ Daṇḍadhāreṇa vadhyatām.
nivartayitvā tu rathaṃ Keśavo 'rjunam abravīt
vāhayann eva turagān Garuḍ'|ânila|raṃhasaḥ:
«Māgadho 'py ativikrānto dvi|radena pramāthinā,
Bhagadattād an|avaraḥ śikṣayā ca balena ca.
enaṃ hatvā nihant" âsi punaḥ saṃśaptakān iti.»
vāky'|ânte prāpayat Pārthaṃ Daṇḍadhār'|ântikaṃ prati.
18.5 sa Māgadhānāṃ pravaro 'ṅkuśa|grahe,
grahe '|prasahyo vikaco yathā grahaḥ;
sapatna|senāṃ pramamātha dāruṇo,
mahīṃ samagrāṃ vikaco yathā grahaḥ.
su|kalpitaṃ, dānava|nāga|saṃnibhaṃ,
mah"|âbhra|nirhrādam, a|mitra|mardanam,
rath'|âśva|mātaṅga|gaṇān sahasraśaḥ
samāsthito hanti śarair, narān api.
rathān adhiṣṭhāya sa|vāji|sārathīn,
narāṃś ca pādair dvi|rado vyapothayat;
dvipāṃś ca padbhyāṃ mamṛde kareṇa

When their opponent Ashvattháman was carried away from the battle by his horses—like a sickness removed from a body with mantras, herbs, medicinal treatments or yoga exercises—Késhava and Árjuna turned towards the oath-bound warriors and advanced with their flag buffeted by the wind and their chariot roaring like floodwaters. 17.25

SÁNJAYA said:

THEN FROM THE north of the Pándava forces came forth the peal of chariots, elephants, horses and foot-soldiers being slaughtered by Danda·dhara. 18.1

Turning their chariot around and driving their horses that had the speed of Gáruda and the wind, Késhava said to Árjuna: "The Mágadha* is incredibly courageous with his destructive elephant, and in skill and power is superior to Bhaga·datta. Once you've killed him, you can return to killing the oath-bound warriors." At the end of this speech he led Pritha's son near to Danda·dhara.

Among the Mágadhas he was the finest at wielding the elephant's hook, just as a *víkacha* comet is irresistible among comets; violent, he destroyed the army of his enemies, like a *víkacha* comet destroying the entire earth. 18.5

Astride his well-equipped and demon-like elephant that thundered like a massive cloud and crushed his enemies, with his arrows he destroyed hordes of chariots, horses and elephants by the thousand, and men as well. With his feet the elephant pulverised men mounted on their chariots, along with their horses and charioteers. And that superb elephant pounded other elephants with his trunk and two feet and killed them as if he was the wheel of time. Throwing

dvip'|ôttamo, hanti ca kāla|cakravat.
narāṃs tu kārṣṇāyasa|varma|bhūṣaṇān
nipātya s'|âśvān api pattibhiḥ saha,
vyapothayad danti|vareṇa śuṣmiṇā
sa śabdavat sthūla|nalaṃ yathā, tathā.
ath' Ârjuno jyā|tala|nemi|nisvane
mṛdaṅga|bherī|bahu|śaṅkha|nādite
nar'|âśva|mātaṅga|sahasra|saṃkule
rath'|ôttamen' âbhyapatad dvip'|ôttamam.
18.10 tato 'rjunaṃ dvādaśabhiḥ śar'|ôttamair,
Janārdanaṃ ṣoḍaśabhiḥ samārpayat
sa Daṇḍadhāras turagāṃs tribhis tribhis,
tato nanāda, prajahāsa c' â|sakṛt.
tato 'sya Pārthaḥ sa|guṇ'|êṣu|kārmukaṃ
cakarta bhallair, dhvajam apy alaṃ|kṛtam
punar niyantṝn saha pāda|goptṛbhis;
tatas tu cukrodha Girivraj'|ēśvaraḥ!
tato 'rjunaṃ bhinna|kaṭena dantinā
ghanāghanen' ânila|tulya|varcasā
atīva cukṣobhayiṣur Janārdanaṃ
Dhanaṃjayaṃ c' âbhijaghāna tomaraiḥ.
ath' âsya bāhū dvipa|hasta|saṃnibhau,
śiraś ca pūrṇ'|êndu|nibh'|ānanaṃ tribhiḥ,
kṣuraiḥ praciccheda sah' âiva Pāṇḍavas;
tato dvipaṃ bāṇa|śataiḥ samārpayat.
sa Pārtha|bāṇais tapanīya|bhūṣaṇaiḥ
samācitaḥ kāñcana|varma|bhṛd dvipaḥ
tathā cakāśe niśi parvato yathā
dav'|âgninā prajvalit'|âuṣadhi|drumaḥ.

down men garbed in armor of black-iron, and their horses and foot-soldiers too, Danda·dhara noisily pulverised them with his superb, excited elephant, as if they were thick reeds.

Then, in that throng of thousands of chariots, horses and elephants reverberating with many conches, *mridánga* drums and kettle-drums and ringing with the sounds of wheels, palms and bow-strings, Árjuna attacked that superb elephant in his superb chariot.

Danda·dhara then struck Árjuna with twelve fine arrows, 18.10
Janárdana with sixteen and their horses with three a piece, and then repeatedly bellowed and laughed.

With his broad arrows Pritha then cut his bow to pieces, with its arrows and bow-string, and his embossed banner as well, and then his elephant's handlers along with the men protecting its legs. At this the lord of Giri·vraja* became furious!

Eager to thoroughly shake up Árjuna with his ruttish elephant that enjoyed killing and whose splendor equalled the wind's, he then struck Janárdana and Dhanan·jaya with lances.

Then, with three razor arrows the Pándava simultaneously severed his arms that seemed like elephant trunks and his head, its face resembling a full moon. Next he wounded his elephant with hundreds of arrows. Covered with the gilded arrows of Pritha's son, that golden-armored elephant glowed like a mountain in the night as its plants and trees burn with a forest fire.

18.15 sa vedan'|ârto 'mbuda|nisvano nadaṃś,
caran, bhraman praskhalit'|ântaro 'dravat;
papāta rugṇaḥ sa|niyantṛkas tathā,
yathā girir vajra|vidāritas, tathā.
him'|âvadātena suvarṇa|mālinā
him'|âdri|kūṭa|pratimena dantinā,
hate raṇe bhrātari Daṇḍa āvrajaj,
jighāṃsur Indr'|âvara|jaṃ Dhanaṃjayam.
sa tomarair arka|kara|prabhais tribhir
Janārdanaṃ pañcabhir Arjunaṃ śitaiḥ
samarpayitvā vinanāda, nardayaṃs
tato 'sya bāhū nicakarta Pāṇḍavaḥ.
kṣurapra|kṛttau su|bhṛśaṃ sa|tomarau
śubh'|âṅgadau candana|rūṣitau bhujau,
gajāt patantau yugapad virejatur,
yath" âdri|śṛṅgād rucirau mah"|ôragau.
tath" ârdha|candreṇa hataṃ Kirīṭinā
papāta Daṇḍasya śiraḥ kṣitiṃ dvipāt;
sa śoṇit'|ārdro nipatan vireje
divākaro 'stād iva paścimāṃ diśam.
18.20 atha dvipaṃ śveta|var'|âbhra|saṃnibhaṃ
divākar'|âṃśu|pratimaiḥ śar'|ôttamaiḥ
bibheda Pārthaḥ; sa papāta nādayan
him'|âdri|kūṭaṃ kuliś'|āhato yathā.
tato 'pare tat|pratimā gaj'|ôttamā
jigīṣavaḥ saṃyati Savyasācinā
tathā kṛtās te ca yath" âiva tau dvipau;
tataḥ prabhagnaṃ su|mahad ripor balam.

In agony and sounding like a rain-cloud, it ran in a stagger as it thundered, roamed and tottered about. Ruined, it collapsed with its handler, like a mountain blown apart by lightning. 18.15

With his snow-white elephant that wore garlands of gold and resembled the summit of the Himalayas, Danda came near once his brother had been killed in battle, intending to kill Indra's younger brother* and Dhanan·jaya. He roared after striking Janárdana with three and Árjuna with five sharp lances that had the radiance of the sun's candescence. At this the bellowing Pándava cut off his arms.

Brutally cut off by razor-edged arrows, his arms looked radiant with their lances and beautiful bracelets and smeared with sandal powder as they fell side by side from that elephant, like two massive serpents falling from the summit of a mountain. And struck off with a half-moon arrow by the Wearer of the crown, Danda's head fell from the elephant to the ground. As it fell damp with blood, it glowed like the sun falling from the western mountain to the western quarter.

Then, with his superb arrows that were like rays from the sun, Pritha's son pierced his elephant that seemed like the finest of white clouds. Bellowing, it collapsed, like a Himalayan summit shattered by a thunderbolt. The Left-handed archer then did what he'd done to that pair of elephants to other superb elephants like them that sought victory in battle. Then his enemy's massive army was crushed! 18.20

gajā, rath'|âśvāḥ, puruṣāś ca saṃghaśaḥ
parasparalghnāḥ paripetur āhave;
parasparaṃ praskhalitāḥ samāhitā
bhṛśaṃ nipetur bahu|bhāṣiṇo hatāḥ.
ath' Ârjunaṃ sve parivārya sainikāḥ,
Puraṃdaraṃ deva|gaṇā iv', âbruvan:
«abhaiṣma yasmān maraṇād iva prajāḥ,
sa, vīra, diṣṭyā nihatas tvayā ripuḥ;
na ced arakṣiṣya imaṃ janaṃ bhayād
dviṣadbhir evaṃ balibhiḥ prapīḍitam,
tath" âbhaviṣyad dviṣatāṃ pramodanaṃ,
yathā hateṣv eṣv iha no, 'ri|sūdana!»
18.25 it' îva bhūyaś ca suhṛdbhir īḍitā;
niśamya vācaḥ su|manās tato 'rjunaḥ
yath" ânurūpaṃ pratipūjya taṃ janaṃ,
jagāma saṃśaptaka|saṃgha|hā punaḥ.

SAṂJAYA uvāca:

19.1 PRATYĀGATYA PUNAR Jiṣṇur jaghne saṃśaptakān bahūn,
vakr'|âtivakra|gamanād Aṅgāraka iva grahaḥ.
Pārtha|bāṇa|hatā, rājan, nar'|âśva|ratha|kuñjarāḥ,
vicelur, babhramur, neśuḥ, petur, mamluś ca, Bhārata.
dhuryān, dhury'|êtarān, sūtān, dhvajāṃś, cāpāni, sāyakān,
pāṇīn, pāṇi|gataṃ śastraṃ, bāhūn api, śirāṃsi ca
bhallaiḥ, kṣurair, ardha|candrair, vatsa|dantaiś ca Pāṇḍavaḥ
cicched' âmitra|vīrāṇāṃ samare pratiyudhyatām.

As one, elephants, chariots, horses and men rushed about striking one another in the battle. Stumbling into one another, they quickly collapsed together, struck down and babbling excessively.

Surrounding him like the hordes of the gods surrounding the Sacker of cities, his own troops said to Árjuna: "Thank god you slaughtered that enemy, hero; we feared him in the same way that people fear death! If you'd been unable to protect the people from that danger, pressed as they were by powerful enemies, our enemies would have been exhilarated, foe-destroyer, just as we are now that they're dead!"

Further praise like this was proffered by his allies. Ár- 18.25
juna listened to these words and, in good spirits, offered similar praise in return to those people, and then left again to slaughter the hordes of oath-bound warriors.

SÁNJAYA said:

RETURNING LIKE the planet Mars from its curved and 19.1
winding orbit, Jishnu* again killed many of the oath-bound warriors. Men, horses, chariots and elephants struck by the arrows of Pritha's son lurched, tottered, gave up, collapsed and perished, Bhárata. With his broad, razor, half-moon and calf-toothed arrows, the Pándava carved through horses yoked and not yoked, charioteers, banners, bows, arrows, hands and weapons clasped in hands, arms and heads too that belonged to the enemy-heroes who fought him in the battle.

19.5 vāśit"|ârthe yuyutsanto vṛṣabhā vṛṣabhaṃ yathā,
āpatanty Arjunaṃ śūrāḥ śataśo 'tha sahasraśaḥ.
teṣāṃ tasya ca tad yuddham abhaval loma|harṣaṇam,
trailokya|vijaye yādṛg daityānāṃ saha Vajriṇā!

tam avidhyat tribhir bāṇair dandaśūkair iv' âhibhiḥ
Ugrāyudha|sutas; tasya śiraḥ kāyād apāharat!
te 'rjunaṃ sarvataḥ kruddhā nānā|śastrair avīvṛṣan,
marudbhiḥ preritā meghā Himavantam iv' ôṣṇa|ge.
astrair astrāṇi saṃvārya dviṣatāṃ sarvato 'rjunaḥ
samyag astaiḥ śaraiḥ sarvān a|hitān ahanad bahūn.
19.10 chinna|tri|veṇu|saṃghātān, hat'|âśvān pārṣṇi|sārathīn,
visrasta|hasta|tūṇīrān, vi|cakra|ratha|ketanān,
saṃchinna|raśmi|yoktr'|âkṣān, vy|anukarṣa|yugān rathān,
vidhvasta|sarva|saṃnāhān bāṇaiś cakre 'rjunas tadā.
te rathās tatra vidhvastāḥ parārdhyā bhānty an|ekaśaḥ,
dhaninām iva veśmāni hatāny agny|anil'|âmbubhiḥ!

dvipāḥ saṃbhinna|varmāṇo vajr'|âśani|samaiḥ śaraiḥ
petur, giry|agra|veśmāni vajra|pāt'|âgnibhir yathā.
s'|ârohās turagāḥ petur bahavo 'rjuna|tāḍitāḥ,
nir|jihv'|ântrāḥ, kṣitau kṣīṇā, rudhir'|ārdrāḥ, su|dur|dṛśaḥ.

Like bulls eager to fight another bull over a cow on heat, 19.5
those heroes rushed at Árjuna by the hundred and then by the thousand. The battle they had with him was as hair-raising as that between the *daityas* and the Thunderbolt-wielder for victory over the triple-world!

Ugráyudha's son pelted him with three arrows that were like deadly snakes. Árjuna removed his head from his body! In rage the warriors rained all over Árjuna with various weapons, like clouds sent by the storm-gods in the hot season to rain all over the Himalayas. After completely obstructing his enemies' missiles with his missiles, Árjuna struck many of his adversaries all over with well-directed
arrows. With his arrows Árjuna then stripped chariots of 19.10
their dragging ballasts and yoking-poles, destroyed all their armor, cut their bridles, yoking-straps and axles to pieces, stripped the chariots of their wheels and flags, severed hands and quivers, slaughtered their horses and charioteers controlling their outer horses* and cut down masses of their three-piece bamboo struts. Those exceptional chariots ruined there in great numbers seemed like houses of the rich destroyed by water, wind and fire!

Elephants collapsed, their armor completely shattered by arrows the equal of Indra's thunderbolts, like houses on mountain summits destroyed by the fire caused by a lightning strike. Many horses struck by Árjuna collapsed with their riders; they looked hideous on the ground with their tongues and entrails hanging out, broken and wet with blood.

19.15 nar'|âśva|nāgā nārācaiḥ saṃsyūtāḥ Savyasācinā,
babhramuś, caskhaluḥ, petur, nedur, mamluś ca, māriṣa.
anekaiś ca śilā|dhautair vajr'|âśani|viṣ'|ôpamaiḥ
śarair nijaghnivān Pārtho, Mahendra iva dānavān.
mah"|ârha|varm'|ābharaṇā, nānā|rūp'|âmbar'|āyudhāḥ,
sa|rathāḥ, sa|dhvajā vīrā hatāḥ Pārthena śerate.
vijitāḥ puṇya|karmāṇo, viśiṣṭ'|âbhijana|śrutāḥ,
gatāḥ śarīrair vasudhām, ūrjitaiḥ karmabhir divam.
ath' Ârjunaṃ ratha|varaṃ tvadīyāḥ samabhidravan
nānā|jana|pad'|âdhyakṣāḥ sa|gaṇā jāta|manyavaḥ.
19.20 uhyamānā rath'|âśv'|êbhaiḥ pattayaś ca jighāṃsavaḥ
samabhyadhāvann asyanto vividhaṃ kṣipram āyudham.
tad" āyudha|mahā|varṣaṃ muktaṃ yodha|mah"|âmbudaiḥ,
vyadhaman niśitair bāṇaiḥ kṣipram Arjuna|mārutaḥ.
s'|âśva|patti|dvipa|rathaṃ mahā|śastr'|âugha|saṃplavam
sahasā saṃtitīrṣantaṃ Pārthaṃ śastr'|âstra|setunā,
ath' âbravīd Vāsudevaḥ: «Pārtha, kiṃ krīḍase, 'nagha?
saṃśaptakān pramathy' âināṃs tataḥ Karṇa|vadhe tvara!»
«tath"! êty» uktv" Ârjunaḥ Kṛṣṇaṃ
śiṣṭān saṃśaptakāṃs tadā
ākṣipya śastreṇa balād,
daityān Indra iv' âvadhīt.
19.25 ādadan, saṃdadhan n' êṣūn dṛṣṭaḥ kaiś cid raṇe 'rjunaḥ,

Pinned with iron arrows by the Left-handed archer, men, 19.15
horses and elephants lurched, stumbled, collapsed, cried out and perished, dear friend. Like mighty Indra destroying the *dánavas*, Pritha's son killed them with many stone-polished arrows equal in venom to the thunderbolts of Indra.

Heroes cased in superb armor and sporting various garments and weapons, lay prone with their chariots and standards, slaughtered by Pritha's son. Defeated heroes whose deeds were meritorious and who were distinguished in family and learning went to the soil with their bodies and to heaven with their courageous deeds.

Then with their hordes chiefs of yours from various regions, their anger roused, attacked Árjuna, the finest of
warriors. Foot-soldiers and warriors conveyed by chariot, 19.20
horse and elephant, all eager to kill, charged at him as they quickly hurled various weapons. With his sharp arrows Árjuna the wind then quickly scattered the massive torrent of weapons released by those huge warrior-clouds.

To Pritha's son—who was suddenly eager to cross over the great deluge of weapons, with its horses, foot-soldiers, elephants and chariots, with a bridge made of his weapons and missiles—Vasudéva then said: "Faultless son of Pritha, why mess about? Destroy these oath-bound warriors! Then quickly go and kill Karna!"

Árjuna said "Very well!" to Krishna and then dispersed the surviving oath-bound warriors and violently killed them
with his weapon, just as Indra killed the *daityas*. No one saw 19.25
Árjuna grabbing or nocking arrows in the battle, and even those who watched closely did not see him release those fast arrows. Go·vinda thought it extraordinary, Bhárata. As

vimuñcan vā śarāñ śīghraṃ dṛśyate 'vahitair api.
āścaryam, iti Govindaḥ samamanyata, Bhārata;
haṃs'|âṃśu|gaurās te senāṃ haṃsāḥ sara iv' âviśan.
tataḥ saṃgrāma|bhūmiṃ ca vartamāne jana|kṣaye
avekṣamāṇo Govindaḥ Savyasācinam abravīt:
«eṣa, Pārtha, mahā|raudro vartate Bharata|kṣayaḥ
pṛthivyāṃ pārthivānāṃ vai Duryodhana|kṛte mahān!
paśya, Bhārata! cāpāni rukma|pṛṣṭhāni dhanvinām,
mahatāṃ c' âpaviddhāni kalāpān, iṣu|dhīṃs tathā!
19.30 jātarūpa|mayaiḥ puṅkhaiḥ śarāṃś ca nata|parvaṇaḥ,
taila|dhautāṃś ca nārācān, nirmuktān iva pannagān,
ākīrṇāṃs tomarāṃś c' âpi vicitrān, hema|bhūṣitān,
carmāṇi c' âpaviddhāni rukma|pṛṣṭhāni, Bhārata,
su|varṇa|vikṛtān prāsāñ, śaktīḥ kanaka|bhūṣitāḥ,
jāmbūnada|mayaiḥ paṭṭair baddhāś ca vipulā gadāḥ,
jātarūpa|mayīś ca' rṣṭīḥ, paṭṭiśān hema|bhūṣitān,
daṇḍaiḥ kanaka|citraiś ca vipraviddhān paraśvadhān,
parighān, bhindipālāṃś ca, bhuśuṇḍīḥ, kuṇapān api,
ayas|kuntāṃś ca patitān, musalāni gurūṇi ca!
19.35 nānā|vidhāni śastrāṇi pragṛhya jaya|gṛddhinaḥ,
jīvanta iva dṛśyante gata|sattvās tarasvinaḥ.
gadā|vimathitair gātrair, musalair bhinna|mastakān,
gaja|vāji|rathaiḥ kṣuṇṇān paśya yodhān sahasraśaḥ!
manuṣya|gaja|vājīnāṃ śara|śakty|ṛṣṭi|tomaraiḥ,
nistriṃśaiḥ, paṭṭiśaiḥ, prāsair, nakharair, laguḍair api,
śarīrair bahudhā chinnaiḥ, śoṇit'|âugha|pariplutaiḥ,
gat'|âsubhir, amitra|ghna, saṃvṛtā raṇa|bhūmayaḥ.
bāhubhiś candan'|ādigdhaiḥ, s'|âṅgadaiḥ, śubha|bhūṣaṇaiḥ,
sa|tala|traiḥ, sa|keyūrair bhāti, Bhārata, medinī,

white as geese, the arrows entered that army like geese into a lake.

Surveying the battleground as the carnage unfolded, Go·vinda then said to the Left-handed archer: "Son of Pritha, this is horrific! This massive massacre of Bharatas and princes has transpired on earth on Duryódhana's account! Look, Bhárata! At the great archers' discarded gilded bows and quivers full of arrows! At those smooth-jointed ar- 19.30
rows with nocks made of gold and the iron arrows shining with sesame oil like snakes that have shed their sloughs! At the brilliant, gold-embossed lances scattered about and the gilded shields cast aside, Bhárata! And at the gold-set darts, gold decorated spears and huge clubs bound with gold strapping! At the golden javelins, gold-embossed tridents and axes with their gold colored handles strewn about! At those fallen iron bludgeons, short javelins, *bhushúndis*,* spears, iron spears and heavy maces!

Grasping their various weapons, eager for victory, those 19.35
bold men seem alive though they are lifeless. Look at those warriors trampled in their thousands by elephants, horses and chariots, their skulls split by heavy maces and with bodies crushed by clubs!

Enemy-destroyer, the battlefields are covered with the lifeless bodies of men, elephants and horses, immersed in rivers of blood and shattered in many ways by arrows, spears, javelins, lances, swords, tridents, darts, claw knives and staffs. Bhárata, the earth is luminous with bold men's arms 19.40
smeared with sandal powder and wearing beautifully decorated armlets, arm-guards and bracelets, their jeweled hands sporting finger-guards scattered about, with their shattered

19.40 s'|âṅguli|trair bhuj'|âgraiś ca vipraviddhair alaṃ|kṛtaiḥ,
hasti|hast'|ôpamaiś chinnair ūrubhiś ca tarasvinām,
baddha|cūḍā|maṇi|varaiḥ śirobhiś ca sa|kuṇḍalaiḥ.
rathāṃś ca bahudhā bhagnān, hema|kiṅkiṇinaḥ, śubhān,
aśvāṃś ca bahudhā paśya śoṇitena pariplutān,
anukarśān, upāsaṅgān, patākā, vividhān dhvajān!
yodhānāṃ ca mahā|śaṅkhān, pāṇḍurāṃś ca prakīrṇakān,
nirasta|jihvān mātaṅgāñ śayānān parvat'|ôpamān,
vaijayantīr vicitrāś ca, hatāṃś ca gaja|yodhinaḥ,
vāraṇānāṃ paristomān, saṃyuktān, eka|kambalān,
19.45 vipāṭita|vicitrāś ca rūpa|citrāḥ kuthās tathā,
bhinnāś ca bahudhā ghaṇṭāḥ patadbhiś cūrṇitā gajaiḥ,
vaidūrya|maṇi|daṇḍāṃś ca, patitāṃś c' âṅkuśān bhuvi,
aśvānāṃ ca yug'|āpīḍān, ratna|citrān uraś|chadān,
viddhāḥ sādi|dhvaj'|âgreṣu su|varṇa|vikṛtāḥ kuthāḥ,
vicitrān maṇi|citrāṃś ca jātarūpa|pariṣkṛtān,
aśv'|āstara|paristomān rāṅkavān patitān bhuvi,
cūḍā|maṇīn nar'|êndrāṇāṃ, vicitrāḥ kāñcana|srajaḥ,
chatrāṇi c' âpaviddhāni cāmara|vyajanāni ca,
candra|nakṣatra|bhāsaiś ca vadanaiś cāru|kuṇḍalaiḥ,
19.50 kḷpta|śmaśrubhir ākīrṇāṃ pūrṇa|candra|nibhair mahīm,
kumud'|ôtpala|padmānāṃ khaṇḍaiḥ phullaṃ yathā saraḥ,
tathā mahī|bhṛtāṃ vaktraiḥ kumud'|ôtpala|saṃnibhaiḥ,
tārā|gaṇa|vicitrasya nirmal'|êndu|dyuti|tviṣaḥ,
paśy' êmāṃ nabhasas tulyāṃ śaran|nakṣatra|mālinīm!

thighs the equal of elephant trunks, and their heads wearing earrings and fine jewels in their braided hair.

And look at the beautiful chariots with golden bells pulverised in various ways, their many horses bathed with blood and their ballasts, chariot-quivers, flags and various banners! And at the warriors' huge conches and white horse plumes, at the elephants with their tongues hanging out lying there like mountains! And at the colorful banners, and the slaughtered elephant-riding warriors, at the elephants' coverings jumbled together, though each is a single blanket! At the var- 19.45
iously colored and shaped cloths ripped to shreds, and the many bells shattered and pulverised by falling elephants! At the staffs with cat's eye gems and the elephant hooks fallen on the ground, and at the horses' yokes and headdresses, and the breast-plates spotted with jewels! At the shredded cloths embroidered with gold attached to the tops of the horseman's standards! At the variously colored horse blankets and cushions made from *ranku* deer hair and spotted with jewels and adorned with gold that have fallen on the ground! At the head-jewels of those lords of men, and at their wonderful golden garlands!

At the discarded parasols and chowries! At the earth scattered with faces adorned with beautiful earrings having the luster of the moon and stars, their beards neatly trimmed 19.50
and appearing like full moons! At the earth covered with the faces of lords of the earth that seemed like white and blue lilies, like a flower covered lake with masses of white and blue lilies and lotuses! Look at it! The equal of a sky ringed with autumnal stars that has the splendor and luster of the spotless moon and is brilliant with clusters of stars!

etat tav' âiv' ânurūpaṃ karm', Ârjuna, mah"|āhave,
divi vā deva|rājasya, tvayā yat kṛtam āhave!»
evaṃ tāṃ darśayan Kṛṣṇo yuddha|bhūmiṃ Kirīṭine,
gacchann ev' âśṛṇoc chabdaṃ Duryodhana|bale mahat,
śaṅkha|dundubhi|nirghoṣaṃ, bherī|paṇava|nisvanam,
19.55 rath'|âśva|gaja|nādāṃś ca, śastra|śabdāṃś ca dāruṇān.
praviśya tad balaṃ Kṛṣṇas turagair vāta|vegibhiḥ
Pāṇḍyen' âbhyarditaṃ sainyaṃ tvadīyāṃ vīkṣya vismitaḥ.
sa hi nānā|vidhair bāṇair iṣv|astra|pravaro yudhi
nyahanad dviṣatāṃ pūgān, gatāsūn Antako yathā.
gaja|vāji|manuṣyāṇāṃ śarīrāṇi śitaiḥ śaraiḥ
bhittvā praharatāṃ śreṣṭho videh'|âsūn apātayat.
śatru|pravīrair astāni nānā|śastrāṇi sāyakaiḥ
chittvā tān avadhīc chatrūn Pāṇḍyaḥ, Śakra iv' âsurān.

DHṚTARĀṢṬRA uvāca:

20.1 PROKTAS TVAYĀ pūrvam eva pravīro loka|viśrutaḥ,
na tv asya karma saṃgrāme tvayā, Saṃjaya, kīrtitam.
tasya vistaraśo brūhi pravīrasy' âdya vikramam,
śikṣāṃ, prabhāvaṃ, vīryaṃ ca, pramāṇaṃ, darpam eva ca!

SAṂJAYA uvāca:

Bhīṣma|Droṇa|Kṛpa|Drauṇi|Karṇ'|Ârjuna|Janārdanān
samāpta|vidyān dhanuṣi śreṣṭhān yān manyase rathān,
yo hy ākṣipati vīryeṇa sarvān etān mahā|rathān,
na mene c' ātmanā tulyaṃ kañ cid eva nar'|ēśvaram.
20.5 tulyatāṃ Droṇa|Bhīṣmābhyām ātmano yo na mṛṣyate;

Árjuna, in this great war, this deed that you did in battle is as befitting of you as it is of the king of the gods in heaven!"

As he moved along showing the battleground to the Wearer of the crown, from within Duryódhana's army Krishna heard a great noise of the clamor of conches and *dú-*
ndubhi drums, the beat of kettle-drums and cymbals, the 19.55
peal of elephants, horses and chariots and the shrill sounds of weapons. Krishna entered that army with his horses as fleet as the wind and was stunned to see your army tormented by the Pandya king. With his various arrows that man who is excellent with his bow massacred multitudes of his enemies in battle, like Death slaying those whose lives have expired. Penetrating the bodies of elephants, horses and men with his sharp arrows, that best of fighters threw those lifeless bodies down. With his arrows the Pandya king shattered the various weapons hurled by enemy-heroes and killed those enemies, like Shakra the demons.

DHRITA·RASHTRA said:

EARLIER YOU mentioned that world famous hero, but 20.1
you did not describe his deeds in battle, Sánjaya. Now tell me at length about that hero's courage, and his skill, power, energy, authority and pride!

SÁNJAYA said:

You believe that Bhishma, Drona, Kripa, Drona's son, Karna, Árjuna and Janárdana are the finest warriors, their learning perfected in the skill of the bow. Yet he who dispersed all those mighty warriors with his strength did not
reckon that any other lord of men was his equal. He did 20.5
not suffer comparison of himself with Drona or Bhishma;

Vāsudev'|Ârjunābhyāṃ ca nyūnatāṃ n' âicchat' ātmani,
sa Pāṇḍyo nṛ|patiḥ śreṣṭhaḥ sarva|śastra|bhṛtāṃ varaḥ
Karṇasy' ânīkam ahanat, parābhūta iv' Ântakaḥ.

tad udīrṇa|rath'|âśvaṃ ca, patti|pravara|saṃkulam,
kulāla|cakravad bhrāntaṃ Pāṇḍyen' âbhyāhataṃ balāt.
vy|aśva|sūta|dhvaja|rathān, vipraviddh'|āyudha|dvipān
samyag astaiḥ śaraiḥ Pāṇḍyo, vāyur meghān iv' âkṣipat.
dviradān, dvirad'|ārohān, vi|patāk'|āyudha|dhvajān,
sa|pāda|rakṣān ahanad, vajreṇ' âdrīn iv' âdri|hā.
20.10 sa|śakti|prāsa|tūṇīrān aśv'|ārohān hayān api,
Pulinda|Khasa|Bāhlīka|Niṣād'|Āndhraka|Kuntalān,
dākṣiṇātyāṃś ca, Bhojāṃś ca śūrān saṃgrāma|karkaśān,
vi|śastra|kavacān bāṇaiḥ kṛtvā c' âiv' âkarod vyasūn.

catur|aṅgaṃ balaṃ bāṇair nighnantaṃ Pāṇḍyam āhave
dṛṣṭvā, Drauṇir a|saṃbhrāntam a|saṃbhrāntas tato 'bhyayāt
ābhāṣya c' âinaṃ madhuram, a|bhītaṃ tam a|bhītavat
prāha praharatāṃ śreṣṭhaḥ smita|pūrvaṃ samāhvayan:

«rājan, kamala|patr'|âkṣa! viśiṣṭ'|âbhijana|śruta!
vajra|saṃhanana|prakhya! prakhyāta|bala|pauruṣa!
20.15 muṣṭi|śliṣṭ'|āyata|jyaṃ ca vyāyatābhyāṃ mahad dhanuḥ
dorbhyāṃ visphārayan bhāsi mahā|jaladavad bhṛśam!
śara|varṣair mahā|vegair amitrān abhivarṣataḥ,

and to himself he conceded no inferiority to Vasudéva or Árjuna. That Pandya king was the best, the finest of all weapon-bearers; and he massacred Karna's army as though he was Death slighted.

Swelling with chariots and horses and crammed with fine foot-soldiers, that army was vigorously struck by the Pandya king as it whirled about like a potter's wheel. With accurately discharged arrows the Pandya king dispersed that army, stripping chariots of their horses, charioteers and standards and scattering elephants and weapons, like the wind dispersing clouds. He killed elephants and the riders of elephants—removing their banners, weapons and standards, as well as the men protecting their legs—just as the mountain-
destroyer* destroys mountains with his thunderbolt. With 20.10
his arrows he removed the weapons and armor—and took the lives!—of horseman wielding spears, darts and quivers, and their horses too, and battle-hardened heroes of the Pulíndas, Khashas, Bahlíkas, Nishádas, Andhras, Kúntalas, southerners and Bhojas.

Seeing the Pandya king destroying the army's four divisions in battle with his arrows, Drona's calm son then calmly attacked him. As if he had no fear, that finest of fighters uttered sweet words to that fearless man and, challenging him with a smile, said:

"King, your eyes are like the petals of a lotus! You're distinguished in family and learning! You're as hard as diamond
and your strength and courage are renowned! You look as 20.15
threatening as a massive cloud with your great bow drawn by your out-stretched arms, its bow-string stretched and held

mad anyaṃ n' ânupaśyāmi prativīraṃ tav' āhave.
ratha|dvirada|patty|aśvān ekaḥ pramathase bahūn,
mṛga|saṃghān iv' âraṇye vibhīr bhīma|balo hariḥ.
mahatā ratha|ghoṣeṇa divaṃ bhūmiṃ ca nādayan
varṣ'|ânte sasya|hā megho bhāsi hrād" îva, pārthiva.
saṃspṛśānaḥ śarāṃs tīkṣṇāṃs tūṇād āśīviṣ'|ôpamān,
may" âiv' âikena yudhyasva, Tryambakeṇ' Ândhako yathā!»

20.20 evam uktas, «tath"! êty» uktvā, «prahar'! êti» ca tāḍitaḥ;
karṇinā Droṇa|tanayaṃ vivyādha Malayadhvajaḥ.
marma|bhedibhir atyugrair bāṇair agni|śikh"|ôpamaiḥ,
smayann abhyahanad Drauṇiḥ Pāṇḍyam ācārya|sattamaḥ.
tato 'parān su|tīkṣṇ'|âgrān nārācān marma|bhedinaḥ
gatyā daśamyā saṃyuktān Aśvatthām" âpy avāsṛjat.

tāñ śarān acchinat Pāṇḍyo navabhir niśitaiḥ śaraiḥ,
caturbhir ardayac c' âśvān, āśu te vy|asavo 'bhavan.
atha Droṇa|sutasy' êṣūṃs tāñ chittvā niśitaiḥ śaraiḥ,
dhanur|jyāṃ vitatāṃ Pāṇḍyaś cicched' âditya|tejasaḥ.

20.25 divyaṃ dhanur ath' âdhijyaṃ kṛtvā Drauṇir amitra|hā,
prekṣya c' āśu rathe yuktān narair anyān hay'|ôttamān,
tataḥ śara|sahasrāṇi preṣayām āsa vai dvijaḥ;
iṣu|saṃbādham ākāśam akarod, diśa eva ca.
tatas tān asyataḥ sarvān Drauṇer bāṇān mah"|ātmanaḥ

in your hand! As you shower your enemies with tremendously fast cascades of arrows, I see no one other than me who can match you in battle. Alone you lay waste to many chariots, elephants, foot-soldiers and horses, like a fearless lion of awesome might laying waste to herds of deer in the forest. Making heaven and earth reverberate with the great thunder of your chariot, prince, you're like a rumbling cloud destroying the crops at the end of the rainy season. Taking from your quiver those sharp arrows that are like poisonous snakes, you must battle with me alone, like Ándhaka with Try·ámbaka!"*

Spoken to like this, Málaya·dhvaja* yelled "So be it!" and 20.20
"Attack!" as he was struck. Then he wounded Drona's son with a barbed arrow. Grimacing, Drona's son, the finest of teachers, struck the Pandya king with his extremely sharp, flesh-piercing arrows that had points like flames. Then Ashvattháman let loose other flesh-piercing iron arrows with extremely sharp points that were endowed with the ten ways of moving.

The Pandya king cut down those arrows with nine sharp arrows and wounded his horses with four. They were immediately lifeless. After cutting down the arrows of Drona's son with sharp arrows, the Pandya king then cut the drawn bow-string of that man who was as fiery as the sun.

A destroyer of enemies, Drona's son restrung his divine 20.25
bow and, seeing that his men had immediately yoked other fine horses to his chariot, that brahmin dispatched thousands of arrows and filled the air and directions with arrows. Then the Pandya king, a bull of a man, knocked down all those arrows of Drona's great son as he shot them though

jānāno 'py a|kṣayān Pāṇḍyo 'śātayat puruṣa'|rṣabhaḥ.
prayuktāṃs tān prayatnena chittvā Drauṇer iṣūn ariḥ
cakra|rakṣau raṇe tasya prāṇudan niśitaiḥ śaraiḥ.
　ath' ârer lāghavaṃ dṛṣṭvā, maṇḍalī|kṛta|kārmukaḥ
prāsyad Droṇa|suto bāṇān, vṛṣṭiṃ Pūṣ'|ânujo yathā.
20.30 aṣṭāv aṣṭa|gavāny ūhuḥ śakaṭāni yad āyudham,
ahnas tad aṣṭa|bhāgena Drauṇiś cikṣepa, māriṣa.
tam Antakam iva kruddham, Antakasy' ântak'|ôpamam,
ye ye dadṛśire tatra, vi|saṃjñāḥ prāyaśo 'bhavan!
parjanya iva gharm'|ânte vṛṣṭyā s'|âdri|drumāṃ mahīm,
ācārya|putras tāṃ senāṃ bāṇa|vṛṣṭyā vyavīvṛṣat.
　Drauṇi|parjanya|muktāṃ tāṃ bāṇa|vṛṣṭiṃ su|duḥ|sahām
Vāyavy'|âstreṇa saṃkṣipya mudā Pāṇḍy'|ânilo 'nudat.
tasya nānadataḥ ketuṃ candan'|âguru|rūṣitam
Malaya|pratimaṃ Drauṇiś chittv" âśvāṃś caturo 'hanat.
20.35 sūtam ek'|êṣuṇā hatvā, mahā|jalada|nisvanam
dhanuś chittv" ârdha|candreṇa, tilaśo vyadhamad ratham.
astrair astrāṇi saṃvārya, chittvā sarv'|āyudhāni ca,
prāptam apy a|hitaṃ Drauṇir na jaghāna raṇ'|ēpsayā.
　etasminn antare Karṇo gaj'|ânīkam upādravat,
drāvayām āsa sa tadā Pāṇḍavānāṃ mahad balam.
vi|rathān rathinaś cakre, gajān, aśvāṃś ca, Bhārata,
gajān bahubhir ānarchac charaiḥ saṃnata|parvabhiḥ.

he knew them to be inexhaustible. Tirelessly cutting down those arrows hurled at him, the enemy of Drona's son drove away his wheel-protectors in the battle with sharp arrows.

Seeing his enemy's skill, Drona's son then bent his bow and discharged arrows like Pushan's younger brother* discharging rain. By the eighth part of the day, dear friend, 20.30
Drona's son had discharged as many weapons as were conveyed in eight carts led by eight bulls. Almost everyone who saw him there like Death enraged, or like the death of Death, went out of their minds! Like a rain-cloud showering the earth and its mountains and trees with rain at the end of the hot season, the teacher's son showered that army with a torrent of arrows.

Destroying with his Wind weapon that irresistible torrent of arrows discharged by Drona's son the rain-cloud, the Pandya wind ecstatically drove him away. As the Pandya king roared hideously, Drona's son shredded his sandal and aloe smeared banner that bore the image of the Málaya
mountain range, and killed his four horses. He killed his 20.35
charioteer with one arrow, split his bow that sounded like a massive rain-cloud with a half-moon arrow and smashed his chariot into pieces the size of sesame seeds. Enveloping his missiles with missiles and shattering all his weapons, Drona's son refrained from killing his enemy, though he'd earned it, due to his eagerness for battle.

In the meantime, Karna hastened towards the elephant division of the Pándavas and then drove away their huge army. He divested the chariot-warriors of their chariots, Bhárata, and assailed the elephants, horses and elephants again with many smooth-jointed arrows.

atha Drauṇir mah"|êṣv|āsaḥ Pāṇḍyaṃ śatru|nibarhaṇam
vi|rathaṃ rathināṃ śreṣṭhaṃ n' âhanad yuddha|kāṅkṣayā.

20.40 hat'|ēśvaro danti|varaḥ su|kalpitas,
tvar"|âbhisṛṣṭaḥ pratiśabda|go, balī
tam ādravad Drauṇi|śar'|āhatas tvaran,
javena kṛtvā pratihasti|garjitam.
taṃ vāraṇaṃ vāraṇa|yuddha|kovido,
dvip'|ôttamaṃ parvata|sānu|saṃnibham,
samabhyatiṣṭhan Malayadhvajas tvaran,
yath" âdri|śṛṅgaṃ harir unnadaṃs tathā.
sa tomaraṃ bhāskara|raśmi|varcasaṃ,
bal'|âstra|sarg'|ôttama|yatna|manyubhiḥ,
sasarja śīghraṃ paripīḍayan gajaṃ
guroḥ sutāy' âdri|pat'|īśvaro nadan.
maṇi|pravek'|ôttama|vajra|hāṭakair
alaṃ|kṛtaṃ c' âṃśuka|mālya|mauktikaiḥ,
«hato! hato 's'! îty» a|sakṛn mudā nadan
parāhanad Drauṇi|var'|âṅga|bhūṣaṇam.
tad arka|candra|graha|pāvaka|tviṣaṃ,
bhṛś'|âtipātāt patitaṃ, vicūrṇitam,
Mahendra|vajr'|âbhihataṃ, mahā|svanaṃ
yath" âdri|śṛṅgaṃ dharaṇī|tale, tathā.

Due to his desire for battle, Drona's son, a mighty archer, had not then slain that enemy destroyer the Pandya king, the finest of chariot-warriors who he'd stripped of his chariot.

A superb, powerful and well-equipped elephant whose 20.40
master had been killed speedily rushed in the direction of a noise and, struck by the arrows of Drona's son, quickly attacked the Pandya king as it bellowed at an opposing elephant.

Málaya·dhvaja was skilled in elephant-combat and quickly mounted that elephant—a superb elephant like the summit of a mountain—and roared like a lion roaring at a mountain peak. As he coerced that elephant, with the fury and supreme effort needed to release a missile with power, the roaring lord of the lord of mountains* quickly hurled his lance that had the splendor of a ray of the sun at the guru's son. Repeatedly and ecstatically yelling "You're dead! You're dead!" he struck the ornament off the head of Drona's son that was decorated with most excellent jewels, fine diamonds, gold, fine cloth, wreaths and pearls. Having the brilliance of the sun, the moon, the planets and fire, it fell because of his violent strike, pulverised like a mountain peak struck by great Indra's lightning bolt making a thunderous noise as it falls to the ground.

20.45 tataḥ prajajvāla pareṇa manyunā,
pād'|āhato nāga|patir yathā, tathā,
samādade c' Ântaka|daṇḍa|saṃnibhān
iṣūn amitr'|ārti|karāṃś catur|daśa.
dvipasya pād'|âgra|karān sa pañcabhir,
nṛpasya bāhū ca, śiro 'tha ca tribhiḥ,
jaghāna ṣaḍbhiḥ ṣaḍ anuttama|tviṣaḥ
sa Pāṇḍya|rāj'|ânucarān mahā|rathān.
su|dīrgha|vṛttau vara|candan'|ôkṣitau
suvarṇa|muktā|maṇi|vajra|bhūṣaṇau,
bhujau dharāyāṃ patitau nṛpasya tau
viceṣṭatus Tārkṣya|hatāv iv' ôragau.
śiraś ca tat pūrṇa|śaśi|prabh'|ānanaṃ
sa|roṣa|tāmr'|āyata|netram, unnasam
kṣitāv api bhrājati tat sa|kuṇḍalaṃ,
viśākhayor madhya|gataḥ śaśī yathā.
sa tu dvipaḥ pañcabhir uttam'|êṣubhiḥ
kṛtaḥ ṣaḍ|aṃśaś caturo nṛpas tribhiḥ,
kṛto daś'|âṃśaḥ kuśalena yudhyatā,
yathā havis tad daśa|daivataṃ, tathā.
20.50 sa pādaśo rākṣasa|bhojanān bahūn
pradāya Pāṇḍyo 'śva|manuṣya|kuñjarān,
svadhām iv' āpya jvalanaḥ pitṛ|priyas
tataḥ praśāntaḥ salila|pravāhataḥ.
samāpta|vidyaṃ tu guroḥ sutaṃ nṛpaḥ
samāpta|karmāṇam upetya te sutaḥ
suhṛd|vṛto 'tyartham apūjayan mudā,
jite Balau Viṣṇum iv' âmar'|ēśvaraḥ.

With great fury Ashvattháman then blazed like the lord of snakes when kicked by a foot, and grabbed fourteen arrows to torture his enemies, each resembling the rod of Death. With five he struck the elephant's feet and trunk and with three the king's arms and head and with six the six mighty warriors—whose brilliance was unsurpassed—following the king of the Pandyas. Like a pair of snakes attacked by Tarkshya,* the king's long and round arms, sprinkled with the best sandal powder and decorated with gold, pearls, jewels and diamonds, thrashed about once they had fallen to the ground. And, its face like a full moon, its eyes wide and red with rage and its nose prominent, his head glitters on the earth with its earrings like the moon between two constellations. 20.45

As if that skilful fighter was cutting an offering into ten portions for ten gods, with five excellent arrows he cut the elephant into six portions and with three he cut the king into four. After offering foot by foot many horses, men 20.50
and elephants as food to demons, the Pandya king was extinguished, just as the fire beloved of the ancestors is extinguished by a stream of water after it has consumed the offering.

After approaching the guru's son, whose learning is perfected and who had completed this deed, your son the king, surrounded by his allies, exuberantly honored him with joy, just as the lord of the immortals* honored Vishnu when he defeated Bali.

DHṚTARĀṢṬRA uvāca:

21.1 PĀṆḌYE HATE kim akarod Arjuno yudhi, Saṃjaya,
eka|vīreṇa Karṇena drāviteṣu pareṣu ca?
samāpta|vidyo, balavān, yukto, vīraḥ sa Pāṇḍavaḥ;
sarva|bhūteṣv anujñātaḥ Śaṃkareṇa mah"|ātmanā!
tasmān mahad bhayaṃ tīvram amitra|ghnād Dhanaṃjayāt!
sa yat tatr' âkarot Pārthas, tan mam' ācakṣva Saṃjaya!

SAṂJAYA uvāca:

hate Pāṇḍye, 'rjunaṃ Kṛṣṇas tvarann āha vaco hitam:
«paśyāmi n' âhaṃ rājānam, apayātāṃś ca Pāṇḍavān;
21.5 nivṛttaiś ca punaḥ Pārthair bhagnaṃ śatru|balaṃ mahat.
Aśvatthāmnaś ca saṃkalpādd hatāḥ Karṇena Sṛñjayāḥ,
tath" âśva|ratha|nāgānāṃ kṛtaṃ ca kadanaṃ mahat!»
sarvam ākhyātavān vīro Vāsudevaḥ Kirīṭine.

etac chrutvā ca dṛṣṭvā ca bhrātur ghoraṃ mahad bhayam,
«vāhay' âśvān, Hṛṣīkeśa, kṣipram! ity» āha Pāṇḍavaḥ.

tataḥ prāyādd Hṛṣīkeśo rathen' â|pratiyodhinā,
dāruṇaś ca punas tatra prādur āsīt samāgamaḥ.
tataḥ punaḥ samājagmur a|bhītāḥ Kuru|Pāṇḍavāḥ,
Bhīmasena|mukhāḥ Pārthāḥ, sūta|putra|mukhā vayam.

21.10 tataḥ pravavṛte bhūyaḥ saṃgrāmo, rāja|sattama,
Karṇasya Pāṇḍavānāṃ ca, Yama|rāṣṭra|vivardhanaḥ.
dhanūṃṣi, bāṇān, parighān, asi|paṭṭiśa|tomarān,
musalāni, bhuśuṇḍīś ca sa|śakty|ṛṣṭi|paraśvadhān,

DHRITA·RASHTRA said:

SÁNJAYA! WHEN the Pandya king had been killed and Karna, that singular hero, had driven away his enemies, what did Árjuna do in the battle? The Pándava is a powerful and skilled hero perfected in learning; among all beings, he was honored by great Shánkara!* Because of this there's terribly intense fear of Dhanan·jaya, a destroyer of enemies! Tell me, Sánjaya, what Pritha's son did then! 21.1

SÁNJAYA said:

When the Pandya king had been killed, Krishna quickly spoke these helpful words to Árjuna: "I can't see either the king or the retreated Pándavas; besides, had they re- 21.5
turned, Pritha's sons would've torn apart that huge hostile army. At Ashvatthámans direction, Karna has slaughtered the Srínjayas and carried out this massive massacre of horses, chariots and elephants!" All this the hero Vasudéva related to the Wearer of the crown.

Hearing this and realizing his brother's great and terrible danger, the Pándava said, "Quickly, Hrishi·kesha,* drive the horses!"

Hrishi·kesha then set out with that unrivalled chariot, and the terrible conflict again came into view there. Once again the fearless Kurus and Pándavas approached one another, the sons of Pritha led by Bhima·sena and us by the charioteer's son.

The battle between Karna and the Pándavas began once 21.10
more, finest of kings, expanding the kingdom of Yama. Grabbing their bows, arrows, iron bludgeons, swords, tridents, lances, maces, *bhushúndis*, spears, javelins, axes, clubs,

gadāḥ, prāsāñ, śitān kuntān, bhindipālān, mah"|âṅkuśān
pragṛhya kṣipram āpetuḥ paraspara|jighāṃsayā.
bāṇa|jyā|tala|śabdena dyāṃ, diśaḥ, pradiśo, viyat,
pṛthivīṃ nemi|ghoṣeṇa nādayanto 'bhyayuḥ parān.
tena śabdena mahatā saṃhṛṣṭāś, cakrur āhavam
vīrā vīrair mahā|ghoraṃ, kalah'|ântaṃ titīrṣavaḥ.
21.15 jyā|talatra|dhanuḥ|śabdāḥ, kuñjarāṇāṃ ca bṛṃhatām,
pādātānāṃ ca patatāṃ nṛṇāṃ nādo mahān abhūt.
tāla|śabdāṃś ca vividhāñ, śūrāṇām c' âbhigarjatām
śrutvā tatra bhṛśaṃ tresuḥ, petur, mamluś ca sainikāḥ.
teṣāṃ ninadatāṃ c' âiva, śastra|varṣaṃ ca muñcatām,
bahūn Ādhirathiḥ vīraḥ pramamāth' êṣubhiḥ parān.
pañca Pañcāla|vīrāṇāṃ rathān daśa ca pañca ca
s'|âśva|sūta|dhvajān Karṇaḥ śarair ninye Yama|kṣayam.
yodha|mukhyā mahā|vīryāḥ Pāṇḍūnāṃ Karṇam āhave
śīghr'|âstrās tūrṇam āvṛtya parivavruḥ samantataḥ.
21.20 tataḥ Karṇo dviṣat|senāṃ śara|varṣair viloḍayan
vijagāh', âṇḍa|j'|ākīrṇāṃ padminīm iva yūtha|paḥ.
dviṣan|madhyam avaskandya Rādheyo dhanur uttamam
vidhunvānaḥ śitair bāṇaiḥ śirāṃsy unmathya pātayat.
carma|varmāṇi saṃchinnāny apatan bhuvi dehinām,
viṣehur n' âsya saṃsparśaṃ dvitīyasya patatriṇaḥ.
varma|deh'|âsu|mathanair dhanuṣaḥ pracyutaiḥ śaraiḥ

darts, sharp *kunta* spears, short javelins and huge elephant hooks, they quickly attacked with eagerness to kill one another. They attacked their enemies, filling the earth, atmosphere, directions and regions with the roar of wheels, the buzz of arrows, the twangs of bow-strings and the sound of hands clapping. Excited by the huge noise, heroes did battle with other heroes, hoping to bring this appalling quarrel
to an end. There were sounds of bow-strings, arm-guards, 21.15
and bows and the massive sound of foot-soldiers, falling men and trumpeting elephants. And hearing the sounds of hands slapped on arms and the varied sounds of heroes savagely crying, troops there became utterly terrified and collapsed and perished.

As those men yelled and released showers of weapons, Ádhiratha's heroic son laid waste to many enemies with his arrows. With arrows Karna led five warriors of the Panchála heroes to Yama's house with their horses, charioteers and standards as well, and then ten and then five more. Courageous warrior chiefs of the Pándavas quickly wheeled about brandishing rapid-flying missiles and hemmed Karna in from all sides in the battle.

Then, as he confounded the army of his enemies with 21.20
showers of arrows, Karna penetrated it like the lead bull of a herd of elephants a lotus pond covered with birds. Storming into the midst of his enemies shaking his excellent bow, Radha's son struck and knocked off their heads with sharp arrows. The shattered armor and shields of men fell to the ground and they didn't survive a second arrow's touch. With arrows streaming from his bow destroying armor, bodies and lives, he struck his arm-guard with his bow-string, like

maurvyā tala|tre nyahanat, kaśayā vājino yathā.
Pāṇḍu|Sṛñjaya|Pañcālāñ śara|gocaram āgatān
mamarda tarasā Karṇaḥ, siṃho mṛga|gaṇān iva.

21.25 tataḥ Pāñcāla|rājaś ca, Draupadeyāś ca, māriṣa,
Yamau ca, Yuyudhānaś ca sahitāḥ Karṇam abhyayuḥ.

teṣu vyāyacchamāneṣu Kuru|Pañcāla|Pāṇḍuṣu,
priyān asūn raṇe tyaktvā yodhā jagmuḥ parasparam.
su|saṃnaddhāḥ, kavacinaḥ, sa|śiras|trāṇa|bhūṣaṇāḥ
gadābhir musalaiś c' ânye, parighaiś ca mahā|balāḥ,
samabhyadhāvanta bhṛśaṃ, Kāla|daṇḍair iv' ôdyataiḥ,
nardantaś c', āhvayantaś ca, pravalgantaś ca, māriṣa.

tato nijaghnur anyonyaṃ, petuś c' ânyonya|tāḍitāḥ,
vamanto rudhiraṃ gātrair, vi|mastiṣk'|ēkṣaṇ'|āyudhāḥ.
21.30 danta|pūrṇaiḥ, sa|rudhirair vaktrair dāḍima|saṃnibhaiḥ,
jīvanta iva c' âpy eke tasthuḥ śastr'|ôpabṛṃhitāḥ.
paraśvadhaiś c' âpy apare, paṭṭiśair, asibhis tathā,
śaktibhir, bhindipālaiś ca, nakhara|prāsa|tomaraiḥ,
tatakṣuś, cicchiduś c' ânye, bibhiduś, cikṣipus tathā,
saṃcakartuś ca, jaghnuś ca kruddhā raṇa|mah"|ârṇave.
petur anyonya|nihatā, vy|asavo, rudhir'|ôkṣitāḥ,
kṣarantaḥ su|rasaṃ raktaṃ, prakṛttāś candanā iva.

horses with a whip. Like a lion ravaging herds of deer, Karna immediately ravaged any Pándava, Srínjaya or Panchála who came within the range of his arrows.

Then, dear friend, the king of the Panchálas, Dráupadi's 21.25
sons, the twins* and Yuyudhána,* attacked Karna together.

As those Kurus, Panchálas and Pándavas fought together, warriors gave up their cherished lives and went at one another in battle. And other powerful and well-equipped warriors sporting armor and helmets and roaring, yelling challenges and leaping about, dear friend, brutally attacked with their clubs, maces and iron bludgeons held high as if they were the staffs of Death.

They struck one another and collapsed, wounded by each other and squirting blood from their limbs, disarmed,
blinded and their brains falling out. With their mouths filled 21.30
with bloody teeth looking like pomegranates, some stood propped up by their weapons as though still living. And in that mighty ocean of a battle, others were hacked apart by axes, cut down by tridents, pierced by swords, struck down by spears or cut to pieces by short javelins, or others in a rage were killed by claw knives, darts and lances. Slain by one another they collapsed, lifeless and sprinkled with blood, like hewn sandal trees oozing brilliant red sap.

rathai rathā vinihatā, hastinaś c' âpi hastibhiḥ,
narair narā hatāḥ petur, aśvāś c' âśvaiḥ sahasraśaḥ.
21.35 dhvajāḥ, śirāṃsi, chatrāṇi, dvipa|hastā, nṛṇāṃ bhujāḥ,
kṣurair, bhall'|ârdha|candraiś ca cchinnāḥ petur mahī|tale.
narāṃś ca, nāgān sa|rathān, hayān mamṛdur āhave,
aśv'|ārohair hatāḥ śūrāś, chinna|hastāś ca dantinaḥ.
sa|patākā dhvajāḥ petur viśīrṇā iva parvatāḥ,
pattibhiś ca samāplutya dvi|radāḥ, syandanās tathā.
hatāś ca, hanyamānāś ca, patitāś c' âiva sarvaśaḥ,
aśv'|ārohāḥ samāsādya tvaritāḥ pattibhir hatāḥ,
sādibhiḥ patti|saṃghāś ca nihatā yudhi śerate.
mṛditān' îva padmāni, pramlānā iva ca srajaḥ,
hatānāṃ vadanāny āsan, gātrāṇi ca mah"|āhave.
21.40 rūpāṇy atyartha|kāntāni dvirad'|âśva|nṛṇāṃ, nṛpa,
samunnān' îva vastrāṇi yayur dur|darśatāṃ param.

SAMJAYA uvāca:

22.1 HASTIBHIS TU mahā|mātrās,
tava putreṇa coditāḥ,
Dhṛṣṭadyumnaṃ jighāṃsantaḥ
kruddhāḥ Pārṣatam abhyayuḥ.
prācyāś ca, dākṣiṇātyāś ca, pravarā gaja|yodhinaḥ,
Aṅgā, Vaṅgāś ca, Puṇḍrāś ca, Māgadhās, Tāmraliptakāḥ,
Mekalāḥ, Kośalā, Madrā, Daśārṇā, Niṣadhās tathā,
gaja|yuddheṣu kuśalāḥ Kaliṅgaiḥ saha, Bhārata.
śara|tomara|nārācair, vṛṣṭimanta iv' âmbu|dāḥ,
siṣicus te tataḥ sarve Pāñcāla|balam āhave.

Chariots destroyed by chariots and elephants by elephants, men slain by men and horses by horses, collapsed by the thousand. Standards, heads, parasols, elephant trunks 21.35
and the arms of men were cut off by razor, broad and half-moon arrows and fell to the ground. In that battle, heroes were slaughtered by horsemen and elephants with their trunks cut off crushed men, elephants and horses together with their chariots. Overwhelmed by foot-soldiers, standards with their insignia and elephants and chariots fell down like shattered mountains. Killed, being killed and completely collapsed, swift horseman who'd been killed by foot-soldiers after attacking them lay prone, as did hordes of foot-soldiers struck down in battle by horsemen. The faces and limbs of those slaughtered in that massive battle were like crushed lotuses and withered garlands. Later, king, the 21.40
incredibly beautiful bodies of elephants, horses and men became hideous to look at, as their clothes became almost completely saturated.

SÁNJAYA said:

INCITED BY YOUR son, angry mahouts attacked Príshata's 22.1
grandson Dhrishta·dyumna with their elephants, eager to kill him. In that battle the finest elephant warriors from the east and south—the Angas, Vangas, Pundras, Mágadhas, Tamra·liptas, Mékalas, Kóshalas, Madras, Dashárnas, Níshadhas and Kalíngas, Bhárata, who were skilled in elephant-combat—showered the Panchála army like clouds raining with arrows, lances and iron arrows.

22.5 tān saṃmimardiṣūn nāgān
pārṣṇy|aṅguṣṭh'|âṅkuśair bhṛśam
coditān Pārṣato bāṇair
nārācair abhyavīvṛṣat.
ek'|âikaṃ daśabhiḥ, ṣaḍbhir, aṣṭābhir api, Bhārata,
dvi|radān abhivivyādha kṣiptair giri|nibhāñ śaraiḥ.

pracchādyamānaṃ dviradair, meghair iva divākaram,
prayayuḥ Pāṇḍu|Pāñcālā nadanto, niśit'|āyudhāḥ.
tān nāgān abhivarṣanto, jyā|tantrī|tala|nāditaiḥ,
vīra|nṛtyaṃ pranṛtyantaḥ, śūra|tāla|pracoditaiḥ,
Nakulaḥ, Sahadevaś ca, Draupadeyāḥ, Prabhadrakāḥ,
Sātyakiś ca, Śikhaṇḍī ca, Cekitānaś ca vīryavān,
samantāt siṣicur vīrā, meghās toyair iv' âcalān.
22.10 te mlecchaiḥ preṣitā nāgā narān, aśvān, rathān api
hastair ākṣipya mamṛduḥ, padbhiś c' âpy atimanyavaḥ.
bibhiduś ca viṣāṇ'|âgraiḥ, samākṣipya ca cikṣipuḥ;
viṣāṇa|lagnāś c' âpy anye paripetur vibhīṣaṇāḥ.

pramukhe vartamānaṃ tu dvipaṃ Aṅgasya Sātyakiḥ
nārācen' ôgra|vegena bhittvā marmāṇy apātayat.
tasy' āvarjita|kāyasya dvi|radād utpatiṣyataḥ,
nārācen' âhanad vakṣaḥ Sātyakiḥ, so 'patad bhuvi.

Puṇḍrasy' āpatato nāgaṃ calantam iva parvatam
Sahadevaḥ prayatn'|âstair nārācair ahanat tribhiḥ.
22.15 vipatākaṃ, viyantāraṃ, vi|varma|dhvaja|jīvitam
taṃ kṛtvā dvi|radaṃ, bhūyaḥ Sahadevo 'ṅgam abhyayāt.

Just as they were about to crush him, Príshata's grandson rained down arrows and iron arrows on those elephants that were brutally steered by heels, elephant hooks and thumbs. One by one he wounded those mountain-like elephants as he dispatched ten then six then eight arrows, Bhárata. 22.5

While he was being surrounded by elephants like the sun by clouds, the Pándavas and Panchálas went to his aid roaring and wielding sharp weapons. Raining on those elephants and dancing the dance of heroes to the sound of their palms on bow-strings and the encouragement of heroes clapping their hands, the heroes Nákula, Saha·deva, Dráupadi's sons, the Prabhádrakas, Sátyaki, Shikhándin and courageous Chekitána completely showered those elephants, like clouds showering mountains with water.

Urged on by barbarians, in utter fury elephants struck men, horses and chariots with their trunks and trampled them with their feet. They pierced them with the tips of their tusks and tossed them about and hurled them aside; others clinging to those tusks were flung about, inspiring terror. 22.10

But with a formidably fast iron arrow Sátyaki gored the elephant of the Anga prince* where it was vulnerable and felled it as it advanced before him. As its rider's body bent over to leap from the elephant, Sátyaki struck him in the chest with an iron arrow and he fell to the ground.

As the Pundra king rushed towards him, Saha·deva struck his elephant that moved like a mountain with three iron arrows shot with precision. After stripping his elephant of its flag, driver, armor and standard and taking its life, Saha·deva once more attacked the Anga prince. 22.15

Sahadevaṃ tu Nakulo vārayitv" Âṅgam ārdayat
nārācair Yama|daṇḍ'|ābhais tribhir nāgaṃ, śatena tam.
divākara|kara|prakhyān Aṅgaś cikṣepa tomarān
Nakulāya śatāny aṣṭau. tridh" âik'|âikaṃ tu so 'cchinat.
tath" ârdha|candreṇa śiras tasya ciccheda Pāṇḍavaḥ.
sa papāta hato mlecchas ten' âiva saha dantinā.

ath' Âṅga|putre nihate hasti|śikṣā|viśārade,
Aṅgāḥ kruddhā mahā|mātrā nāgair Nakulam abhyayuḥ,
22.20 calat|patākaiḥ su|mukhair, hema|kakṣ"|tanu|cchadaiḥ,
mimardiśantas tvaritāḥ, pradīptair iva parvataiḥ.
Mekal'|Ôtkala|Kāliṅgā, Niṣadhās, Tāmraliptakāḥ
śara|tomara|varṣāṇi vimuñcanto jighāṃsavaḥ.

taiś chādyamānaṃ Nakulaṃ, divākaram iv' âmbudaiḥ,
paripetuḥ su|saṃrabdhāḥ Pāṇḍu|Pañcāla|Somakāḥ.
tatas tad abhavad yuddhaṃ rathināṃ hastibhiḥ saha,
sṛjatāṃ śara|varṣāṇi, tomarāṃś ca sahasraśaḥ.
nāgānāṃ prāsphuṭan kumbhā, marmāṇi vividhāni ca,
dantāś c' âiv' âtividdhānāṃ nārācair, bhūṣaṇāni ca.
22.25 teṣām aṣṭau mahā|nāgāṃś catuḥ|ṣaṣṭyā su|tejanaiḥ
Sahadevo jaghān' āśu; te 'patan saha sādibhiḥ.
añjo|gatibhir āyamya prayatnād dhanur uttamam,
nārācair ahanan nāgān Nakulaḥ kula|nandanaḥ.
tataḥ Pāñcālya|Śaineyau, Draupadeyāḥ, Prabhadrakāḥ,
Śikhaṇḍī ca mahā|nāgān siṣicuḥ śara|vṛṣṭibhiḥ.
te Pāṇḍu|yodh'|âmbu|dharaiḥ śatru|dvirada|parvatāḥ

But Nákula held Saha·deva back and wounded the Anga prince with three iron arrows that appeared like Yama's staff, and his elephant with a hundred. The Anga prince hurled eight hundred lances at Nákula that seeming like rays of the sun. But one by one he split them in three. And with a half-moon arrow the Pándava cut off his head. Killed, the barbarian collapsed together with his elephant.

Once that son of Anga skilled in elephant craft had been 22.20
slain, the enraged Anga mahouts attacked Nákula hoping to quickly crush him with their elephants that were like burning mountains with their flapping banners, magnificent mouths and golden girdles and armor. And, eager to kill him off, Mékalas, Útkalas, Kalíngas, Níshadhas and Tamra·liptas released showers of arrows and lances.

The Pándavas, Panchálas and Sómakas were furious and rushed towards Nákula who was surrounded by enemies like the sun by clouds. Then the chariot-warriors began to fight with those elephants, releasing torrents of arrows and lances by the thousand. The foreheads, various exposed areas, tusks and adornments of those elephants that were deeply wounded by iron arrows burst apart. From among 22.25
them Saha·deva immediately struck eight huge elephants with sixty-four well-sharpened arrows; they collapsed with their riders. Drawing back his excellent bow with fast movements and great effort, Nákula, the joy of his family, slaughtered those elephants with iron arrows. Then the Panchálas, Shainéyas, Dráupadi's sons, Prabhádrakas and Shikhándin rained torrents of arrows on those massive elephants. Struck by the Pándava warrior-clouds with their torrents of arrows,

bāṇa|varṣair hatāḥ petur, vajra|varṣair iv' âcalāḥ.
evaṃ hatvā tava gajāṃs te Pāṇḍu|nara|kuñjarāḥ
drutāṃ senām avaikṣanta, bhinna|kūlām iv' āpagām.
22.30 tāṃ te senām samāloḍya Pāṇḍu|putrasya sainikāḥ
vikṣobhayitvā ca, punaḥ Karṇam ev' âbhidudruvuḥ.

SAMJAYA uvāca:

23.1 SAHADEVAṂ TATHĀ kruddhaṃ dahantaṃ tava vāhinīm
Duḥśāsano, mahā|rāja, bhrātā bhrātaram abhyayāt.
tau sametau mahā|yuddhe dṛṣṭvā, tatra mahā|rathāḥ
siṃha|nāda|ravāṃś cakrur, vāsāṃsy ādudhuvuś ca ha.
tato, Bhārata, kruddhena tava putreṇa dhanvinā
Pāṇḍu|putras tribhir bāṇair vakṣasy abhihato balī.
Sahadevas tato, rājan, nārācena tav' ātmajam
viddhvā vivyādha saptatyā, sārathiṃ ca tribhiḥ śaraiḥ.
23.5 Duḥśāsanas tataś cāpaṃ chittvā, rājan, mah"|āhave
Sahadevaṃ tri|saptatyā bāhvor urasi c' ārdayat.
Sahadevas tu saṃkruddhaḥ khaḍgaṃ gṛhya mah"|āhave
āvidhya prāsṛjat tūrṇaṃ tava putra|rathaṃ prati.
sa|mārgaṇa|guṇaṃ cāpaṃ chittvā tasya mahān asiḥ
nipapāta tato bhūmau, cyutaḥ sarpa iv' âmbarāt.
ath' ânyad dhanur ādāya, Sahadevaḥ pratāpavān
Duḥśāsanāya cikṣepa bāṇam anta|karaṃ tataḥ.
tam āpatantaṃ viśikhaṃ, Yama|daṇḍ'|ôpama|tviṣam
khaḍgena śita|dhāreṇa dvidhā ciccheda Kauravaḥ.

those hostile elephant-mountains collapsed, like mountains struck by torrents of lightning bolts.

Destroying your elephants like this, the men and elephants of the Pándavas watched your army retreat like a river with a breached embankment. The troops of Pandu's 22.30
son, having stirred up that army and thrown it into confusion, again attacked Karna.

SÁNJAYA said:

As SAHA·DEVA furiously scorched your army, great king, 23.1
Duhshásana attacked him, brother against brother. Seeing those two come together for a great fight, the mighty warriors there thundered lions' roars and waved their clothes about. Then, Bhárata, your angry son armed with a bow struck Pandu's powerful son in the chest with three arrows. Next, king, Saha·deva wounded your son with an iron arrow and then wounded him with seventy more and his charioteer with three.

After splintering his bow in the great battle, king, Duh- 23.5
shásana wounded Saha·deva in the chest and arms with seventy-three arrows. But Saha·deva was incensed and grabbed his sword in that great battle and, whirling it around, quickly hurled it at your son's chariot. His massive sword sliced through his bow and its arrow and bow-string and then fell to earth like a snake falling from the sky.

Glorious Saha·deva seized another bow and sent a death-bringing arrow towards Duhshásana. With his sharp-edged sword the Káurava split that arrow in two as it flew towards him as majestic as Yama's staff. Then, hastily flinging his 23.10
sharp sword in the fight, that powerful man grasped another

23.10 tatas taṃ niśitaṃ khaḍgaṃ āvidhya yudhi sa|tvaraḥ,
dhanuś c' ânyat samādāya śaraṃ jagrāha vīryavān.
tam āpatantaṃ sahasā nistriṃśaṃ niśitaiḥ śaraiḥ
pātayām āsa samare Sahadevo hasann iva.

tato bāṇāṃś catuḥ|ṣaṣṭiṃ tava putro mahā|raṇe
Sahadeva|rathaṃ tūrṇaṃ preṣayām āsa, Bhārata.
tāñ śarān samare, rājan, vegen' āpatato bahūn
ek'|âikaṃ pañcabhir bāṇaiḥ Sahadevo nyakṛntata.
saṃnivārya mahā|bāṇāṃs tava putreṇa preṣitān,
ath' âsmai su|bahūn bāṇān preṣayām āsa saṃyuge.
23.15 tān bāṇāṃs tava putro 'pi chittv" âik'|âikaṃ tribhiḥ śaraiḥ
nanāda su|mahā|nādaṃ, dārayāṇo vasuṃ|dharān.

tato Duḥśāsano, rājan, viddhvā Pāṇḍu|sutaṃ raṇe,
sārathiṃ navabhir bāṇair Mādreyasya samārpayat.
tataḥ kruddho, mahā|rāja, Sahadevaḥ pratāpavān
samādhatta śaraṃ ghoraṃ mṛtyu|kāl'|Ântak'|ôpamam.
vikṛṣya balavac cāpaṃ tava putrāya so 'sṛjat;
sa taṃ nirbhidya vegena, bhittvā ca kavacaṃ mahat,
prāviśad dharaṇīṃ, rājan, valmīkam iva pannagaḥ.

tataḥ saṃmumuhe, rājaṃs, tava putro mahā|rathaḥ,
23.20 mūḍhaṃ c' âinaṃ samālokya sārathis tvarito ratham
apovāha bhṛśaṃ trasto vadhyamānaṃ śitaiḥ śaraiḥ.

parājitya raṇe taṃ tu Kauravyaṃ Pāṇḍu|nandanaḥ
Duryodhana|balaṃ dṛṣṭvā pramamātha samantataḥ.
pipīlika|puṭaṃ, rājan, yathā mṛdnan naro ruṣā,
tathā sā Kauravī senā mṛditā tena, Bhārata.

bow and seized an arrow. Saha·deva almost laughed and immediately felled that sword with sharp arrows as it flew towards him during the struggle.

Then in that great battle, Bhárata, your son quickly shot sixty-four arrows at Saha·deva's chariot. As numerous arrows speedily flew towards him in the battle, king, Saha·deva cut down every one of them with five arrows. Once he'd repelled the many arrows shot by your son, he then shot a huge number of arrows at him in the battle. Your son, having 23.15
also cut down every one of those arrows with three of his arrows, bellowed a massive roar, tearing apart the earth.

After that, king, Duhshásana wounded Pandu's son in the conflict and struck the charioteer of Madri's son with nine arrows. Enraged, great king, glorious Saha·deva nocked a dreadful arrow that was like Death at the hour of death. Powerfully bending his bow, he discharged it at your son. Piercing him through with a violent jolt and shattering his great armor, it penetrated the earth, king, like a snake an ant-hill.

King, your son the mighty warrior then lost consciousness. And as soon as he saw that he was unconscious, his 23.20
terrified charioteer quickly drove his chariot away while sharp arrows brutally harried it.

After overcoming that Kaurávya in battle, Pandu's son looked towards Duryódhana's army and assaulted it from all sides. Bhárata, he crushed that Káurava army like a man furiously trampling an ant-hill.

SAMJAYA uvāca:

24.1 NAKULAM RABHASAM yuddhe drāvayantaṃ varūthinīm
Karṇo Vaikartano, rājan, vārayām āsa vai ruṣā.
Nakulas tu tataḥ Karṇaṃ prahasann idam abravīt:
«cirasya, bata, dṛṣṭo 'haṃ daivataiḥ saumya|cakṣuṣā!
paśya māṃ tvaṃ raṇe, pāpa, cakṣur|viṣayam āgataḥ!
tvaṃ hi mūlam an|arthānāṃ, vairasya, kalahasya ca;
tvad|doṣāt Kuravaḥ kṣīṇāḥ samāsādya parasparam.
tvām adya samare hatvā kṛta|kṛtyo 'smi, vijvaraḥ!»
24.5 evam uktaḥ pratyuvāca Nakulaṃ sūta|nandanaḥ
sadṛśaṃ rāja|putrasya, dhanvinaś ca viśeṣataḥ:
«praharasva ca me, vīra! paśyāmas tava pauruṣam!
karma kṛtvā raṇe, śūra, tataḥ katthitum arhasi!
an|uktvā samare, tāta, śūrā yudhyanti śaktitaḥ.
prayudhyasva mayā śaktyā! haniṣye darpam eva te!»
ity uktvā prāharat tūrṇaṃ Pāṇḍu|putrāya sūta|jaḥ,
vivyādha c' âinaṃ samare tri|saptatyā śilīmukhaiḥ.
Nakulas tu tato viddhaḥ sūta|putreṇa, Bhārata,
aśīty" āśīviṣa|prakhyaiḥ sūta|putram avidhyata.
24.10 tasya Karṇo dhanuś chittvā svarṇa|puṅkhaiḥ, śilā|śitaiḥ
triṃśatā param'|êṣv|āsaḥ śaraiḥ Pāṇḍavam ārdayat.
te tasya kavacaṃ bhittvā papuḥ śoṇitam āhave,
āśī|viṣā yathā nāgā bhittvā gāṃ salilaṃ papuḥ.

SÁNJAYA said:

KING, KARNA Vaikártana furiously repelled fierce Nákula 24.1
who was driving away his army in the battle. But, laughing, Nákula said this to Karna:

"Ah! At last the gods have looked on me with their gentle eye! You can see me in this battle, wretch, and you've come within the range of my sight! You're the root of all the bad things that've happened, of this hostility and this quarrel. Because of your failings the Kurus have attacked one another and are on the wane. Once I've killed you in battle today, I will have accomplished my goal and shall be free from this fever!"

Spoken to like this, the charioteer's son replied to Nákula 24.5
in a way fitting for a prince and especially for a bowman. "Attack me, hero! We'll see your courage! Once you've done this deed in battle, champion, then you can boast! Dear boy, champions fight in battle to the best of their ability without uttering a word. Fight with me to the best of your ability! I'll destroy your conceit!"

Once he had said this, the charioteer's son quickly assailed Pandu's son and pelted him in battle with seventy-three arrows. Though wounded by the charioteer's son, Nákula then pelted the charioteer's son with eighty arrows that resembled
poisonous snakes. Karna, a superb archer, splintered his bow 24.10
and pummeled the Pándava with thirty stone-sharpened arrows with golden nocks. They pierced his armor and drank his blood in the battle, like venomous snakes that have penetrated the earth and drunk its water.

ath' ânyad dhanur ādāya hema|pṛṣṭhaṃ, dur|āsadam,
Karṇaṃ vivyādha saptatyā, sārathiṃ ca tribhiḥ śaraiḥ.
tataḥ kruddho, mahā|rāja, Nakulaḥ para|vīra|hā
kṣurapreṇa su|tīkṣṇena Karṇasya dhanur ācchinat.
ath' âinaṃ chinna|dhanvānaṃ sāyakānāṃ śatais tribhiḥ
ājaghne prahasan vīraḥ sarva|loka|mahā|ratham.
24.15 Karṇam abhyarditaṃ dṛṣṭvā Pāṇḍu|putreṇa, māriṣa,
vismayaṃ paramaṃ jagmū rathinaḥ saha daivataiḥ.

ath' ânyad dhanur ādāya, Karṇo Vaikartanas tadā
Nakulaṃ pañcabhir bāṇair jatru|deśe samārpayat.
tatra|sthair atha tair bāṇair, Mādrī|putro vyarocayat,
sva|raśmibhir iv' ādityo bhuvane visṛjan prabhām.

Nakulas tu tataḥ Karṇaṃ viddhvā saptabhir āśu|gaiḥ
ath' âsya dhanuṣaḥ koṭiṃ punaś ciccheda, māriṣa.
so 'nyat kārmukam ādāya samare vegavattaram
Nakulasya tato bāṇaiḥ samantāc chādayad diśaḥ.
24.20 saṃchādyamānaḥ sahasā Karṇa|cāpa|cyutaiḥ śaraiḥ,
ciccheda sa śarāṃs tūrṇaṃ śarair eva mahā|rathaḥ.

tato bāṇa|mayaṃ jālaṃ vitataṃ vyomni dṛśyate,
kha|dyotānām iva vrātair saṃpatadbhir yathā nabhaḥ.
tair vimuktaiḥ śara|śataiś chāditaṃ gaganaṃ tadā,
śalabhānāṃ yathā vrātais tadvad āsīd, viśāṃ pate.
te śarā hema|vikṛtāḥ saṃpatanto muhur muhuḥ
śreṇī|kṛtā vyakāśanta, krauñcāḥ śreṇī|kṛtā iva.
bāṇa|jāl'|āvṛte vyomni, cchādite ca divākare,

Then grabbing another insurmountable gilded bow, Nákula wounded Karna with seventy arrows and his charioteer with three. A destroyer of enemy-heroes, Nákula was enraged, great king, and cut down Karna's bow with an exceedingly sharp razor-edged arrow. With three-hundred arrows that hero, laughing all the while, then struck the mightiest warrior in all the worlds whose bow had been splintered. When they saw Karna tormented by Pandu's 24.15
son, dear friend, the chariot-warriors were astonished, as were the gods.

Grabbing another bow, Karna Vaikártana then struck Nákula around the collar-bone with five arrows. With those arrows embedded there Madri's son looked as radiant as the sun casting light on the earth with its own rays.

But Nákula then wounded Karna with seven arrows and again splintered the curved tip of his bow, dear friend. In that contest, Karna seized another even faster bow and completely shrouded the directions on all sides of Nákula with arrows. Suddenly enveloped by those arrows streaming forth 24.20
from Karna's bow, that mighty warrior quickly cut down those arrows with his own arrows.

A mass of arrows then became visible spread out in the air, as though the sky was filled with swarms of flying fireflies. The sky was then covered with hundreds of discharged arrows, lord of the people, as though with swarms of locusts. Those gold-embellished arrows flying incessantly onwards aligned in rows, looked like curlews aligned in rows. With that spread of arrows enclosing the sky and covering the sun, not a single bird flew down to the ground. With the 24.25
way there obstructed on all sides by masses of arrows, those

na sma sampatate bhūmyāṃ kiṃ cid apy antarikṣa|gam.
24.25 niruddhe tatra mārge ca śara|saṃghaiḥ samantataḥ,
vyarocatāṃ mah"|ātmānau, kāla|sūryāv iv' ôditau.
Karṇa|cāpa|cyutair bāṇair vadhyamānās tu Somakāḥ
avālīyanta, rāj'|êndra, vedan'|ârtā, bhṛś'|ârditāḥ.
Nakulasya tathā bāṇair hanyamānā camūs tava
vyaśīryata diśo, rājan, vāta|nunnā iv' âmbu|dāḥ.
te sene hanyamāne tu tābhyāṃ divyair mahā|śaraiḥ
śara|pātam apākramya tasthatuḥ prekṣike tadā.
protsārita|jane tasmin Karṇa|Pāṇḍavayoḥ śaraiḥ,
avidhyetāṃ mah"|ātmānāv anyonyaṃ śara|vṛṣṭibhiḥ.
24.30 vidarśayantau divyāni śastrāṇi raṇa|mūrdhani,
chādayantau ca sahasā paraspara|vadh'|âiṣiṇau,
Nakulena śarā muktāḥ kaṅka|barhiṇa|vāsasaḥ
sūta|putram avacchādya vyatiṣṭhanta yath" âmbare.
tath" âiva sūta|putreṇa preṣitāḥ param'|āhave
Pāṇḍu|putram avacchādya vyatiṣṭhant' âmbare śarāḥ.
śara|veśma|praviṣṭau tau dadṛśāte na kaiś cana,
sūryā|candram asau, rājañ, chādyamānau dhanair iva.
tataḥ kruddho raṇe Karṇaḥ kṛtvā ghorataraṃ vapuḥ
Pāṇḍavaṃ chādayām āsa samantāc chara|vṛṣṭibhiḥ.
24.35 so 'ticchanno, mahā|rāja, sūta|putreṇa Pāṇḍavaḥ
na cakāra vyathāṃ, rājan, bhāskaro jaladair yathā.
tataḥ prahasy' Ādhirathiḥ śara|jālāni, māriṣa,
preṣayām āsa samare śataśo 'tha sahasraśaḥ.

two great men were radiant like a pair of rising suns at the end of the world.

As they were slaughtered by the arrows streaming forth from Karna's bow, the Sómakas cowered down, lord of kings, racked with pain and badly wounded. And as it was being destroyed by Nákula's arrows, king, your army dispersed from that place like clouds scattered by the wind. Being destroyed by those two with their huge divine arrows, both armies retreated from the range of their arrows and then stood by looking on.

Once those people had been dispersed by the arrows of
Karna and the Pándava, the two great men pelted one another with torrents of arrows. As they displayed their di- 24.30
vine weapons at the front of the battle and ferociously enveloped one another, each eager to kill the other, heron-
and peacock-feathered arrows released by Nákula and enveloping the charioteer's son seemed to be suspended in the
sky. Similarly, arrows dispatched by the charioteer's son and
enveloping Pandu's son in that extraordinary battle seeemed
to be suspended in the sky. Lost in a house of arrows, no one
could see those two, king, like the sun and moon concealed
by clouds.

Then in a rage Karna took on a more dreadful appearance in the battle and completely enveloped the Pándava
with showers of arrows. Totally enveloped by the chario- 24.35
teer's son, great king, the Pándava felt no dread like the sun
when enveloped by clouds. Ádhiratha's son then burst into
laughter and sent forth multitudes of arrows in the battle,
dear friend, by the hundred and then by the thousand. Everywhere was quite dark with the arrows of that great man.

ekaǀcchāyam abhūt sarvaṃ tasya bāṇair mah"ǀātmanaḥ;
abhraǀcchāy" êva saṃjajñe saṃpatadbhiḥ śar'ǀôttamaiḥ.
tataḥ Karṇo, mahāǀrāja, dhanuś chittvā mah"ǀātmanaḥ
sārathiṃ pātayām āsa rathaǀnīḍādd hasann iva.
tato 'śvāṃś caturaś c' âsya caturbhir niśitaiḥ śaraiḥ
Yamasya bhavanaṃ tūrṇaṃ preṣayām āsa, Bhārata.
24.40 ath' âsya taṃ rathaṃ divyaṃ tilaśo vyadhamac charaiḥ,
patākāṃ, cakraǀrakṣāṃś ca, gadāṃ, khaḍgaṃ ca, māriṣa,
śataǀcandraṃ ca tac carma, sarv'ǀôpakaraṇāni ca.
hat'ǀâśvo, virathaś c' âiva, vivarmā ca, viśāṃ pate,
avatīrya rathāt tūrṇaṃ, parighaṃ gṛhya dhiṣṭhitaḥ.
tam udyataṃ mahāǀghoraṃ parighaṃ tasya sūtaǀjaḥ
vyahanat sāyakai, rājañ, suǀtīkṣṇair bhāraǀsādhanaiḥ.
vyāyudhaṃ c' âinam ālakṣya, śaraiḥ saṃnataǀparvabhiḥ
ārpayad bahubhiḥ Karṇo, na c' âinaṃ samapīḍayat.
sa hanyamānaḥ samare kṛt'ǀâstreṇa balīyasā,
24.45 prādravat sahasā, rājan, Nakulo vyākul'ǀêndriyaḥ.
tam abhidrutya Rādheyaḥ prahasan vai punaḥ punaḥ,
saǀjyam asya dhanuḥ kaṇṭhe vyavāsṛjata, Bhārata.
tataḥ sa śuśubhe, rājan, kaṇṭh'ǀāsaktaǀmahāǀdhanuḥ,
pariveṣam anuprāpto yathā syād vyomni candramāḥ,
yath" âiva c' âsito meghaḥ śakraǀcāpena śobhitaḥ.
tam abravīt tataḥ Karṇo: «vyarthaṃ vyāhṛtavān asi!
vad' êdānīṃ punar hṛṣṭo vadhyamānaḥ punaḥ punaḥ!
mā yotsīḥ Kurubhiḥ sārdhaṃ balavadbhiś ca, Pāṇḍava!
sadṛśais, tāta, yudhyasva! vrīḍāṃ mā kuru, Pāṇḍava!
24.50 gṛhaṃ vā gaccha, Mādreya, yatra vā KṛṣṇaǀPhālgunau!»

With those superb arrows flying forth a shadow appeared as if from clouds.

Great king, Karna then splintered that great man's bow and, smirking, knocked his charioteer from the chariot box. Next he quickly sent his four horses to Yama's house with four sharp arrows, Bhárata. Then with arrows he smashed 24.40
his divine chariot into pieces as small as sesame seeds, and his flag, wheel-guards, club and sword as well, dear friend, and his shield that was adorned with a hundred moons and all his other implements. His horses dead and stripped of his chariot and armor, lord of people, Nákula suddenly leapt from his chariot and stood clutching his bludgeon. King, with his terribly sharp and extremely effective arrows the charioteer's son destroyed his horrifying bludgeon as he raised it high. Seeing that he had no weapons, Karna tormented him with many smooth-jointed arrows, but did not crush him.

About to be slaughtered in battle by that stronger man who was skilled with his weapons, Nákula suddenly fled, 24.45
king, his mind in disarray. Laughing manically, Radha's son pursued him and slung his stringed bow around Nákula's neck, Bhárata. With that great bow circling his neck, king, he looked brilliant like the moon when encircled by a halo in the sky, or like a dark cloud resplendent with a rainbow.

Karna then said to him: "You spoke in vain! Now speak once more if you're happy to be thrashed again and again! You can't fight with powerful Kurus, Pándava! Fight only those whose might is similar to your own, boy! Don't feel shame, Pándava! Go home, son of Madri! Or to where Kri- 24.50

evam uktvā, mahā|rāja, vyasarjayata taṃ tadā.

vadha|prāptaṃ tu taṃ śūro n' âhanad dharma|vit tadā,
smṛtvā Kuntyā vaco, rājaṃs, tata enaṃ vyasarjayat.
visṛṣṭaḥ Pāṇḍavo, rājan, sūta|putreṇa dhanvinā,
vrīḍann iva jagām' âtha Yudhiṣṭhira|rathaṃ prati.
āruroha rathaṃ c' âpi sūta|putra|pratāpitaḥ,
niḥśvasan, duḥkha|saṃtaptaḥ, kumbha|stha iva pannagaḥ.

taṃ vijity', âtha Karṇo 'pi Pañcālāṃs tvarito yayau
rathen' âtipatākena, candra|varṇa|hayena ca.
24.55 tatr' ākrando mahān āsīt Pāṇḍavānāṃ, viśāṃ pate,
dṛṣṭvā senā|patiṃ yāntaṃ Pañcālānāṃ ratha|vrajān.
tatr' âkaron, mahā|rāja, kadanaṃ sūta|nandanaḥ,
madhyaṃ prāpte dina|kare cakravad vicaran prabhuḥ.

bhagna|cakrai rathaiḥ kaiś cic chinna|dhvaja|patākibhiḥ
hat'|âśvair, hata|sūtaiś ca, bhagn'|âkṣaiś c' âiva, māriṣa,
hriyamāṇān apaśyāma Pāñcālānāṃ ratha|vrajān.
tatra tatra ca saṃbhrāntā vicerur atha kuñjarāḥ,
dav'|âgni|paridagdh'|âṅgā yath" âiva syur mahā|vane.
bhinna|kumbh'|ārdra|rudhirāś, chinna|hastāś ca vāraṇāḥ,
24.60 chinna|gātr'|âvarāś c' âiva, cchinna|vāladhayo 'pare;
chinn'|âbhrāṇ' îva saṃpetur hanyamānā mah"|ātmanā.
apare trāsitā nāgā nārāca|śara|tomaraiḥ
tam ev' âbhimukhaṃ jagmuḥ, śalabhā iva pāvakam.
apare niṣṭanantaś ca vyadṛśyanta mahā|dvipāḥ

shna and Phálguna are!" Once he had said this, great king, he released him.

Though Nákula had arrived at his death, that hero who knew the law did not then kill him, dear king, for he had remembered Kunti's words and let him go.* Released by the charioteer's bow-wielding son, king, in some shame the Pándava then went to Yudhi·shthira's chariot. Scorched by the charioteer's son and burning with distress, he ascended the chariot hissing like a snake in a pot.

After defeating him, Karna then quickly advanced on the Panchálas, with his chariot proudly flying its flag and its horses the color of the moon. There was a great cry 24.55
there among the Pándavas, lord of the people, as they saw that general advancing on squadrons of Panchála warriors. Careering like a wheel, great king, the powerful son of the charioteer created carnage there by the time the sun had reached the middle of its course.

We saw squadrons of Panchála warriors being carried away by chariots that had busted wheels, shredded banners and standards, slaughtered horses and charioteers and busted axles, dear friend. And their elephants then went astray, whirling about here and there, as if their limbs were scorched by a forest-fire in a great wood. Some elephants had split foreheads wet with blood, others had severed trunks, some had lacerated fore and hindquarters, others had sev- 24.60
ered tails. Like clouds broken up they collapsed as they were slaughtered by that great man. Other elephants terrorised by lances, arrows and iron arrows, moved closer to him like moths to a flame. And other massive elephants, trumpeting

kṣarantaḥ śoṇitaṃ gātrair, nagā iva jala|sravāḥ.
uraś|chadair viyuktāś ca, vāla|bandhaiś ca vājinaḥ,
rājataiś ca, tathā kāṃsyaiḥ, sauvarṇaiś c' âiva bhūṣaṇaiḥ,
hīnāṃś c' ābharaṇaiś c' âiva, khalīnaiś ca vivarjitān,
cāmaraiś ca, kuthābhiś ca, tūṇīraiḥ patitair api,
24.65 nihataiḥ sādibhiś c' âiva, śūrair āhava|śobhitaiḥ,
apaśyāma raṇe tatra bhrāmyamāṇān hay'|ôttamān.
prāsaiḥ, khaḍgaiś ca rahitān, ṛṣṭibhiś c' âpi, Bhārata,
haya|sādīn apaśyāma kañcuk'|ôṣṇīṣa|dhāriṇaḥ,
nihatān, vadhyamānāṃś ca, vepamānāṃś ca, Bhārata,
nān"|âṅg'|âvayavair hīnāṃs tatra tatr' âiva, Bhārata.
rathān hema|pariṣkārān, saṃyuktāñ javanair hayaiḥ,
bhrāmyamāṇān apaśyāma hateṣu rathiṣu drutam,
bhagn'|âkṣa|kūbarān kāṃś cid, bhagna|cakrāṃś ca, Bhārata,
vi|patāka|dhvajāṃś c' ânyāñ, chinn'|ēṣā|daṇḍa|bandhurān.
24.70 vihatān rathinas tatra, dhāvamānāṃs tatas tataḥ,
sūta|putra|śarais tīkṣṇair hanyamānān, viśāṃ pate,
viśastrāṃś ca tath" âiv' ânyān, sa|śastrāṃś ca bahūn hatān;
tārakā|jāla|saṃchannān, vara|ghaṇṭā|viśobhitān,
nānā|varṇa|vicitrābhiḥ patākābhir alaṃ|kṛtān,
vāraṇān anupaśyāma dhāvamānān samantataḥ.
śirāṃsi, bāhūn, ūrūṃś ca cchinnān, anyāṃs tath" âiva ca
Karṇa|cāpa|cyutair bāṇair apaśyāma samantataḥ.

and oozing blood from their limbs, looked like mountains streaming with water.

And in that battle we saw the finest war horses, stripped of 24.65
their mail and cruppers and their silver, copper and golden ornaments, and without their decorations and deprived of their bridles, and with their plumes, rugs and quivers fallen aside, roaming about deranged with their riders slaughtered, though they be heroes brilliant in battle. We saw horse-riders sporting mail and turbans without their darts, swords and javelins, Bhárata, slaughtered, being killed and shaking fearfully, Bhárata, and missing various limbs and body parts here and there, Bhárata. We saw chariots decorated with gold and harnessed to swift horses rapidly careering out of control with their chariot-warriors killed. Some had busted axles and yoking-poles and some busted wheels, Bhárata, others were stripped of their flags and banners, their poles, banner-staffs and seats smashed. And we saw many chariot- 24.70
warriors killed there, some quickly running off here and there, and others being slaughtered by the charioteer's son with sharp arrows, lord of people, and many others who'd been slaughtered with or without their weapons. We saw elephants running about all over the place, decorated with banners motley with various colors, covered by star-studded mail-coats and adorned with the finest bells. And we saw heads, arms and shins and other limbs completely cut off by arrows shot from Karna's bow.

mahān vyatikaro raudro yodhānām anvapadyata,
Karṇa|sāyaka|nunnānāṃ, yudhyatāṃ ca śitaiḥ śaraiḥ.
24.75 te vadhyamānāḥ samare sūta|putreṇa Sṛñjayāḥ
tam ev' âbhimukhaṃ yānti, pataṃgā iva pāvakam.
taṃ dahantam anīkāni tatra tatra mahā|ratham
kṣatriyā varjayām āsur, yug'|ânt'|âgnim iv' ôlbaṇam.
hata|śeṣās tu ye vīrāḥ Pāñcālānāṃ mahā|rathāḥ,
tān prabhagnān drutān vīraḥ pṛṣṭha|to vikirañ śaraiḥ
abhyadhāvata tejasvī viśīrṇa|kavaca|dhvajān.
tāpayām āsa tān bāṇaiḥ sūta|putro mahā|balaḥ,
madhyaṃ|dinam anuprāpto bhūtān' îva tamo|nudaḥ.

SAṂJAYA uvāca:

25.1 YUYUTSUṂ TAVA putrasya drāvayantaṃ balaṃ mahat
Ulūko nyapatat tūrṇaṃ, «tiṣṭha! tiṣṭh'! êti» c' âbravīt.
Yuyutsuś ca tato, rājañ, śita|dhāreṇa patriṇā
Ulūkaṃ tāḍayām āsa vajreṇ' êva mahā|balam.
Ulūkas tu tataḥ kruddhas tava putrasya saṃyuge
kṣurapreṇa dhanuś chittvā, tāḍayām āsa karṇinā.
tad apāsya dhanuś chinnaṃ Yuyutsur vegavattaram
anyad ādatta su|mahac cāpaṃ saṃrakta|locanaḥ.
25.5 śākuniṃ tu tataḥ ṣaṣṭyā vivyādha, Bharata'|rṣabha,
sārathiṃ tribhir ānarchat, taṃ ca bhūyo vyavidhyata.

A huge and dreadful catastrophe followed for those warriors as they fought with sharp arrows and were driven away by Karna's arrows. As the charioteer's son slaughtered them 24.75
in battle, the Sríñjayas drew closer to him like an insect to a flame. The kshatriyas avoided that mighty warrior as he scorched the forces here and there, like the immense fire at the end of an epoch. But that brilliant hero attacked those Panchála heroes who survived the slaughter from behind, destroying mighty warriors with his arrows as they fled defeated, their armor and standards ruined. The immensely powerful son of the charioteer scorched them with arrows, just as the sun scorches all living things when it arrives at midday.

SÁNJAYA said:

ULÚKA SUDDENLY rushed upon Yuyútsu, who was driv- 25.1
ing away your son's huge army, and yelled, "Stand! Stand your ground!" But with a winged and sharp-bladed arrow, Yuyútsu then struck the very powerful Ulúka as if with a thunderbolt. Ulúka was then enraged and splintered your son's bow in battle with a razor-edged arrow and struck him with a barbed arrow.

Discarding his splintered bow, Yuyútsu seized another huge and much faster bow, his eyes red with rage. And then 25.5
he pelted Shákuni's son* with sixty arrows, bull of Bharatas, attacked his charioteer with three and wounded Ulúka some more.

Ulūkas taṃ tu viṃśatyā viddhvā svarṇa|vibhūṣitaiḥ,
ath' âsya samare kruddho dhvajaṃ ciccheda kāñcanam.
sa cchinna|yaṣṭiḥ su|mahāñ śīryamāṇo mahā|dhvajaḥ,
papāta pramukhe, rājan, Yuyutsoḥ kāñcana|dhvajaḥ.
dhvajam unmathitaṃ dṛṣṭvā, Yuyutsuḥ krodha|mūrcchitaḥ
Ulūkaṃ pañcabhir bāṇair ājaghāna stan'|ântare.

Ulūkas tasya samare taila|dhautena, māriṣa,
śiraś ciccheda bhallena yantur, Bharata|sattama.
25.10 tac chinnam apatad bhūmau Yuyutsoḥ sārathes tadā,
tārā|rūpaṃ yathā citraṃ nipapāta mahī|tale.
jaghāna caturo 'śvāṃś ca, taṃ ca vivyādha pañcabhiḥ;
so 'tividdho balavatā pratyapāyād rath'|ântaram.
taṃ nirjitya raṇe, rājann, Ulūkas tvarito yayau
Pāñcālān Sṛñjayāṃś c' âiva vinighnan niśitaiḥ śaraiḥ.

Śatānīkaṃ, mahā|rāja, Śrutakarmā sutas tava
vy|aśva|sūta|rathaṃ cakre nimeṣ'|ârdhād a|saṃbhramaḥ.
hat'|âśve tu rathe tiṣṭhañ, Śatānīko mahā|rathaḥ
gadāṃ cikṣepa saṃkruddhas tava putrasya, māriṣa.
25.15 sā kṛtvā syandanaṃ bhasma, hayāṃś c' âiva sa|sārathīn,
papāta dharaṇīṃ tūrṇaṃ dārayant" îva, Bhārata.

tāv ubhau virathau vīrau Kurūṇāṃ kīrti|vardhanau
vyapākrametāṃ yuddhāt tu prekṣamāṇau parasparam.
putras tu tava saṃbhrānto Viviṃśo ratham āruhat;
Śatānīko 'pi tvaritaḥ Prativindhya|rathaṃ gataḥ.

Ulúka pelted him with twenty gold-plated arrows and then angrily cut down his golden standard. Its huge pole broken and the massive standard torn to shreds, Yuyútsu's golden standard fell before him, king. Seeing his standard torn to shreds, Yuyútsu seethed with rage and struck Ulúka in the center of his chest with five arrows.

In that encounter, dear friend and foremost Bharata, Ulúka cut off the head of Yuyútsu's charioteer with a broad
arrow daubed in sesame oil. The decapitated head of Yuyú- 25.10
tsu's driver then fell on the ground as if a brilliant star-like
object had fallen to the earth's surface. Ulúka slaughtered
his four horses and wounded him with five arrows. Horrifically wounded by that powerful man, Yuyútsu retreated to
another chariot. After defeating him in battle, king, Ulúka
quickly advanced on the Panchálas and Srínjayas, slaying
them with sharp arrows.

Your unflustered son Shruta·karman, great king, stripped
Shataníka of his horses, charioteer and chariot in half the
twinkling of an eye. But standing in his chariot with its
horses dead, dear friend, the mighty warrior Shataníka
hurled his club in fury at your son. Pulverising his char- 25.15
iot and horses along with their driver, Bhárata, it quickly
fell to earth and almost tore it apart.

Stripped of their chariots, both heroes, who enhanced the fame of the Kurus, retired from battle, staring back at one another. Flustered, your son mounted the chariot of Vivímshu. Shataníka also quickly went to Prativíndhya's chariot.

Sutasomaṃ tu Śakunir viddhvā tu niśitaiḥ śaraiḥ
n' âkampayata saṃkruddho, vāry|augha iva parvatam.
Sutasomas tu taṃ dṛṣṭvā pitur atyanta|vairiṇam
śarair aneka|sāhasraiś chādayām āsa, Bhārata.

25.20 tāñ śarāñ Śakunis tūrṇaṃ ciccheď ânyaiḥ patatribhiḥ,
laghv|astraś, citra|yodhī ca, jita|kāśī ca saṃyuge.
nivārya samare c' âpi śarāṃs tān niśitaiḥ śaraiḥ,
ājaghāna su|saṃkruddhaḥ Sutasomaṃ tribhiḥ śaraiḥ.
tasy' âśvān, ketanaṃ, sūtaṃ tilaśo vyadhamac charaiḥ
syālas tava, mahā|rāja. tata uccukruśur janāḥ.

hat'|âśvo, virathaś c' âiva, cchinna|ketuś ca, māriṣa,
dhanvī dhanur|varaṃ gṛhya rathād bhūmāv atiṣṭhata.
vyasṛjat sāyakāṃś c' âiva svarṇa|puṅkhāñ śilā|śitān,
chādayām āsa samare tava syālasya taṃ ratham.

25.25 śalabhānām iva vrātāñ, śara|vrātān mahā|rathaḥ
rath'|ôpagān samīkṣy' âivaṃ vivyathe n' âiva Saubalaḥ.
pramamātha śarāṃs tasya śara|vrātair mahā|yaśāḥ.

tatr' âtuṣyanta yodhāś ca siddhāś c' âpi divi sthitāḥ,
Sutasomasya tat karma dṛṣṭv" â|śraddheyam adbhutam,
ratha|sthaṃ Śakuniṃ yas tu padātiḥ samayodhayat.

tasya tīkṣṇair mahā|vegair bhallaiḥ saṃnata|parvabhiḥ
vyahanat kārmukaṃ, rājaṃs, tūṇīrāṃś c' âiva sarvaśaḥ.
sa cchinna|dhanvā virathaḥ khaḍgam udyamya c' ânadat,
vaidūry'|ôtpala|varṇ'|ābhaṃ danti|danta|maya|tsarum.

Though pelting Suta·soma with sharp arrows, in his rage Shákuni could not make him tremble, like a flood of water against a mountain. As soon as Suta·soma saw his father's perpetual enemy, Bhárata, he enveloped him with many thousands of arrows. Quick with his weapons, fighting in 25.20
various ways and behaving like a conqueror in that battle, Shákuni quickly cut down those arrows with other feathered arrows. And after deflecting those arrows in the battle with sharp arrows, he furiously struck Suta·soma with three arrows. With arrows your brother-in-law cut up Suta·soma's horses, banner and charioteer into pieces as small as sesame seeds. At that, great king, the people screamed.

His horses dead, stripped of his chariot and his flag shredded, dear friend, the bowman Suta·soma grabbed a fine bow and stood down from his chariot onto the ground. He discharged stone-sharpened arrows with nocks of gold and enveloped your brother-in-law's chariot in the battle.

Seeing those swarms of arrows approaching his chariot 25.25
like swarms of locusts, Súbala's son, a mighty warrior, didn't even tremble. That much celebrated man destroyed those arrows with swarms of his own arrows.

And the warriors there and the *siddha*s abiding in heaven were impressed after seeing Suta·soma's incredible and extraordinary deed, as he did battle with Shákuni standing in his chariot while he was on foot.

Shákuni completely destroyed his bow and quivers, king, with sharp broad arrows that were exceedingly fast and had smooth-joints. His bow shattered and stripped of his chariot, Suta·soma roared as he raised his sword high, its color that of the blue lotus and cat's eye gems and its hilt made of

25.30 bhrāmyamāṇaṃ tatas taṃ tu vimal'|âmbara|varcasam
Kāla|daṇḍ'|ôpamaṃ mene Sutasomasya dhīmataḥ.
so 'carat sahasā khaḍgī maṇḍalāni sahasraśaḥ
catur|daśa, mahā|rāja, śikṣā|bala|samanvitaḥ,
bhrāntam, udbhrāntam, āviddham,
āplutaṃ, viplutaṃ, sṛtam,
saṃpāta|samudīrṇe ca
darśayām āsa saṃyuge.
Saubalas tu tatas tasya śarāṃś cikṣepa vīryavān;
tān āpatata ev' āśu ciccheda param'|âsinā.
tataḥ kruddho, mahā|rāja, Saubalaḥ para|vīra|hā
prāhiṇot Sutasomāya śarān āśīviṣ'|ôpamān.
25.35 ciccheda tāṃś tu khaḍgena śikṣayā ca balena ca,
darśayal̄ lāghavaṃ yuddhe Tārkṣya|tulya|parākramaḥ.
tasya saṃcarato, rājan, maṇḍal'|āvartane tadā,
kṣurapreṇa su|tīkṣṇena khaḍgaṃ ciccheda su|prabham.
sa cchinnaḥ sahasā bhūmau nipapāta mahān asiḥ,
ardham asya sthitaṃ haste su|tsaros tatra, Bhārata.
chinnam ājñāya nistriṃśam, avaplutya padāni ṣaṭ,
prāvidhyata tataḥ śeṣaṃ Sutasomo mahā|rathaḥ.
tac chittvā sa|guṇaṃ cāpaṃ raṇe tasya mah"|ātmanaḥ,
papāta dharaṇīṃ tūrṇaṃ svarṇa|vajra|vibhūṣitam.

ivory. Shákuni then reckoned that, as it was swung about, 25.30
wise Suta·soma's sword had the splendor of a clear sky and the likeness of the staff of Time.*

Endowed with skill and power and wielding his sword, great king, Suta·soma suddenly moved about in circles by the thousand and displayed in the battle the fourteen different maneuvers—whirling, waving, swinging, springing forward, scattering, running, rushing and hurling and so on. But Súbala's powerful son then dispatched his arrows at him. But as they rushed towards him Suta·soma immediately cut them down with his excellent sword.

Great king, Súbala's son, a killer of enemy-heroes, was then furious and discharged arrows at Suta·soma that were
like venomous snakes. With skill and strength Suta·soma cut 25.35
them down with his sword, displaying speed in the battle and his courage the equal of Tarkshya's. As he roamed in circles first one way and then the other, king, Shákuni then cut down his immensely powerful sword with a very sharp razor-edged arrow. That huge, broken sword immediately fell to the ground, Bhárata, while half its fine hilt remained in his hand.

Realizing his sword was broken, the mighty warrior Suta·soma leapt back six steps and hurled what was left of it. After smashing that great man's bow together with its bow-string in the battle, that gold and diamond decorated remnant immediately fell to ground.

25.40 Sutasomas tato 'gacchac Chrutakīrter mahā|ratham.
Saubalo 'pi dhanur gṛhya ghoram anyat su|dur|jayam,
abhyayāt Pāṇḍav'|ânīkaṃ nighnañ śatru|gaṇān bahūn.
tatra nādo mahān āsīt Pāṇḍavānāṃ, viśāṃ pate,
Saubalaṃ samare dṛṣṭvā vicarantam a|bhītavat.
tāny anīkāni dṛptāni, śastravanti, mahānti ca,
drāvyamāṇāny adṛśyanta Saubalena mah"|ātmanā.
yathā daitya|camūṃ, rājan, deva|rājo mamarda ha,
tath" âiva Pāṇḍavīṃ senāṃ Saubaleyo vyanāśayat.

SAṂJAYA UVĀCA:

26.1 DHṚṢṬADYUMNAṂ Kṛpo, rājan, vārayām āsa saṃyuge,
yathā dṛṣṭvā vane siṃhaṃ śarabho vārayed yudhi.
niruddhaḥ Pārṣatas tena Gautamena balīyasā,
padāt padaṃ vicalituṃ n' âśakat tatra, Bhārata.

Gautamasya rathaṃ dṛṣṭvā Dhṛṣṭadyumna|rathaṃ prati,
vitresuḥ sarva|bhūtāni kṣayaṃ prāptaṃ ca menire.
tatr' âvocan vimanaso rathinaḥ sādinas tathā:
«Droṇasya nidhanān nūnaṃ saṃkruddho dvipadāṃ varaḥ;
26.5 Śāradvato mahā|tejā, divy'|âstra|vid, udāra|dhīḥ;
api svasti bhaved adya Dhṛṣṭadyumnasya Gautamāt?
ap' îyaṃ vāhinī kṛtsnā mucyeta mahato bhayāt?
apy ayaṃ brāhmaṇaḥ sarvān na no hanyāt samāgatān?
yādṛśaṃ dṛśyate rūpam Antaka|pratimaṃ bhṛśam,
gamiṣyaty adya padavīṃ Bhāradvājasya Gautamaḥ.
ācāryaḥ kṣipra|hastaś ca, vijayī ca sadā yudhi,

Suta·soma then went to Shruta·kirti's great chariot. And Súbala's son grabbed another horrifying and unbeatable bow and attacked the Pándava army, slaughtering many enemy units. A huge roar rose from the Pándavas there, lord of the people, after they saw the son of Súbala roaming about fearless in battle. Those proud and mighty troops wielding their weapons were seen being driven away by that great man the son of Súbala. Just as the king of the gods laid waste to the army of the *daityas*, king, so Súbala's son devastated the Pándava army. 25.40

SÁNJAYA said:

KRIPA KEPT Dhrishta·dyumna back in the battle, king, just as a *shárabha** spotting a lion in a forest would keep it back in a fight. Held back by Gáutama,* who was more powerful then he, Príshata's grandson* couldn't even move from one foot to the other there, Bhárata. 26.1

Seeing Gáutama's chariot hard against the chariot of Dhrishta·dyumna, all living things were terrified and believed that the end had come. The dejected chariot-warriors and horsemen there said: "That finest of men is still furious at Drona's death. Sharádvat's very fiery son* knows the divine weapons and is very astute. Shall Dhrishta·dyumna be safe from Gáutama today? Shall any of the army escape his immense rage? Shall not this brahmin slaughter us all together? His appearance is very much like that of Death and suggests that today Gáutama will follow the lead of Bharad·vaja's son. The teacher* is quick of hand, armed with weapons, endowed with courage, filled with rage and always victorious in battle. And Príshata's grandson now 26.5

astravān, vīrya|sampannaḥ, krodhena ca samanvitaḥ;
Pārṣataś ca mahā|yuddhe vimukho 'dy' âbhilakṣyate.»
ity evaṃ vividhā vācas tāvakānāṃ paraiḥ saha
26.10 vyaśrūyanta, mahā|rāja, tayos tatra samāgame.
vinihśvasya tataḥ krodhāt Kṛpaḥ Śāradvato, nṛpa,
Pārṣataṃ c' ârdayām āsa niśceṣṭaṃ sarva|marmasu.
sa hanyamānaḥ samare Gautamena mah"|ātmanā,
kartavyaṃ na sma jānāti mohena mahat" āvṛtaḥ.
tam abravīt tato yantā: «kac cit kṣemaṃ tu, Pārṣata?
īdṛśaṃ vyasanaṃ yuddhe na te dṛṣṭaṃ mayā kvacit!
daiva|yogāt tu te bāṇā n' âpatan marma|bhedinaḥ
preṣitā dvija|mukhyena marmāṇy uddiśya sarvataḥ.
vyāvartaye rathaṃ tūrṇaṃ, nadī|vegam iv' ârṇavāt.
26.15 a|vadhyaṃ brāhmaṇaṃ manye yena te vikramo hataḥ!»
Dhṛṣṭadyumnas tato, rājañ, śanakair abravīd vacaḥ:
«muhyate me manas, tāta, gātra|svedaś ca jāyate.
vepathuś ca śarīre me, roma|harṣaś ca, sārathe.
varjayan brāhmaṇaṃ yuddhe śanair yāhi yato 'rjunaḥ!
Arjunaṃ Bhīmasenaṃ vā samare prāpya, sārathe,
kṣemam adya bhaved evam. eṣā me naiṣṭhikī matiḥ!»
tataḥ prāyān, mahā|rāja, sārathis tvarayan hayān,
yato Bhīmo mah"|êṣv|āso yuyudhe tava sainikaiḥ.
pradrutaṃ tu rathaṃ dṛṣṭvā Dhṛṣṭadyumnasya, māriṣa,
26.20 kirañ śata|śatāny eva Gautamo 'nuyayau tadā.
śaṅkhaṃ ca pūrayām āsa muhur muhur ariṃ|damaḥ,
Pārṣataṃ trāsayām āsa, Mahendro Namuciṃ yathā.

seems less than keen for a great battle." Such were the various discussions of your troops with their enemies, great 26.10 king, that were heard when those two came together there.

Breathing deeply with anger, king, Sharádvat's son Kripa then struck Príshata's helpless grandson wherever he was exposed. As great Gáutama struck him in battle, Dhrishta·dyumna was filled with great confusion and didn't know what to do. Then his charioteer said to him: "Is this safe, grandson of Príshata? Never have I seen you have a crisis in battle like this! It's only by chance that the mortally wounding arrows aimed at all your exposed areas and discharged by that foremost brahmin haven't overwhelmed you. I'll quickly separate our chariot, just as the current of a river separates from the sea. I reckon that this brahmin who's 26.15 destroyed your courage cannot be killed!"

Dhrishta·dyumna then quietly said these words, king: "I'm confused, dear friend, and my body's begun to sweat. Driver, I'm shaking and the hairs on my body are on end. Avoid that brahmin in the battle and go quietly to where Árjuna is! Once we find Árjuna or Bhima·sena in the battle, driver, then we'll be safe today. I'm completely convinced of this!"

Urging the horses forward, great king, his driver departed from there to where the mighty archer Bhima fought with your troops. But Gáutama saw Dhrishta·dyumna's chariot flee, dear friend, and then pursued him, releasing hundreds 26.20 and hundreds of arrows. That enemy-destroyer blew his conch again and again and terrified Príshata's grandson just as great Indra had terrified Námuchi.

Śikhaṇḍinaṃ tu samare Bhīṣma|mṛtyuṃ dur|āsadam
Hārdikyo vārayām āsa, smayann iva muhur muhuḥ.
Śikhaṇḍī ca samāsādya Hṛdikānāṃ mahā|ratham
pañcabhir niśitair bhallair jatru|deśe samāhanat.
Kṛtavarmā tu saṃkruddho bhittvā ṣaṣṭyā patatribhiḥ
dhanur ekena ciccheda hasan, rājan, mahā|rathaḥ.
ath' ânyad dhanur ādāya, Drupadasy' ātmajo balī,
26.25 «tiṣṭha! tiṣṭh'! êti» saṃkruddho Hārdikyaṃ pratyabhāṣata.
tato 'sya navatiṃ bāṇān rukma|puṅkhān su|tejanān
preṣayām āsa, rāj'|êndra; te 'sy' âbhraśyanta varmaṇaḥ!
vitathāṃs tān samālakṣya patitāṃś ca mahī|tale,
kṣurapreṇa su|tīkṣṇena kārmukaṃ cicchide bhṛśam.
ath' âinaṃ chinna|dhanvānaṃ, bhagna|śṛṅgam iva' rṣabham
aśītyā mārgaṇaiḥ kruddho bāhvor urasi c' ārpayat.
Kṛtavarmā tu saṃkruddho mārgaṇaiḥ kṣata|vikṣataḥ
vavāma rudhiraṃ gātraiḥ, kumbha|vaktrād iv' ôdakam.
rudhireṇa pariklinnaḥ Kṛtavarmā tv arājata,
26.30 varṣeṇa kledito, rājan, yathā gairika|parvataḥ.
ath' ânyad dhanur ādāya sa|mārgaṇa|guṇaṃ prabhuḥ,
Śikhaṇḍinaṃ bāṇa|gaṇaiḥ skandha|deśe vyatāḍayat.
skandha|deśa|sthitair bāṇaiḥ Śikhaṇḍī tu vyarājata,
śākhā|praśākhā|vipulaḥ su|mahān pādapo yathā.

In that battle, Hrídika's son* snarled manically and forced back indomitable Shikhándin who had brought about Bhishma's death. Yet Shikhándin assailed that mighty warrior of the Hrídikas and struck him with five sharp broad arrows around his collar-bone. In rage the great warrior Krita·varman wounded him with sixty arrows and splintered his bow with one as he laughed, king.

Drúpada's powerful son* then grabbed another bow and angrily yelled at Hrídika's son, "Stand! Stand your ground!" 26.25
Then he dispatched at him ninety sharp-pointed arrows with nocks of gold, lord of kings. But they rebounded from his armor! Watching those futile arrows fall to the ground, he quickly split Krita·varman's bow with a very sharp razor-edged arrow. Enraged, Shikhándin struck Krita·varman—who with his bow splintered was like a bull with a broken horn—in the chest and arms with eighty arrows.

Furious and covered in wounds due to those arrows, Krita·varman squirted blood from his body like water poured from the spout of a jug. Saturated with blood, king, Krita·varman looked as magnificent as a red ochre mountain 26.30
soaked with rain. That powerful man then grabbed another bow with an arrow and bow-string and wounded Shikhándin around his shoulder with numerous arrows. With those arrows sticking out from around his shoulder, Shikhándin was as magnificant as a gigantic tree bristling with branches and twigs.

tāv anyonyaṃ bhṛśaṃ viddhvā rudhireṇa samukṣitau,
anyonya|śṛṅg'|âbhihatau rejatur vṛṣabhāv iva.
anyonyasya vadhe yatnaṃ kurvāṇau tau mahā|rathau
rathābhyāṃ ceratus tatra maṇḍalāni sahasraśaḥ.
Kṛtavarmā, mahā|rāja, Pārṣataṃ niśitaiḥ śaraiḥ
26.35 raṇe vivyādha saptatyā svarṇa|puṅkhaiḥ śilā|śitaiḥ.
tato 'sya samare bāṇaṃ Bhojaḥ praharatāṃ varaḥ
jīvit'|ânta|karaṃ ghoraṃ vyasṛjat tvaray" ânvitaḥ.
sa ten' âbhihato, rājan, mūrchām āśu samāviśat,
dhvaja|yaṣṭiṃ ca sahasā śiśriye kaśmal'|āvṛtaḥ.
apovāha raṇāt tūrṇaṃ sārathī rathināṃ varam,
Hārdikya|śara|saṃtaptaṃ, niḥśvasantaṃ punaḥ punaḥ.
parājite tataḥ śūre Drupadasya sute prabho
vyadravat Pāṇḍavī senā vadhyamānā samantataḥ.

SAMJAYA uvāca:

27.1 ŚVET'|ÂŚVO 'THA, mahā|rāja, vyadhamat tāvakaṃ balam,
yathā vāyuḥ samāsādya tūla|rāśiṃ samantataḥ.
pratyudyayus Trigartās taṃ, Śibayaḥ Kauravaiḥ saha,
Śālvāḥ, saṃśaptakāś c' âiva, Nārāyaṇa|balaṃ ca tat.
Satyasenaś, Candradevo, Mitradevaḥ, Sutaṃjayaḥ,
Sauśrutiś, Citrasenaś ca, Mitravarmā ca, Bhārata,
Trigarta|rājaḥ samare bhrātṛbhiḥ parivāritaḥ,
putraiś c' âiva mah"|êṣv|āsair nānā|śastra|viśāradair,
27.5 vyasṛjanta śara|vrātān kiranto 'rjunam āhave;
abhyavartanta sahasā, vāry|oghā iva sāgaram.

Drenched with blood after brutally wounding one another, they appeared like a pair of bulls who'd struck one another with their horns. Expending great effort to kill one another, both mighty warriors moved about on their chariots there in thousands of circular maneuvers. In that battle, great king, Krita·varman pounded Príshata's grandson* with seventy stone-sharpened arrows with golden nocks. Next 26.35
in that clash the Bhoja,* the finest of champions, speedily shot his terrible, life-ending arrow. It struck Shikhándin and he immediately fell into a stupor and suddenly collapsed against the pole of his banner in a thorough daze. Scorched by the arrows of Hrídika's son and gasping again and again, that fine chariot-warrior was quickly carried away from the battle by his chariot driver.

After Drúpada's heroic son had been defeated, powerful lord, the Pándava army fled as they were struck from all sides.

SÁNJAYA said:

THE MAN WITH white horses* then broke up your army, 27.1
great king, like the wind assailing a pile of cotton and scattering it everywhere. The Tri·gartas and Shibis with the Káuravas alongside, and the Shalvas, oath-bound warriors and the Naráyana division, counter-attacked. Satya·sena, Chandra·deva, Mitra·deva, Sutan·jaya, Sáushruti, Chitra·sena, Mitra·varman, and the king of the Tri·gartas* surrounded in the conflict by his brothers and sons who were mighty archers skilled with various weapons, Bhárata, sent 27.5
forth swarms of arrows and covered Árjuna in the battle. Quickly they attacked him, like a flood of water the sea.

te tv Arjunaṃ samāsādya yodhāḥ śata|sahasraśaḥ
agacchan vilayaṃ sarve, Tārkṣyaṃ dṛṣṭv" êva pannagāḥ.
te hanyamānāḥ samare n' ājahuḥ Pāṇḍavaṃ raṇe,
hanyamānā, mahā|rāja, śalabhā iva pāvakam.
Satyasenas tribhir bāṇair vivyādha yudhi Pāṇḍavam,
Mitradevas tri|ṣaṣṭyā tu, Candrasenaś tu saptabhiḥ,
Mitravarmā tri|saptatyā, Sauśrutiś c' âpi saptabhiḥ,
Śatruṃjayas tu viṃśatyā, Suśarmā navabhiḥ śaraiḥ.
27.10 sa viddho bahubhiḥ saṃkhye prativivyādha tān nṛpān.
Sauśrutiṃ saptabhir viddhvā, Satyasenaṃ tribhiḥ śaraiḥ,
Śatruṃjayaṃ ca viṃśatyā, Candradevaṃ tath" âṣṭabhiḥ,
Mitradevaṃ śaten' âiva, Śrutasenaṃ tribhiḥ śaraiḥ,
navabhir Mitravarmāṇaṃ, Suśarmāṇaṃ tath" âṣṭabhiḥ,
Śatruṃjayaṃ ca rājānaṃ hatvā tatra śilā|śitaiḥ,
Sauśruteḥ sa|śiras|trāṇaṃ śiraḥ kāyād apāharat.
tvaritaś Candradevaṃ ca śarair ninye Yama|kṣayam.
tath" êtarān, mahā|rāja, yatamānān mahā|rathān
pañcabhiḥ pañcabhir bāṇair ek'|âikaṃ pratyavārayat.
27.15 Satyasenas tu saṃkruddhas tomaraṃ vyasṛjan mahat
samuddiśya raṇe Kṛṣṇaṃ, siṃha|nādaṃ nanāda ca.
sa nirbhidya bhujaṃ savyaṃ Mādhavasya mah"|ātmanaḥ,
ayas|mayo hema|daṇḍo jagāma dharaṇīṃ tadā.
Mādhavasya tu viddhasya tomareṇa mahā|raṇe
pratodaḥ prāpatadd hastād, raśmayaś ca, viśāṃ pate.
Vāsudevaṃ vibhinn'|âṅgaṃ dṛṣṭvā, Pārtho Dhanaṃjayaḥ
krodham āhārayat tīvraṃ Kṛṣṇaṃ c' êdam uvāca ha:
«prāpay' âśvān, mahā|bāho, Satyasenaṃ prati, prabho,
yāvad enaṃ śarais tīkṣṇair nayāmi Yama|sādanam!»

But after attacking Árjuna in the hundreds and thousands, all those warriors melted away like snakes after spying Tarkshya. Though they were being massacred in combat, they did not leave Árjuna in the battle, great king, just as moths can't leave a fire though it kills them.

Satya·sena wounded the Pándava in battle with three arrows, Mitra·deva with sixty-three, Chandra·sena with seven,
Mitra·varman with seventy-three, Sáushruti with seven,
Shatrun·jaya with twenty and Sushárman with nine arrows.
Wounded in battle by many arrows, Árjuna wounded those 27.10
princes in return. Having wounded Sáushruti with seven arrows, Satya·sena with three, Shatrun·jaya with twenty, Cha-
ndra·deva with eight, Mitra·deva with a hundred, Shruta·
sena with three, Mitra·varman with nine, Sushárman with
eight, and after killing King Shatrun·jaya there with his
stone-sharpened arrows, he removed Sáushruti's head from
his body along with its helmet. Moving quickly, he sent
Chandra·deva to Yama's house with arrows. And one by
one he warded off those other mighty warriors attacking
him, great king, with five arrows each.

But Satya·sena was furious and, pointing his massive 27.15
lance at Krishna in the battle, hurled it at him and roared
a lion's roar. That golden staff made of iron wounded great
Mádhava's left hand and then fell to earth. Wounded in
the great battle by that lance, Mádhava's whip fell from
his hand, as did his reins, lord of the people. Seeing Vasudéva's arm torn open, Pritha's son Dhanan·jaya marshalled
his anger and impulsively said this to Krishna: "Direct the
horses closer to Satya·sena, powerful man of mighty arms,
so that I can send him to Yama's house with sharp arrows!"

27.20 pratodaṃ gṛhya so 'nyat tu, raśmīn api yathā purā,
vāhayām āsa tān aśvān Satyasena|rathaṃ prati.
Viṣvaksenaṃ tu nirbhinnaṃ dṛṣṭvā, Pārtho Dhanaṃjayaḥ
Satyasenaṃ śarais tīkṣṇair vārayitvā mahā|rathaḥ,
tataḥ su|niśitair bhallai rājñas tasya mahac chiraḥ
kuṇḍal'|ôpacitaṃ kāyāc cakarta pṛtan"|ântare.
tan nikṛtya śitair bāṇair Mitravarmāṇam ākṣipat,
vatsa|dantena tīkṣṇena, sārathiṃ c' âsya, māriṣa.
  tataḥ śara|śatair bhūyaḥ saṃśaptaka|gaṇān balī
pātayām āsa saṃkruddhaḥ śataśo 'tha sahasraśaḥ.
27.25 tato rajata|puṅkhena, rājañ, śīrṣaṃ mah"|ātmanaḥ
Mitrasenasya ciccheda kṣurapreṇa mahā|rathaḥ,
Suśarmāṇaṃ su|saṃkruddho jatru|deśe samāhanat.
  tataḥ saṃśaptakāḥ sarve parivārya Dhanaṃjayam
śastr'|âughair mamṛduḥ kruddhā, nādayanto diśo daśa.
abhyarditas tu taj Jiṣṇuḥ Śakra|tulya|parākramaḥ
Aindram astram a|mey'|ātmā prāduś cakre mahā|rathaḥ.
tataḥ śara|sahasrāṇi prādur āsan, viśāṃ pate.
  dhvajānāṃ chidyamānānāṃ, kārmukāṇāṃ ca, mariṣa,
rathānāṃ sa|patākānāṃ, tūṇīrāṇāṃ yugaiḥ saha,
27.30 akṣāṇām, atha yoktrāṇāṃ, cakrāṇāṃ raśmibhiḥ saha,
kūbarāṇāṃ, varūthānāṃ, pṛṣatkānāṃ ca saṃyuge,
aśvānāṃ patatāṃ c' âpi, prāsānām ṛṣṭibhiḥ saha,
gadānāṃ, parighāṇāṃ ca śakti|tomara|paṭṭiśaiḥ,
śata|ghnīnāṃ sa|cakrāṇāṃ, bhujānām c' ōrubhiḥ saha,

Grabbing another whip, as he had already reins, he drove 27.20
their horses close to Satya·sena's chariot. Looking at Vi-
shvak·sena* wounded, Pritha's son Dhanan·jaya, a mighty
warrior, enveloped Satya·sena with his sharp arrows. With
very sharp broad arrows he then cut the king's massive
earring-covered head from his body in the midst of his army.
Humiliating him, he struck Mitra·varman with sharp arrows and his chariot-driver with a sharp calf-toothed arrow,
dear friend.

Thereafter, with hundreds more arrows, that enraged and
powerful man felled hordes of oath-bound warriors by the
hundreds and then by the thousands. Next, king, the mighty 27.25
warrior severed the head of great Mitra·sena with a razor-
edged arrow having a nock of silver and, thoroughly enraged, struck Sushárman around his collar-bone.

All the oath-bound warriors then surrounded Dhanan·
jaya and pounded him in rage with waves of their weapons,
filling all areas with their cries. But, punished by them, Jishnu, a mighty warrior with courage the equal of Shakra's
and a soul beyond measure, revealed his Aindra weapon and
thousands of arrows appeared from it, lord of the people.

Then a massive noise could be heard all over the place, 27.30
lord of the people, of banners and bows breaking up as
well as chariots with their flags, quivers and yokes, dear
friend, and their axles, yoking-straps, wheels, reins, yoking-
poles and guards, and of arrows in the battle, of falling
horses, darts, javelins, clubs, iron bludgeons, spears, lances
and tridents, and *shata·ghni*s with discusses and arms along
with shins, of necklaces and *ángada* and *keyúra* armlets, dear
friend, of pearl necklaces and gold collars, and of armor,

kaṇṭha|sūtr'|âṅgadānāṃ ca, keyūrāṇāṃ ca, māriṣa,
hārāṇām, atha niṣkāṇāṃ, tanu|trāṇāṃ ca, Bhārata,
chatrāṇāṃ, vyajanānāṃ ca, śirasāṃ mukuṭaiḥ saha,
aśrūyata mahāñ śabdas tatra tatra, viśāṃ pate.
sa|kuṇḍalāni, sv|akṣīṇi, pūrṇa|candra|nibhāni ca
27.35 śirāṃsy urvyām adṛśyanta, tārā|jālam iv' âmbare.
su|sragvīṇi, su|vāsāṃsi, candanen' ôkṣitāni ca
śarīrāṇi vyadṛśyanta nihatānāṃ mahī|tale,
gandharva|nagar'|ākāraṃ ghoram āyodhanaṃ tadā.
nihatai rāja|putraiś ca, kṣatriyaiś ca mahā|balaiḥ,
hastibhiḥ patitaiś c' âiva, turaṃgaiś c' âbhavan mahī
a|gamya|rūpā samare, viśīrṇair iva parvataiḥ.
n' āsīc cakra|pathaś tatra Pāṇḍavasya mah"|ātmanaḥ,
nighnataḥ śātravān bhallair, hasty|aśvaṃ c' āsyato mahat.
ā tuṅgād iva sīdanti ratha|cakrāṇi, māriṣa,
27.40 caratas tasya saṃgrāme tasmil̃ lohita|kardame.
sīdamānāni cakrāṇi samūhus turagā bhṛśam
śrameṇa mahatā yuktā, mano|māruta|raṃhasaḥ.
vadhyamānaṃ tu tat sainyaṃ Pāṇḍu|putreṇa dhanvinā
prāyaśo vimukhaṃ sarvaṃ n' âvatiṣṭhata saṃyuge.
tāñ jitvā samare Jiṣṇuḥ saṃśaptaka|gaṇān bahūn,
virarāja tadā Pārtho, vidhūmo 'gnir iva jvalan.

Bhárata, and of parasols and fans, and of heads along with their crowns.

Resembling full moons with their earrings and beautiful eyes, the heads lying on the ground appeared like a constel- 27.35
lation of stars in the sky. Wearing beautiful garlands, beautiful clothes and sprinkled with sandal powder, the bodies of those slaughtered were clearly visible on the ground, the horrific battlefield appearing like a city of the *gandhárvas*.

The ground became impassable in the battle with slain princes and immensely powerful kshatriyas, and with fallen elephants and horses, as though it were covered with crumbling mountains. There was no way through there for the
wheels of the great Pándava as he slaughtered enemies and 27.40
shot massive elephants and horses with broad arrows. As he careered about in the battle, the wheels of his chariot sunk down into that red soil nearly to their highest points, dear friend. His horses, that were as fast as wind and thought, powerfully dragged those sinking wheels, working together with great effort.

But, while it was being slaughtered by Pandu's bow-wielding son, almost the entire army turned away and didn't remain in the battle, Bhárata. After conquering many divisions of the oath-bound warriors in battle, Pritha's son Jishnu then shone forth like a burning smokeless fire.

SAMJAYA uvāca:

28.1 YUDHIṢṬHIRAM, mahā|rāja, visṛjantaṃ śarān bahūn
svayaṃ Duryodhano rājā pratyagṛhṇād a|bhītavat.
tam āpatantaṃ sahasā tava putraṃ mahā|ratham
Dharma|rājo drutaṃ viddhvā, «tiṣṭha! tiṣṭh'! êti» c' âbravīt.
sa tu taṃ prativivyādha navabhir niśitaiḥ śaraiḥ,
sārathiṃ c' âsya bhallena bhṛśaṃ kruddho 'bhyatāḍayat.
tato Yudhiṣṭhiro, rājan, svarṇa|puṅkhāñ śilīmukhān
Duryodhanāya cikṣepa trayo|daśa śilā|śitān.
28.5 caturbhiś caturo vāhāṃs tasya hatvā mahā|rathaḥ
pañcamena śiraḥ kāyāt sāratheś ca samākṣipat.
ṣaṣṭhena tu dhvajaṃ rājñaḥ, saptamena tu kārmukam,
aṣṭamena tathā khaḍgaṃ pātayām āsa bhū|tale;
pañcabhir nṛ|patiṃ c' âpi Dharma|rājo 'rdayad bhṛśam.
hat'|âśvāt tu rathāt tasmād avaplutya sutas tava
uttamaṃ vyasanaṃ prāpto bhūmāv ev' âvatiṣṭhata.
taṃ tu kṛcchra|gataṃ dṛṣṭvā, Karṇa|Drauṇi|Kṛp'|âdayaḥ
abhyavartanta sahasā, parīpsanto nar'|âdhipam.
atha Pāṇḍu|sutāḥ sarve parivārya Yudhiṣṭhiram
28.10 abhyayuḥ samare, rājaṃs. tato yuddham avartata!
tatas tūrya|sahasrāṇi prāvādyanta mahā|mṛdhe;
tataḥ kilakilā|śabdāḥ prādur āsan, mahī|pate,
yatr' âbhyagacchan samare Pañcālāḥ Kauravaiḥ saha.
narā naraiḥ samājagmur, vāraṇā vara|vāraṇaiḥ,
rathāś ca rathibhiḥ sārdhaṃ, hayāś ca haya|sādibhiḥ.
dvaṃdvāny āsan, mahā|rāja, prekṣaṇīyāni saṃyuge,
vividhāny apy a|cintyāni, śastravanty uttamāni ca.

SÁNJAYA said:

GREAT KING, King Duryódhana himself fearlessly opposed Yudhi·shthira, who was releasing many arrows at him. The King of Law immediately wounded your son, as that mighty warrior abruptly attacked him, and yelled "Stand! Stand your ground!" But Duryódhana wounded him in return with nine sharp arrows and, in rage, brutally wounded Yudhi·shthira's charioteer with a broad arrow. 28.1

Then, king, Yudhi·shthira dispatched thirteen stone-
sharpened arrows with nocks of gold at Duryódhana. That 28.5
mighty warrior slaughtered his four horses with four arrows and with a fifth cut the head from his driver's body. With a sixth he dropped the king's banner to the ground, with a seventh his bow and with an eighth his sword. What's more, the King of Law brutally struck the king with five arrows.

Its horses slain, your son leapt from his chariot and stood on the ground in a most dangerous predicament. But Karna, Drona's son, Kripa and others saw that he was in danger and suddenly attacked aiming to reach that ruler of men. All of
Pandu's sons then surrounded Yudhi·shthira and followed 28.10
him into battle, king. Then the battle began!

Thousands of instruments were played in that great battle, lord of the earth, and sounds of battle cries then became audible where the Panchálas met with the Káuravas in battle. Men collided with men, elephants with fine elephants, chariots with chariot-warriors, and horses with horse-riders. There were various spectacular weapon duels in that battle, great king, that were inconceivable and of the highest quality. All those super-fast heroes fought brilliantly, nimbly and properly in combat as they tried to kill one another.

te śūrāḥ samare sarve citraṃ, laghu ca, suṣṭhu ca
ayudhyanta mahā|vegāḥ paraspara|vadh'|âiṣiṇaḥ.
28.15 anyonyaṃ samare jaghnur yodha|vratam anuṣṭhitāḥ,
na hi te samaraṃ cakruḥ pṛṣṭha|to vai kathaṃ cana.
muhūrtam eva tad yuddham āsīn madhura|darśanam;
tata unmattavad, rājan, nirmaryādam avartata!
rathī nāgaṃ samāsādya, dārayan niśitaiḥ śaraiḥ,
preṣayām āsa Kālāya śaraiḥ saṃnata|parvabhiḥ.
nāgā hayān samāsādya, vikṣipanto bahūn raṇe,
dārayām āsur atyugraṃ tatra tatra tadā tadā.
hay'|ārohāś ca bahavaḥ parivārya hay'|ôttamān,
tala|śabda|ravāṃś cakruḥ saṃpatantas tatas tataḥ.
28.20 dhāvamānāṃs tatas tāṃs tu dravamāṇān mahā|gajān
pārśvataḥ pṛṣṭhataś c' âiva nijaghnur haya|sādinaḥ.
vidrāvya ca bahūn aśvān nāgā, rājan, mad'|ôtkaṭāḥ;
viṣāṇaiś c' âpare jaghnur, mamṛduś c' âpare bhṛśam.
s'|âśv'|ārohāṃś ca turagān viṣāṇair vivyadhū ruṣā,
apare cikṣipur vegāt pragṛhy' âtibalās tadā.
pādātair āhatā nāgā vivareṣu samantataḥ
cakrur ārta|svaraṃ ghoraṃ, dudruvuś ca diśo daśa.
padātīnāṃ tu sahasā pradrutānāṃ mah"|āhave,
utsṛjy' ābharaṇaṃ tūrṇam avavavrū raṇ'|âjire;
28.25 nimittaṃ manyamānās tu pariṇāmya mahā|gajāḥ,
jagṛhur bibhiduś c' âiva citrāṇy ābharaṇāni ca.
tāṃs tu tatra prasaktān vai parivārya padātayaḥ
hasty|ārohān nijaghnus te mahā|vegā bal'|ôtkaṭāḥ.

They killed one another in combat observing the vow of 28.15
the warrior, for never did they do battle from behind.

For a brief period the battle had seemed amiable. Then, as if through madness, king, it turned lawless! A chariot-warrior assailed an elephant and, tearing it apart with sharp arrows, sent it to Death with smooth-jointed arrows. Elephants attacked horses, throwing many aside in the battle, and time and again fiercely tore them to shreds all over the place. And many horsemen surrounding the most superb horses yelled and clapped their hands as they rushed
at them from every direction. As those horses fled and huge 28.20
elephants ran off as well, horsemen slaughtered them from the side and from behind. And ruttish elephants dispersed many horses, king; some slaughtered them with their tusks and others brutally trampled them. Some elephants furiously pierced horses and horsemen with their tusks, and then other very powerful elephants seized them and wildly threw them about. Struck by foot-soldiers where they were exposed on all sides, elephants trumpeted horrific bellows of pain and fled to the ten directions.

Massive elephants quickly surrounded the ornaments of foot-soldiers who'd suddenly fled and left them behind on
the battlefield. Their riders regarding this as an omen, they 28.25
bent down, pierced and grabbed those beautiful ornaments. Very fast foot-soldiers proud of their strength surrounded them while they were engrossed in those ornaments and slaughtered their elephant-riders.

apare hastibhir hastaiḥ khaṃ vikṣiptā mah"|āhave,
nipatanto viṣāṇ'|âgrair bhṛśaṃ viddhāḥ su|śikṣitaiḥ.
apare sahasā gṛhya viṣāṇair eva sūditāḥ;
sen"|ântaraṃ samāsādya ke cit tatra mahā|gajaiḥ
kṣuṇṇa|gātrā, mahā|rāja, vikṣipya ca punaḥ punaḥ,
apare vyajanān' îva vibhrāmya nihatā mṛdhe.
28.30 puraḥ|sarāś ca nāgānām apareṣāṃ, viṣāṃ pate,
śarīrāṇy atividdhāni tatra tatra raṇ'|âjire.

pratimāneṣu, kumbheṣu, danta|veṣṭeṣu c' âpare
nigṛhītā bhṛśaṃ nāgāḥ prāsa|tomara|śaktibhiḥ;
nigṛhya ca gadāḥ ke cit pārśva|sthair bhṛśa|dāruṇaiḥ
rath'|âśva|sādibhis tatra saṃbhinnā nyapatan bhuvi.

sa|hayāḥ sādinās tatra tomareṇa mahā|mṛdhe
bhūmāv amṛdnan vegena sa|carmāṇaṃ padātinam.
tathā s'|āvaraṇān kāṃś cit tatra tatra, viśāṃ pate,
rathān nāgāḥ samāsādya parigṛhya ca, māriṣa,
28.35 vyākṣipan sahasā tatra ghora|rūpe bhayānake.
nārācair nihatāś c' âpi gajāḥ petur mahā|balaḥ,
parvatasy' êva śikharaṃ vajra|rugnaṃ mahī|tale.

yodhā yodhān samāsādya muṣṭibhir vyahanan yudhi;
keśeṣv anyonyam ākṣipya cikṣipur bibhiduś ca ha.
udyamya ca bhujān anye, nikṣipya ca mahī|tale
padā c' ôraḥ samākramya sphurato 'pāharac chiraḥ.

In that huge battle, others were flung into the sky by well-trained elephants with their trunks and brutally pierced as they fell with the points of their tusks. Others were violently seized and killed with their tusks. Some there sailing into the midst of the army had their bodies trampled by massive elephants and were thrown about again and again. Others were whirled about like fans and slaughtered in the battle.
And some here and there on the battlefield who attended 28.30
to other elephants, lord of the people, had badly lacerated bodies.

And other elephants were brutally curtailed by darts, lances and spears in the area between their tusks, in their globes and in their gums. And after being so curtailed and deeply wounded by the terribly brutal chariots, horses and horsemen positioned at their flanks, some elephants collapsed onto the ground.

In that great battle, horsemen on horses violently pounded shield-bearing foot-soldiers into the earth with their lances. Similarly, lord of the earth, after attacking some armored warriors here and there and seizing them, dear
friend, elephants ferociously stretched them out into terri- 28.35
ble, hideous shapes. Moreover, powerful elephants struck by iron arrows fell down like a mountain peak shattered by a thunderbolt falling to the surface of the earth.

Warriors assailing warriors in the battle struck out with their fists. Dragging one another down by the hair, they struck and stabbed each other. And others raised their arms and threw their struggling enemies down on the ground and, stepping on their chests with a foot, removed their heads.

patataś c' âparo, rājan, vijahār' âsinā śiraḥ;
jīvataś ca tath" âiv' ânyaḥ śastraṃ kāye nyamajjayat.
muṣṭi|yuddhaṃ mahac c' āsīd yodhānāṃ tatra, Bhārata,
28.40 tathā keśa|grahaś c' ôgro, bāhu|yuddhaṃ ca bhairavam.

samāsaktasya c' ânyena, a|vijñātas tath" âparaḥ
jahāra samare prāṇān nānā|śastrair an|ekadhā.
saṃsakteṣu ca yodheṣu, vartamāne ca saṃkule,
kabandhāny utthitāni syuḥ śataśo 'tha sahasraśaḥ.
śoṇitaiḥ sicyamānāni śastrāṇi kavacāni ca
mahā|raṅg'|ânuraktāni vastrāṇ' îva cakāśire.

evam etan mahā|yuddhaṃ dāruṇaṃ, śastra|saṃkulam,
unmatta|Gaṅgā|pratimaṃ śabden' āpūrayaj jagat.
n' âiva sve, na pare, rājan, vijñāyante śar'|āturāḥ;
28.45 yoddhavyam, iti yudhyante rājāno jaya|gṛddhinaḥ.
svān sve jaghnur, mahā|rāja, parāṃś c' âiva samāgatān.
ubhayoḥ senayor vīrair vyākulaṃ samapadyata.

rathair bhagnair, mahā|rāja, vāraṇaiś ca nipātitaiḥ,
hayaiś ca patitais tatra, naraiś ca vinipātitaiḥ,
a|gamya|rūpā pṛthivī kṣaṇena samapadyata;
kṣaṇen' āsīn, mahī|pāla, kṣata|j'|âugha|pravartinī.

Pāñcālān ahanat Karṇas, Trigartāṃś ca Dhanaṃjayaḥ,
Bhīmasenaḥ Kurūn, rājan, hasty|anīkaṃ ca sarvaśaḥ.
evam eṣa kṣayo vṛttaḥ Kuru|Pāṇḍava|senayoḥ
apar'|âhṇe, mahā|rāja, kāṅkṣatāṃ vipulaṃ yaśaḥ.

And another warrior severed the head of a fallen warrior with his sword, king. Similarly another plunged his weapon into the body of a warrior who still lived. There was a tremendous fist fight among the warriors there, Bhárata, and there was savage hair pulling and terrible arm to arm 28.40
combat.

And a warrior took the life of another in battle with many various weapons while he was occupied with someone else and didn't notice him. And while those warriors thronged together and that battle unfolded, headless trunks were mounting by the hundred and then by the thousand. Weapons and armor soaked with blood shone brilliantly like cloth dyed deep red.

This massive and cruel battle teeming with weapons filled the world with its sound, like the roaring Ganga. Tormented by arrows, king, warriors could make out neither their own men nor their enemies. Eager for victory, kings fought 28.45
whom they reckoned ought to be fought. They slaughtered whomever they encountered, great king, whether they were their own men or their enemies. The earth became filled with heroes of both armies.

With broken chariots, destroyed elephants, fallen horses and annihilated men, great king, in an instant the ground became impassable. In an instant, king, it flowed with rivers of blood.

Karna slaughtered the Panchálas, Dhanan·jaya the Tri·gartas and Bhima·sena the Kurus and a complete elephant division, king. This massacre of the Kuru and Pándava armies took place in that afternoon, great king, as both sought to extend their fame.

DHṚTARĀṢṬRA uvāca:

29.1 ATITĪVRĀṆI DUḤKHĀNI duḥ|sahāni bahūni ca
tvatto 'haṃ, Saṃjay', âśrauṣaṃ putrāṇāṃ c' âiva saṃkṣayam
yathā tvaṃ me kathayase, yathā yuddham avartata,
na santi, sūta, Kauravyā iti me niścitā matiḥ.
Duryodhanaś ca virathaḥ kṛtas tatra mahā|rathaḥ;
Dharma|putraḥ kathaṃ cakre? tasya vā nṛ|patiḥ katham?
apar'|âhṇe kathaṃ yuddham abhaval loma|harṣaṇam?
tan mam' ācakṣva tattvena, kuśalo hy asi, Saṃjaya!

SAṂJAYA uvāca:

29.5 saṃsakteṣu tu sainyeṣu vadhyamāneṣu bhāgaśaḥ,
ratham anyaṃ samāsthāya putras tava, viśāṃ pate,
krodhena mahatā yuktaḥ, sa|viṣo bhuja|go yathā,
Duryodhanaḥ samālakṣya Dharma|rājaṃ Yudhiṣṭhiram,
provāca sūtaṃ, «tvarito yāhi! yāh'! îti» Bhārata,
«tatra māṃ prāpaya kṣipraṃ, sārathe, yatra Pāṇḍavaḥ
dhriyamāṇ'|ātapatreṇa rājā rājati daṃśitaḥ!»
sa sūtaś codito rājñā rājñaḥ syandanam uttamam
Yudhiṣṭhirasy' âbhimukhaṃ preṣayām āsa saṃyuge.
tato Yudhiṣṭhiraḥ kruddhaḥ, prabhinna iva kuñjaraḥ,
29.10 sārathiṃ codayām āsa, «yāhi yatra Suyodhanaḥ!»
tau samājagmatur vīrau bhrātarau ratha|sattamau!
sametya ca mahā|vīrau saṃrabdhau, yuddha|dur|madau,
vavarṣatur mah"|êṣv|āsau śarair anyonyam āhave.

DHRITA·RASHTRA said:

I HAVE HEARD from you, Sánjaya, about many exceedingly bitter and unbearable difficulties, and about the annihilation of my sons. In as much as this battle took place as you related it to me, herald, I am convinced that the Kaurávyas are no more. The mighty warrior Duryódhana was stripped of his chariot there. How did Dharma's son* do that? And what did the king do to him? Was the battle that afternoon hair-raising? Explain this to me truthfully, Sánjaya, for you're good at this! 29.1

SÁNJAYA said:

While those armies massed together were being slaughtered bit by bit, your son, mounting another chariot, lord of the people, was filled with enormous anger like a snake with poison. Bhárata, Duryódhana spotted Yudhi·shthira, the King of Law, and said to his charioteer, "Go! Go quickly! Driver, take me immediately to where the armor-clad Pándava king shimmers with his umbrella remaining above him!" 29.5

As directed by the king, the charioteer drove the king's superb chariot towards Yudhi·shthira in the battle. Then Yudhi·shthira, raging like an elephant in rut, urged his charioteer, "Go to where Suyódhana is!" 29.10

That pair of heroes came together, brothers and superb warriors! And once they'd come together in battle, those great heroes—furious and mighty battle-mad archers!—showered one another with arrows.

tato Duryodhano rājā dharma|śīlasya, māriṣa,
śilā|śitena bhallena dhanuś ciccheda saṃyuge.
taṃ n' âmṛṣyata saṃkruddho hy avamānaṃ Yudhiṣṭhiraḥ.
apavidhya dhanuś chinnaṃ krodha|saṃrakta|locanaḥ,
anyat kārmukam ādāya Dharma|putraś camū|mukhe,
Duryodhanasya ciccheda dhvajaṃ kārmukam eva ca.

29.15 ath' ânyad dhanur ādāya
prāvidhyata Yudhiṣṭhiram.
tāv anyonyaṃ su|saṃkruddhau
śastra|varṣāṇy amuñcatām,
siṃhāv iva su|saṃrabdhau paraspara|jigīṣayā.
jaghnatus tau raṇe 'nyonyaṃ, nardamānau vṛṣāv iva,
antaraṃ mārgamāṇau ca ceratus tau mahā|rathau.
tataḥ pūrṇ'|āyat'|ôtsṛṣṭaih śarais tau tu kṛta|vraṇau
virejatur, mahā|rāja, kiṃśukāv iva puṣpitau.

tato, rājan, vimuñcantau siṃha|nādān muhur muhuḥ,
talayoś ca tathā śabdān, dhanuṣaś ca mah"|āhave,
śaṅkha|śabda|varāṃś c' âiva cakratus tau nar'|ēśvarau.

29.20 anyonyaṃ tau, mahā|rāja, pīḍayāṃ cakratur bhṛśam.
tato Yudhiṣṭhiro rājā tava putraṃ śarais tribhiḥ
ājaghān' ôrasi kruddho vajra|vegair, dur|āsadaiḥ.

prativivyādha taṃ tūrṇaṃ tava putro mahī|patiḥ
pañcabhir niśitair bāṇaiḥ svarṇa|puṅkhaiḥ śilā|śitaiḥ.
tato Duryodhano rājā śaktiṃ cikṣepa, Bhārata,
sarva|pārasavīṃ, tīkṣṇāṃ, mah"|ôlkā|pratimāṃ tadā.
tām āpatantīṃ sahasā Dharma|rājaḥ śitaiḥ śaraiḥ
tribhiś ciccheda sahasā, taṃ ca vivyādha pañcabhiḥ.

Then in that encounter, dear friend, King Duryódhana splintered the bow of that man who was disposed towards the law* with a stone-sharpened broad arrow. Enraged, Yu-dhi·shthira didn't put up with this humiliation. Discarding his splintered bow and his eyes red with rage, in the vanguard of his army Dharma's son grabbed another bow and cut down Duryódhana's banner and his bow as well. Duryódha- 29.15
na then grabbed another bow and wounded Yudhi·shthira.

Infuriated, those two let loose showers of weapons at one another; they were like a pair of furious lions, each desperate to defeat the other. Bellowing like a pair of bulls, the mighty warriors struck one another in the battle and careered about searching for an opening. Wounded by arrows released from their fully bent bows, great king, the pair of them glowed like *kínshuka* trees in blossom.

Then, letting go lions' roars again and again, king, the two lords of men in that colossal battle clapped their hands, twanged their bows and blew excellent sounds from their conches. Great king, they brutally punished one another. 29.20
Then in fury King Yudhi·shthira struck your son in the chest with three irresistible arrows that were as fast as lightning bolts.

Your son the king quickly wounded him in return with five sharp stone-sharpened arrows with nocks of gold. Then, Bhárata, King Duryódhana hurled his keen spear that was made entirely of iron and was like a massive meteor. With three sharp arrows the King of Law immediately cut down that spear as it speedily flew towards him and wounded Duryódhana with five. That noisy, golden-shafted spear then fell

nipapāta tataḥ s" âtha svarṇa|daṇḍā mahā|svanā,
29.25 nipatantī mah"|ôlk" êva vyarājac chikhi|saṃnibhā.
śaktiṃ vinihatāṃ dṛṣṭvā putras tava, viśāṃ pate,
navabhir niśitair bhallair nijaghāna Yudhiṣṭhiram.
so 'tividdho balavatā śatruṇā śatru|tāpanaḥ
Duryodhanaṃ samuddiśya bāṇaṃ jagrāha sa|tvaraḥ.
samādhatta ca taṃ bāṇaṃ dhanur|madhye mahā|balaḥ,
cikṣepa ca, mahā|rāja, tataḥ kruddhaḥ parākramī.
sa tu bāṇaḥ samāsādya tava putraṃ mahā|ratham,
vyāmohayata rājānaṃ, dharaṇīṃ ca dadāra ha.
tato Duryodhanaḥ kruddho gadām udyamya vegitaḥ
29.30 vidhitsuḥ kalahasy' ântam Dharma|rājam upādravat.
tam udyata|gadaṃ dṛṣṭvā, daṇḍa|hastam iv' Ântakam,
Dharma|rājo mahā|śaktiṃ prāhiṇot tava sūnave,
dīpyamānāṃ, mahā|vegāṃ, mah"|ôlkāṃ jvalitām iva.
ratha|sthaḥ sa tayā viddho varma bhittvā stan'|ântare,
bhṛśaṃ saṃvigna|hṛdayaḥ papāta ca mumoha ca.
Bhīmas tam āha ca tataḥ pratijñām anucintayan,
«n' âyaṃ vadhyas tava nṛpa! ity» uktaḥ sa nyavartata.
tatas tvaritam āgamya Kṛtavarmā tav' ātmajam
pratyapadyata rājānaṃ nimagnaṃ vyasan'|ârṇave.
29.35 gadām ādāya Bhīmo 'pi hema|paṭṭa|pariṣkṛtām
abhidudrāva vegena Kṛtavarmāṇam āhave.
evaṃ tad abhavad yuddhaṃ tvadīyānāṃ paraiḥ saha
apar'|âhṇe, mahā|rāja, kāṅksatāṃ vijayaṃ yudhi.

down and, as it fell like a massive meteor, it glowed like the fire-god. 29.25

Seeing that spear struck down, lord of the people, your son pelted Yudhi·shthira with nine sharp broad arrows. Severely wounded by his enemy who was stronger than he, that enemy-scorcher hastily grabbed an arrow and aimed it at Duryódhana. That immensely powerful man fixed the arrow in the middle of his bow and then, great king, furious and showing his courage, dispatched it. After striking your son the king and stunning that mighty warrior, the arrow tore up the earth.

In rage Duryódhana impetuously raised his club and, 29.30
intending to bring the fight to an end, ran at the King of Law. Seeing him with his club raised like Death holding his staff aloft, the King of Law hurled his massive spear at your son. It was tremendously fast and blazed like a huge burning meteor. It penetrated his armor and wounded Duryódhana in the center of the chest as he stood in his chariot. His heart palpitating wildly, he collapsed and fell unconscious.

Then Bhima recalled his vow* and said to him, "The king is not yours to kill!" Once this had been said, Yudhi·shthira turned away.

Krita·varman quickly arrived and then brought back your
son, the king, who'd sunk into a sea of distress. Grabbing 29.35
his club that was fitted with golden binding, Bhima quickly pursued Krita·varman in the battle.

In this fashion, your men fought with their enemies on that afternoon, great king, seeking victory in battle.

SAMJAYA uvāca:

30.1 TATAḤ KARṆAṂ puras|kṛtya tvadīyā yuddha|dur|madāḥ
punar āvṛtya saṃgrāmaṃ cakrur dev'|âsur'|ôpamam.
dvirada|nara|rath'|âśva|śaṅkha|śabdaiḥ
parihṛṣitā, vividhaiś ca śastra|pātaiḥ,
dvirada|ratha|padāti|sādi|saṃghāḥ
parikupit'|âbhimukhāḥ prajaghnire te.
śita|paraśu|var'|âsi|paṭṭiśair,
iṣubhir aneka|vidhaiś ca sūditāḥ
dvirada|ratha|hayā mah"|āhave
vara|puruṣaiḥ; puruṣāś ca vāhanaiḥ.
kamala|dina|kar'|êndu|saṃnibhaiḥ
sita|daśanaiḥ su|mukh'|âkṣi|nāsikaiḥ
rucira|mukuṭa|kuṇḍalair mahī
puruṣa|śirobhir upastṛtā babhau.
30.5 parigha|musala|śakti|tomarair,
nakhara|bhuśuṇḍi|gadā|śatair hatāḥ,
dvirada|nara|hayāḥ sahasraśo
rudhira|nadī|pravahās tad" âbhavan.
prahata|ratha|nar'|âśva|kuñjaraṃ
pratibhaya|darśanam ulbaṇa|vraṇam
tad a|hita|hataṃ ābabhau balaṃ
pitṛ|pati|rāṣṭram iva prajā|kṣaye.

SÁNJAYA said:

THEN YOUR TROOPS saluted Karna and, mad for battle, turned about again and engaged in a fight like that of the gods and demons. 30.1

Excited by the sounds of elephants, men, chariots, horses and conches, the divisions of elephants, chariots, foot-soldiers and horsemen faced their enemy in anger and struck out with blows from their various weapons. In that tremendous battle, elephants, chariots and horses were destroyed by excellent men with sharp axes, fine swords, tridents and many different arrows; and men too were killed by these vehicles of war.

The earth was luminous, strewn over with heads of men that were like lotus-flowers, the sun or the moon with their beautiful mouths, eyes and noses, brilliant crowns and ear-rings and their white teeth. Slaughtered by hundreds of 30.5
iron bludgeons, maces, spears, lances, claw knives, *bhushú-ndis* and clubs, elephants, men and horses were carried away in their thousands by rivers of blood.

Its chariots, men, horses and elephants destroyed, its appearance exciting fear and its wounds immense, the army looked like the realm of the lord of ancestors* at the end of living things.

atha tava, nara|deva, sainikās,
tava ca sutāḥ sura|sūnu|saṃnibhāḥ,
a|mita|bala|puraḥ|sarā raṇe
Kuru|vṛṣabhāḥ Śini|putram abhyayuḥ.
tad atirucira|bhīmam ābabhau
puruṣa|var'|âśva|ratha|dvip'|ākulam,
lavaṇa|jala|samuddhata|svanaṃ
balam asur'|âmara|sainya|sa|prabham.
sura|pati|sama|vikramas tatas
tridaśa|var'|âvaraj'|ôpamaṃ yudhi
dina|kara|kiraṇa|prabhaiḥ pṛṣatkai
ravi|tanayo 'bhyahanac Chini|pravīram.
30.10 tam api sa|ratha|vāji|sārathiṃ
Śini|vṛṣabho vividhaiḥ śarais tvaran
bhujaga|viṣa|sama|prabhai raṇe
puruṣa|varaṃ samavāstṛṇot tadā.
Śini|vṛṣabha|śarair nipīḍitaṃ
tava suhṛdo Vasuṣeṇam abhyayuḥ
tvaritam atirathā ratha'|rṣabhaṃ
dvirada|rath'|âśva|padātibhiḥ saha.
tad udadhi|nibham ādravad balaṃ
tvaritataraiḥ samabhidrutaṃ paraiḥ
Drupada|suta|mukhais; tad" âbhavat
puruṣa|rath'|âśva|gaja|kṣayo mahān.
atha puruṣa|varau kṛt'|āhnikau
Bhavam abhipūjya yathā|vidhi prabhum
ari|vadha|kṛta|niścayau drutaṃ
tava balam Arjuna|Keśavau sṛtau.
jalada|ninada|nisvanaṃ rathaṃ
pavana|vidhūta|patāka|ketanam

Then, preceded by their immense army in the battle, god among men, those Kuru-bulls—your troops and your sons who seemed like sons of gods—attacked the son of a Shini.* Teeming with elephants, chariots, horses and the finest men, its noise like an ocean swell and as magnificent as the immortal army of the gods, that army was luminous, its immense beauty terrible.

Then in that battle, with arrows that were as fabulous as the rays of the sun, the son of the Sun,* who was equal in courage to the lord of the gods, struck the hero of the Shinis who resembled the younger brother of the best of the gods.*

Then, moving quickly in the battle, the bull of the Shinis completely covered that excellent man, and his chariot, horses and charioteer as well, with various kinds of arrows that were equal in beauty to poisonous snakes. 30.10

With their elephants, chariots, horses and foot-soldiers, your great warrior allies quickly went over to Vasu·shena,* that bull among warriors who'd been hurt by arrows from the bull of the Shinis. Resembling a cloud, that army ran towards him as it was attacked by even faster enemies led by Drúpada's son.* Then there was a great massacre of men, chariots, horses and elephants.

Those excellent men Késhava and Árjuna, their daily rites completed after properly worshipping the lord Bhava, then quickly ran at your army, determined to destroy their enemies. With resolved minds their enemies watched that chariot approaching nearby with its white horses, sounding like the rumble of a cloud and its flag and banner blowing about in the wind.

sita|hayam upayāntam antikaṃ
    kṛta|manaso dadṛśus tad" ârayaḥ.

30.15 atha visphārya Gāṇḍīvaṃ rathe nṛtyann iv' Ârjunaḥ
śara|saṃbādham akarot khaṃ, diśaḥ, pradiśas tathā.
rathān vimāna|pratimān majjayan s'|āyudha|dhvajān,
sa|sārathīṃs tadā bāṇair, abhrāṇ' îv' ânilo, 'vadhīt.
gajān gaja|prayantṝṃś ca vaijayanty|āyudha|dhvajān,
sādino 'śvāṃś ca, pattīṃś ca, śarair ninye Yama|kṣayam.
tam Antakam iva kruddham a|nivāryaṃ mahā|ratham
Duryodhano 'bhyayād eko, nighnan bāṇair ajihma|gaiḥ.
tasy' Ârjuno dhanuḥ, sūtaṃ, aśvān, ketum ca sāyakaiḥ
hatvā saptabhir, ekena cchatraṃ ciccheda patriṇā.

30.20 navamaṃ ca samādhāya vyasṛjat prāṇa|ghātinam
Duryodhanāy'; êṣu|varaṃ taṃ Drauṇiḥ saptadh" âcchinat.
tato Drauṇer dhanuś chittvā, hatvā c' âśva|rathāñ śaraiḥ,
Kṛpasy' âpi tad atyugraṃ dhanuś ciccheda Pāṇḍavaḥ.
Hārdikyasya dhanuś chittvā,
    dhvajaṃ c' âśvāṃs tad" âvadhīt,
Duḥśāsanasy' êṣv|asanaṃ
    chittvā Rādheyam abhyayāt.

atha Sātyakim utsṛjya tvaran Karṇo 'rjunaṃ tribhiḥ
viddhvā, vivyādha viṃśatyā Kṛṣṇaṃ Pārthaṃ punaḥ punaḥ.
na glānir āsīt Karṇasya kṣipataḥ sāyakān bahūn,
raṇe vinighnataḥ śatrūn, kruddhasy' êva Śatakratoḥ.

As if dancing in his chariot, Árjuna then drew his Gandíva 30.15
bow and filled the sky and all directions with arrows. With his bolts he immersed those chariots that were like the chariots of the gods, along with their charioteers, weapons and banners, and destroyed them just as the wind destroys clouds. With his arrows he sent elephants and their guides, and horseman, horses and foot-soldiers, to Yama's house, along with their their flags, weapons and banners.

Lashing out with his straight-flying bolts, Duryódhana alone attacked that mighty warrior who, enraged and unstoppable, was like Death.

Árjuna devastated his bow, charioteer, horses and flag with seven arrows, and lopped off his parasol with one arrow. Fixing a ninth life-destroying arrow, he released it at 30.20
Duryódhana. Drona's son, however, chopped down that fine arrow with seven. After splintering the bow of Drona's son and destroying his horses and chariot with his arrows, the Pándava splintered Kripa's terribly formidable bow as well. Once he'd splintered the bow of Hrídika's son he then destroyed his banner and horses and, after splintering Duhshásana's bow, attacked Radha's son.

Leaving Sátyaki behind and quickly wounding Árjuna with three arrows, Karna pelted Krishna with twenty and then Pritha's son again and again. Karna did not tire as he dispatched many arrows, striking his enemies in battle like Shata·kratu enraged.

30.25 atha Sātyakir āgatya Karṇaṃ viddhvā śitaiḥ śaraiḥ
navatyā navabhiś c' ôgraiḥ, śatena punar ārpayat.
tataḥ pravīrāḥ Pārthānāṃ sarve Karṇam apīḍayan.
Yudhāmanyuḥ, Śikhaṇḍī ca, Draupadeyāḥ, Prabhadrakāḥ,
Uttamaujā, Yuyutsuś ca, yamau, Pārṣata eva ca,
Cedi|Kārūṣa|Matsyānāṃ, Kaikayānāṃ ca yad balam,
Cekitānaś ca balavān, Dharma|rājaś ca su|vrataḥ,
ete rath'|âśva|dviradaiḥ pattibhiś c' ôgra|vikramaiḥ
parivārya raṇe Karṇaṃ nānā|śastrair avākiran.
bhāṣanto vāgbhir ugrābhiḥ, sarve Karṇa|vadhe dhṛtāḥ.
30.30 tāṃ śastra|vṛṣṭiṃ bahudhā Karṇaś chittvā śitaiḥ śaraiḥ,
apovāh' âstra|vīryeṇa, drumaṃ bhaṅktv" êva mārutaḥ.
rathinaḥ, sa|mahā|mātrān gajān, aśvān sa|sādinaḥ,
patti|vrātāṃś ca saṃkruddho nighnan Karṇo vyadṛśyata.
tad vadhyamānaṃ Pāṇḍūnāṃ balaṃ Karṇ'|âstra|tejasā
vi|śastra|patra|deh'|âsu, prāya āsīt parāṅ|mukham.
atha Karṇ'|âstram astreṇa pratihaty' Ârjunaḥ smayan,
diśaṃ, khaṃ c' âiva, bhūmiṃ ca prāvṛṇoc chara|vṛṣṭibhiḥ.
musalān' îva saṃpetuḥ, parighā iva c' êṣavaḥ,
śata|ghnya iva c' âpy anye, vajrāṇy ugrāṇi v" âpare.
30.35 tair vadhyamānaṃ tat sainyaṃ sa|patty|aśva|ratha|dvipam
nimīlit'|âkṣam atyarthaṃ babhrāma ca nanāda ca.
niṣkaivalyaṃ tadā yuddhaṃ prāpur aśva|nara|dvipāḥ;
hanyamānāḥ śarair ārtās tadā bhītāḥ pradudruvuḥ.

Then Sátyaki turned up and, after pummeling Karna 30.25
with ninety-nine formidable arrows, struck him with a hundred more. Next all the heroes among the Parthas* pounded
Karna. Yudha·manyu, Shikhándin, Dráupadi's sons, the
Prabhádrakas, Uttamáujas, Yuyútsu, the twins and Príshata's
grandson, and the forces of the Káikayas, Chedis, Karúshas
and Matsyas, powerful Chekitána and the King of Law who
is strict in his vows, surrounded Karna in battle with their
chariots, horses, elephants and terribly courageous foot-
soldiers and covered him with their various weapons. Yelling
with ferocious sounds, they were all determined to kill Karna.

Cutting down that torrent of weapons with many sharp 30.30
arrows, Karna drove them away with the power of his missile, like the wind after breaking apart a tree. Karna could
be seen furiously slaughtering chariot-warriors, elephants
with their mahouts, horses with their riders and droves of
foot-soldiers.

The army of the Pándavas that was being slaughtered by
the brilliance of Karna's missile, losing weapons, chariots,
body-parts and lives, mostly turned away. Smiling, Árjuna then struck back at Karna's missile with his missile and
filled the directions, the sky and the earth with showers of
arrows. Some of his arrows fell like maces, some like iron
bludgeons, others like *shata·ghnis* and some like formidable
thunderbolts. As it was destroyed by those arrows, the entire 30.35
army with its foot-soldiers, horses, chariots and elephants

tvadīyānāṃ tadā yuddhe saṃsaktānāṃ, jay'|âiṣiṇām,
girim astaṃ samāsādya pratyapadyata bhānumān.
tamasā ca, mahā|rāja, rajasā ca viśeṣataḥ,
na kiṃ cit pratyapaśyāma, śubhaṃ vā yadi v" âśubham.
te trasyanto mah"|êṣv|āsā rātri|yuddhasya, Bhārata,
apayānaṃ tataś cakruḥ sahitāḥ sarva|yodhibhiḥ.

30.40 Kauraveṣv apayāteṣu tadā, rājan, dina|kṣaye,
jayaṃ su|manasaḥ prāpya Pārthāḥ sva|śibiraṃ yayuḥ.
vāditra|śabdair vividhaiḥ, siṃha|nādaiḥ sa|garjitaiḥ
parān upahasantaś ca stuvantaś c' Âcyut'|Ârjunau.
kṛte 'vahāre tair vīraiḥ, sainikāḥ sarva eva te
āśīr vācaḥ Pāṇḍaveṣu prāyuñjanta nar'|ēśvarāḥ.
tataḥ kṛte 'vahāre ca prahṛṣṭās tatra Pāṇḍavāḥ
niśāyāṃ śibiraṃ gatvā, nyavasanta nar'|ēśvarāḥ.

tato rakṣaḥ|piśācāś ca, śvāpadāś c' âiva saṃghaśaḥ
jagmur āyodhanaṃ ghoraṃ Rudrasy' ākrīḍa|saṃnibham.

closed its eyes and rambled about and bellowed tremendously. Horses, men and elephants joined in that incomparable battle; even as they were slaughtered by arrows, they fled injured and terrified.

The sun drew near the western mountain and then set while your troops, eager for victory, were engrossed in the battle. Because of the darkness, great king, and even more so because of the dust, we couldn't see a thing, whether it be good or bad. The mighty archers, Bhárata, terrified of fighting during the night, retreated from there together with all their warriors.

When those Káuravas retreated at the end of the day, king, 30.40
Pritha's sons, well pleased at achieving victory, went to their own encampment, ridiculing their enemies with lions' roars, howls and the sounds of various instruments, and lauding Áchyuta and Árjuna. When the heroes had ceased fighting, all the troops and lords of men recited benedictions to the Pándavas. And once they had ceased fighting, the Pándavas rejoiced there, and then those lords of men returned to their encampment and passed the night.

Then *rákshasa* and *pishácha* demons and wild animals went by the horde to that horrific battlefield that seemed like one of Rudra's playgrounds.*

31–36

SHALYA BECOMES KARNA'S CHARIOTEER

DHṚTARĀṢṬRA uvāca:

31.1 SVENA CCHANDENA naḥ sarvān
avadhīd vyaktam Arjunaḥ,
na hy asya samare mucyed
Antako 'py ātatāyinaḥ!
Pārthaś c' âiko 'harad Bhadrām, ekaś c' Âgnim atarpayat,
ekaś c' êmāṃ mahīṃ jitvā cakre bali|bhṛto nṛpān.
eko Nivātakavacān ahanad divya|kārmukaḥ,
ekaḥ Kirāta|rūpeṇa sthitaṃ Śarvam ayodhayat.
eko hy arakṣad Bharatān, eko Bhavam atoṣayat.
ten' âikena jitāḥ sarve mahī|pā hy ugra|tejasaḥ.
31.5 te na nindyāḥ; praśasyās te! yat te cakrur, bravīhi tat!
tato Duryodhanaḥ, sūta, paścāt kim akarot tadā?

SAMJAYA uvāca:

hata|prahata|vidhvastā, vi|varm'|āyudha|vāhanāḥ,
dīna|svarā, dūyamānā, māninaḥ, śatru|nirjitāḥ,
śibira|sthāḥ punar mantraṃ mantrayanti sma Kauravāḥ,
bhagna|daṃṣṭrā, hata|viṣāḥ, pād'|ākrāntā iv' ôragāḥ.
tān abravīt tataḥ Karṇaḥ kruddhaḥ, sarpa iva śvasan,
karaṃ kareṇa niṣpīḍya, prekṣamāṇas tav' ātmajam:
«yatto, dṛḍhaś ca, dakṣaś ca, dhṛti|mān Arjunaḥ sadā;
saṃbodhayati c' âpy enaṃ yathā|kālam Adhokṣajaḥ.
31.10 sahas" âstra|visargeṇa vayaṃ ten' âdya vañcitāḥ;
śvas tv ahaṃ tasya saṃkalpaṃ sarvaṃ hantā, mahī|pate!»
evam uktas, «tath"! êty» uktvā so 'nujajñe nṛp'|ôttamān.
te 'nujñātā nṛpā sarve svāni veśmāni bhejire.

DHRITA·RASHTRA said:

OF COURSE ÁRJUNA slaughtered all our troops at will, 31.1
for not even Death could escape him in battle once his bow has been drawn! Alone Pritha's son carried off Bhadra,* alone he satisfied Agni, and alone he conquered the earth and made the kings tributaries. With his divine bow he alone destroyed the Niváta·kávacha demons, and alone he fought Sharva* who'd assumed the form of a mountain man. Alone he protected the Bharatas and alone he gratified Bhava. All the princes were conquered by him alone with
his formidable power. They cannot be blamed; they ought 31.5
to be praised! Tell me what they did! Then, herald, what did Duryódhana do next?

SÁNJAYA said:

Beaten, killed and scattered, stripped of their armor, weapons and chariots, their voices deflated and consumed with sadness, the proud Káuravas who'd been defeated by their enemy gathered again at their encampment and deliberated over their plan, like snakes trampled by feet, their fangs destroyed and venom ruined.

Hissing like a snake and squeezing one hand in the other as he looked at your son, Karna furiously addressed them: "Árjuna is always careful, strong, clever and intelligent. Furthermore Adhókshaja* advises him at the right times. Today 31.10
he deceived us by suddenly releasing his missile. But tomorrow, lord of the earth, I'll destroy all his conviction!"

Spoken to in this way and responding, "So be it!" Duryódhana dismissed those excellent kings. Once he'd dismissed them, all the kings turned to their own tents.

sukh'|ôṣitās tāṃ rajanīṃ hṛṣṭā yuddhāya niryayuḥ.
te 'paśyan vihitaṃ vyūhaṃ Dharma|rājena dur|jayam
prayatnāt Kuru|mukhyena Bṛhaspaty|Uśano|mate.
atha pratīpa|kartāraṃ pravīraṃ para|vīra|hā
sasmāra vṛṣabha|skandhaṃ Karṇaṃ Duryodhanas tadā.
Puraṃdara|samaṃ yuddhe, Marud|gaṇa|samaṃ bale,
31.15 Kārtavīrya|samaṃ vīrye, Karṇaṃ rājño 'gaman manaḥ.
sarveṣāṃ c' âiva sainyānāṃ Karṇam ev' âgaman manaḥ,
sūta|putraṃ mah"|êṣv|āsaṃ, bandhum ātyayikeṣv iva.

DHṚTARĀṢṬRA uvāca:

tato Duryodhanaḥ, sūta, paścāt kim akarot tadā?
yad vo 'gaman mano, mandāḥ, Karṇaṃ Vaikartanaṃ prati,
apy apaśyata Rādheyaṃ, śīt'|ârtā iva bhāskaram?
kṛte 'vahāre sainyānāṃ, pravṛtte ca raṇe punaḥ,
kathaṃ Vaikartanaḥ Karṇas tatr' âyudhyata, Saṃjaya?
kathaṃ ca Pāṇḍavāḥ sarve yuyudhus tatra sūta|jam?
Karṇo hy eko mahā|bāhur hanyāt Pārthān sa|Sṛñjayān.
Karṇasya bhujayor vīryaṃ Śakra|Viṣṇu|samaṃ yudhi,
31.20 tasya śastrāṇi ghorāṇi, vikramaś ca mah"|ātmanaḥ.
Karṇam āśritya saṃgrāme matto Duryodhano nṛpaḥ.

They spent the night comfortably and then excitedly set out for battle. They saw the invincible army carefully arrayed by the King of Law, the foremost of the Kurus, in accordance with the doctrine of Brihas·pati and Úshanas.

Then Duryódhana, a killer of enemy-heroes, called Karna to mind, a hero who took on adversaries and whose shoulders were as broad as a bull's. The king's thoughts turned to Karna, who was the equal of the Sacker of cities in battle, the equal of the horde of Maruts in strength and the equal of Kartavírya in courage. The thoughts of all the troops turned to Karna alone, the son of the charioteer, a mighty archer, just as one's thoughts turn to family when help is needed. 31.15

DHRITA·RASHTRA said:

Then, herald, what did Duryódhana do next? When your thoughts turned to Karna Vaikártana, depressed people, did you look to Radha's son like someone suffering from a chill looks to the sun? When the battle resumed again after the withdrawal of the armies, Sánjaya, how did Karna Vaikártana fight then? And how did all the Pándavas fight the charioteer's son then? On his own mighty-armed Karna could have killed Pritha's sons along with the Srínjayas. For the strength of Karna's arms in battle was the equal of Shakra's and Vishnu's, his weapons were terrible and that great 31.20
man had courage. Relying on Karna in battle, King Duryódhana was excited.

Duryodhanaṃ tato dṛṣṭvā Pāṇḍavena bhṛś'|ârditam,
parākrāntān Pāṇḍu|sutān dṛṣṭvā c' âpi mahā|rathaḥ,
Karṇam āśritya saṃgrāme, mando Duryodhano punaḥ
jetum utsahate Pārthān sa|putrān saha|Keśavān.
aho bata! mahad duḥkhaṃ, yatra Pāṇḍu|sutān raṇe
n' âtarad rabhasaḥ Karṇo. daivaṃ nūnaṃ parāyaṇam!
aho! dyūtasya niṣṭh" êyaṃ ghorā saṃprati vartate.
aho! tīvrāṇi duḥkhāni Duryodhana|kṛtāny aham
31.25 soḍhā ghorāṇi bahuśaḥ śalya|bhūtāni, Saṃjaya.
Saubalaṃ ca tadā, tāta, nīti|mān iti manyate
Karṇaś ca rabhaso nityaṃ, rājā taṃ c' âpy anuvrataḥ.
yad evaṃ vartamāneṣu mahā|yuddheṣu, Saṃjaya,
aśrauṣaṃ nihatān putrān nityam eva vinirjitān.
na Pāṇḍavānāṃ samare kaś cid asti nivārakaḥ;
strī|madhyam iva gāhante! daivaṃ tu balavattaram!

SAṂJAYA uvāca:

rājan, pūrva|nimittāni dharmiṣṭhāni vicintaya!
atikrāntaṃ hi yat kāryaṃ, paścāc cintayate naraḥ
tac c' âsya na bhavet kāryaṃ; cintayā ca vinaśyati.
31.30 tad idaṃ tava kāryaṃ tu dūra|prāptaṃ vijānatā,
na kṛtaṃ yat tvayā pūrvaṃ prāpt'|âprāpta|vicāraṇam.
ukto 'si bahudhā, rājan, «mā yudhyasv' êti Pāṇḍavaiḥ!»
gṛhṇīṣe na ca tan mohād vacanaṃ ca, viśāṃ pate.
tvayā pāpāni ghorāṇi samācīrṇāni Pāṇḍuṣu.
tvat|kṛte vartate ghoraḥ pārthivānāṃ jana|kṣayaḥ.
tat tv idānīm atikrāntaṃ mā śuco, Bharata'|rṣabha!
śṛṇu sarvaṃ yathā|vṛttaṃ, ghoraṃ vaiśasam ucyate!

That mighty warrior saw Duryódhana horribly wounded by the Pándava and saw Pandu's courageous sons. Relying on Karna in battle, foolish Duryódhana still had the power to defeat Pritha's sons with their sons and Késhava.

Damn it! It's utterly devastating that ferocious Karna couldn't overcome Pandu's sons in battle. Fate is now the last resort! Oh! This truly is the terrible consequence of the dice 31.25
game. Oh! I have to endure intense miseries wrought by Duryódhana, Sánjaya, that are like so many terrible thorns! Dear fellow, ferocious Karna always regarded Súbala's son as shrewd, and the king was devoted to him. Yet Sánjaya, I've learned that as these tremendous battles unfolded my sons were always defeated and killed. There's no way to fend off the Pándavas in battle; it's as if they plunge deep into the midst of women! But fate is more powerful!

SÁNJAYA said:

King, consider the merits of those prior factors! A man later reflects that he should not have done what has long since been done. But by thinking like this he becomes utterly lost. Long ago you earned this outcome of yours, since, 31.30
though you are wise, you acted earlier without considering what may or may not have resulted. Often you were advised, king, "Don't fight with the Pándavas!" But, out of confusion, you didn't grasp this advice, lord of the people. You committed terrible sins against Pandu's sons; in consequence of what you did, this horrific massacre of princes unfolds. But now that too much time has passed, bull of Bharatas, don't grieve! Listen as I describe all the terrible butchery just as it happened!

prabhātāyāṃ rajanyāṃ tu, Karṇo rājānam abhyayāt.
sametya ca mahā|bāhur Duryodhanam ath' âbravīt.

KARNA uvāca:

31.35 «adya, rājan, sameṣyāmi Pāṇḍavena yaśasvinā;
nihaniṣyāmi taṃ vīraṃ, sa vā māṃ nihaniṣyati.
bahutvān mama kāryāṇāṃ, tathā Pārthasya, Bhārata,
n' âbhūt samāgamo, rājan, mama c' âiv' Ârjunasya ca.
idaṃ tu me yathā|prajñaṃ śṛṇu vākyaṃ, viśāṃ pate!
a|nihatya raṇe Pārthaṃ n' âham eṣyāmi, Bhārata.
hata|pravīre sainye 'smin, mayi c' âvasthite yudhi,
abhiyāsyati māṃ Pārthaḥ Śakra|śakti|vinā|kṛtam.
tataḥ śreyas|karaṃ yac ca tan nibodha, jan'|ēśvara,
āyudhānāṃ ca me vīryaṃ divyāṇām, Arjunasya ca!
31.40 kāryasya mahato bhede, lāghave, dūra|pātane,
sauṣṭhave c', âstra|pāte ca, Savyasācī na mat|samaḥ.
prāṇe, śaurye, 'tha vijñāne, vikrame c' âpi, Bhārata,
nimitta|jñāna|yoge ca Savyasācī na mat|samaḥ.
sarv'|āyudha|mahā|mātraṃ Vijayaṃ nāma tad dhanuḥ,
Indr'|ârtham priya|kāmena nirmitaṃ Viśvakarmaṇā;
yena daitya|gaṇān, rājañ, jitavān vai Śatakratuḥ;
yasya ghoṣeṇa daityānāṃ vyāmuhyanta diśo daśa.
tad Bhārgavāya prāyacchac Chakraḥ parama|saṃmatam;
tad divyaṃ Bhārgavo mahyam adadad dhanur uttamam.
31.45 tena yotsye mahā|bāhum Arjunaṃ jayatāṃ varam,
yath" Êndraḥ samare sarvān daiteyān vai samāgatān.
dhanur ghoraṃ Rāma|dattaṃ Gāṇḍīvāt tad viśiṣyate;

When night began to become light, mighty-armed Karna went up to the king. After joining him, he spoke to Duryódhana.

KARNA said:

"Today, king, I will meet the famous Pándava. I'll kill that hero or he'll kill me. Because of my own and Pritha's son's many deeds, Bhárata, Árjuna and I have not yet confronted one another, king. But, lord of the people, listen to this suggestion that is in line with how I understand things! 31.35

If I don't kill Pritha's son in battle I will not return, Bhárata. When this army has lost its heroes and yet I remain in battle, Pritha's son will attack me, since I've lost Shakra's spear.* Listen, lord of people, to what will then bring success, to the power of Árjuna's and my own divine weapons!

In the thwarting of great deeds, deftness, long-range shooting, skill and the discharging of missiles, the Left-handed archer is no match for me. In vitality, valor, intelligence, power and the application of the knowledge of omens, Bhárata, the Left-handed archer is no match for me. 31.40

My bow called Víjaya is the very best of all weapons. It was fashioned for Indra by Vishva·karman, who wanted to do him a favor. It was with it, king, that Shata·kratu conquered hordes of *daitya*s. It was by its sound that the ten directions of *daitya*s were bewildered. Shakra gave this highly renowned weapon to Bhárgava,* and Bhárgava gave that superb, divine bow to me. With it I will fight mighty-armed Árjuna, the most excellent of conquerors, just as Indra fought all the *daitya*s united together in battle. That terrible bow given to me by Rama* is better than Gandíva; 31.45

triḥ|sapta|kṛtvaḥ pṛthivī dhanuṣā yena nirjitā!
dhanuṣo hy asya karmāṇi divyāni prāha Bhārgavaḥ,
tad Rāmo hy adadan mahyaṃ. tena yotsyāmi Pāṇḍavam!

adya, Duryodhan', âhaṃ tvāṃ nandayiṣye sa|bāndhavam
nihatya samare vīram Arjunaṃ jayatāṃ varam.
sa|parvata|vana|dvīpā, hata|dviḍ, bhūḥ sa|sāgarā
putra|pautra|pratiṣṭhā te bhaviṣyaty adya, pārthiva.
31.50 n' âśakyaṃ vidyate me 'dya, tvat|priy'|ârthaṃ viśeṣataḥ,
samyag dharm'|ânuraktasya siddhir ātmavato yathā.
na hi māṃ samare soḍhuṃ saṃśakto, 'gniṃ tarur yathā.

avaśyaṃ tu mayā vācyaṃ yena hīno 'smi Phālgunāt.
jyā tasya dhanuṣo divyā, tath" âkṣayye mah"|êṣu|dhī,
sārathis tasya Govindo; mama tādṛṅ na vidyate.
tasya divyaṃ dhanuḥ śreṣṭhaṃ Gāṇḍīvam a|jitaṃ yudhi;
Vijayaṃ ca mahad divyaṃ mam' âpi dhanur uttamam.
tatr' âham adhikaḥ Pārthād dhanuṣā tena, pārthiva,

yena c' âpy adhiko vīraḥ Pāṇḍavas, tan nibodha me!
31.55 raśmi|grāhaś ca Dāśārhaḥ sarva|loka|namas|kṛtaḥ;
Agni|dattaś ca vai divyo rathaḥ kāñcana|bhūṣaṇaḥ,
a|cchedyaḥ sarvato, vīra; vājinaś ca mano|javāḥ;
dhvajaś ca divyo dyutimān vānaro vismayaṃ|karaḥ.
Kṛṣṇaś ca sraṣṭā jagato rathaṃ tam abhirakṣati.
etair dravyair ahaṃ hīno, yoddhum icchāmi Pāṇḍavam!

twenty-one times the earth has been conquered by this bow! Rama Bhárgava gave to me this bow whose divine deeds he explained. With it I will fight the Pándava!

Today, Duryódhana, I will gladden you as well as your kin after destroying in battle the hero Árjuna, the most excellent of conquerors. Today, king, with its enemies slain, the earth with its mountains, forests, islands and seas shall become
the foundation of your sons and grandsons. Because of my 31.50
fondness for you above all else, nothing is impossible for me today, just as perfection is not impossible for a scrupulous man who's completely devoted to the law. For no one can prevail against me in battle, just as a tree cannot prevail against fire.

But, of course, I will admit how I am inferior to Phálguna. The divine bow-string of his bow, his massive quiver in its inexhaustibleness and his charioteer Go·vinda; the like of these I do not have. He has the divine Gandíva, a superb bow that is invincible in battle; and I also have the divine Víjaya, a tremendous and massive bow. In this case I am superior to Pritha's son with this bow, king.

And listen to me for how the Pándava hero is superior!
The holder of his horses' reins, Dashárha,* who is adored 31.55
by all people; his divine chariot decorated with gold given to him by Agni, hero, that is utterly impossible to smash; his horses that are as fast as thought; and his divine and splendid standard that induces astonishment. And Krishna, the creator of the world, protects his chariot. By these things I'm inferior, yet I want to fight the Pándava!

ayaṃ tu sadṛśaḥ Śaureḥ Śalyaḥ samiti|śobhanaḥ;
sārathyaṃ yadi me kuryād, dhruvas te vijayo bhavet.
tasya me sārathiḥ Śalyo bhavatv a|sukaraḥ paraiḥ!
nārācān, gārdhra|patrāṃś ca śakaṭāni vahantu me!
31.60 rathāś ca mukhyā, rāj'|êndra, yuktā vājibhir uttamaiḥ
āyāntu paścāt satataṃ mām eva, Bharata'|rṣabha!
evam abhyadhikaḥ Pārthād bhaviṣyāmi guṇair aham.
Śalyo 'py abhyadhikaḥ Kṛṣṇād, Arjunād api c' âpy aham.
yath" âśva|hṛdayaṃ veda Dāśārhaḥ para|vīra|hā,
tathā Śalyo vijānīte haya|jñānaṃ mahā|rathaḥ.
bāhu|vīrye samo n' âsti Madra|rājasya kaś cana;
tath" âstre mat|samo n' âsti kaś cid eva dhanur|dharaḥ;
tathā Śalya|samo n' âsti haya|jñāne hi kaś cana;
so 'yam abhyadhikaḥ Kṛṣṇād bhaviṣyati ratho mama!
31.65 evaṃ kṛte, ratha|stho 'haṃ guṇair abhyadhiko 'rjunā,
bhave yudhi, jayeyaṃ ca Phālgunaṃ, Kuru|sattama.
samudyātuṃ na śakṣyanti devā api sa|Vāsavāḥ.
etat kṛtaṃ, mahā|rāja, tvay" êcchāmi, paraṃ|tapa!
kriyatām eṣa kāmo me! mā vaḥ kālo 'tyagād ayam!
evaṃ kṛte, kṛtaṃ sahyaṃ sarva|kāmair bhaviṣyati.
tato drakṣyasi saṃgrāme yat kariṣyāmi, Bhārata.
sarvathā Pāṇḍavān saṃkhye vijeṣye vai samāgatān.
na hi me samare śaktāḥ samudyātuṃ sur'|âsurāḥ.
kim u Pāṇḍu|sutā, rājan, raṇe, mānuṣa|yonayaḥ?»

But Shalya, who is brilliant in battle, is the like of Shura's grandson.* If he would become my charioteer then your victory would be certain. Let Shalya become my charioteer, enemies find him difficult to cope with! Let my carts carry iron and vulture-feathered arrows! Lord of kings, let 31.60
the finest chariots harnessed to superb steeds always follow behind me, bull of Bharatas! With these things I'll be superior to Pritha's son. Shalya is superior to Krishna as I too am to Árjuna. Just as Dashárha, a killer of enemy-heroes, knows the heart of a horse, so too Shalya, a mighty warrior, is erudite in horse lore. In strength of arms no one is the equal of the king of the Madras; in missiles no bowman is the equal of me, and in horse lore no one is the equal of Shalya. My chariot shall certainly be superior to Krishna's!

When this has been done, standing in my chariot with 31.65
these enhancements I'll be superior to Árjuna. And when the battle commences I shall defeat Phálguna, most excellent of Kurus. Even the gods with Vásava could not rise against me. Great king, foe-destroyer, I want you to do this! Please do what I want. Don't let this chance pass us by! When this is done, you shall have granted support for all my needs. Then you'll see what I can do in battle, Bhárata. I'll completely defeat the Pándavas united together in combat. For not even the gods and demons can rise up against me in battle. What more could Pandu's sons do in battle, king, being of merely human stock?"

SAṂJAYA uvāca:

31.70 evam uktas tava sutaḥ Karṇen' âhava|śobhinā
saṃpūjya saṃprahṛṣṭ'|ātmā tato Rādheyam abravīt.

DURYODHANA uvāca:

«evam etat kariṣyāmi yathā tvaṃ, Karṇa, manyase
s'|ôpāsaṅgā rathāḥ s'|âśvāḥ svanuyāsyanti saṃyuge.
nārācān, gārdhra|pattrāṃś ca śakaṭāni vahantu te;
anuyāsyāma, Karṇa, tvāṃ vayaṃ, sarve ca pārthivāḥ.»

SAṂJAYA uvāca:

evam uktvā, mahā|rāja, tava putraḥ pratāpavān
abhigamy' âbravīd rājā Madra|rājam idaṃ vacaḥ.

SAṂJAYA uvāca:

32.1 PUTRAS TAVA, mahā|rāja, Madra|rājam mahā|ratham
vinayen' ôpasaṃgamya praṇayād vākyam abravīt:
«satya|vrata, mahā|bhāga, dviṣatām tāpa|vardhana,
Madr'|ēśvara, raṇe śūra, para|sainya|bhayaṃ|kara!
śrutavān asi Karṇasya bruvato, vadatāṃ vara!
yathā nṛ|pati|siṃhānāṃ madhye tvāṃ varaye svayam,
tat tvām, a|prativīry', âdya, śatru|pakṣa|kṣay'|āvaha,
Madr'|ēśvara, prayāce 'ham śirasā vinayena ca!
32.5 tasmāt Pārtha|vināś'|ârthaṃ, hit'|ârthaṃ mama c' âiva hi,
sārathyaṃ, rathināṃ śreṣṭha, praṇayāt kartum arhasi!

SÁNJAYA said:

Once Karna, who was brilliant in battle, had said this, 31.70
your son respectfully saluted him and, his body rippling with excitement, spoke to Radha's son.

DURYÓDHANA said:

"I will do this in the way you think fit, Karna. Chariots with quivers and horses will quickly follow you in the battle. Your wagons shall bear iron and vulture-feathered arrows. And we and all the kings shall follow you, Karna."

SÁNJAYA said:

Once he had said this, great king, your powerful son the king approached the king of the Madras and uttered these words to him.

SÁNJAYA said:

YOUR SON APPROACHED the king of the Madras with hu- 32.1
mility, great king, and affectionately spoke these words to that mighty warrior:

"You're highly distinguished and true to your vows! You intensify the suffering of enemies! You're a hero in battle, lord of the Madras, and you rouse fear amongst enemy troops! You listened while Karna spoke, finest of speakers. Accordingly, I myself choose you amidst these lions of kings. You have no equal and bring about the destruction of opponents! Lord of the Madras, with humility and deference
I beg you now! Therefore, finest of chariot-warriors, please, 32.5
as a favor, become the chariot-driver for my well-being and for the destruction of Pritha's sons!

tvayi yantari Rādheyo vidviṣo me vijeṣyate.
abhīśūṇāṃ hi Karṇasya grahit" ânyo na vidyate
ṛte hi tvāṃ, mahā|bhāga, Vāsudeva|samaṃ yudhi.
sa pāhi sarvathā Karṇaṃ, yathā Brahmā Maheśvaram!
yathā ca sarvath" āpatsu Vārṣṇeyaḥ pāti Pāṇḍavam,
tathā, Madr'|ēśvar', âdya tvaṃ Rādheyaṃ pratipālaya!
Bhīṣmo, Droṇaḥ, Kṛpaḥ, Karṇo,
bhavān, Bhojaś ca vīryavān,
Śakuniḥ Saubalo, Drauṇir,
aham eva ca no balam
32.10 evam eṣa kṛto bhāgo nava|dhā, pṛthivī|pate.
na ca bhāgo 'tra Bhīṣmasya, Droṇasya ca mah"|ātmanaḥ;
tābhyām atītya tau bhāgau nihatā mama śatravaḥ.
vṛddhau hi tau mah"|êṣv|āsau chalena nihatau yudhi;
kṛtvā na|sukaraṃ karma gatau svargam ito, 'nagha.
tath" ânye puruṣa|vyāghrāḥ parair vinihatā yudhi,
asmadīyāś ca bahavaḥ svargāy' ôpagatā raṇe
tyaktvā prāṇān, yathā|śakti ceṣṭāṃ kṛtvā ca puṣkalām.
tad idaṃ hata|bhūyiṣṭhaṃ balaṃ mama, nar'|âdhipa,
pūrvam apy alpakaiḥ Pārthair hataṃ. kim uta sāṃpratam?
32.15 balavanto, mah"|ātmānaḥ Kaunteyāḥ, satya|vikramāḥ
balaṃ śeṣaṃ na hanyur me yathā, tat kuru, pārthiva!
hata|vīram idaṃ sainyaṃ Pāṇḍavaiḥ samare, vibho;
Karṇo hy eko mahā|bāhur asmat|priya|hite rataḥ,
bhavāṃś ca, puruṣa|vyāghra, sarva|loka|mahā|rathaḥ;
Śalya, Karṇo 'rjunen' âdya yoddhum icchati saṃyuge,

With you as his driver, Radha's son will overwhelm my enemies. For, apart from you, distinguished man, there's no one else to hold Karna's reins who is Vasudéva's equal in battle. You must protect Karna by every means, just as Brahma protected Mahéshvara!* Just as in crises the Varshnéya* protects the Pándava by every means, so today, lord of the Madras, you must protect Radha's son!

Bhishma, Drona, Kripa, Karna, you, the powerful Bhoja, 32.10
Súbala's son Shákuni, Drona's son and I as well, amongst us that army was divided into nine shares,* lord of the earth. And of these, the shares of Bhishma and great Drona are no more. Going beyond their two shares, those two destroyed my enemies. Yet those two mighty archers were old and were deceitfully struck down in battle. After performing terribly difficult feats, those two went from this world to heaven, faultless man.

Other tigers of men too were slaughtered by enemies in battle, and many of our men went to heaven in the war, giving up their lives after performing numerous deeds to the best of their abilities. This army of mine has almost been completely decimated, ruler of men. It was destroyed by those sons of Pritha, though they were the fewer before. How many more are they now? So that Kunti's powerful 32.15
sons—mighty men of true courage!—cannot destroy what is left of my army, king, you must do this!

The army's heroes have been killed in battle by the Pándavas, powerful man. Mighty-armed Karna is one who is still devoted to our welfare and friendship, and you, tiger of a man, are a mighty warrior in all the worlds. Shalya, Karna wants to fight with Árjuna in battle today. On him

tasmiñ jay'|āśā vipulā, Madra|rāja, nar'|âdhipa.
tasy' âbhīṣu|graha|varo n' ânyo 'sti bhuvi kaś cana.
Pārthasya samare Kṛṣṇo yath" âbhīṣu|graho varaḥ,
tathā tvam api Karṇasya rathe 'bhīṣu|graho bhava!
32.20 tena yukto raṇe Pārtho rakṣyamāṇaś ca, pārthiva,
yāni karmāṇi kurute pratyakṣāṇi ca tāni te.
pūrvaṃ na samare hy evam avadhīd Arjuno ripūn;
idānīṃ vikramo hy asya Kṛṣṇena sahitasya ca.
Kṛṣṇena sahitaḥ Pārtho Dhārtarāṣṭrīṃ mahā|camūm
ahany ahani, Madr'|ēśa, drāvayan dṛśyate yudhi.
bhāgo 'vaśiṣṭaḥ Karṇasya, tava c' âiva, mahā|dyute.
taṃ bhāgaṃ saha Karṇena yugapan nāśay' âdya hi!
aruṇena yathā sārdhaṃ tamaḥ sūryo vyapohati,
tathā Karṇena sahito jahi Pārthaṃ mah"|āhave.
32.25 udyantau ca yathā sūryau bāla|sūrya|sama|prabhau
Karṇa|Śalyau raṇe dṛṣṭvā vidravantu mahā|rathāḥ!
sūry'|âruṇau yathā dṛṣṭvā tamo naśyati, māriṣa,
tathā naśyantu Kaunteyāḥ sa|Pañcālāḥ sa|Sṛñjayāḥ!
rathināṃ pravaraḥ Karṇo, yantṝṇāṃ pravaro bhavān.
saṃyogo yuvayor loke n' âbhūn, na ca bhaviṣyati.
yathā sarvāsv avasthāsu Vārṣṇeyaḥ pāti Pāṇḍavam,
tathā bhavān paritrātu Karṇaṃ Vaikartanaṃ raṇe!
tvayā sārathinā hy eṣa a|pradhṛṣyo bhaviṣyati,
devatānām api raṇe sa|Śakrāṇāṃ, mahī|pate.

rests our great hope for victory, king of the Madras, ruler of men. There is no one else on earth who would be better at grasping his reins. Just as Krishna is the best at holding the reins for Pritha's son in battle, so you also are the best at holding the reins in Karna's chariot!

Joined with Krishna and protected by him in battle, 32.20
prince, the deeds that Pritha's son can do should be obvious to you. Previously Árjuna never destroyed his enemies like this in battle. Now he has courage and is joined by Krishna as well. Joined with Krishna, lord of the Madras, day after day Pritha's son can be seen scattering the Dhartaráshtra army in battle.

Karna's share survives, as does yours, man of great splendor. Together with Karna, today you must destroy that share! Just as the sun together with the dawn drives away the darkness, so you together with Karna must destroy Pritha's son in this great battle.

Seeing Karna and Shalya in battle like a pair of rising 32.25
suns, their radiance like an early morning sun, those mighty warriors could only flee! Just as darkness perishes after seeing the dawn and the sun, dear friend, so Kunti's sons and the Panchálas and Srínjayas could only perish after seeing the two of you!

Karna is the finest chariot-warrior and you are the finest driver. In this world there has been no and shall be no combination like the two of you. Just as the Varshnéya protects the Pándava in all situations, so you, sir, must protect Karna Vaikártana in battle! For with you as his chariot-driver, lord of the earth, he will be invincible, even in battle with the

kiṃ punaḥ Pāṇḍaveyānāṃ? mā viśaṅkīr vaco mama!»

SAMJAYA uvāca:

32.30 Duryodhana|vacaḥ śrutvā, Śalyaḥ krodha|samanvitaḥ
tri|śikhāṃ bhrukuṭiṃ kṛtvā, dhunvan hastau punaḥ punaḥ,
krodha|rakte mahā|netre parivṛtya, mahā|bhujaḥ
kul'|āiśvarya|śruta|balair dṛptaḥ Śalyo 'bravīd idam.

ŚALYA uvāca:

«avamanyasi, Gāndhāre, dhruvaṃ ca pariśaṅkase,
yan māṃ bravīṣi viśrabdhaṃ, ‹sārathyaṃ kriyatām, iti!›
asmatto 'bhyadhikaṃ Karṇaṃ manyamānaḥ praśaṃsasi;
na c' âhaṃ yudhi Rādheyaṃ gaṇaye tulyam ātmanā.
ādiśyatām abhyadhiko mam' âṃśaḥ, pṛthivī|pate!
tam ahaṃ samare jitvā gamiṣyāmi yath"|āgatam.
32.35 atha v" âpy eka ev' âhaṃ yotsyāmi, Kuru|nandana.
paśya vīryaṃ mam' âdya tvaṃ saṃgrāme dahato ripūn!
yath" âbhimānaṃ, Kauravya, vidhāya hṛdaye pumān
asmad|vidhaḥ pravarteta, mā māṃ tvam abhiśaṅkithāḥ!
yudhi c' âpy avamāno me na kartavyaḥ kathaṃ cana;
paśya pīnau mama bhujau vajra|saṃhanan'|ôpamau!
dhanuḥ paśya ca me citraṃ, śarāṃś c' āśīviṣ'|ôpamān!
rathaṃ paśya ca me kḷptaṃ sad|aśvair vāta|vegitaiḥ!
gadāṃ ca paśya, Gāndhāre, hema|paṭṭa|vibhūṣitām!
dārayeyaṃ mahīṃ kṛtsnāṃ, vikireyaṃ ca parvatān,
32.40 śoṣayeyaṃ samudrāṃś ca tejasā svena, pārthiva.
taṃ māṃ evaṃ|vidhaṃ, rājan, samartham ari|nigrahe

gods and Shakra. How much more then with the Pándavas? Do not doubt my words!"

SÁNJAYA said:

After listening to Duryódhana's words, Shalya was filled 32.30
with rage. Contracting his brow into three lines, he shook his hands again and again and rolled his huge, rage-reddened eyes. Proud of his family, sovereignty, learning and strength, mighty-armed Shalya said this.

SHALYA said:

"You insult and surely distrust me, son of Gandhári, since you brazenly say to me, 'Please become the chariot-driver'! You praise Karna, thinking him better than us. But I don't consider Radha's son my equal in battle. Assign a superior share to me, lord of the earth! After defeating it in battle,
I will go the way I came. Or I could fight alone, joy of 32.35
the Kurus. You must watch my valor today as I scorch our enemies in battle!

Since a man like us would depart after taking an insult to heart, Kaurávya, you shouldn't doubt me! And there shouldn't be any contempt for me in battle. Look at my thick arms; they're as hard as diamond! Look at my beautiful bow and my arrows that are like poisonous snakes! And look at my chariot complete with good horses as fast as the wind! And, son of Gandhári, look at my club decorated with golden binding!

I could tear apart the entire earth, split apart the mountains and parch the oceans with my power, king. Why ap- 32.40
point someone like me who can overwhelm enemies, king, as chariot-driver in battle for Ádhiratha's son, who's of such

kasmād yunaṅkṣi sārathye nīcasy' Ādhirathe raṇe?
na mām a|dhuri, rāj'|êndra, niyoktuṃ tvam ih' ârhasi;
na hi pāpīyasaḥ śreyān bhūtvā preṣyatvam utsahe!
yo hy abhyupagataṃ prītyā garīyāṃsaṃ vaśe sthitam
vaśe pāpīyaso dhatte, tat pāpam adhar'|ôttaram!

Brahmaṇā brāhmaṇāḥ sṛṣṭā mukhāt, kṣatraṃ ca bāhutaḥ,
ūrubhyām asṛjad vaiśyāñ, śūdrān padbhyām, iti śrutiḥ!
tebhyo varṇa|viśeṣāś ca pratilom'|ânuloma|jāḥ,
32.45 ath' ânyonyasya saṃyogāc cāturvarṇyasya, Bhārata.
goptāraḥ, saṃgrahītāro, dātāraḥ kṣatriyāḥ smṛtāḥ;
yājan'|âdhyāpanair viprā, viśuddhaiś ca pratigrahaiḥ,
lokasy' ânugrah'|ârthāya sthāpitā brāhmaṇā bhuvi;
kṛṣiś ca, pāśupālyaṃ ca viśāṃ, dānaṃ ca dharmataḥ;
brahma|kṣatra|viśāṃ śūdrā vihitāḥ paricārakāḥ.
brahma|kṣatrasya vihitāḥ sūtā vai paricārakāḥ,
na kṣatriyo vai sūtānāṃ śṛṇuyāc ca kathaṃ cana!

ahaṃ mūrdh'|âbhiṣikto hi rāja'|rṣi|kula|jo nṛpaḥ,
mahā|rathaḥ samākhyātaḥ, sevyaḥ, stutyaś ca bandinām!
32.50 so 'ham etādṛśo bhūtvā n' êh' âri|bala|sūdanaḥ
sūta|putrasya saṃgrāme sārathyaṃ kartum utsahe!
avamānam ahaṃ prāpya na yotsyāmi kathaṃ cana!
āpṛcche tv" âdya, Gāndhāre, gamiṣyāmi gṛhāya vai!»

inferior status? Please, lord of kings, don't appoint me here in this position that has no honor. For having been higher than that lowly man, I can't become his servant. For when the man lower in authority accepts under his power the higher man who assents out of friendship, that evil has it back to front!

Brahma emitted brahmins from his mouth and kshatriyas from his arms. He emitted vaishyas from his thighs and shudras from his feet. This is sacred learning! And from them then came the special social classes—those born against the
grain and those with the grain—because of the intermixture 32.45
of the four social classes with one another, Bhárata. Kshatriyas are traditionally regarded as protectors, gatherers of wealth and benefactors. Learned brahmins were deposited on earth in order to assist people by offering sacrifices, teaching and accepting pure gifts. According to the law, vaishyas have agriculture, animal husbandry and giving. And shudras have been decreed as the servants of brahmins, kshatriyas and vaishyas. Charioteers have been decreed as the servants of brahmins and kshatriyas. In no way should a kshatriya listen to anything from charioteers!

I am a king! I was anointed on the head and born in a family of royal sages. I am celebrated as a great warrior.
I should be served and praised by bards! Having been one 32.50
such as this, a destroyer of enemy armies, I can't now become the chariot-driver in battle for the charioteer's son! Receiving this insult, I will not fight at all! I bid you farewell, son of Gandhári, now I go home!"

SAMJAYA uvāca:

evam uktvā, mahā|rāja, Śalyaḥ samiti|śobhanaḥ
utthāya prayayau tūrṇaṃ rāja|madhyād a|marṣitaḥ.
praṇayād, bahu|mānāc ca tan nigṛhya sutas tava
abravīn madhuraṃ vākyaṃ sāmnā sarv'|ârtha|sādhakam:
«yathā, Śalya, vijānīṣe, evam etad a|saṃśayam.
abhiprāyas tu me kaś cit. tan nibodha, jan'|ēśvara!
32.55 na Karṇo 'bhyadhikas tvatto; na śaṃke tvāṃ ca, pārthiva;
na hi Madr'|ēśvaro rājā kuryād yad an|ṛtaṃ bhavet.
ṛtam eva hi pūrvās te vadanti puruṣ'|ôttamāḥ,
tasmād Ārtāyaniḥ prokto bhavān, iti matir mama.
śalya|bhūtaś ca śatrūṇāṃ yasmāt tvaṃ yudhi, māna|da,
tasmāc Chalyo hi te nāma kathyate pṛthivī|tale.
yad etad vyāhṛtaṃ pūrvaṃ bhavatā, bhūri|dakṣiṇa,
tad eva kuru, dharma|jña, mad|arthaṃ yad yad ucyate.
na ca tvatto hi Rādheyo, na c' âham api vīryavān,
vṛṇe 'ham tvāṃ hay'|âgryāṇāṃ yantāram iha saṃyuge.
32.60 manye c' âbhyadhikaṃ, Śalya,
guṇaiḥ Karṇaṃ Dhanaṃjayāt,
bhavantaṃ Vāsudevāc ca
loko 'yam iti manyate.
Karṇo hy abhyadhikaḥ Pārthād astrair eva, nara'|ṛṣabha,
bhavān abhyadhikaḥ Kṛṣṇād aśva|jñāne bale tathā.
yath" âśva|hṛdayaṃ veda Vāsudevo mahā|manāḥ,
dvi|guṇaṃ tvaṃ tathā vetsi, Madra|rāj' ēśvar'|ātmaja.»

SÁNJAYA said:

Having said this, great king, Shalya, who was brilliant in battle, rose quickly and indignantly and departed from the midst of the kings. Holding him back out of his affection and great respect for him, in a conciliatory way your son spoke these soothing words that could accomplish every purpose:

"Shalya, it is as you understand it, without a doubt. But I had a point. Listen to it, lord of people! Karna is not 32.55
superior to you and I do not distrust you, king. For a lord of the Madras, a king, could not do what would be false. Your ancestors were the most excellent of men and spoke the truth alone; I reckon it's for this that you're known as Artáyani.*

But because in battle you're a thorn to your enemies, giver of honor, on earth your name is regarded as Shalya.* Giver of rich gifts, do what you previously said you would, knower of the law, whatever you say now for my sake. Since neither Radha's son nor I is more powerful than you, I choose you as the driver of these most excellent horses for this battle. Shalya, I regard Karna as superior to Dhanan·jaya in merits, 32.60
and the world regards you as superior to Vasudéva. Karna is certainly superior to Pritha's son in weapons, bull of a man, and you're superior to Krishna in horse lore and strength. Just as proud Vasudéva understands the heart of a horse, so you understand it twice as much, lord's son and king of the Madras."

ŚALYA uvāca:

«yan māṃ bravīṣi, Gāndhāre,
madhye sainyasya, Kaurava,
viśiṣṭaṃ Devakī|putrāt,
prītimān asmy ahaṃ tvayi.
eṣa sārathyam ātiṣṭhe Rādheyasya yaśasvinaḥ
yudhyataḥ Pāṇḍav'|âgryeṇa, yathā tvaṃ, vīra, manyase.
32.65 samayaś ca hi me, vīra, kaś cid Vaikartanaṃ prati
utsṛjeyaṃ yathā|śraddham ahaṃ vāco 'sya saṃnidhau.»

SAṂJAYA uvāca:

«tath"! êti» rājan, putras te saha Karṇena, Bhārata,
abravīn Madra|rājasya mataṃ, Bharata|sattama.

DURYODHANA uvāca:

33.1 «BHŪYA EVA TU, Madr'|ēśa, yat te vakṣyāmi tac chṛṇu,
yathā purā vṛttam idaṃ yuddhe dev'|âsure, vibho!
yad uktavān pitur mahyaṃ Mārkaṇḍeyo mahān ṛṣiḥ,
tad a|śeṣeṇa bruvato mama, rāja'|rṣi|sattama,
nibodha manasā, c' âtra na te kāryā vicāraṇā!
devānām asurāṇāṃ ca paraspara|jigīṣayā
babhūva prathamo, rājan, saṃgrāmas Tārakā|mayaḥ.
nirjitāś ca tadā daityā daivatair, iti naḥ śrutam.
33.5 nirjiteṣu ca daityeṣu Tārakasya sutās trayaḥ,
Tārākṣaḥ, Kamalākṣaś ca, Vidyunmālī ca, pārthiva,
tapa ugraṃ samāsthāya niyame parame sthitāḥ,
tapasā karśayām āsur dehān svāñ, śatru|tāpana.
damena, tapasā c' âiva, niyamena, samādhinā
teṣāṃ Pitā|mahaḥ prīto vara|daḥ pradadau varam.
a|vadhyatvaṃ ca te, rājan, sarva|bhūtasya sarvadā

SHALYA said:

"Son of Gandhári, since you describe me in the midst of this army as better than Dévaki's son,* I am pleased with you, Káurava. I will act as chariot-driver for Radha's famous son while he battles with the foremost of the Pándavas, hero,
just as you wish. And my only condition, hero, is that in 32.65
his presence I can sling any words I want at Vaikártana."

SÁNJAYA said:

"Fine!" said your son together with Karna to that wish of the king of the Madras, King Bhárata, finest of Bharatas.

DURYÓDHANA said:

"MIGHTY LORD OF the Madras, listen! I will tell you some- 33.1
thing else. Namely, what happened long ago in the battle of the gods and demons. The great sage Markandéya related this to my father, who related it to me. Listen as I relate it in full, finest of royal sages, and have no doubts in your mind as regards it!

The first battle of the gods and demons, each seeking to defeat the other, took place on account of Taraká.* We are taught that the demons were then conquered by the
gods. And once the demons were conquered, king, Tára- 33.5
ka's three sons, Táraksha, Kamaláksha and Vidyun·malin, undertaking terrible austerity and remaining in the most extreme penance, tormented their own bodies with austerity, scorcher of enemies.

The Grandfather* was pleased with their self-control, austerity, penance and meditation, and that giver of boons gave them a boon. Together, king, they asked the Grandfather of all the worlds for the inability to be killed by any be-

sahitā varayām āsuḥ sarva|loka|Pitā|maham.
tān abravīt tadā devo lokānāṃ prabhur īśvaraḥ:
‹n' âsti sarv'|âmaratvaṃ vai, nivartadhvam ito, 'surāḥ!
33.10 anyaṃ varaṃ vṛṇīdhvaṃ vai, yādṛśaṃ saṃprarocate!›
tatas te sahitā, rājan, saṃpradhāry' â|sakṛt, prabhum
sarva|lok'|ēśvaraṃ vākyaṃ
praṇamy' êdam ath' âbruvan:
‹asmabhyaṃ tvaṃ varaṃ, Deva,
saṃprayaccha, Pitā|maha.
vayaṃ purāṇi trīṇy eva samāsthāya mahīm imām
vicariṣyāma loke 'smiṃs tvat|prasāda|puras|kṛtāḥ.
tato varṣa|sahasre tu sameṣyāmaḥ parasparam;
ekī|bhāvaṃ gamiṣyanti purāṇy etāni c', ânagha.
samāgatāni c' âitāni yo hanyād, Bhagavaṃs, tadā
ek'|êṣuṇā deva|varaḥ, sa no mṛtyur bhaviṣyati!›
33.15 ‹evam astv! iti› tān devaḥ pratyuktvā prāviśad divam.
te tu labdha|varāḥ prītāḥ, saṃpradhārya parasparam
pura|traya|visṛṣṭy|arthaṃ Mayaṃ vavrur mah'|âsuram
viśva|karmāṇam ajaraṃ, daitya|dānava|pūjitam.
tato Mayaḥ sva|tapasā cakre dhīmān purāṇi ca
trīṇi, kāñcanam ekaṃ vai, raupyaṃ, kārṣṇāyasaṃ tathā.
kāñcanaṃ divi tatr' āsīd, antarikṣe ca rājatam,
āyasaṃ c' âbhavad bhaumaṃ, cakra|sthaṃ, pṛthivī|pate.
ek'|âikaṃ yojana|śataṃ vistār'|āyāmataḥ samam,
gṛh'|âṭṭālaka|saṃyuktaṃ, bahu|prākāra|toraṇam,
33.20 gṛha|pravara|saṃbādham, a|saṃbādha|mahā|patham,
prāsādair vividhaiś c' âiva, dvāraiś c' âpy upaśobhitam.
pureṣu c' âbhavan, rājan, rājāno vai pṛthak pṛthak;

ing at any time. That god, the powerful lord of worlds, then said to them: 'There is no absolute immortality, demons,
you must turn away from this! Choose another boon the 33.10
like of which pleases you!'

After deliberating together over and over again, king, and after bowing to the powerful lord of all the worlds, they then spoke this speech:

'Grandfather, God, you offered us a boon. We will live in three cities and wander the earth preceded in this world by your grace. In a thousand years we will meet one another. And those cities, faultless one, will have become one. Lord, the best of the gods who with one arrow can then destroy them combined together will be our death!'

The god replied to them, 'Let it be so!' and entered 33.15
heaven. With their boon obtained the demons were delighted. After deliberating with one another, they chose the mighty demon Maya to create the three cities, the never-ageing all-creator worshipped by the *daitya* and *dánava* demons.

Learned Maya then created three cities through his own austerity. One was made of gold, one of silver and one of black iron. Forming a circle, the golden city was in heaven, the silver in the space between heaven and earth, and the iron city was on earth, lord of the earth. Each on its own was equal to a hundred *yójanas** in length and breadth. Each was filled with houses and watchtowers, and had many walls
with arched doorways. Each was crowded with mansions 33.20
and had wide and huge roads. Each was adorned with gateways and various palaces. And in each of the cities there were different kings, king. The beautiful golden city was

kāñcanaṃ Tārakākṣasya citram āsīn mah"|ātmanaḥ,
rājataṃ Kamalākṣasya, Vidyunmālina āyasam.
trayas te daitya|rājānas trīl lokān astra|tejasā
ākramya tasthur, ūcuś ca, ‹kaś ca nāma Prajāpatiḥ?›
teṣāṃ dānava|mukhyānāṃ prayutāny, arbudāni ca,
koṭyaś c' â|prativīrāṇāṃ samājagmus tatas tataḥ,
māṃs'|âśinaḥ su|dṛptāś ca surair vinikṛtāḥ purā,
33.25 mahad aiśvaryam icchantas, tri|puraṃ durgam āśritāḥ.
sarveṣāṃ ca punaś c' âiṣāṃ sarva|yoga|vaho Mayaḥ;
tam āśritya hi te sarve vartayante '|kuto|bhayāḥ.
yo hi yan manasā kāmaṃ dadhyau tri|pura|saṃśrayaḥ,
tasmai kāmaṃ Mayas taṃ taṃ vidadhe māyayā tadā.
Tārakākṣa|suto vīro Harir nāma mahā|balaḥ
tapas tepe paramakaṃ, yen' âtuṣyat Pitā|mahaḥ.
saṃtuṣṭam avṛṇod devaṃ, ‹vāpī bhavatu naḥ pure,
śastrair vinihatā yatra kṣiptāḥ, syur balavattarāḥ.›
sa tu labdhvā varaṃ, vīras Tārakākṣa|suto Hariḥ
33.30 sasṛje tatra vāpīṃ tāṃ mṛtānāṃ jīvanīṃ, prabho.
yena rūpeṇa daityas tu, yena veṣeṇa c' âiva ha
mṛtas tasyāṃ parikṣiptas, tādṛśen' âiva jajñivān.
tāṃ prāpya te punas tāṃs tu lokān sarvān babādhire,
mahatā tapasā siddhāḥ, surāṇāṃ bhaya|vardhanāḥ.
na teṣām abhavad, rājan, kṣayo yuddhe kadā cana.
tatas te lobha|mohābhyām abhibhūtā, vicetasaḥ,

great Tarakáksha's,* the silver Kamaláksha's and the iron Vidyun·malin's.

Those three demon-kings, after attacking the three worlds with the fiery power of their missiles, remained there and said, 'Who's called the Lord of beings?' Millions, ten million and tens of millions of the foremost demons who were without rival—immensely proud flesh-eaters who'd previously been mistreated by the gods—gathered together from all over the place and, seeking great power, took refuge in 33.25
the three impenetrable cities.

And furthermore, Maya brought everything to them all there. Relying on him, they all lived without fear from anyone. Whatever wish anyone taking refuge in the three cities could imagine Maya fulfilled for him with his magic.

Tarakáksha's son, an immensely powerful hero called Hari, underwent the most extreme austerity with which the Grandfather was pleased. He requested of that well satisfied god, 'Please, let us have a lake in our city where those who've been killed by weapons can be sent to become more powerful.'

After receiving that boon, powerful man, Tarakáksha's
heroic son Hari created a lake there that could revive the 33.30
dead. With whatever form and whatever garment a demon died, once he'd been thrown into it he was reborn with exactly the same appearance.

After obtaining the lake, the demons again oppressed all the worlds. Made powerful by their great austerity and provoking fear among the gods, there was no way at all to destroy them in battle, king. Overcome with greed and delusion, arrogant and foolish, they all then tore the established

nir|hrīkāḥ saṃsthitiṃ sarve sthāpitāṃ samalūlupan.
vidrāvya sa|gaṇān devāṃs tatra tatra tadā tadā
viceruḥ svena kāmena, vara|dānena darpitāḥ.
33.35 dev'|ôdyānāni sarvāṇi, priyāṇi ca div'|âukasām,
ṛṣīṇām āśramān puṇyān, ramyāñ jana|padāṃs tathā,
vyanāśayann a|maryādā dānavā duṣṭa|cāriṇaḥ.
pīḍyamāneṣu lokeṣu, tataḥ Śakro Marud|vṛtaḥ
purāṇy āyodhayāṃ cakre vajra|pātaiḥ samantataḥ.
n' âśakat tāny a|bhedyāni yadā bettuṃ Puraṃdaraḥ
purāṇi vara|dattāni dhātrā tena, nar'|âdhipa,
tadā bhītaḥ sura|patir muktvā tāni purāṇy atha
tair eva vibudhaiḥ sārdhaṃ Pitā|maham, ariṃ|dama,
jagām' âtha tad ākhyātuṃ viprakāraṃ sur'|êtaraiḥ.
33.40 te tattvaṃ sarvam ākhyāya, śirobhiḥ saṃpraṇamya ca,
vadh'|ôpāyam apṛcchanta bhagavantaṃ Pitā|maham.
śrutvā tad bhagavān devo devān idam uvāca ha:
‹mam' âpi so 'parādhnoti yo yuṣmākam a|saumya|kṛt.
asurā hi dur|ātmānaḥ sarva eva sura|dviṣaḥ
aparādhyanti satataṃ ye yuṣmān pīḍayanty uta.
ahaṃ hi tulyaḥ sarveṣāṃ bhūtānāṃ n' âtra saṃśayaḥ;
a|dhārmikās tu hantavyā! iti me vratam āhitam!
ek'|êṣuṇā vibhedyāni tāni durgāṇi, n' ânyathā.
na ca Sthāṇum ṛte śakto bhettum ek'|êṣuṇā puraḥ.
33.45 te yūyaṃ Sthāṇum īśānaṃ, jiṣṇum, a|kliṣṭa|kāriṇam
yoddhāraṃ vṛṇut', ādityāḥ. sa tān hantā sur'|êtarān!›

order to pieces. Made proud by the granting of the boon,
time and again they drove away the gods and their hordes in
all directions and roamed about at will. Those lawless and 33.35
evil demons destroyed all the sacred gardens held dear by the
gods, and the sacred ashrams and delightful communities
of sages.

As they oppressed the worlds, Shakra, surrounded by the
Maruts, made war against those cities by hurling lightning
bolts from all sides. When the Sacker of cities could not
destroy those indestructible cities that had been granted a
boon by the creator, ruler of men, the lord of the gods was
terrified. After quitting the cities, foe-conqueror, together
with the gods he went to the Grandfather to explain the
wicked things done by those opposed to the gods. They 33.40
explained everything truthfully to him and, bowing their
heads, asked the illustrious Grandfather for a way to destroy
them.

Once he'd heard this, the illustrious god said this to the
gods: 'Whoever brings displeasure to you also offends me.
Since those demons, all wicked enemies of the gods, always
oppress you, they offend me. There's no doubt that I'm
equitable to all beings; yet those who are unlawful should
be killed! That's the vow I've given! Those citadels can only
be destroyed by one arrow, in no other way. And none other
than Sthanu* can destroy that city with a single arrow. Gods, 33.45
you must choose lord Sthanu as your warrior. He's a winner
and never tires of doing deeds. He will kill those who are
opposed to the gods!'

iti tasya vacaḥ śrutvā devāḥ Śakra|puro|gamāḥ
Brahmāṇam agrataḥ kṛtvā Vṛṣāṅkaṃ śaraṇaṃ yayuḥ.
tapo|niyamam āsthāya, gṛṇanto Brahma śāśvatam
ṛṣibhiḥ saha dharma|jñā Bhavaṃ sarv'|ātmanā gatāḥ.
tuṣṭuvur vāgbhir ugrābhir bhayeṣv abhaya|daṃ, nṛpa,
Sarvātmānaṃ mah"|ātmānaṃ, yen' āptaṃ sarvam ātmanā.
tapo|viśeṣair vividhair yogaṃ yo veda c' ātmanaḥ,
yaḥ sāṃkhyam ātmano vetti, yasya c' ātmā vaśe sadā,
33.50 te taṃ dadṛśur Īśānaṃ, tejo|rāśim Umā|patim,
an|anya|sadṛśaṃ loke bhagavantam a|kalmaṣam.
ekaṃ ca bhagavantaṃ te nānā|rūpam akalpayan;
ātmanaḥ pratirūpāṇi rūpāṇy atha mah"|ātmani
parasparasya c' âpaśyan sarve parama|vismitāḥ.
sarva|bhūta|mayaṃ dṛṣṭvā tam a|jaṃ jagataḥ patim
devā brahma'|rṣayaś c' âiva śirobhir dharaṇīṃ gatāḥ.
tān svasti|vāden' âbhyarcya samutthāpya ca Śaṃkaraḥ
‹brūta! brūt'! êti› bhagavān smayamāno 'bhyabhāṣata.
Tryaṃbakeṇ' âbhyanujñātās tatas te svastha|cetasaḥ:
33.55 ‹namo! namo! namas te 'stu, prabho! ity› abruvan vacaḥ.
‹namo dev'|âdhidevāya, dhanvine vana|māline,
Prajāpati|makha|ghnāya Prajāpatibhir īḍyate!*
namaḥ stutāya, stutyāya, stūyamānāya Śaṃbhave,
vilohitāya, rudrāya, nīla|grīvāya, śūline,
a|moghāya, mṛg'|âkṣāya, pravar'|āyudha|yodhine,

After hearing his words, the gods, led by Shakra and placing Brahma at their head, went to Vrishánka* to seek protection. Once they'd performed the obligatory penance, those law-knowing gods recited the eternal Veda with the sages and, with complete conviction, went to Bhava.*

With powerful words they praised magnanimous Sarvátman,* king, who offered safety in crises and by whom all is filled with his soul. He who understands the cultivation of the soul through various kind of austerity, he who understands the discrimination of the soul, he who always has his soul under control, they saw him, Ishána, a mass of splen- 33.50
dor, the husband of Uma, illustrious and blemish free like no other in the world. Though he is one, they considered that lord to have many forms; and they saw the images that one another had of that soul as images in the great soul, and they were all immensely surprised. After seeing him, the non-born lord of the universe, as consisting of all beings, the gods and brahmin-sages touched the ground with their heads.

Honoring them with a benediction and raising them up, lord Shánkara smiled and said to them, 'Speak! Speak!'

As commanded by Try·ámbaka, their minds at ease, they
then spoke these words: 'Powerful lord, homage! Homage! 33.55
Let there be homage to you! Homage to the supreme god of gods, the archer garlanded with wildflowers, the destroyer of the sacrifice of the Lord of creatures* who is praised by the Praja·patis! Homage to Shambhu* who is praised, should be praised and is being praised, who is deep-red, who is fierce, whose neck is blue, who holds the trident, who never fails, whose are eyes like a deer's, who is a warrior with the

arhāya c' âiva, śuddhāya, kṣayāya krathanāya ca,
dur|vāraṇāya, krāthāya, brahmaṇe, brahma|cāriṇe,
Īśānāy' â|prameyāya, niyantre, carma|vāsase,
tapo|ratāya, piṃgāya, vratine, kṛtti|vāsase,
33.60 Kumāra|pitre, try|akṣāya, pravar'|āyudha|dhāriṇe,
prapann'|ārti|vināśāya, brahma|dviṭ|saṃgha|ghātine!
vanas|patīnāṃ pataye, narāṇāṃ pataye namaḥ!
gavāṃ ca pataye nityaṃ, yajñānāṃ pataye namaḥ!
namo 'stu te sa|sainyāya Tryambakāy' âmit'|âujase!
mano|vāk|karmabhir, Deva, tvāṃ prapannān bhajasva naḥ!›
tataḥ prasanno bhagavān sv|āgaten' âbhinandya ca
provāca, ‹vyetu vas trāso! brūta! kiṃ karavāṇi vaḥ?›»

DURYODHANA uvāca:

34.1 «PITṚ|DEVA'|ṚṢI|saṃghebhyo '|bhaye datte mah"|ātmanā,
sat|kṛtya Śaṃkaraṃ prāha Brahmā loka|hitaṃ vacaḥ:
‹tav' âtisargād, dev'|ēśa, prājāpatyam idaṃ padam
may" âdhitiṣṭhatā datto dānavebhyo mahān varaḥ.
tān atikrānta|maryādān n' ânyaḥ saṃhartum arhati
tvām ṛte, bhūta|bhavy'|ēśa, tvaṃ hy eṣāṃ pratyarir vadhe.
sa tvaṃ, Deva, prapannānāṃ yācatāṃ ca div'|âukasām
kuru prasādaṃ, dev'|ēśa! dānavāñ jahi, Śaṃkara!
34.5 tvat|prasādāj jagat sarvaṃ sukham aidhata, māna|da;
śaraṇyas tvaṃ hi, lok'|ēśa, te vayaṃ śaraṇaṃ gatāḥ.›

most excellent weapons, who is worthy and pure, who is destruction and a destroyer, who is irrepressible, a killer, a brahmin and a celibate, who is immeasurable Ishána, who is restrained, who wears a hide, who is intent on austerity,
who is yellow, who observes his vows, who wears a skin, who 33.60
is the father of Kumára,* who has three eyes, who holds excellent weapons, who is the destroyer of the distress of those who petition for it and who slaughters heretic groups! Homage to the lord of trees and the lord of men! Homage to the eternal lord of cows and lord of sacrifices! Let there be homage to you along with your army, to Try·ámbaka, whose energy has no limit! God, be gracious to us who entreat you with thought, speech and action!'

After greeting them with welcome, the gracious lord said, 'Let your fear go! Speak! What can I do for you?'"

DURYÓDHANA said:

"ONCE THAT GREAT soul had granted safety to the bands 34.1
of ancestors, gods and sages, Brahma honored Shánkara and spoke these words for the benefit of the worlds:

'I gave a great boon to the demons while in the position of lord of creatures at your behest, lord of the gods. Apart from you, lord of past and future, no one else could destroy those law violating demons. For when it comes to killing, you're an opponent well-matched for them. God, you must do this favor for the gods who've come to you and are begging you,
lord of the gods! Shánkara, destroy the demons! Because of 34.5
your grace the entire world became happy, giver of honor. You provide protection, lord of the worlds, so we've come to you for protection.'

STHĀṆUR uvāca:

‹hantavyāḥ śatravaḥ sarve yuṣmākam, iti me matiḥ!
na tv eka utsahe hantuṃ, bala|sthā hi sura|dviṣaḥ.
te yūyaṃ saṃhatāḥ sarve madīyen' ârdha|tejasā
jayadhvaṃ yudhi tāñ śatrūn, saṃhatā hi mahā|balāḥ!›

DEVĀ ūcuḥ:

‹asmat|tejo|balaṃ yāvat, tāvad dvi|guṇam āhave
teṣām, iti hi manyāmo; dṛṣṭa|tejo|balā hi te.›

STHĀṆUR uvāca:

‹vadhyās te sarvataḥ pāpā ye yuṣmāsv aparādhinaḥ!
mama tejo|bal'|ârdhena sarvān nighnata śātravān!›

DEVĀ ūcuḥ:

34.10 ‹bibhartuṃ bhavato 'rdhaṃ tu na śakṣyāmo, Maheśvara.
sarveṣāṃ no bal'|ârdhena tvam eva jahi śātravān!›

STHĀṆUR uvāca:

‹yadi śaktir na vaḥ kā cid bibhartuṃ māmakaṃ balam,
aham etān haniṣyāmi yuṣmat|tejo|'rdha|bṛṃhitaḥ!›
tatas ‹tath"! êti› dev'|ēśas tair ukto, rāja|sattama,
ardham ādāya sarveṣāṃ tejas" âbhyadhiko 'bhavat.
sa tu devo balen' āsīt sarvebhyo balavattaraḥ.
Mahādeva iti khyātas tataḥ|prabhṛti Śaṃkaraḥ.

STHANU said:

'All your enemies should be killed, that's what I think! But I can't kill them alone, for those enemies of the gods are powerful. All of you, united together with half my power, must conquer those enemies in battle, for there is great strength in being united!'

THE GODS said:

'As great as the strength of our power is, in battle theirs is twice that. That's what we believe, for we've seen the strength of their power.'

STHANU said:

'Those wretches offending against you should be completely annihilated! With half the strength of my power, destroy all those enemies!'

THE GODS said:

'But we can't bear half of you, Mahéshvara. Alone you 34.10
must destroy our enemies with half the power of all of us!'

STHANU said:

'If you don't have the ability to bear my power, then, enhanced by half your power, I'll slaughter them!'

'Yes!' they then said to the lord of the gods, finest of kings. Grabbing half of all their power, he became more extraordinary with their power. And with that power the god was more powerful than all of them. From this point on Shánkara was known as Maha·deva.*

tato 'bravīn Mahādevo, ‹dhanur|bāṇa|dharo hy aham
haniṣyāmi rathen' ājau tān ripūn vo, div'|âukasaḥ.
34.15 te yūyaṃ me rathaṃ c' âiva, dhanur, bāṇaṃ tath" âiva ca
paśyadhvaṃ, yāvad ady' âitān pātayāmi mahī|tale!›

DEVĀ ūcuḥ:

‹mūrtīḥ sarvāḥ samādhāya trailokyasya tatas tataḥ,
rathaṃ te kalpayiṣyāma, dev'|ēśvara, su|varcasam.›
tath" âiva buddhyā vihitaṃ, Viśvakarma|kṛtaṃ śubham
tato vibudha|śārdūlās te rathaṃ samakalpayan.
Viṣṇuṃ, Somaṃ, Hutāśaṃ ca tasy' êṣuṃ samakalpayan.
śṛṅgam Agnir babhūv' âsya, bhallaḥ Somo, viśāṃ pate,
kuḍmalaś c' âbhavad Viṣṇus tasminn iṣu|vare tadā.
rathaṃ vasuṃ|dharāṃ devīṃ viśāla|pura|mālinīm,
34.20 sa|parvata|vana|dvīpāṃ cakrur bhūta|dharāṃ tadā.
Mandaraḥ parvataś c' âkṣo, jaṃghā tasya Mahānadī,
diśaś ca pradiśaś c' âiva parivāro rathasya tu.
īṣā nakṣatra|vaṃśaś ca, yugaḥ Kṛta|yugo 'bhavat.
kūbaraś ca rathasy' āsīd Vāsukir bhujag'|ôttamaḥ.
apaskaram adhiṣṭhāne Himavān, Vindhya|parvataḥ,
uday'|âstāv adhiṣṭhāne girī cakruḥ sur'|ôttamāḥ.
samudram akṣam asṛjan dānav'|ālayam uttamam.
sapta'|rṣi|maṇḍalaṃ c' âiva rathasy' āsīt pariṣkaraḥ.
Gaṅgā, Sarasvatī, Sindhur dhuram, ākāśam eva ca,
upaskaro rathasy' āsann āpaḥ sarvāś ca nimna|gāḥ.
34.25 aho|rātraṃ, kalāś c' âiva, kāṣṭhāś ca, ṛtavas* tathā

Maha·deva then said, 'Brandishing my bow and arrows on my chariot in combat, gods, I will destroy those enemies of yours. You must watch my chariot, as well as my bow 34.15
and arrow, and how many that I drop to the ground today!'

THE GODS said:

'After collecting together all the manifestations of the triple-world from all over the place, we will put together a magnificent and beautiful chariot for you, lord of gods.'

Then, exactly as it was astutely designed and made by Vishva·karman, those tigers of gods prepared his beautiful chariot. They prepared his arrow from Vishnu, Soma and Agni. Agni became its horn-shaft, Soma its broad arrowhead, lord of the people, and Vishnu became the tip on that excellent arrow.

Then they made the chariot out of the goddess earth— 34.20
who sustains living things and is garlanded by enormous cities—along with her mountains, forests and islands. The Mándara mountain became an axle, the Great River* its shank and the regions and directions became the chariots's covering. A multitude of stars became its pole and the Krita epoch* its yoke. Vásuki, the most excellent serpent, became the chariot's railing. Those excellent gods made the Himalayan and the Vindhya ranges a pair of standing positions, and the eastern and western ranges standing positions as well. They made the ocean, that tremendous domicile of demons, an axle. The circle of seven sages became the chariot's wheel-guard. The Ganga, Sarásvati and Sindhu rivers,

anukarṣaṃ, grahā dīptā varūthaṃ, c' âpi tārakāḥ.
dharm'|ârtha|kāmaṃ saṃyuktaṃ tri|veṇu, dāru bandhuram
oṣadhīr, vīrudhāś c' âiva ghaṇṭāḥ puṣpa|phal'|ôpagāḥ.

sūryā|candramasau kṛtvā cakre ratha|var'|ôttame,
pakṣau pūrv'|âparau tatra kṛte rātry|ahanī śubhe.
daśa nāga|patīn īṣāṃ Dhṛtarāṣṭra|mukhāṃs tadā,
yoktrāṇi cakrur nāgāṃś ca niḥśvasanto mah"|ôragān;
dyāṃ yugaṃ, yuga|carmāṇi saṃvartaka|balāhakān.
Kālapṛṣṭho, 'tha Nahuṣaḥ, Karkoṭaka|Dhanaṃjayau,
34.30 itare c' âbhavan nāgā hayānāṃ vāla|bandhanāḥ.
diśaś ca pradiśaś c' âiva raśmayo ratha|vājinām.
Saṃdhyāṃ, Dhṛtiṃ ca, Medhāṃ ca,
Sthitiṃ, Saṃnatim eva ca,
graham|nakṣatra|tārābhiś
carma citraṃ, nabhas|talam.

sur'|âmbu|preta|vittānāṃ patīl lok'|ēśvarān hayān;
Sinīvālīm, Anumatiṃ, Kuhūṃ, Rākāṃ ca su|vratām
yoktrāṇi cakrur, vāhānāṃ rohakāṃs tatra kaṇṭakān.
dharmaḥ, satyaṃ, tapo, 'rthaś ca vihitās tatra raśmayaḥ,
adhiṣṭhānaṃ manaś c' āsīt, parirathyā Sarasvatī.

and the sky too, became its pole. All the rivers and waters became the chariot's furnishings. Day and night, min- 34.25
utes, instances and seasons, became its drag, and the blazing planets and stars became its bumper. Law, wealth and love together became the three bamboo pieces connecting the pole to the chariot. The wood became its seat. The herbs and creepers covered in fruits and flowers became its bells.

After the Sun and Moon were made the wheels of that exceptional chariot, day and night were made the wings on either side. They made the ten serpent chiefs led by Dhrita·rashtra* its pole, and those hissing great serpents the *nagas* the yoking-thongs. The sky was made the yoke and rolling clouds the leather pads attached to the yoke. Then
Kala·prishtha, Náhusha, Karkótaka, Dhanan·jaya and other 34.30
serpents became the cruppers for the horses. All the directions and regions became the chariot horses' reins. Twilight, Constancy, Intelligence, Rectitude and Humility, and the firmament decorated with the planets, constellations and stars, became its armor.

The masters of the worlds—the lords of the gods,* the waters, the dead and wealth—became the horses. They made the very auspicious moon-phases Siniváli, Ánumati, Kuhu and Raka the yoking-thongs of those horses, and those who ride on those moon-phases the pins securing them in. Law, truth, austerity and prosperity became the reins in that chariot, mind its base and Sarásvati its track.

nānā|varṇāś ca citrāś ca patākāḥ pavan'|eritāḥ,
34.35 vidyud|indradhanur|naddhaṃ rathaṃ dīptaṃ vyadīpayan.
vaṣaṭ|kāraḥ pratodo 'bhūd, Gāyatrī śīrṣa|bandhanā.
yo yajñe vihitaḥ pūrvam Īśānasya mah"|ātmanaḥ
saṃvatsaro, dhanus tad vai, Sāvitrī jyā mahā|svanā.
divyaṃ ca varma vihitaṃ mah"|ârhaṃ, ratna|bhūṣitam,
a|bhedyaṃ, virajaskaṃ vai, kāla|cakra|bahiṣ|kṛtam.
dhvaja|yaṣṭir abhūn Meruḥ śrīmān kanaka|parvataḥ,
patākāś c' âbhavan meghās taḍidbhiḥ samalaṃkṛtāḥ.

rejur adhvaryu|madhya|sthā jvalanta iva pāvakāḥ,
kḷptaṃ tu taṃ rathaṃ dṛṣṭvā, vismitā devat" âbhavan!
34.40 sarva|lokasya tejāṃsi dṛṣṭv" âika|sthāni, māriṣa,
yuktaṃ nivedayām āsur devās tasmai mah"|ātmane.

evaṃ tasmin, mahā|rāja, kalpite ratha|sattame
devair, manu|ja|śārdūla, dviṣatām abhimardane,
svāny āyudhāni mukhyāni nyadadhāc Chaṃkaro rathe.
dhvaja|yaṣṭiṃ viyat kṛtvā sthāpayām āsa go|vṛṣam.
Brahma|daṇḍaḥ, Kāla|daṇḍo, Rudra|daṇḍas, tathā jvaraḥ
pariskandā rathasy' āsan, sarvato|diśam udyatāḥ.
Atharv'|Âṅgirasāv āstāṃ cakra|rakṣau mah"|ātmanaḥ.
Ṛg|vedaḥ, Sāma|vedaś ca, purāṇaṃ ca puraḥ|sarāḥ.
34.45 itihāsa|Yajur|vedau pṛṣṭha|rakṣau babhūvatuḥ,
divyā vācaś ca vidyāś ca paripārśva|carāḥ sthitāḥ.
stotr'|âdayaś ca, rāj'|êndra, vaṣaṭ|kāras tath" âiva ca,
oṃ|kāraś ca mukhe, rājann, ati|śobhā|karo 'bhavat.

With its beautiful and variously colored flags buffeted by the wind, the gods illuminated that blazing chariot, binding 34.35
it with a rainbow and lightning. The exclamation "*vashat*" became the whip, the Gayátri chant the strap at its tip. The year as previously determined in the sacrifice of that great soul Ishána became the bow, and the Savítri chant its deafening bow-string. And valuable and divine armor was made. Adorned with jewels, impenetrable and unsullied, it was not subject to the wheel of time. The magnificent, golden mountain Meru became the flagpole, and the clouds, decorated by lightning, became the flags.

After seeing that chariot so prepared, the gods were amazed; they glowed like the fires blazing amidst Adhváryu priests!* After seeing the powers of the entire world assem- 34.40
bled together, dear friend, the gods gave that well-prepared chariot to the great soul.

Great king, once the gods had so put together that superb chariot for the suppression of their enemies, tiger of a man, Shánkara placed his own remarkable weapons in the chariot. After making the sky his flagpole, he raised up his bull banner. The rod of Brahma, the rod of Death, the rod of Rudra and fever became his servants at the flanks of the chariot, raised towards every direction. Athárvan and Ángiras became the wheel-protectors of that great soul. The *Rig·veda*,
Sama·veda and *puránas** became his advance runners. The 34.45
historical tales and the *Yajur·veda** became the protectors at his back and the divine utterances and sciences were situated at his sides. The eulogies and so on, lord of kings, the exclamation "*vashat*" and the sound "*Om*" were in the front of the chariot, king, making it extremely beautiful.

vicitram ṛtubhiḥ ṣaḍbhiḥ kṛtvā saṃvatsaraṃ dhanuḥ,
chāyām ev' ātmanaś cakre dhanur|jyām a|kṣayāṃ raṇe.
Kālo hi bhagavān Rudras, tasya saṃvatsaro dhanuḥ,
tasmād raudrī Kāla|rātrir jyā kṛtā dhanuṣo '|jarā.
iṣuś c' âpy abhavad Viṣṇur, Jvalanaḥ, Soma eva ca.
Agnī|Ṣomau jagat kṛtsnaṃ, Vaiṣṇavaṃ c' ôcyate jagat.
34.50 Viṣṇuś c' ātmā bhagavato Bhavasy' âmita|tejasaḥ,
tasmād dhanur|jyā|saṃsparśaṃ na viṣehur Harasya te.
tasmiñ śare tigma|manyuṃ mumoc' âsahyaṃ īśvaraḥ
Bhṛgv|Aṅgiro|manyu|bhavaṃ krodh'|âgnim ati|duḥ|saham.
sa Nīlalohito dhūmraḥ, kṛtti|vāsā, bhayaṃ|karaḥ,
ādity'|âyuta|saṃkāśas, tejo|jvāl'|āvṛto jvalan,
duś|cyāva|cyāvano, jetā, hantā, Brahma|dviṣāṃ haraḥ,
nityaṃ trātā ca, hantā ca dharm'|âdharm'|āśritān narān.
pramāthibhir bhīma|balair, bhīma|rūpair, mano|javaiḥ
vibhāti bhagavān Sthāṇus tair ev' ātma|guṇair vṛtaḥ.
34.55 tasy' âṅgāni samāśritya sthitaṃ viśvam idaṃ jagat
jaṅgam'|â|jaṅgamaṃ, rājañ, śuśubhe 'dbhuta|darśanam!
dṛṣṭvā tu taṃ rathaṃ yuktaṃ, kavacī sa śar'|âsanī
bāṇam ādāya taṃ divyaṃ Soma|Viṣṇv|Agni|saṃbhavam,
tasya, rājaṃs, tadā devāḥ kalpayāṃ cakrire, prabho,
puṇya|gandha|vahaṃ, rājañ, Śvasanaṃ deva|sattamam.
tam āsthāya Mahādevas trāsayan daivatāny api
āruroha tadā yattaḥ, kampayann iva medinīm.

After making the year with the six seasons his spectacular bow, he made his own shadow its bow-string, and it never failed in battle. Since Time* is lord Rudra and his bow is the year, therefore the terrible night of Time was formed into the never-flagging bow-string of his bow. And further, Vishnu, Agni and Soma became his arrow. Agni and Soma are the entire universe; and the universe is said to consist of Vishnu. Vishnu is the soul of the lord Bhava whose power 34.50
is without measure. Consequently, they* could not bear the touch of the bow-string of Hara's* bow. The lord released on to that arrow his unbearable, violent rage, the utterly insufferable fire of anger that arose from the rage of Bhrigu and Ángiras.

Wearing only a skin, inciting fear and encompassed by the flames of his power, dark red Nila·lóhita* blazed like ten-thousand suns. Felling those who are difficult to fell, a vanquisher, a killer, the destroyer of Brahma's enemies, he always protects men devoted to law and kills those devoted to its opposite. Lord Sthanu was resplendent surrounded by his own virtues and by destructive beings of terrible power and appearance that were as quick as thought. Taking refuge in 34.55
his limbs, the entire universe—moving and non-moving—remained there, king. It was beautiful. A spectacular sight!

Once he'd seen that the chariot had been finished, donning his armor and picking up his bow, he grabbed the divine arrow born from Soma, Vishnu and Agni. Then, powerful king, the gods made the Wind, the most excellent of the gods, convey a sweet scent to him, king. Maha·deva climbed and then keenly mounted the chariot, terrifying even the gods and almost making the earth tremble.

tam āruruksụm dev'|ēśaṃ tuṣṭuvuḥ parama'|rṣayaḥ,
gandharvā, deva|saṃghāś ca, tath" âiv' âpsarasāṃ gaṇāḥ.
34.60 brahma'|rṣibhiḥ stūyamāno vandyamānaś ca bandhibhiḥ,
tath" âiv' âpsarasāṃ vṛndair nṛtyadbhir nṛtya|kovidaiḥ,
sa śobhamāno, vara|daḥ, khaḍgī, bāṇī, śar'|âsanī
hasann iv' âbravīd devān, ‹sārathiḥ ko bhaviṣyati?›
tam abruvan deva|gaṇā, ‹yaṃ bhavān saṃniyokṣyate,
sa bhaviṣyati, dev'|ēśa, sārathis te, na saṃśayaḥ!›
tān abravīt punar devo, ‹mattaḥ śreṣṭhataro hi yaḥ,
taṃ sārathiṃ kurudhvaṃ me svayaṃ saṃcintya mā|ciram!›
etac chrutvā tato devā vākyam uktaṃ mah"|ātmanā
gatvā Pitā|mahaṃ devāḥ prasādy' êdaṃ vaco 'bruvan:
34.65 ‹yathā tvat|kathitaṃ, Deva, tri|daś'|âri|vinigrahe,
tathā ca kṛtam asmābhiḥ. prasanno no vṛṣa|dhvajaḥ.
rathaś ca vihito 'smābhir vicitr'|āyudha|saṃvṛtaḥ.
sārathiṃ ca na jānīmaḥ. kaḥ syāt tasmin rath'|ôttame?
tasmād vidhīyatāṃ kaś cit sārathir, deva|sattama.
sa|phalāṃ tāṃ giraṃ, Deva, kartum arhasi no, vibho.
evam asmāsu hi purā, bhagavann, uktavān asi,
«hita|kart" âsmi bhavatām! iti» tat kartum arhasi!

The eminent sages, the *gandhárvas*, the bands of gods and the hordes of *ápsarases* sung the praises of the lord of the gods as he eagerly ascended the chariot. While he was 34.60
praised by the brahmin-sages and venerated by the bards and the dancing dancing-troops of the *ápsarases* too, the boon-giver, looking brilliant and bearing his sword, arrow and bow, said to the gods as he nearly laughed, 'Who'll be my chariot-driver?'

The hordes of gods said to him, 'Lord of gods, whomever you appoint will become your chariot-driver, without a doubt!'

The god again spoke to them. 'Quickly think it over among yourselves and then make whoever is better than me my chariot-driver!'

After hearing those words uttered by that great soul and approaching the Grandfather, the gods reverently spoke this speech: 'We did just as you told us, God, to suppress the en- 34.65
emies of the gods. The one whose emblem is a bull* was gracious to us. We prepared his chariot and furnished him with various weapons. But we do not know who his chariot-driver is. Who should be his chariot-driver in that superb chariot? Therefore, please appoint someone as chariot-driver, most excellent of the gods. Powerful God, please make your words bear fruit for us. For previously, lord, you said to us, "I'll promote your interests!" Please do so now!

sa, Deva, yukto ratha|sattamo no
durādharo, drāvaṇaḥ śātravāṇām;
Pināka|pāṇir vihito 'tra yoddhā
vibhīṣayan dānavān udyato 'sau!
34.70 tath" âiva vedāś caturo hay'|âgryā,
dharā sa|śailā ca ratho mah"|ātmanaḥ,
nakṣatra|vaṃś'|ânugato, varūthī;
Haro yoddhā, sārathir n' âbhilakṣyaḥ!
tatra sārathir eṣṭavyaḥ sarvair etair viśeṣavān;
tat|pratiṣṭho ratho, Deva, hayā, yoddhā tath" âiva ca,
kavacāni sa|śastrāṇi, kārmukaṃ ca, Pitā|maha.
tvām ṛte sārathiṃ tatra n' ânyaṃ paśyāmahe vayam,
tvaṃ hi sarva|guṇair yukto, daivatābhyo 'dhikaḥ, prabho.
sa rathaṃ tūrṇam āruhya saṃyaccha paramān hayān
jayāya tri|div'|ēśānāṃ, vadhāya tri|daśa|dviṣām!›
iti te śirasā gatvā tri|lok'|ēśaṃ Pitā|maham,
devāḥ prasādayām āsuḥ sārathyāy', êti naḥ śrutam!

PITĀ|MAHA UVĀCA:

34.75 ‹n' âtra kiṃ cin mṛṣā vākyaṃ yad uktaṃ, tri|div'|âukasaḥ.
saṃyacchāmi hayān eṣa yudhyato vai Kapardinaḥ!›

We've prepared the most excellent of chariots, God,
That is invincible and shall put our enemies to flight.
The god wielding the Pináka bow was determined its warrior;
Terrifying the demons, he is ready to go!
The earth with its mountains is the chariot of that great soul, 34.70
Likewise the four Vedas are its foremost horses
And its armor was acquired from a multitude of stars.
Hara is the warrior; but the chariot-driver has yet to be determined!

It's desirable that the chariot-driver is better than all these. The chariot and the horses—and the warrior as well—rely upon him, God, as do the warrior's armor, weapons and bow, Grandfather. We see no one other than you as its chariot-driver. For you possess all the qualities and are superior to the other gods, master. You must quickly mount that chariot and guide those superb horses to victory for the lords of heaven and for the destruction of the gods' enemies!'

Bowing to the Grandfather, the lord of the triple-world, the gods asked him to assume the station of chariot-driver. This is what we're taught!

THE GRANDFATHER said:

'On this matter, gods, you've not spoken these words in 34.75
vain. I shall control the horses while Kapárdin* fights!'

tataḥ sa bhagavān devo loka|sraṣṭā Pitā|mahaḥ
sārathye kalpito devair Īśānasya mah"|ātmanaḥ.
tasminn ārohati kṣipraṃ syandane loka|pūjite,
śirobhir agaman bhūmiṃ te hayā vāta|raṃhasaḥ.
āruhya bhagavān devo dīpyamānaḥ sva|tejasā
abhīśūn hi pratodaṃ ca saṃjagrāha Pitā|mahaḥ.
tata utthāya bhagavāṃs tān hayān anil'|ôpamān
babhāṣe ca tadā Sthāṇum, ‹āroh'! êti› sur'|ôttamaḥ.
tatas tam iṣum ādāya Viṣṇu|Som'|Âgni|saṃbhavam,
34.80 āruroha tadā Sthāṇur dhanuṣā kampayan parān.
tam ārūḍhaṃ tu dev'|ēśaṃ tuṣṭuvuḥ parama'|rṣayaḥ,
gandharvā, deva|saṃghāś ca, tath" âiv' âpsarasāṃ gaṇāḥ.
sa śobhamāno vara|daḥ, khaḍgī, bāṇī, śar'|âsanī
pradīpayan rathe tasthau trīl lokān svena tejasā.
tato bhūyo 'bravīd devo devān Indra|purogamān:
‹«na hanyād! iti» kartavyo na śoko vaḥ kathaṃ cana;
hatān ity eva jānīta bānen' ânena c' âsurān!›
te devāḥ ‹satyam! ity› āhur, ‹nihatā! iti› c' âbruvan.
‹na ca tad vacanaṃ mithyā yad āha bhagavān prabhuḥ!›
34.85 iti saṃcintya vai devāḥ parāṃ tuṣṭim avāpnuvan.
tataḥ prayāto dev'|ēśaḥ sarvair deva|gaṇair vṛtaḥ
rathena mahatā, rājann, upamā n' âsti yasya ha.
svaiś ca pāriṣadair devaḥ pūjyamāno mahā|yaśāḥ,
nṛtyadbhir aparaiś c' âiva māṃsa|bhakṣair dur|āsadaiḥ,

Then the Grandfather, that illustrious god who created the worlds, was confirmed in the position of chariot-driver for that great soul Ishána. As he who is honored in all the worlds quickly mounted that chariot, the horses that were as swift as wind touched their heads to the ground. After mounting the chariot, the Grandfather, the illustrious god who was luminous with his own fiery energy, took hold of the reins and the whip. The illustrious, most excellent of the gods, then raised those horses that were the equal of the wind and called out to Sthanu, 'Mount!'

Once he'd grabbed the arrow born from Vishnu, Soma
and Agni, Sthanu then mounted the chariot with his bow, 34.80
making his enemies tremble. And the pre-eminent sages praised the lord of the gods as he mounted, as did the *gandhárvas*, the groups of gods and the hordes of *ápsaras*es. That giver of boons, shining brilliantly with his sword, arrow and bow, stood in the chariot lighting the triple-world with his own fiery energy. Once more that god spoke to the gods who were led by Indra:

'Don't at all feel glum, thinking, "He can't kill them!" Know that the demons have already been slaughtered with this arrow!'

The gods exclaimed, 'It's true!' and said, 'They're dead!' 34.85
The gods became quite content, thinking, 'The words that the powerful lord spoke are not false!'

Surrounded by all the hordes of the gods, the lord of the gods then set out on that great chariot which had no equal, king. That much celebrated god was worshipped by his own retinue and by other dangerous flesh-eaters who danced and ran about on all sides threatening one another. And highly

dhāvamānaiḥ samantāc ca, tarjamānaiḥ parasparam,
ṛṣayaś ca mahā|bhāgās, tapo|yuktā, mahā|guṇāḥ
āśaṃsur vai jayaṃ devā Mahādevasya sarvaśaḥ.
evaṃ prayāte dev'|ēśe lokānām abhayaṃ|kare,
tuṣṭam āsīj jagat sarvaṃ, devatāś ca, nar'|ôttama.
34.90 ṛṣayas tatra dev'|ēśaṃ stuvanto bahubhiḥ stavaiḥ,
tejaś c' âsmai vardhayanto, rājann, āsan punaḥ punaḥ,
gandharvāṇām sahasrāṇi, prayutāny, arbudāni ca
vādayanti prayāṇe 'sya vādyāni vividhāni ca.
tato 'dhirūḍhe vara|de, prayāte c' âsurān prati,
‹sādhu! sādhv! iti› viśv'|ēśaḥ smayamāno 'bhyabhāṣata.
‹yāhi, Deva, yato daityāś! coday' âśvān a|tandritaḥ!
paśya bāhvor balaṃ me 'dya nighnataḥ śātravān raṇe!›
tato 'śvāṃś codayām āsa mano|māruta|raṃhasaḥ,
yena tat tri|puraṃ, rājan, daitya|dānava|rakṣitam.
34.95 pibadbhir iva c' ākāśaṃ tair hayair loka|pūjitaiḥ
jagāma bhagavān kṣipraṃ jayāya tri|div'|âukasām.
prayāte ratham āsthāya tri|pur'|âbhimukhe Bhave,
nanāda su|mahā|nādaṃ vṛṣabhaḥ, pūrayan diśaḥ.
vṛṣabhasy' âsya ninadaṃ śrutvā bhaya|karaṃ mahat,
vināśam agamaṃs tatra Tārakāḥ sura|śatravaḥ.
apare 'vasthitās tatra yuddhāy' âbhimukhās tadā.
tataḥ Sthāṇur, mahā|rāja, śūla|dhṛk, krodha|mūrchitaḥ.
trastāni sarva|bhūtāni, trailokyaṃ bhūḥ prakampate,
nimittāni ca ghorāṇi tatra saṃdadhataḥ śaram.

distinguished sages who were intent upon austerities and had great qualities, and all the gods as well, hoped wholeheartedly for the victory of Maha·deva.

When the lord of the gods, who brought security to the worlds, set out in this way, the entire universe was content,
finest of men, as were the gods. The sages there praised him 34.90
with many eulogies, increasing his fiery energy again and again, and thousands, millions and tens of millions of *gandhárvas* played various instruments for him as he departed.

After the boon-giver had mounted his chariot and headed for the demons, the lord of the universe* said with a grin, 'Excellent! Excellent! Go, God, to where the demons are! Drive those horses without rest! Watch the strength of my arms today as I strike down our enemies in battle!'

Then he drove those horses that were as swift as thought and wind to the three cities that were protected by the *daitya*
tya and *dánava* demons. With those horses honored in all 34.95
the worlds that seemed to drink in the sky, the lord quickly set out intent on victory for the gods.

When Bhava arrived before the three cities after mounting his chariot, his bull bellowed a mighty bellow, filling the directions. Hearing the bull's massive fear-provoking bellow, Táraka's sons, the gods' enemies, became utterly lost there. Others who stood there then prepared for battle.

Then, great king, Sthanu brandished his trident and swelled with rage. All beings trembled and the triple-world and the ground shook. And there were terrible omens as he fixed his arrow.

34.100 tasmin Som'|Âgni|Viṣṇūnāṃ
kṣobheṇa Brahma|Rudrayoḥ
sa ratho dhanuṣaḥ kṣobhād
atīva hy avasīdati.
tato Nārāyaṇas tasmāc chara|bhāgād viniḥsṛtaḥ,
vṛṣa|rūpaṃ samāsthāya ujjahāra mahā|ratham.
sīdamāne rathe c' âiva, nardamāneṣu śatruṣu,
sa saṃbhramāt tu bhagavān nādaṃ cakre mahā|balaḥ.
vṛṣabhasya sthito mūrdhni, haya|pṛṣṭhe ca, māna|da,
tadā sa bhagavān Rudro niraikṣad dānavaṃ puram.
vṛṣbhasy' āsthito, Rudro hayasya ca, nar'|ôttama,
stanāṃs tad" âśātayata, khurāṃś c' âiva dvidh" âkarot.
34.105 tataḥ|prabhṛti, bhadraṃ te, gavāṃ dvaidhī|kṛtāḥ khurāḥ!
hayānāṃ ca stanā, rājaṃs, tadā|prabhṛti n' âbhavan,
pīḍitānāṃ balavatā Rudreṇ' âdbhuta|karmaṇā!
ath' âdhijyaṃ dhanuḥ kṛtvā Śarvaḥ saṃdhāya taṃ śaram
yuktvā Pāśupat'|âstreṇa, tri|puraṃ samacintayat.
tasmin sthite, mahā|rāja, Rudre vidhṛta|kārmuke,
purāṇi tāni kālena jagmur ev' âikatāṃ tadā!
ekī|bhāvaṃ gate c' âiva, Tripuratvam upāgate,
babhūva tumulo harṣo devatānāṃ mah"|ātmanām.
tato deva|gaṇāḥ sarve, siddhāś ca, parama'|rṣayaḥ,
34.110 ‹jay'! êti› vāco mumucuḥ saṃstuvanto Maheśvaram.
tato 'grataḥ prādur abhūt Tripuraṃ nighnato 'surān
a|nirdeśy'|ôgra|vapuṣo devasy' â|sahya|tejasaḥ.
sa tad vikṛṣya bhagavān divyaṃ lok'|ēśvaro dhanuḥ,
trailokya|sāraṃ tam iṣuṃ mumoca Tri|puraṃ prati.

But due to the agitation of Soma, Agni and Vishnu in that 34.100
arrow and because of the frenzied agitation of Brahma and Rudra and his bow, the chariot sunk down. Then Naráyana* emerged from a section of that arrow and, assuming the form of a bull, extricated that great chariot. As the chariot sank and his enemies shrieked, the powerful lord roared impatiently. Standing on the head of his bull and the back of his horse, giver of honor, illustrious Rudra then surveyed the demon city.

Standing tall, Rudra cut off the horses' teats and split the
bulls' hooves in two, excellent man. From that point on—if 34.105
you please!—cows had cloven hooves! And from that point on, king, the teats of horses—mutilated by powerful Rudra as he behaved miraculously—were no more!

Stringing his bow, nocking the arrow and joining it with the Páshupata weapon, Sharva carefully considered the three cities. As Rudra stood there holding his bow, great king, at that moment the cities became one! Once they had become one and turned into Triple-city, tumultuous joy came forth from the great gods. Then all the hordes of gods, *siddha*s
and distinguished sages lauded Mahéshvara and let loose 34.110
the word 'Victory!'

Then Triple-city rose up before that god as he struck down demons, his terrible form incomparable and his vitality insufferable. Bending his divine bow, the illustrious lord of the world released the arrow that was the essence of the triple-world at Triple-city.

utsṛṣṭe vai, mahā|bhāga, tasminn iṣu|vare tadā
mahān ārta|svaro hy āsīt purāṇāṃ patatāṃ bhuvi.
tān so 'sura|gaṇaṃ dagdhvā prākṣipat paścim'|ârṇave.
evaṃ tu Tri|puraṃ dagdhaṃ, dānavāś c' âpy a|śeṣataḥ,
Maheśvareṇa kruddhena trailokyasya hit'|âiṣiṇā.
34.115 sa c' ātma|krodha|jo vahnir, ‹hāh"! êty› uktvā nivāritaḥ,
‹mā kārṣīr bhasmasāl lokān! iti› Tryakṣo 'bravīc ca tam.
tataḥ prakṛtim āpannā devā, lokās tv, atha' rṣayaḥ
tuṣṭuvur vāgbhir agryābhiḥ Sthāṇum a|pratim'|âujasam.
te 'nujñātā bhagavatā jagmuḥ sarve yath"|āgatam,
kṛta|kāmāḥ prayatnena Prajāpati|mukhāḥ surāḥ.
evaṃ sa bhagavān devo loka|sraṣṭā Maheśvaraḥ
dev'|âsura|gaṇ'|âdhyakṣo lokānāṃ vidadhe śivam.
yath" âiva bhagavān Brahmā loka|dhātā Pitā|mahaḥ
sārathyam akarot tatra Rudrasya paramo 'vyayaḥ,
34.120 tathā bhavān api kṣipraṃ, Rudrasy' êva Pitā|mahaḥ,
saṃyacchatu hayān asya Rādheyasya mah"|ātmanaḥ.
tvaṃ hi Kṛṣṇāc ca, Karṇāc ca, Phalgunāc ca viśeṣataḥ
viśiṣṭo, rāja|śārdūla, n' âsti tatra vicāraṇā.
yuddhe hy ayaṃ Rudra|kalpas, tvaṃ ca Brahma|samo naye;
tasmāc chakto bhavāñ jetuṃ mac|chatrūṃs, tān iv' âsurān.
yathā, Śaly', âdya Karṇo 'yaṃ śvet'|âśvaṃ Kṛṣṇa|sārathim
pramathya hanyāt Kaunteyaṃ, tathā śīghraṃ vidhīyatām.
tvayi, Madr'|ēśa, rājy'|āśā, jīvit'|āśā tath" âiva ca,

When that superb arrow was released, eminent man, a massive cry of pain came from those cities as they crashed to earth. After he had burnt hordes of demons he tossed them into the western sea.

In this way furious Mahéshvara, desiring prosperity for the triple-world, burnt Triple-city and left the demons with no survivors. Yelling 'Ha! Ha!' Tryáksha* quelled the fire 34.115
born from his own rage and said to it, 'Don't reduce the worlds to ashes!'

The gods, worlds and sages then regained their original dispositions and, with the finest words, praised Sthanu whose power had no measure. Dismissed by the lord, all the gods departed as they had come with Praja·pati in their lead, their desires fulfilled through this endeavor.

In this way, that illustrious god Mahéshvara, the creator of the worlds and overseer of the hordes of gods and demons, did what was best for the worlds.

Just as the supreme, undecaying and illustrious Brahma, creator of the worlds, the Grandfather, became Rudra's driver then, so you also must take immediate control of the 34.120
steeds of Radha's great son like the Grandfather took control of Rudra's. For without a doubt, tiger of a king, you above all are better than Krishna, Karna and Phálguna. In battle Karna is the equal of Rudra and in prudent conduct you are the equal of Brahma. You, therefore, can defeat my enemies just as they defeated the demons. Please do this quickly, Shalya, so that today Karna can crush and kill Kunti's son whose horses are white and whose chariot-driver is Krishna. On you, lord of Madra, rest the hopes of the kingdom; on you also rest the hopes for life. Equally, victory today

vijayaś ca tath" âiv' âdya Karna|sācivya|kāritaḥ.
34.125 tvayi Karṇaś ca, rājyaṃ ca, vayaṃ c' âiva pratiṣṭhitāḥ,
vijayaś c' âiva saṃgrāme; saṃyacch' âdya hay'|ôttamān!

imaṃ c' âpy aparaṃ bhūya itihāsaṃ nibodha me,
pitur mama sakāśe yad brāhmaṇaḥ prāha dharma|vit!
śrutvā c' âitad vacaś citraṃ hetu|kāry'|ârtha|saṃhitam,
kuru, Śalya, viniścitya! mā bhūd atra vicāraṇā!

Bhārgavāṇāṃ kule jāto Jamadagnir mahā|yaśāḥ,
tasya Rām' êti vikhyātaḥ putras tejo|guṇ'|ânvitaḥ.
sa tīvraṃ tapa āsthāya prasādayitavān Bhavam
astra|hetoḥ, prasann'|ātmā, niyataḥ, saṃyat'|êndriyaḥ.
34.130 tasya tuṣṭo mahā|devo bhaktyā ca, praśamena ca,
hṛd|gataṃ c' âsya vijñāya darśayām āsa Śaṃkaraḥ.

MAHEŚVARA uvāca:

‹Rāma, tuṣṭo 'smi! bhadraṃ te! viditaṃ me tav' ēpsitam.
kuruṣva pūtam ātmānaṃ. sarvam etad avāpsyasi!
dāsyāmi te tad" âstrāṇi, yadā pūto bhaviṣyasi;
a|pātram a|samarthaṃ ca dahanty astrāṇi, Bhārgava!›

ity ukto Jāmadagnyas tu deva|devena śūlinā
pratyuvāca mah"|ātmānaṃ śiras" âvanataḥ prabhum:
‹yadā jānāti dev'|ēśaḥ pātraṃ mām astra|dhāraṇe,
tadā śuśrūṣave 'strāṇi bhavān me dātum arhati.›»

shall come down to the assistance you give Karna. On you depends Karna, the kingdom and us too, as does victory in battle; today you must lead these superb horses! 34.125

Listen to me once again about this other story that a law-knowing brahmin related in my father's presence! After hearing these beautiful words endowed with reason and purpose, feeling reassured, you must act, Shalya! In this there can be no hesitation!

Famous Jamad·agni who was born in the lineage of the Bhárgavas had a son called Rama who was filled with merit and vigor. After enduring terrible austerity, with his senses under control, self-disciplined and his body purified, he asked Bhava for his weapons. The great god Shánkara was 34.130
pleased with his devotion and tranquility and, recognising what he cherished in his heart, revealed himself to him.

MAHÉSHVARA said:

'Rama, I am pleased! Good fortune to you! I know what you want. Make yourself pure and you'll receive everything! I will give you weapons once you're purified; weapons that burn the unworthy and the unsuitable, Bhárgava!'

So spoken to by the trident-wielding god of gods, Jamad·agni's son bowed his head and replied to that powerful great soul: 'When you, the lord of the gods, recognise me as worthy to bear these weapons, then please give the weapons to me who serves you well.'"

DURYODHANA uvāca:

34.135 «tataḥ sa tapasā c' âiva, damena, niyamena ca,
pūj"|ôpahāra|balibhir homa|mantra|puras|kṛtaiḥ,
ārādhayitavāñ Śarvaṃ bahūn varṣa|gaṇāṃs tadā.
prasannaś ca Mahādevo Bhārgavasya mah"|ātmanaḥ
abravīt tasya bahuśo guṇān Devyāḥ samīpataḥ:
‹bhakti|mān eṣa satataṃ mayi Rāmo, dṛḍha|vrataḥ!›
evaṃ tasya guṇān prīto bahuśo 'kathayat prabhuḥ
devatānāṃ pitṝṇāṃ ca samakṣam, ari|sūdana.
etasminn eva kāle tu, daityā āsan mahā|balāḥ.
tais tadā darpa|moh'|ândhair abādhyanta div'|âukasaḥ.
34.140 tataḥ saṃbhūya vibudhās tān hantuṃ kṛta|niścayāḥ,
cakruḥ śatru|vadhe yatnaṃ, na śekur jetum eva tān.
abhigamya tato devā Maheśvaram Umā|patim
prāsādayaṃs tadā bhaktyā, ‹jahi śatru|gaṇān! iti.›
pratijñāya tato devo devatānāṃ ripu|kṣayam,
Rāmaṃ Bhārgavam āhūya so 'bhyabhāṣata Śaṃkaraḥ,
‹ripūn, Bhārgava, devānāṃ jahi sarvān samāgatān,
lokānāṃ hita|kām'|ârthaṃ, mat|prīty|arthaṃ tath" âiva ca!›
evam uktaḥ pratyuvāca Tryaṃbakaṃ vara|daṃ prabhum.

RĀMA uvāca:

‹kā śaktir mama, dev'|ēśa, a|kṛt'|âstrasya saṃyuge
34.145 nihantuṃ dānavān sarvān kṛt'|âstrān, yuddha|dur|madān?›

DURYÓDHANA said:

"Then, for a long sequence of years, he worshipped Sharva with austerity, self-control and discipline, and with offerings, oblations and homage preceded by mantras and sacrifices. Maha·deva was pleased with the great Bhárgava and said of his many merits before his wife Devi, 'Rama's vows are firm and he is constant in his devotion to me!' In this way that delighted god described his merits in the presence of the gods and ancestors, destroyer of enemies. 34.135

In the meantime, however, the demons had become immensely powerful. Then, blind with conceit and stupidity, they oppressed the gods. Uniting together, the wise gods resolved to kill them. But though they expended great effort to kill their enemies, they could not defeat them. 34.140

After approaching Mahéshvara, the husband of Uma, they begged of him with devotion, 'Destroy the hordes of our enemies!'

The god Shánkara promised to destroy the enemies of the gods and, summoning Rama Bhárgava, said, 'Bhárgava, out of a desire for the well-being of the world and for your love of me, destroy all those enemies of the gods that have assembled together!'

Spoken to like this, he replied to Try·ámbaka the powerful boon-giver.

RAMA said:

'Ill-equipped with weapons, lord of gods, what capacity do I have to kill all those battle-mad demons in combat when they're equipped with weapons?' 34.145

MAHEŚVARA uvāca:

‹gaccha tvaṃ mad|anujñāto! nihaniṣyasi śātravān.
vijitya ca ripūn sarvān, guṇān prāpsyasi puṣkalān.›
etac chrutvā ca vacanaṃ, pratigṛhya ca sarvaśaḥ,
Rāmaḥ kṛta|svasty|ayanaḥ prayayau dānavān prati.
abravīd deva|śatrūṃs tān mahā|darpa|bal'|ânvitān:
‹mama yuddhaṃ prayacchadhvaṃ,
daityā yuddha|mad'|ôtkaṭāḥ!
preṣito deva|devena
vo vijetuṃ, mah'|âsurāḥ!›
ity uktā Bhārgaveṇ' âtha daityā yuddhaṃ pracakramuḥ.
sa tān nihatya samare daityān Bhārgava|nandanaḥ
34.150 vajr'|âśani|sama|sparśaiḥ prahārair eva Bhārgavaḥ,
sa dānavaiḥ kṣata|tanur Jāmadagnyo dvij'|ôttamaḥ
saṃspṛṣṭaḥ Sthāṇunā sadyo nirvraṇaḥ samajāyata.
prītaś ca bhagavān devaḥ karmaṇā tena tasya vai,
varān prādād bahu|vidhān Bhārgavāya mah"|ātmane.
uktaś ca deva|devena prīti|yuktena śūlinā:
‹nipātāt tava śastrāṇāṃ śarīre y" âbhavad rujā,
tayā te mānuṣaṃ karma vyapoḍhaṃ, Bhṛgu|nandana.
gṛhāṇ' âstrāṇi divyāni mat|sakāśād, yath" ēpsitam!›»

DURYODHANA uvāca:

«tato 'strāṇi samastāni, varāṃś ca manas" ēpsitān
34.155 labdhvā bahu|vidhān Rāmaḥ, praṇamya śirasā Bhavam,
anujñāṃ prāpya dev'|ēśāj jagāma sa mahā|tapāḥ.

MAHÉSHVARA said:

'You must go as I commanded! You will kill those enemies. Once you defeat all those enemies you will earn many merits.'

Rama heard and completely grasped this speech and, commended to the protection of the gods, advanced towards the demons. He said to those enemies of the gods who were filled with great conceit and power: 'Fight with me, demons, if you're furious for a fight! I've been sent by the god of gods to defeat you, mighty demons!'

So spoken to by Bhárgava, the demons began to fight.
Once he'd destroyed those demons in battle with blows that 34.150
were equal in touch to Indra's thunderbolts, Jamad·agni's son, that descendent of Bhrigu and joy of the Bhárgavas, that fine brahmin whose body had been wounded by demons, was touched by Sthanu and immediatedly became free of wounds.

And the illustrious god, pleased with that deed of his, offered the great Bhárgava many kinds of boons. And the trident-wielding god of gods, filled with gratification, said to him: 'That wound of yours which is the result of weapons falling on your body has rid you of your human karma, joy of the Bhrigus. Take these divine weapons from me, just as you wished!'"

DURYÓDHANA said:

"After receiving all the weapons and as many kinds of 34.155
boons as he could ever imagine wanting, that great ascetic Rama bowed his head to Bhava and, granted leave, departed from the lord of gods.

evam etat purā|vṛttaṃ tadā kathitavān ṛṣiḥ.
Bhārgavo 'pi dadau divyaṃ dhanur|vedaṃ mah"|ātmane
Karṇāya, puruṣa|vyāghra, su|prīten' ântar|ātmanā.
vṛjinaṃ hi bhavet kiṃ cid yadi Karṇasya, pārthiva,
n' âsmai hy astrāṇi divyāni prādāsyad Bhṛgu|nandanaḥ.
n' âpi sūta|kule jātaṃ Karṇaṃ manye kathaṃ cana.
deva|putram ahaṃ manye kṣatriyāṇāṃ kul'|ôdbhavam,
visṛṣṭam avabodh'|ârthaṃ kulasy', êti matir mama!
34.160 sarvathā na hy ayaṃ, Śalya, Karṇaḥ sūta|kul'|ôdbhavaḥ.
sa|kuṇḍalaṃ, sa|kavacaṃ, dīrgha|bāhuṃ, mahā|ratham,
katham āditya|sadṛśaṃ mṛgī vyāghraṃ janiṣyati?
yathā hy asya bhujau pīnau, nāga|rāja|kar'|ôpamau,
vakṣaḥ paśya viśālaṃ ca sarva|śatru|nibarhaṇam!
na tv eṣa prākṛtaḥ kaś cit Karṇo Vaikartano vṛṣaḥ;
mah"|ātmā hy eṣa, rāj'|êndra, Rāma|śiṣyaḥ pratāpavān!»

DURYODHANA uvāca:

35.1 «EVAṂ SA BHAGAVĀN devaḥ sarva|loka|Pitā|mahaḥ
sārathyam akarot tatra Brahmā, Rudro 'bhavad rathī.
rathino 'bhyadhiko vīraḥ kartavyo ratha|sārathiḥ;
tasmāt tvaṃ, puruṣa|vyāghra, niyaccha turagān yudhi!
yathā deva|gaṇais tatra vṛto yatnāt Pitā|mahaḥ,
tath" âsmābhir bhavān yatnāt Karṇād abhyadhiko vṛtaḥ;
yathā devair, mahā|rāja, Īśvarād adhiko vṛtaḥ,
tathā bhavān api kṣipraṃ, Rudrasy' êva Pitā|mahaḥ,
35.5 niyaccha turagān yuddhe Rādheyasya, mahā|dyute!»

This is what happened long ago as that sage* described it back then.

Bhárgava too gave the divine knowledge of weapons to great Karna with feelings of great joy, tiger of a man. If Karna had been wicked in any way, prince, the joy of the Bhrigus would not have given him the divine weapons. I don't at all believe that Karna was born into a family of charioteers. I reckon that he's the son of a god and was born into a family of kshatriyas. He was thrown out so that his lineage could be correctly recognized,* that's what I reckon! Because, Shalya, in no way was Karna born into the family 34.160 of a charioteer. How could a doe give birth to a sun-like tiger, a mighty warrior with earrings, armor and long arms? Equally, look at his arms that are as round as the trunks of regal elephants and his broad chest that destroys all enemies! The bull Karna Vaikártana is no vulgar man. He is a great man, lord of kings, a glorious pupil of Rama!"

DURYÓDHANA said:

"IN THIS WAY the illustrious god Brahma, Grandfather of 35.1 all the worlds, became the chariot-driver when Rudra was a chariot-warrior. A hero superior to the chariot-warrior should be made driver of the chariot. Therefore, tiger of a man, you must assume control of these horses in battle! Just as the Grandfather was carefully chosen then by the hordes of gods, so we carefully choose you who are superior to Karna; just as he who was chosen by the gods is superior 35.5 to Íshvara,* great king, so you too must quickly assume control of the horses of Radha's son in battle, glorious man, like the Grandfather assumed control of Rudra's!"

ŚALYA uvāca:

«may" âpy etan, nara|śreṣṭha, bahuśo nara|siṃhayoḥ
kathyamānaṃ śrutaṃ divyam ākhyānam atimānuṣam,
yathā ca cakre sārathyaṃ Bhavasya Prapitāmahaḥ,
yath" âsurāś ca nihatā iṣuṇ" âikena, Bhārata.
Kṛṣṇasya c' âpi viditaṃ sarvam etat purā hy abhūt,
yathā Pitā|maho jajñe bhagavān sārathis tadā.
an|āgatam, atikrāntaṃ veda Kṛṣṇo 'pi tattvataḥ!
etad arthaṃ viditv" âpi sārathyam upajagmivān,
Svayaṃ|bhūr iva Rudrasya, Kṛṣṇaḥ Pārthasya, Bhārata.
35.10 yadi hanyāc ca Kaunteyaṃ sūta|putraḥ kathaṃ cana,
dṛṣṭvā Pārthaṃ hi nihataṃ, svayaṃ yotsyati Keśavaḥ.
śaṅkha|cakra|gadā|pāṇir dhakṣyate tava vāhinīm.
na c' âpi tasya kruddhasya Vārṣṇeyasya mah"|ātmanaḥ
sthāsyate pratyanīkeṣu kaś cid atra nṛpas tava.»

SAṂJAYA uvāca:

taṃ tathā bhāṣamāṇaṃ tu Madra|rājam ariṃ|damaḥ
pratyuvāca mahā|bāhur a|dīn'|ātmā sutas tava.
«m" âvamaṃsthā, mahā|bāho, Karṇaṃ Vaikartanaṃ raṇe
sarva|śastra|bhṛtāṃ śreṣṭhaṃ sarva|śāstr'|ârtha|pāra|gam!
yasya jyā|tala|nirghoṣaṃ śrutvā bhayaṃ|karaṃ mahat,
35.15 Pāṇḍaveyāni sainyāni vidravanti diśo daśa.
pratyakṣaṃ te, mahā|bāho, yathā rātrau Ghaṭotkacaḥ
māyā|śatāni kurvāṇo hato māyā|puras|kṛtaḥ.
na c' âtiṣṭhata Bībhatsuḥ pratyanīke kathaṃ cana,
etāṃś ca divasān sarvān bhayena mahatā vṛtaḥ.
Bhīmasenaś ca balavān dhanuṣ|koṭy" âbhicoditaḥ

SHALYA said:

"Finest of men, many times have I heard the divine, superhuman tale of these two lions of men that you've just now told me, how the Grandfather became Bhava's chariot-driver and how the demons were killed by that single arrow, Bhárata. Moreover Krishna already knew all this, how the illustrious Grandfather became chariot-driver back then. Krishna truly knows what has passed and what is yet to happen! Understanding its import, Krishna also became chariot-driver for Pritha's son, just as Svayam·bhu* had for Rudra, Bhárata. If the charioteer's son should somehow kill 35.10
Kunti's son, after seeing the son of Pritha slain Késhava himself will fight. Brandishing his conch, discus and club, he will torch your chariot. What is more, no king of yours will stand opposed to that great and furious Varshnéya."

SÁNJAYA said:

But your mighty-armed son the foe destroyer was not discouraged and replied to the Madra king who had said this.

"Man of mighty arms, don't be contemptuous of Karna Vaikártana in battle! He is the finest of all those who bear weapons and has mastered the meaning of all learned treatises. It's after hearing the sound of his huge, fear instilling bow-string that the Pándava troops flee in every 35.15
direction. Just so it was he who at night—as you witnessed, mighty-armed man!—killed Ghatótkacha though he made hundreds of illusions and was shielded by illusion. And not once for all those days did Bibhátsu stand opposed to him, for he was filled with great fear. And, king, it was he who

uktaś ca saṃjñayā, rājan, mūḍha, audariko yathā.
Mādrī|putrau tathā śūrau yena jitvā mahā|raṇe
kam apy arthaṃ puras|kṛtya na hatau yudhi, māriṣa.
yena Vṛṣṇi|pravīras tu Sātyakiḥ Sātvatāṃ varaḥ
35.20 nirjitya samare śūro virathaś ca balāt kṛtaḥ.
Sṛñjayāś c' êtare sarve Dhṛṣṭadyumna|puro|gamāḥ
a|sakṛn nirjitāḥ saṃkhye smayamānena saṃyuge.
taṃ kathaṃ Pāṇḍavā yuddhe vijeṣyanti mahā|ratham,
yo hanyāt samare kruddho vajra|hastaṃ Puraṃdaram?
tvaṃ ca sarv'|âstra|vid, vīraḥ, sarva|vidy"|âstra|pāra|gaḥ;
bāhu|vīryeṇa te tulyaḥ pṛthivyāṃ n' âsti kaś cana.
tvaṃ śalya|bhūtaḥ śatrūṇām, a|viṣahyaḥ parākrame;
tatas tvam ucyase, rājañ, Śalya ity, ari|sūdana.
tava bāhu|balaṃ prāpya na śekuḥ sarva|Sātvatāḥ;
35.25 tava bāhu|balād, rājan, kiṃ nu Kṛṣṇo bal'|âdhikaḥ?
yathā hi Kṛṣṇena balaṃ dhāryaṃ vai Phālgune hate,
tathā Karṇ'|âtyayī|bhāve tvayā dhāryaṃ mahad balam.
kim|arthaṃ samare sainyaṃ Vāsudevo nyavārayat?
kim|arthaṃ ca bhavān sainyaṃ na haniṣyati, māriṣa?
tvat|kṛte padavīṃ gantum iccheyaṃ yudhi, māriṣa,
s'|ôdarāṇāṃ ca vīrāṇāṃ sarveṣāṃ ca mahī|kṣitām!»

goaded powerful Bhima·sena with the curved end of his bow and referred to him with names such as 'Stupid' and 'Glut- 35.20
ton.' So also, dear friend, it was he who for some reason did not kill Madri's champion sons in combat after defeating them in a terrific battle. It was he who overpowered and stripped the champion Sátyaki of his chariot after defeating that Vrishni hero, the best of the Sátvatas, in a skirmish. It was by him that the Srínjayas, and all the others led by Dhrishta·dyumna, were repeatedly defeated in the war while he laughed in battle. How will the Pándavas overcome that mighty warrior in battle when, in his fury, he could kill in combat Indra, the thunderbolt-wielding Sacker of cities?

And you are a hero who knows all the missiles and have mastered all learning and weapons. There's no one on earth the equal of you in strength of arms. Irresistible in attack, you've become a thorn for your enemies; it is for this, king, destroyer of enemies, that you're known as Shalya.* All the Sátvatas were inept when they encountered the power of
your arms. How could Krishna possibly surpass in power 35.25
the power of your arms, king? Just as Krishna shall sustain their army once Phálguna has been slain, so, in the event of Karna's death, you'll sustain this great army. Why should Vasudéva be able to resist our troops in battle? And why could you not destroy their army, dear friend? For your sake, dear friend, I would endeavor to go the way of my brothers in battle, and of all royal heroes!"

ŚALYA uvāca:

«yan māṃ bravīṣi, Gāndhāre, agre sainyasya, māna|da,
viśiṣṭaṃ Devakī|putrāt, prītimān asmy ahaṃ tvayi.
eṣa sārathyam ātiṣṭhe Rādheyasya yaśasvinaḥ,
yudhyataḥ Pāṇḍav'|âgryeṇa, yathā tvaṃ, vīra, manyase.
35.30 samayaś ca hi me, vīra, kaś cid Vaikartanaṃ prati:
utsṛjeyaṃ yathā|śraddham ahaṃ vāco 'sya saṃnidhau.»

SAṂJAYA uvāca:

«tath"! êti» rājan, putras te saha Karṇena, māriṣa,
abravīn Madra|rājānaṃ sarva|kṣatrasya saṃnidhau.
sārathyasy' âbhyupagamāc Chalyen' āśvāsitas tadā
Duryodhanas tadā hṛṣṭaḥ Karṇaṃ tam abhiṣasvaje.
abravīc ca punaḥ Karṇaṃ stūyamānaḥ sutas tava:
«jahi Pārthān raṇe sarvān, Mahendro dānavān iva!»
sa Śalyen' âbhyupagate hayānāṃ saṃniyacchane,
Karṇo hṛṣṭa|manā bhūyo Duryodhanam abhāṣata:
35.35 «n' âtihṛṣṭa|manā hy eṣa Madra|rājo 'bhibhāṣate.
rājan, madhurayā vācā punar enaṃ bravīhi vai!»
tato rājā mahā|prājñaḥ sarv'|âstra|kuśalo balī
Duryodhano 'bravīc Chalyaṃ Madra|rājaṃ mahī|patim,
pūrayann iva ghoṣeṇa megha|gambhīrayā girā.
«Śalya, Karṇo ‹'rjunen' âdya yoddhavyam, iti› manyate.
tasya tvaṃ, puruṣa|vyāghra, niyaccha turagān yudhi!
Karṇo hatv" êtarān sarvān Phālgunaṃ hantum icchati.
tasy' âbhīṣu|grahe, rājan, prayāce tvāṃ punaḥ punaḥ!
Pārthasya sacivaḥ Kṛṣṇo yath" âbhīṣu|graho varaḥ,

SHALYA said:

"Son of Gandhári, since you describe me in the midst of this army as better than Dévaki's son, I am pleased with you, giver of honor. I will act as chariot-driver for Radha's famous son while he battles with the foremost of the Pándavas, just as you wish, hero. And my only condition, hero, is that in 35.30
his presence I can sling any words I want at Vaikártana."

SÁNJAYA said:

"Fine!" said your son along with Karna to the Madra king, dear friend, in the presence of all the warriors, king.

Relieved by Shalya agreeing to become the chariot-driver, Duryódhana was then thrilled and embraced Karna. As he was being euologised, your son again said to Karna: "Defeat all Pritha's sons in battle, just as great Indra defeated the demons!"

Once Shalya had agreed to guide his horses, Karna became excited and spoke further to Duryódhana: "The king 35.35
of Madra did not speak with much enthusiasm. King, speak to him again with charming words!"

Then Duryódhana, the very wise and powerful king who was skilled in all weapons, spoke to Shalya, a lord of the earth and the king of the Madras, in a voice as deep as a cloud's, as if filling everywhere with its sound.

"Shalya, Karna thinks that there should be combat with Árjuna today. Tiger of a man, you must guide his horses in battle! Once he's killed all the others, Karna wants to kill Phálguna. I emphatically implore you to take his reins, king! Just as Krishna, who's the best at grasping reins, is

tathā tvam api Rādheyaṃ sarvataḥ paripālaya!»

SAṂJAYA uvāca:

35.40 tataḥ Śalyaḥ pariṣvajya sutaṃ te vākyam abravīt
Duryodhanam amitra|ghnaṃ prīto Madr'|âdhipas tadā.

ŚALYA uvāca:

«evaṃ cen manyase, rājan, Gāndhāre, priya|darśana,
tasmāt te yat priyaṃ kiṃ cit, tat sarvaṃ karavāṇy aham!
yatr' âsmi, Bharata|śreṣṭha, yogyaḥ karmaṇi karhi cit,
tatra sarv'|ātmanā yukto vakṣye kāryaṃ, paraṃ|tapa.
yat tu Karṇam ahaṃ brūyāṃ hita|kāmaḥ priy'|âpriye,
mama tat kṣamatāṃ sarvaṃ bhavān, Karṇaś ca sarvaśaḥ!»

KARNA uvāca:

«Īśānasya yathā Brahmā, yathā Pārthasya Keśavaḥ,
tathā nityaṃ hite yukto, Madra|rāja, bhajasva naḥ!»

ŚALYA uvāca:

35.45 «ātma|nind", ātma|pūjā ca, para|nindā, para|stavaḥ,
an|ācaritam āryāṇāṃ vṛttam etac catur|vidham.
yat tu, vidvan, pravakṣyāmi pratyay'|ârtham ahaṃ tava,
ātmanas tava saṃyuktaṃ. tan nibodha yathā|tatham!
ahaṃ Śakrasya sārathye yogyo Mātalivat, prabho,
a|pramāda|prayogāc ca jñāna|vidyā|cikitsanaiḥ.
tataḥ Pārthena saṃgrāme yudhyamānasya te, 'nagha,
vāhayiṣyāmi turagān! vijvaro bhava, sūta|ja!»

counsellor to Pritha's son, you also must protect Radha's son in every way!"

SÁNJAYA said:

Shalya was satisfied and, after embracing your son, the 35.40
ruler of the Madras spoke this speech to Duryódhana, a destroyer of enemies.

SHALYA said:

"If this is what you think, king, handsome son of Gandhári, then I must do whatever pleases you! Where I'm capable of any particular deed, best of Bharatas, then I will carry out what must be done with total conviction, enemy-scorcher. But whatever I might say to Karna in seeking his well-being—whether it be good or bad—for all of it you and Karna must completely forgive me!"

KARNA said:

"Like Brahma for Ishána and Késhava for Pritha's son, king of Madra, you must always be intent on our well-being!"

SHALYA said:

"Noble people do not practise these four kinds of behav- 35.45
ior: self-abuse, self-worship, abuse of others and praise of others. However, learned man, whatever I say to convince you shall concern me or you. Listen to it carefully! Like Mátali,* powerful man, I'm fit to be Shakra's chariot-driver with my knowledge, learning and curative skill and because I'm careful and capable. Relax, son of a charioteer! From now on, faultless man, I'll drive your horses while you're fighting in battle with Pritha's son!"

DURYODHANA uvāca:

36.1 «AYAṂ TE, KARṆA, sārathyaṃ Madra|rājaḥ kariṣyati,
Kṛṣṇād abhyadhiko yantā, dev'|ēśasy' êva Mātaliḥ.
yathā hari|hayair yuktaṃ saṃgṛhṇāti sa Mātaliḥ,
Śalyas tathā tav' âdy' âyaṃ saṃyantā ratha|vājinām.
yodhe tvayi ratha|sthe ca Madra|rāje ca sārathau,
ratha|śreṣṭho dhruvaṃ saṃkhye Pārthān abhibhaviṣyati.»

SAṂJAYA uvāca:

tato Duryodhano bhūyo Madra|rājaṃ tarasvinam
uvāca, rājan, saṃgrāme 'dhyuṣite paryupasthite.
36.5 «Karṇasya yaccha saṃgrāme, Madra|rāja, hay'|ôttamān!
tvay" âbhigupto Rādheyo vijeṣyati Dhanaṃjayam!»
ity ukto ratham āsthāya, «tath"! êti» prāha, Bhārata.
Śalye 'bhyupagate Karṇaḥ sārathiṃ su|man" âbravīt,
«tvaṃ, sūta, syandanaṃ mahyaṃ
kalpay'! êty» a|sakṛt, tvaran.
tato jaitraṃ ratha|varaṃ,
gandharva|nagar'|ôpamam,
vidhivat kalpitaṃ, bhartre «jay'! êty» uktvā nyavedayat.
taṃ rathaṃ rathināṃ śreṣṭhaḥ Karṇo 'bhyarcya yathā|vidhi,
saṃpāditaṃ brahma|vidā pūrvam eva purodhasā,
kṛtvā pradakṣiṇaṃ yatnād, upasthāya ca bhāskaram,
36.10 samīpa|sthaṃ Madra|rājaṃ, «āroha tvam!» ath' âbravīt.

DURYÓDHANA said:

"THE KING OF Madra will become your chariot-driver, Karna. He's a much better driver than Krishna and is like Mátali, the charioteer of the lord of gods. Just as Mátali controls his chariot yoked to bay-colored horses, so Shalya is now the driver of your chariot's horses. With you as the warrior standing in the chariot and the Madra king as your chariot-driver, this excellent chariot will surely humiliate Pritha's sons in battle." 36.1

SÁNJAYA said:

Later at daybreak when the battle was about to begin, king, Duryódhana spoke further with the bold king of Madra.

"King of Madra, control Karna's superb horses in the battle! Protected by you, Radha's son will defeat Dhanan·jaya!" Addressed in this way, Bhárata, he mounted the chariot and said "So it shall be!" 36.5

When Shalya arrived, Karna was pleased and urgently and repeatedly said to him, "Charioteer, get the chariot ready for me!"

Shouting, "Victory!" Shalya presented to the master that superb, triumphant chariot appropriately fitted out like a city of the *gandhárvas*. Karna, the finest of chariot-warriors, praised that chariot according to rule—as had earlier been carried out by a royal priest who knew the sacred texts—and carefully circumambulated it and worshipped the sun. Then he said to the king of Madra who stood nearby, "You, mount!" 36.10

tataḥ Karṇasya dur|dharṣaṃ syandana|pravaraṃ mahat
āruroha mahā|tejāḥ Śalyaḥ, siṃha iv' âcalam.
tataḥ Śaly'|āśritaṃ dṛṣṭvā Karṇaḥ svaṃ ratham uttamam
adhyatiṣṭhad, yath" âmbho|daṃ vidyutvantaṃ divākaraḥ.

tāv eka|ratham ārūḍhāv ādity'|âgni|sama|tviṣau
abhrājetāṃ, yathā meghaṃ Sūry'|Âgnī sahitau divi.
saṃstūyamānau tau vīrau tad" âstāṃ dyutimattamau,
ṛtvik|sadasyair Indr'|Âgnī stūyamānāv iv' âdhvare.

sa Śalya|saṃgṛhīt'|âśve rathe Karṇaḥ sthito babhau
36.15 dhanur visphārayan ghoraṃ, pariveṣ" îva bhāskaraḥ.
āsthitaḥ sa ratha|śreṣṭhaṃ Karṇaḥ śara|gabhastimān
prababhau, puruṣa|vyāghro, Mandara|stha iv' âṃśumān.

taṃ ratha|sthaṃ mahā|bāhuṃ yuddhāy' âmita|tejasam
Duryodhanas tu Rādheyam idaṃ vacanam abravīt:

«a|kṛtaṃ Droṇa|Bhīṣmābhyāṃ duṣ|karaṃ karma saṃyuge
kuruṣv', Ādhirathe vīra, miṣatāṃ sarva|dhanvinām!
mano|gataṃ mama hy āsīd Bhīṣma|Droṇau mahā|rathau
Arjunaṃ Bhīmasenaṃ ca nihantārāv, iti dhruvam.
tābhyāṃ yad a|kṛtaṃ, vīra, vīra|karma mahā|mṛdhe,
36.20 tat karma kuru, Rādheya, Vajrapāṇir iv' âparaḥ!
gṛhāṇa Dharma|rājaṃ vā, jahi vā tvaṃ Dhanaṃjayam,
Bhīmasenaṃ ca, Rādheya, Mādrī|putrau yamāv api!

Then the very fiery Shalya mounted Karna's massive, unassailable and marvellous chariot like a lion climbing a mountain. After seeing his superb chariot occupied by Shalya, Karna ascended it like the sun rising over a cloud filled with lightning.

Their brilliance equal to the sun and fire, those two mounted on the one chariot glittered like Surya* and Agni together in the sky shining through a cloud. And while being euologised, those most majestic heroes were like Indra and Agni being praised by the sacrificial and supervising priests during a sacrifice.

Drawing his terrible bow as he stood in the chariot, its 36.15
horses restrained by Shalya, Karna shone brilliantly like the sun surrounded by a halo. Standing on that superb chariot with his arrows like shafts of sunlight, Karna, a tiger among men, shone brilliantly like the sun on top of Mount Mándara.

Duryódhana spoke this speech to Radha's son, that mighty-armed man standing in the chariot, his verve for battle without limit:

"Heroic son of Ádhiratha, before the eyes of all the bowmen you must complete that terribly difficult task that Bhishma and Drona left incomplete in the war! It was my firm
hope that Bhishma and Drona, mighty warriors, would kill 36.20
Árjuna and Bhima·sena. Like another Thunderbolt-wielder, son of Radha, you must complete that task, hero, that heroic deed which those two did not do in the great battle! Son of Radha, you must capture the King of Law and kill Dhanan·jaya, Bhima·sena and Madri's twin sons too! May victory be

jayaś ca te 'stu! bhadraṃ te! prayāhi, puruṣa'|rṣabha!
Pāṇḍu|putrasya sainyāni kuru sarvāṇi bhasmasāt!»
tatas tūrya|sahasrāṇi, bherīṇām ayutāni ca
vādyamānāny arājanta megha|śabdo yathā divi.
pratigṛhya tu tad vākyaṃ ratha|stho ratha|sattamaḥ
abhyabhāṣata Rādheyaḥ Śalyaṃ yuddha|viśāradam:
«coday' âśvān, mahā|bāho, yāvadd hanmi Dhanaṃjayam,
36.25 Bhīmasenaṃ, yamau c' ôbhau, rājānaṃ ca Yudhiṣṭhiram!
adya paśyatu me, Śalya, bāhu|vīryaṃ Dhanaṃjayaḥ
asyataḥ kaṅka|patrāṇāṃ sahasrāṇi śatāni ca!
adya kṣepsyāmy ahaṃ, Śalya, śarān parama|tejanān
Pāṇḍavānāṃ vināśāya, Duryodhana|jayāya ca!»

ŚALYA uvāca:

«sūta|putra, kathaṃ nu tvaṃ Pāṇḍavān avamanyase,
sarv'|âstra|jñān, mah"|êṣv|āsān, sarvān eva mahā|balān?
a|nivartino, mahā|bhāgān, a|jayyān, satya|vikramān
api saṃjanayeyur ye bhayaṃ sākṣāc Chatakratoḥ?
yadā śroṣyasi nirghoṣaṃ, visphūrjitam iv' âśaneḥ,
36.30 Rādheya, Gāṇḍivasy' ājau, tadā n' âivaṃ vadiṣyasi.
yadā drakṣyasi Bhīmena kuñjar'|ânīkam āhave
viśīrṇa|dantaṃ nihataṃ, tadā n' âivaṃ vadiṣyasi.
yadā drakṣyasi saṃgrāme Dharma|putraṃ, yamau tathā,
śitaiḥ pṛṣatkaiḥ kurvāṇān abhra|cchāyām iv' âmbare,
asyataḥ kṣiṇvataś c' ârīn, laghu|hastān, dur|āsadān
pārthivān api c' ânyāṃs, tvaṃ tadā n' âivaṃ vadiṣyasi.»

yours! Good luck to you! Go forth, bull of a man! Reduce to ashes all the troops of Pandu's son!"

The thousands of musical instruments and tens of thousands of kettle-drums that were being played sounded like the rumble of clouds in the sky.

Radha's son accepted this speech and that magnificent warrior standing in the chariot addressed Shalya, who was skilled in battle:

"Drive those horses, man of mighty arms, while I kill
Dhanan·jaya, Bhima·sena, both twins and King Yudhi·sh- 36.25
thira! Shalya, let Dhanan·jaya see the might of my arms today as I shoot hundreds and thousands of heron-feathered arrows! Today I'll discharge razor sharp arrows for the Pándavas' destruction and for Duryódhana's victory!"

SHALYA said:

"Son of a charioteer, how can you regard the Pándavas with contempt? Those mighty archers know all weapons and are immensely powerful. Never retreating, highly distinguished, invincible, their courage true, could it be they 36.30
who inspire fear in Shata·kratu himself? Son of Radha, you won't speak this way when you hear the sound of Gándiva in battle like the clap of a thunderbolt. You won't speak this way when you see the elephant division destroyed by Bhima, their tusks shattered in battle. You won't speak this way when you see Dharma's son and the twins in battle, and other princes too, fleet of hand and dangerous to approach, shooting and injuring their enemies as if making a blanket of clouds in the sky with their sharp arrows."

SAMJAYA uvāca:

an|ādṛtya tu tad vākyaṃ Madra|rājena bhāṣitam
«yāh'! îty» ev' âbravīt Karṇo Madra|rājaṃ tarasvinam.

SÁNJAYA said:

Ignoring that speech spoken by the king of the Madras,
to the bold Madra king Karna said only, "Move off!"

37–45

THE WRANGLING OF KARNA AND SHALYA

SAMJAYA uvāca:

37.1 DṚṢṬVĀ KARṆAṂ mah"|êṣv|āsaṃ
yuyutsuṃ samavasthitam,
cukruśuḥ Kuravaḥ sarve
hṛṣṭa|rūpāḥ samantataḥ.
tato dundubhi|nirghoṣair, bherīṇāṃ ninadena ca,
bāṇa|śabdaiś ca vividhair, garjitaiś ca tarasvinām,
niryayus tāvakā yuddhe, mṛtyuṃ kṛtvā nivartanam.
prayāte tu tataḥ Karṇe, yodheṣu muditeṣu ca,
cacāla pṛthivī, rājan, vavāśa ca su|vistaram.
niḥsaranto vyadṛśyanta sūryāt sapta mahā|grahāḥ.
37.5 ulkā|pātāś ca saṃjajñur, diśāṃ dāhās tath" âiva ca.
śuṣk'|âśanyaś ca saṃpetur, vavur vātāś ca bhairavāḥ.
mṛga|pakṣi|gaṇāś c' âiva pṛtanāṃ bahuśas tava
apasavyaṃ tadā cakrur, vedayanto mahā|bhayam.
prathitasya ca Karṇasya nipetus turagā bhuvi,
asthi|varṣaṃ ca patitam antarikṣād bhayānakam!
jajvaluś c' âiva śastrāṇi, dhvajāś c' âiva cakampire,
aśrūṇi ca vyamuñcanta vāhanāni, viśāṃ pate.
ete c' ânye ca bahava utpātās tatra, māriṣa,
samutpetur vināśāya Kauravāṇāṃ su|dāruṇāḥ.
37.10 na ca tān gaṇayām āsuḥ, sarve daivena mohitāḥ,
prasthitaṃ sūta|putraṃ ca, «jay'! êty» ūcur nar'|âdhipāḥ.
nirjitān Pāṇḍavāṃś c' âiva menire tatra Kauravāḥ!

SÁNJAYA said:

SEEING THE MIGHTY archer Karna standing on that chariot eager for battle, all the Kurus were ecstatic and shouted from everywhere. To the rattling of *dúndubhi* drums, the rumble of kettle-drums, the various sounds of arrows and the cries of bold heroes, your troops went forth into battle, determined to flee only in death. 37.1

And then as Karna advanced and the warriors rejoiced, king, the earth shook and rumbled at length. The seven great planets became visible surging forward from the sun.
Meteors plunged down and regions burnt as well. Thunderbolts fell, despite it being dry, and terrible winds blew. Herds of animals and flocks of birds then continually circled your army from right to left, heralding great peril. And while Karna was being celebrated his horses stumbled to the ground, and a terrifying shower of bones fell from the sky! Weapons shone brightly, banners flapped and draught animals shed tears, lord of people. These and many other dreadful portents, dear friend, appeared there foretelling the destruction of the Káuravas. 37.5

But, deluded by divine fate, all those rulers of men paid no heed to them and shouted out "Victory!" to the charioteer's son as he departed. The Káuravas then thought the Pándavas defeated already! 37.10

tato ratha|sthaḥ para|vīra|hantā
Bhīṣma|Droṇāv ativīryau samīkṣya,
samujjvalan bhāskara|pāvak'|ābho
Vaikartano 'sau ratha|kuñjaro, nṛpa,
sa Śalyam ābhāṣya jagāda vākyaṃ,
Pārthasya karm'|âtiśayaṃ vicintya,
mānena, darpeṇa vidahyamānaḥ,
krodhena dīpyann iva, niḥśvasaṃś ca:
«n' âhaṃ Mahendrād api vajra|pāṇeḥ
kruddhād bibhemy āyudhavān, ratha|sthaḥ!
dṛṣṭvā hi Bhīṣma|pramukhāñ śayānān,
atīva māṃ hy a|sthiratā jahāti.
Mahendra|Viṣṇu|pratimāv aninditau
rath'|âśva|nāga|pravara|pramāthinau;
a|vadhya|kalpau nihatau yadā parais;
tato na me 'py asti raṇe 'dya sādhvasam.
37.15 samīkṣya saṃkhye 'tibalān nar'|âdhipān
sa|sūta|mātaṅga|rathān parair hatān,
kathaṃ na sarvān a|hitān raṇe 'vadhīn
mah"|âstra|vid brāhmaṇa|puṃgavo guruḥ.
sa saṃsmaran Droṇam ahaṃ mah"|āhave,
bravīmi satyaṃ; Kuravo nibodhata!
na vā mad|anyaḥ prasahed raṇe 'rjunaṃ
samāgataṃ Mṛtyum iv' ôgra|rūpiṇam.

Standing in his chariot, Vaikártana, that killer of enemy-heroes, then reflected on Bhishma and Drona whose courage was tremendous. Blazing like the fire of the sun, king, that superb warrior reflected on the excellence of Pritha's son's deeds and, consumed by arrogance and pride and snorting as if burning with fury, shouted out to Shalya and spoke this speech:

"Standing in this chariot with my weapons I have no fear even of mighty Indra wielding his thunderbolt in rage! For seeing those who were led by Bhishma lying prone, doubt has completely left me. Like great Indra and Vishnu those two could not be faulted as they lay waste to the finest chariots, horses and elephants. They had seemed invincible when their enemies killed them. Yet still I have no fear of battle today.

After seeing those extremely powerful rulers of men with 37.15
their charioteers, elephants and chariots struck down in battle by their enemies, how was it that the guru, the brahmin-hero,* expert in the great weapons, didn't kill all those enemies in battle? I remember Drona in the great battle and I speak the truth! Listen Kurus! No one other than me can match Árjuna in battle once he's attacked like Death in wrathful form.

śikṣā, prasādaś ca, balaṃ, dhṛtiś ca
Droṇe, mah"|âstrāṇi ca, saṃnatiś ca,
sa ced agān mṛtyu|vaśaṃ mah"|ātmā,
sarvān anyān āturān adya manye!
n' êha dhruvaṃ kiṃ cid api pracintayan
vidyāṃ loke karmaṇo daiva|yogāt.
sūry'|ôdaye ko hi vimukta|saṃśayo
bhāvaṃ kurvīt' âdya gurau nipātite?
na nūnam astrāṇi, balaṃ, parākramaḥ,
kriyāḥ, su|nītaṃ, param'|āyudhāni vā
alaṃ manuṣyasya sukhāya vartituṃ;
tathā hi yuddhe nihataḥ parair guruḥ.
37.20 hutāśan'|āditya|samāna|tejasaṃ,
parākrame Viṣṇu|Puraṃdar'|ôpamam,
naye Bṛhaspaty|Uśanoḥ* sadā samaṃ,
na c' âinam astraṃ tad upāsta duḥ|saham.
saṃprākruṣṭe rudita|strī|kumāre
parābhūte pauruṣe Dhārtarāṣṭre,
mayā kṛtyam iti jānāmi, Śalya!
prayāhi tasmād dviṣatām anīkam!
yatra rājā Pāṇḍavaḥ satya|saṃdho
vyavasthito, Bhīmasen'|Ârjunau ca,
Vāsudevaḥ, Sātyakiḥ, Sṛñjayāś ca,
yamau ca, kas tān viṣahen mad|anyaḥ?
tasmāt kṣipraṃ, Madra|pate, prayāhi
raṇe Pañcālān, Pāṇḍavān, Sṛñjayāṃś ca!
tān vā haniṣyāmi sametya saṃkhye,
yāsyāmi vā Droṇa|pathā Yamāya.
nanv ev' âhaṃ na gamiṣyāmi madhye
teṣāṃ śūrāṇām iti mā, Śalya, viddhi!

Learning, kindness, strength, tenacity, the great weapons and humility were found in Drona. If this great man could fall under the sway of death, then I reckon all others shall suffer today!

Thinking it over, I can't find a thing that is certain in this world because of the divine workings of past acts. With the guru felled, could anyone, free of doubt, now look forward to sunrise? Assuredly not missiles, strength, courage, ritual acts, prudent conduct nor the most excellent weapons are enough to ensure the happiness of a man, for still the guru was felled in battle by his enemies. In fiery energy he was 37.20
the equal of the sun or fire, in courage he was the equal of Vishnu and the Sacker of cities, in prudent conduct he was always equal to Brihas·pati and Úshanas, but his irresistible missile did not serve him well.

With the courage of the Dhartaráshtras humbled and their women and children weeping and wailing, Shalya, I know what I must do! So attack our enemies' army! Other than me, who's a match for those among whom stands Bhima·sena, Árjuna, Vasudéva, Sátyaki, the Srínjayas, the twins and the Pándava king who is true to his promises? So quickly, lord of Madra, attack the Panchálas, Pándavas and Srínjayas in the battle! Once I've met with them in battle either I'll kill them or I'll go by Drona's path to Yama.

Shalya, certainly don't think that I will not go into the midst of those heroes! Such a betrayal of a friend I could

mitra|droho marṣaṇīyo na me 'yaṃ;
tyaktvā prāṇān anuyāsyāmi Droṇam.
37.25 prājñasya mūḍhasya ca jīvit'|ânte
n' âsti pramokṣo 'ntaka|sat|kṛtasya.
ato, vidvann, abhiyāsyāmi Pārthaṃ;
diṣṭaṃ na śakyaṃ vyativartituṃ vai!
kalyāṇa|vṛttaḥ satataṃ hi, rājan,
Vaicitravīryasya suto mam' āsīt.
tasy' ârtha|siddhy|artham ahaṃ tyajāmi
priyān bhogān dus|tyajaṃ jīvitaṃ ca.
vaiyāghra|carmāṇam, a|kūjan'|âkṣaṃ,
haimaṃ, tri|kośaṃ, rajata|tri|veṇum
ratha|prabarhaṃ turaga|prabarhair
yuktaṃ prādān mahyam idaṃ hi Rāmaḥ.
dhanūṃṣi citrāṇi nirīkṣya, Śalya,
dhvajān, gadāḥ, sāyakāṃś c' ôgra|rūpān,
asiṃ ca dīptaṃ param'|āyudhaṃ ca,
śaṅkhaṃ ca śubhraṃ svanavantam ugram,
patākinaṃ, vajra|nipāta|nisvanaṃ,
sit'|âśva|yuktaṃ, śubha|tūṇa|śobhitam,
imaṃ samāsthāya rathaṃ, ratha'|rṣabhaṃ
raṇe haniṣyāmy aham Arjunaṃ balāt.

not pardon; giving up my life, I'll follow Drona. At the end 37.25
of life, there's no escape for a man, wise or stupid, who's been honored by Death. Therefore, wise man, I will attack Pritha's sons. Destiny can't be avoided!

King, the son of Vichítra·virya's son* has always acted well towards me. To fulfil his objectives I surrender my favorite pleasures and my treasured life. Rama gave me the finest chariot yoked to the finest horses, its three-piece bamboo struts silver and three scabbards gold, its axle silent and shield covered in tiger-skin. Looking over my beautiful bows, Shalya, my banners, clubs and formidable arrows, and my brilliant sword and superb weapon and my white conch reverberating threateningly, and mounting this flag-bearing chariot that is adorned with beautiful quivers, yoked to white horses and sounding like a falling thunderbolt, in battle I'll brutally kill Árjuna, a bull of a warrior.

37.30 taṃ cen Mṛtyuḥ sarva|haro 'bhirakṣet
sad" âpramattaḥ samare Pāṇḍu|putram,
taṃ vā haniṣyāmi sametya yuddhe,
yāsyāmi vā Bhīṣma|mukho Yamāya.
Yama|Varuṇa|Kubéra|Vāsavā vā
yadi yugapat sa|gaṇā mah"|āhave
jugupiṣava ih' âdya Pāṇḍavaṃ,
kim u bahunā saha tair jayāmi tam!»

SAṂJAYA said:

iti raṇa|rabhasasya katthatas
tad uta niśamya vacaḥ sa Madra|rāṭ
avahasad avamanya vīryavān
pratiṣiṣidhe ca, jagāda c' ôttaram.

ŚALYA uvāca:

«virama! virama, Karṇa, katthanād!
atirabhaso 'py ativācam uktavān.
kva ca hi nara|varo Dhanaṃjayaḥ,
kva punar aho puruṣ'|âdhamo bhavān!
Yadu|sadanam Upendra|pālitaṃ
tri|daśam iv' âmara|rāja|rakṣitam
prasabham ativiloḍya, ko haret
puruṣa|var'|âvara|jām ṛte 'rjunāt?
37.35 tri|bhuvana|vibhum īśvar'|ēśvaraṃ
ka iha pumān Bhavam āhvayed yudhi
mṛga|vadha|kalahe ṛte 'rjunāt
sura|pati|vīrya|sama|prabhāvataḥ?

If all-destroying, ever-vigilant Death should protect Pandu's son in the war, after meeting him in battle either I'll kill him or, preceded by Bhishma, I'll go to Yama. Or if together with their attendants Yama, Váruna, Kubéra and Vásava intend to protect the Pándava here today in this great battle—what more need be said?—I'll kill him along with them!" 37.30

SÁNJAYA said:

Hearing Karna's words as he boasted eager for war, laughing contemptuously the courageous king of Madra stopped him and spoke this response.

SHALYA said:

"Stop it Karna! Stop this boasting! You're too impetuous and the words you spoke were over the top. For on the one hand we have Dhanan·jaya, a fine man, and on the other we have you, a vile man!

Who other than Árjuna could have destroyed the city of Yadus while it was protected by Indra's younger brother like heaven guarded by the king of the immortals,* and carried
off the younger sister of that excellent man?*What man in 37.35
this world other than Árjuna, whose power is equal to the strength of the lord of the gods, could challenge Bhava in battle, the lord of lords, the lord of the triple-world, in that quarrel over the killing of an animal?

asura|sura|mah"|ôragān, narān,
Garuḍa|piśāca|sa|yakṣa|rākṣasān
iṣubhir ajayad Agni|gauravāt
sv|abhilaṣitaṃ ca havir dadau Jayaḥ.
smarasi nanu yadā parair hṛtaḥ
sa ca Dhṛtarāṣṭra|suto 'pi mokṣitaḥ
dina|kara|sadṛśaiḥ śar'|ôttamair*
Kuruṣu bahūn vinihatya tān arīn.
prathamam api palāyite tvayi,
priya|kalahā Dhṛtarāṣṭra|sūnavaḥ
smarasi nanu yadā pramocitāḥ
kha|cara|gaṇān avajitya Pāṇḍavaiḥ.
samudita|bala|vāhanāḥ punaḥ
puruṣa|vareṇa jitāḥ stha go|grahe
sa|guru|guru|sutāḥ sa|Bhīṣmakāḥ;
kim u na jitaḥ sa tadā tvay" Ârjunaḥ?
37.40 idam aparam upasthitaṃ punas
tava nidhanāya su|yuddham adya vai;
yadi na ripu|bhayāt palāyase,
samaragato 'dya hato 'si, sūta|ja!»

SAMJAYA uvāca:

iti bahu paruṣaṃ prabhāṣati
pramanasi Madra|patau ripu|stavam,
bhṛśam abhiruṣitaḥ paraṃ|tapaḥ
Kuru|pṛtanā|patir āha Madra|pam.

Out of his respect for Agni, Jaya defeated demons, gods, great serpents, men, Gáruda, *pishácha*s, *yaksha*s and *rák-shasa*s with his arrows and offered him his eagerly desired oblation.

No doubt you remember when, after he'd slaughtered many enemies for the Kurus with his superb arrows that resemble the sun, he freed Dhrita·rashtra's son who'd been captured by his enemies. No doubt you remember when, after you were the first to flee, Dhrita·rashtra's quarrelsome sons were released by the Pándavas after they'd conquered hordes of those that travel through the sky.* During the cattle raid,* the armies and their vehicles gathered with Bhishma—the guru and the guru's son among them—were again defeated by that excellent man. Why didn't you defeat
Árjuna then? Now again another extraordinary battle is at 37.40
hand for your destruction. If you do not flee out of fear of your enemy, son of a charioteer, you'll be killed once you engage in battle!"

SÁNJAYA said:

While the cheerful lord of the Madras uttered this devastating rebuke and praised their enemy, the general of the Kuru army, a scorcher of enemies, became tremendously angry and spoke to the lord of the Madras.

KARNA uvāca:

«bhavatu! bhavatu! kiṃ vikatthase?
nanu mama tasya ca yuddham udyatam;
yadi sa jayati māṃ ih' āhave,
tata idam astu su|katthitaṃ tava!»

SAṂJAYA uvāca:

«evam astv! iti» Madr'|ēśa uktvā n' ôttaram uktavān.
«yāhi, Śaly'! êti» c' âpy enaṃ Karṇaḥ prāha yuyutsayā.
sa rathaḥ prayayau śatrūñ śvet'|âśvaḥ Śalya|sārathiḥ,
nighnann amitrān samare, tamo ghnan savitā yathā.
37.45 tataḥ prāyāt prītimān vai rathena
vaiyāghreṇa śveta|yuj" âtha Karṇaḥ.
sa c' ālokya dhvajinīṃ Pāṇḍavānāṃ,
Dhanaṃjayaṃ tvarayā paryapṛcchat.

SAṂJAYA uvāca:

38.1 PRAYĀṆE CA tataḥ Karṇo harṣayan vāhinīṃ tava,
ek'|âikaṃ samare dṛṣṭvā Pāṇḍavaṃ paryapṛcchata.
«yo māṃ adya mah"|ātmānaṃ darśayec chveta|vāhanam,
tasmai dadyām abhipretaṃ dhanaṃ yan manas" êcchati.
na cet tad abhimanyeta, tasmai dadyām ahaṃ punaḥ,
śakaṭaṃ ratna|saṃpūrṇaṃ, yo me brūyād Dhanaṃjayam.
na cet tad abhimanyeta puruṣo 'rjuna|darśivān,
śataṃ dadyāṃ gavāṃ tasmai naityakaṃ kāṃsya|dohanam.
38.5 śataṃ grāma|varāṃś c' âiva dadyām Arjuna|darśine.
tathā tasmai punar dadyāṃ śvetam aśvatarī|ratham,
yuktam añjana|keśībhir, yo me brūyād Dhanaṃjayam.

KARNA said:

"Enough! Enough! Why do you taunt me? Without any doubt the battle between him and me shall take place. If he defeats me in this battle, then shall this boast of yours be fair!"

SÁNJAYA said:

After saying, "Let it be so!" the lord of Madra said no more. And then, with eagerness to fight, Karna said to him, "Shalya, charge!"

With his white horses and Shalya as his chariot-driver, that warrior attacked his enemies, destroying his adversaries in battle just as the sun destroys the darkness.

Karna was then pleased and advanced with his chariot 37.45
covered in tiger-skin and drawn by white horses. When he caught sight of the army of the Pándavas, he quickly asked after Dhanan·jaya.

SÁNJAYA said:

THEN KARNA roused your army as he advanced and asked 38.1
each combatant who he saw in the battle about the Pándava.

"Whoever can point out to me today the great man with the white horses, I shall give any precious reward that he desires. If he doesn't agree to that, I shall still give whoever can tell me about Dhanan·jaya a wagon filled with jewels. If he doesn't want that, I shall give the man who's seen Árjuna a hundred cows along with the obligatory copper milk-pails.

To whoever's seen Árjuna I shall give a hundred of the 38.5
best villages. And further, to whoever can tell me about Dhanan·jaya I shall give a white cart pulled by black-maned she-mules. If he doesn't want that, I shall further give the

na cet tad abhimanyeta puruṣo 'rjuna|darśivān,
anyaṃ v" âsmai punar dadyāṃ sauvarṇaṃ hasti|ṣaḍ|gavam.
tath" âpy asmai punar dadyāṃ strīṇāṃ śatam alaṃ|kṛtam,
śyāmānāṃ, niṣka|kaṇṭhīnāṃ, gīta|vādya|vipaścitām.
na cet tad abhimanyeta puruṣo 'rjuna|darśivān,
tasmai dadyāṃ śataṃ nāgāñ, śataṃ grāmāñ, śataṃ rathān,
su|varṇasya ca mukhyasya hay'|âgryāṇāṃ śataṃ śatān,
38.10 ṛddhyā guṇaiḥ su|dāntāṃś ca, dhurya|vāhān, su|śikṣitān.
tathā su|varṇa|śṛṅgīṇāṃ go|dhenūnāṃ catuḥ|śatam
dadyāṃ tasmai sa|vatsānāṃ, yo me brūyād Dhanaṃjayam.
na cet tad abhimanyeta puruṣo 'rjuna|darśivān,
anyad asmai varaṃ dadyāṃ śvetān pañca|śatān hayān.
hema|bhāṇḍa|paricchannān, su|mṛṣṭa|maṇi|bhūṣaṇān,
su|dāntān api c' âiv' âhaṃ
dadyām aṣṭā|daś'|âparān.
rathaṃ ca śubhraṃ sauvarṇaṃ
dadyāṃ tasmai sv|alaṃ|kṛtam,
yuktaṃ parama|Kāmbojair, yo me brūyād Dhanaṃjayam.
na cet tad abhimanyeta puruṣo 'rjuna|darśivān,
38.15 anyad asmai varaṃ dadyāṃ kuñjarāṇāṃ śatāni ṣaṭ,
kāñcanair vividhair bhāṇḍair ācchannān, hema|mālinaḥ,
utpannān apar'|ânteṣu, vinītān hasti|śikṣakaiḥ.
na cet tad abhimanyeta puruṣo 'rjuna|darśivān,
anyad asmai varaṃ dadyāṃ vaiśya|grāmāṃś catur|daśa,
su|sphītān, dhana|saṃyuktān, pratyāsanna|van'|ôdakān;
a|kuto|bhayān su|sampannān rāja|bhojyāṃś catur|daśa!

man who's seen Árjuna another chariot made of gold and pulled by six oxen the size of elephants. And I'll give him still more! A hundred women of dark complexion, covered in ornaments, wearing gold collars and skilled in songs and musical instruments. If he doesn't want that, I shall give the man who's seen Árjuna a hundred elephants, a hundred villages, a hundred chariots and ten thousand superb horses of the finest gold color that are in good health, have good 38.10
qualities, are well tamed and trained and can be used as draught horses. To whoever can tell me about Dhanan·jaya I shall give four hundred golden-horned milk-cows along with their calves. If he doesn't want that, I shall give the man who's seen Árjuna another reward, five hundred white horses.

And I shall also give him eighteen other very placid horses with golden harnesses and blankets and decorated with highly polished jewels. And to whoever can tell me about Dhanan·jaya I shall give a beautiful chariot, brilliantly decorated and yoked to the finest Kambójan horses. If he doesn't want that, I shall give the man who's seen Árjuna another 38.15
reward, six hundred elephants bred in the west, clothed with various gold trappings, wearing golden garlands and led by elephant trainers. If he doesn't want that, I shall give the man who's seen Árjuna another reward, fourteen flourishing villages of vaishyas that are filled with wealth and have forests and water nearby—fourteen danger free and well supplied villages fit to be enjoyed by kings!

dāsīnāṃ niṣka|kaṇṭhīnām Māgadhīnām śataṃ tathā
praty|agra|vayasāṃ dadyāṃ, yo me brūyād Dhanaṃjayam.
na cet tad abhimanyeta puruṣo 'rjuna|darśivān,
anyaṃ tasmai varaṃ dadyāṃ, yam asau kāmayet svayam!
38.20 putra|dārān, vihārāṃś ca yad anyad vittam asti me,
tac ca tasmai punar dadyāṃ, yad yac ca manas" êcchati.
hatvā ca sahitau Kṛṣṇau, tayor vittāni sarvaśaḥ
tasmai dadyām ahaṃ yo me prabrūyāt Keśav'|Ârjunau!»
etā vācaḥ su|bahuśaḥ Karṇa uccārayan yudhi
dadhmau sāgara|saṃbhūtaṃ su|svanaṃ śaṅkham uttamam.
tā vācaḥ sūta|putrasya tathā yuktā niśamya tu,
Duryodhano, mahā|rāja, prahṛṣṭaḥ s'|ânugo 'bhavat.
tato dundubhi|nirghoṣo, mṛdaṅgānāṃ ca sarvaśaḥ
siṃha|nādaḥ sa|vāditraḥ, kuñjarāṇāṃ ca nisvanaḥ
38.25 prādur āsīt tadā, rājan, sainyeṣu, puruṣa'|rṣabha,
yodhānāṃ saṃprahṛṣṭānāṃ tathā samabhavat svanaḥ.
tathā prahṛṣṭe sainye tu plavamānaṃ mahā|ratham,
vikatthamānaṃ ca tadā Rādheyam ari|karṣaṇam,
Madra|rājaḥ prahasy' êdaṃ vacanaṃ pratyabhāṣata.

ŚALYA uvāca:

39.1 «MĀ, SŪTA|PUTRA, dānena sauvarṇaṃ hasti|ṣaḍ|gavam
prayaccha puruṣāy'; âdya drakṣyasi tvaṃ Dhanaṃjayam!
bālyād iha tvaṃ tyajasi vasu Vaiśravaṇo yathā;
a|yatnen' âiva, Rādheya, draṣṭ" âsy adya Dhanaṃjayam.
parān sṛjasi yad vittaṃ kiṃ cit tvaṃ bahu mūḍhavat;
a|pātra|dāne ye doṣās tān mohān n' âvabudhyase.

And whoever can tell me about Dhanan·jaya I shall give a hundred young Mágadhi slave girls wearing golden collars. And if he doesn't want that, I shall give the man who's seen Árjuna another reward, whatever he would desire for himself! Sons, wives or pleasures, or whatever other possessions 38.20
I have, and whatever he desires in his heart, I will give to him. Once I've killed the two Krishnas together, I will give everything they owned to whoever tells me about Késhava and Árjuna!"

Whilst uttering these many words in the battle, Karna blew his superb conch that came from the ocean and had a beautiful tone. And when they heard these fitting words of the charioteer's son, great king, Duryódhana and his attendants were thrilled.

Then, king, the sound of *dúndubhi* and *mridánga* drums, 38.25
lion roars, musical instruments and elephants trumpeting became audible everywere among the troops, bull of a man, as did the clamor of soldiers celebrating.

But as that mighty warrior Radha's son, a tormenter of enemies, bragged as he sailed into that excited army, the king of the Madras responded with this speech.

SHALYA said:

"SON OF A charioteer, don't reward a man by offering a 39.1
golden cart pulled by six elephant-like oxen. You will see Dhanan·jaya today! Foolishly you give away riches here as if you were Váishravana. With no effort, son of Radha, you will see Dhanan·jaya today. Like a sucker you give away much wealth to others. In giving to the unworthy, stupidly you don't recognise those who are wicked. With these vast

yat tvaṃ prerayase vittaṃ, bahu tena khalu tvayā
śakyaṃ bahu|vidhair yajñair yaṣṭuṃ. sūta, yajasva taiḥ!
39.5 yac ca prārthayase hantuṃ Kṛṣṇau mohād, vṛth" âiva tat!
na hi śuśruma saṃmarde kroṣṭrā siṃhau nipātitau!
a|prārthitaṃ prārthayase; suhṛdo na hi santi te
ye tvāṃ nivārayanty āśu prapatantaṃ hut'|âśane.
kāry'|â|kāryaṃ na jānīṣe; kāla|pakvo 'sy a|saṃśayam!
bahv a|baddham a|karṇīyaṃ ko hi brūyāj jijīviṣuḥ?
samudra|taraṇaṃ dorbhyāṃ kaṇṭhe baddhvā yathā śilām,
giry|agrād vā nipatanaṃ, tādṛk tava cikīrṣitam.
sahitaḥ sarva|yodhais tvaṃ vyūḍh'|ânīkaiḥ su|rakṣitaḥ
Dhanaṃjayena yudhyasva, śreyaś cet prāptum icchasi.
39.10 hit'|ârthaṃ Dhārtarāṣṭrasya bravīmi tvāṃ, na hiṃsayā.
śraddhasv' âivaṃ mayā proktaṃ yadi te 'sti jijīviṣā!»

KARNA uvāca:

«sva|bāhu|vīryaṃ āśritya, prārthayāmy Arjunaṃ raṇe.
tvaṃ tu mitra|mukhaḥ śatrur māṃ bhīṣayitum icchasi!
na mām asmād abhiprāyāt kaś cid adya nivartayet,
ap' Îndro vajram udyamya! kiṃ nu martyaḥ kathaṃ cana?»

SAMJAYA uvāca:

iti Karṇasya vāky'|ânte Śalyaḥ prāh' ôttaraṃ vacaḥ
cukopayiṣur atyarthaṃ Karṇaṃ Madr'|ēśvaraḥ punaḥ.

riches that you send away, truly you could offer many different sacrifices. And you must offer those sacrifices, *suta*!*

Stupidly, you long to kill the two Krishnas; this is point- 39.5
less! For we've never heard of a pair of lions destroyed by a jackal! You long for what should not be longed for; there are no friends who can stop you tumbling directly into fire. You don't understand what should and shouldn't be done. Without doubt you've been cooked by time!* Who that wants to live would say so much that's meaningless and not worth listening to? Your plan is like crossing the ocean by the arms after tying a rock around one's neck. Or like leaping from the summit of a mountain. If you want to find success, you must fight with Dhanan·jaya together with all your warriors
and well protected by your arrayed forces. Without malice I 39.10
speak to you for the good of Dhrita·rashtra's son. You must trust what I say if you want to live!"

KARNA said:

"Relying upon the strength of my own arms, I long for Árjuna in battle. But you, an enemy with the face of a friend, want to intimidate me! No one could stop me from my objective today, not even Indra with his thunderbolt raised! How much less then could some mere mortal?"

SÁNJAYA said:

At the end of Karna's speech, Shalya, the lord of the Madras, hoping to utterly infuriate Karna, again spoke these words in reply.

«yadā vai tvāṃ Phalguna|vega|yuktā
jyā|coditā, hastavatā visṛṣṭāḥ,
anvetāraḥ, kaṅka|patrāḥ, śit'|âgrās,
tadā tapsyasy Arjunasy' âbhiyogāt.
39.15 yadā divyaṃ dhanur ādāya Pārthaḥ
pratāpayan pṛtanāṃ Savyasācī
tvām mardayiṣyan niśitaiḥ pṛṣatkais,
tadā paścāt tapsyase, sūta|putra.
bālaś candraṃ mātur aṅke śayāno
yathā kaś cit prārthayate 'pahartum,
tadvan mohād dyotamānaṃ ratha|sthaṃ
saṃprārthayasy Arjunaṃ jetum adya.
tri|śūlam āśritya su|tīkṣṇa|dhāraṃ
sarvāṇi gātrāṇi vigharṣasi tvam,
su|tīkṣṇa|dhār'|ôpama|karmaṇā tvaṃ
yuyutsase yo 'rjunen' âdya, Karṇa.
kruddhaṃ siṃhaṃ kesariṇaṃ bṛhantaṃ
bālo mūḍhaḥ kṣudra|mṛgas tarasvī
samāhvayet, tadvad etat tav' âdya
samāhvānaṃ, sūta|putr', Ârjunasya.
mā, sūta|putr', āhvaya rāja|putraṃ,
mahā|vīryaṃ kesariṇaṃ yath" âiva
vane śṛgālaḥ piśitena tṛpto!
mā Pārtham āsādya vinaṅkṣyasi tvam.
39.20 īṣā|dantaṃ mahā|nāgaṃ prabhinna|karaṭā|mukham
śaśako hvayase yuddhe, Karṇa, Pārthaṃ Dhanaṃjayam.
bila|sthaṃ kṛṣṇa|sarpaṃ tvaṃ bālyāt kāṣṭhena vidhyasi
mahā|viṣaṃ, pūrṇa|kopaṃ, yat Pārthaṃ yoddhum icchasi.
siṃhaṃ kesariṇaṃ kruddham atikramy' âbhinardase,
śṛgāla iva mūḍhas, tvaṃ nṛ|siṃhaṃ, Karṇa, Pāṇḍavam.

"When heron-feathered arrows with sharp points are released by his skilled hand and impelled by his bow-string and, filled with Phálguna's speed, seek you out, then you'll be mortified because of Árjuna's assault. When Pritha's son 39.15
the Left-handed archer grabs his divine bow and crushes you with his sharp arrows as he torments your army, then later, son of a charioteer, you'll feel mortified.

Just as a child lying in his mother's lap likes to carry away the moon, similarly it is absurd that you ask after Árjuna today in order to defeat him as he stands in his chariot in brilliant radiance. Choosing a sharp-bladed trident, you grind yourself against it, Karna, since it is you who wants to fight with Árjuna today whose deeds are like sharp blades. Son of a charioteer, your challenge of Árjuna today is like a small, young deer—impulsive yet confused—challenging a huge and furious maned lion. Son of a charioteer, just as a jackal sated with meat does not challenge a mighty lion in the forest, you must not challenge that prince! Then when you meet Pritha's son you will not perish.

Karna, your challenge to Pritha's son Dhanan·jaya in bat- 39.20
tle is like a hare challenging a huge elephant with tusks as long as a pole and the cleft on its head flowing with ruttish secretions. In desiring to fight Pritha's son, you childishly poke a black snake with a stick as it rests in its hole, potently poisonous and filled with anger. Like a stupid jackal roaring at an enraged, maned lion after passing him by, Karna,

Suparṇaṃ patagalśreṣṭhaṃ Vainateyaṃ tarasvinam
bhogī vā, hvayase pāte, Karṇa, Pārthaṃ Dhanaṃjayam.
sarv'|âmbhasāṃ nidhiṃ bhīmaṃ
mūrtimantaṃ, jhaṣ'|āyutam,
candr'|ôdaye vivardhantam
a|plavaḥ san titīrṣasi.
39.25 ṛṣabhaṃ dundubhi|grīvaṃ, tīkṣṇa|śṛṅgaṃ, prahāriṇam,
vatsa, āhvayase yuddhe, Karṇa, Pārthaṃ Dhanaṃjayam.
mahā|meghaṃ mahā|ghoraṃ darduraḥ pratinardasi
kāma|toya|pradaṃ loke nara|parjanyam Arjunam.
yathā ca sva|gṛha|sthaḥ śvā vyāghraṃ vana|gataṃ bhaṣet,
tathā tvaṃ bhaṣase, Karṇa, nara|vyāghraṃ Dhanaṃjayam!
sṛgālo 'pi vane, Karṇa, śaśaiḥ parivṛto vasan
manyate siṃham ātmānaṃ yāvat siṃhaṃ na paśyati.
tathā tvam api, Rādheya, siṃham ātmānam icchasi,
a|paśyañ śatru|damanaṃ nara|vyāghraṃ Dhanaṃjayam.
39.30 vyāghraṃ tvaṃ manyase "tmānaṃ, yāvat Kṛṣṇau na paśyasi
samāsthitāv eka|rathe, sūryā|candramasāv iva.
yāvad Gāṇḍīva|ghoṣaṃ tvaṃ na śṛṇoṣi mah"|āhave,
tāvad eva tvayā, Karṇa, śakyaṃ vaktuṃ yath" êcchasi.
ratha|śabda|dhanuḥ|śabdair nādayantaṃ diśo daśa,
nardantam iva śārdūlaṃ dṛṣṭvā kroṣṭā bhaviṣyasi!
nityam eva sṛgālas tvaṃ, nityaṃ siṃho Dhanaṃjayaḥ;
vīra|pradveṣaṇān, mūḍha, nityaṃ kroṣṭ" êva lakṣyase!

you roar at the Pándava, a lion of a man. Karna, you challenge Pritha's son Dhanan·jaya in a shoot-out like a snake challenging Vínata's bold son Supárna, the finest of birds. It is as though, despite not having a boat, you hope to cross a formidable ocean that's taken bodily form, as that fish-crowded receptacle for all waters swells during the moon's rise.

Karna, you challenge Pritha's son Dhanan·jaya in battle 39.25
like a calf taking on a fighting bull whose horn is sharp and whose neck is like a *dúndubhi* drum. Like a frog chirping at a massive and terrifying cloud to shed water needed for the world, you cry out at Árjuna, a rain-cloud of a man. Just as a dog remaining in his own house might bark at a forest-roaming tiger, Karna, so you speak to Dhanan·jaya, a tiger of a man!

Karna, even a jackal living in a forest surrounded by rabbits thinks himself a lion until he sees a lion. You too, son of Radha, regard yourself as a lion while you're yet to see
the enemy tamer Dhanan·jaya, a tiger among men. You'll 39.30
think yourself a tiger until you see the two Krishnas standing on the one chariot like the sun and the moon. As long as you can't hear the sound of Gandíva in the great war, Karna, you can say whatever you like. When you see him filling the ten directions with the twangs of his bow and the rumble of his chariot like a roaring tiger, you will become a jackal! You'll always be a jackal and Dhanan·jaya will always be a lion. Because of your hatred for that hero, you've always
been regarded as a jackal, stupid! Just as a mouse and cat are 39.35
weak and strong, or a dog and tiger, or a jackal and lion, or a rabbit and elephant, or untruth and truth or poison and

yath" ākhuḥ syād biḍālaś ca, śvā vyāghraś ca bal'|â|bale,
yathā sṛgālaḥ siṃhaś ca, yathā ca śaśa|kuñjarau,
39.35 yath" ân|ṛtaṃ ca satyaṃ ca, yathā c' âpi viṣ'|âmṛte,
tathā tvam api Pārthaś ca prakhyātāv ātma|karmabhiḥ.»

SAMJAYA uvāca:

40.1 ADHIKṢIPTAS TU Rādheyaḥ Śalyen' âmita|tejasā
Śalyam āha su|saṃkruddho vāk|śalyam avadhārayan.

KARNA uvāca:

«guṇān guṇavatāṃ, Śalya, guṇavān vetti, n' â|guṇaḥ.
tvaṃ tu, Śalya, guṇair hīnaḥ kiṃ jñāsyasi guṇ'|â|guṇam?
Arjunasya mah"|âstrāṇi, krodhaṃ, vīryaṃ, dhanuḥ, śarān
ahaṃ, Śaly', âbhijānāmi, vikramaṃ ca mah"|ātmanaḥ.
tathā Kṛṣṇasya māhātmyam ṛṣbhasya mahī|kṣitām
yath" âhaṃ, Śalya, jānāmi, na tvaṃ jānāsi tat tathā.
40.5 evam ev' ātmano vīryam ahaṃ, vīryaṃ ca Pāṇḍave,
jānann ev' āhvaye yuddhe, Śalya, Gāṇḍīva|dhāriṇam.
asti v" âyam iṣuḥ, Śalya, su|puṅkho, rakta|bhojanaḥ,
eka|tūṇī|śayaḥ, patrī, su|dhautaḥ, samalaṃkṛtaḥ.
śete candana|cūrṇeṣu pūjito bahulāḥ samāḥ,
āheyo, viṣavān, ugro, nar'|âśva|dvipa|saṃgha|hā.
ghora|rūpo, mahā|raudras, tanutr'|âsthi|vidāraṇaḥ;
nirbhindyāṃ yena ruṣṭo 'ham api Meruṃ mahā|girim.
tam ahaṃ jātu n' âsyeyam anyasmin Phalgunād ṛte,
Kṛṣṇād vā Devakī|putrāt. satyaṃ c' âtra śṛṇuṣva me!

nectar, in this very way you and Pritha's son have come to be recognized through your deeds."

SÁNJAYA said:

But Radha's son had been insulted by Shalya, whose fiery energy had no limit, and he was absolutely furious. After mulling over that verbal barb,* he spoke to Shalya. 40.1

KARNA said:

"Only someone endowed with good qualities can recognise the qualities of someone with good qualities, Shalya, not someone without qualities. You, Shalya, have no qualities. How could you recognise whether someone has good or bad qualities?

I'm aware of Árjuna's great missiles, of his anger, courage, bow and arrows, Shalya, and of that great man's heroism. Equally, you don't know Krishna's greatness, a bull among
princes, the way I know it, Shalya. Even knowing in this 40.5
way the Pándava's strength and my own strength, Shalya, I still challenge the wielder of the Gandíva bow in battle.

This arrow with the fine nock, Shalya, is a devourer of blood. Lying alone in this quiver it has wings and is well-polished and beautifully decorated. For many years it has lain revered in sandal powder, snake-like and poisonous, a formidable destroyer of hordes of men, horses and elephants. It's horrendous and terribly fearsome as it shatters bone and armor; if affronted, I could split huge Mount Meru with it. But I shall shoot it at no one else other than Árjuna or Dévaki's son Krishna. Hear me regarding the truth of this!

40.10 ten' âham iṣuṇā, Śalya, Vāsudeva|Dhanaṃjayau
yotsye parama|saṃkruddhas, tat karma sadṛśaṃ mama.
sarveṣāṃ Vṛṣṇi|vīrāṇāṃ Kṛṣṇe lakṣmīḥ pratiṣṭhitā;
sarveṣāṃ Pāṇḍu|putrāṇāṃ jayaḥ Pārthe pratiṣṭhitaḥ.
ubhayaṃ tat samāsādya ko nivartitum arhati?
tāv etau puruṣa|vyāghrau sametau syandane sthitau
mām ekam abhisaṃyātau, su|jātaṃ paśya, Śalya, me!
pitṛ|ṣvasā|mātula|jau bhrātarāv a|parājitau,
maṇī sūtra iva protau, draṣṭ" âsi nihatau mayā.

Arjune Gāṇḍivaṃ, Kṛṣṇe cakraṃ, Tārkṣya|kapi|dhvajau,
40.15 bhīrūṇāṃ trāsa|jananaṃ, Śalya, harṣa|karaṃ mama.
tvaṃ tu duṣ|prakṛtir, mūḍho, mahā|yuddheṣv a|kovidaḥ,
bhay'|âvadīrṇaḥ saṃtrāsād a|baddhaṃ bahu bhāṣase.

saṃstauṣi tau tu ken' âpi hetunā tvaṃ, ku|deśa|ja.
tau hatvā samare hantā tvām adya saha|bāndhavam!
pāpa|deśa|ja! dur|buddhe! kṣudra! kṣatriya|pāṃsana!
suhṛd bhūtvā ripuḥ, kiṃ māṃ Kṛṣṇābhyāṃ bhīṣayiṣyasi?
tau vā mām adya hantārau, haniṣye v" âpi tāv aham.
n' âhaṃ bibhemi Kṛṣṇābhyāṃ, vijānann ātmano balam.
Vāsudeva|sahasraṃ vā Phālgunānāṃ śatāni vā
40.20 aham eko haniṣyāmi. joṣam āssva, ku|deśa|ja!

striyo, bālāś ca, vṛddhāś ca prāyaḥ krīḍā|gatā janāḥ,
yā gāthāḥ saṃpragāyanti kurvanto 'dhyayanaṃ yathā;
tā gāthāḥ śṛṇu me, Śalya, Madrakeṣu dur|ātmasu
brāhmaṇaiḥ kathitāḥ pūrvaṃ yathāvad rāja|saṃnidhau!

In utter rage I will fight Vasudéva and Dhanan·jaya with this arrow, a deed that is worthy of me. On Krishna depends the fortune of all the Vrishni heroes; on Pritha's son* depends the triumph of all Pandu's sons. After attacking both of them, who could return? As those two tigers of men stand together on their chariot and attack me on my own, Shalya, behold the nobility of my birth!* Those two brothers, the sons of one another's paternal aunt and maternal uncle, are indomitable. You'll see me destroy those two; they'll be like a pair of pearls threaded on a string. 40.10

Árjuna's Gándiva bow, Krishna's discus and their banners
bearing the monkey and Tarkshya inspire fear among the 40.15
timid but excite me, Shalya. But you are evil by nature; you're stupid and know nothing of great battles. Torn apart by fear, you blabber on so much because you're terrified.

You're from a wretched country! For some reason you praise those two. Once I've killed them in battle, I'll kill you today along with your relatives! You're from an evil country! You're dumb! You're mean and a disgrace to the kshatriya ethos! Why do you—a friend who's become an enemy!—menace me with the two Krishnas? Either they will kill
me today, or I'll kill them. I know my own strength and 40.20
do not fear the two Krishnas. Alone I could kill a thousand Vasudévas and hundreds of Phálgunas. Shut up! You're from a wretched country!

It's common for people amusing themselves—women, children and the aged—to sing these verses as if they were commencing study. Hear from me these verses about the wretched Madras! In times past brahmins fittingly related

śrutvā c' âika|manā, mūḍha, kṣama vā, brūhi c' ôttaram!

mitra|dhruṅ Madrako nityaṃ; yo no dveṣṭi sa Madrakaḥ.
Madrake saṃgataṃ n' âsti kṣudra|vākye nar'|âdhame.
dur|ātmā Madrako nityaṃ, nityam ānṛtiko, 'n|ṛjuḥ,
yāvad|antyaṃ hi daurātmyaṃ Madrakeṣv. iti naḥ śrutam!
40.25 pitā, putraś ca, mātā ca, śvaśrū|śvaśura|mātulāḥ,
jāmātā, duhitā, bhrātā, napt", ânye te cabāndhavāḥ,
vayasy'|âbhyāgatāś c' ânye, dāsī|dāsaṃ ca saṃgatam;
puṃbhir vimiśrā nāryaś ca jñāt'|âjñātāḥ svay" êcchayā.

yeṣāṃ gṛheṣv a|śiṣṭānāṃ saktu|matsy'|āśināṃ tathā,
pītvā sīdhu sa|go|māṃsaṃ, krandanti ca hasanti ca,
gāyanti c' âpy a|baddhāni, pravartante ca kāmataḥ,
kāma|pralāpino 'nyonyaṃ—teṣu dharmaḥ kathaṃ bhavet
Madrakeṣv avalipteṣu prakhyāt'|âśubha|karmasu?

n' âpi vairaṃ na sauhārdaṃ Madrakeṇa samācaret.
40.30 Madrake saṃgataṃ n' âsti, Madrako hi sadā malaḥ;
Madrakeṣu ca saṃsṛṣṭaṃ, śaucaṃ Gāndhārakeṣu ca.

rāja|yājaka|yājye ca naṣṭaṃ dattaṃ havir bhavet.

śūdra|saṃskārako vipro yathā yāti parābhavam,
yathā brahma|dviṣo nityaṃ gacchant' îha parābhavam,
tath" âiva saṃgataṃ kṛtvā naraḥ patati Madrakaiḥ.

these in the presence of kings. Listen with your mind focused, fool, and suffer it or voice a response!

A Madra is always treacherous to friends; whoever hates us is a Madra. There's no friendship with a Madra; he's a callous speaking wretch. A Madra is always wicked and always untruthful and crooked, for wickedness among the Madras lasts their entire lives. That's what we've been taught!

Fathers, sons, mothers, mothers- and fathers-in-law, ma- 40.25
ternal uncles, sons-in-law, daughters, brothers, grandsons, various relatives, other friends and uninvited guests, and slave men and women, associate together. Women mingle with men as they please, whether they know them or not.

In the houses of the uncouth Madras—who eat fish mixed with meal!—people indulge in rum and beef, and then shriek, laugh and sing senseless songs. They behave however they want and babble to one another about their lusts. How could law exist among these arrogant Madras, famous for their wicked deeds?

Neither enmity nor friendship should be pursued with a
Madra. There's no friendship with a Madra, for a Madra is 40.30
always dirt; among the Madra there's no camaraderie, and there's no purity among the Gandháras.

Given that their king is both sacrificer and patron of the sacrifice, whatever oblation is offered shall be ruined.

Just as a brahmin who consecrates a shudra becomes ruined, and just as enemies of brahmins are always ruined in this world, so truly a man falls after associating with Madras.

Madrake saṃgataṃ n' âsti! ‹hataṃ, vṛścika, te viṣam!›
ātharvaṇena mantreṇa yathā śāntiḥ kṛtā mayā,
iti vṛścika|daṣṭasya viṣa|vega|hatasya ca
kurvanti bheṣajaṃ prājñāḥ, satyaṃ tac c' âpi dṛśyate!
40.35 evaṃ, vidvañ, joṣam āssva, śṛṇu c' âtr' ôttaraṃ vacaḥ!
vāsāṃsy utsṛjya nṛtyanti striyo yā madya|mohitāḥ,
maithune '|saṃyatāś c' âpi, yathā|kāma|varāś ca tāḥ;
tāsāṃ putraḥ kathaṃ dharmaṃ Madrako vaktum arhati?
yās tiṣṭhantyaḥ pramehanti yath" âiv' ôṣṭrī|daśerakāḥ,
tāsāṃ vibhraṣṭa|dharmāṇāṃ nirlajjānāṃ tatas tataḥ
tvaṃ putras tādṛśīnāṃ hi dharmaṃ vaktum ih' êcchasi!
suvīrakaṃ yācyamānā Madrikā karṣati sphicau.
a|dātu|kāmā vacanam idaṃ vadati dāruṇam:
‹mā māṃ suvīrakaṃ kaś cid yācatāṃ dayitaṃ mama.
40.40 putraṃ dadyāṃ, patiṃ dadyāṃ, na tu dadyāṃ suvīrakam!›
gauryo bṛhatyo, nir|hrīkā Madrikāḥ kambal'|āvṛtāḥ,
ghasmarā, naṣṭa|śaucāś ca prāya, ity anuśuśruma.
evam|ādi may" ânyair vā śakyaṃ vaktuṃ bhaved bahu,
ā keś'|âgrān nakh'|âgrāc ca, vaktavyeṣu ku|karmasu!
Madrakāḥ Sindhu|Sauvīrā dharmaṃ vidyuḥ kathaṃ tv iha?
pāpa|deś'|ôdbhavā, mlecchā, dharmāṇām a|vicakṣaṇāḥ!

There's no friendship with a Madra! And so I ward him off as if with the Athárvan mantra, 'Scorpion, your poison has been destroyed!' by which it's truly seen that learned men make an antidote for a person bitten by a scorpion and struck by the force of its poison!

Accordingly, smart-arse,* shut up and listen to this next 40.35
revelation! When drunk, Madra women strip off their clothes and dance about. Uninhibited in sex, they choose whoever they lust after. How can a Madra son of theirs speak about morality?

Like camels and asses they piss while standing; their laws have vanished and they're everywhere shameless. You, the son of women such as these, want to speak here about morality!

When she is asked for her fermented gruel,* a Madra woman scratches at her buttocks. Not wanting to give it up, she speaks these awful words: 'No one can ask me for my
precious brew. I'd give up my son, I'd give up my husband, 40.40
but I couldn't give up my brew!'

We hear that most of the shameless Madra women are voracious fat cows covered only in blankets and devoid of purity.

I could say more about such things, as could others, regarding their reprehensible and wicked behavior, from the tips of their hair to the ends of their toenails! How then could the Madra women, these Sindhus and Sauvíras, understand morality here? These barbarians are from an evil country and are ignorant of the laws!

eṣa mukhyatamo dharmaḥ kṣatriyasy', êti naḥ śrutam:
‹yad" ājau nihataḥ śete, sadbhiḥ samabhipūjitaḥ.›
āyudhānāṃ sāṃparāye yan mucyeyam ahaṃ tataḥ,
40.45 mam' âiṣa prathamaḥ kalpo nidhane svargam icchataḥ.
so' haṃ priyaḥ sakhā c' âsmi Dhārtarāṣṭrasya dhīmataḥ;
tad|arthe hi mama prāṇā, yac ca me vidyate vasu.
vyaktaṃ tvam apy upahitaḥ Pāṇḍavaiḥ, pāpa|deśa|ja,
yathā c' âmitravat sarvaṃ tvam asmāsu pravartase.
kāmaṃ na khalu śakyo 'haṃ tvad|vidhānāṃ śatair api
saṃgrāmād vimukhaḥ kartuṃ, dharma|jña iva nāstikaiḥ.
sāraṅga iva gharm'|ârtaḥ, kāmaṃ vilapa, śuṣya ca!
n' âhaṃ bhīṣayituṃ śakyaḥ kṣatra|vṛtte vyavasthitaḥ.
tanu|tyajāṃ nṛ|siṃhānām āhaveṣv a|nivartinām
40.50 yā gatir guruṇā proktā purā Rāmeṇa, tāṃ smare.
teṣāṃ trāṇ'|ârtham udyantaṃ, vadh'|ârthaṃ dviṣatām api,
viddhi mām āsthitaṃ vṛttaṃ Paurūravasam uttamam!
na tad bhūtaṃ prapaśyāmi triṣu lokeṣu, Madra|pa,
yo mām asmād abhiprāyād vārayed, iti me matiḥ.
evaṃ, vidvañ, joṣam āssva! trāsāt kiṃ bahu bhāṣase?
na tvā hatvā pradāsyāmi kravy'|âdbhyo, Madrak'|âdhama,
mitra|pratīkṣayā, Śalya, Dhṛtarāṣṭrasya c' ôbhayoḥ,
apavāda|titikṣābhis, tribhir etair hi jīvasi.
punaś ced īdṛśaṃ vākyaṃ, Madra|rāja, vadiṣyasi,
40.55 śiras te pātayiṣyāmi gadayā vajra|kalpayā!
śrotāras tv idam ady' êha, draṣṭāro vā, ku|deśa|ja,

This is the most important law for a kshatriya as it was taught to us: 'Once killed in battle he lies prone honored by good people.' I shall, then, give myself up to this in a battle of weapons! This is my principal rule, since I seek heaven 40.45
in death.

I'm a dear friend to Dhrita·rashtra's wise son; my life and whatever wealth I have are for his cause. You're from an evil country! Clearly you've been planted by the Pándavas since, like an enemy, you always act against us. In any case, by no means could even a hundred of the like of you avert me from battle, just as one who knows the law cannot be swayed by heretics. Like an antelope suffering from the heat, bleat as much as you want and fade away! I'm committed to 40.50
a warrior's way of life and cannot be intimidated. For I recall the path that guru Rama taught long ago, of those lions of men who relinquished their bodies and never retreated in battles.

Understand this: As I strive to safeguard the Dhartaráshtras and destroy their enemies I follow that excellent course of conduct derived from Puru·ravas!* I see no being in the three worlds, lord of the Madras, who could hold me back from this plan. That's what I think. So shut up, smart-arse! Why do you fearfully speak so much?

I will not kill you and give you to carnivorous beasts, vile Madra. In consideration for my friend,* for Dhrita·rashtra and due to forbearing to speak ill of either; for these three reasons you remain alive, Shalya. If you again utter a speech like that, king of Madra, I'll knock your head off with my 40.55
diamond-hard club! You're from a wretched country! Today

Karṇaṃ vā jaghnatuḥ Kṛṣṇau, Karṇo vā nijaghāna tau.»
evam uktvā tu Rādheyaḥ punar eva, viśāṃ pate,
abravīn Madra|rājānaṃ «yāhi! yāh'! îty» a|saṃbhramam.

SAMJAYA uvāca:

41.1 MĀRIṢ', ĀDHIRATHEH śrutvā vāco yuddh'|âbhinandinaḥ,
Śalyo 'bravīt punaḥ Karṇaṃ nidarśanam idaṃ vacaḥ:
«jāto 'ham yajvanāṃ vaṃśe, saṃgrāmeṣv a|nivartinām,
rājñāṃ mūrdh'|âbhiṣiktānām, svayam dharma|parāyaṇaḥ.
yath" âiva matto madyena, tvaṃ tathā lakṣyase, Vṛṣa,
tath" âdya tvāṃ pramādyantaṃ cikitseyaṃ suhṛttayā.
imāṃ kāk'|ôpamāṃ, Karṇa, procyamānāṃ nibodha me!
śrutvā yath"|êṣṭaṃ kuryās tvaṃ, nihīna, kula|pāṃsana!
41.5 n' âham ātmani kiṃ cid vai kilbiṣaṃ, Karṇa, saṃsmare,
yena māṃ tvaṃ, mahā|bāho, hantum icchasy an|āgasam.
avaśyaṃ tu mayā vācyaṃ budhyatā tvadd|hit'|â|hitam,
viśeṣato ratha|sthena rājñaś c' âiva hit'|âiṣiṇā.
samaṃ ca viṣamaṃ c' âiva; rathinaś ca bal'|âbalam;
śramaḥ khedaś ca satataṃ hayānāṃ rathinā saha;
āyudhasya parijñānaṃ rutaṃ ca mṛga|pakṣiṇām;
bhāraś c' âpy atibhāraś ca; śalyānāṃ ca pratikriyā;
astra|yogaś ca yuddhaṃ ca, nimittāni tath" âiva ca;
sarvam etan mayā jñeyaṃ rathasy' âsya kuṭumbinā.
41.10 atas tvāṃ kathaye, Karṇa, nidarśanam idaṃ punaḥ.

people here will hear or see that either the two Krishnas killed Karna or Karna killed them."

After speaking this, lord of people, Radha's son coolly said again to the king of Madra, "Go! Go!"

SÁNJAYA said:

DEAR FRIEND, after hearing those words of Ádhiratha's 41.1
battle-eager son, Shalya further spoke these instructive words to Karna:

"I was born in a lineage of sacrificers who never retreated in wars, of kings anointed on their heads. I myself am utterly devoted to the law. You seem as though pissed on booze, Vrisha, so, out of friendship, I'll take care of you today while you're being so rash.

Karna, listen to me as I narrate this parable of the crow. After hearing it you can do what you want, vile man, disgrace of your family! I don't recall my offence, mighty armed 41.5
Karna, for which you want to kill me, innocent as I am. It's necessary that I say this, informing you of what's to your advantage and what's not, especially since I stand in this chariot and seek the advantage of my king.

Smooth ground and rough ground; the strength and weakness of a chariot-warrior; at every moment the exhaustion and distress of the horses as well as of the chariot-warrior; a knowledge of weapons and the sounds of animals and birds; burdens and excessive burdens; the treatment of weapon wounds; the deployment of weapons, and battle and omens; all this I know as custodian of this chariot.
Therefore, Karna, I narrate to you this parable once more. 41.10

vaiśyaḥ kila samudr'|ânte prabhūta|dhana|dhānyavān;
yajvā, dāna|patiḥ, kṣāntaḥ, sva|karma|stho 'bhavac chuciḥ.
bahu|putraḥ, priy'|âpatyaḥ, sarva|bhūt'|ânukampakaḥ;
rājño dharma|pradhānasya rāṣṭre vasati nirbhayaḥ.
putrāṇāṃ tasya bālānāṃ kumārāṇāṃ yaśasvinām
kāko bahūnām abhavad ucchiṣṭa|kṛta|bhojanaḥ.
tasmai sadā prayacchanti vaiśya|putrāḥ kumārakāḥ
māṃs'|odanaṃ, dadhi, kṣīraṃ, pāyasaṃ, madhu|sarpiṣī.
sa c' ôcchiṣṭa|bhṛtaḥ kāko vaiśya|putraiḥ kumārakaiḥ,
41.15 sadṛśān pakṣiṇo dṛptaḥ śreyasaś c' âdhicikṣipe.
atha haṃsāḥ samudr'|ânte kadā cid atipātinaḥ,
Garuḍasya gatau tulyāś, cakr'|âṅgā, hṛṣṭa|cetasaḥ.
kumārakās tato haṃsān dṛṣṭvā kākam ath' âbruvan,
‹bhavān eva viśiṣṭo hi patatribhyo, vihaṃ|gama!›
pratāryamāṇas taiḥ sarvair alpa|buddhibhir aṇḍa|jaḥ,
‹tad vacaḥ satyam! ity› eva maurkhyād darpāc ca manyate.
tān so 'bhipatya jijñāsuḥ, ‹ka eṣāṃ śreṣṭha|bhāg? iti›
ucchiṣṭa|darpitaḥ kāko bahūnāṃ dūra|pātinām.
teṣāṃ yaṃ pravaraṃ mene haṃsānāṃ dūra|pātinām,
41.20 tam āhvayata dur|buddhiḥ, ‹patāva! iti› pakṣiṇam.
tac chrutvā prāhasan haṃsā ye tatr' āsan samāgatāḥ,
bhāṣato bahu kākasya balinaḥ patatāṃ varāḥ.
idam ūcuḥ sma cakr'|âṅgā vacaḥ kākaṃ vihaṃ|gamāḥ.

On the coast there was a vaishya who was rich in wealth and corn. A sacrificer, he was a generous man, patient, pure, and preoccupied with his own duties. He had many sons, loved his children and was compassionate to all beings. He lived without fear in the kingdom of a king who put the law first.

There was a crow there that ate the leftovers provided by his many sons, who were strong and famous youths. Those youths, the sons of the vaishya, always gave him meat and boiled rice, sour milk, milk, rice pudding, honey and ghee. Nourished with leftovers by those youthful sons
of the vaishya, the crow became proud and scorned birds 41.15
similar to him and better too.

Then one day fast flying geese arrived on that coast, excited birds with curved necks the equal of Gáruda in their bearing.

Once they spotted the geese, the youths then said to the crow, 'Bird, you're surely better than those birds!'

Taken in by all those inane boys, from pride and stupidity 41.20
the bird thought, 'Those words are true!' The crow flew towards them and, made haughty by the leftovers, wanted to know of those many far-flying birds, 'Who among them is the best?' The daft crow challenged the bird that he regarded as the best of those far-flying geese, 'We must fly together!'

When they heard this as the crow prattled on, the geese who were gathered there, powerful and superb birds, laughed. Those curved-necked birds then spoke this speech to the crow.

HAṂSĀ ūcuḥ:

‹vayaṃ haṃsāś carām' êmāṃ pṛthivīṃ Mānas'|âukasaḥ;
pakṣiṇāṃ ca vayaṃ nityaṃ dūra|pātena pūjitāḥ.
kathaṃ haṃsaṃ nu balinaṃ, cakr'|âṅgaṃ, dūra|pātinam
kāko bhūtvā nipatane samāhvayasi, dur|mate?
kathaṃ tvaṃ patitā, kāka, sah' âsmābhir? bravīhi tat.›

atha haṃsa|vaco mūḍhaḥ kutsayitvā punaḥ punaḥ,
prajagād' ôttaraṃ kākaḥ katthano jāti|lāghavāt.

KĀKA uvāca:

41.25 ‹śatam ekaṃ ca pātānāṃ patit" âsmi, na saṃśayaḥ!
śata|yojanam ek'|âikaṃ vicitraṃ, vividhaṃ tathā.
uḍḍīnam, avaḍīnaṃ ca, praḍīnaṃ, ḍīnam eva ca,
niḍīnam, atha saṃḍīnaṃ, tiryag|ḍīna|gatāni ca,
viḍīnaṃ, pariḍīnaṃ ca, parāḍīnaṃ, su|ḍīnakam,
abhiḍīnaṃ, mahā|ḍīnaṃ, nirḍīnam, atiḍīnakam,
avaḍīnaṃ, praḍīnaṃ ca, saṃḍīnaṃm ḍīna|ḍīnakam,
saṃḍīn'|ôḍḍīna|ḍīnaṃ ca, punar ḍīna|viḍīnakam,
saṃpātaṃ, samudīṣaṃ ca, tato 'nyad vyatiriktakam,
gat'|āgata|pratigataṃ, bahvīś ca nikulīnikāḥ
41.30 kart" âsmi miṣatāṃ vo 'dya, tato drakṣyatha me balam!
teṣām anyatamen' âhaṃ patiṣyāmi vihāyasam.
pradiśadhvaṃ yathā|nyāyaṃ! Kena, haṃsāḥ, patāmy aham?
te vai dhruvaṃ viniścitya, patadhvaṃ tu mayā saha
pātair ebhiḥ khalu, kha|gāḥ, patituṃ khe nir|āśraye!›

THE GEESE said:

'We geese live on Lake Mánasa and wander the earth. We are always honored among birds due to the distance we fly. Being a crow, moron, how could you challenge a powerful, curved-necked and far-flying goose in a flying contest? Explain, crow, how you will fly with us?'

Rebuking these words of the geese again and again, the stupid crow, boasting due to the impulsiveness of his kind, then uttered this response.

THE CROW said:

'Without a doubt I will fly a hundred and one kinds of 41.25
flight! Each of a hundred *yójana*s will be surprising and diverse. Flying up, flying down, flying forwards and just plain flying, then flying in downward swoops, flying in formation and drifting sideways in flight, flying at angles, flying in circles, flying away, flying gracefully, flying towards another, flying powerfully, gliding and flying ostentatiously, flying down and forwards, flying repeated maneuvers in formation, flying upwards in formation and flying backwards at an angle, swift descents and then rising upwards, withdrawing from another, wheeling about and flying backwards then
forwards, and many other modes of flying I will do before 41.30
your eyes today and you will then see my strength! I will fly through the sky with any one of these. Select one according to the rule! Geese, with which shall I fly? Once you've come to a final decision, you must fly with me, birds, with those ways of flying you fly through the sky that has no haven!'

evam ukte tu kākena, prahasy' âiko vihaṃ|gamaḥ
uvāca kākaṃ, Rādheya, vacanaṃ. tan nibodha me!

HAṂSA uvāca:

‹śatam ekaṃ ca pātānāṃ tvaṃ, kāka, patitā dhruvam.
ekam eva tu yaṃ pātaṃ viduḥ sarve vihaṃ|gamāḥ,
tam ahaṃ patitā, kāka, n' ânyaṃ jānāmi kañ cana.
41.35 pata tvam api, tāmr'|âkṣa, yena pātena manyase!›
atha kākāḥ prajahasur ye tatr' āsan samāgatāḥ:
‹katham ekena pātena haṃsaḥ pāta|śataṃ jayet?
eken' âiva śatasy' âiṣa pāten', âbhipatiṣyati
haṃsasya patitaṃ kāko balavān, āśu|vikramaḥ!›
prapetatuḥ spardhayā ca tatas tau haṃsa|vāyasau,
eka|pātī ca cakr'|âṅgaḥ, kākaḥ pāta|śatena ca.
patitā v" âtha cakr'|âṅgaḥ, patitā v" âtha vāyasaḥ,
visismāpayiṣuḥ pātair, ācakṣāṇo "tmanaḥ kriyāḥ.
atha kākasya citrāṇi patitāni muhur muhuḥ
41.40 dṛṣṭvā, pramuditāḥ kākā vinedur adhikaiḥ svaraiḥ,
haṃsāṃś c' âvahasanti sma prāvadann a|priyāṇi ca.
utpaty' ôtpatya ca muhur muhūrtam iti c' êti ca
vṛkṣ'|âgrebhyaḥ, sthalebhyaś ca nipatanty utpatanti ca,
kurvāṇā vividhān rāvān āśaṃsanto jayam tathā.
haṃsas tu mṛdun' âikena vikrāntum upacakrame,
pratyahīyata kākāc ca muhūrtam iva, māriṣa.
avamanya ca haṃsāṃs tān idaṃ vacanam abruvan:
‹yo 'sāv utpatito haṃsaḥ, so 'sāv evaṃ prahīyate!›

Once this had been spoken by the crow, one bird laughed and addressed the crow. Son of Radha, listen to those words from me!

THE GOOSE said:

'Crow, you surely will fly a hundred and one ways of flying. But I will fly just the one way of flying that all birds know, crow; I know no other. You too must fly, red-eyed 41.35
crow, with whatever way of flying you think right!'

The crows that had gathered there then laughed: 'How can the goose with just one way of flying defeat the crow who has a hundred ways of flying? With only one of his hundred ways of flying, the powerful, fast moving crow will out-fly the flight of the goose!'

Then the goose and the crow flew in competition, the goose with his one way of flying and the crow with his hundred. Either the goose would fly or the crow would fly, each hoping to dazzle with their ways of flying and bragging about their own feats.

As they again and again saw the crow's various flights, 41.40
the excited crows shrieked with splendid cries and, making unpleasant sounds, mocked the geese. Ascending repeatedly and momentarily, and so on and so on, they descended and then rose up from tree-tops and the ground, making various cries and hoping for victory.

But the goose began to move with one gentle wave and, for an instant, seemed to fall behind the crow, dear friend. Regarding the geese with contempt, the crows said these words to them: 'So the rising goose has been left behind!'

atha haṃsaḥ sa tac chrutvā prāpatat paścimāṃ diśam
41.45 upary upari vegena sāgaraṃ makar'|ālayam.
tato bhīḥ prāviśat kākaṃ tadā tatra vicetasam,
dvīpa|drumān a|paśyantaṃ nipāt'|ârthe śram'|ânvitam,
‹nipateyaṃ kva nu śrānta? iti› tasmiñ jal'|ârṇave.
a|viṣahyaḥ samudro hi bahu|sattva|gaṇ'|ālayaḥ;
mahā|sattva|śat'|ôdbhāsī nabhaso 'pi viśiṣyate.
gāṃbhīryādd hi samudrasya na viśeṣaṃ hi, sūta|ja,
dig|ambar'|âmbhasaḥ, Karṇa, samudra|sthā vidur janāḥ.
vidūra|pātāt toyasya, kiṃ punaḥ, Karṇa, vāyasaḥ?
atha haṃso 'py atikramya muhūrtam iti c' êti ca,
41.50 avekṣamāṇas taṃ kākaṃ, n' âśakad vyapasarpitum.
atikramya ca cakr'|âṅgaḥ kākaṃ taṃ samudaikṣata,
‹yāvad gatvā pataty eṣa kāko mām! iti› cintayan.
tataḥ kāko bhṛśaṃ śrānto haṃsam abhyāgamat tadā.
taṃ tathā hīyamānaṃ tu haṃso dṛṣṭv" âbravīd idam,
ujjihīrṣur nimajjantaṃ, smaran sat|puruṣa|vratam.

HAṂSA uvāca:

‹bahūni patanāni tvam ācakṣāṇo muhur muhuḥ
pātasya vyāharaṃś c' êdaṃ na no guhyaṃ prabhāṣase.
kiṃ nāma patitaṃ, kāka, yat tvaṃ patasi sāṃpratam?
jalaṃ spṛśasi pakṣābhyāṃ tuṇḍena ca punaḥ punaḥ.
41.55 prabrūhi, katame tatra pāte vartasi, vāyasa?
ehy! ehi, kāka, śīghraṃ tvam! eṣa tvāṃ pratipālaye!›»

Hearing this, the goose then rapidly flew away to the west over and beyond the ocean, the habitat of sea-monsters. 41.45

Because of this, fear entered the stupid crow and, filled with exhaustion and seeing neither trees nor islands in the ocean suitable for landing, he thought, 'I'm exhausted, where can I land?'

For the ocean is unfathomable and home to innumerable kinds of creatures. Graced with hundreds of massive creatures, it is more impressive even than the sky. Son of a charioteer, Karna, people who live by the ocean know that there's nothing deeper than the depth of the ocean. Its waters encompass the sky. Because he had flown so far over the water, Karna, what more could the crow do?

Then, sweeping past him in an instant or so, the goose
saw the crow and could not slink away. Once he swept past 41.50
him, the goose looked carefully at the crow, thinking, 'The crow's gone this far, he can fly to me!' Utterly exhausted, the crow then came near the goose. But seeing him fall behind, the goose, remembering a good man's oath and wanting to rescue him, said this as the crow sank down.

THE GOOSE said:

'When you named and bragged repeatedly about your many ways of flying, you didn't disclose to us the secret of this way of flying. What do you call this way of flying that you fly now, crow, as you touch the water again and again
with your wings and beak? Explain, crow, what's this mode 41.55
of flying you're employing? Come here! Come here quickly crow! I'll take care of you!'"

ŚALYA uvāca:

«sa pakṣābhyāṃ spṛśann ārtas tuṇḍena ca jalaṃ tadā
dṛṣṭo haṃsena, duṣṭ'|ātmann, idaṃ haṃsaṃ tato 'bravīt.
a|paśyann ambhasaḥ pāraṃ, nipataṃś ca śram'|ânvitaḥ,
pāta|vega|pramathito, haṃsaṃ kāko 'bravīd idam:

‹vayaṃ kākāḥ. kuto nāma? carāmaḥ kāka|vāśikāḥ.
haṃsa, prāṇaiḥ prapadye tvām, udak'|ântaṃ nayasva mām!›

sa pakṣābhyāṃ spṛśann ārtas tuṇḍena ca mah"|ârṇave,
kāko dṛḍha|pariśrāntaḥ sahasā nipapāta ha.
41.60 sāgar'|âmbhasi taṃ dṛṣṭvā patitaṃ dīna|cetasam,
mriyamāṇam idaṃ kākaṃ haṃso vākyam uvāca ha:

‹«śatam ekaṃ ca pātānāṃ patāmy aham!» anusmara!
ślāghamānas tvam ātmānaṃ, kāka, bhāṣitavān asi.
sa tvam eka|śataṃ pātaṃ patann abhyadhiko mayā,
katham evaṃ pariśrāntaḥ patito 'si mah"|ârṇave?›

pratyuvāca tataḥ kākaḥ sīdamāna idaṃ vacaḥ
upari|ṣṭhaṃ tadā haṃsam abhivīkṣya prasādayan.

KĀKA uvāca:

‹ucchiṣṭa|darpito, haṃsa, manye "tmānaṃ Suparṇavat,
avamanya bahūṃś c' âhaṃ kākān, anyāṃś ca pakṣiṇaḥ.
41.65 prāṇair, haṃsa, prapadye tvāṃ,
dvīp'|ântaṃ prāpayasva mām!
yady ahaṃ svastimān, haṃsa,
sva deśaṃ prāpnuyāṃ, vibho,
na kañ cid avamanye 'ham. āpado māṃ samuddhara!›

SHALYA said:

"Distressed and touching the water with his wings and beak while the goose watched him, malicious man, the crow then spoke to the goose. Seeing no end to the water, falling and filled with exhaustion and dragged down by the momentum of his descent, the crow said this to the goose:

'We are crows. Why this name? Because we roam about crying "*kaka.*"* Goose, I implore you with my life, lead me to shore!'

Distressed and dipping his wings and beak into the great ocean, the completely exhausted crow suddenly dropped. Seeing him utterly wretched as he fell into the waters of the 41.60
ocean, the goose spoke this speech to the crow as he was dying:

'You must remember, "I fly a hundred and one ways of flying!" You said this about yourself while bragging, crow. You're the one who flies a hundred more ways of flying than me; how is it then that, exhausted like this, you fall into the great ocean?'

As he sank down the crow saw the goose above him and, seeking to appease him, then responded with this speech.

THE CROW said:

'Made cocky by being fed leftovers, goose, I treated many crows and other birds with contempt and thought myself like Supárna.* I implore you with my life, goose, help me 41.65
reach the shore of an island! If I should reach my own country in good health, powerful goose, I will not treat anyone with contempt. Save me from this disaster!'

tam evaṃ|vādinaṃ, dīnaṃ, vilapantam, a|cetanam,
‹kāka! kāk'! êti› vāśantaṃ, nimajjantaṃ mah"|ârṇave,
kṛpay" ādāya haṃsas taṃ jala|klinnaṃ su|dur|daśam
padbhyām utkṣipya vegena, pṛṣṭham āropayac chanaiḥ.
āropya pṛṣṭhaṃ haṃsas taṃ kākaṃ tūrṇaṃ vicetanam,
ājagāma punar dvīpaṃ spardhayā petatur yataḥ.
saṃsthāpya taṃ c' âpi punaḥ, samāśvāsya ca khe|caram,
41.70 gato yath"|ēpsitaṃ deśaṃ haṃso, mana iv' āśu|gaḥ.
evam ucchiṣṭa|puṣṭaḥ sa kāko haṃsa|parājitaḥ;
balaṃ, vīryaṃ mahat, Karṇa, tyaktvā kṣāntim upāgataḥ.
ucchiṣṭa|bhojanaḥ kāko yathā vaiśya|kule purā,
evaṃ tvam ucchiṣṭa|bhṛto Dhārtarāṣṭrair na saṃśayaḥ!
sadṛśāñ, śreyasaś c' âpi sarvān, Karṇ', âvamanyase.
Droṇa|Drauṇi|Kṛpair gupto,
Bhīṣmeṇ', ânyaiś ca Kauravaiḥ
Virāṭa|nagare, Pārtham
ekaṃ kiṃ n' âvadhīs tadā?
yatra vyastāḥ samastāś ca nirjitāḥ stha Kirīṭinā,
sṛgālā iva siṃhena, kva te vīryam abhūt tadā?
41.75 bhrātaraṃ nihataṃ dṛṣṭvā samare Savyasācinā,
paśyatāṃ Kuru|vīrāṇāṃ prathamaṃ tvaṃ palāyitaḥ.
tathā Dvaita|vane, Karṇa, gandharvaiḥ samabhidrutaḥ
kurūn samagrān utsṛjya, prathamaṃ tvaṃ palāyitaḥ.

As he said this while he moaned senselessly and shrieked '*kaka*! *kaka*!' and sank into the deep sea, out of compassion the goose grasped that miserable bird. Quickly raising that bird with his wings, he gently placed him on his back, soaked with water and in a very bad way.

Once he had quickly placed the senseless crow onto his back, the goose returned to the island where they had flown in competition. And, after placing that bird down and reviving him again, the goose departed moving as fast as thought 41.70
for whatever place he wished.

In this way the crow, fattened by leftovers, was defeated by the goose. Giving up his excessive bravado and vigor, Karna, he began a life of temperance.

Just as before the crow had lived off leftovers in the family of vaishyas, so—without any doubt!—the Dhartáshtras support you with their leftovers. Moreover you treat everyone—those like you and better than you—with contempt, Karna.

When you were protected by Drona, Drona's son, Kripa, Bhishma and other Káuravas in Viráta's city, why didn't you kill Pritha's son while he was alone then? When you were all torn apart and defeated by the Wearer of the crown, like jackals by a lion, where was your courage then? After see- 41.75
ing your brother killed in battle by the Left-handed archer, you were the first to flee while the Kuru heroes watched.* Similary, Karna, when you were attacked by the *gandhárvas* in the Dvaita forest, abandoning all the Kurus, you were the first to flee. After defeating and killing in battle the *gandhárvas* led by Chitra·sena, Karna, Pritha's son freed Duryódhana along with his wife. Besides, Rama related the

hatvā jitvā ca gandharvāṃś Citrasena|mukhān raṇe,
Karṇa, Duryodhanaṃ Pārthaḥ sa|bhāryaṃ samamokṣayat.
punaḥ prabhāvaḥ Pārthasya, paurāṇaḥ Keśavasya ca
kathitaḥ, Karṇa, Rāmeṇa sabhāyāṃ rāja|saṃsadi.
satataṃ ca tvam aśrauṣīr vacanaṃ Droṇa|Bhīṣmayoḥ,
a|vadhyau vadataḥ Kṛṣṇau saṃnidhau ca mahī|kṣitām.

41.80 kiyat tat tat pravakṣyāmi, yena yena Dhanaṃjayaḥ
tvatto 'tiriktaḥ, sarvebhyo bhūtebhyo brāhmaṇo yathā.
idānīm eva draṣṭ" âsi pradhāne syandane sthitau,
putraṃ ca Vasudevasya, Kuntī|putraṃ ca Pāṇḍavam.
yath" āśrayata cakr'|âṅgaṃ vāyaso buddhim āsthitaḥ,
tath" āśrayasva Vārṣṇeyaṃ Pāṇḍavaṃ ca Dhanaṃjayam!

yadā tvaṃ yudhi vikrāntau Vāsudeva|Dhanaṃjayau
draṣṭ" âsy eka|rathe, Karṇa, tadā n' âivaṃ vadiṣyasi.
yadā śara|śataiḥ Pārtho darpaṃ tava vadhiṣyati,
tadā tvam antaraṃ draṣṭā ātmanaś c' Ârjunasya ca.

41.85 dev'|âsura|manuṣyeṣu prakhyātau yau nara'|rṣabhau,
tau m" âvamaṃsthā maurkhyāt tvaṃ, kha|dyota iva rocanau!
sūryā|candramasau yadvat, tadvad Arjuna|Keśavau
prākāśyen' âbhivikhyātau, tvaṃ tu kha|dyotavan nṛṣu.
evaṃ, vidvan, m" âvamaṃsthāḥ, sūta|putr', Âcyut'|Ârjunau
nṛ|siṃhau tau mah"|ātmānau! joṣam āssva vikatthane!»

magnificence of Pritha's son and the ancient lore of Ké-shava in the assembly hall at the king's court.* And you always heard the words of Drona and Bhishma, who said* in the presence of the kings that the two Krishnas couldn't be defeated.

I will tell you in how many ways Dhanan·jaya is better 41.80
than you, just as a brahmin is better than all other beings. Right now you will see those two standing in that foremost chariot, the son of Vasu·deva and Kunti's son the Pándava. Just as the crow used his intellect and sought refuge with the goose, so you must seek refuge with Varshnéya and the Pándava Dhanan·jaya!

When you see courageous Vasudéva and Dhanan·jaya in battle on the same chariot, Karna, then you will not speak like this. When Pritha's son destroys your arrogance with hundreds of arrows, then you'll see the difference between yourself and Árjuna. Don't stupidly show contempt 41.85
for those brilliant men who are famed among gods, demons and men; you're like a fire-fly and they're like two shining stars! Árjuna and Késhava are renowned for their fame like the sun and moon, but you're like a fire-fly among men. So, smart-arse son of a charioteer, don't show contempt for Áchyuta and Árjuna! They are great lions of men. Quit this boasting!"

SAMJAYA uvāca:

42.1 MADR'|ÂDHIPASY' Ādhirathir mah"|ātmā
vaco niśamy' âpriyam a|pratītaḥ
uvāca Śalyaṃ: «viditaṃ mam' âitad,
yathā|vidhāv Arjuna|Vāsudevau.
Śaure rathaṃ vāhayato, 'rjunasya
balaṃ, mah"|âstrāṇi ca Pāṇḍavasya,
ahaṃ vijānāmi yathāvad adya;
parokṣa|bhūtaṃ tava tat tu, Śalya.
tau c' âpy ahaṃ śastra|bhṛtāṃ variṣṭhau
vyapeta|bhīr yodhayiṣyāmi Kṛṣṇau.
saṃtāpayaty abhyadhikaṃ nu Rāmāc
chāpo 'dya māṃ brāhmaṇa|sattamāc ca.
avasaṃ vai brāhmaṇa|cchadman" âhaṃ
Rāme purā divyam astraṃ cikīrṣuḥ.
tatr' âpi me deva|rājena vighno,
hit'|ârthinā Phalgunasy' âiva, Śalya,
42.5 kṛto vibhedena mam' ōrum etya,
praviśya kīṭasya tanuṃ virūpām.
mam' ōrum etya prabibheda kīṭaḥ,
supte gurau tatra śiro nidhāya.
ūru|prabhedāc ca mahān babhūva
śarīrato me ghana|śoṇit'|âughaḥ,
guror bhayāc c' âpi na celivān ahaṃ.
tato vibuddho dadṛśe sa vipraḥ.
sa dhairya|yuktaṃ prasamīkṣya māṃ vai,
‹na tvaṃ vipraḥ; ko 'si? satyaṃ vad'! êti.›
tasmai tad" ātmānam ahaṃ yathāvad
ākhyātavān, ‹sūta! ity› eva, Śalya.

SÁNJAYA said:

HAVING HEARD the antagonistic words of the lord of the Madras, Ádhiratha's great son was unimpressed. He said to Shalya: "I understand what kind of people Árjuna and Késhava are. Today I know well the chariot of Shauri* and his driving of it, and the strength and great missiles of the Pándava Árjuna. But these are imperceptible to you, Shalya. Moreover I will fearlessly fight the two Krishnas, the finest weapon-bearers. Still, the curse from Rama, that finest of brahmins, troubles me greatly today. 42.1

Hoping to gain access to a divine weapon, some time ago I lived with Rama in disguise as a brahmin. In this also I was thwarted by the king of the gods who sought Phálguna's advantage, Shalya, which he did by approaching and 42.5
piercing my thigh, having entered the hideous body of a worm.

Once it had approached, the worm pierced my thigh while the guru rested his head on it and slept. From the incision in my thigh, a huge torrent of thick blood welled up from my body, but, because of my fear of the guru, I dared not move.

Waking up, the brahmin looked up from there. Seeing me holding firm, he asked, 'You're no brahmin, are you? Tell me the truth!' Then, Shalya, I myself truthfully confessed to him, 'I'm a *suta*!'*

sa māṃ niśamy' âtha mahā|tapasvī
samśaptavān roṣa|parīta|cetāḥ:
‹sūt', ôpadhāv āptam idaṃ tav' âstraṃ,
na karma|kāle pratibhāsyati tvām.
anyatra tasmāt tava mṛtyu|kālād,
a|brāhmaṇe Brahma na hi dhruvaṃ syāt!›
tad adya paryāptam atīva c' âstram
asmin saṃgrāme tumule 'tīva bhīme.
42.10 yo 'yaṃ, Śalya, Bharateṣ' ûpapannaḥ,
prakarṣaṇaḥ, sarva|haro, 'tibhīmaḥ;
so 'bhimanye kṣatriyāṇāṃ pravīrān
pratāpitā balavān vai vimardaḥ.
Śaly', ôgra|dhanvānam ahaṃ variṣṭhaṃ,
tarasvinaṃ, bhīmam, a|sahya|vīryam,
satya|pratijñaṃ yudhi Pāṇḍaveyaṃ
Dhanaṃjayaṃ mṛtyu|mukhaṃ nayiṣye.
astraṃ hi me tat|pratipannam adya,
yena kṣepsye samare śatru|pūgān.
pratāpinaṃ, balavantaṃ, kṛt'|âstraṃ
tam ugra|dhanvānam, amit'|âujasaṃ ca,
krūraṃ, śūraṃ, raudram, amitra|sāhaṃ,
Dhanaṃjayaṃ saṃyuge 'haṃ haniṣye!
apāṃ patir vegavān, a|prameyo,
nimajjayiṣyan bahulāḥ prajāś ca
mahā|vegaṃ saṃkurute samudraḥ;
velā c' âinaṃ dhārayaty a|prameyam.
pramuñcantaṃ bāṇa|saṃghān a|meyān
marma|cchido, vīra|haṇaḥ, su|patrān
42.15 Kuntī|putraṃ yatra yotsyāmi yuddhe
jyāṃ karṣatām uttamam adya loke.

After hearing me, the great ascetic then cursed me, his mind seized by rage: '*Suta*, you've acquired this weapon dishonestly. When the time comes for it to perform, it won't appear to you. On occasions other than the time of your death, it will. For the Brahma weapon shall not always be reliable for a non-brahmin!' Yet today this weapon is quite sufficient for this utterly terrible and tumultuous battle.

Among the Bharatas, Árjuna is fit for this occasion, Sha- 42.10
lya. He's troublesome, destroys everything and is utterly formidable. Powerful and devastating, I reckon he'll scorch the heroes among the kshatriyas. Shalya, I will lead the bold Pándava Dhanan·jaya into the jaws of death in battle. He is the best, his bow is awesome, his courage unendurable and his promise true. With my weapon that I obtained from him,* today I will strike down masses of enemies in battle.

I will kill Dhanan·jaya in battle. Majestic, powerful, 42.15
skilled with his weapons and bearing a formidable bow, his strength has no limit; he is a ferocious hero, an awesome subduer of enemies. The lord of waters—the volatile and immeasurable ocean—generates a massive flood sinking many people, yet the shoreline holds fast against that immeasurable force. In this world I will fight Kunti's son today in a battle in which the finest of those who draw a bow-string shall release innumerable volleys of lethally wounding arrows, hero-killers with fine wings. In this way, like the shoreline, I will resist Pritha's ocean-like son with my

evaṃ balen' âtibalaṃ, mah"|âstraṃ,
samudra|kalpaṃ, su|dur|āpam, ugram,
śar'|âughiṇaṃ, pārthivān majjayantaṃ,
vel" êva Pārtham iṣubhiḥ saṃsahiṣye.
ady' āhave yasya na tulyam anyaṃ
manye manuṣyaṃ dhanur ādadānam.
sur'|âsurān yudhi vai yo jayeta.
ten' âdya me paśya yuddhaṃ su|ghoram!
atīva mānī Pāṇḍavo yuddha|kāmo;
hy a|mānuṣair eṣyati me mah"|âstraiḥ.
tasy' âstram astraiḥ pratihatya saṃkhye,
bāṇ'|ôttamaiḥ pātayiṣyāmi Pārtham.
sahasra|raśmi|pratimaṃ jvalantaṃ,
diśaś ca sarvāḥ pratapantam, ugram,
tamo|nudaṃ megha iv', âtimātraṃ
Dhanaṃjayaṃ chādayiṣyāmi bāṇaiḥ.
Vaiśvānaraṃ dhūma|śikhaṃ jvalantaṃ,
tejasvinaṃ lokam imaṃ dahantam,
42.20 parjanya|bhūtaḥ śara|varṣair yath" Âgniṃ,
tathā Pārthaṃ śamayiṣyāmi yuddhe.
āśī|viṣaṃ dur|dharam, a|prameyaṃ,
su|tīkṣṇa|daṃṣṭraṃ, jvalana|prabhāvam,
krodha|pradīptaṃ tv, a|hitaṃ, mahāntaṃ,
Kuntī|putraṃ śamayiṣyāmi bhallaiḥ.
pramāthinaṃ, balavantaṃ, prahāriṇaṃ,
prabhañjanaṃ, mātariśvānam ugram,

arrows, as he powerfully sinks the princes, his waves of arrows formidable and unfathomable and his mighty weapon awesomely powerful.

I reckon that there's no other man holding a bow today who's his equal in battle. He could defeat the gods and demons in battle. Watch as I have this utterly horrendous battle with him today! The Pándava is immensely proud and wants a fight; he'll come at me today with his mighty, inhuman weapons. After repelling his weapon with my weapons in the battle, I'll fell Pritha's son with my superb arrows.

He is formidable, burning like a thousand shafts of sunlight and scorching all directions. Like a cloud concealing 42.20
the sun, I will completely cover Dhanan·jaya with arrows. I'll extinguish Pritha's son with torrents of arrows as if I were a rain-cloud extinguishing powerful Agni Vaishvánara as he burns the world blazing with plumes of smoke. With broad arrows I'll extinguish Kunti's son, a mighty adversary, an untrappable and immeasurable poisonous snake with razor-sharp fangs and the power of a fire burning with anger.

yuddhe sahiṣye, Himavān iv' âcalo,
Dhanaṃjayaṃ kruddham a|mṛṣyamāṇam,
viśāradaṃ ratha|mārgeṣu śaktaṃ,
dhuryaṃ nityaṃ samareṣu, pravīram,
loke varaṃ sarva|dhanur|dharāṇāṃ,
Dhanaṃjayaṃ saṃyuge saṃsahiṣye.
ady' āhave yasya na tulyam anyaṃ
manye manuṣyaṃ dhanur ādadānam,
sarvām imāṃ yaḥ pṛthivīṃ vijigye,
tena prayoddh" âsmi sametya saṃkhye.
yaḥ sarva|bhūtāni sa|daivatāni
prasthe 'jayat Khāṇḍave Savyasācī;
42.25 ko jīvitaṃ rakṣyamāṇo hi tena
yuyutsed vai mām ṛte mānuṣo 'nyaḥ?
mānī, kṛt'|âstraḥ, kṛta|hasta|yogo,
divy'|âstra|vic, chveta|hayaḥ, pramāthī,
tasy' âham ady' âtirathasya kāyāc
chiro hariṣyāmi śitaiḥ pṛṣatkaiḥ!
yotsyāmy enaṃ, Śalya, Dhanaṃjayaṃ vai,
mṛtyuṃ puras|kṛtya raṇe, jayaṃ vā;
anyo hi na hy eka|rathena martyo
yudhyeta yaḥ Pāṇḍavam Indra|kalpam.
tasy' āhave pauruṣaṃ Pāṇḍavasya
brūyāṃ hṛṣṭaḥ samitau kṣatriyāṇām.
kiṃ tvaṃ mūrkhaḥ prasabhaṃ mūḍha|cetā
mām avocaḥ pauruṣam Phālgunasya?
a|priyo yaḥ puruṣo niṣṭhuro hi,
kṣudraḥ, kṣeptā, kṣamiṇaś c' â|kṣamāvān;
hanyām ahaṃ tvādṛśānāṃ śatāni,
kṣamāmi tvāṃ kṣamayā Kāla|yogāt.

Like the Himalayas I'll resist in battle the enraged and unforgiving Dhanan·jaya, who is powerful like a formidable gale, harassing, beating and crushing. I will resist Dhanan·jaya in battle, the best of all bowmen in this world, a clever hero skilled in the ways of chariots who always leads from the front in battles.

I reckon that there's no other man holding a bow today who's his equal in battle. After meeting him in battle, I'll fight with that man who conquered this entire earth. The Left-handed archer defeated all beings along with the gods in the clearing in the Khándava forest. Other than me, 42.25
which man keen to preserve his own life would want to fight with him? The man with white horses is proud, skilled with his weapon and in the methods of hand combat, knows the divine weapons and is capable of destroying; yet today with sharp arrows I'll sever the head from the great warrior's body! I will fight Dhanan·jaya, Shalya, honoring death or victory in battle above all else. For there's no other mortal who, with just a single chariot, could fight the Indra-like Pándava.

In an assembly of kshatriyas I would gladly testify to the courage of the Pándava in battle. Why did you, stupid as you are and your mind utterly confused, recount to me Phálguna's courage? You're no friend! You're a cruel man; a pathetic, intolerant abuser of one who tolerates you. I 42.30
could kill hundreds of the like of you, but I suffer you with tolerance because of the workings of Time. Reprobate, you spoke antagonistically to me for the Pándava's benefit, attacking me like a fool. In all honesty, I should have killed you; your intentions dishonest, you sought to betray an ally,

avocas tvaṃ Pāṇḍav'|ârthe '|priyāṇi,
pradharṣayan māṃ mūḍhavat, pāpa|karman.
42.30 may" ārjave jihma|matir hatas tvaṃ
mitra|drohī, sāpta|padaṃ hi maitram.
kālas tv ayaṃ pratyupayāti dāruṇo,
Duryodhano yuddham upāgamad yat.
asy' ârtha|siddhim tv abhikāṅkṣamāṇas,
tam manyase yatra n' āikāntyam asti.
mitraṃ minder, nandateḥ, prīyater vā,
saṃtrāyater, minuter, modater vā.
bravīmi te, sarvam idaṃ mam' âsti;
tac c' âpi sarvaṃ mama vetti rājā.
śatruḥ śadeḥ, śāsater vā, śyater vā,
śṛṇāter vā, śvasateḥ, sīdater vā;
upasargād bahudhā sūdateś ca.
prāyeṇa sarvaṃ tvayi, tac ca mahyam.
Duryodhan'|ârthaṃ, tava ca priy'|ârthaṃ,
yaśo|'rtham ātm'|ârtham ap' Īśvar'|ârtham,
tasmād ahaṃ Pāṇḍava|Vāsudevau
yotsye yatnāt. karma tat paśya me 'dya!
astrāṇi paśy' âdya mam' ôttamāni,
Brāhmāṇi, divyāny, atha mānuṣāṇi!
42.35 āsādayiṣyāmy aham ugra|vīryaṃ,
dvipo dvipaṃ mattaṃ iv' âtimattaḥ.
astraṃ Brāhmaṃ manasā yudhy a|jeyaṃ
kṣepsye Pārthāy' â|prameyaṃ Jayāya.
ten' âpi me n' âiva mucyeta yuddhe,
na cet pated viṣame me 'dya cakram.

and an alliance is ratified in seven steps.* But the cruel hour returns again now that Duryódhana has arrived for battle. As I strive for the success of his cause, you worry that there's nothing certain about it.

'Friend'* is derived from the verbs 'to fatten,' 'to gladden,' 'to love,' 'to protect,' 'to build' or 'to give pleasure.' I tell you, I have all these traits. Moreover the king* knows I have all these traits.

'Enemy' is derived from the verbs 'to destroy,' 'to punish,' 'to sharpen,' 'to crush,' 'to hiss' or 'to exhaust,' and, in various ways depending on the prefix, from 'to kill.' Almost all these are in you; and you see them in me.

For Duryódhana, for your affection, for fame, for myself and for god, doggedly I'll fight the Pándava and Vasudéva. Watch this feat of mine today! Watch my superb weapons today—those coming from Brahma, other divine weapons and those made by man! I'll floor Árjuna whose courage 42.35
is formidable, like an incredibly ruttish elephant flooring a ruttish elephant. With my mind I'll release the invincible and immeasurable Brahma weapon at Pritha's son Jaya in the battle. He cannot escape from this weapon of mine in battle today as long as my wheel doesn't sink in the rugged ground.

Vaivasvatād daṇḍa|hastād, Varuṇād v" âpi pāśinaḥ,
sa|gadād vā dhana|pateḥ, sa|vajrād v" âpi Vāsavāt,
anyasmād api kasmāc cid amitrād ātatāyinaḥ,
iti, Śalya, vijānīhi yathā n' âhaṃ bibhemy ataḥ.
tasmān na me bhayaṃ Pārthān, n' âpi c' âiva Janārdanāt;
saha yuddhaṃ hi me tābhyāṃ sāṃparāye bhaviṣyati.

kadā cid Vijayasy' âham astra|hetor aṭan, nṛpa,
ajñānādd hi kṣipan bāṇān ghora|rūpān bhayānakān,
homa|dhenvā vatsam asya pramatta iṣuṇ" âhanam
42.40 carantam vijane. Śalya, tato 'nuvyājahāra mām.

‹yasmāt tvayā pramattena homa|dhenvā hataḥ sutaḥ,
śvabhre te patatāṃ cakram, iti› māṃ brāhmaṇo 'bravīt,
‹yudhyamānasya saṃgrāme prāptasy' âik'|âyanaṃ bhayam!›

tasmād bibhemi balavad brāhmaṇa|vyāhṛtād aham,
ete hi soma|rājāna īśvarāḥ sukha|duḥkhayoḥ.
adāṃ tasmai go|sahasraṃ, balīvardāṃś ca ṣaṭ|śatān,
prasādaṃ na lebhe, Śalya, brāhmaṇān, Madrak'|ēśvara.
īṣā|dantān sapta|śatān, dāsī|dāsa|śatāni ca
dadato dvija|mukhyo me prasādaṃ na cakāra saḥ.
42.45 kṛṣṇānāṃ śveta|vatsānāṃ sahasrāṇi catur|daśa
āharaṃ, na labhe tasmāt prasādaṃ dvija|sattamāt.
ṛddhaṃ gṛhaṃ sarva|kāmair, yac ca me vasu kiñ cana,
tat sarvam asmai sat|kṛtya prayacchāmi; na c' êcchati.

Vaivásvata* with staff in hand, Váruna with his noose, the lord of wealth with his club, Vásava with his thunderbolt and any other enemy drawing his bow, Shalya, you must know that I have no fear of them. Therefore, I fear neither Pritha's son nor even Janárdana. My fight with those two shall take place in this battle.

One day, king, while wandering about in order to practise my weapon Víjaya and obliviously shooting formidable arrows of hideous appearance, with an arrow I carelessly killed the calf of a brahmin's cow that provided milk for his sacrifice as it wandered in a deserted place. Consequently, 42.40
Shalya, he cursed me.

The brahmin said to me, 'Since you carelessly killed the issue of my cow that provides milk for my sacrifices, the wheel of your chariot shall fall into a hole as you fight in battle and meet a terror that's all your own!'

Because of this I'm terribly afraid of what the brahmin said, for the kings of *soma** are the lords of joy and despair. I gave him a thousand cows and six hundred bulls, but I gained no favor from the brahmin, Shalya, lord of the Madras. That foremost of brahmins did me no favors though I gave him seven hundred elephants with tusks as long as poles and hundreds of male and female slaves. I 42.45
gained no favor from that most excellent brahmin, though I fetched him fourteen thousand black cows with white calves. An oppulent house with everything desirable and all the wealth that I had I respectfully gave to him; but he did not want it.

tato 'bravīn māṃ yācantam aparādhaṃ prayatnataḥ:
‹vyāhṛtaṃ yan mayā, sūta, tat tathā, na tad anyathā.
an|ṛt'|ôktaṃ prajā hanyāt; tataḥ pāpam avāpnuyām.
tasmād dharm'|âbhirakṣ'|ârthaṃ n' ân|ṛtaṃ vaktum utsahe.
mā tvaṃ brahma|gatiṃ hiṃsyāḥ. prāyaścittaṃ kṛtaṃ tvayā.
mad|vākyaṃ n' ân|ṛtaṃ loke kaś cit kuryāt. samāpnuhi!›
42.50 ity etat te mayā proktaṃ kṣipten' âpi suhṛttayā.
jānāmi tvāṃ vikṣipantaṃ! joṣam āssv', ôttaraṃ śṛṇu!»

SAṂJAYA uvāca:

43.1 TATAḤ PUNAR, mahā|rāja, Madra|rājam ariṃ|damaḥ
abhyabhāṣata Rādheyaḥ saṃnivāry' ôttaraṃ vacaḥ:
«yat tvaṃ nidarśan'|ârthaṃ māṃ, Śalya, jalpitavān asi,
n' âhaṃ śakyas tvayā vācā vibhīṣayitum āhave!
yadi māṃ devatāḥ sarvā yodhayeyuḥ sa|Vāsavāḥ,
tath" âpi me bhayaṃ na syāt. kim u Pārthāt sa|Keśavāt?
n' âhaṃ bhīṣayituṃ śakyo vāṅ|mātreṇa kathaṃ cana.
anyaṃ jānīhi yaḥ śakyas tvayā bhīṣayituṃ raṇe.
43.5 nīcasya balam etāvat pāruṣyaṃ, yat tvam āttha mām.
a|śakto mad|guṇān vaktuṃ, valgase bahu, dur|mate!
na hi Karṇaḥ samudbhūto bhay'|ârtham iha, Madraka,
vikram'|ârtham ahaṃ jāto yaśo|'rthaṃ ca tath" ātmanaḥ!

sakhi|bhāvena, sauhārdān, mitra|bhāvena c' âiva hi—
kāraṇais tribhir etais tvaṃ, Śalya, jīvasi sāṃpratam.
rājñaś ca Dhārtarāṣṭrasya kāryaṃ su|mahad udyatam,
mayi tac c' āhitaṃ, Śalya; tena jīvasi me kṣaṇam.

Then he said to me as I tirelessly pleaded with him about my offence: 'What I said to you, *suta*, so it shall be. It can be no other way. A false statement would destroy living things; because of this I would earn guilt. Therefore, in order to preserve the law, I cannot speak untruly. Never again should you destroy a brahmin's means of living. You must undertake penance. No one in this world can make my words untrue. Accept them!'

I've said this with friendship even though you revile me. 42.50
I know you're insulting me! Shut up and listen further!"

SÁNJAYA said:

AFTER THIS, great king, Radha's son, a conqueror of en- 43.1
emies, stopped the king of Madra from replying and said further: "Though you rattled off that parable* to me, Shalya, you can't intimidate me in battle with words! Even if all the gods along with Vásava were to do battle with me, still I'd have no fear. How much less would I fear Pritha's son joined together with Késhava? Mere words could never intimidate me. You must know someone else who you can intimidate in battle.

What you said to me was an insult; as such it is the power 43.5
of a weak man. Unable to speak about my qualities, moron, you go over the top! For Karna wasn't born into this world to be frightened, Madra, I was born to be heroic and to further my own fame!

For these three reasons—friendship,* my goodwill and my alliance—you remain alive now, Shalya. And there's a massive task still to be completed for Dhrita·rashtra's son

kṛtaś ca samayaḥ pūrvaṃ, kṣantavyaṃ vipriyaṃ tava.
ṛte Śalya|sahasreṇa, vijayeyam ahaṃ parān.
mitra|drohas tu pāpīyān, iti jīvasi sāṃpratam.»

ŚALYA uvāca:

44.1 «NANU PRALĀPĀḤ, Karṇ', âite yān bravīṣi parān prati.
ṛte Karṇa|sahasreṇa śakyā jetuṃ pare yudhi!»

SAṂJAYA uvāca:

tathā bruvantaṃ paruṣaṃ Karṇo Madr'|âdhipaṃ tadā
paruṣaṃ dvi|guṇaṃ bhūyaḥ provāc' âpriya|darśanam.

KARNA uvāca:

«idaṃ tu me tvam ek'|âgraḥ śṛṇu, Madra|jan'|âdhipa!
saṃnidhau Dhṛtarāṣṭrasya procyamānaṃ mayā śrutam.
deśāṃś ca vividhāṃś citrān, pūrva|vṛttāṃś ca pārthivān
brāhmaṇāḥ kathayanti sma Dhṛtarāṣṭra|niveśane.
44.5 tatra vṛddhaḥ purā|vṛttāḥ kathāḥ kaś cid dvij'|ôttamaḥ
Vāhīka|deśaṃ, Madrāṃś ca kutsayan vākyam abravīt:
‹bahiṣ|kṛtā Himavatā, Gaṅgayā ca bahiṣ|kṛtāḥ,
Sarasvatyā, Yamunayā, Kurukṣetreṇa c' âpi ye,
pañcānāṃ Sindhu|ṣaṣṭhānāṃ nadīnāṃ ye 'ntar'|āśritāḥ,
tān dharma|bāhyān, aśucīn Vāhīkān api varjayet.
Govardhano nāma vaṭaḥ, Subhadraṃ nāma catvaram,
etad rāja|kula|dvāram ā kumārāt smarāmy aham.
kāryeṇ' âtyartha|gūḍhena Vāhīkeṣ' ûṣitaṃ mayā,

the king, and it rests on me. Because of this, I've let you live for the moment.

Previously we agreed that your abuse should be forgiven. Without a thousand Shalyas I could still defeat my enemies. But since injuring an ally is thought a greater evil, you remain alive now."

SHALYA said:

"KARNA, THESE certainly are idle rants that you speak 44.1
against our enemies. These enemies could be defeated in battle without a thousand Karnas!"

SÁNJAYA said:

As the lord of the Madras uttered this abuse, Karna then spoke to that ugly man, doubling the abuse still further.

KARNA said:

"Lord of the Madra people, carefully listen to this from me! I heard this when it was voiced before Dhrita·rashtra. In Dhrita·rashtra's palace brahmins described various amazing places and princes of long ago. One admirable old brahmin 44.5
who was there told tales of long ago and spoke this speech, belittling the Madras and the country of the Vahíkas:

'They who live beyond the Himalayas, beyond the rivers Ganga, Sarásvati and Yámuna, and beyond Kuru·kshetra, and who live among the five rivers which have the Sindhu River* as their sixth, live outside the law. One should avoid these impure Vahíkas. From my youth I recall a fig tree called Go·várdhana, a meeting place called Subhádra and the entrance to the king's palace there. On very secret business, I lived among the Vahíkas and came to know their

tata eṣāṃ samācāraḥ saṃvāsād vidito mama.
44.10 Śākalaṃ nāma nagaram, Āpagā nāma nimna|gā,
Jartikā nāma Vāhīkās, teṣāṃ vṛttaṃ su|ninditam.
dhānā|gauḍy|āsavaṃ pītvā go|māṃsaṃ laśunaiḥ saha,
apūpa|māṃsa|vāṭyānām āśinaḥ, śīla|varjitāḥ
gāyanty atha ca nṛtyanti striyo mattā vivāsasaḥ
nagar'|āgāra|vapreṣu, bahir|māly'|ânulepanāḥ,
matt'|âvagītair vividhaiḥ khar'|ôṣṭra|ninad'|ôpamaiḥ.
an|āvṛtā maithune tāḥ, kāma|cārāś ca sarvaśaḥ.
āhur anyonya|sūktāni prabruvāṇā mad'|ôtkaṭāḥ.
«he! hate! he! hatety» evaṃ, «svāmi|bhartṛ|hateti» ca*
44.15 ākrośantyaḥ pranṛtyanti vrātyāḥ parvasv a|saṃyatāḥ.
tāsāṃ kil' âvaliptānāṃ nivasan Kuru|jāṅgale
kaś cid Vāhīka|duṣṭānāṃ n' âtihṛṣṭa|manā jagau:
«sā nūnaṃ bṛhatī gaurī sūkṣma|kambala|vāsinī
mām anusmaratī śete Vāhīkaṃ Kuru|jāṅgale.
Śatadrukām ahaṃ tīrtvā, tāṃ ca ramyām Irāvatīm,
gatvā sva|deśaṃ, drakṣyāmi sthūla|śaṅkhāḥ śubhāḥ striyaḥ,
manaḥ|śil'|ôjjval'|āpāṅgyo gauryas tri|kakud|āñjanāḥ
kambal'|âjina|saṃvītāḥ, krandantyaḥ, priya|darśanāḥ.
mṛdaṅg'|ānaka|śaṅkhānāṃ mardalānāṃ ca nisvanaiḥ
44.20 khar'|ôṣṭr'|âśvataraiś c' âiva mattā yāsyāmahe sukham.
śamī|pīlu|karīrāṇāṃ vaneṣu sukha|vartmasu
apūpān, saktu|piṇḍāṃś ca prāśnanto mathit'|ânvitān,

customs from living with them. There was a town called 44.10
Shákala and a river called Ápaga and the Vahíkas there were called the Jártikas. They had a particularly despicable way of living.

After gorging on grains, molasses spirit, beef and garlic, and eating bread, meat and fried barley, their depraved women sing and dance drunk and naked along the walls and in the houses of the town, without garlands and oils, and with their drunken bawdy singing like the sounds of asses and camels. Uninhibited when having sex they always behaved however they wanted. They uttered witticisms to one another and told stories while pissed. Shrieking abuse like, "Ah! Whore! Ah! Whore!" and "You've been whoring
with your king and your husband!" these vagrants dance 44.15
about without restraint during moon day festivals.

One of the vile Vahíkas living on the plain of the Kurus who belonged to those arrogant women sang despondently: "That fat cow wearing but a thin blanket sleeps recalling me, the Vahíka on the plain of the Kurus. Once I've crossed the Shata·druka River* and the beautiful Irávati River* and returned to my own country, I will see those beautiful thick-browed women, those lowing cows, the corners of their eyes blazing with red arsenic and black ointment on their three humps, looking lovely wrapped in blankets and antelope skins. Intoxicated by the din of conches and *ánaka*, *mridánga* and *márdala* drums, we will happily travel by ass, 44.20
camel and mule. Enjoying meal cakes and barley balls with buttermilk on excellent roads in forests of *shami*, *pilu* and *karíra* trees, once we've become very powerful on the road,

pathi su|prabalā bhūtvā, kadā sampatato 'dhva|gān
cel'|âpahāraṃ kurvāṇās tāḍayiṣyāma bhūyasaḥ?»
evaṃ|śīleṣu vrātyeṣu Vāhīkeṣu dur|ātmasu
kaś cetayāno nivasen muhūrtam api mānavaḥ?›
īdṛśā brāhmaṇen' ôktā Vāhīkā mogha|cāriṇaḥ;
yeṣāṃ ṣaḍ|bhāga|hartā tvam ubhayoḥ śubha|pāpayoḥ!
ity uktvā brāhmaṇaḥ sādhur uttaraṃ punar uktavān.
44.25 Vāhīkeṣv a|vinīteṣu procyamānaṃ nibodha tat!
‹tatra sma rākṣasī gāti sadā kṛṣṇa|catur|daśīm
nagare Śākale sphīte, āhatya niśi dundubhim:
«kadā Vāheyikā gāthāḥ punar gāsyāmi Śākale,
gavyasya tṛptā māṃsasya, pītvā gauḍaṃ sur"|āsavam,
gaurībhiḥ saha nārībhir bṛhatībhiḥ, sv|alaṃ|kṛtāḥ,
palāṇḍu|gaṇḍūṣa|yutān
khādantī c' âiḍakān bahūn?
vārāhaṃ, kaukkuṭaṃ māṃsaṃ,
gavyaṃ, gārdabham, auṣṭrikam,
aiḍaṃ ca ye na khādanti, teṣāṃ janma nirarthakam!»
iti gāyanti ye mattāḥ sīdhunā Śākalāś ca ye
44.30 sa|bāla|vṛddhāḥ krandantas. teṣu dharmaḥ kathaṃ bhavet?›
iti, Śalya, vijānīhi! hanta! bhūyo bravīmi te!
yad anyo 'py uktavān asmān brāhmaṇaḥ Kuru|saṃsadi:
‹pañca nadyo vahanty etā yatra pīlu|vanāny uta:
Śatadruś ca, Vipāśā ca, tṛtīy" Āirāvatī tathā,
Candrabhāgā, Vitastā ca; Sindhu|ṣaṣṭhā bahir|gireḥ.
Āraṭṭā nāma te deśā naṣṭa|dharmā; na tān vrajet.
vrātyānāṃ, Dāsamīyānāṃ, Vāhīkānām a|yajvanām
na devāḥ pratigṛhṇanti, pitaro, brāhmaṇās tathā,

will we meet travelers and make off with their clothes and beat them up many times?"

What sensible man would live for even an instant among the wicked, vagrant Vahíkas, whose customs are like this?'

In such a way the brahmin described the Vahíkas, whose behavior is ridiculous. You collect a sixth of both their merit and evil!

After saying this, the virtuous brahmin spoke further still. 44.25
Listen to what he said about the boorish Vahíkas!

'In the flourishing city of Shákala, a demoness always sung during the night on the fourteenth day of the dark half of the month while beating a *dúndubhi* drum: "When will I again sing those delightfully embellished Vahíka songs in Shákala, sated with beef and drinking spirit distilled from molasses and, with those cows the fat women there,
devouring many sheep with onions and water for rinsing 44.30
the mouth? For those who don't eat boar, chicken, beef, ass, camel and mutton, life is pointless!" The Shákalas—both the young and the aged too—sing this while they shriek, pissed on rum. How can there be law among them?'

Shalya, come on! You know this! I'll tell you more!

This is what another brahmin said to us at the Kuru's court: 'Five rivers flow where the forests of *pilu* trees are: the Shata·dru, the Vipásha,* the Airávati* is the third, the Chandra·bhaga* and the Vitásta.* A sixth, the Sindhu, flows from the other side of the mountain. These lands, called the Aráttas, are lawless and one should avoid them. The gods, ancestors and brahmins do not accept anything from

teṣāṃ pranaṣṭa|dharmāṇāṃ Vāhīkānām, iti śrutiḥ.›
44.35 brāhmaṇena tathā proktaṃ viduṣā sādhu|saṃsadi:
‹kāṣṭha|kuṇḍeṣu Vāhīkā mṛṇ|mayeṣu ca bhuñjate
saktu|mady'|âvalipteṣu, śv'|âvalīḍheṣu nirghṛṇāḥ.
āvikaṃ c' āuṣṭrikaṃ c' âiva kṣīraṃ, gārdabham eva ca,
tad|vikārāṃś ca Vāhīkāḥ khādanti ca pibanti ca.
putra|saṃkariṇo jālmāḥ sarv'|ânna|kṣīra|bhojanāḥ,
Āraṭṭā nāma Vāhīkā varjanīyā vipaścitā!›

hanta, Śalya! vijānīhi! hanta! bhūyo bravīmi te!

yad anyo 'py uktavān mahyaṃ brāhmaṇaḥ Kuru|saṃsadi:
‹Yugaṃdhare payaḥ pītvā, proṣya c' âpy Acyutasthale,
44.40 tadvad Bhūtilaye snātvā, kathaṃ svargaṃ gamiṣyati?
pañca nadyo vahanty etā yatra niḥsṛtya parvatāt
Āraṭṭā nāma Vāhīkā. na teṣv āryo dvy|ahaṃ vaset!

Vahiś ca nāma Hīkaś ca Vipāśāyāṃ piśācakau,
tayor apatyaṃ Vāhīkā, n' âiṣā sṛṣṭiḥ Prajāpateḥ;
te kathaṃ vividhān dharmāñ jñāsyante hīna|yonayaḥ?
Kāraskarān, Mahiṣakān, Kāliṅgān, Keralāṃs tathā,
Karkoṭakān, Vīrakāṃś ca, dur|dharmāṃś ca vivarjayet.›
iti tīrth'|ânusartāraṃ rākṣasī kā cid abravīt
eka|rātra|śayī gehe mah"|ôlūkhala|mekhalā.

vagrants, from the Dasamíyas, from Vahíkas who don't perform sacrifices and from Vahíkas who have no law. This is what's taught.'

A wise brahmin uttered this at the court of a virtuous man: 'Without the slightest disgust Vahíkas eat in wooden and earthen bowls licked by dogs and smeared with grain and spirit. And Vahíkas drink the milk of the camel, ass and sheep, and eat their by-products. These wretches screw their own children and eat all types of food and milk. A wise man should avoid these Vahíkas known as the Aráttas!' 44.35

Come on, Shalya! You know this! Come on! I'll tell you more!

This is what another brahmin also said to me at the court of the Kurus: 'How can a man go to heaven once he's drunk milk in Yugan·dhara, lived in Áchyuta·sthala and bathed in Bhuti·laya? Where the five rivers flow after surging from the mountain the Vahíkas are known as the Aráttas. A noble man should not live among them for even two days! 44.40

There were two *pishácha* demons on the Vipásha River called Vahi and Hika. Their offspring was Vahiká* and she was no creation of Praja·pati. How could the Vahíkas, being of such low birth, comprehend the various laws? One should avoid the Karáskaras, Máhishakas, Kalíngas, Kéralas, Karkótakas, Vírakas and they who follow bad laws.' A demoness, wearing a large earring and girdle and sleeping for one night in his house, told this to that brahmin who followed pilgrimage routes.

44.45 Āraṭṭā nāma te deśā, Vāhīkā nāma te janāḥ;
brāhmaṇ'|âpasadā yatra, tulya|kālāḥ Prajāpateḥ,
vedā na teṣāṃ, vedyaś ca, yajñā, yajanam eva ca.
vrātyānāṃ Dāsamīyānām annaṃ devā na bhuñjate.
Prasthalā, Madra|Gāndhārā, Āraṭṭā nāmataḥ, Khaśāḥ
Vasāti|Sindhu|Sauvīrā iti prāyo 'tikutsitāḥ.»

KARNA uvāca:

45.1 «HANTA, ŚALYA! vijānīhi! hanta! bhūyo bravīmi te!
ucyamānaṃ mayā samyak tvam ek'|âgra|manāḥ śṛṇu!
brāhmaṇaḥ kila no geham abhyagacchat pur" âtithiḥ.
ācāraṃ tatra saṃprekṣya, prīto vacanam abravīt:
‹mayā Himavataḥ śṛṅgam eken' âdhyuṣitaṃ ciram,
dṛṣṭāś ca bahavo deśā nānā|dharma|samāvṛtāḥ.
na ca kena ca dharmeṇa virudhyante prajā imāḥ?
sarvaṃ hi te 'bruvan dharmaṃ yad uktaṃ veda|pāra|gaiḥ.
45.5 aṭatā tu tato deśān nānā|dharma|samākulān
āgacchatā, mahā|rāja, Vāhīkeṣu niśāmitam,
tatra vai brāhmaṇo bhūtvā tato bhavati kṣatriyaḥ,
vaiśyaḥ, śūdraś ca Vāhīkas, tato bhavati nāpitaḥ.
nāpitaś ca tato bhūtvā, punar bhavati brāhmaṇaḥ.
dvijo bhūtvā ca tatr' âiva punar dāso 'bhijāyate.
bhavaty ekaḥ kule vipraḥ, śiṣṭ" ânye kāma|cāriṇaḥ.
Gāndhārā, Madrakāś c' âiva, Vāhīkāś c' âlpa|cetasaḥ;

These places are called the Aráttas; the people are called the Vahíkas. There were outcaste brahmins in these places, contemporaries of Praja·pati, who had no Vedas, no knowledge, no sacrifices and no worship. The gods consume no food from vagrants or from the Dasamíyas. The Prásthalas, Madras, Gandháras, Khashas, Vasátis and Sindhus and Sauvíras are known as Aráttas, they are despised almost as much." 44.45

KARNA said:

"COME ON, SHALYA! You know this! Come on! I'll tell you some more! With a focused mind, listen to everything I say! 45.1

Some time ago a brahmin guest arrived at our house. After carefully observing the customs there he was delighted and made this speech:

'For a long time I lived alone on a Himalayan peak and observed many countries protected by many different laws. By what law were these people regulated? And by what law were they not? For they spoke the entire law as it was uttered
by brahmins learned in the Vedas. But, wandering about 45.5
and visiting these countries abounding in various laws, great king, among the Vahíkas I learned that once a Vahíka has been a brahmin he then becomes a kshatriya, and then a vaishya and a shudra. Then he becomes a barber. After being a barber he then becomes a brahmin again. And, after being a brahmin, he is reborn there as a slave. One brahmin is born in each family; the others that remain do as they please. The Gandháras, Madras and Vahíkas have very small intellects.

etan mayā śrutaṃ tatra dharma|saṃkara|kārakam,
kṛtsnām aṭitvā pṛthivīṃ; Vāhīkeṣu viparyayaḥ!›
45.10 hanta, Śalya! vijānīhi! hanta! bhūyo bravīmi te!
yad apy anyo 'bravīd vākyaṃ Vāhīkānāṃ ca kutsitam:
‹satī purā hṛtā kā cid Āraṭṭāt kila dasyubhiḥ;
a|dharmataś c' ôpayātā; sā tān abhyaśapat tataḥ:
«bālāṃ bandhumatīṃ yan mām a|dharmeṇ' ôpagacchatha,
tasmān nāryo bhaviṣyanti bandhakyo vai kulasya ca,
na c' âiv' âsmāt pramokṣyadhvaṃ
ghorāt pāpān, nar'|âdhamāḥ!»
tasmāt teṣāṃ bhāga|harā
bhāgineyā, na sūnavaḥ.
Kuravaḥ saha|Pāñcālāḥ, Śālvā, Matsyāḥ sa|Naimiṣāḥ,
Kosalāḥ, Kāśapauṇḍrāś ca, Kaliṅgā, Magadhās tathā,
45.15 Cedayaś ca mahā|bhāgā dharmaṃ jānanti śāśvatam.
nānā|deśeṣv a|santaś ca prāyo Vāhya|nayād ṛte.
ā Matsyebhyaḥ Kuru|Pāñcāla|deśyā,
ā Naimiṣāc Cedayo ye viśiṣṭāḥ,
dharmaṃ purāṇam upajīvanti santo,
Madrād ṛte, pāñca|nadāṃś ca jihmān.›
evaṃ vidvān dharma|kathāsu, rājaṃs,
tūṣṇīṃ|bhūto jaḍavac, Chalya, bhūyaḥ;
tvaṃ tasya goptā ca janasya rājā,
ṣaḍ|bhāga|hartā śubha|duṣ|kṛtasya!
atha vā duṣ|kṛtasya tvaṃ hartā, teṣām a|rakṣitā;
rakṣitā puṇya|bhāg rājā prajānāṃ; tvaṃ tv a|puṇya|bhāk!

After wandering the entire earth I learned that the laws are mingled there. Things are perverse among the Vahíkas!'

Come on, Shalya! You know this! Come on! I'll tell you 45.10
some more! These are the disgraceful words someone else said regarding the Vahíkas:

'It's said that, long ago, bandits from Arátta kidnapped a virtuous woman and sinfully raped her. Later she cursed them: "Since you raped me with no regard for law—a young woman with relatives!—the women of your clan will be whores and, because of this, vile men, you'll never be released from this hideous evil!" As a consequence their sisters' sons are their heirs, not their own children.

The Kurus and Panchálas, the Shalvas, Matsyas and Náimishas, the Kósalas, Kasha·paundras, Kalíngas, Mágadhas
and Chedis—all of whom are much celebrated—know that 45.15
the law is constant. And even most of the bad people in these various countries take exception to the conduct of Vahíkas. Especially those native to Kuru and Panchála—as far as the Matsyas, the Chedis and the Náimishas—are good people who live under the ancient law, except for the Madras and the wretches from the land of the five rivers.'

The man learned in these tales about law then fell silent once more as if paralysed, King Shalya. You're these people's protector, their king, incurring a sixth portion of their good and bad deeds! Then again, in not protecting them you share in only their bad deeds. Since only a king who protects his people shares in their merits, you have no share of their merits!

pūjyamāne purā dharme sarva|deśeṣu śāśvate,
dharmaṃ pāñca|nadaṃ dṛṣṭvā, ‹dhig! ity› āha Pitā|mahaḥ.
45.20 vrātyānāṃ, Dāsamīyānāṃ Kṛte 'py a|śubha|karmaṇām
Brahmaṇā nindite dharme, sa tvaṃ loke kim abravīḥ?
iti pāñca|nadaṃ dharmam avamene Pitā|mahaḥ.
sva|dharma|stheṣu varṣeṣu, so 'py etān n' âbhipūjayat.
hanta, Śalya! vijānīhi! hanta! bhūyo bravīmi te!
Kalmāṣapādaḥ sarasi nimajjan rākṣaso 'bravīt:
‹kṣatriyasya malaṃ bhaikṣyaṃ;
brāhmaṇasy' â|śrutaṃ malam;
malaṃ pṛthivyāṃ Vāhīkāḥ;
strīṇāṃ Madra|striyo malam.›
nimajjamānam uddhṛtya kaś cid rājā niśā|caram
apṛcchat, tena c' ākhyātaṃ. proktavāṃs tan nibodha me!
45.25 ‹mānuṣāṇāṃ malaṃ mlecchā;
mlecchānāṃ auṣṭrikā malam;
auṣṭrikānāṃ malaṃ ṣaṇḍhāḥ;
ṣaṇḍhānāṃ rāja|yājakāḥ.
rāja|yājaka|yājyānāṃ Madrakāṇāṃ ca yan malam,
tad bhaved vai tava malaṃ yady asmān na vimuñcasi!›
iti rakṣopasṛṣṭeṣu,* viṣa|vīrya|hateṣu ca
rākṣasaṃ bhaiṣajaṃ proktaṃ saṃsiddha|vacan'|ôttaram.
brāhmaṃ Pāñcālāḥ, Kauraveyās tu dharmyaṃ,
satyaṃ Matsyāḥ, Śūrasenāś ca yajñam,
prācyā dāsā, vṛṣalā dākṣiṇātyāḥ,
stenā Vāhīkāḥ, saṃkarā vai Surāṣṭrāḥ.

Long ago when the eternal law was honored in all countries, the Grandfather observed the law in the region of the
five rivers and cried out, 'Scandalous!' Given that, even in 45.20
the Krita epoch, Brahma scorned the law of the evil-acting vagrants and Dasamíyas, how can you speak out in this world? The Grandfather regarded such law from the land of the five rivers with contempt. Even after they had followed their own proper laws for years he did not approve of them.

Come on, Shalya! You know this! Come on! I'll tell you some more!

While drowning in a lake, the demon Kalmásha·pada said: 'Begging is dirt to a kshatriya; lack of learning is dirt to a brahmin; Vahíkas are the dirt of the earth; Madra women are the dirt of women.' A king rescued that drowning night-walker and questioned him and it was explained by him. Listen from me what he told him!

'Among men barbarians are dirt; among barbarians 45.25
camel-herders are dirt; among camel-herders eunuchs are dirt; among eunuchs kings who act as sacrificer are dirt.* And whatever dirt there is of the Madras whose king acts as both sacrificer and patron of the sacrifice shall become your dirt if you don't let us go!' These excellent restorative words were commended as a demonic charm for those possessed by demons or struck down by virulent poison.

The Panchálas hold to the Veda; the Kurus are law-abiding; the Matsyas are truthful and the Shura·senas perform sacrifices. The easterners are slaves; the southerners are contemptible; the Vahíkas are thieves and the Suráshtras are interbred.

kṛta|ghnatā, para|vitt'|âpahāro,
madya|pānaṃ, guru|dār'|âvamardaḥ,
vāk|pāruṣyaṃ, go|vadho, rātri|caryā
bahir|gehaṃ, para|vastr'|ôpabhogaḥ
45.30 yeṣāṃ dharmas, tān prati n' âsty a|dharmo!
hy Ārattānāṃ pañca|nadān dhig astu!
ā Pāñcālebhyaḥ Kuravo, Naimiṣāś ca,
Matsyāś c' âite 'py atha jānanti dharmam.
ath' ôdīcyāś c' Āṅgakā, Māgadhāś ca
śiṣṭān dharmān upajīvanti vṛddhāḥ.

prācīṃ diśaṃ śritā devā Jātavedaḥ|puro|gamāḥ;
dakṣiṇāṃ pitaro, guptāṃ Yamena śubha|karmaṇā;
pratīcīṃ Varuṇaḥ pāti pālayānaḥ surān balī;
udīcīṃ bhagavān Somo brāhmaṇaiḥ saha rakṣati;
tathā rakṣaḥ|piśācāś ca Himavantaṃ nag'|ôttamam;
guhyakāś ca, mahā|rāja, parvataṃ Gandhamādanam;
dhruvaḥ sarvāṇi bhūtāni Viṣṇuḥ pāti Janārdanaḥ.

iṅgita|jñāś ca Magadhāḥ; prekṣita|jñāś ca Kosalāḥ;
45.35 ardh'|ôktāḥ Kuru|Pāñcālāḥ; Śālvāḥ kṛtsn'|ânuśāsanāḥ;
pārvatīyāś ca viṣamā, yath" âiva Śibayas tathā;
sarva|jñā Yavanā, rājañ, Śūrāś c' âiva viśeṣataḥ;
mlecchāḥ sva|saṃjñā|niyatā, n' ân|uktam itare janāḥ;
pratirathās tu Vāhīkā, na ca ke cana Madrakāḥ.
sa tvam etādṛśaḥ, Śalya, n' ôttaraṃ vaktum arhasi!

Ingratitude, stealing another's wealth, drinking spirits, touching up a guru's wife, abusive language, killing cows, wandering around during the night outside of the house, using another's clothes; for whom these are law nothing is 45.30
immoral! Damn those who live along the five rivers of the Aráttas!

The Kurus and Náimishas up to and including the Panchálas, and the Matsyas also, understand the law. The elders among the northerners, Angas and Mágadhas live according to the laws as they are taught.

Led by Agni, the gods remain in the east; the ancestors in the south, which is governed by Yama acting with virtue; powerful Váruna governs the west protecting the gods; illustrious Soma guards the north with the brahmins; similarly the *rákshasa* and *pishácha* demons govern the superb Himalayan range; and, great king, the *gúhyaka*s govern the mountain Gandha·mádana; and, as Janárdana, immovable Vishnu governs all beings.

The Mágadhas are skilled in the ways of gestures; Kósalas
are skilled in the ways of glances; the Kurus and Panchálas in 45.35
speeches only half uttered; the Shalvas in entire commands; the mountain people are difficult to understand, as are the Shibis. The Greeks are experts in everthing, king, as are the Shuras above all. Barbarians are focused upon their own conceptions; other people don't understand their strange speech. The Vahíkas are adversaries in war, but some Madras are not. You're such a one, Shalya. Please, say no more!

pṛthivyāṃ sarva|deśānāṃ Madrako malam ucyate.
sīdhoḥ pānaṃ, guru|talp'|âvamardo,
bhrūṇa|hatyā, para|vitt'|âpahāraḥ
yeṣāṃ dharmas tān prati n' âsty a|dharma!
Āraṭṭa|jān pañca|nadān dhig astu!
etaj jñātvā joṣam āssva! pratīpaṃ mā sma vai kṛthāḥ!
mā tvāṃ pūrvam ahaṃ hatvā haniṣye Keśav'|Ârjunau!»

ŚALYA uvāca:

45.40 «āturāṇāṃ parityāgaḥ, sva|dāra|sūta|vikrayaḥ
Aṅge pravartate, Karṇa, yeṣām adhipatir bhavān.
rath'|âtiratha|saṃkhyāyāṃ yat tvāṃ Bhīṣmas tad" âbravīt:
‹tān viditv" ātmano doṣān nirmanyur bhava, mā krudhaḥ!›
sarvatra brāhmaṇāḥ santi; santi sarvatra kṣatriyāḥ;
vaiśyāḥ, śūdrās tathā, Karṇa, striyaḥ sādhvyaś ca su|vratāḥ;
ramante c' ôpahāsena puruṣāḥ puruṣaiḥ saha
anyonyam abhibhartsanto; deśe deśe sa|maithunāḥ;
para|vācyeṣu nipuṇaḥ sarvo bhavati sarvadā,
ātma|vācyaṃ na jānīte, jānann api ca muhyati.
45.45 sarvatra santi rājānaḥ svaṃ svaṃ dharmam anuvratāḥ,
dur|manuṣyān nigṛhṇanti. santi sarvatra dhārmikāḥ.
na, Karṇa, deśa|sāmānyāt sarvaḥ pāpaṃ niṣevate.
yādṛśāḥ sva|svabhāvena, devā api na tādṛśāḥ.»

Among all countries on earth the Madra are regarded as dirt. Drinking spirit, violating a guru's bed, murdering brahmins, stealing another's wealth; for whom these are law nothing is immoral! Damn those born in Arátta in the land of the five rivers! Once you've understood this, shut up! Stop being antagonistic lest I kill Késhava and Árjuna after killing you first!"

SHALYA said:

"Abandoning the sick and selling one's wife and children 45.40
occurs in Anga, Karna, whose ruler you are. In enumerating the warriors and great warriors, Bhishma said to you: 'Understand your own faults and be neither malicious nor angry!' Brahmins are everywhere; kshatriyas are everywhere, Karna, as are vaishyas and shudras, and devout women firm in their vows. And for fun men sport with men, ridiculing one another; in every country there are men who fornicate. Everyone is always familiar with another's defects but don't recognise their own defects. Even when they do recognise
them, they get confused. Everywhere are kings who follow 45.45
their own law and stifle bad men. Everywhere are the righteous. Not everyone incurs evil because of the vulgarity of their country, Karna. Even they who, by their very natures, are like gods, are not really so."

SAMJAYA uvāca:

tato Duryodhano rājā Karṇa|Śalyāv avārayat;
sakhi|bhāvena Rādheyaṃ, Śalyaṃ svāñjalyakena ca.
tato nivāritaḥ Karṇo Dhārtarāṣṭreṇa, māriṣa,
Karṇo 'pi n' ôttaraṃ prāha, Śalyo 'py abhimukhaḥ parān.
tataḥ prahasya Rādheyaḥ punar, «yāh'! îty» acodayat.

SÁNJAYA said:

King Duryódhana then restrained Karna and Shalya; Radha's son through their friendship and Shalya by joining his hands in supplication. Then, restrained by Dhrita·rashtra's son, dear friend, Karna spoke no further and Shalya turned his face towards the enemy. Bursting into laughter, Radha's son again urged, "Advance!"

46–54

KARNA THE GENERAL, DAY TWO

SAMJAYA uvāca:

46.1 TATAḤ PAR'|ÂNĪKA|saham
vyūham a|pratimam kṛtam
samīkṣya Karṇaḥ Pārthānām
Dhṛṣṭadyumn'|âbhirakṣitam,
prayayau ratha|ghoṣeṇa, siṃha|nāda|raveṇa ca,
vāditrāṇāṃ ca ninadaiḥ kampayann iva medinīm!
vepamāna iva krodhād yuddha|śauṇḍaḥ, paraṃ|tapaḥ,
prativyūhya mahā|tejā yathāvad, Bharata'|rṣabha,
vyadhamat Pāṇḍavīṃ senām, āsurīṃ Maghavān iva.
Yudhiṣṭhiraṃ c' âbhyahanad, apasavyaṃ cakāra ha.

DHṚTARĀṢṬRA uvāca:

46.5 kathaṃ, Saṃjaya, Rādheyaḥ pratyavyūhata Pāṇḍavān
Dhṛṣṭadyumna|mukhān sarvān, Bhīmasen' âbhirakṣitān,
sarvān eva mah"|êṣv|āsān a|jayyān amarair api?
ke ca prapakṣau pakṣau vā mama sainyasya, Saṃjaya?
pravibhajya yathā|nyāyaṃ kathaṃ vā samavasthitāḥ?
kathaṃ Pāṇḍu|sutāś c' âpi pratyavyūhanta māmakān?
kathaṃ c' âiva mahad yuddhaṃ prāvartata su|dāruṇam?
kva ca Bībhatsur abhavad, yat Karṇo 'yād Yudhiṣṭhiram?
ko hy Arjunasya sāṃnidhye śakto 'bhyetuṃ Yudhiṣṭhiram?
sarva|bhūtāni yo hy ekaḥ Khāṇḍave jitavān purā;
kas tam anyas tu Rādheyāt pratiyudhyej jijīviṣuḥ?

SÁNJAYA said:

SEEING PRITHA'S sons' incomparable battle array— 46.1
readied and commanded by Dhrishta·dyumna and the equal of their enemies' army—Karna advanced to the rumbling sound of his chariot, the thunder of lions' roars and the sounds of musical instruments, almost making the earth quake! Keen to fight and shaking from rage, that tremendously potent enemy-destroyer promptly arrayed his forces against them, bull of Bharatas, and scattered the Pándava army like Mághavan* scattering the army of demons. He struck out at Yudhi·shthira and circled him from right to left.

DHRITA·RASHTRA said:

Sánjaya, how did Radha's son array his forces against all 46.5
those Pándavas led by Dhrishta·dyumna and guarded by Bhima·sena? Surely all those mighty archers were unbeatable, even by the gods! Who were at the flanks and outer flanks of my army, Sánjaya? Once they were appropriately assigned, how were they positioned? Moreover, how were the sons of Pandu arrayed against my forces? And how did that massive and appalling battle begin? And where was Bibhátsu when Karna closed on Yudhi·shthira? And who was able to loom on Yudhi·shthira so near to Árjuna? For some time back he was the one who conquered all living things in the Khándava forest. Who that wants to remain alive would fight him, other than Radha's son?

SAMJAYA uvāca:

46.10 śṛṇu vyūhasya racanām, Arjunaś ca yathā gataḥ,
parivārya nṛpaṃ svaṃ svaṃ saṃgrāmaś c' âbhavad yathā!
Kṛpaḥ Śāradvato, rājan, Māgadhāś ca tarasvinaḥ,
Sātvataḥ Kṛtavarmā ca dakṣiṇaṃ pakṣam āśritāḥ.
teṣāṃ prapakṣe Śakunir, Ulūkaś ca mahā|rathaḥ
sādibhir vimala|prāsais tav' ânīkam arakṣatām
Gāndhāribhir a|saṃbhrāntaiḥ, pārvatīyaiś ca dur|jayaiḥ,
śalabhānām iva vrātaiḥ, piśācair iva dur|dṛśaiḥ.
catur|viṃśat sahasrāṇi rathānām a|nivartinām,
saṃśaptakā yuddha|śauṇḍā, vāmaṃ pārśvam apālayan.
46.15 samanvitās tava sutaiḥ Kṛṣṇ'|Ârjuna|jighāṃsavaḥ.
teṣāṃ prapakṣāḥ Kāmbojāḥ, Śakāś ca Yavanaiḥ saha,
nideśāt sūta|putrasya sa|rathāḥ, s'|âśva|pattayaḥ
āhvayanto 'rjunaṃ tasthuḥ, Keśavaṃ ca mahā|balam.
madhye senā|mukhe Karṇo 'py avātiṣṭhata daṃśitaḥ,
citra|varm'|âṅgadaḥ, sragvī, pālayan vāhinī|mukham.
rakṣamāṇaiḥ su|saṃrabdhaiḥ putraiḥ śastra|bhṛtāṃ varaḥ
vāhinīṃ pramukhe vīraḥ saṃprakarṣann aśobhata.
abhyavartan mahā|bāhuḥ sūrya|vaiśvānara|prabhaḥ,
mahā|dvipa|skandha|gataḥ, piṅg'|âkṣaḥ, priya|darśanaḥ
46.20 Duḥśāsano vṛtaḥ sainyaiḥ sthito vyūhasya pṛṣṭhataḥ.

SÁNJAYA said:

Listen to how the battle array was arranged, how Árjuna went and how the battle transpired after each king was surrounded! 46.10

Sharádvat's son Kripa, king, the bold Mágadhas and the Sátvata Krita·varman were positioned on the right flank. On their outer flank was Shákuni and the mighty warrior Ulúka. Those two protected your army with unflappable Gandhári horsemen wielding gleaming lances and unconquerable mountain men who were like swarms of locusts or clandestine *pishácha* demons.

Twenty four thousand warriors refusing to retreat—oath-bound warriors that were keen for a fight—protected the left
flank. They allied with your sons in the hope of killing Kri- 46.15
shna and Árjuna. On their outer flank were positioned the Kambójas and the Shakas along with the Greeks, challenging Árjuna and powerful Késhava at the command of the charioteer's son with their chariots, horses and foot-soldiers.

In the middle at the head of the army stood Karna, too, clad in mail, garlanded and sporting beautiful armor and bracelets, protecting the head of the array. With his ferocious sons guarding him, that hero, the finest of weapon-bearers, looked brilliant at the head of his army as he bent his bow.

Surrounded by his troops and stationed at the rear of the 46.20
array, mighty-armed Duhshásana advanced with his power like the sun and fire, his eyes red and his appearance dazzling as he rode on the shoulders of a massive elephant.

tam anvayān, mahā|rāja, svayaṃ Duryodhano nṛpaḥ,
citr'|âstraiś, citra|saṃnāhaiḥ s'|ôdaryair abhirakṣitaḥ.
rakṣyamāṇo mahā|vīryaiḥ sahitair Madra|Kekayaiḥ,
aśobhata, mahā|rāja, devair iva Śatakratuḥ.
Aśvatthāmā, Kurūṇāṃ ca ye pravīrā mahā|rathāḥ,
nitya|mattāś ca mātaṅgāḥ śūrair mlecchaiḥ samanvitāḥ
anvayus tad rath'|ânīkaṃ, kṣaranta iva toya|dāḥ.
te dhvajair, vaijayantībhir, jvaladbhiḥ param'|āyudhaiḥ,
sādibhiś c' āsthitā rejur, drumavanta iv' âcalāḥ.
46.25 teṣāṃ padāti|nāgānāṃ pāda|rakṣāḥ sahasraśaḥ
paṭṭiś'|âsi|dharāḥ śūrā babhūvur a|nivartinaḥ.
sādibhiḥ, syandanair, nāgair adhikaṃ samalaṃkṛtaiḥ
sa vyūha|rājo vibabhau dev'|âsura|cam"|ûpamaḥ.
Bārhaspatyaḥ su|vihito nāyakena vipaścitā
nṛtyat' îva mahā|vyūhaḥ, pareṣām bhayam ādadhat.
tasya pakṣa|prapakṣebhyo niṣpatanti yuyutsavaḥ
patty|aśva|ratha|mātaṅgāḥ, prāvṛṣ' îva balāhakāḥ.
tataḥ senā|mukhe Karṇaṃ dṛṣṭvā rājā Yudhiṣṭhiraḥ
Dhanaṃjayam amitra|ghnam eka|vīram uvāca ha:
46.30 «paśy', Ârjuna, mahā|vyūhaṃ Karṇena vihitaṃ raṇe!
yuktaṃ pakṣaiḥ prapakṣaiś ca par'|ânīkaṃ prakāśate.
tad etad vai samālokya pratyamitraṃ mahad balam,
yathā n' âbhibhavaty asmāṃs, tathā nītir vidhīyatām!»

King Duryódhana himself followed him, great king, guarded by his brothers with their beautiful weapons and coats of mail. Protected by the tremendously potent combination of the Madras and Kékayas, he looked magnificent, great king, like Shata·kratu protected by the gods.

Ashvattháman, heroic mighty warriors of the Kurus, and elephants in constant rut seeping like rain-clouds and attended by brave barbarians, followed that army of warriors. Standing with their banners, flags, riders and brilliant weapons flashing, they looked magnificent, like mountains covered in trees. Among those foot-soldiers and elephants 46.25
were foot-guards by the thousand, heroes wielding swords and tridents and refusing to retreat.

That king of battle arrays with its lavishly decorated chariots, elephants and horsemen was astonishing, like the armies of the gods and demons. That great battle array perfectly arranged by the inspired commander—just as it was devised by Brihas·pati—seemed to dance, imbuing their enemy with terror. Like thunder-clouds in the wet season, foot-soldiers, horses, chariots and elephants, hurtled from its flanks and outer flanks, eager for battle.

After seeing Karna at the head of his army, King Yudhi·shthira called out to that singular hero, the enemy-destroyer
Dhanan·jaya: "Look, Árjuna, at the great battle array Karna 46.30
has arranged for battle! The enemy's army with its flanks and outer flanks is on display. Once you've had a look at that massive and hostile army, proceed astutely so that it doesn't overwhelm us!"

evam ukto 'rjuno rājñā prāñjalir nṛpam abravīt:
«yathā bhavān āha, tathā tat sarvaṃ, na tad anyathā.
yas tv asya vihito ghātas, taṃ kariṣyāmi, Bhārata.
pradhāna|vadha ev' âsya vināśas; taṃ karomy aham!»

YUDHIṢṬHIRA uvāca:

«tasmāt tvam eva Rādheyaṃ, Bhīmasenaḥ Suyodhanam,
Vṛṣasenaṃ ca Nakulaḥ, Sahadevo 'pi Saubalam,
46.35 Duḥśāsanaṃ Śatānīko,
Hārdikyaṃ Śini|puṃgavaḥ,
Dhṛṣṭadyumno Droṇa|sutaṃ,
svayaṃ yotsyāmy ahaṃ Kṛpam.
Draupadeyā Dhārtarāṣṭrāñ śiṣṭān saha Śikhaṇḍinā.
te te ca tāṃs tān ahitān asmākaṃ ghnantu māmakāḥ!»

SAṂJAYA uvāca:

ity ukto Dharma|rājena, «tath"! êty» uktvā Dhanaṃjayaḥ
vyādideśa sva|sainyāni, svayaṃ c' âgāc camū|mukham.
Agnir Vaiśvānaraḥ pūrvo Brahm"|ênduḥ saptitāṃ gataḥ.
tasmād yaḥ prathamaṃ jātas taṃ devā brāhmaṇaṃ viduḥ.
Brahm"|Ēśān'|Êndra|Varuṇān kramaśo yo 'vahat purā,
tam ādyaṃ ratham āsthāya prayātau Keśav'|Ârjunau.
46.40 atha taṃ ratham āyāntaṃ dṛṣṭv" âtyadbhuta|darśanam,
uvāc' Ādhirathiṃ Śalyaḥ punas taṃ yuddha|dur|madam:
«ayaṃ sa ratha āyātaḥ śvet'|âśvaḥ, Kṛṣṇa|sārathiḥ,
dur|vāraḥ sarva|sainyānāṃ, vipākaḥ karmaṇām iva.
nighnann amitrān Kaunteyo, yaṃ, Karṇa, paripṛcchasi.

Once the king had uttered this to him, Árjuna joined his hands together and said to the king: "Everything shall be just as you said, and in no other way. I will do whatever is necessary to destroy it, Bhárata. Only the death of its commander will lead to its destruction; that I will do!"

YUDHI·SHTHIRA said:

"In that case, you alone will fight Radha's son, Bhima·sena will fight Suyódhana, Nákula Vrisha·sena, Saha·deva Súbala's son, Shataníka Duhshásana, the hero of the Shinis* 46.35
Hrídika's son, Dhrishta·dyumna Drona's son, and I myself will fight Kripa. Dráupadi's boys and Shikhándin will fight Dhrita·rashtra's remaining sons. May countless of my men kill countless of our enemies!"

SÁNJAYA said:

So addressed by the King of Law and replying "So it shall be!" Dhanan·jaya distributed his own forces and took himself to the head of the army.

Previously Agni Vaishvánara, a portion of Brahma, became the horse. Because he was born first from Brahma, the gods understand that he is a brahmin.* After mounting their unparalleled chariot—that had previously borne, in turn, Brahma, Ishána, Indra and Váruna—Késhava and Árjuna set out.

Seeing that chariot approaching—an absolutely spectac- 46.40
ular sight!—Shalya again spoke to Ádhiratha's battle-mad son: "The warrior has approached with his white horses and Krishna as his charioteer. Like the ripening of actions, none of the troops can resist him. Kunti's son—after whom you ask, Karna!—is overwhelming his enemies.

śrūyate tumulaḥ śabdo, yathā megha|svano mahān;
dhruvam etau mah"|ātmānau Vāsudeva|Dhanaṃjayau!
eṣa reṇuḥ samudbhūto divam āvṛtya tiṣṭhati.
cakra|nemi|praṇunn" êva kampate, Karṇa, medinī!
pravāty eṣa mahā|vāyur abhitas tava vāhinīm.
46.45 kravy'|âdā vyāharanty ete, mṛgāḥ krandanti bhairavam.
paśya, Karṇa! mahā|ghoraṃ bhaya|daṃ loma|harṣaṇam
kabandhaṃ megha|saṃkāśaṃ bhānum āvṛtya saṃsthitam!
paśya! yūthair bahu|vidhair mṛgāṇāṃ sarvato|diśam
balibhir dṛpta|śārdūlair ādityo 'bhinirīkṣyate!
paśya kaṅkāṃś ca gṛdhrāṃś ca samavetān sahasraśaḥ,
sthitān abhimukhān ghorān anyonyam abhibhāṣataḥ!
rañjitāś cāmarā yuktās tava, Karṇa, mahā|rathe
pravarāḥ prajvalanty ete, dhvajaś c' âiva prakampate.
sa|vepathūn hayān paśya mahā|kāyān, mahā|javān,
46.50 plavamānān, darśanīyān, ākāśe Garuḍān iva!
dhruvam eṣu nimitteṣu bhūmim āśritya pārthivāḥ
svapsyanti nihatāḥ, Karṇa, śataśo 'tha sahasraśaḥ!
śaṅkhānāṃ tumulaḥ śabdaḥ śrūyate loma|harṣaṇaḥ,
ānakānāṃ ca, Rādheya, mṛdaṅgānāṃ ca sarvaśaḥ.
bāṇa|śabdān bahu|vidhān, nar'|âśva|gaja|nisvanān,
jyā|talatr'|êṣu|śabdāṃś ca śṛṇu, Karṇa, mah"|ātmanām!
hema|rūpya|prasṛṣṭānāṃ vāsasāṃ śilpi|nirmitāḥ
nānā|varṇā rathe bhānti śvasanena prakampitāḥ
sa|hema|candra|tār"|ârkāḥ patākāḥ kiṅkiṇī|yutāḥ,
46.55 paśya, Karṇ', Ârjunasy' âitāḥ, saudāmanya iv' âmbu|de!

A tumultuous sound can be heard, like the massive rumble of a cloud; surely it's those great men Vasudéva and Dhanan·jaya! The dust that's risen envelops the sky and remains there. Karna, the earth trembles as if shaking from his wheel rims. The mighty wind buffets your army on all sides. Carrion-eaters howl and wild animals cry horribly. 46.45
Look, Karna! That utterly dreadful, fear-inspiring and hair-raising dust-cloud remains, obscuring the sun like a cloud! Look! In every direction various packs of wild animals and powerful and proud tigers stare at the sun! Look! Horrible herons and vultures have gathered by the thousands and remain still, facing one another as they screech!

The excellent colored plumes fastened to your great chariot shimmer, Karna, and your banner flutters. Look at the horses quivering, their bodies immense and their speed awesome like beautiful Gárudas soaring in the sky! Surely on 46.50
account of these omens, Karna, the princes will sleep resting on the earth, struck down in their hundreds and then thousands!

Everywhere can be heard the tumultuous and hair-raising clamor of conches, son of Radha, as can the boom of *ánaka* and *mridánga* drums. Karna, listen to the many distinct sounds of arrows, to the noises of the men, horses and elephants, and to the twangs of bow-strings, the thwacks of arm-guards and the buzzing of the arrows of great men!

Karna, look at Árjuna's multi-colored flags! Fashioned 46.55
by craftsmen from cloth threaded with gold and silver and covered with small bells and golden moons, stars and suns, they look brilliant buffeted by the wind on his chariot, like lightning in a cloud! His banners make flapping sounds

dhvajāḥ kaṇakaṇāyante vāten' âbhisamīritāḥ.
vibhrājanti rathe, Karṇa, vimāne daivate yathā,
sa|patākā rathāś c' âite Pāñcālānāṃ mah"|ātmanām.

paśya Kuntī|sutaṃ vīraṃ Bībhatsum a|parājitam,
pradharṣayitum āyāntaṃ kapi|pravara|ketanam!
eṣa dhvaj'|âgre Pārthasya prekṣaṇīyaḥ samantataḥ
dṛśyate vānaro bhīmo, dviṣatām agha|vardhanaḥ.

etac cakraṃ, gadā, Śārṅgaṃ, śaṅkhaḥ Kṛṣṇasya dhīmataḥ
atyarthaṃ bhrājate Kṛṣṇe, Kaustubhas tu maṇis tataḥ.
46.60 eṣa Śārṅga|gadā|pāṇir Vāsudevo 'tivīryavān
vāhayann eti turagān pāṇḍurān vāta|raṃhasaḥ.
etat kūjati Gāṇḍīvaṃ vikṛṣṭaṃ Savyasācinā;
ete hastavatā muktā ghnanty amitrāñ śitāḥ śarāḥ.

viśāl'|āyata|tāmr'|âkṣaiḥ, pūrṇa|candra|nibh'|ānanaiḥ,
eṣā bhūḥ kīryate rājñāṃ śirobhir a|palāyinām.
ete su|parigh'|ākārāḥ, puṇya|gandh'|ânulepanāḥ,
udyat'|āyudha|śauṇḍānāṃ pātyante s'|āyudhā bhujāḥ.
nirasta|netra|jihvāś ca vājinaḥ saha sādibhiḥ
patitāḥ pātyamānāś ca kṣitau kṣīṇāś ca śerate.
46.65 ete parvata|śṛṅgāṇāṃ tulya|rūpā hatā dvipāḥ
saṃchinna|bhinnāḥ Pārthena pracaranty, adrayo yathā.
gandharva|nagar'|ākārā rathā hata|nar'|ēśvarāḥ
vimānān' îva puṇyāni svargiṇāṃ nipatanty amī.

as they're tossed by the wind. The warriors of those great Panchálas are dazzling with their flags on their chariots, as if they're on divine chariots, Karna.

Look at Kunti's son Bibhátsu as that unsurpassed hero approaches to destroy us, his banner displaying a superb monkey! From everywhere can be seen that formidable and striking monkey on top Pritha's son's banner, instilling a sense of danger among his enemies.

Wise Krishna's discus, club, conch and his bow Sharnga sparkle astonishingly, as does the jewel on Krishna called Káustubha. Vasudéva is immensely powerful and has come 46.60
near, wielding his club and his bow Sharnga and driving the white horses as fast as wind. The Gandíva bow groans as the Left-handed archer draws it. Sharp arrows released by that dexterous man kill their enemies.

The earth is littered with the heads of kings who didn't flee, their faces like full moons and their red eyes stretched wide. Daubed in pleasant perfumes and shaped like superb iron clubs, the arms of men feverishly raising their weapons fall down together with their weapons. Their tongues and eyes hanging out, collapsed and collapsing along with their riders, horses lie prone on the ground, destroyed. Cut to 46.65
pieces and ruined by Pritha's son, slaughtered elephants tumble onwards like rocks, their bulk equal to mountain peaks. Chariots seeming like cities of the *gandhárva*s, their lords of men dead, hurtle onwards like sacred chariots of the gods.

vyākulī|kṛtam atyartham paśya sainyaṃ Kirīṭinā,
nānā|mṛga|sahasrāṇāṃ yūthaṃ kesariṇā yathā!
ghnanty ete pārthivān vīrāḥ Pāṇḍavāḥ samabhidrutāḥ,
nāg'|âśva|ratha|patty|oghāṃs tāvakān samabhighnataḥ.
eṣa, sūrya iv' âmbho|daiś channaḥ, Pārtho na dṛśyate;
dhvaj'|âgraṃ dṛśyate tv asya, jyā|śabdaś c' âpi śrūyate.
46.70 adya drakṣyasi taṃ vīraṃ śvet'|âśvaṃ Kṛṣṇa|sārathim
nighnantaṃ śātravān saṃkhye, yaṃ, Karṇa, paripṛcchasi!
adya tau puruṣa|vyāghrau lohit'|âkṣau, paraṃ|tapau
Vāsudev'|Ârjunau, Karṇa, draṣṭ" âsy eka|ratha|sthitau!

sārathir yasya Vārṣṇeyo; Gāṇḍīvaṃ yasya kārmukam;
taṃ cedd hant" âsi, Rādheya, tvaṃ no rājā bhaviṣyasi!
eṣa saṃśaptak'|āhūtas, tān ev' âbhimukho gataḥ
karoti kadanaṃ c' âiṣāṃ saṃgrāme dviṣatāṃ balī.»

iti bruvāṇaṃ Madr'|ēśaṃ Karṇaḥ prāh' âtimanyunā:
«paśya! saṃśaptakaiḥ kruddhaiḥ sarvataḥ samabhidrutaḥ;
46.75 eṣa, sūrya iv' âmbho|daiś channaḥ, Pārtho na dṛśyate!
etad|anto 'rjunaḥ, Śalya, nimagno yodha|sāgare!»

ŚALYA uvāca:

«Varuṇaṃ ko 'mbhasā, hanyād indhanena ca pāvakam?
ko v" ânilaṃ nigṛhṇīyāt? pibed vā ko mah"|ârṇavam?
īdṛg|rūpam ahaṃ manye Pārthasya yudhi vigraham.
na hi śakyo 'rjuno jetuṃ yudhi s'|Êndraiḥ sur'|âsuraiḥ!
atha vā paritoṣas te vāc" ôktvā, su|manā bhava!

Look at the Wearer of the crown completely confound that army, like a lion confounding a herd of thousands of different animals! As they attack, the Pándava heroes kill your kings and torrents of your elephants, horses, chariots and foot-soldiers, though they fight back. Like the sun obscured by clouds, Pritha's son is invisible. But the top of his standard is visible and the twang of his bow-string is audible.

Now you'll see that hero after whom you ask, Karna, with 46.70
his white horses and Krishna as his charioteer, slaughtering his enemies in battle! Now, Karna, you'll see that pair of enemy-scorchers, those red-eyed tigers of men Vasudéva and Árjuna, standing on a single chariot!

His chariot-driver is Varshnéya; his bow is Gandíva. If you can kill him, son of Radha, you will become our king! Summoned by the oath-bound warriors, that powerful man went to face them and massacres those enemies in the battle."

As the lord of Madra spoke this, Karna said to him with great passion: "Look! The furious oath-bound warriors have
attacked him from all sides. Like the sun obscured by clouds, 46.75
that son of Pritha can't be seen. Árjuna is finished, Shalya, submerged in a sea of warriors!"

SHALYA said:

"Who could kill Váruna with water and fire with fuel? Or who could catch the wind? Or who could swallow a massive ocean? In battle I reckon Pritha's son has a body similar to these. For the gods and demons with Indra alongside couldn't defeat Árjuna in battle! Now that you've spoken

na sa śakyo yudhā jetum. anyaṃ kuru mano|ratham!
bāhubhyām uddhared bhūmiṃ,
dahet kruddha imāḥ prajāḥ,
pātayet tri|divād devān,
yo 'rjunaṃ samare jayet.
46.80 paśya Kuntī|sutaṃ vīraṃ, Bhīmam a|kliṣṭa|kāriṇam,
prabhāsantaṃ, mahā|bāhuṃ, sthitaṃ Merum iv' âparam!
amarṣī, nitya|saṃrabdhaś, ciraṃ vairam anusmaran,
eṣa Bhīmo jaya|prepsur yudhi tiṣṭhati vīryavān.
eṣa dharma|bhṛtāṃ śreṣṭho Dharma|rājo Yudhiṣṭhiraḥ
tiṣṭhaty a|sukaraḥ saṃkhye paraiḥ, para|puraṃ|jayaḥ.
etau ca puruṣa|vyāghrāv, Aśvināv iva s'|ôdarau,
Nakulaḥ Sahadevaś ca tiṣṭhato yudhi dur|jayau.
amī sthitā Draupadeyāḥ pañca, pañc' âcalā iva,
vyavasthitā, yoddhu|kāmāḥ sarve 'rjuna|samā yudhi.
46.85 ete Drupada|putrāś ca Dhṛṣṭadyumna|puro|gamāḥ
sphītāḥ, satya|jitā, vīrās tiṣṭhanti param'|âujasaḥ.
asāv Indra iv' âsahyaḥ Sātyakiḥ Sātvatāṃ varaḥ
yuyutsur upayāty asmān, kruddh'|Ântaka|samaḥ puraḥ.»
iti saṃvadator eva tayoḥ puruṣa|siṃhayoḥ
te sene samasajjetāṃ Gaṅgā|Yamunavad bhṛśam!

DHṚTARĀṢṬRA uvāca:

47.1 TATHĀ VYŪḌHEṢV anīkeṣu, saṃsakteṣu ca, Saṃjaya,
saṃśaptakān kathaṃ Pārtho gataḥ, Karṇaś ca Pāṇḍavān?
etad vistaraśo yuddhaṃ prabrūhi, kuśalo hy asi!
na hi tṛpyāmi vīrāṇāṃ śṛṇvāno vikramān raṇe!

these words, relax and be satisfied! A warrior can't defeat him. Make another wish! Only whoever could raise the earth with his arms, burn these people in a rage or bring the gods down from heaven, could defeat Árjuna in battle.

Look at Kunti's son Bhima, an unrelenting hero, a 46.80
mighty-armed man standing there without rival as brilliant as Mount Meru! Passionate, always livid and holding grudges for ages, powerful Bhima remains striving for victory in battle. The best of those who uphold the law and a conqueror of his enemies' cities, the King of Law Yudhi·shthira remains in battle as a nuisance to his enemies. Tigers of men who shared the same womb like the Ashvins, Nákula and Saha·deva remain undefeated in the battle. Standing like five mountains, Dráupadi's five sons—all the equal of Árjuna in battle—are in position eager to
fight. Drúpada's prosperous sons, truly victorious heroes led 46.85
by Dhrishta·dyumna, remain with their vigor at its height. Insurmountable like Indra and the best of the Sátvatas, Sátyaki approaches us in the vanguard eager to fight like Death enraged."

While those lions of men conversed, the two armies violently crashed together like the Ganga and Yámuna rivers!

DHRITA·RASHTRA said:

ONCE THOSE ARMIES had been arrayed and then clashed 47.1
together, Sánjaya, how did Árjuna attack the oath-bound warriors? And how did Karna attack the Pándavas? Report on the battle in detail, for you know it well! I'm yet to hear enough about the courage of those heroes in battle!

SAMJAYA uvāca:

tad āsthitam avajñāya pratyamitra|balaṃ mahat,
avyūhat' Ârjuno vyūhaṃ, putrasya tava dur|naye.
tat sādi|nāga|kalilaṃ, padāti|ratha|saṃkulam,
Dhṛṣṭadyumna|mukhaṃ vyūham, aśobhata mahad balam!
47.5 pārāvata|sa|varṇ'|âśvaś, candr'|āditya|sama|dyutiḥ
Pārṣataḥ prababhau dhanvī, Kālo vigrahavān iva.
Pārṣataṃ jugupuḥ sarve Draupadeyā yuyutsavaḥ,
divya|varm'|āyudha|dharāḥ śārdūla|sama|vikramāḥ,
s'|ânugā, dīpta|vapuṣaś, candraṃ tārā|gaṇā iva.

atha vyūḍheṣv anīkeṣu prekṣya saṃśaptakān raṇe,
kruddho 'rjuno 'bhidudrāva vyākṣipan Gāṇḍivaṃ dhanuḥ.
atha saṃśaptakāḥ Pārtham abhyadhāvan vadh'|âiṣiṇaḥ,
vijaye dhṛta|saṃkalpā, mṛtyuṃ kṛtvā nivartanam.
tan nar'|âśv'|âugha|bahulaṃ, matta|nāga|rath'|ākulam,
47.10 pattimac, chūra|vīr'|âughaṃ, drutam Arjunam ārdayat.
sa saṃprahāras tumulas teṣām āsīt Kirīṭinā,
tasy' âiva naḥ śruto yādṛṅ Nivāta|kavacaiḥ saha!

rathān, aśvān, dhvajān, nāgān, pattīn, raṇa|gatān api,
iṣūn, dhanūṃṣi, khaḍgāṃś ca, cakrāṇi ca, paraśvadhān,
s'|āyudhān udyatān bāhūn, vividhāny āyudhāni ca
ciccheda dviṣatāṃ Pārthaḥ, śirāṃsi ca sahasraśaḥ.

SÁNJAYA said:

In consequence of your son's poor policy, Árjuna had little regard for his enemy's massive army that stood before him and drew his army into battle array. Thick with horsemen and elephants, crowded with foot-soldiers and chariots and led in formation by Dhrishta·dyumna, that massive army
looked spectacular! Príshata's grandson, a bowman whose 47.5
radiance was the equal of the sun and moon and whose horses were the color of doves, shone forth like Time incarnate. Along with their followers, all Dráupadi's boys—eager for battle and sporting divine armor and weapons and their courage equal to that of tigers—guarded Príshata's grandson, their bodies ablaze like the constellations of stars surrounding the moon.

Then, seeing the oath-bound warriors in the battle among those arrayed armies, Árjuna drew his bow Gándiva and attacked them in fury. The oath-bound warriors then rushed
upon Pritha's son, striving to kill him with their hearts 47.10
firmly on victory and resolved to flee only in death. That onslaught of valiant heroes, dense with waves of men and horses, crowded with maddened elephants and chariots and including foot-soldiers, speedily struck Árjuna. The tumultuous battle that they had with the Wearer of the crown was just like the one that we've been told he had with the Niváta·kávacha demons!

Pritha's son hacked apart the chariots, horses, banners, elephants and foot-soldiers that had gone into battle, and the arrows, bows, swords, discuses, axes and arms raised with weapons, and many other various weapons and the heads of his enemies by the thousand. Thinking that that warrior was

tasmin sainya|mah"|āvarte pātāla|tala|saṃnibhe
nimagnaṃ taṃ rathaṃ matvā neduḥ saṃśaptakās tathā.
sa punas tān arīn hatvā, punar uttarato 'vadhīt,
47.15 dakṣiṇena ca, paścāc ca, kruddho Rudraḥ paśūn iva.
atha Pāñcāla|Cedīnāṃ, Sṛñjayānāṃ ca, māriṣa,
tvadīyaiḥ saha saṃgrāma āsīt parama|dāruṇaḥ.
Kṛpaś ca, Kṛtavarmā ca, Śakuniś c' âpi Saubalaḥ,
hṛṣṭa|senāḥ, su|saṃrabdhā rath'|ânīka|prahāriṇaḥ,
Kosalaiḥ, Kāśya|Matsyaiś ca, Kārūṣaiḥ, Kekayair api,
Śūrasenaiḥ śūra|varair yuyudhur yuddha|dur|madāḥ.
teṣām anta|karaṃ yuddhaṃ deha|pāpm'|âsu|nāśanam
kṣatra|viṭ|śūdra|vīrāṇāṃ dharmyaṃ, svargyaṃ, yaśas|karam.
Duryodhano 'tha sahito bhrātṛbhir, Bharata'|rṣabha,
47.20 guptaḥ Kuru|pravīraiś ca, Madrāṇāṃ ca mahā|rathaiḥ,
Pāṇḍavaiḥ saha, Pāñcālaiś, Cedibhiḥ, Sātyakena ca
yudhyamānaṃ raṇe Karṇaṃ Kuru|vīro 'bhyapālayat.
Karṇo 'pi niśitair bāṇair vinihatya mahā|camūm,
pramṛdya ca ratha|śreṣṭhān, Yudhiṣṭhiram apīḍayat.
vi|vastr'|āyudha|deh'|âsūn kṛtvā śatrūn sahasraśaḥ,
yuktvā svarga|yaśobhyāṃ ca, svebhyo mudam udāvahat.
evaṃ, māriṣa, saṃgrāmo nara|vāji|gaja|kṣayaḥ
Kurūṇāṃ Sṛñjayānāṃ ca dev'|âsura|samo 'bhavat!

sinking into the great maelstrom of troops which seemed like the pit of hell, the oath-bound warriors rejoiced. Continually striking his enemies, he repeatedly killed those to
his left, those to his right and those behind him, like Rudra 47.15
slaughtering animals in rage.

Then there was an incredibly violent battle between the Panchálas, Chedis and Srínjayas and your troops, dear friend. Mad for battle, Kripa, Krita·varman and Súbala's son Shákuni, and their ferocious and excited forces attacking with their chariot divisions, fought with those brilliant heroes the Shura·senas, Kósalas, Kashis, Matsyas, Karúshas and Kékayas. Their death-causing battle, destroying body, sin and life, generated merit, heaven and fame for the kshatriya, vaishya and shudra heroes.

Then the Kuru hero Duryódhana, together with his 47.20
brothers, bull of Bharatas, and guarded by Kuru heroes and mighty warriors of the Madras, protected Karna as he fought with the Pándavas, Panchálas, Chedis and Sátyaki in the battle. Karna too, after destroying a massive division with sharp arrows and crushing the finest chariots, bore down on Yudhi·shthira. Stripping his enemies by the thousands of their garments, weapons, bodies and lives, and uniting them with fame and heaven, he brought joy to his own people.

In this way, dear friend, this battle of the Kurus and Srínjayas, the end for men, horses and elephants, was the equal of the battle of the gods and demons!

DHṚTARĀṢṬRA uvāca:

48.1 YAT TAT PRAVIŚYA Pārthānāṃ
sainyaṃ, kurvañ jana|kṣayam,
Karṇo rājānam abhyetya,
tan mam' ācakṣva, Saṃjaya!
ke ca pravīrāḥ Pārthānāṃ yudhi Karṇam avārayan?
kāṃś ca pramathy' Ādhirathir Yudhiṣṭhiram apīḍayat?

SAṂJAYA uvāca:

Dhṛṣṭadyumna|mukhān Pārthān
dṛṣṭvā Karṇo vyavasthitān
samabhyadhāvat tvaritaḥ
Pañcālāñ śatru|karṣiṇaḥ.
taṃ tūrṇam abhidhāvantaṃ Pāñcālā jita|kāśinaḥ
pratyudyayur mah"|ātmānaṃ, haṃsā iva mah"|ârṇavam.
48.5 tataḥ śaṅkha|sahasrāṇāṃ nisvano hṛdayaṃ|gamaḥ
prādur āsīd ubhayato, bherī|śabdaś ca dāruṇaḥ.
nānā|bāṇa|nipātāś ca, dvip'|âśva|ratha|nisvanaḥ,
siṃha|nādaś ca vīrāṇām abhavad dāruṇas tadā.
s'|âdri|drum'|ârṇavā bhūmiḥ, sa|vāt'|âmbu|dam ambaram,
s'|ârk'|êndu|graha|nakṣatrā dyauś ca, vyaktaṃ vighūrṇitā.
iti bhūtāni taṃ śabdaṃ menire, te ca vivyathuḥ,
yāni c' âpy alpa|sattvāni, prāyas tāni mṛtāni ca.

DHRITA·RASHTRA said:

SÁNJAYA! TELL ME how Karna breached the army of Pritha's sons, laid waste to its men and attacked the king. Who were the heroes among Pritha's sons that thwarted Karna in the battle? And who did Ádhiratha's son destroy so he could bear down on Yudhi·shthira? 48.1

SÁNJAYA said:

Seeing the Dhrishta·dyumna led forces of Pritha's sons positioned for battle, Karna quickly attacked the Panchálas, scourges of their enemies. Like geese rising to meet the ocean, the Panchálas rose like conquerors to meet that great man who had attacked them so suddenly.

The heart-stirring sound of thousands of conches and the 48.5
raucous sound of kettle-drums then became audible from both sides. And then various arrows began to fall, the sound of elephants, horses and chariots arose, and the guttural roar of a lion came forth from the heroes. The earth with the mountains, trees and oceans, the atmosphere with the wind and clouds, and the sky with the sun, moon, planets and stars, shook visibly. Living beings pondered that sound and trembled; most of those that had little courage perished.

atha Karṇo bhṛśaṃ kruddhaḥ, śīghram astram udīrayan,
jaghāna Pāṇḍavīṃ senām, āsurīṃ Maghavān iva.
48.10 sa Pāṇḍava|balaṃ Karṇaḥ praviśya visṛjañ charān
Prabhadrakāṇāṃ pravarān ahanat sapta|saptatim.
tataḥ su|puṅkhair niśitai ratha|śreṣṭho rath'|êṣubhiḥ
avadhīt pañca|viṃśatyā Pañcālān pañca|viṃśatim.
su|varṇa|puṅkhair nārācaiḥ para|kāya|vidāraṇaiḥ
Cedikān avadhīd vīraḥ śataśo 'tha sahasraśaḥ.

tam tathā samare karma kurvāṇam atimānuṣam,
parivavrur, mahā|rāja, Pañcālānāṃ ratha|vrajāḥ.
tataḥ saṃdhāya viśikhān pañca, Bhārata, duḥ|sahān,
Pañcālān avadhīt pañca Karṇo Vaikartano vṛṣaḥ.
48.15 Bhānudevaṃ, Citrasenaṃ, Senābinduṃ ca, Bhārata,
Tapanaṃ, Śūrasenaṃ ca Pañcālān ahanad raṇe.
Pañcāleṣu ca śūreṣu vadhyamāneṣu sāyakaiḥ,
hāhā|kāro mahān āsīt Pañcālānāṃ mah''|āhave.
parivavrur, mahā|rāja, Pañcālānāṃ rathā daśa,
punar eva ca tān Karṇo jaghān' āśu patatribhiḥ.
cakra|rakṣau tu Karṇasya putrau, māriṣa, dur|jayau
Suṣeṇaḥ Satyasenaś ca tyaktvā prāṇān ayudhyatām.
pṛṣṭha|goptā tu Karṇasya jyeṣṭhaḥ putro mahā|rathaḥ
Vṛṣasenaḥ svayaṃ Karṇaṃ pṛṣṭhataḥ paryapālayat.
48.20 Dhṛṣṭadyumnaḥ, Sātyakiś ca, Draupadeyā, Vṛkodaraḥ,
Janamejayaḥ, Śikhaṇḍī ca, pravīrāś ca Prabhadrakāḥ,
Cedi|Kekaya|Pañcālā, yamau, Matsyāś ca daṃśitāḥ
samabhyadhāvan Rādheyaṃ jighāṃsantaḥ prahāriṇam.
ta enaṃ vividhaiḥ śastraiḥ, śara|dhārābhir eva ca

Quickly raising his swift missile in a terrible rage, Karna
then struck the Pándava army like Mághavan the army of
demons. Breaching the army of the Pándavas and discharg- 48.10
ing his arrows, he slaughtered seventy-seven heroes of the
Prabhádrakas. Then that superior warrior killed twenty-five
Panchálas with twenty-five sharp arrows with superb nocks.
With iron arrows sporting golden nocks lacerating the bodies of his enemies, that hero killed Chedis by the hundred
and then by the thousand.

Masses of Panchála chariots surrounded him, great king, as he carried out this superhuman deed in the battle. After nocking five irresistible arrows, Bhárata, that bull Karna Vaikártana then killed five Panchálas.

Bhanu·deva, Chitra·sena, Sena·bindu, Tápana and Shura· 48.15
sena were the Panchálas he killed in combat, Bhárata. And
when his arrows killed those Panchála heroes, there were
great sounds of astonishment from the Panchálas in that
great battle. Ten Panchála warriors surrounded him, great
king, and again Karna immediately killed them with his
arrows. Karna's indomitable sons and wheel-protectors Sushéna and Satya·sena, dear friend, fought without regard
for their lives. And Karna's rear-guard and eldest son, the
mighty warrior Vrisha·sena himself, protected Karna from
behind.

Dhrishta·dyumna, Sátyaki, Dráupadi's sons, Wolf-belly, 48.20
Janam·éjaya, Shikhándin, the Prabhádraka heroes, the
Chedis, Kékayas and Panchálas, the twins and the Matsyas, all clad in mail, attacked Radha's son together, striving
to kill him as he fought back. Like clouds in the wet season
raining down on a mountain, they rained down on him

abhyavarṣan vimardantaṃ, prāvṛṣ' îv' âmbu|dā girim.
pitaraṃ tu parīpsantaḥ Karṇa|putrāḥ prahāriṇaḥ,
tvadīyāś c' âpare, rājan, vīrā vīrān avārayan.
Suṣeṇo Bhīmasenasya chittvā bhallena kārmukam
nārācaiḥ saptabhir viddhvā hṛdi Bhīmaṃ nanāda ha.
48.25 ath' ânyad dhanur ādāya su|dṛḍhaṃ bhīma|vikramaḥ
sa|jyaṃ Vṛkodaraḥ kṛtvā Suṣeṇasy' âcchinad dhanuḥ.
vivyādha c' âinaṃ daśabhiḥ kruddho nṛtyann iv' êṣubhiḥ,
Karṇaṃ ca tūrṇaṃ vivyādha tri|saptatyā śitaiḥ śaraiḥ.
Bhānusenaṃ ca daśabhiḥ s'|âśva|sūt'|āyudha|dhvajam
paśyatāṃ suhṛdāṃ madhye Karṇa|putram apātayat.
kṣurapra|ṇunnaṃ tat tasya śiraś candra|nibh'|ānanam
śubha|darśanam ev' āsīn, nāla|bhraṣṭam iv' âmbu|jam.
hatvā Karṇa|sutaṃ Bhīmas tāvakān punar ārdayat.
Kṛpa|Hārdikyayoś chittvā cāpau tāv apy ath' ārdayat.
48.30 Duḥśāsanaṃ tribhir viddhvā, Śakuniṃ ṣaḍbhir āyasaiḥ,
Ulūkaṃ ca Patatriṃ ca cakāra virathāv ubhau.
Suṣeṇaṃ ca, «hato 's'! îti» bruvann ādatta sāyakam;
tam asya Karṇaś ciccheda, tribhiś c' âinam atāḍayat.
ath' ânyam parijagrāha su|parvāṇaṃ, su|tejanam,
Suṣeṇāy' âsṛjad Bhīmas. tam apy asy' âcchinad Vṛṣaḥ.
punaḥ Karṇas tri|saptatyā Bhīmasenam ath' êṣubhiḥ
putraṃ parīpsan vivyādha krūraṃ krūrair jighāṃsayā.

with various weapons and sheets of arrows as he pounded them.

But Karna's attacking sons striving to save their father, and other heroes of your army, king, thwarted those heroes. After splintering Bhima's bow with a broad arrow and wounding him in the chest with seven iron arrows, Sushéna roared at Bhima.

Grabbing another very stiff bow and stringing it, with 48.25
formidable force Wolf-belly then splintered Sushéna's bow. And as if dancing in rage he wounded him with ten arrows and quickly wounded Karna with seventy-three sharp arrows. With ten he felled Karna's son Bhanu·sena amid his watching allies, along with his horses, charioteer, weapons and banner. Dispatched by a razor-edged arrow, his head—its face like the moon—was as beautiful as a lotus flower fallen from its stalk.

Bhima resumed tormenting your men after killing Karna's son. Splintering the bows of Kripa and Hrídika's son,
he then tormented them, too. Wounding Duhshásana with 48.30
three iron arrows and Shákuni with six, he stripped both Ulúka and Patátri of their chariots. He seized an arrow as he yelled at Sushéna, "You're dead!" But Karna split his arrow and wounded him with three arrows.

Then Bhima seized another neatly jointed and well-pointed arrow and discharged it at Sushéna. But Vrisha split that arrow of his as well. Protecting his son and with the intention of killing him, Karna again wounded fierce Bhima·sena with seventy-three fierce arrows.

Suṣeṇas tu dhanur gṛhya bhāra|sādhanam uttamam
Nakulaṃ pañcabhir bāṇair bāhvor urasi c' ārpayat.
48.35 Nakulas taṃ tu viṃśatyā viddhvā bhāra|sahair dṛḍhaiḥ
nanāda balavan nādaṃ, Karṇasya bhayam ādadhat.
taṃ Suṣeṇo, mahā|rāja, viddhvā daśabhir āśu|gaiḥ
ciccheda ca dhanuḥ śīghraṃ kṣurapreṇa mahā|rathaḥ.
ath' ânyad dhanur ādāya Nakulaḥ krodha|mūrchitaḥ
Suṣeṇaṃ navabhir bāṇair vārayām āsa saṃyuge.
sa tu bāṇair diśo, rājann, ācchādya para|vīra|hā
ājaghne sārathiṃ c' âsya, Suṣeṇaṃ ca tatas tribhiḥ,
ciccheda c' âsya su|dṛḍhaṃ dhanur bhallais tribhis tridhā.
ath' ânyad dhanur ādāya Suṣeṇaḥ krodha|mūrchitaḥ
48.40 āvidhyan Nakulaṃ ṣaṣṭyā, Sahadevaṃ ca saptabhiḥ.
tad yuddhaṃ su|mahad, ghoram āsīd, dev'|âsur'|ôpamam,
nighnatāṃ sāyakais tūrṇam anyonyasya vadhaṃ prati.
Sātyakir Vṛṣasenasya sūtaṃ hatvā tribhiḥ śaraiḥ
dhanuś ciccheda bhallena, jaghān' âśvāṃś ca saptabhiḥ.
dhvajam ek'|êṣuṇ' ônmathya tribhis taṃ hṛdy atāḍayat.
ath' âvasannaḥ sva|rathe muhūrtāt punar utthitaḥ;
sa raṇe Yuyudhānena vi|sūt'|âśva|ratha|dhvajaḥ
kṛto, jighāṃsuḥ Śaineyaṃ khaḍga|carma|dhṛg abhyayāt.
tasya c' āpatataḥ śīghraṃ Vṛṣasenasya, Sātyakiḥ
48.45 vārāha|karṇair daśabhir avidhyad asi|carmaṇī.

Sushéna grabbed a superb and extremely effective bow and wounded Nákula in the chest and arms with five arrows. But powerful Nákula, after wounding him with twenty very 48.35
strong and solid arrows, roared a roar and roused fear in Karna. After wounding him with ten arrows, great king, the mighty warrior Sushéna quickly split his bow with a razor-edged arrow.

Seething with rage, Nákula then grabbed another bow and enveloped Sushéna in battle with nine arrows. Covering the directions with arrows, king, that killer of enemy-heroes struck his driver and then Sushéna with three arrows, and split his very stiff bow in three places with three broad arrows.

Seething with rage, Sushéna then grabbed another bow and wounded Nákula with sixty arrows and Saha·deva with 48.40
seven. Like the battle of the gods and demons, the battle between those men was magnificent and horrific as they attacked quickly with arrows in order to kill one another.

Once he'd killed Vrisha·sena's charioteer with three arrows, Sátyaki split his bow with a broad arrow and killed his horses with seven arrows. After tearing his banner apart with one arrow, he wounded him in the chest with three.

Sinking into his chariot, after a moment Vrisha·sena rose up again. Stripped in battle of his driver, horses, chariot and banner by Yuyudhána, he attacked Shini's grandson wielding his sword and shield and hoping to kill him. As Vrisha·sena rapidly rushed at him, Sátyaki pummelled his 48.45
sword and shield with ten boar-eared arrows.

Duḥśāsanas tu taṃ dṛṣṭvā virathaṃ, vy|āyudhaṃ kṛtam,
āropya sva|rathaṃ tūrṇam apovāha raṇ'|āturam.
ath' ânyaṃ ratham āsthāya, Vṛṣaseno mahā|rathaḥ,
Draupadeyāṃs tri|saptatyā, Yuyudhānaṃ ca pañcabhiḥ,
Bhīmasenaṃ catuḥ|ṣaṣṭyā, Sahadevaṃ ca pañcabhiḥ,
Nakulaṃ triṃśatā bāṇaiḥ, Śatānīkaṃ ca saptabhiḥ,
Śikhaṇḍinaṃ ca daśabhir, Dharma|rājaṃ śatena ca,
etāṃś c' ânyāṃś ca, rāj'|êndra, pravīrāñ jaya|gṛddhinaḥ,
abhyardayan mah"|êṣv|āsaḥ Karṇa|putro, viśāṃ pate,
48.50 Karṇasya yudhi dur|dharṣas tataḥ pṛṣṭham apālayat.

Duḥśāsanaṃ tu Śaineyo navair navabhir āyasaiḥ
vi|sūt'|âśva|rathaṃ kṛtvā lalāṭe tribhir ārpayat.
sa tv anyaṃ ratham āsthāya vidhivat kalpitaṃ punaḥ
yuyudhe Pāṇḍubhiḥ sārdhaṃ Karṇasy' āpyāyayan balam.

Dhṛṣṭadyumnas tataḥ Karṇam avidhyad daśabhiḥ śaraiḥ,
Draupadeyās tri|saptatyā, Yuyudhānas tu saptabhiḥ,
Bhīmasenaś catuḥ|ṣaṣṭyā, Sahadevaś ca saptabhiḥ,
Nakulas triṃśatā bāṇaiḥ, Śatānīkas tu saptabhiḥ,
Śikhaṇḍī daśabhir, vīro Dharma|rājaḥ śatena tu.
48.55 ete c' ânye ca, rāj'|êndra, pravīrā jaya|gṛddhinaḥ
abhyardayan mah"|êṣv|āsaṃ sūta|putraṃ mahā|mṛdhe.

tān sūta|putro viśikhair daśabhir daśabhiḥ śaraiḥ
rathen' ânucaran vīraḥ pratyavidhyad ariṃ|damaḥ.
tatr' âstra|vīryaṃ Karṇasya, lāghavaṃ ca mah"|ātmanaḥ
apaśyāma, mahā|bhāga; tad adbhutam iv' âbhavat!
na hy ādadānaṃ dadṛśuḥ, saṃdadhānaṃ ca sāyakān,

But, seeing Vrisha·sena stripped of his chariot and weapon and injured in battle, Duhshásana pulled him onto his chariot and quickly carried him away. Mounting another chariot, lord of the people, and tormenting Dráupadi's sons with seventy-three arrows, Yuyudhána with five, Bhima·sena with sixty-four, Saha·deva with five, Nákula with thirty, Shataníka with seven, Shikhándin with ten and the King of Law with a hundred arrows—these and other heroes eager for victory, lord of kings—Karna's indomitable son Vrisha·sena, a mighty warrior and archer, thereby protected Karna's 48.50
rear in the battle.

But Shini's grandson stripped Duhshásana of his charioteer, horses and chariot with nine new iron arrows and wounded him in the forehead with three. But mounting another well-prepared chariot, Duhshásana continued battling with the Pándavas, bolstering Karna's army.

Dhrishta·dyumna then wounded Karna with ten arrows, Dráupadi's sons wounded him with seventy-three, Yuyudhána with seven, Bhima·sena with sixty-four, Saha·deva with seven, Nákula with thirty arrows, Shataníka with seven, Shikhándin with ten and the heroic King of Law with a hundred. These and other heroes eager for victory, lord of 48.55
kings, tormented that mighty archer the charioteer's son in that great battle.

That enemy-subduing hero, the son of the charioteer, pursued them in his chariot and wounded them in return with ten arrows each. Distinguished man, we saw there the prowess of Karna's weapon and the speed of that great man; it was miraculous! They saw him neither grab, nock nor release his arrows; but they saw his enemies killed from

vimuñcantaṃ ca, saṃraṃbhād; apaśyanta hatān arīn.
dyaur, viyad, bhūr, diśaś c' âiva prapūrṇāni śitaiḥ śaraiḥ,
aruṇ'|âbhr'|āvṛt'|ākāraṃ tasmin deśe babhau viyat.
48.60 nṛtyann iva hi Rādheyaś cāpa|hastaḥ pratāpavān
yair viddhaḥ, pratyaviddhyat tān ek'|âikaṃ tri|guṇaiḥ śaraiḥ.
śataiś ca daśabhiś c' âitān punar viddhvā nanāda ca.
s'|âśva|sūta|rathāś channās tatas te vivaraṃ daduḥ.
tān pramathya mah"|êṣv|āsān Rādheyaḥ śara|vṛṣṭibhiḥ
gaj'|ânīkam a|saṃbādhaṃ prāviśac chatru|karśanaḥ.
sa rathāṃs tri|śataṃ hatvā Cedīnām a|nivartinām,
Rādheyo niśitair bāṇais tato 'bhyārchad Yudhiṣṭhiram.
tatas te Pāṇḍavā, rājañ, Chikhaṇḍī ca sa|Sātyakiḥ
Rādheyāt parirakṣanto rājānaṃ paryavārayan.
48.65 tath" âiva tāvakāḥ sarve Karṇaṃ dur|vāraṇaṃ raṇe
yattāḥ śūrā mah"|êṣv|āsāḥ paryarakṣanta sarvaśaḥ.
nānā|vāditra|ghoṣāś ca prādur āsan, viśāṃ pate,
siṃha|nādaś ca saṃjajñe śūrāṇām abhigarjatām.
tataḥ punaḥ samājagmur a|bhītāḥ Kuru|Pāṇḍavāḥ,
Yudhiṣṭhira|mukhāḥ Pārthāḥ, sūta|putra|mukhā vayam.

SAṂJAYA uvāca:

49.1 VIDĀRYA KARṆAS tāṃ senāṃ Yudhiṣṭhiram ath' âdravat
ratha|hasty|aśva|pattīnāṃ sahasraiḥ parivāritaḥ.
nān"|āyudha|sahasrāṇi preritāny aribhir Vṛṣaḥ
chittvā bāṇa|śatair ugrais tān avidhyad a|saṃbhramāt.

his rage. The sky, the air, the earth and the directions were completely filled with sharp arrows, and the air in that place glowed like it was filled with red clouds.

As if dancing with bow in hand, one by one and with 48.60
three times as many arrows, Radha's powerful son wounded in return those who had wounded him. And he roared after wounding them again with a hundred and ten arrows. Covered along with their horses, charioteers and chariots, they then offered him an opening. Crushing mighty archers with showers of arrows, Radha's son, withering his enemies, breached the gaping elephant division. Once he'd killed thirty warriors of the unwavering Chedis, Radha's son then reached Yudhi·shthira with his sharp arrows.

So, king, the Pándavas and Shikhándin with Sátyaki alongside surrounded the king, protecting him from Radha's son. Similarly, all the heroes and mighty archers from 48.65
your army readied themselves and protected irrepressible Karna in every way in the battle.

And sounds from various instruments became audible, lord of the people, and a lion's roar rose from those heroes as they savagely howled. Then the fearless Kurus and Pándavas clashed together, Pritha's sons led by Yudhi·shthira and us led by the charioteer's son.

SÁNJAYA said:

SURROUNDED BY thousands of chariots, elephants, horses 49.1
and foot-soldiers and tearing open that army, Karna then attacked Yudhi·shthira. Vrisha shattered the thousands of different weapons hurled by his enemies and coolly pelted them with hundreds of formidable arrows. The charioteer's

nicakarta śirāṃsy eṣāṃ, bāhūn, ūrūṃś ca sūta|jaḥ;
te hatā vasudhāṃ petur, bhagnāś c' ânye vidudruvuḥ.

Drāviḍās tu, Niṣādās tu punaḥ Sātyaki|coditāḥ
abhyadravañ jighāṃsantaḥ pattayaḥ Karṇam āhave.
49.5 te vi|bāhu|śirastrāṇāḥ prahatāḥ Karṇa|sāyakaiḥ,
petuḥ pṛthivyāṃ yugapac, chinnaṃ śāla|vanaṃ yathā.
evaṃ yodha|śatāny ājau, sahasrāṇy, ayutāni ca
hatān' īyur mahīṃ dehair, yaśas" âpūrayan diśaḥ.

atha Vaikartanaṃ Karṇaṃ raṇe kruddham iv' Ântakam
rurudhuḥ Pāṇḍu|Pañcālā, vyādhiṃ mantr'|āuṣadhair iva.
sa tān pramṛdy' âbhyapatat punar eva Yudhiṣṭhiram,
mantr'|âuṣadhi|kriy"|âtīto vyādhir atyulbaṇo yathā.
sa rāja|gṛddhibhī ruddhaḥ Pāṇḍu|Pañcāla|Kekayaiḥ,
n' âśakat tān atikrāntuṃ, mṛtyur Brahma|vido yathā.
49.10 tato Yudhiṣṭhiraḥ Karṇam a|dūra|sthaṃ nivāritam
abravīt para|vīra|ghnaṃ krodha|saṃrakta|locanaḥ:
«Karṇa! Karṇa! vṛthā|dṛṣṭe, sūta|putra! vacaḥ śṛṇu!
sadā spardhasi saṃgrāme Phālgunena tarasvinā.
tath" âsmān bādhase nityaṃ Dhārtarāṣṭra|mate sthitaḥ.
yad balaṃ, yac ca te vīryaṃ, pradveṣo yaś ca Pāṇḍuṣu,
tat sarvaṃ darśayasv' âdya pauruṣaṃ mahad āsthitaḥ!
yuddha|śraddhāṃ ca te 'dy' âhaṃ vineṣyāmi mah"|āhave!»

son cut off their heads, arms and shins; those killed collapsed on the ground and others fled in defeat.

But, egged on by Sátyaki, Dravidian and Nisháda foot-soldiers attacked Karna aiming to kill him in the battle. Stripped of their arms and helmets and slain by Karna's 49.5
arrows, as one they fell to the earth like a clear-felled forest of *shala* trees. In this way, hundreds, thousands and tens of thousands of warriors killed in combat spread the earth with their bodies and filled the directions with their fame.

Then, just as a disease is repelled with mantras and medicinal herbs, the Pándavas and Panchálas repelled Karna Vai·kártana who in battle was like Death in a fury. Like a powerful disease beyond the effects of mantras, medicinal herbs and remedies, he crushed them and again fell on Yudhi·shthira. But, repelled by the Pándavas, Panchálas and Kékayas who hankered for their king, he couldn't overcome them just as death can't overcome those who know Brahman.

His eyes inflamed with rage, Yudhi·shthira then spoke 49.10
to Karna, that killer of enemy-heroes who, held back, remained nearby: "Karna! Karna! You're insight is pathetic, charioteer's son! Listen to these words! You always vie in battle with bold Phálguna. Devoted to the will of Dhrita·rashtra's son, you always oppose us. Drawing on your enormous courage, you must put everything on display today: your strength, your courage and your hostility for the Pándavas! In this great battle today I will dispel your faith in combat!"

evam uktvā, mahā|rāja, Karṇaṃ Pāṇḍu|sutas tadā
su|varṇa|puṅkhair daśabhir vivyādh' âyas|mayaiḥ śitaiḥ.
49.15 taṃ sūta|putro daśabhiḥ pratyaviddhyad ariṃ|damaḥ
vatsa|dantair mah"|êṣv|āsaḥ prahasann iva, Bhārata.
so 'vajñāya tu nirviddhaḥ sūta|putreṇa, māriṣa,
prajajvāla tataḥ krodhādd, haviṣ" êva hut'|âśanaḥ.
jvālā|mālā|parikṣipto rājño deho vyadṛśyata,
yug'|ânte dagdhu|kāmasya saṃvart'|âgner iv' âparaḥ.
tato visphārya su|mahac cāpaṃ hema|pariṣkṛtam,
samādhatta śitaṃ bāṇaṃ girīṇām api dāraṇam.
tataḥ pūrṇ'|āyat'|ôtkṛṣṭaṃ Yama|daṇḍa|nibhaṃ śaram
mumoca tvarito rājā sūta|putra|jighāṃsayā.
49.20 sa tu vegavatā mukto bāṇo vajr'|âśani|svanaḥ
viveśa sahasā Karṇaṃ savye pārśve mahā|ratham.
sa tu tena prahāreṇa pīḍitaḥ pramumoha vai.
srasta|gātro mahā|bāhur dhanur utsṛjya syandane
gat'|âsur iva niścetāḥ Śalyasy' âbhimukho 'patat.
rāj" âpi bhūyo n' ājaghne Karṇaṃ Pārtha|hit'|ēpsayā.
tato hāhā|kṛtaṃ sarvaṃ Dhārtarāṣṭra|balaṃ mahat
vivarṇa|mukha|bhūyiṣṭhaṃ Karṇaṃ dṛṣṭvā tathā|gatam.
siṃha|nādaś ca saṃjajñe, kṣvelāḥ, kilakilās tathā
Pāṇḍavānāṃ, mahā|rāja, dṛṣṭvā rājñaḥ parākramam.

Once he'd said this to Karna, great king, Pandu's son pelted him with ten iron arrows with nocks of gold. Sneer- 49.15
ing, the charioteer's son, an enemy-destroyer and mighty archer, pelted him in return with ten calf-toothed arrows, Bhárata.

Contemptuously wounded by the charioteer's son, dear friend, Yudhi·shthira then flared up with anger like a sacrifical fire with an oblation. The king's body seemed surrounded by a garland of flames, as if he rivalled the world-destroying fire eager to burn at the end of an epoch. Then, drawing his massive, gold-embossed bow, he nocked a sharp arrow able to split even mountains. With the aim of killing the charioteer's son, the king quickly released that arrow which seemed like Yama's staff drawn up in his fully extended bow.

Released by the dynamic king, that arrow which sounded 49.20
like Indra's thunderbolt brutally penetrated the mighty warrior Karna in his left side. Badly injured by that blow, he became dazed. His limbs hanging limply and losing grip on his bow, he fell senseless before Shalya in the chariot as if he were dead. Yet still the king did not kill Karna because he wanted to do what was right by Pritha's son.*

The entire massive army of the Dhartaráshtras exclaimed in horror after seeing Karna in such a state, his face almost completely devoid of color. A lion's roar came forth from the Pándavas, great king, as did whistles and cries of joy, after they had witnessed the courage of their king.

49.25 pratilabhya tu Rādheyaḥ saṃjñāṃ n' âticirād iva
dadhre rāja|vināśāya manaḥ krūra|parākramaḥ.
sa hema|vikṛtaṃ cāpaṃ visphārya Vijayaṃ mahat,
avākirad a|mey'|ātmā Pāṇḍavaṃ niśitaiḥ śaraiḥ.
tataḥ kṣurābhyāṃ Pāñcālyau cakra|rakṣau mah"|ātmanaḥ
jaghāna Candradevaṃ ca, Daṇḍadhāraṃ ca saṃyuge.
tāv ubhau Dharma|rājasya pravīrau paripārśvataḥ
rath'|âbhyāśe cakāśete, candrasy' êva punar|vasū.
Yudhiṣṭhiraḥ punaḥ Karṇam aviddhyat triṃśatā śaraiḥ,
Suṣeṇaṃ, Satyasenaṃ ca tribhis tribhir atāḍayat.
49.30 Śalyaṃ navatyā vivyādha, tri|saptatyā ca sūta|jam,
tāṃś c' âsya goptṝn vivyādha tribhis tribhir a|jihma|gaiḥ.
tataḥ prahasy' Ādhirathir vidhunvānaḥ sa kārmukam
bhittvā bhallena, rājānaṃ viddhvā ṣaṣṭy" ânadat tadā.
tataḥ pravīrāḥ Pāṇḍūnām abhyadhāvann a|marṣitāḥ,
Yudhiṣṭhiraṃ parīpsantaḥ, Karṇam abhyardayañ śaraiḥ.
Sātyakiś, Cekitānaś ca,
Yuyutsuḥ, Pāṇḍya eva ca,
Dhṛṣṭadyumnaḥ, Śikhaṇḍī ca,
Draupadeyāḥ, Prabhadrakāḥ,
yamau ca, Bhīmasenaś ca, Śiśupālasya c' ātmajaḥ,
Kārūṣā, Matsya|śeṣāś ca, Kekayāḥ, Kāśi|Kosalāḥ,
49.35 ete ca tvaritā vīrā Vasuṣeṇam atāḍayan.
Janamejayaś ca Pāñcālyaḥ Karṇaṃ vivyādha sāyakaiḥ.
vārāha|karṇa|nārācair, nālīkair niśitaiḥ śaraiḥ,
vatsa|dantair, vipāṭhaiś ca, kṣurapraiś, caṭakā|mukhaiḥ,
nānā|praharaṇaiś c' ôgrai, ratha|hasty|aśva|sādibhiḥ,
sarvato 'bhyādravat Karṇaṃ parivārya jighāṃsayā.

After almost no time at all Radha's son recovered consciousness and, his courage formidable, focused his mind on the king's destruction. Drawing his huge gilded bow Víjaya, Karna, whose soul had no measure, covered the Pándava with sharp arrows. With two sharp blades he then killed in battle that great man's wheel-protectors, the Panchálas Chandra·deva and Danda·dhara. Both those heroes on either side of the King of Law close by his chariot were radiant like the pair of lunar mansions either side of the moon. 49.25

Yudhi·shthira again pelted Karna with thirty arrows, and wounded Sushéna and Satya·sena with three each. He pelted 49.30
Shalya with ninety arrows and the charioteer's son with seventy-three, and he pelted his guards with three straight-flying arrows each.

Laughing, Ádhiratha's son bellowed as he shook his bow after wounding the king with a broad arrow and pelting him with sixty more.

Keeping Karna at bay with their arrows, the infuriated heroes of the Pándavas rushed forward hoping to reach Yudhi·shthira. Sátyaki, Chekitána, Yuyútsu, the Pandya king, Dhrishta·dyumna, Shikhándin, Dráupadi's sons, the Prabhádrakas, the twins, Bhima·sena, Shishu·pala's son, the Karúshas, the surviving Matsyas, the Kékayas, Kashis and Kósalas—all those quick heroes punished Vasu·shena. 49.35

And Janam·éjaya, grandson of the Panchála princess,* wounded Karna with his arrows. Surrounding him on all sides with chariots, elephants, horses and horsemen, he attacked Karna eager to kill him with sharp boar-eared iron arrows, tubular arrows, calf-toothed arrows, large arrows,

sa Pāṇḍavānāṃ pravaraiḥ sarvataḥ samabhidrutaḥ.
udīrayan Brāhmam astraṃ, śaraiḥ āpūrayan diśaḥ;
tataḥ śara|mahā|jvālo, vīry'|ôṣmā Karṇa|pāvakaḥ
nirdahan Pāṇḍava|vanaṃ, vīraḥ paryacarad raṇe!
49.40 sa saṃdhāya mah"|âstrāṇi mah"|êṣv|āso mahā|manāḥ
prahasya puruṣ'|êndrasya śaraiś ciccheda kārmukam.
tataḥ saṃdhāya navatiṃ nimeṣān nata|parvaṇām,
bibheda kavacaṃ rājño raṇe Karṇaḥ śitaiḥ śaraiḥ.

tad varma hema|vikṛtaṃ, ratna|citraṃ babhau patat,
sa|vidyud abhraṃ savituḥ śliṣṭaṃ vāta|hataṃ yathā.
tad aṅgāt puruṣ'|êndrasya bhraṣṭaṃ varma vyarocata
ratnair alaṃ|kṛtaṃ citrair, vy|abhraṃ niśi yathā nabhaḥ.
chinna|varmā śaraiḥ Pārtho, rudhireṇa samukṣitaḥ,
tataḥ sarv'|āyasīṃ śaktiṃ cikṣep' Ādhirathiṃ prati.
49.45 tāṃ jvalantīm iv' ākāśe śaraiś ciccheda saptabhiḥ.
sā chinnā bhūmim agaman mah"|êṣv|āsasya sāyakaiḥ.

tato bāhvọr, lalāṭe ca, hṛdi c' âiva Yudhiṣṭhiraḥ
caturbhis tomaraiḥ Karṇaṃ tāḍayitv" ânadan mudā.

udbhinna|rudhiraḥ Karṇaḥ kruddhaḥ sarpa iva śvasan
dhvajaṃ ciccheda bhallena, tribhir vivyādha Pāṇḍavam,
iṣu|dhī c' âsya ciccheda, rathaṃ ca tilaśo 'cchinat.

razor-edged arrows, sparrow-faced arrows and various other formidable weapons.

Rushed upon from all sides by the best of the Pándavas, the hero maneuvered in battle as he discharged his Brahma weapon and filled the directions with his arrows; his courage the heat and his arrows the massive blaze, Karna was a fire burning the Pándavaforest! Nocking his great missiles and 49.40
laughing, that proud and mighty archer splintered the bow of that lord of men* with his arrows. Then, nocking ninety smooth-jointed arrows in a flash, Karna smashed through the king's armor in the battle with sharp arrows.

That gilded and jewel-speckled armor looked beautiful as it fell, like a lightning-filled cloud near the sun blown apart by the wind. Falling from the body of the lord of men, that armor decorated with colorful gems looked as beautiful as a cloudless sky in the night. His armor shattered and sprinkled with blood, Pritha's son then hurled his iron spear at Ádhiratha's son.

With seven arrows Karna shattered that spear that seemed 49.45
to blaze in the sky and, shattered by the arrows of that mighty archer, it dropped to the ground.

Then after wounding him in the arms, forehead and heart with four lances, Yudhi·shthira bellowed with excitement.

Spouting blood, hissing like a snake and infuriated, Karna shredded his banner with a broad arrow, wounded the Pándava with three more, cut off both his quivers and smashed his chariot into pieces the size of sesame seeds.

kāla|vālās tu ye Pārthaṃ danta|varṇ" âvahan hayāḥ,
tair yuktaṃ ratham āsthāya, prāyād rājā parāṅ|mukhaḥ.
evaṃ Pārtho 'py apāyāt sa nihataḥ pārṣṇi|sārathiḥ,
49.50 a|śaknuvan pramukhataḥ sthātuṃ Karṇasya dur|manāḥ.
abhidrutya tu Rādheyaḥ Pāṇḍu|putraṃ Yudhiṣṭhiram,
vajra|cchatr'|âṅkuśair, matsyair,
dhvaja|kūrm'|âmbu|j'|âdibhiḥ
lakṣaṇair upapannena
pāṇḍunā Pāṇḍu|nandanam,
pavitrī|kartum ātmānaṃ, skandhe saṃspṛśya pāṇinā,
grahītum icchan sa balāt Kuntī|vākyaṃ ca so 'smarat.
taṃ Śalyaḥ prāha, «mā, Karṇa,
gṛhṇīthāḥ pārthiv'|ôttamam!
gṛhīta|mātro, hatvā tvāṃ,
mā kariṣyati bhasmasāt!»
abravīt prahasan, rājan, kutsayann iva Pāṇḍavam:
«kathaṃ nāma kule jātaḥ, kṣatra|dharme vyavasthitaḥ,
49.55 prajahyāt samaraṃ bhītaḥ, prāṇān rakṣan mah"|āhave?
na bhavān kṣatra|dharmeṣu kuśalo h' îti me matiḥ!
brāhme bale bhavān yuktaḥ, svādhyāye, yajña|karmaṇi.
mā sma yudhyasva, Kaunteya! mā ca vīrān samāsadaḥ!
mā c' âitān a|priyaṃ brūhi! mā vai vraja mahā|raṇam!
vaktavyā, māriṣ', ânye tu; na vaktavyās tu mādṛśāḥ;
mādṛśān vibruvan yuddhe etad anyac ca lapsyase.
sva|gṛhaṃ gaccha, Kaunteya, yatra tau Keśav'|Ârjunau!
na hi tvāṃ samare, rājan, hanyāt Karṇaḥ kathaṃ cana!»

After mounting a chariot that was yoked to those black-tailed and teeth-colored horses that had just now drawn Pritha's son, the king sped off in the opposite direction. In this way, with the charioteers that drove his outer horses dead, Pritha's son retired in low spirits, unable to stand 49.50
before Karna.

Running after Pandu's son Yudhi·shthira, to purify himself Radha's son touched the son of Pandu on the shoulder with his pale hand that was adorned with tattoos such as lightning bolts, parasols, hooks, fish, flags, tortoises and lotuses. As he endeavored to seize him with force, he recalled Kunti's words.*

Shalya said to him, "Karna, don't capture that excellent prince lest he kills you as soon as you capture him and reduces you to ashes!"

Laughing as if to scorn the Pándava, king, he said to Yudhi·shthira: "How is it that, born in a noble family and
adhering to warrior law, you can abandon battle terrified, 49.55
preserving your life in this great war? You're incapable of the duties of a warrior, that's what I think! Dedicated to sacred power, the recitation of mantras and sacrificial rites, you mustn't fight, son of Kunti! Don't advance against heroes, don't abuse them and don't go into the great battle! Dear friend, you can abuse others, but you shouldn't abuse the likes of us. If you do speak that way to the likes of us, you'll meet with this or some other fate in battle. Go home, son of Kunti! Or to wherever Késhava and Árjuna are! For, king, Karna would never kill you in battle!"

evam uktvā tataḥ Pārthaṃ visṛjya ca mahā|balaḥ
49.60 nyahanat Pāṇḍavīṃ senāṃ, Vajrahasta iv' âsurīm.
tato 'pāyād drutaṃ, rājan, vrīḍann iva nar'|ēśvaraḥ.
ath' âpayātaṃ rājānam matv" ânvīyus tam acyutam
Cedi|Pāṇḍava|Pañcālāḥ, Sātyakiś ca mahā|rathaḥ,
Draupadeyās, tathā Śūrā, Mādrī|putrau ca Pāṇḍavau.
tato Yudhiṣṭhir'|ânīkaṃ dṛṣṭvā, Karṇaḥ parāṅ|mukham,
Kurubhiḥ sahito vīraḥ prahṛṣṭaḥ pṛṣṭha|to 'nvagāt.
bherī|śaṅkha|mṛdaṃgānāṃ kārmukāṇāṃ ca nisvanaḥ
babhūva Dhārtarāṣṭrāṇāṃ, siṃha|nāda|ravas tathā.
Yudhiṣṭhiras tu, Kauravya, ratham āruhya sa|tvaram
49.65 Śrutakīrter, mahā|rāja, dṛṣṭavān Karṇa|vikramam.
kālyamānaṃ balaṃ dṛṣṭvā, Dharma|rājo Yudhiṣṭhiraḥ
tān yodhān abravīt kruddho, «nighnat' âitān! kim āsata?»
tato rājñ" âbhyanujñātāḥ Pāṇḍavānāṃ mahā|rathāḥ
Bhīmasena|mukhāḥ sarve putrāṃs te pratyupādravan.
abhavat tumulaḥ śabdo yodhānāṃ tatra, Bhārata,
ratha|hasty|aśva|pattīnāṃ, śastrāṇāṃ ca tatas tataḥ.
«uttiṣṭhata!» «praharata!» «prait'!» «âbhipatat'! êti» ca
iti bruvāṇā anyonyaṃ jaghnur yodhā mahā|raṇe.
abhra|cchāy" êva tatr' āsīc chara|vṛṣṭibhir ambare
49.70 samāvṛtair nara|varair nighnadbhir itar'|êtaram.
vi|patākā|dhvaja|cchatrā, vy|aśva|sūt'|āyudhā raṇe
vy|aṅg'|âṅg'|âvayavāḥ, petuḥ kṣitau kṣīṇā kṣit'|īśvarāḥ.

Once he'd said this, the powerful man released Pritha's son and assailed the Pándava army just as the Thunderbolt-wielder assailed the army of demons. 49.60

That lord of men, king, then quickly departed from there as if in shame. Realizing he was in retreat, the Chedis, Pándavas, Panchálas, the mighty warrior Sátyaki, Dráupadi's boys, the Shuras and the two Pándava sons of Madri, followed that imperishable king.

Seeing Yudhi·shthira's army turn away from there, the hero Karna was elated and followed from behind together with the Kurus. The sound of bows, kettle-drums, conches and *mridánga* drums arose from among the Dhartaráshtras, as did the thunder of lion roars.

But, Kaurávya, Yudhi·shthira quickly mounted Shruta·kirti's chariot and saw Karna's procession, great king. Seeing 49.65 that army driven on, the King of Law Yudhi·shthira was furious and said to his warriors, "Why do you rest? Kill them!"

As commanded by the king, all the mighty warriors of the Pándavas led by Bhima·sena then rushed on your sons. A chaotic clamor arose from the warriors there, Bhárata, and from the chariots, elephants, horses, foot-soldiers and 49.70 weapons all over the place. Yelling "Stand your ground!" "Attack!" "Die!" and "Rush forward!" the warriors killed one another in the great battle. Enveloped by showers of arrows in the sky, it was as if there was a shadow from a cloud there as those excellent men struck one another. Stripped of their flags, banners, parasols, horses, charioteers and weapons in the battle, and losing limbs and portions of

pravaṇād iva śailānāṃ śikharāṇi, dvip'|ôttamāḥ
s'|ârohā nihatāḥ petur, vajra|bhinnā iv' âdrayaḥ.
chinna|bhinna|viparyastair varm'|âlaṃkāra|bhūṣaṇaiḥ
s'|ârohās turagāḥ petur hata|vīrāḥ sahasraśaḥ.
vipraviddh'|āyudhāś c' âiva virathāś ca rathair hatāḥ;
prativīraiś ca saṃmarde patti|saṃghāḥ sahasraśaḥ.
viśāl'|āyata|tāmr'|âkṣaiḥ padm'|êndu|sadṛś'|ānanaiḥ,
49.75 śirobhir yuddha|śauṇḍānāṃ sarvataḥ saṃvṛtā mahī.

yathā bhuvi, tathā vyomni nisvanaṃ śuśruvur janāḥ
vimānair, apsaraḥ|saṃghair, gīta|vāditra|nisvanaiḥ.
hatān abhimukhān vīrān vīraiḥ śata|sahasraśaḥ
āropy' āropya gacchanti vimāneṣv apsaro|gaṇāḥ.

tad dṛṣṭvā mahad āścaryaṃ pratyakṣaṃ, svarga|lipsayā
prahṛṣṭa|manasaḥ śūrāḥ kṣipraṃ jaghnuḥ parasparam.
rathino rathibhiḥ sārdhaṃ citraṃ yuyudhur āhave,
pattayaḥ pattibhir, nāgāḥ saha nāgair, hayair hayāḥ.
evaṃ pravṛtte saṃgrāme gaja|vāji|nara|kṣaye,
49.80 sainyena rajasā vṛtte, sve svāñ jaghnuḥ, pare parān.
kacā|kaci yuddham āsīd, dantā|danti, nakhā|nakhi,
muṣṭi|yuddhaṃ, niyuddhaṃ ca deha|pāpm'|âsu|nāśanam!

their limbs, those lords of the earth collapsed on the earth dead.

Like peaks falling down the slopes of mountains, superb elephants were slaughtered with their riders and collapsed like mountains struck by thunderbolts. Horses collapsed with their riders—these heroes were killed by the thousand!—their armor, ornaments and decorations torn, broken and inverted. Their weapons scattered, those stripped of their chariots were killed by others still in their
chariots; and in that melee opposing forces killed divisions 49.75
of foot-soldiers by the thousand. The earth was completely covered with the heads of those battle-keen warriors, their eyes red and stretched wide and their faces like a lotus or the moon.

In the sky and on earth people heard the sound made by the hordes of *ápsaras*es in their celestial vehicles and the sounds of their songs and musical instruments. The bands of *ápsaras*es still move along, continually raising onto their celestial chariots those heroes killed in hundreds and thousands by other heroes that they faced.

Seeing that great miracle before their eyes, the heroes were elated and immediatelty struck at one another with eagerness to reach heaven. Chariot-warriors fought brilliantly in battle with chariot-warriors, foot-soldiers with foot-soldier, elephants with elephants and horses with horses. In the battle that unfolded like so, destroying elephants, horses and
men and whirling with dust kicked up by the troops, al- 49.80
lies killed allies and enemies killed enemies. Yanking one another's hair and fighting tooth to tooth and nail to nail,

tathā vartati saṃgrāme gaja|vāji|nara|kṣaye,
nar'|âśva|nāga|dehebhyaḥ prasṛtā lohit'|āpagā
gaj'|âśva|nara|dehān sā vyuvāha patitān bahūn.
nar'|âśva|gaja|sambādhe nar'|âśva|gaja|sādinām
lohit'|ôdā mahā|ghorā, māṃsa|śoṇita|kardamā,
nar'|âśva|gaja|dehānāṃ vahantī, bhīru|bhīṣaṇā.
tasyāḥ pāram apāraṃ ca vrajanti vijay'|âiṣiṇaḥ;
49.85 gādhena c' ôtplavantaś ca, nimajjy', ônmajjya c' âpare,
te tu lohita|digdh'|âṅgā rakta|varm'|āyudh'|âmbarāḥ,
sasnus tasyāṃ, papuś c' âsyāṃ, mamluś ca, Bharata'|rṣabha.
rathān, aśvān, narān, nāgān, āyudh'|ābharaṇāni ca,
vasanāny atha varmāṇi
vadhyamānān, hatān api
bhūmiṃ, khaṃ, dyāṃ, diśaś c' âiva
prāyaḥ paśyāma lohitam.
lohitasya tu gandhena, sparśena ca, rasena ca,
rūpeṇa c' âtiraktena, śabdena ca visarpatā,
viṣādaḥ su|mahān āsīt prāyaḥ sainyasya, Bhārata.
tat tu viprahataṃ sainyaṃ Bhīmasena|mukhās tadā
49.90 bhūyaḥ samādravan vīrāḥ Sātyaki|pramukhā tadā.
teṣām āpatatāṃ vegam a|viṣahyaṃ nirīkṣya ca,
putrāṇāṃ te mahā|sainyam āsīd, rājan, parāṅ|mukham.
tat prakīrṇa|rath'|âśv'|êbhaṃ, nara|vāji|samākulam,
vidhvasta|varma|kavacaṃ, praviddh'|āyudha|kārmukam
vyadravat tāvakaṃ sainyaṃ loḍyamānaṃ samantataḥ,
siṃh'|ârditam iv' âraṇye yathā gaja|kulaṃ, tathā.

battling with fists and fighting hand to hand, this battle destroyed bodies, sins and life!

As this battle unfolded, destroying elephants, horses and men, a river of blood flowing with the bodies of men, horses and elephants carried away the many fallen bodies of elephants, horses and men. In that mob of men, horses and elephants, that flowing river of the bodies of men, horses and elephants was horrifying, its utterly horrendous water the blood of men and horses, elephants and their riders, and its mud their flesh and blood. Those eager for victory moved along its near and distant bank; but others, after sinking 49.85
and bobbing up again and emerging by its shallows, their limbs smeared with blood and their clothes, weapons and armor reddened, wallowed in it, swallowed it and died in it, bull of Bharatas. We could only stare as chariots, horses, men, elephants, weapons and ornaments, clothes, armor, those being killed and those killed already too, the earth, the atmosphere, the sky and the directions became almost completely blood-red. With the smell, touch and taste of blood, with its intense red color and its gliding sound, a heavy despair infected almost all the troops, Bhárata.

Then heroes led by Bhima·sena, and still more led by 49.90
Sátyaki, charged at that defeated army. And when they saw that unbearable flood of men rushing towards them, your sons' massive army turned away, king, its chariots, horses and elephants dispersing and its men and horses in disarray. Their armor and mail falling to pieces and their weapons and bows hurled aside, your troops fled in all directions while being harried, as if stalked by a lion like a herd of elephants in the forest.

SAMJAYA uvāca:

50.1 TĀN ABHIDRAVATO dṛṣṭvā Pāṇḍavāṃs tāvakaṃ balam,
Duryodhano, mahā|rāja, vārayām āsa sarvaśaḥ.
yodhāṃś ca, sva|balaṃ c' âiva samantād, Bharata'|rṣabha,
krośatas tava putrasya na sma, rājan, nyavartata.
tataḥ pakṣaḥ, prapakṣaḥ ca, Śakuniś c' âpi Saubalaḥ,
tadā sa|śastrāḥ Kuravo Bhīmam abhyadravan raṇe.
Karṇo 'pi dṛṣṭvā dravato Dhārtarāṣṭrān sa|rājakān
Madra|rājaṃ uvāc' êdaṃ, «yāhi Bhīma|rathaṃ prati!»
50.5 evam uktaś ca Karṇena, Śalyo Madr'|âdhipas tadā
haṃsa|varṇān hayān agryān praiṣīd, yatra Vṛkodaraḥ.
te preritā, mahā|rāja, Śalyen' āhava|śobhinā
Bhīmasena|rathaṃ prāpya samasajjanta vājinaḥ.
dṛṣṭvā Karṇaṃ samāyāntaṃ Bhīmaḥ krodha|samanvitaḥ
matiṃ cakre vināśāya Karṇasya, Bharata'|rṣabha.
so 'bravīt Sātyakiṃ vīraṃ, Dhṛṣṭadyumnaṃ ca Pārṣatam:
«yūyaṃ rakṣata rājānaṃ dharm'|ātmānaṃ Yudhiṣṭhiram!
saṃśayān mahato muktaṃ kathaṅ cit prekṣato mama.
agrato me kṛto rājā chinna|sarva|paricchadaḥ
50.10 Duryodhanasya prīty|arthaṃ Rādheyena dur|ātmanā.
antam adya gamiṣyāmi tasya duḥkhasya, Pārṣata.
hant" âsmy adya raṇe Karṇaṃ, sa vā māṃ nihaniṣyati,
saṃgrāmeṇa su|ghoreṇa. satyam etad bravīmi te!
rājānam adya bhavatāṃ nyāsa|bhūtaṃ dadāni vai.
tasya saṃrakṣaṇe sarve yatadhvaṃ vigata|jvarāḥ!»

SÁNJAYA said:

SEEING THE PÁNDAVAS overrunning your army, great 50.1
king, Duryódhana demanded it hold its ground as one. But despite your son's bellowing, king, he could not completely stop those warriors and his army, bull of Bharatas. Then Súbala's son Shákuni, the flank and outer flank—those well-armed Kurus—attacked Bhima in the battle. Karna, too, seeing the Dhartaráshtra troops fleeing with their kings, said this to the Madra king, "Charge Bhima's chariot!"

Once Karna had said this to him, the Madra lord Shal- 50.5
ya then drove his superb horses the color of geese to where Wolf-belly was. Driven by Shalya who was brilliant in battle, great king, those horses joined in the attack after reaching Bhima·sena's chariot.

When he saw Karna approach, Bhima was completely overcome with rage and set his mind on destroying Karna, bull of Bharatas. He said to the hero Sátyaki and to Príshata's grandson Dhrishta·dyumna:

"You must protect King Yudhi·shthira, the soul of law!
Somehow he escaped from great peril as I looked on. In front 50.10
of me, Radha's appalling son completely shredded the king's attire for Duryódhana's gratification. I will bring about the end of this misery, grandson of Príshata. By fierce combat, today I'll kill Karna in battle or he will kill me. I speak the truth to you! I must now hand over the king to you as a pledge. Free from other concerns, all of you must make every effort for his protection!"

evam uktvā mahā|bāhuḥ prāyād Ādhirathiṃ prati,
siṃha|nādena mahatā sarvāḥ saṃnādayan diśaḥ.
dṛṣṭvā tvaritam āyāntaṃ Bhīmaṃ yuddh'|âbhinandinam,
sūta|putram ath' ôvāca Madrāṇām īśvaro vibhuḥ.

ŚALYA uvāca:

50.15 «paśya, Karṇa, mahā|bāhuṃ
saṃkruddhaṃ Pāṇḍu|nandanam!
dīrgha|kāl'|ârjitaṃ krodhaṃ
moktu|kāmaṃ tvayi dhruvam!
īdṛśaṃ n' âsya rūpaṃ me dṛṣṭa|pūrvaṃ kadā cana,
Abhimanyau hate, Karṇa, rākṣase vā Ghaṭotkace.
trailokyasya samastasya śaktaḥ kruddho nivāraṇe,
bibharti sadṛśaṃ rūpaṃ yug'|ânt'|âgni|sama|prabham!»

SAṂJAYA uvāca:

iti bruvati Rādheyaṃ Madrāṇām īśvare, nṛpa,
abhyavartata vai Karṇaṃ krodha|dīpto Vṛkodaraḥ.
ath' āgataṃ tu saṃprekṣya Bhīmaṃ yuddh'|âbhinandinam,
abravīd vacanaṃ Śalyaṃ Rādheyaḥ prahasann iva:
50.20 «yad uktaṃ vacanaṃ me 'dya tvayā, Madra|jan'|ēśvara,
Bhīmasenaṃ prati, vibho, tat satyaṃ, n' âtra saṃśayaḥ!
eṣa śūraś ca, vīraś ca, krodhanaś ca Vṛkodaraḥ,
nirapekṣaḥ śarīre ca, prāṇataś ca bal'|âdhikaḥ.
a|jñāta|vāsaṃ vasatā Virāṭa|nagare tadā,
Draupadyāḥ priya|kāmena, kevalaṃ bāhu|saṃśrayāt,
gūḍha|bhāvaṃ samāśritya, Kīcakaḥ sa|gaṇo hataḥ.
so 'dya saṃgrāma|śirasi saṃnaddhaḥ krodha|mūrcchitaḥ,

Once he'd said this, the mighty-armed man advanced on Ádhiratha's son, filling all directions with a colossal lion's roar.

Seeing Bhima quickly approaching eager for a fight, the powerful lord of the Madras then spoke to the charioteer's son.

SHALYA said:

"Karna, look at that furious mighty-armed son of Pan- 50.15
du! Surely the anger he's long since gathered he wants to dump on you! I've never seen him look like this before, Karna, even when Abhimányu or the demon Ghatótkacha was killed. Enraged and able to resist the entire triple world, he bears an appearance that is equal in brilliance to a fire at the end of an epoch!"

SÁNJAYA said:

While the lord of the Madras was saying this to Radha's son, king, Wolf-belly drew near Karna burning with rage. Then, seeing that Bhima had approached eager for a fight, Radha's son sneered and spoke this speech to Shalya:

"Those words you spoke to me just now regarding Bhima· 50.20
sena are true, powerful lord of the Madra people. There's no doubt about it! Wolf-belly is passionate, a champion and a hero. He's indifferent to his body and, because of his vitality, is superior in strength. In wanting to show his love for Dráupadi while living unrecognised in Viráta's city, he assumed a disguise and, relying only on his arms, killed Kíchaka along with his tribe.* Armed and seething with rage at the head of the battle, he would even do combat today with Death for raising his staff against a slave! My deepest

kiṃ|kar'|ôdyata|daṇḍena Mṛtyun" âpi vrajed raṇam!
cira|kāl'|âbhilaṣito mam' âyaṃ tu mano|rathaḥ,
50.25 Arjunaṃ samare hanyāṃ, māṃ vā hanyād Dhanaṃjayaḥ.
sa me kadā cid ady' âiva bhaved Bhīma|samāgamāt!
nihate Bhīmasene vā, yadi vā virathī|kṛte,
abhiyāsyati māṃ Pārthas; tan me sādhu bhaviṣyati!
atra yan manyase prāptaṃ, tac chīghraṃ saṃpradhāraya!»
etac chrutvā tu vacanaṃ Rādheyasy' âmit'|âujasaḥ,
uvāca vacanaṃ Śalyaḥ sūta|putraṃ tathā|gatam:
«abhiyāhi, mahā|bāho, Bhīmasenaṃ mahā|balam!
nirasya Bhīmasenaṃ tu tataḥ prāpsyasi Phalgunam.
yas te kāmo 'bhilaṣitaś cirāt prabhṛti hṛd|gataḥ,
50.30 sa vai saṃpatsyate, Karṇa! satyam etad bravīmi te!»
evam ukte tataḥ Karṇaḥ Śalyaṃ punar abhāṣata:
«hant" âham Arjunaṃ saṃkhye,
māṃ vā hanyād Dhanaṃjayaḥ.
yuddhe manaḥ samādhāya
yāhi yatra Vṛkodaraḥ!»

SAMJAYA uvāca:

tataḥ prāyād rathen' āśu Śalyas tatra, viśāṃ pate,
yatra Bhīmo mah"|êṣv|āso vyadrāvayata vāhinīm.
tatas tūrya|ninādaś ca bherīṇāṃ ca mahā|svanaḥ
udatiṣṭhac ca, rāj'|êndra, Karṇa|Bhīma|samāgame.
Bhīmaseno 'tha saṃkruddhas tasya sainyaṃ dur|āsadam
nārācair vimalais tīkṣṇair diśaḥ prādrāvayad balī.
50.35 sa saṃnipātas tumulo ghora|rūpo, viśāṃ pate,
āsīd raudro, mahā|rāja, Karṇa|Pāṇḍavayor mṛdhe!

desire, a hope I've held for a long time, is that I shall kill Ár- 50.25
juna in battle or Dhanan·jaya shall kill me. Some time today this shall come to be for me as a result of Bhima attacking us! If Bhima·sena is killed or stripped of his chariot, Pritha's son will attack me; that'll be good for me! Quickly consider whatever you think shall make this happen!"

Once he'd heard that speech of Radha's son whose vigor has no limit, Shalya spoke this speech to the charioteer's son who was in such a state: "Man of mighty-arms, attack
mighty Bhima·sena! Once you've driven Bhima·sena away, 50.30
then you'll meet Phálguna. Your desire, that wish you've long since had in your heart, will come to pass, Karna! I speak the truth to you!"

Addressed in this way, Karna again said to Shalya: "I'll kill Árjuna in battle or Dhanan·jaya shall kill me. Focus your mind on battle and go to where Wolf-belly is!"

SÁNJAYA said:

Immediately after that, lord of the people, Shalya set out with the chariot to that place where Bhima the mighty archer had scattered the army. Lord of kings, the sound of musical instruments and the huge boom of kettle-drums then came forth in that encounter between Karna and Bhima. With sharp and gleaming iron arrows, powerful and furious Bhima·sena then drove away Karna's unparalleled
troops to all directions. Great king, lord of the people, the 50.35
collision between Karna and the Pándava in that battle was chaotic, horrific and violent!

tato muhūrtād, rāj'|êndra, Pāṇḍavaḥ Karṇam ādravat.
tam āpatantaṃ saṃprekṣya, Karṇo Vaikartano vṛṣaḥ
ājaghāna su|saṃkruddho nārācena stan'|ântare,
punaś c' âinam a|mey'|ātmā śara|varṣair avākirat.
sa viddhaḥ sūta|putreṇa, cchādayām āsa pattribhiḥ,
vivyādha niśitaiḥ Karṇaṃ navabhir nata|parvabhiḥ.
tasya Karṇo dhanur madhye dvidhā ciccheda pattribhiḥ,
ath' âinaṃ chinna|dhanvānaṃ pratyavidhyat stan'|ântare
50.40 nārācena su|tīkṣṇena sarv'|āvaraṇa|bhedinā.
so 'nyat kārmukam ādāya, sūta|putraṃ Vṛkodaraḥ,
rājan, marmasu marma|jño vivyādha niśitaiḥ śaraiḥ.
nanāda balavan nādaṃ, kampayann iva rodasī!
taṃ Karṇaḥ pañca|viṃśatyā nārācena samārpayat,
mad'|ôtkaṭaṃ vane dṛptam ulkābhir iva kuñjaram.
tataḥ sāyaka|bhinn'|âṅgaḥ Pāṇḍavaḥ krodha|mūrcchitaḥ,
saṃrambh'|âmarṣa|tāmr'|âkṣaḥ sūta|putra|vadh'|ēpsayā,
sa kārmuke mahā|vegaṃ bhāra|sādhanam uttamam
girīṇām api bhettāraṃ sāyakaṃ samayojayat.
50.45 vikṛṣya balavac cāpam ā karṇād atimārutiḥ
taṃ mumoca mah"|êṣv|āsaḥ kruddhaḥ Karṇa|jighāṃsayā.

In an instant, lord of kings, the Pándava charged Karna. Seeing him rush at him, the bull Karna Vaikártana, whose soul had no measure, furiously struck him in the middle of the chest with an iron arrow and, what's more, covered him with showers of arrows.

Wounded by the son of the charioteer, Bhima covered Karna with winged arrows and wounded him with nine sharp smooth-jointed arrows. Karna split his bow in two 50.40
down the middle with winged arrows and then, with an extremely sharp iron arrow able to penetrate all armor, wounded that warrior whose bow had been split in the center of his chest.

Grabbing another bow, king, Wolf-belly, who knows where a man's vulnerable, wounded the charioteer's son in his vulnerable areas with sharp arrows, and then the powerful man roared a roar that almost made heaven and earth tremble!

Karna struck him with twenty-five iron arrows as if striking a proud and ruttish elephant in the forest with burning torches. Then the Pándava, his limbs punctured by arrows and seething with rage, his eyes red with anger and passion out of his desire to kill the charioteer's son, fixed an excellent, exceedingly fast and very effective arrow to his bow that could even split mountains. Drawing his powerful bow 50.45
as far back as his ear, the son of the powerful Wind,* that mighty archer, released it in rage, yearning to kill Karna.

sa visṛṣṭo balavatā bāṇo vajr'|âśani|svanaḥ
adārayad raṇe Karṇaṃ, vajra|vega iv' âcalam.
sa Bhīmasen' âbhihato, sūta|putraḥ, Kur'|ûdvaha,
niṣasāda rath'|ôpasthe visaṃjñaḥ pṛtanā|patiḥ.
tato Madr'|âdhipo dṛṣṭvā visaṃjñaṃ sūta|nandanam
apovāha rathen' ājau Karṇam āhava|śobhinam.
tataḥ parājite Karṇe, Dhārtarāṣṭrīṃ mahā|camūm
vyadrāvayad Bhīmaseno, yath" Êndro dānavān purā.

DHṚTARĀṢṬRA uvāca:

51.1 SU|DUṢ|KARAM idaṃ karma kṛtaṃ Bhīmena, Saṃjaya,
yena Karṇo mahā|bāhū rath'|ôpasthe nipātitaḥ.
«Karṇo hy eko raṇe hantā Pāṇḍavān Sṛñjayaiḥ saha!»
iti Duryodhanaḥ, sūta, prābravīn māṃ muhur muhuḥ.
parājitaṃ tu Rādheyaṃ dṛṣṭvā Bhīmena saṃyuge,
tataḥ paraṃ kim akarot putro Duryodhano mama?

SAṂJAYA uvāca:

vi|mukhaṃ prekṣya Rādheyaṃ sūta|putraṃ mah"|āhave,
putras tava, mahā|rāja, s'|ôdaryān samabhāṣata:
51.5 «śīghraṃ gacchata! bhadraṃ vo! Rādheyaṃ parirakṣata!
Bhīmasena|bhay'|âgādhe majjantaṃ vyasan'|ârṇave!»
te tu rājñā samādiṣṭā, Bhīmasenaṃ jighāṃsavaḥ
abhyavartanta saṃkruddhāḥ, pataṃ|gāḥ pāvakaṃ yathā.
Śrutarvā, Durdharaḥ, Krātho, Vivitsur, Vikaṭaḥ, Samaḥ,

Its sound like Indra's thunderbolt, the arrow released by that powerful bow tore Karna apart in the battle, like the force of a thunderbolt tearing apart a mountain. Struck by Bhima·sena, descendent of Kuru, the commander of the army, that son of the charioteer, slid down senseless onto the floor of his chariot. Seeing the charioteer's son lose consciousness in that battle, the lord of the Madras carried away Karna on the chariot though he was brilliant in combat.

After he had defeated Karna, Bhima·sena drove away the huge army of the Dhartaráshtras, just as Indra had driven away the *dánava*s long ago.

DHRITA·RASHTRA said:

BHIMA PERFORMED a tremendously difficult deed, Sán- 51.1
jaya, in dropping mighty-armed Karna onto the floor of his chariot. Herald, Duryódhana said to me time and time again, "For Karna is the one who will kill the Pándavas and Sríñjayas in battle!" But once he saw Bhima defeat Radha's son in combat, what did my son Duryódhana do next?

SÁNJAYA said:

Seeing Radha's son, the son of the charioteer, lose face in that immense battle, great king, your son addressed his
brothers: "Quickly go! Good luck! Save Radha's son! He's 51.5
sinking in an ocean of misfortune, its depths the danger of Bhima·sena!"

As commanded by their king, they approached Bhima·sena—furious and eager to kill him—like moths to fire. Shrutárvan, Dúrdhara, Kratha, Vivítsu, Víkata, Sama, Nishángin, Kávachin, Pashin, Nanda and Upanándaka, Dushpra-

Niṣaṅgī, Kavacī, Pāśī, tathā Nand'|Ôpanandakau,
Duṣpradharṣaḥ, Subāhuś ca, Vātavega|Suvarcasau,
Dhanurgrāho, Durmadaś ca, Jalasaṃdhaḥ, Śalaḥ, Sahaḥ,
ete rathaiḥ parivṛtā vīryavanto mahā|balāḥ,
Bhīmasenaṃ samāsādya, samantāt paryavārayan,
51.10 te vyamuñcañ śara|vrātān nānā|liṅgān samantataḥ.
sa tair abhyardyamānas tu Bhīmaseno mahā|balaḥ,
teṣām āpatatāṃ kṣipraṃ sutānāṃ te, jan'|âdhipa,
rathaiḥ pañca|daśaiḥ sārdhaṃ pañcāśad ahanad rathān.
Vivitsos tu tataḥ kruddho bhallen' âpāharac chiraḥ
Bhīmaseno, mahā|rāja. tat papāta hataṃ bhuvi
sa|kuṇḍala|śiras|trāṇaṃ pūrṇa|candr'|ôpamaṃ tadā.
taṃ dṛṣṭvā nihataṃ śūraṃ bhrātaraḥ sarvataḥ, prabho,
abhyadravanta samare Bhīmaṃ bhīma|parākramam.
tato 'parābhyāṃ bhallābhyāṃ putrayos te mah"|āhave
51.15 jahāra samare prāṇān Bhīmo bhīma|parākramaḥ.
tau dharām anvapadyetāṃ, vāta|rugṇāv iva drumau,
Vikaṭaś ca Sahaś c' ôbhau deva|putr'|ôpamau, nṛpa.
tatas tu tvarito Bhīmaḥ Krāthaṃ ninye Yama|kṣayam;
nārācena su|tīkṣṇena sa hato nyapatad bhuvi.
hāhā|kāras tatas tīvraḥ saṃbabhūva, jan'|ēśvara,
vadhyamāneṣu vīreṣu tava putreṣu dhanviṣu.
teṣāṃ su|lulite sainye, punar Bhīmo mahā|balaḥ
Nand'|Ôpanandau samare praiṣayad Yama|sādanam.
tatas te prādravan bhītāḥ putrās te vihvalī|kṛtāḥ
51.20 Bhīmasenaṃ raṇe dṛṣṭvā Kāl'|ântaka|Yam'|ôpamam.

dhársha, Subáhu, Vata·vega and Suvárchas, Dhanur·graha,
Dúrmada, Jala·sandha, Shala and Saha, once these vigorous
and powerful men surrounded by chariots had reached Bhi-
ma·sena, they surrounded him on every side and released 51.10
swarms of different arrows from every direction.

But, though tormented by them, mighty Bhima·sena killed fifty warriors together with fifteen chariots from among your sons as they quickly charged him, lord of the people. In a fury Bhima·sena then removed Vivítsu's head with a broad arrow, great king. Struck off, it fell to the ground with its earrings and helmet, looking like a full moon.

Seeing that hero killed, lord, from every direction in
that clash his brothers attacked Bhima whose courage was 51.15
formidable. Next in that great battle, with two other broad
arrows Bhima—his courage formidable—took the lives of
two of your sons in combat. Both Víkata and Saha, king,
who were like sons of the gods, fell to the earth side by side
like a pair of trees levelled by the wind.

Then Bhima quickly sent Kratha to Yama's house. Killed
by an extremely sharp iron arrow, he collapsed to the ground.
Horrendous sounds of astonishment arose from there, lord
of the people, as your sons—those bow wielding heroes—
were killed. And while their troops were thoroughly unset-
tled, mighty Bhima further dispatched Nanda and Upaná-
nda to Yama's place in the battle. Then your sons fled in
bewilderment, terrified after seeing Bhima·sena in the battle 51.20
resembling Yama as all-destroying Time.

putrāṃs te nihatān dṛṣṭvā, sūta|putraḥ su|durmanāḥ
haṃsa|varṇān hayān bhūyaḥ prāhiṇod, yatra Pāṇḍavaḥ.
te preṣitā, mahā|rāja, Madra|rājena vājinaḥ
Bhīmasena|rathaṃ prāpya samasajjanta vegitāḥ.
sa saṃnipātas tumulo ghora|rūpo, viśāṃ pate,
āsīd raudro, mahā|rāja, Karṇa|Pāṇḍavayor mṛdhe!
dṛṣṭvā mama, mahā|rāja, tau sametau mahā|rathau,
āsīd buddhiḥ, «kathaṃ yuddham etad adya bhaviṣyati?»
tato Bhīmo raṇa|ślāghī chādayām āsa patribhiḥ
51.25 Karṇaṃ raṇe, mahā|rāja, putrāṇāṃ tava paśyatām.
tataḥ Karṇo bhṛśaṃ kruddho Bhīmaṃ navabhir āyasaiḥ
vivyādha param'|âstra|jño bhallaiḥ saṃnata|parvabhiḥ.
āhataḥ sa mahā|bāhur Bhīmo bhīma|parākramaḥ
ākarṇa|pūrṇair viśikhaiḥ Karṇaṃ vivyādha saptabhiḥ.
tataḥ Karṇo, mahā|rāja, āśī|viṣa iva śvasan,
śara|varṣeṇa mahatā chādayām āsa Pāṇḍavam.
Bhīmo 'pi taṃ śara|vrātaiś chādayitvā mahā|ratham,
paśyatāṃ Kauraveyāṇāṃ, vinanarda mahā|balaḥ.
tataḥ Karṇo bhṛśaṃ kruddho dṛḍham ādāya kārmukam
51.30 Bhīmaṃ vivyādha daśabhiḥ kaṅka|patraiḥ śilā|śitaiḥ,
kārmukaṃ c' âsya ciccheda bhallena niśitena ca.
tato Bhīmo mahā|bāhur hema|paṭṭa|vibhūṣitam
parighaṃ ghoram ādāya, Mṛtyu|daṇḍam iv' âparam,
Karṇasya nidhan'|ākāṅkṣī cikṣep' âtibalo nadan.
tam āpatantaṃ parighaṃ vajr'|âśani|sama|svanam
ciccheda bahudhā Karṇaḥ śarair āśīviṣ'|ôpamaiḥ.
tataḥ kārmukam ādāya Bhīmo dṛḍhataraṃ tadā,

After seeing your sons killed, the charioteer's son felt especially glum and once more directed his goose-colored horses to where the Pándava was. Driven by the king of the Madras, great king, those swift horses reached Bhima's chariot and engaged him in combat. The collision of Karna and the Pándava in that battle was chaotic, violent and horrifying, lord of the people! When I saw those two come together, great king, I wondered how the battle would unfold!

Then Bhima, who was celebrated for combat, enveloped Karna in the battle with arrows while your sons looked on. 51.25
Soon after Karna, who knew the finest missiles, pummeled Bhima in a furious rage with nine smooth-jointed broad arrows made of iron.

Mighty-armed Bhima was wounded but his courage was formidable and he wounded Karna with seven arrows that he'd drawn back to his ear. Then, great king, hissing like a venomous snake, Karna enveloped the Pándava with a massive shower of arrows. Bhima also enveloped that mighty warrior with swarms of arrows as the Káuravas watched on, and then that powerful man roared. Karna was then in a furious rage and, grabbing his stiff bow, wounded Bhima 51.30
with ten heron-feathered arrows sharpened on stone and splintered his bow with a sharp broad arrow.

Then, grabbing his unrivalled and horrendous iron bludgeon that was decorated with golden binding and like the staff of Death, mighty-armed Bhima roared and, his strength immense, hurled it with the intention of killing Karna. As it flew towards him with a sound equal to Indra's thunderbolt, Karna splintered that bludgeon into many pieces with arrows resembling venomous snakes. Grabbing an even stiffer

chādayām āsa viśikhaiḥ Karṇaṃ para|bal'|ârdanam.
tato yuddham abhūd ghoraṃ Karṇa|Pāṇḍavayor mṛdhe,
51.35 har'|îndrayor iva, muhuḥ paraspara|vadh'|âiṣiṇoḥ.
tataḥ Karṇo, mahā|rāja, Bhīmasenaṃ tribhiḥ śaraiḥ
ā|karṇa|mūlaṃ vivyādha, dṛḍham āyamya kārmukam.
so 'tividdho mah"|êṣv|āsaḥ Karṇena balināṃ varaḥ
ghoram ādatta viśikhaṃ Karṇa|kāy'|âvadāraṇam.
tasya bhittvā tanu|trāṇaṃ, bhittvā kāyaṃ ca, sāyakaḥ
prāviśad dharaṇīṃ, rājan, valmīkam iva pannagaḥ.
sa ten' âtiprahāreṇa vyathito vihvalann iva
saṃcacāla rathe Karṇaḥ, kṣiti|kampe yath" âcalaḥ.
tataḥ Karṇo, mahā|rāja, roṣ'|âmarṣa|samanvitaḥ
51.40 Pāṇḍavaṃ pañca|viṃśatyā nārācānāṃ samārpayat.
ājaghne bahubhir bāṇair, dhvajam ek'|êṣuṇ" âhanat,
sārathiṃ c' âsya bhallena preṣayām āsa mṛtyave.
chittvā ca kārmukaṃ tūrṇaṃ Pāṇḍavasy' āśu patriṇā,
tato muhūrtād, rāj'|êndra, n' âtikṛcchrādd hasann iva,
vi|rathaṃ bhīma|karmāṇaṃ Bhīmaṃ Karṇaś cakāra ha.
vi|ratho, Bharata|śreṣṭha, prahasann Anil'|ôpamaḥ
gadāṃ gṛhya mahā|bāhur apatat syandan'|ôttamāt.
avaplutya ca vegena, tava sainyaṃ, viśāṃ pate,
vyadhamad gadayā Bhīmaḥ, śaran|meghān iv' ânilaḥ.
51.45 nāgān sapta|śatān, rājann, īṣā|dantān, prahāriṇaḥ
vyadhamat sahasā Bhīmaḥ kruddha|rūpaḥ paraṃ|tapaḥ.

bow, with arrows Bhima then enveloped Karna, a tormenter of enemy armies.

The fight between Karna and the Pándava in that battle was horrific; endeavoring to kill each other at every chance, 51.35
they were like a pair of lordly lions.*

Karna stretched his stiff bow to his ear, great king, and wounded Bhima·sena with three arrows. Deeply wounded by Karna, that mighty archer—the best of powerful men—grabbed a horrific arrow capable of tearing Karna's body apart. Piercing through his armor and piercing through his body, that arrow penetrated the ground, king, like a snake an ant-hill.

Reeling and nearly staggering with that powerful blow, Karna wavered on his chariot like a mountain shuddering in an earthquake. Filled with rage and indignation, great
king, Karna then struck the Pándava with twenty-five iron 51.40
arrows. He attacked with many more arrows, ruined his banner with a single shaft and sent his charioteer to his death with a broad arrow. Suddenly and quickly splitting the Pándava's bow with an arrow and then sneering momentarily for the little effort he needed, lord of kings, Karna stripped Bhima, whose deeds were formidable, of his chariot.

Stripped of his chariot, best of Bharatas, that mighty-armed man who resembled the Wind-god grabbed his club with a laugh and leapt from his superb chariot. After nimbly jumping down, lord of the people, Bhima scattered your troops with his club, like the wind autumnal clouds.
A furious scorcher of enemies, king, Bhima vigorously scat- 51.45
tered seven hundred long-tusked elephants as they fought. Knowing where they were vulnerable, that mighty man

danta|veṣṭeṣu, netreṣu, kumbheṣu ca, kaṭeṣu ca,
marmasv api ca marma|jño tān nāgān avadhīd balī.
tatas te prādravan bhītāḥ. pratīpaṃ prahitāḥ punaḥ
mahā|mātrais, tam āvavrur, meghā iva divākaram.
tān sa sapta|śatān nāgān s'|âroh'|āyudha|ketanān
bhūmi|ṣṭho gadayā jaghne, vajreṇ' Êndra iv' âcalān.
tataḥ Subala|putrasya nāgān atibalān punaḥ
pothayām āsa Kaunteyo dvi|pañcāśad ariṃ|damaḥ.
51.50 tathā ratha|śataṃ sāgraṃ, pattīṃś ca śataśo 'parān
nyahanat Pāṇḍavo yuddhe tāpayaṃs tava vāhinīm.

pratāpyamānaṃ sūryeṇa Bhīmena ca mah"|ātmanā,
tava sainyaṃ saṃcukoca, carm' âgnāv āhitaṃ yathā.
te Bhīma|bhaya|saṃtrastās tāvakā, Bharata'|rṣabha,
vihāya samare Bhīmaṃ dudruvur vai diśo daśa.

rathāḥ pañca|śatāś c' ânye hrādinaś carma|varmiṇaḥ
Bhīmam abhyadravan, ghnantaḥ śara|pūgaiḥ samantataḥ.
tān sa pañca|śatān vīrān sa|patākā|dhvaj'|āyudhān
pothayām āsa gadayā Bhīmo, Viṣṇur iv' âsurān.
51.55 tataḥ Śakuni|nirdiṣṭāḥ sādinaḥ śūra|saṃmatāḥ
tri|sāhasr" âbhyayur* Bhīmaṃ śakty|ṛṣṭi|prāsa|pāṇayaḥ.
pratyudgamya javen' āśu s'|âśv'|ārohāṃs tad" âri|hā
vividhān vicaran mārgān, gadayā samapothayat.
teṣām āsīn mahāñ chabdas tāḍitānāṃ ca sarvaśaḥ,
aśmabhir vidhyamānānāṃ nagānām iva, Bhārata.
evaṃ Subala|putrasya tri|sāhasrān hay'|ôttamān

struck those elephants in their vulnerable parts as well: in their gums, eyes, temples and just above their hips. They fled from him in terror. But, compelled to turn back by their mahouts, they surrounded him like clouds the sun. Standing on the ground with his club he destroyed those seven hundred elephants and their riders, weapons and banners, like Indra destroying mountains with his thunderbolt. Next Kunti's enemy-conquering son further crushed fifty-two immensely powerful elephants belonging to Súbala's
son. Scorching your army in battle, the Pándava completely 51.50
destroyed a hundred chariots and hundreds of unrivalled foot-soldiers as well.

Scorched by mighty Bhima and the sun, your army shrivelled like skin placed on a fire. Trembling with dread for Bhima, bull of Bharatas, your men left Bhima behind in the battle and fled to the ten directions.

Another five hundred noisy warriors sporting shields and clad in armor assaulted Bhima, striking him from all sides with clusters of arrows. With his club Bhima crushed those five hundred heroes, with their flags, banners and weapons, like Vishnu crushing demons.

Then Shákuni dispatched three thousand horsemen cel- 51.55
ebrated by heroes, who charged Bhima wielding spears, javelins and darts. Taking various lines as he immediately charged out at pace to meet those horsemen on their horses, that killer of enemies crushed them with his club. A thunderous sound came from them as they were comprehensively beaten, Bhárata, like trees pelted with rocks. Once he'd so

hatv", ânyaṃ ratham āsthāya kruddho Rādheyam abhyayāt.

Karṇo 'pi samare, rājan, Dharma|putram ariṃ|damam
sa śaraiś chādayām āsa, sārathiṃ c' âpy apātayat.
51.60 tataḥ sa pradrutaḥ saṃkhye; rathaṃ dṛṣṭvā, mahā|rathaḥ
anvadhāvat kiran bāṇaiḥ kaṅka|patrair ajihma|gaiḥ.
rājānam abhidhāvantaṃ śarair āvṛtya rodasī
kruddhaḥ pracchādayām āsa śara|jālena Mārutiḥ.
saṃnivṛttas tatas tūrṇaṃ Rādheyaḥ śatru|karśanaḥ
Bhīmaṃ pracchādayām āsa samantān niśitaiḥ śaraiḥ.

Bhīmasena|ratha|vyagraṃ Karṇaṃ, Bhārata, Sātyakiḥ
abhyardayad a|mey'|ātmā pārṣṇi|grahaṇa|kāraṇāt.
abhyavartata Karṇas tam ardito 'pi śarair bhṛśam.
tāv anyonyaṃ samāsādya, vṛṣabhau sarva|dhanvinām,
51.65 visṛjantau śarān dīptān vibhrājetāṃ manasvinau.
tābhyāṃ viyati, rāj'|êndra, vitataṃ, bhīma|darśanam,
krauñca|pṛṣṭh'|âruṇaṃ, raudraṃ bāṇa|jālaṃ vyadṛśyata.
n' âiva sūrya|prabhā, rājan, na diśaḥ, pradiśaḥ tathā
prājñāsiṣma vayaṃ, te vā, śarair muktaiḥ sahasraśaḥ.
madhy'|âhne tapato, rājan, bhāskarasya mahā|prabhāḥ
hṛtāḥ sarvāḥ śar'|âughais
    taiḥ Karṇa|Pāṇḍavayos tadā.

killed the three thousand superb horses belonging to Súbala's son and then mounted another chariot, he attacked Radha's son in a fury.

Meanwhile, king, in that battle Karna had enveloped Dharma's enemy-destroying son with arrows and felled his charioteer. Yudhi·shthira then fled in the battle. Keeping 51.60
an eye on his chariot, the mighty warrior pursued him as he covered him with heron-feathered and straight-flying arrows. Enraged, the son of the Wind enveloped Karna with a spread of arrows as he chased the king and covered heaven and earth with arrows. Immediately turning from Yudhi·shthira, Radha's son, withering his enemies, completely enveloped Bhima with sharp arrows.

While Karna was distracted by Bhima's chariot, Sátyaki, whose soul has no measure, harried Karna by attacking him from behind, Bhárata. Though he was badly wounded by arrows, Karna continued to attack Bhima. As they attacked one another, those brilliant bulls were radiant among all the 51.65
archers as they let fly with blazing arrows. Lord of kings, the hideous expanse of arrows that spread in the sky from those two looked as ominous as blood on the backs of curlews. Neither we nor they could make out the sun's brightness, nor the regions or directions, king, owing to those arrows released by the thousand. All the vast splendor of the burning midday sun had been taken away, king, by the arrows streaming from Karna and the Pándava.

Saubalaṃ, Kṛtavarmāṇaṃ,
Drauṇim, Ādhirathiṃ, Kṛpam
saṃsaktān Pāṇḍavair dṛṣṭvā, nivṛttāḥ Kuravaḥ punaḥ.
teṣām āpatatāṃ śabdas tīvra āsīd, viśāṃ pate,
51.70 udvṛttānāṃ yathā vṛṣṭyā sāgarāṇāṃ bhay'|āvahaḥ.
te sene bhṛśa|saṃsakte dṛṣṭv" ânyonyaṃ mah"|āhave
harṣeṇa mahatā yukte parigṛhya parasparam.
tataḥ pravavṛte yuddhaṃ madhyaṃ prāpte divākare.
tādṛśaṃ na kadā cidd hi dṛṣṭa|pūrvaṃ, na ca śrutam.
bal'|âughas tu samāsādya bal'|âughaṃ sahasā raṇe
upāsarpata vegena, vāry|ogha iva sāgaram.
āsīn ninādaḥ su|mahān bāṇ'|âughānāṃ parasparam
garjatāṃ, sāgar'|âughāṇāṃ yathā syān nisvano mahān.
te tu sene samāsādya vegavatyau parasparam
51.75 ekī|bhāvam anuprāpte, nadyāv iva samāgame.
tataḥ pravavṛte yuddhaṃ ghora|rūpaṃ, viśāṃ pate,
Kurūṇāṃ Pāṇḍavānāṃ ca, lipsatāṃ su|mahad yaśaḥ.
śūrāṇāṃ garjatāṃ tatra hy a|viccheda|kṛtā giraḥ
śrūyante vividhā, rājan, nāmāny uddiśya, Bhārata.
yasya yadd hi raṇe vyaṅgaṃ, pitṛto, mātṛto 'pi vā,
karmataḥ, śīlato v" âpi, sa tac chrāvayate yudhi.
tān dṛṣṭvā samare śūrāṃs tarjamānān parasparam,
abhavan me matī, rājan, «n' âiṣām ast' îti jīvitam!»
teṣāṃ dṛṣṭvā tu kruddhānāṃ vapūṃṣy a|mita|tejasām,
51.80 abhavan me bhayaṃ tīvraṃ, «katham etad bhaviṣyati?»

Noticing that Súbala's son, Krita·varman, Drona's son, Ádhiratha's son and Kripa had closed in on the Pándavas, the Kurus turned back again. A horrific sound came from them as they approached, lord of the people, like the terrifying 51.70
sound of the oceans swollen with rain. Violently engaging together after seeing one another, both armies were filled with great exhilaration as they enveloped one another in that great battle.

Then, as the sun reached midday, a battle unfolded the likes of which had never been seen or heard before. In that battle, the wave of one army immediately advanced on the wave of the other army, and rapildy streamed towards it like a torrent of water streaming towards the ocean. A massive hum arose of waves of arrows thundering towards one another, like the huge roar of waves in the ocean. And once they'd collided together, the two charging armies became 51.75
one like two rivers at a confluence.

Lord of people, a horrifying battle then unfolded between the Kurus and Pándavas, all wishing to earn immense fame. The voices of those roaring heroes could be heard there with barely a pause, king, as they yelled one another's names, Bhárata. For in that battle whatever flaw that anyone had—on account of his father or even his mother or his deeds or even his character—was proclaimed in combat.

As I saw those heroes ridiculing one another in battle, king, I wondered if their lives were no more! As I saw the beautiful bodies of those furious men whose power had no limit, I was terribly alarmed about how it would turn out! 51.80

tatas te Pāṇḍavā, rājan, Kauravāś ca mahā|rathāḥ
tatakṣuḥ sāyakais tīkṣṇair, nighnanto hi parasparam!

SAMJAYA uvāca:

52.1 KṢATRIYĀS TE, mahā|rāja, paraspara|vadh'|âiṣiṇaḥ
anyonyaṃ samare jaghnuḥ kṛta|vairāḥ parasparam.
rath'|âughāś ca, hay'|âughāś ca, nar'|âughāś ca samantataḥ,
gaj'|âughāś ca, mahā|rāja, saṃsaktāḥ sma parasparam.
gadānāṃ, parighāṇāṃ ca, kaṇapānāṃ ca kṣipyatām,
prāsānāṃ, bhindipālānāṃ, bhuśuṇḍīnāṃ ca sarvaśaḥ
saṃpātaṃ c' ânvapaśyāma saṃgrāme bhṛśa|dāruṇe.
śalabhā iva saṃpetuḥ śara|vṛṣṭyaḥ samantataḥ.
52.5 nāgān nāgāḥ samāsādya vyadhamanta parasparam,
hayā hayāṃś ca samare, rathino rathinas tathā,
pattayaḥ patti|saṃghāṃś ca, haya|saṃghāṃś ca pattayaḥ,
pattayo ratha|mātaṅgān, rathā hasty|aśvam eva ca.
nāgāś ca samare try|aṅgaṃ mamṛduḥ śīghra|gā, nṛpa.
vadhyatāṃ tatra śūrāṇāṃ, krośatāṃ ca parasparam,
ghoram āyodhanaṃ jajñe, paśūnāṃ vaiśasaṃ yathā.
rudhireṇa samāstīrṇā bhāti, Bhārata, medinī,
śakra|gopa|gaṇ'|ākīrṇā prāvṛṣ' îva yathā dharā;
yathā vā vāsasī śukle mahā|rañjana|rañjite
52.10 bibhṛyād yuvatiḥ śyāmā, tadvad āsīd vasuṃ|dharā;
māṃsa|śoṇita|citr" êva śātakaumbha|may" îva ca.
bhinnānāṃ c' ôttam'|âṅgānāṃ, bāhūnāṃ c' ōrubhiḥ saha,
kuṇḍalānāṃ pravṛddhānāṃ, bhūṣaṇānāṃ ca, Bhārata,
niṣkāṇām, atha śūrāṇāṃ śarīrāṇāṃ ca dhanvinām,
carmaṇāṃ sa|patākānāṃ saṃghās tatr' âpatan bhuvi.

Then, king, those mighty Pándava and Káurava warriors attacked and cut one another apart with sharp arrows.

SÁNJAYA said:

GREAT KING, feuding with one another and endeavor- 52.1
ing to destroy each other, the kshatriyas killed one another in the battle. Waves of chariots, waves of horses, waves of men and waves of elephants, great king, closed in on one another from all sides. In that vicious battle we saw *bhu-shúndis*, short javelins, darts, *kánapas*, iron bludgeons and clubs fly everywhere as they were hurled. Torrents of arrows flew from all sides like moths. Elephants attacking ele- 52.5
phants destroyed one another, as did horses attacking horses in the battle, chariot-warriors attacking chariot-warriors, foot-soldiers attacking squads of foot-soldiers, foot-soldiers attacking squads of horses, foot-soldiers attacking chariots and elephants, and chariots attacking elephants and horses. Elephants stampeding in the battle, king, crushed the armies' other three divisions.

As those heroes there bawled at one another and were killed, the battlefield became as horrific as an animal slaughterhouse. Coated with blood, the ground was luminous,
Bhárata, like the soil covered with red beetles in the wet sea- 52.10
son; or, the earth was like a darkly beautiful young woman who might wear, above and below, white garments died with safflower. Brilliantly colored with flesh and blood, it was as though the earth was made of gold. Heaps of severed heads, arms and shins, of large earrings and ornaments, of gold collars, of the bodies of heroes and archers, and of shields with their insignia, Bhárata, had fallen onto the ground.

gajā gajān samāsādya viṣāṇair ārdayan, nṛpa;
viṣāṇ'|âbhihatās tatra bhrājante dvi|radā tathā
rudhireṇ' âvasikt'|âṅgā, gairika|prasravā iva
yathā bhrājanti syandantaḥ parvatā dhātu|maṇḍitāḥ.
52.15 tomarān sādhibhir muktān, pratīpān āsthitān bahūn
hastair vicerus te nāgā, babhañjuś c' âpare tathā.
nārācaiś chinna|varmāṇo bhrājante sma gaj'|ôttamāḥ,
him'|āgame yathā, rājan, vyabhrā iva mahī|dharāḥ.
śaraiḥ kanaka|puṅkhais tu citrā rejur gaj'|ôttamāḥ,
ulkābhiḥ saṃpradīpt'|âgrāḥ parvatā iva, Bhārata.
ke cid abhyāhatā nāgair nāgā naga|nibhā bhuvi
nipetuḥ samare tasmin, pakṣavanta iv' âdrayaḥ.
apare prādravan nāgāḥ śaly'|ârtā vraṇa|pīḍitāḥ
pratimānaiś ca kumbhaiś ca petur urvyāṃ mah"|āhave.
52.20 vineduḥ siṃhavac c' ânye, nadanto bhairavān ravān
babhramur bahavo, rājaṃś, cukruśuś c' âpare gajāḥ.

hayāś ca nihatā bāṇair hema|bhāṇḍa|vibhūṣitāḥ
niṣeduś c' âiva, mamluś ca, babhramuś ca diśo daśa.
apare kṛṣyamāṇāś ca viceṣṭanto mahī|tale,
bhāvān bahu|vidhāṃś cakrus tāḍitāḥ śara|tomaraiḥ.

narās tu nihatā bhūmau kūjantas tatra, māriṣa;
dṛṣṭvā ca bāndhavān anye, pitṝn anye, pitā|mahān,
dhāvamānān parāṃś c' ânye dṛṣṭv" ânye tatra, Bhārata,
gotra|nāmāni khyātāni śaśaṃsur itar'|êtaram.

Elephants attacking elephants, king, struck out with their tusks; and those elephants struck by tusks still glitter there with their limbs bathed in blood, just as mountains festooned with minerals glitter, oozing as if with streams of red ochre. With their trunks some elephants evaded, and 52.15
others shattered, the lances slung by horsemen and the many held fast that remained opposed to them, too. Their armor smashed by iron arrows, the finest elephants were radiant, king, like mountains free of clouds at the onset of winter. Speckled with arrows with nocks of gold, Bhárata, the finest elephants glittered like mountains as their summits burn with grass-fires. Some mountain-like elephants wounded by other elephants collapsed on the ground in that battle, like mountains with wings.* Tormented by darts and traumatized by wounds, other fleeing elephants collapsed in that great battle, with their temples and areas between their tusks on the ground. Some elephants roared like lions, 52.20
many roamed unsteadily trumpeting terrible roars, king, and others cried out in pain.

And struck by arrows, horses adorned with gold harnesses sank down and faltered and unsteadily roamed the ten directions. Others became feeble and thrashed on the ground. Wounded by lances and arrows, they assumed many different states.

And wounded men groaned on the ground there, dear friend. Others seeing their relatives and others their fathers and others their grandfathers and others seeing their enemies advancing there, Bhárata, yelled to one another their common names and the names of their families.

52.25 teṣāṃ chinnā, mahā|rāja, bhujāḥ kanaka|bhūṣaṇāḥ
udveṣṭante, viceṣṭante, patante c', ôtpatanti ca.
nipatanti tath" âiv' ânye, sphuranti ca sahasraśaḥ,
vegāṃś c' ânye raṇe cakruḥ pañc'|āsyā iva pannagāḥ.
te bhujā bhogi|bhog'|ābhāś, candan'|âktā, viśāṃ pate,
lohit'|ārdrā bhṛśaṃ rejus, tapanīya|dhvajā iva.
vartamāne tathā ghore saṃkule sarvato|diśam,
a|vijñātāḥ sma yudhyante vinighnantaḥ parasparam.
bhaumena rajasā kīrṇe śastra|saṃpāta|saṃkule,
n' âiva sve, na pare, rājan, vyajñāyanta tamo|vṛtāḥ.
52.30 tathā tad abhavad yuddhaṃ ghora|rūpaṃ bhayānakam.
lohit'|ôdā mahā|nadyaḥ prasasrus tatra c' â|sakṛt.
śīrṣa|pāṣāṇa|saṃchannāḥ, keśa|śaivala|śādvalāḥ,
asthi|mīna|samākīrṇā, dhanuḥ|śara|gad"|ôḍupāḥ,
māṃsa|śoṇita|paṅkinyo, ghora|rūpāḥ, su|dāruṇāḥ
nadīḥ pravartayām āsur, śoṇit'|âugha|vivardhanīḥ.
bhīru|vitrāsa|kāriṇyaḥ, śūrāṇāṃ harṣa|vardhanāḥ,
tā nadyo ghora|rūpāś tu nayantyo Yama|sādanam,
avagāḍhān majjayantyaḥ, kṣatrasy' âjanayan bhayam.
kravy'|âdānāṃ, nara|vyāghra, nardatāṃ tatra tatra ha,
52.35 ghoram āyodhanaṃ jajñe preta|rāja|pur'|ôpamam.
utthitāny a|gaṇeyāni kabandhāni samantataḥ
nṛtyanti vai bhūta|gaṇāḥ su|tṛptā māṃsa|śoṇitaiḥ.
pītvā ca śoṇitaṃ tatra, vasāṃ pītvā ca, Bhārata,
medo|majjā|vasā|mattās tṛptā, māṃsasya c' âiva ha,
dhāvamānāḥ sma dṛśyante kāka|gṛdhra|bakās tathā.

Great king, their hacked off arms decorated with gold writhed about, thrashed around, fell down and rose up again. Similarly others fell down and twitched by the thousand, and others jerked violently in that battle like five-headed snakes. Smeared with sandal and dripping with blood, lord of the people, those arms that resembled coiled snakes glittered superbly like banners of refined gold. 52.25

As that horrific battle unfolded in every direction, they fought one another not knowing who they slaughtered. Covered in darkness in that maelstrom of flying weapons filled with dust kicked up from the earth, neither friends nor enemies could distinguish a thing.

Along these lines that horrific and terrifying battle took place. Mighty rivers with blood for water flowed there continually. Covered in skulls for stones and hair for grasses and algae, chock full of bones for fish, their driftwood bows, arrows and clubs, and their mud flesh and blood, those horrifying and terrible rivers poured onwards, swelling with rivulets of blood. Provoking terror among the timid and escalating the excitement of the heroes, those horrific rivers that led to Yama's house and drowned those who plunged in them, instilled dread among the kshatriyas. 52.30

With carrion-eaters shrieking here and there, tiger of a man, that hideous battlefield became like the city of the king of the dead. Well satisfied with flesh and blood, herds of beasts danced about the incalculable headless torsos that had surfaced everywhere. After drinking blood and consuming fat there, Bhárata, crows, vultures and cranes could be seen scuttling about, intoxicated by lymph, marrow and fat and sated with flesh. 52.35

śūrās tu samare, rājan, bhayaṃ tyaktvā su|dus|tyajam
yodha|vrata|samākhyātāś cakruḥ karmāṇy a|bhītavat.
śara|śakti|samākīrṇe kravy'|âda|gaṇa|saṃkule
vyacaranta raṇe śūrāḥ khyāpayantaḥ sva|pauruṣam.
52.40 anyonyaṃ śrāvayanti sma nāma|gotrāṇi, Bhārata;
pitṛ|nāmāni ca raṇe, gotra|nāmāni vā, vibho,
śrāvayantaś ca bahavas tatra yodhā, viśāṃ pate,
anyonyam avamṛdnantaḥ śakti|tomara|paṭṭiśaiḥ.
vartamāne tadā yuddhe ghora|rūpe su|dāruṇe,
vyaṣīdat Kauravī senā, bhinnā naur iva sāgare.

SAṂJAYA uvāca:

53.1 VARTAMĀNE TADĀ yuddhe kṣatriyāṇāṃ nimajjane,
Gāṇḍīvasya mahā|ghoṣaḥ śrūyate yudhi, māriṣa,
saṃśaptakānāṃ kadanam akarod yatra Pāṇḍavaḥ,
Kosalānāṃ tathā, rājan, Nārāyaṇa|balasya ca.
saṃśaptakās tu samare śara|vṛṣṭīḥ samantataḥ
apātayan Pārtha|mūrdhni jaya|gṛddhāḥ pramanyavaḥ.
tā vṛṣṭīḥ sahasā, rājaṃs, tarasā dhārayan prabhuḥ
vyagāhata raṇe Pārtho vinighnan rathināṃ varān.
53.5 vigāhya tad rath'|ânīkaṃ kaṅka|patraiḥ śilā|śitaiḥ,
āsasāda tataḥ Pārthaḥ Suśarmāṇaṃ var'|āyudham.
sa tasya śara|varṣāṇi vavarṣa rathināṃ varaḥ,
tathā saṃśaptakāś c' âiva Pārthaṃ bāṇaiḥ samārpayan.
Suśarmā tu tataḥ Pārthaṃ viddhvā navabhir āśu|gaiḥ,
Janārdanaṃ tribhir bāṇair ahanad dakṣiṇe bhuje,

But in that battle, king, heroes celebrated for their warrior vows let go of their deep-seated fears and performed deeds as if they were fearless. Into that battle that teemed with arrows and spears and swarmed with carrion-eaters, those heroes went forth and put their manliness on display.
In that battle, Bhárata, they declared to one another their 52.40
personal and family names. And, lord, in making known the names of their fathers and the names of their families, the many warriors there, lord of the people, crushed one another with spears, lances and tridents. Then, as that dreadful and horribly brutal battle unfolded, the Káurava army sank in despair, like a shattered boat in the ocean.

SÁNJAYA said:

THEN AS THAT battle unfolded that had immersed the 53.1
kshatriyas, the massive sound of the Gandíva bow was heard amid the fracas, dear friend, where the Pándava butchered the oath-bound warriors, the Kósalas and the army of the Naráyanas. But, incensed and longing for victory, from all sides the oath-bound warriors let fly showers of arrows at the head of Pritha's son. Quickly and abruptly repelling those showers, king, Pritha's powerful son plunged into those excellent chariot warriors, striking them down in combat.

Once he'd plunged into that chariot division with heron- 53.5
feathered arrows sharpened on stone, Pritha's son then attacked Sushárman who wielded superb weapons. That excellent chariot warrior rained down showers of arrows on Árjuna at the same time as the oath-bound warriors struck Pritha's son with arrows. But after Sushárman wounded Pritha's son with nine arrows, he struck Janárdana in the

tato ’pareṇa bhallena ketuṃ vivyādha, māriṣa.
sa vānara|varo, rājan, Viśvakarma|kṛto mahān
nanāda su|mahā|nādaṃ, bhīṣayāṇo jagarja ca.
kapes tu ninadaṃ śrutvā saṃtrastā tava vāhinī,
53.10 bhayaṃ vipulam ādhāya niśceṣṭā samapadyata.
tataḥ sā śuśubhe senā niśceṣṭ” âvasthitā, nṛpa,
nānā|puṣpa|samākīrṇaṃ yathā Caitrarathaṃ vanam.
pratilabhya tataḥ saṃjñāṃ, yodhās te, Kuru|sattama,
Arjunaṃ siṣicur bāṇaiḥ, parvataṃ jaladā iva,
parivavrus tadā sarve Pāṇḍavasya mahā|ratham.
nigṛhya taṃ pracukruśur vadhyamānāḥ śitaiḥ śaraiḥ.
te hayān, ratha|cakre ca, rath’|ēṣāṃ c’ âpi, māriṣa,
nigrahītum upākrāman krodh’|āviṣṭāḥ samantataḥ.
nigṛhya taṃ rathaṃ tasya yodhās te tu sahasraśaḥ
53.15 nigṛhya balavat sarve siṃha|nādam ath’ ânadan.
apare jagṛhuś c’ âiva Keśavasya mahā|bhujau,
Pārtham anye, mahā|rāja, ratha|sthaṃ jagṛhur mudā.
Keśavas tu tato bāhū vidhunvan raṇa|mūrdhani,
pātayām āsa tān sarvān, duṣṭa|hast” îva hasti|pān.
tataḥ kruddho raṇe Pārthaḥ saṃvṛtas tair mahā|rathaiḥ,
nigṛhītaṃ rathaṃ dṛṣṭvā, Keśavaṃ c’ âpy abhidrutam,
rath’|ārūḍhāṃs tu su|bahūn padātīṃś c’ âpy apātayat.
āsannāṃś ca tathā yodhāñ śarair āsanna|yodhibhiḥ
chādayām āsa samare. Keśavaṃ c’ êdam abravīt:

right arm with three arrows and then, with another broad arrow, pierced his monkey banner, dear friend. That excellent, massive monkey fashioned by Vishva·karman, king, roared a massive roar and growled chillingly.

Hearing the roar of the monkey and permeated with pro- 53.10
found terror, your traumatized army became motionless. As it stood motionless, king, that army looked brilliant, like the Cháitraratha forest carpeted with assorted flowers. Once they recovering their senses, finest of Kurus, your warriors showered Árjuna with arrows, like clouds showering a mountain, and then they all circled the mighty warrior of the Pándavas. Holding him back, they shrieked as they were struck by sharp arrows. Possessed by rage, from all sides they ventured to sieze his horses, his chariot's wheels and his chariot's pole, dear friend. Once those thousands
of warriors had siezed these and siezed his chariot, they 53.15
all powerfully roared a lion's roar. Others grabbed Késhava's mighty arms, and others joyfully grabbed Pritha's son standing in the chariot, great king.

But, flailing his arms at the head of the battle, Késhava then felled them all like a rogue elephant its drivers. Then, surrounded by those mighty warriors in the battle and watching in rage as his chariot was captured and Késhava was attacked, Pritha's son felled very many of those mounted on chariots as well as those on foot. At the same time, he enveloped the warriors close by in the battle with arrows designed for close combat. Then he said this to Késhava:

53.20 «paśya, Kṛṣṇa, mahā|bāho! saṃśaptaka|gaṇān bahūn,
kurvāṇān dāruṇaṃ karma, vadhyamānān sahasraśaḥ!
ratha|bandham imaṃ ghoraṃ pṛthivyāṃ n' âsti kaś cana
yaḥ saheta pumāl̃ loke mad anyo, Yadu|puṃgava!»
ity evam uktvā Bībhatsur Devadattam ath' âdhamat,
Pāñcajanyaṃ ca Kṛṣṇo 'pi, pūrayann iva rodasī.
taṃ tu śaṅkha|svanaṃ śrutvā, saṃśaptaka|varūthinī
saṃcacāla, mahā|rāja, vitrastā c' âdravad bhṛśam.
pāda|bandhaṃ tataś cakre Pāṇḍavaḥ para|vīra|hā,
Nāgam astraṃ, mahā|rāja, saṃprakīrya muhur muhuḥ.
53.25 te baddhāḥ pāda|bandhena Pāṇḍavena mah"|ātmanā,
niśceṣṭāś c' âbhavan, rājann, aśma|sāra|mayā iva.
niśceṣṭāṃs tu tato yodhān avadhīt Pāṇḍu|nandanaḥ,
yath" Êndraḥ samare daityāṃs Tārakasya vadhe purā.
te vadhyamānāḥ samare, mumucus taṃ rath'|ôttamam,
āyudhāni ca sarvāṇi visraṣṭum upacakramuḥ.
te baddhāḥ pāda|bandhena na śekuś ceṣṭituṃ, nṛpa.
tatas tān avadhīt Pārthaḥ śaraiḥ saṃnata|parvabhiḥ.
sarva|yodhā hi samare bhujagair veṣṭit" âbhavan,*
yān uddiśya raṇe Pārthaḥ pāda|bandhaṃ cakāra ha!
53.30 tataḥ Suśarmā, rāj'|êndra, gṛhītāṃ vīkṣya vāhinīm,
Sauparṇam astraṃ tvaritaḥ prāduś cakre mahā|rathaḥ.
tataḥ suparṇāḥ saṃpetur bhakṣayanto bhujaṃgamān;
te vai vidudruvur nāgā dṛṣṭvā tān kha|carān, nṛpa.
babhau balaṃ tad vimuktaṃ pāda|bandhād, viśāṃ pate,
megha|vṛndād yathā mukto bhāskaras tāpayan prajāḥ!

"Look, mighty-armed Krishna! At the umpteen hordes of 53.20
oath-bound warriors doing dreadful deeds as they're killed by the thousand! Other than me, chief of Yadus, there's no man on earth who could prevail against this violent band of warriors!"

Once he'd said this, Bibhátsu then blew his conch Deva·datta, and Krishna also his conch Panchajánya, almost filling heaven and earth with their sound. When they heard the sound of their conches, the army of oath-bound warriors wavered and suddenly fled in terror, great king.

Then the Pándava, a destroyer of enemy-heroes, repeatedly summoned his Snake weapon and made a leg shackle.
Bound by the mighty Pándava with the leg shackle, the war- 53.25
riors were motionless, king, as if they were made of iron. Pandu's son then slaughtered those motionless warriors, just as Indra slaughtered the *daityas* during the killing of Táraka in a battle long ago. As they were slaughtered in the battle, they released that superb chariot and began to lose grip on all their weapons. Bound by the leg shackle, they could not move, king, and Pritha's son then slaughtered them with smooth-jointed arrows. In that struggle, all the warriors at whom Pritha's son aimed the leg shackle that he'd made in the battle were bound by snakes!

Then the mighty warrior Sushárman, lord of kings, who'd 53.30
seen the army captured, hastily revealed his Bird-of-prey weapon. Birds of prey then swooped down, devouring those snakes; and when they saw those birds, king, the snakes scattered. Freed from the leg shackle, lord of people, that army was as glorious as the sun as it scorches people when freed from a bank of clouds! Once freed, those warriors

vipramuktās tu te yodhāḥ Phālgunasya rathaṃ prati
sasṛjur bāṇa|saṃghāṃś ca, śastra|saṃghāṃś ca, māriṣa,
vividhāni ca śastrāṇi pratyavidhyanta sarvaśaḥ.

tāṃ mah"|âstra|mayīṃ vṛṣṭiṃ saṃchidya śara|vṛṣṭibhiḥ
53.35 nyavadhīc ca tato yodhān Vāsaviḥ para|vīra|hā.
Suśarmā tu tato, rājan, bāṇen' ānata|parvaṇā
Arjunaṃ hṛdaye viddhvā, vivyādh' ânyais tribhiḥ śaraiḥ.
sa gāḍha|viddho vyathito rath'|ôpastha upāviśat.
tata uccukruśuḥ sarve, «hataḥ Pārtha! iti» sma ha.
tataḥ śaṅkha|ninādāś ca, bherī|śabdāś ca puṣkalāḥ,
nānā|vāditra|ninadāḥ, siṃha|nādāś ca jajñire.

pratilabhya tataḥ saṃjñāṃ, śvet'|âśvaḥ Kṛṣṇa|sārathiḥ
Aindram astram a|mey'|ātmā prāduś cakre tvar"|ânvitaḥ.
tato bāṇa|sahasrāṇi samutpannāni, māriṣa.
53.40 sarva|dikṣu vyadṛśyanta nighnanti tava vāhinīm;
hayān rathāṃś ca samare śastraiḥ śata|sahasraśaḥ.

vadhyamāne tataḥ sainye, bhayaṃ su|mahad āviśat
saṃśaptaka|gaṇānāṃ ca, Gopālānāṃ ca, Bhārata,
na hi tatra pumān kaś cid yo 'rjunaṃ pratyayudhyata.
paśyatāṃ tatra vīrāṇām ahanyata mahad balam.
hanyamānam apaśyaṃś ca niśceṣṭaṃ sma parākrame.

discharged clusters of arrows and clusters of weapons at Phálguna's chariot, dear friend, and all at once they hurled their various weapons.

But with showers of arrows Indra's son,* a killer of enemy-heroes, cut down that shower comprising massive missiles
and then killed those warriors. However Susharman, king, 53.35
wounded Árjuna in the heart with a smooth-jointed shaft and then wounded him with three other arrows. Deeply wounded and reeling, he plonked down on the floor of his chariot. They all then cried out, "Pritha's son's been killed!" Then the reverberation of conches, the booming sounds of kettle-drums, the sounds of various musical instruments and lions' roars came forth from there.

Recovering his senses, he whose horses are white, whose charioteer is Krishna, whose soul has no measure and who is endowed with speed, revealed his Aindra weapon and thousands of arrows sprang forward from it, dear friend.
They appeared in all directions and destroyed your army; 53.40
with these weapons, he killed horses and warriors in the hundreds and thousands in that battle.

As the troops were massacred, profound fear took possession of the hordes of oath-bound warriors and the Go·palas, Bhárata, for there was no man there who was a match for Árjuna in battle. While the heroes looked on there, that mighty army was destroyed. They watched as it was destroyed, powerless to counterattack.

ayutaṃ tatra yodhānāṃ hatvā, Pāṇḍu|suto raṇe
vyabhrājata, mahā|rāja, vidhūmo 'gnir iva jvalan.
catur|daśa sahasrāṇi yāni śiṣṭāni, Bhārata,
53.45 rathānām ayutaṃ c' âiva, tri|sāhasrāś ca dantinaḥ.
tataḥ saṃśaptakā bhūyaḥ parivavrur Dhanaṃjayam,
martavyam, iti niścitya, jayaṃ v" âpy, a|nivartanam.
tatra yuddhaṃ mahac c' āsīt tāvakānāṃ, viśāṃ pate,
śūreṇa balinā sārdhaṃ Pāṇḍavena kirīṭinā!

SAṂJAYA uvāca:

54.1 KṚTAVARMĀ, KṚPO, Drauṇiḥ, sūta|putraś ca, māriṣa,
Ulūkaḥ, Saubalaś c' âiva, rājā ca saha s'|ôdaraiḥ,
sīdamānāṃ camūṃ dṛṣṭvā Pāṇḍu|putra|bhay'|ârditām,
samujjahruḥ sma vegena, bhinnāṃ nāvam iv' ârṇave.
tato yuddham atīv' āsīn muhūrtam iva, Bhārata,
bhīrūṇāṃ trāsa|jananaṃ, śūrāṇāṃ harṣa|vardhanam.
Kṛpeṇa śara|varṣāṇi pratimuktāni saṃyuge
Sṛñjayāṃś chādayām āsuḥ, śalabhānāṃ vrajā iva.
54.5 Śikhaṇḍī ca tataḥ kruddho Gautamaṃ tvarito yayau;
vavarṣa śara|varṣāṇi samantād dvija|puṃgavam.
Kṛpas tu śara|varṣaṃ tad vinihatya mah"|âstra|vit
Śikhaṇḍinaṃ raṇe kruddho vivyādha daśabhiḥ śaraiḥ.
tataḥ Śikhaṇḍī kupitaḥ śaraiḥ saptabhir āhave
Kṛpaṃ vivyādha kupitaṃ kaṅka|patrair a|jihma|gaiḥ.
tataḥ Kṛpaḥ śarais tīkṣṇaiḥ so 'tividdho mahā|rathaḥ
vy|aśva|sūta|rathaṃ cakre Śikhaṇḍinam atho dvijaḥ.

Killing ten thousand warriors in that battle, Pandu's son was radiant, great king, like a fire blazing without smoke. Then he massacred fourteen thousand survivors from those warriors, Bhárata, then ten thousand more and three thou- 53.45
sand elephants.

The oath-bound warriors then surrounded Dhanan·jaya once again, resolving on either death or victory and to never retreat.

Then there was a massive battle, lord of people, of your troops with that powerful hero, the crown wearing Pándava!

SÁNJAYA said:

DEAR FRIEND, Krita·varman, Kripa, Drona's son, the 54.1
charioteer's son, Ulúka, Súbala's son, and the king along with his brothers, seeing their army perishing and traumatized with fear of Pandu's son, quickly rescued it as they would a leaky boat in the ocean. Almost in an instant, a prodigious battle then began that incited fear among the timid but provoked excitement among the heroes.

Torrents of arrows released by Kripa in the battle enveloped the Srínjayas like swarms of locusts. And Shikhá- 54.5
ndin then quickly attacked Gáutama in a fury and rained showers of arrows all over that brahmin-chief. But Kripa, who knew the great missiles, destroyed that shower of arrows and furiously wounded Shikhándin in battle with ten arrows.

Then in fury Shikhándin wounded fuious Kripa in battle with seven heron-feathered and straight-flying arrows. Severely wounded by those sharp arrows, the mighty warrior brahmin Kripa then stripped Shikhándin of his horses,

hat'|âśvāt tu tato yānād avaplutya mahā|rathaḥ,
khaḍgaṃ, carma tathā gṛhya sa|tvaraṃ brāhmaṇaṃ yayau.
54.10 tam āpatantaṃ sahasā śaraiḥ saṃnata|parvabhiḥ
chādayām āsa samare. tad adbhutam iv'| âbhavat!
tatr' âdbhutam apaśyāma, śilānāṃ plavanaṃ yathā!
niśceṣṭas tad raṇe, rājañ, Chikhaṇḍī samatiṣṭhata.

Kṛpeṇa cchāditaṃ dṛṣṭvā, nṛp'|ôttama, Śikhaṇḍinam,
pratyudyayau Kṛpaṃ tūrṇaṃ Dhṛṣṭadyumno mahā|rathaḥ.
Dhṛṣṭadyumnaṃ tato yāntaṃ Śāradvata|rathaṃ prati
pratijagrāha vegena Kṛtavarmā mahā|rathaḥ.
Yudhiṣṭhiram ath' āyāntaṃ Śāradvata|rathaṃ prati
sa|putraṃ saha|sainyaṃ ca Droṇa|putro nyavārayat.
54.15 Nakulaṃ Sahadevaṃ ca tvaramāṇau mahā|rathau
pratijagrāha te putraḥ, śara|varṣeṇa vārayan.
Bhīmasenaṃ, Karūṣāṃś ca, Kekayān saha|Sṛñjayān
Karṇo Vaikartano yuddhe vārayām āsa, Bhārata.

Śikhaṇḍinas tato bāṇān Kṛpaḥ Śāradvato yudhi
prāhiṇot tvarayā yukto, didhakṣur iva, māriṣa.
tāñ śarān preṣitāṃs tena samantāt svarṇa|bhūṣitān
ciccheda khaḍgam āvidhya, bhrāmayaṃś ca punaḥ punaḥ.
śata|candraṃ ca tac carma Gautamas tasya, Bhārata,
vyadhamat sāyakais tūrṇaṃ. tata uccukruśur janāḥ!
54.20 sa vicarmā, mahā|rāja, khaḍga|pāṇir upādravat
Kṛpasya vaśam āpanno, mṛtyor āsyam iv' āturaḥ.

charioteer and chariot. Its horses killed, the mighty warrior jumped down from his chariot and, grabbing his sword and shield, charged the quick brahmin.

As Shikhándin suddenly rushed towards him, Kripa en- 54.10
veloped him in the battle with smooth-jointed arrows. It was like a miracle! It was a miracle what we saw there, as if rocks were flying! Powerless, Shikhándin remained still in that battle, king.

Seeing Shikhándin enveloped by Kripa, excellent man, the mighty warrior Dhrishta·dyumna quickly counter-attacked Kripa. But the mighty warrior Krita·varman hastily opposed Dhrishta·dyumna as he rushed at the chariot of Sharádvat's son. Then Drona's son repelled Yudhi·shthira as he charged with his sons and army alongside at the chariot
of Sharádvat's son. Your son opposed Nákula and Saha·deva 54.15
as those mighty warriors surged forward, enveloping them in a shower of arrows. In that battle, Bhárata, Karna Vai-kártana drove back Bhima·sena, the Karúshas, Kékayas and Srínjayas.

Next Sharádvat's son Kripa, filled with haste, dispatched arrows at Shikhándin in the battle as if he wanted to burn him, dear friend. Swinging and twirling his sword again and again, Shikhándin completely cut down those gold-embossed arrows that had been dispatched at him. With his arrows Gáutama suddenly destroyed his shield decorated with a hundred moons, Bhárata. The people then howled!
Without his shield and with sword in hand, great king, he 54.20
rushed at Kripa like a sick man rushing at the jaws of death; he'd fallen under Kripa's sway!

Śāradvata|śarair grastaṃ kliśyamānaṃ mahā|balaḥ
Citraketu|suto, rājan, Suketus tvarito yayau.
vikiran brāhmaṇaṃ yuddhe bahubhir niśitaiḥ śaraiḥ,
abhyāpatad a|mey'|ātmā Gautamasya rathaṃ prati.
dṛṣṭvā ca yuktaṃ taṃ yuddhe brāhmaṇaṃ carita|vratam,
apayātas tatas tūrṇaṃ Śikhaṇḍī, rāja|sattama.

Suketus tu tato, rājan, Gautamaṃ navabhiḥ śaraiḥ
viddhvā vivyādha saptatyā punaś c' âinaṃ tribhiḥ śaraiḥ.
54.25 ath' âsya sa|śaraṃ cāpaṃ punaś ciccheda, māriṣa,
sārathiṃ ca śareṇ' âsya bhṛśaṃ marmasv atāḍayat.

Gautamas tu tataḥ kruddho dhanur gṛhya navaṃ dṛḍham
Suketuṃ triṃśatā bāṇaiḥ sarva|marmasv atāḍayat.
sa vihvalita|sarv'|âṅgaḥ pracacāla rath'|ôttame,
bhūmi|kampe yathā vṛkṣaś cacāla kampito bhṛśam.
calatas tasya kāyāt tu śiro jvalita|kuṇḍalam
s'|ôṣṇīṣaṃ, sa|śiras|trāṇaṃ kṣurapreṇa tv apātayat.
tac chiraḥ prāpatad bhūmau śyen'|āhṛtam iv' āmiṣam;
tato 'sya kāyo vasudhāṃ paścāt prāpatad, acyuta.
54.30 tasmin hate, mahā|rāja, trastās tasya puro|gamāḥ
Gautamaṃ samare tyaktvā dudruvus te diśo daśa.

Dhṛṣṭadyumnaṃ tu samare saṃnivārya, mahā|rathaḥ
Kṛtavarm" âbravīdd hṛṣṭas, «tiṣṭha! tiṣṭh'! êti» Bhārata.
tad abhūt tumulaṃ yuddhaṃ Vṛṣṇi|Pārṣatayo raṇe,
āmiṣ'|ârthe yathā yuddhaṃ śyenayoḥ kruddhayor, nṛpa.

Chitra·ketu's powerful son Sukétu, king, hastily went to him as he was devoured and traumatized by the arrows of Sharádvat's son. Covering the brahmin in the battle with many sharp arrows, he whose soul had no measure charged Gáutama's chariot. Seeing that the vow-observant brahmin had been engaged in combat, best of kings, Shikhándin quickly retreated from there.

But then Sukétu wounded Gáutama with nine arrows, king, and then wounded him with seven and then once more with three arrows. Then he further splintered his bow 54.25
and its arrows as well, dear friend, and with an arrow he brutally wounded his charioteer where he was vulnerable.

But in a rage, Gáutama grabbed a new stiff bow and wounded Sukétu wherever he was exposed with thirty arrows. With all his limbs trembling, he floundered in his superb chariot just as a violently swaying tree flounders during an earthquake. As he floundered, Kripa knocked his head from his body with a razor-edged arrow, together with its turban, flashy earrings and helmet. His head fell to the ground like meat dropped by a bird of prey; then later, imperishable man, his body dropped to the earth. When 54.30
he had been killed, great king, his chiefs fled to the ten directions in terror, leaving Gáutama behind in the battle.

But forcing Dhrishta·dyumna back in the struggle, Bhárata, the mighty warrior Krita·varman excitedly yelled, "Stand! Stand your ground!" Then in that battle there was a tumultuous tussle between the Vrishni and Príshata's grandson, king, like a pair of furious birds of prey fighting over meat.

Dhṛṣṭadyumnas tu samare Hārdikyaṃ navabhiḥ śaraiḥ
ājaghān' ôrasi kruddhaḥ, pīḍayan Hṛdik'|ātmajam.
Kṛtavarmā tu samare Pārṣatena dṛḍh'|āhataḥ
Pārṣataṃ sa|rathaṃ s'|âśvaṃ chādayām āsa sāyakaiḥ.
54.35 sa|rathaś chādito, rājan, Dhṛṣṭadyumno na dṛśyate,
meghair iva paricchanno bhāskaro jala|dhāribhiḥ.
vidhūya taṃ bāṇa|gaṇaṃ śaraiḥ kanaka|bhūṣaṇaiḥ,
vyarocata raṇe, rājan, Dhṛṣṭadyumnaḥ kṛta|vraṇaḥ.
tatas tu Pārṣataḥ kruddhaḥ śastra|vṛṣṭiṃ su|dāruṇām
Kṛtavarmāṇam āsādya vyasṛjat pṛtanā|patiḥ.
tām āpatantīṃ sahasā śastra|vṛṣṭiṃ nirantarām
śarair aneka|sāhasrair Hārdikyo 'vārayad yudhi.
dṛṣṭvā tu vāritāṃ yuddhe śastra|vṛṣṭiṃ dur|āsadām,
Kṛtavarmāṇam āsādya vārayām āsa Pārṣataḥ.
54.40 sārathiṃ c' âsya tarasā prāhiṇod Yama|sādanam
bhallena śita|dhāreṇa; sa hataḥ prāpatad rathāt.
Dhṛṣṭadyumnas tu balavāñ jitvā śatruṃ mahā|balam
Kauravān samare tūrṇaṃ vārayām āsa sāyakaiḥ.
tatas te tāvakā yodhā Dhṛṣṭadyumnam upādravan
siṃha|nāda|ravaṃ kṛtvā. tato yuddham avartata!

In a rage, Dhrishta·dyumna struck Hrídika's son with nine arrows in the battle, wounding Hrídika's progeny in the chest. But Krita·varman, though badly wounded in the battle by Príshata's grandson, enveloped Príshata's grandson
along with his chariot and horses with arrows. Covered 54.35
along with his chariot, Dhrishta·dyumna could not be seen, king, like the sun obscured by water-bearing clouds. After scattering that cluster of arrows with arrows embossed with gold, king, Dhrishta·dyumna became visible, wounded in the battle.

Next, Príshata's grandson, the commander of the army, attacked Krita·varman in rage and let loose a dreadful shower of arrows. As that incessant stream of arrows flew quickly towards him, Hrídika's son repelled them in the battle with many thousands of arrows. Seeing that dangerous shower of arrows repelled in the battle, Príshata's grandson attacked
Krita·varman and pinned him down. He sent his charioteer 54.40
directly to Yama's house with a sharp-bladed broad arrow; dead, he plummeted from his chariot.

As soon as he defeated his mighty enemy, powerful Dhrishta·dyumna enveloped the Káuravas in the battle with his arrows. Then your warriors attacked Dhrishta·dyumna thundering lions' roars. The battle resumed!

NOTES

Bold *references are to the English text;* ***bold italic*** *references are to the Sanskrit text. An asterisk (*) in the body of the text marks the word or passage being annotated.*

1.1 **Drona's son**: Ashvattháman.

1.2 **Sharádvat's daughter**: Kripi, Drona's wife and Ashvattháman's mother.

1.5 **Charioteer's son**: Karna. The word translated here as charioteer is ***sūta***, a person reputedly born from the mixed union of a brahmin and kshatriya. A *sūta* also functions as a herald, bard or panegyrist for the warrior whose chariot he drives. Thus *sūta* has a more complex sense than any single translation can convey. Another significant *sūta* is Sánjaya, Dhrita·rashtra's charioteer, whose chief function in the *Karṇa/parvan* is to report the events of the war to his king. In most cases where it refers to Sánjaya, therefore, I translate *sūta* as "herald." **Suyódhana**: Duryódhana.

1.7 **Krishná**: Dráupadi. The accent on the final syllable distinguishes this name, with its long vowel feminine ending, from its masculine counterpart, Krishna.

1.16 **Vrisha**: Karna, literally "bull." **Phálguna** is Árjuna. **Dhartaráshtras** are the sons of Dhrita·rashtra.

1.17 **Naga·pura**: The city Hástina·pura.

1.18 **Son of the river**: Bhishma.

1.22 **Shántanu's son**: Bhishma.

2.1 **Gaválgana's son**: Sánjaya.

2.5 **I am Sánjaya:** Though it may seem odd that Sánjaya introduces himself to Dhrita·rashtra, who of course knows him well since Sánjaya is his *sūta*, this is explained by Dhrita·rashtra's blindness.

2.6 **Ganga's son**: Bhishma. **Késhava**: Krishna.

2.9 **Charioteer's son**: Sánjaya. See also note to 1.5 above.

2.11 **Vasus' offspring**: Bhishma. There are two accounts of Bhishma's divine origin, both of which concur on the point that he has been born as a result of the divine Vasus being cursed to be reborn on earth. In one he is produced from portions of each of the eight Vasus. In the other, he is the earthly incarnation of one Vasu, Dyaus. The account alluded to here is likely to be the former.

2.12 **The Pándava**: Árjuna.

2.13 **Bhárgava; Rama**: Rama Jamadágnya, sometimes known as Párashu·rama.

2.14 **Kunti**: Pritha. **Kunti's sons**: the Pándavas.

2.18 **Dhanan·jaya**: Árjuna. **Oath-bound warriors**: warriors bound by an oath to kill Árjuna.

3.12 **Fighting by ordinary means alone**: i.e. not using the divine weapons, or other means of non-human origin.

3.15 **Radha's son**: Karna.

4.3 **Bharatas**: The first syllable of the Sanskrit *Bharata* is stressed, but to distinguish it from the patronymic *Bhārata* it has been left unstressed in translation. The transcription of *Bhārata* is marked with stress, giving "Bhárata."

4.8 **Whose eyes were wisdom**: A common epithet for the blind Dhrita·rashtra.

4.15 **Vaikártana**: An epithet given to Karna when he cut away (*vikartana*) the armor with which he was born, an episode recounted in *Vana/parvan*, MBh CE III.294.38 (CSL III.310.25, Johnson 2005: 271, though a slightly different version from the Critical Edition). See also *Ādi/parvan*, MBh CE I.104.21. But since *vikartana* can also mean "the sun," Vaikártana accrues the additional meaning of "son of the Sun."

5.12 **Aksháuhini army**: A massive army reputedly consisting of 21,870 elephants, the same number of chariots, 65,610 horses and 109,350 foot-soldiers.

5.18 **Left-handed archer**: Árjuna.

5.26 **Pritha's son**: Árjuna.

5.42 **Fierce**: his name is Ugra·karman, lit. "of fierce deeds."

5.55 **Kartavírya**: Árjuna Kartavírya.

6.4 **Wearer of the crown**: Árjuna.

6.9 **Bibhátsu**: Árjuna.

6.10 **Son of Subhádra**: Abhimányu.

6.15 **Bharad·vaja's son**: Drona.

6.18 **Wolf-belly**: Bhima.

6.32 The hemistich *senābinduḥ kuruśreṣṭhaḥ kṛtvā kadanam āhave*, a subordinate clause without an obvious main clause, has been omitted from the text.

7.9 **Artáyani**: Shalya. For an explanation of this name see MBh CSL VIII.32.56. **Shalya's sister**: Madri.

7.10 **Ajáta·shatru**: Yudhi·shthira. **Shakra**: Indra.

8.10 **Ádhiratha's son**: Karna.

8.15 **Áchyuta**: Krishna.

8.17 **The bearers of the Gandíva and Sharnga bows**: Árjuna and Krishna.

8.24 **Uchchaih·shravas**: Indra's horse. **Váishravana**: Kubéra, the god of wealth.

9.1 **Yayáti**: a famous ancestor of the Bháratas.

9.5 **Pritha's sons**: the Pándavas. **The thunderbolt-wielder**: Indra.

9.26 **The war must end with me**: see *Bhīṣma/parvan* ('Bhishma') 116.46.

9.43 **Sacker of cities**: Indra.

9.45 **Jamadágnya**: Rama Jamadágnya.

9.50 *ye āhvayanta*: Irregular sandhi. For the general type (-e ā-), see Oberlies 2003: 16–17.

9.59 **My son**: Duryódhana. **The Pándavas' wife**: Dráupadi.

9.66 **Janárdana**: Krishna.

9.67 **Vásava**: Indra.

9.70 **Stupid fool**: Duryódhana.

9.71 **Vasudéva**: Krishna.

10.12 **Teacher's son**: Ashvattháman.

10.42 **Shata·kratu**: Indra, so named for having performed a hundred sacrifices.

10.49 **Go·vinda**: Krishna.

10.56 **Taraká**: Tara, the wife of the god Brihas·pati who was stolen by Soma, resulting in a war between the gods and demons (who allied with Soma). The accent on the last syllable serves to distinguish this name, with its feminine long vowel ending, from its masculine counterpart, Táraka, a demon who features in this volume as well.

11.4 *yogeti*: Double sandhi (-e- < /-as i-/); see OBERLIES 2003: 36.

11.9 **Shata·ghni**: A type of weapon, literally "hundred killers."

11.22 **King of Law**: Yudhi·shthira.

11.26 *Kínnara*: A half-human half-animal creature.

11.28 **The Pándava with the white horses**: Árjuna.

11.34 **Dhrita·rashtra's son**: Duryódhana.

12.35 **Ruler of the Kulútas**: Kshema·dhurti.

12.38 **Like a cloud stirred by the wind attacking a cloud driven by a mighty wind**: The simile is not merely metaphoric but metonymic as well; Bhima, as the son of Vayu, the wind god, embodies the wind.

13.15 **Shini's grandson**: Sátyaki (Yuyudhána).

13.16 **Shauri**: Sátyaki.

13.20 **The Sátvata**: Sátyaki.

13.30 **Jambha**: A demon-lord defeated by Indra.

14.2 **The Abhisára**: Chitra·sena.

14.17 **King of the dead**: Yama.

15.16 ***abhrajālena Aṅgāraka/Budhāv***: with hiatus.

15.27 **Siddhas**: Semi-divine beings possessing supernatural abilities. *Siddha* literally means "one who is perfected."

16.16 **Jaya**: Árjuna.

16.19 **Ishána**: Shiva.

16.22 **The two Krishnas**: Krishna and Árjuna.

16.24 ***'rjuno "tmānam***: Irregular sandhi (-o "- < /-as ā-/); see OBERLIES 2003: 24–25.

16.23 **Teacher's son**: Ashvattháman.

16.25 **Mádhava**: Krishna.

16.37 **The guru**: Drona.

16.38 **I'll destroy his plan**: *asmi* would seem to be used here in the sense of *aham*, a usage apparently common in Prakrits and found also in Puranic Sanskrit. See OBERLIES 1997: 11 n. 23.

17.6 **Death**: Yama.

17.19 **Dhánada**: Literally "giver of wealth," Kubéra, the god of wealth.

17.20 **Lord of the Dashárhas**: Krishna.

17.23 **Vrishni hero**: Krishna.

18.3 **The Mágadha**: Danda·dhara.

18.11 **Lord of Giri·vraja**: Danda·dhara.

18.16 **Indra's younger brother**: Krishna.

19.1 **Jishnu**: Árjuna.

19.11 **Charioteers controlling their outer horses**: The two outer horses of a four horse chariot.

19.34 **Bhushúndi**: A weapon of uncertain type, variously suggested as being a catapult, a flame-thrower, a kind of projectile or a club.

20.9 **Mountain-destroyer**: Indra.

20.19 **Try·ámbaka**: Shiva.

20.20 **Málaya·dhvaja**: The Pandya king.

20.29 **Pushan's younger brother**: Parjánya, the god of rain, often identified with Indra.

20.42 **Lord of the lord of mountains**: Málaya·dhvaja, the Pandya king.

20.47 **Tarkshya**: Gáruda.

20.51 **Lord of the immortals**: Indra.

21.2 **Shánkara**: Shiva.

21.7 **Hrishi·kesha**: Krishna.

21.25 **The twins**: Nákula and Sahadeva. **Yuyudhána**: Sátyaki.

22.12 **The Anga prince**: To be distinguished from Karna, the Anga king.

24.51 **For he had remembered Kunti's words and let him go**: See note to 49.52 below.

25.5 **Shákuni's son**: Ulúka.

25.30 **Time**: Yama (Death).

26.1 **Shárabha**: A fabulous animal.

26.2 **Gáutama**: Kripa. **Príshata's grandson**: Dhrishta·dyumna.

26.5 **Sharádvat's son**: Kripa.

26.8 **The teacher**: Kripa.

26.22 **Hrídika's son**: Krita·varman.

26.24 **Drúpada's son**: Shikhándin.

26.34 **Príshata's grandson**: Shikhándin.

26.35 **The Bhoja**: Krita·varman.

27.1 **The man with white horses**: Árjuna.

27.4 **King of the Tri·gartas**: Sushárman.

27.21 **Vishvak·sena**: Krishna.

29.4 **Dharma's son**: Yudhi·shthira.

29.12 **Man who was disposed towards the law**: Yudhi·shthira.

29.33 **Recalled his vow**: Bhima vowed to kill Duryódhana in *Sabhā/parvan*, MBh CE II.68.26 (Wilmot 2006: CSL II.68.50).

30.6 **Lord of ancestors**: Yama.

30.7 **Son of a Shini**: Sátyaki.

30.9 **Son of the Sun**: Karna. **Younger brother of the best of the gods (Indra)**: Vishnu.

30.11 **Vasu·shena**: Karna.

30.12 **Drúpada's son**: Dhrishta·dyumna.

30.26 **The Parthas**: Literally "the sons of Pritha," i.e. the Pándavas and, more generally, their followers.

30.44 **One of Rudra's playgrounds**: A cemetery or cremation ground.

31.2 **Bhadra**: Subhádra, younger sister of Krishna and Árjuna's second wife.

31.3 **Sharva**: Shiva.

31.9 **Adhókshaja**: Krishna.

31.39 **Since I've lost Shakra's spear**: In return for his divine armor and earrings, Indra gave Karna a divine spear on the condition that it could be used just once. Though Karna intends to use it against Árjuna, he is forced into using it against Bhima's semi-demonic son Ghatótkacha. For this episode see *Droṇa/parvan*, MBh CE VII.147–154.

31.44 **Bhárgava**: Rama Jamadágnya.

31.46 **Rama**: Rama Jamadágnya.

31.55 **Dashárha**: Krishna.

31.58 **Shura's grandson**: Krishna.

32.7 **Mahéshvara**: Shiva.

32.8 **Varshnéya**: Krishna.

32.10 **That army was divided into nine shares**: The army referred to here is the Pándavas' army. It was the practice for opposing armies to divide their enemy's armies amongst themselves as their "shares" to fight in battle. The same practice is followed in the case of individual champions.

32.56 **Artáyani** means something like "the one who sticks to the truth."

32.57 **Shalya** means "thorn."

32.63 **Dévaki's son**: Krishna.

33.4 **Taraká**: See note to 10.56 above.

33.7 **Grandfather**: Brahma.

33.19 **Yójana**: Supposedly anywhere from 2.5 to 9 miles.

33.21 **Tarakáksha**: Taráksha.

33.44 **Sthanu**: Shiva.

33.46 **Vrishánka**: Shiva.

33.47 **Bhava**: Shiva.

33.48 **Sarvátman**: Shiva.

33.56 Following Nīlakaṇṭha, ***īḍyate*** is taken as an irregular form of the present participle. The Critical Edition reads *īḍyase*. **The Lord of creatures (Praja·pati)**: Daksha. **Shambhu**: Shiva.

33.60 **Kumára**: Skanda.

34.13 **Maha·deva**: Literally "Great God."

34.25 ***ca ṛtavas***: Irregular sandhi; see OBERLIES 2003: 9–11.

34.20 **Great River**: The river Ganga.

34.21 **Krita epoch**: The first and most exalted of the four epochs of the world.

34.28 **Dhrita·rashtra**: Obviously not the same as King Dhrita·rashtra.

34.32 **Lord of the gods**: Indra. **Lord of the waters**: Váruna. **Lord of the dead**: Yama. **Lord of wealth**: Kubéra.

34.39 **Adhváryu priest**: A Vedic priest specializing in the *Yajur·veda* and responsible for performing many of the manual tasks of a sacrifice while muttering *yajus* formulas.

34.44 **Rig·veda, Sama·veda and puránas**: The *Rig·veda* and *Sama·veda* are two of the four Vedas. The former, the oldest, consists of hymns or verses (*ṛc*) in praise of the gods; the latter consists of hymns primarily from the *Rig·veda* set to music. A *purána* is a type of text that typically contains "old" (*purāṇa*) tales and lore.

34.45 **Yajur·veda**: One of the four collections that make up the Veda, consisting of hymns and formulas used in sacrifices.

34.48 **Time**: Death.

34.50 **They**: As the commentator Nīlakaṇṭha notes, most likely referring to the demons. **Hara**: Shiva.

34.52 **Nila·lóhita**: Shiva.

34.65 **The one whose emblem is a bull**: Shiva.

34.75 **Kapárdin**: Shiva.

34.92 **Lord of the universe**: Shiva.

34.101 **Naráyana**: Vishnu.

34.115 **Tryáksha**: Shiva.

34.156 **That sage**: Markandéya (see also MBh CSL VIII.33.2).

34.159 **So that his lineage could be correctly recognized**: The fact that he is a kshatriya is demonstrated by the way he acts.

35.5 **Íshvara**: Shiva.

35.9 **Svayam·bhu**: Brahma.

35.24 **Shalya** means "thorn."

35.47 **Mátali**: Indra's charioteer.

36.13 **Surya**: The Sun god (and Karna's father).

37.15 **The brahmin-hero**: Drona.

37.20 ***bṛhaspatyuśanoḥ***: An irregular form of genitive dual; see OBERLIES 2003: 91.

37.26 **The son of Vichítra·virya's son**: Duryódhana.

37.34 **King of the immortals**: Indra. **Younger sister of that excellent man**: Subhádra, sister of Krishna.

37.37 The word *yudhā* has been removed from KINJAWADEKAR's *śarottamair yudhā*, a reading which, besides inflating the meter by two syllables, has no support in the manuscript record as recorded in the critical notes of the Critical Edition.

37.38 **Those that travel through the sky**: *gandhárvas*. For this episode, see *Vana/parvan*, MBh CE III.226–243.

37.39 **Cattle raid**: An episode found in *Virāṭa/parvan*, MBh CE IV.24–62.

39.4 See note to 42.7.

39.7 **Cooked by time**: I.e. destined for death.

40.1 **Verbal barb**: A play on Shalya's name, where "barb" translates *śalya*.

40.11 **Pritha's son**: Árjuna.

40.13 **Behold the nobility of my birth**: This is a pointed statement by Karna, who is, as ever, sensitive of his supposedly low birth.

40.35 **Smart-arse**: ***vidvan***. More typically understood as "learned, wise man," "smart-arse" draws out the sarcastic implications of *vidvan* in the present context.

40.38 **Fermented gruel/brew**: ***su/vīraka***. It is not entirely clear what *su/vīraka* means. Given the context, however, it is unlikely that Monier-Williams' "collyrium" is correct. The commentator Nīlakaṇṭha suggests *kāñjika*, a fermented sour gruel. Fermented gruel also goes by the names *sauvīraka* (or *sauvīra*) and *su/vīr'/âmla*, suggesting that Nīlakaṇṭha is most likely correct. (Some manuscripts have *sauvīraka* for *su/vīraka*.) Fermented gruel was a common remedy in traditional Indian medicine. It appears that in the present context, the Madra woman has become addicted to fermented brew (something akin to beer); essentially she is an alcoholic.

40.51 **Puru·ravas**: An ancient king, ancestor of the Kurus and Pándavas.

40.53 **For my friend**: Duryódhana.

41.58 In Sanskrit crows are known by the onomatopoeic name *kāka*.

41.64 **Supárna**: Gáruda.

41.75 For this episode see *Virāṭa/parvan*, MBh CE IV.24–62.

41.78 For this episode see *Vana/parvan*, MBh CE III.226–243.

41.79 **Who said:** The reading ***vadataḥ*** is certainly awkward here. Though the Critical Edition's *vadatoḥ* is a better reading and makes the sense clear, I have retained KINJAWADEKAR's reading because it is attested in many manuscripts.

42.2 **Shauri**: Krishna.

42.7 **Suta**, "Charioteer," is not translated here and in subsequent verses because it denotes a caste name—I am aware of no example where Karna actually fills the occupation of charioteer.

42.12 **Obtained from him**: "him" is Rama Jamadágnya.

42.30 **An alliance is ratified in seven steps**: Probably referring to a contractual ritual, similar to the seven steps of a marriage rite.

42.31 The folk etymologies in these verses are based on a combination of their semantic and phonetic echoes of the words in question. Any phonetic resemblance is, however, lost in translation.

42.32 **The king**: Duryódhana.

42.36 **Vaivásvata**: Yama.

42.42 **Kings of soma**: Brahmins.

43.2 **That parable**: the fable from Canto 41.

43.7 **Because of friendship**: Probably his friendship for Duryódhana, cf. 40.53–54.

44.7 **The Sindhu river**: the Indus River.

44.14 ***hateti . . . -hateti***: Double sandhi (-e- < /-e i-/); see Oberlies 2003: 47.

44.17 **The Shata·druka River**: The Sutlej, the most easterly of the five tributaries of the Indus. **The Irávati River**: The Ravi River.

44.32 **The Vipásha River**: The Beas River. **The Airávati River**: The Ravi River. **The Chandra·bhaga river**: The Chenab River. **The Vitásta River**: The Jhelum River.

44.42 **Vahiká**: I.e the female progenitor from whom the Vahíka descend. Although the stress falls on the second syllable, the accent on the last syllable serves to distinguish her feminine gender (marked by a long final vowel) from the masculine gender of the Vahíka people.

45.27 *rakṣopasṛṣṭeṣu*: Double sandhi (-o- < /-as u-/); see Oberlies 2003: 39.

45.25 **Kings who act as sacrificer are dirt**: The king should be the patron of the sacrifice; the sacrificer should be a brahmin.

46.4 **Mághavan**: Indra.

46.35 **Hero of the Shinis**: Sátyaki.

46.38 **Previously Agni Vaishva·nara. . .** : The meaning of this verse is not entirely clear. Probably (following in part the commentator Nīlakaṇṭha) it is meant as praise for the horse leading Árjuna's chariot, the subject of the subsequent verse. This stanza has been omitted from the Critical Edition.

49.22 **Because he wanted to do what was right by Pritha's son**: Árjuna (Pritha's son) was assigned Karna as his "share" (*bhāga*) to kill in the war.

49.35 **Panchála princess**: Dráupadi.

49.40 **Lord of men**: Yudhi·shthira.

49.52 **He recalled Kunti's words**: In *Udyoga/parvan*, MBh CE V.144. 15–25, Karna promises Kunti that he will not kill her sons, barring Árjuna. Consequently, on each occasion that he has been in a position to kill one of the other Pándavas, he holds back "recalling Kunti's words." The KINJAWADEKAR edition has a slightly embellished rendering of this incident in regard to Yudhi·shthira, turning his touching of Yudhi·shthira's shoulder into an act of purification, as well as a near thing for Yudhi·shthira. In *Karṇa/parvan*, MBh CE VIII.17.90–94 (CSL VIII.24.45–50, above), Bhima is accorded similar restraint (a recollection of a scene occurring in *Droṇa/parvan*, MBh CE VII.114.67–8), as is Saha·deva in VII.142.15 (Critical Edition) and Nákula in MBh CSL VIII.24.45–50 above.

50.23 For the killing of Kíchaka, see *Virāṭa/parvan*, MBh CE IV.13–23.

50.45 **Son of the Wind**: Bhima.

51.35 **They were like a pair of lordly lions**: *har'/îndra iva*, one could also understand this as "like Vishnu and Indra."

51.55 ***tri/sāhasr" âbhyayur***: Double sandhi (-ā- < /-ās a-/).

52.18 **Like mountains with wings**: A reference to an old myth in which Indra cuts the wings off a flying mountain.

53.29 ***veṣṭitābhavan***: Likely to be a case of double sandhi (-ā- < /-ās a-/), though KINJAWADEKAR gives *veṣṭitā bhavan*, suggesting an augmentless imperfect.

53.34 **Indra's son**: Árjuna.

PROPER NAMES AND EPITHETS

ABHIMÁNYU Son of Árjuna and Subhádra; father of Paríkshit and grandfather of Janam·éjaya.

ÁCHYUTA Krishna, literally "imperishable, not fallen."

ÁDHIRATHA Karna's adoptive father, a charioteer (*sūta*) and friend of Dhrita·rashtra.

AGNI The god of fire.

AJÁTA·SHATRU Yudhi·shthira, literally "he whose enemy has not been born."

ALÁMBUSHA A *rákshasa* demon fighting on the side of the Dhartarásh-tras killed by Bhima's half-demon son Ghatótkacha.

AMBÁSHTHA Name of a country and its king.

ÁMBIKA Dhrita·rashtra's mother.

ÁNDHAKA Name of a demon killed by Rudra-Shiva.

ANGA An area roughly corresponding to modern south-east Bihar over which Karna is made king by Dur·yódhana.

ÁNGIRAS Name of an ancient sage who lends his name to his descen-dants. Often coupled with Athárvan.

ÁPSARAS A class of beautiful semi-divine women that inhabit the sky, singing, dancing and playing instruments.

ARÁTTA An area in the Punjab around the five rivers feeding the Indus.

ÁRJUNA Literally "white, clear." The third of the five Pándavas, son of Pritha (Kunti) and Indra (as substitute for Pandu). Also known as Bibhátsu, Dhanan·jaya, Jaya, Jishnu, the Left-handed archer, Nara, Pándava, Phálguna and the Wearer of the crown.

ARTÁYANI Shalya.

ASHVATTHAMAN son of Drona and Kripi, literally "as strong as a horse."

ASHVIN Name of twin deities who fathered Nákula and Saha·deva.

ATHÁRVAN Name of an ancient sage and priest who lends his name to his descendants, specialists in the *Athárva·veda*. Often coupled with Ángiras.

BÁHLIKA Name of a king fighting on the side of the Pándavas, brother of Shántanu (father of Bhishma) and father of Soma·datta. In the plural, name of his people.

BALA·DEVA Brother of Krishna, also known as Bala·rama.

BHAGA·DATTA King of Prag·jyótisha (roughly equivalent to modern day Assam), on the side of the Dhartaráshtras.

BHANU·SENA Name of a son of Karna.

BHARAD·VAJA An ancient sage and father of Drona.

BHARATA Ancient king and ancestor of most of the key participants in the 'Maha·bhárata.' In the plural, his descendants.

BHÁRATA Descendant of Bharata. Commonly used for many of the heroes of the 'Maha·bhárata.'

BHÁRGAVA A descendant of the sage Bhrigu, usually Rama Bhárgava. See also Jamadágnya.

BHIMA Literally "terrible, formidable." Second of the Pándavas. Son of the wind-god Vayu (as substitute for Pandu) and Pritha (Kunti). Also known as Wolf-belly, Bhima·sena and Pándava.

BHIMA·SENA Bhima, literally "he who has a terrifying army."

BHISHMA Son of Shántanu and the river Ganga. Referred to as "grandfather" by both the Dhartaráshtras and Pándavas. Fights on the side of the Dhartaráshtras as their general for the first ten days before he was deceitfully struck down by Árjuna.

BHOJA Name of a country and a prince, king or the people of that country. Typically refers to the warrior Krita·varman who fights on the side of the Dhartaráshtras.

BHRIGU Name of an ancient sage and, in the plural, his descendants.

BHURI·SHRAVAS Son of Soma·datta fighting on the side of the Dhartaráshtras.

BIBHÁTSU Árjuna, literally "loathing, feeling disgust."

BRAHMA A god, typically responsible for creation. Often called grandfather.

BRIHAS·PATI Divine priest of the gods and expert in law (*dharma*), policy (*nīti*) and military affairs. Often coupled with Úshanas.

CHEDI Name of a people fighting on the side of the Pándavas.

CHEKITÁNA A warrior fighting on the side of the Pándavas.

CHITRA A son of Dhrita·rashtra.

CHITRA·SENA Name of a son of Dhrita·rashtra; of a warrior on the Pándavas' side; and of a leader of the gandhárvas.

DAITYA A class of demons whose mother was Diti and father Káshyapa.

DÁNAVA A class of demons whose mother was Danu and father Káshyapa.

DANDA Brother of Danda·dhara fighting on the side of the Dhartaráshtras and killed by Árjuna.

DANDA·DHARA Name of a number of warriors; most prominently a warrior on the side of the Dhartaráshtras killed by Árjuna.

DASAMÍYA Name of a people.

DASHÁRHA Name of Krishna and of a people.

DEVA·DATTA Árjuna's conch.

DÉVAKI Krishna's mother.

DHANAN·JAYA Árjuna, literally "winner of wealth."

DHARTARÁSHTRA The sons of Dhrita·rashtra; the forces of the Dhartaráshtras in general.

DHRISHTA·DYUMNA Son of the Panchála king Drúpada, grandson of Príshata and brother of Dráupadi and Shikhándin. Principal general of the Pándava army.

DHRITA·RASHTRA Literally "he whose rule is firm." The blind king of the Kurus; father of a 100 sons and one daughter with Gandhári, and with a vaishya woman of another son, Yuyútsu, who fought for the Pándavas. Brother of Pandu, nominal father of the Pándavas, and Vídura.

DRÁUPADI Daughter of Drúpada and wife of the Pándavas. Also known as Krishná.

DRONA Son of Bharad·vaja and father of Ashva·tthaman. A brahmin and expert in weaponry who taught the Pándavas and Dhartaráshtras the arts of war. Fights on the side of the Dhartaráshtras, assuming the generalship upon Bhishma's death, and killed in deceptive circumstances by Dhrishta·dyumna on the fifteenth day of battle.

DRÚPADA King of Panchála and father of Dhrishta·dyumna, Dráupadi and Shikhándin.

DUHSHÁSANA Second son of Dhrita·rashtra and Gandhári. Close confidant of his brother Dur·yódhana.

DURMÁRSHANA A son of Dhrita·rashtra.

DÚRMUKHA A son of Dhrita·rashtra.

DUR·YÓDHANA Eldest son of Dhrita·rashtra and Gandhári, literally "he who's difficult to fight." Also known as Su·yódhana.

GANDHÁRA Name of a place and its people.

GANDHÁRI Wife of Dhrita·rashtra, mother of the Dhartaráshtras and sister of Shákuni. Literally "princess of Gandhára."

GANDHÁRVA Sky-dwelling beings considered skillful musicians.

GANDÍVA/GÁNDIVA Árjuna's bow.

GANGA The Ganges River, personified as the mother of Bhishma.

GÁRUDA Name of a mythical bird.

GÁUTAMA A patronymic of Gótama, Sharádvat's father and Kripa's grandfather. Typically refers to Kripa.

GAVÁLGANA Father of Sánjaya.

GHATÓTKACHA Son of Bhima and the *rákshasi* demon Hidímba. Fights on the side of the Pándavas.

GO·VINDA Krishna, literally "herdsman."

GÚHYAKA A type of semi-divine being, attendants of Kubéra.

HÁSTINA·PURA Capital of the Kuru realm, literally "city of elephants."

HRÍDIKA Father of Krita·varman.

HRISHI·KESHA Krishna.

INDRA King of the gods and father of Árjuna. The lord of the rains. Also known as Mághavan, Sacker of cities, Shakra, Shata·kratu, thunderbolt-wielder and Vásava.

ISHÁNA Shiva, literally "master, lord."

ÍSHVARA Shiva, literally "master, lord."

JAMAD·AGNI Name of a sage of the Bhrigu line; father of Párashu·rama (Rama Bhárgava).

JAMADÁGNYA Name of Rama Bhárgava, the son of Jamad·agni; a brahmin sage otherwise known as Párashu·rama.

JANAM·ÉJAYA Literally "making people tremble," the son of Paríkshit and Mádravati; grandson of Abhimányu; great-grandson of Árjuna. Janam·éjaya's snake sacrifice provides the setting for Vaiśampáyana's recitation of the 'Maha·bhárata.'

JANÁRDANA Krishna, literally "tormentor of men."

JAYA Árjuna, literally "victory, triumph."

JISHNU Árjuna, literally "conquering, victorious."

KÁIKAYA/KAIKÉYA/KÉKAYA Name of a people who, apart from five brothers who joined the Pándavas, fought on the side of the Dhartaráshtras.

KALÍNGA Name of a people from a region roughly corresponding to present day Orissa.

KAMALÁKSHA Name of a demon, literally "lotus-eyed." A son of the demon Táraka who, with his two brothers, had the cities that came to form Tri·pura ("Triple-city") built.

KAMBÓJA Name of a people.

KAPÁRDIN Shiva, literally "having hair matted into a shape like a cowrie shell."

KARNA Adopted son of the charioteer Ádhiratha and Radha; birth son of Kunti by the sun-god Surya; half-brother to the Pándavas. Ally of the Dhartaráshtras and close friend of Dur·yódhana, by whom he was made king of Anga. Often referred to as the charioteer's son, Vaikártana, Vasu·shena and Vrisha.

KARTAVÍRYA Árjuna Kartavírya, name of an ancient warrior killed by Rama Jamadágnya (Párashu·rama).

KARÚSHA Name of a people.

KASHI Name of a people from a region roughly corresponding to modern day Benares (also known as Kashi).

KÁURAVA/ KAURÁVYA Literally "descendant of Kuru," patronymics typically used for the Dhartaráshtras, but occasionally used for the Pándavas too (since they too are "descendants of Kuru").

KÉKAYA See entry for Káikaya.

KÉSHAVA Krishna, literally "having much hair."

KING OF LAW Yudhi·shthira, translation of *Dharma/rāja*.

KÓSALA/KÓSHALA Name of a country and its people situated to the east of Kuru/Panchála heartland in the 'Maḥa·bhárata.'

KRATHA A son of Dhrita·rashtra.

KRIPA Son of Sharádvat, grandson of Gótama, brother of Kripi. A teacher of both the Dhartaráshtras and Pándavas; fights on the side of the Dhartaráshtras.

KRIPI Daughter of Sharádvat, sister of Kripa, wife of Drona and mother of Ashva·tthaman.

KRISHNA Literally "dark, black." Son of Vasu·deva and Dévaki. Identified with the god Vishnu. Also known as Áchyuta, Adhókshaja, Dashárha, Go·vinda, Hrishi·kesha, Janárdana, Késhava, Mádhava, Naráyana, Sátvata, Shauri, Varshnéya, Vasudéva, Vrishni and Yádava.

KRISHNÁ Dráupadi, the wife of the Pándavas, daughter of Drúpada.

KRITA·VARMAN Vrishni prince, son of Hrídika; often referred to as "the Bhoja." A leading warrior on the side of the Dhartaráshtras.

KSHEMA·DHURTI A warrior fighting for the Dhartaráshtras.

KUBÉRA God of wealth.

KUNTI Pritha, adopted daughter of Kunti·bhoja. Wife of Pandu and mother of Yudhi·shthira, Bhima and Árjuna by the gods Dharma, Vayu and Indra respectively; birth mother of Karna by the sun god

Surya. Birth sister to Krishna's father.

KUNTI·BHOJA Adoptive father of Kunti. Sides with the Pándavas.

KURU Ancestor of the Dhartaráshtras and Pándavas. "Kurus" typically refers to the Dhartaráshtras and their followers.

KURU·KSHETRA "The field of the Kurus." Name of a plain upon which take place the battles of the 'Maha·bhárata' war.

LÁKSHMANA Son of Dur·yódhana.

LEFT-HANDED ARCHER Árjuna, translation of the common epithet *Sa-vya/sācin*. A reference to Árjuna's ambidextrous skills with the bow.

MÁDHAVA Krishna, literally "descendant of Madhu."

MADRA/MÁDRAKA Name of a people whose king is Shalya.

MADRI Second wife of Pandu and mother of Nákula and Saha·deva by the two Ashvins. Literally "princess of the Madras." Sister of Shalya.

MÁGADHA Name of a people.

MÁGHAVAN Indra, literally "bountiful, generous."

MAHA·DEVA Shiva, literally "great god."

MAHÉSHVARA Shiva, literally "great lord."

MÁHISHA Name of a demon slain by Skanda.

MÁLAYA·DHVAJA Name of a king of the Pandyas. Literally "he whose banner bears the Málaya mountain range."

MARKANDÉYA Name of an ancient sage.

MÁTALI Name of Indra's charioteer.

MATSYA Name of a people.

MERU A mountain situated at the center of the cosmos.

MITRA·DEVA A warrior fighting for the Dhartaráshtras.

MITRA·VARMAN Name of both a warrior fighting for the Dhartarásh-tras, and a Panchála warrior fighting for the Pándavas.

NAGA·PURA Hástina·pura, literally "city of elephants."

NÁIMISHA Name of a people.

NÁKULA One of the Pándavas, twin of Saha·deva. Son of Madri by one of the Ashvin gods.

NÁMUCHI Name of a demon killed by Indra.

NARA "Man," an ancient deity identified with Árjuna and associated with Naráyana (Vishnu/Krishna).

NÁRADA Name of a revered divine sage.

NÁRAKA Name of a demon killed by Krishna.

NARÁYANA A god, often considered as identical with Vishnu, who manifests as Krishna, usually in association with Nara manifesting as Árjuna.

NISHÁDA Name of a people.

NIVÁTA·KÁVACHA Literally "whose armor is impenetrable," name of a group of demons killed by Árjuna.

OATH-BOUND WARRIORS Warriors from Tri·garta sworn to kill Árjuna.

PANCHAJÁNYA Name of Krishna's conch which he seized from the demon Pancha·jana.

PANCHÁLA Name of a people who were key allies to the Pándavas, an alliance established through the marriage of the Pándava brothers to Dráupadi, the daughter of Drúpada, the king of the Panchálas.

PÁNDAVA Literally "son of Pandu." A patronymic for Yudhi·shthira, Bhima, Árjuna, Nákula and Saha·deva. Occasionally referring to the Pándavas and their followers in toto.

PANDU Literally "the pale one." Nominal father of the Pándavas; husband of Pritha (Kunti) and Madri; half-brother to Dhrita·rashtra and Vídura.

PANDYA Name of a country, its people and, in the singular, its king. The Pandyas fought on the side of the Pándavas.

PHÁLGUNA Árjuna.

PINÁKA Shiva's bow.

PISHÁCHA Name of a class of demons.

PRABHÁDRAKA Name of a group of warriors fighting on the side of the Pándavas.

PRAJA·PATI Literally "lord of creatures." The creator god usually identified as Brahma. Also refers to a number of "creators," themselves the first creations of Brahma, who produced the different living beings.

PRATIVÍNDHYA A son of Yudhi·shthira.

PRÍSHATA Father of Drúpada; grandfather of Shikhándin, Dhrishta·dyumna and Dráupadi.

PRITHA Kunti. Birth-daughter of the Vrishni prince Shura; sister of Vasu·deva and aunt of Krishna. The first wife of Pandu and mother of the three elder Pándavas Yudhi·shthira, Bhima and Árjuna; birth mother of Karna.

PURU·RAVAS Name of an ancient king; distant ancestor of the Dhartaráshtras and Pándavas.

RADHA Adoptive mother of Karna and wife of Ádhiratha.

RÁKSHASA Name of a class of demons.

RAMA Usually Rama Jamadágnya (Bhárgava), son of Jamad·agni. A brahmin who was a famous warrior, slaughtering the world's kshatriyas twenty-one times over. He became Karna's guru and gave him the Brahma weapon. Occasionally also refers to Rama Dásharathi, the hero of the 'Ramáyana.'

RÁVANA A *rákshasa* demon killed by Rama, as told in the 'Ramáyana.'

RUDRA The "howler." An ancient Vedic god later identified with Shiva.

SACKER OF CITIES Indra, translation of Puraṃdara.

SAHA·DEVA One of the Pándavas; twin of Nákula and son of Madri by one of the Ashvin gods.

SÁNJAYA Son of Gaválgana and Dhrita·rashtra's charioteer and personal bard (*sūta*). Narrator of the great battle to Dhrita·rashtra.

SARÁSVATI Name of a river, sometimes personified as a goddess.

SÁTVATA Name of the Yádava people. Refers specifically to Krita·varman, Sátyaki and Krishna.

SÁTYAKI A Vrishni warrior, the son of Sátyaka and grandson of Shini. Also known as Yuyudhána. Fights on the side of the Pándavas.

SATYA·SENA A son of Karna.

SAUVÍRA Name of a people from the area around the Indus and its tributaries.

SHAKRA Indra, literally "strong, mighty."

SHÁKUNI Literally "bird," son of Súbala, the king of Gandhára, and father of Ulúka. Brother of Gandhári and counselor and close confidant of her son Dur·yódhana.

SHALVA Name of a people.

SHALYA Literally "thorn." The king of Madra; brother of Madri and hence maternal-uncle of the Nákula and Saha·deva and by extension the other Pándavas. Allied with the Dhartaráshtras and commander of their army upon Karna's death. Also known as Artáyani.

SHÁNKARA Shiva, literally "bringing prosperity."

SHÁNTANU Bhishma's father.

SHARÁDVAT Father of Kripa and Kripi.

SHARNGA Name of Krishna's bow.

SHARVA Shiva.

SHATA·KRATU Indra, literally "he of a hundred sacrifices."

SHATANÍKA Son of Nákula and Dráupadi.

SHAURI A patronymic ("son or descendant of Shura") used for Krishna (Shura's grandson) and Sátyaki (Krishna's cousin).

SHIKHÁNDIN Son of King Drúpada of Panchála, born as a girl, Shikhándini, and miraculously transformed into a man. Plays a key role in Bhishma's defeat.

SHINI Grandfather of Sátyaki. In the plural refers to a people descending from Shini.

SHIVA "The benevolent one." A god associated with destructive forces. Also known as Ishána, Íshvara, Kapárdin, Maha·deva, Mahéshvara, Rudra, Shánkara, Sharva, Sthanu and Try·ambaka.

SHRUTA·KARMAN Son of Saha·deva and Dráupadi.

SHRUTA·KIRTI Son of Árjuna and Dráupadi.

SHURA Father of Vasu·deva and grandfather of Krishna. In the plural, name of a people.

SIDDHA Literally "perfected." A type of being who has attained supernatural powers.

SINDHU Name of the country around the Indus river and, in the plural, the people who live there.

SÓMAKA A sub-group of the Panchálas.

SRÍNJAYA A sub-group of the Panchálas.

STHANU Shiva, literally "immovable, pillar, tree trunk."

SÚBALA King of Gandhára and father of Shákuni and Gandhári.

SUBHÁDRA Sister of Krishna, wife of Árjuna and mother of Abhimányu.

SUPÁRNA A mythical bird identified with Gáruda.

SURYA The sun god and father of Karna.

SUSHÁRMAN King of the Tri·gartas, fighting on the side of the Dhartaráshtras.

SUSHÉNA Name of a son of Karna and a son of Dhrita·rashtra.

SUTA·SOMA Son of Bhima and Dráupadi.

SU·YÓDHANA Dur·yódhana, literally "fighting well."

TÁRAKA Father of the demons Taráksha, Kamaláksha and Vidyun·malin.

TARÁKSHA Name of a demon, literally "star-eyed." A son of the demon Táraka who, with his two brothers, had three cities built that came to form Tri·pura ("Triple-city").

TARKSHYA Name of a mythical bird identified with Gáruda.

THUNDERBOLT-WIELDER Indra, for *Vajrin*, *Vajra/hasta* and *Vajra/pāṇi*.

TRI·GARTA Name of a people.

TRY·ÁMBAKA Shiva, literally "three-eyed."

ULÚKA Literally "owl." Shákuni's son, fights for the Dhartaráshtras.

UMA Shiva's wife, also known as Párvati.

ÚSHANAS An ancient sage. Considered an expert in political matters (*nīti*) and military affairs. Often coupled with Brihas·pati.

UTTAMÁUJAS A Panchála warrior fighting for the Pándavas. Brother of Yudha·manyu.

VAHÍKA Name of a people.

VAIKÁRTANA Name of Karna in reference to his "cutting away" (*vikartana*) of the armor with which he was born.

VAISHAMPÁYANA A sage and pupil of Krishna Dvaipáyana Vyasa, whose 'Maha·bhárata' he recites to Janam·éjaya.

VÁISHRAVANA Kubéra.

VAISHVÁNARA A name for the ancient fire god Agni.

VARSHNÉYA Literally "descendant of Vrishni," name of Krishna.

VÁRUNA An ancient Vedic god especially associated in the 'Maha·bhárata' with the waters.

VÁSAVA Indra.

VASU·DEVA Krishna's father, brother of Pritha (Kunti).

VASUDÉVA Krishna, literally "son of Vasu·deva."

VASU·SHENA A name given to Karna by his adoptive father Ádhiratha.

VAYU The ancient god of wind and father of Bhima.

VEDA Ancient, sacred and culturally authoritative bodies of "knowledge" (*veda*), consisting chiefly of the four collections known as the *Rig·veda*, *Sama·veda*, *Yajur·veda* and *Athárva·veda*, but including some historically later bodies of literature as well. The 'Maha·bhárata' is sometimes referred too as the "fifth Veda."

VÍDURA Half-brother of Dhrita·rashtra and Pandu. Expert on law (*dharma*).

VIDYUN·MALIN Name of a demon, literally "wreathed with lightning." A son of the demon Táraka who, with his two brothers, had three cities built that came to form Tri·pura ("Triple-city").

VÍJAYA Name of Karna's bow.

VIKÁRNA A son of Dhrita·rashtra.

VIRÁTA The king of the Matsyas and ally of the Pándavas.

VISHNU Name of a god associated with preservation. Often considered the supreme god in the 'Maha·bhárata' and identified with Naráyana. He incarnates as Krishna.

VISHVA·KARMAN The "all-maker," name of the divine architect and craftsman.

VIVÍTSU A son of Dhrita·rashtra.

VRISHA Karna, literally "bull."

VRISHA·SENA A son of Karna.

VRISHNI Name of a people. Sátyaki, Krita·varman and Krishna are Vrishnis.

VRITRA Name of a demon slain by Indra.

WEARER OF THE CROWN Árjuna, translation of *Kirīṭin*. So named for the crown given to him by Indra.

WOLF-BELLY Bhima, translation of *Vṛk'|ôdara*. So called for his large appetite.

YÁDAVA "Descendants of Yadu," Krishna's tribe.

YAJNA·SENA Drúpada.

YAKSHA A type of a semi-divine being. Attendants of Kubéra.

YAMA The god of the dead.

YUDHA·MANYU A Panchála warrior fighting for the Pándavas. Brother of Uttamáujas.

YUDHI·SHTHIRA Literally "steady in battle." Eldest of the five Pándava brothers; son of Pritha (Kunti) and the god Dharma (as substitute for Pandu). Famous for his learning and virtue. Also known as Ajáta·shatru, the King of Law and Pándava.

YUYUDHÁNA Sátyaki.

YUYÚTSU Literally, "eager to fight." A son of Dhrita·rashtra and a vaishya woman who fought on the side of the Pándavas.

INDEX

Sanskrit words are given in the English alphabetical order, according to the accented CSL pronuncuation aid. They are followed by the conventional diacritics in brackets.

Permitted finals:							(Except āḥ/aḥ)			
k	ṭ	t	p	ṅ	n	m	ḥ/r	āḥ	aḥ	*Initial letters:*
k	ṭ	t	p	ṅ	n	ṃ	ḥ	āḥ	aḥ	k/kh
g	ḍ	d	b	ṅ	n	ṃ	r	ā	o	g/gh
k	ṭ	c	p	ṅ	ṃś	ṃ	ś	āś	aś	c/ch
g	ḍ	j	b	ṅ	ñ	ṃ	r	ā	o	j/jh
k	ṭ	ṭ	p	ṅ	ṃṣ	ṃ	ṣ	āṣ	aṣ	ṭ/ṭh
g	ḍ	ḍ	b	ṅ	ṇ	ṃ	r	ā	o	ḍ/ḍh
k	ṭ	t	p	ṅ	ṃs	ṃ	s	ās	as	t/th
g	ḍ	d	b	ṅ	n	ṃ	r	ā	o	d/dh
k	ṭ	t	p	ṅ	n	ṃ	ḥ	ā	aḥ	p/ph
g	ḍ	d	b	ṅ	n	ṃ	r	ā	o	b/bh
ṅ	ṇ	n	m	ṅ	n	ṃ	r	ā	o	*nasals* (n/m)
g	ḍ	d	b	ṅ	n	ṃ	r	ā	o	y/v
g	ḍ	d	b	ṅ	n	ṃ	*zero*[1]	ā	o	r
g	ḍ	l	b	ṅ	l̃[2]	ṃ	r	ā	o	l
k	ṭ	c ch	p	ṅ	ñ ś/ch	ṃ	ḥ	āḥ	aḥ	ś
k	ṭ	t	p	ṅ	n	ṃ	ḥ	āḥ	aḥ	ṣ/s
gg h	ḍḍ h	dd h	bb h	ṅ	n	ṃ	r	ā	o	h
g	ḍ	d	b	ṅ/ṅṅ[3]	n/nn[3]	m	r	ā	a[4]	*vowels*
k	ṭ	t	p	ṅ	n	m	ḥ	āḥ	aḥ	*zero*

[1]ḥ or r disappears, and if a/i/u precedes, this lengthens to ā/ī/ū. [2]e.g. tān+lokān=tāl̃ lokān.
[3]The doubling occurs if the preceding vowel is short. [4]Except: aḥ+a=o '.

Final vowels:

a	ā	i	ī	u	ū	ṛ	e	ai	o	au	*Initial vowels:*
' â	" â	y a	y a	v a	v a	r a	e '	ā a	o '	āv a	a
' ā	" ā	y ā	y ā	v ā	v ā	r ā	a ā	ā ā	a ā	āv ā	ā
' ê	" ê	' î	" î	v i	v i	r i	a i	ā i	a i	āv i	i
' ē	" ē	' ī	" ī	v ī	v ī	r ī	a ī	ā ī	a ī	āv ī	ī
' ô	" ô	y u	y u	' û	" û	r u	a u	ā u	a u	āv u	u
' ō	" ō	y ū	y ū	' ū	" ū	r ū	a ū	ā ū	a ū	āv ū	ū
a' r	a" r	y ṛ	y ṛ	v ṛ	v ṛ	' ṛ̂	a ṛ	ā ṛ	a ṛ	āv ṛ	ṛ
' âi	" âi	y e	y e	v e	v e	r e	a e	ā e	a e	āv e	e
' āi	" āi	y ai	y ai	v ai	v ai	r ai	a ai	ā ai	a ai	āv ai	ai
' âu	" âu	y o	y o	v o	v o	r o	a o	ā o	a o	āv o	o
' āu	" āu	y au	y au	v au	v au	r au	a au	ā au	a au	āv au	au